PIERS PLOWMAN

The B-Version Archetype (Bx)

PIERS PLOWMAN

The B-Version Archetype (Bx)

Edited by
John A. Burrow and Thorlac Turville-Petre

 SEENET

Raleigh, North Carolina, 2018

Piers Plowman: The B-Version Archetype (Bx)
Edited by John A. Burrow and Thorlac Turville-Petre

PPEA Print Series, vol. 1

Published by the Society for Early English and Norse Electronic Texts
Post Office Box 33142, Raleigh, North Carolina 27636
https://www.seenet.org/

Distributed by the University of North Carolina Press

Library of Congress Cataloging-in-Publication Data
Names: Langland, William, 1330?-1400?, author. | Burrow, J. A. (John
    Anthony), editor. | Turville-Petre, Thorlac, editor.
Title: Piers Plowman : the b-version archetype (bx) / edited by John Burrow
    and Thorlac Turville-Petre.
Description: Raleigh, NC : SEENET, [2018]
Identifiers: LCCN 2018017879| ISBN 9781941331132 (cloth) | ISBN 9781941331149
    (pbk) | ISBN 9781941331156 (ebook)
Classification: LCC PR2010 .B87 2018 | DDC 821/.1–dc23
LC record available at https://lccn.loc.gov/2018017879

Typeset in Junicode, by Peter S. Baker. Headings in Signika, by Anna Giedryś.

Version information:
Introduction corresponds to XML version 2.0.
Text corresponds to XML version 2.0.

Contents

About the Series

The PPEA Print Series provides printed counterparts to editions published by the *Piers Plowman Electronic Archive* (http://piers.chass.ncsu.edu). Since its inception in the early 1990s, the PPEA has pursued the goal of creating an open access digital archive of the full medieval and early modern textual tradition of *Piers Plowman*. When complete, the Archive will include documentary editions of all manuscript copies and early printed texts of the poem, along with critical editions of the canonic A, B, and C versions and their archetypes. The Print Series furthers these goals by meeting the research and classroom needs of those who prefer to work with printed versions of these texts.

Both the PPEA and this series owe debts of gratitude to many institutions and individuals for making these volumes possible. The project began at the University of Virginia and for many years was hosted and facilitated by UVA's Institute for Advanced Technology in the Humanities. Since 2014, PPEA has been based at North Carolina State University, where it is supported by the Research Office of the College of Humanities and Social Sciences, the CHASS IT department, and the Department of English. Our editorial work has been made possible by generous backing from the National Endowment for the Humanities, and the PPEA Print Series was launched with the support of a Thomas W. Ross Fund Publishing Grant from the University of North Carolina Press. We have also benefited enormously from two Postdoctoral Fellowships in Data Curation for Medieval Studies funded in full by the Council on Library and Information Resources.

Above all we are indebted to Hoyt Duggan, founder and guiding light of the PPEA, and Gail Duggan, unsung hero of the Archive whose many expert transcriptions constitute the textual foundation upon which much subsequent work is built. We could not do what we do today without their decades of visionary leadership, and dedicate this series to them.

Paul A. Broyles, Jim Knowles, and Timothy L. Stinson, Series Editors
Raleigh, North Carolina
April 2018

Preface to the Online Edition

This edition of the archetypal B-text (Bx) does not, of course, claim to represent what Langland wrote, and indeed our annotations comment on a number of readings we have preserved that are certainly scribal corruptions. We aim to reconstruct the text of the lost copy from which, we argue, all surviving manuscripts descend. We are unpersuaded by the notion that readings in some of the manuscripts are pre-archetypal, and conclude that such readings have no place in future editions of the **B** text except as conjectural emendations. We have set out all the material from which our reconstruction is based so that readers can judge our decisions; but we believe that the readings of **Bx** can usually be determined with confidence. Furthermore we think that its text was much closer to what Langland wrote than recent editors have supposed; that **Bx** was an unsupervised or a loosely-supervised fair copy of Langland's foul papers; furthermore that it may have been the copy from which Langland made his C revision and to that extent was sanctioned by the poet.

A great many people have made substantial contributions to this edition, both formally and in informal discussions. Chief among these is Hoyt Duggan, to whom we dedicate this edition. It was his initiative to set up the *Piers Plowman Electronic Archive*, and he has seen through the production of all its diplomatic editions, as joint editor of most of them. We have relied on such editions as were available for the establishment of the archetype. Together with Ralph Hanna (who has always been on hand to offer valuable advice), Dug edited the Laud copy which we have used as our base text. He worked with JAB on a first draft of Bx, and nobly undertook the transformation into XML of the word-processed material of two editors too idle to learn tagging. Together with his team at Charlottesville, Dug developed the internet programs that will be used in future SEENET editions. This task itself posed unexpected difficulties and considerable delays, compounded in this case by the complication of needing to display with the archetypal text the parallel lines from ten manuscripts. In this task Paul Broyles played a leading part, with the able assistance of Chelsea Lambert Skalak and Christine Schott.

J.A.B. and T.T-P.
2014

Preface to the Print Edition

In preparing the online edition of Bx for print, I have taken the opportunity to correct a handful of errors in the presentation of the text that did not represent our intentions, mostly to supply or move mid-line points we had overlooked or misplaced, and to insert square brackets around emendations. Otherwise the text is unaltered. A valuable feature of the online edition enabled the user to call up the parallel lines of the ten important manuscripts, and from there to move to any of the edited texts with the manuscript images. Since this is not possible in this edition, I have added to the notes more details of the variant readings where it was practical, so that the reader can get along without continually switching to the online text. I have also revised a few notes that seemed to me not entirely clear. Before his death in October 2017, John Burrow worked with me to update references and revise a few passages in the Introduction. Changes are included in the revised edition online.

This print edition would never have got off the ground if it had not been for the perseverance of Tim Stinson and James Knowles, who have helped and encouraged at every stage. Paul Broyles developed software to transform XML into LaTeX, a language designed for publishing and the production of camera-ready copy, and he and James Knowles have seen the edition through to publication and have always been on hand to answer my ignorant queries.

I dedicate this book to the memory of John Burrow, who would have dearly liked to have seen the text as "a real book".

T.T-P.
January 2018

INTRODUCTION

I Nature of the Edition

The edition presents our reconstruction of the archetypal text of the B-version of *Piers Plowman* (henceforth **Bx**). We differ from the great edition by Kane and Donaldson in that we believe the readings of **Bx** can be established with certainty in the majority of lines; nor do we share their belief that the archetype was itself a highly corrupt text of Langland's poem. It is not our purpose to correct **Bx**, and we only comment where corruption there has a bearing on the interpretation of the text or to offer justification for accepting a manifestly wrong reading. We are of the opinion that **Bx**, though containing its share of errors,[1] is not a hopeless representative of Langland's B-version, and that determining its text, as here, may serve as preparation for a final step of establishing an inevitably controversial critical text of **B**.[2]

II The Stemma

II.1 Alpha and Beta

The practice of recension as the basis of editing is sometimes called into question on two principal grounds. The first is purely practical: that the relationship between witnesses may be so thoroughly obscured by contamination and coincidental variation that it is impossible to establish the stemma. The second is a more fundamental objection: that since the relationships can only be established on the basis of identifying erroneous readings, the stemma is not a tool for the editor but a product of the edition. We find the first objection surmountable and the second invalid. A number of scribes of *Piers Plowman* certainly consulted more than one text of the poem, leading to contamination, and scribes tended to make the same kinds of mistake, leading to coincidental error. However, L and R, being the best representatives of the two hyparchetypes, respectively beta and alpha, establish, where

---

1 For examples see notes to **Bx**.13.429, 15.387, 18.323–6. Contrast Schmidt (2008), 154: "The archetypal B-Text contains some 600 major and minor errors." Both KD and Schmidt dismiss many readings on metrical grounds.

2 On the value of **Bx** for establishing a critical text see Turville-Petre (2013).

they agree, many unquestionably **Bx** readings, and this gives us confidence that we can identify non-archetypal readings in most cases. Having thus established the manuscript relationships on the basis of shared error, we can use the stemma to guide us in cases where the direction of error is less certain. We differ from Kane and Donaldson in that we find no evidence that any manuscript offers readings derived from a putative pre-archetypal stage.

In its essential features, the stemma of the B-version was in fact established by Kane and Donaldson (1975), and their collations were refined by Schmidt (1995, 2008),[3] and further by Adams (2000). It has two independent branches, alpha (represented by R and F) and beta (the remaining manuscripts). The majority of the beta witnesses derive from a hyparchetype, beta1, and may be grouped as [BmBoCot][GY(OC^2)C][Cr(WHm)]. L is independent of beta1, while M, though corrected from a CrWHm-family exemplar, is essentially an independent witness for the first part of the poem (see III.2). Beta2 consists of CrWHm, beta3 of WHm alone, beta4 of GYOC^{2}CBmBoCot, beta5 of BmBoCot. Although some of the details are uncertain, Adams supplies us with the following stemma (modifying Schmidt's and slightly revising his own published version):

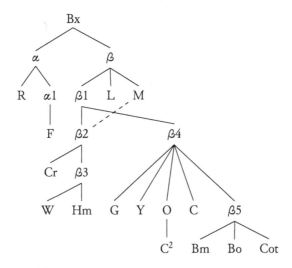

Stemma of the **B**-version. With acknowledgments to Robert Adams, *Studies in Bibliography* 53 (2000), 174.

---

3 Schmidt (2008) appeared at a late stage in our editing. While we have taken account of the relevant sections of the Introduction, we continue to cite the textual notes from Schmidt (1995) on the grounds that these are easier for the reader to use, since they refer to the **B**-text alone, and in any case are more widely accessible. We comment occasionally on substantive revisions to the notes.

Although Kane and Donaldson's collations actually establish a stemma, their view was that "the extreme frequency of convergent variation in the transmission of *Piers Plowman* manuscripts" obliged them to adopt the "direct method" of editing. They maintained that such frequent convergent variation "is the only possible explanation of the many random agreements of these manuscripts" (p. 63). We believe, on the contrary, that the majority of agreements in error are genetic. Like Kane and Donaldson, Schmidt is in principle (though less so in practice) committed to the "direct method," so that, even though he gives a diagram of the stemma, he says that it "has no claim to be a stemma," and again refers to "extensive contamination" (Schmidt [1995], p. lvi, and cf. Schmidt [2008], 126–7). We have found that convergent variation by coincidental substitution is no more or less prevalent than in the scribal traditions of other Middle English texts, and that contamination is not a feature of the best manuscripts and is generally identifiable in the others. In short, establishing the text of **Bx** presents no difficulties peculiar to *Piers Plowman*.

As demonstrated by Adams (2000), the two key witnesses are L and R. Skeat was so impressed by the quality of L that he at first thought it might be Langland's holograph, and Kane and Donaldson, though choosing W as their copy-text, recognised the "superior originality" of L (p. 214). We believe the L scribe to be a remarkably accurate copyist of the beta hyparchetype, uncontaminated by either of the other versions of the poem. Of the only two alpha manuscripts, F is a very eccentric text that reflects the activity of a scribe reshaping his text in both broad features and individual details, and one who had access at certain points to a text of **A** and probably also of **C**. We see no evidence to support the view that F had access to a manuscript of **B** anterior to **Bx** as argued by Kane and Donaldson (pp. 165–72); see e.g. note to **Bx**.14.25. Luckily R is as accurate a representation of alpha as L is of beta, and one mark of this is the occasional willingness of the scribe to transmit nonsense from the alpha hyparchetype. As with L, we see no evidence of contamination from **AC** versions. It follows that agreement of L and R is very strong evidence for **Bx**.[4] Unfortunately R has three major gaps as a result of lost leaves, and here F stands alone. Where R has lost text, we have to fall back on F as a very insecure witness to the alpha hyparchetype.

Where the text of R conflicts with that of F, the only other alpha witness, its reading can often be seen to be the origin of F's invention or misunderstanding (see notes to **Bx**.10.388, 13.110, 14.151, 17.110, 20.265), so confirming R's fidelity to alpha. In the beta tradition, agreement of L with M's original text against all other witnesses is generally sufficient to establish the hyparchetypal reading, though M is heavily corrected from another

---

4 For an extreme case of this, see note to **Bx**.2.121.

beta manuscript, so that its original readings, where they can be recovered, need to be distinguished from its revisions. In principle the single witness of either L or M can represent beta against all the other manuscripts. Disagreement between L and M brings the remaining beta manuscripts into play. CrWHm form a close group derived from a reasonably good text, beta2, with Crowley's print Cr as its most reliable witness, although account has to be taken of its modernisations and Crowley's access to C-text manuscripts. The much less faithful beta4 is represented by GYOC as well as C^2, probably a direct copy of O. Apart from C^2, which has no independent authority, G is the least useful of this group, a sixteenth-century manuscript showing conflation with AC and introducing quite a number of independent revisions and modernisations. We have not found that the beta5 derivatives BmBoCot offer useful evidence in constructing **Bx**. Although we have examined the variant readings of all the **Bx** witnesses, in general we cite the readings of the ten manuscripts LMCrWHmCGORF, in that order. The variant lines are displayed in the electronic version of this edition by clicking on the line-numbers.

In addition to evidence drawn from stemmatic relationships, readings that are scribal can generally be identified by the usual characteristics of reversion to a commonplace or easier reading, adoption of a prose word-order, omission and misunderstanding. By the use of this "direct method" as well as genetic evidence, the establishment of the alpha and beta hyparchetypes is generally pretty straightforward except where R's text is lost and the determination of alpha depends upon the very unreliable F. We have taken agreement of alpha and beta as conclusive evidence for the readings of **Bx**.

II.2   Rolling Revision?

The difficulty is greater where alpha and beta lections are divided, since they are of equal standing for the establishment of **Bx**. In these circumstances, corroboration of one or other may be provided by the support of one or both of the other versions of the poem. This needs to be distinguished from the process for which the Athlone edition has been criticised, that is, importing readings of A and/or C into their critical text of the B-version. Only in those cases where alpha and beta, the two prime witnesses of the B tradition, are in disagreement are we justified in looking in the other traditions for support for one over the other so far as **Bx** is concerned.

A significant difference between alpha and beta is the absence of lines and longer passages from one or the other: alpha lacks 37 such units that are recorded in beta, and beta lacks 45 in alpha, a total of nearly 200 lines absent from each. See Burrow and Turville-Petre (2012). All but one are listed in Kane and Donaldson, pp. 66–9, who regard them as accidental omissions usually caused by eyeskip (p. 65). Kane and Donaldson point to the likelihood of scribes skipping from paraph to paraph, which we regard as a major factor in very many cases, but, since they do not record paraphs in their edition, critics have focussed on their additional explanations of other kinds of eyeskip, some of which are unconvincing (Hanna [1996], 219–22, Schmidt [2008], 148–9). Partly for this reason, the view that at least some of these alpha- and beta-only passages represent "rolling revision" has gained currency.

Advocates of "rolling revision," that is, sporadic alteration by the author over a period of time, might argue that a **B**-text containing both these alpha and beta passages conflates (as traditional editions of *King Lear* are said to do) two distinct states of the text into a single version that never existed. However, the **C** reviser quite certainly had both in the **B**-text on which he worked. Of the 37 alpha-only lines and passages listed by Kane and Donaldson, 27 are either reproduced or developed in **C**; of the remaining 10, most are lost in more extensive cuts. The figures for beta-only passages are similar: 36 are reproduced or developed, nine are lost. It appears that for the **C**-poet these materials were all simply part of his **B**-text, to be preserved, changed or dropped like the rest.

This seems a strong argument in favour of the Athlone interpretation of the evidence, *viz.* that both alpha-only and beta-only passages were present in **Bx**, with some of them lost in the alpha hyparchetype and some in that of beta. But there are difficulties. It has been objected that such extensive omissions in both alpha and beta posit two copyists more careless than any of the *Piers* scribes whose work is extant. Furthermore, the distribution of the alpha-only passages is remarkable, since the first of them occurs as late as **Bx**.10.82–3. Kane informed us in a private communication that he and Donaldson once entertained, on other grounds, the possibility that a second scribe took over in the copying of the beta hyparchetype, and that such a change of scribe might explain the distribution of omissions. There are other possible ways of explaining this. Since almost all the alpha-only passages occur in the **B** continuation, it may be that this part of the archetypal manuscript was in a much more rough and ready state, having revisions entered in margins and on loose sheets, so that the alpha and beta copyists each overlooked some of the additions. It must be significant that none of the alpha- and beta-only passages represent *alternative* versions, for surely this is an argument against "rolling revision"?

On the other hand, there is nothing inherently improbable about "rolling revision," as Hanna (1996), 222–3, describes it: "even after **B** version 'publication,' but before embarking on the major overhaul that produced the **C** version, Langland continued to tinker." If he thus altered his house-copy bit by bit over a period of time, this manuscript might have served the scribes of alpha and beta and the poet of **C** as copy-text at different stages of its revision. Hanna (1996), 215–29, in a discussion that makes a powerful argument for "rolling revision," offers a detailed hypothesis as to how this might have happened (esp. 223–5). It is not a new idea. Skeat (1869), xii, first suggested that beta was the earlier copy of the text, while Donaldson (1955) initially argued that the alpha copy came first, in an article that makes some shrewd points. More recent interest in the *mouvance* of texts has given added impetus to such hypotheses, though Schmidt (2008), 149–51, opposes it with considerable vehemence. The curious fact of the late entry of beta's omitted passages might be explained as a consequence of "rolling revision": the passages were not part of the text when the beta scribe had access to the house-copy, and he copied faithfully enough; but the more careless alpha scribe, making his copy at a stage when revisions had been entered, lost (by eyeskip, loose sheets that had been mislaid, or whatever) passages distributed throughout the text.

In whatever way the alpha- and beta-only passages are explained, the fact remains that both types of passages figure in the **B**-text upon which the C-poet worked, and to that extent the editor of **Bx** is justified in including them all.

This issue of the additional passages in either alpha or beta needs to be kept distinct from a matter more troubling for the editor: the variant alpha and beta readings of a word or phrase. In this case the editor is faced with *alternatives* rather than additions. Some, no doubt the majority, represent misreadings in one hyparchetype or the other, and comparison with AC versions will provide evidence of support for one or the other. However, in a small number of cases the readings of one hyparchetype will be supported by one of the other versions, and that of the other text by the other version. Alpha may thus be supported by **Ax** and beta by **Cx**, or more commonly vice versa. Since we see no evidence for contamination of either hyparchetype with the other versions, such shared readings must represent either coincidental error or authorial revision.

To take a clear example: in **Bx**.1.46, beta (L) reads:

Ac the moneye of þis molde . þat men so faste holdeth

Alpha (R) has the same line but with *kepeth* in place of *holdeth*. Such variation of synonyms looks typically scribal, except that **AC** have exactly the same line, with A agreeing with beta and C with alpha. Of course, alpha and C could share coincidental error, especially as it is not easy to see Langland as the sort of poet who would fuss over such an apparently inconsequential change. Yet the whole passage is full of such small alterations to C, especially in b-verses; indeed the very next line presents another example:

Telle me to whom Madame . þat tresore appendeth (**Bx**.1.47; so also K.1.43)

The last word corresponds to *bylongeth* in **C**. In this line, however, alpha shares the beta reading so that **Bx** is not in doubt. **Bx**.1.84 is in **A** and beta, but is dropped in alpha and **C**. Most apparent instances of **A**/beta agreements against alpha/**C** are far more trivial, with such variation as *bouȝte / he bouȝte* (**Bx**.5.225), *He is / is* (5.602), and *for / of* (5.620).

Perhaps **Bx**.10.198 provides an example of the reverse, **A**/alpha agreement against beta/**C**. **A** has a b-verse deficient in alliteration:

Leue lelly þeron ȝif þou þenke do wel (K.11.144).

Alpha's b-verse is almost identical:

Loue þou loue lelly · if þou thenke do wel (as R; F reads *þynke to*).

Beta, however, has b-verse alliteration:

Loke þow loue lelly · ȝif þe lyketh dowel.

This seems to lie behind the revised **C**-version:

Lerne for to louie yf þe like dowel (RK.11.133).

Yet there are so few instances of **A**/alpha agreements against beta/**C**, and the **A**/alpha reading is so obviously inferior, that we suppose it more likely that alpha presents a coincidental error here.

In theory the editor is presented with an insoluble problem in such cases: once "rolling revision" of individual lections is admitted, it must follow that any alpha reading could be a revision and, especially after passus 10 when the **A**-text ends, "all unique RF readings present in C could be argued to reflect the intermediate version" (Hanna [1996], 229).[5] Hanna goes on to point out that though this is a logical possibility, it is not in practice a serious problem for the editor of the **B** continuation, who must inevitably take agreement of either alpha or beta variant with **Cx** as strong evidence in its favour. Also inevitably, there may be a few occasions when the editor of **B** will be rejecting an unrevised reading and adopting a lection from the later version. Yet Hanna, who is an advocate for "rolling revision," concludes: "The poet made some extensive additions to his fair-copy version, but in doing so, he seems almost never to have queried its standing

---

5   So, too, Adams (2002), 115: "Conservative editors might see the situation as theoretically hopeless: that is, if R/F were to be regarded as embodying a distinctive, somewhat later (or earlier), authorial moment than *beta*, we would not be able to draw the line at the few large patches of apparently added or deleted materials but would have to accept every tiny pair of *alpha/beta* variants as potential evidence of fluctuating authorial purposes. Nevertheless, whatever may be true in theory, in actuality the vast majority of small variations between R/F and *beta* are readily distinguishable (i.e. not textually neutral at all)."

readings" (Hanna [1996], 229). In fact to the end of Passus 10 we find no convincing instances of A/alpha agreement against beta/C, and fewer than thirty instances of A/beta agreement against alpha/C, and many of these can easily be explained as coincidental variation.[6]

III   The Bx Witnesses

The manuscripts are described in order of their citation, LMCrWHmCG ORF, followed more briefly by those not regularly cited, YC²BmBoCotHS. Dates and dialects are from Hanna (1993), 39–40. See also Doyle (1986), 35–48.

III.1   L: Oxford, Bodleian Library, MS Laud Misc. 581, ff. 1r–91r.

Edited Hoyt N. Duggan and Ralph Hanna, PPEA, vol. 4 (2004) <http:// piers.chass.ncsu.edu/texts/L>.

s. xiv ex.; SW Worcs relict forms. Duggan-Hanna (Introduction, section III) suggest that the manuscript was actually written in London.

The text is divided by blue paraphs with blank lines between them. (There are no paraphs on f. 1r because there is a red and blue spray along the left margin.) Latin lines and words are boxed in red. The half-line is generally marked with a raised point, though with a punctus elevatus in the opening 25 lines and occasionally thereafter. The punctuation is quite often overlooked by the scribe.

L evidently offers a very careful and accurate copy of beta; in passus 6, for instance, we identify only three certain (**Bx.**6.9, 32, 207) and three probable (**Bx.**6.139, 247, 332) departures from beta, all of them minor. Sometimes (but not as often as R) the scribe is content to copy obvious nonsense (e.g. **Bx.**11.357). The scribe has corrected his own mistakes and supplied omissions at the time of copying. A supervisor has subsequently marked lines for correction with a small <+> in the margin for the attention of the original scribe, although on many occasions the correction was never made. Some of these marks apparently record objection to spellings such as *a* for *as* and *an* for *and*. Later hands have for some reason marked lines or passages with

---

6   For beta = **Ax** / alpha = **Cx**, see notes to **Bx.**1.46, 1.73, 1.84, 1.126, 1.139, 2.110, 2.156, 2.202, 3.8, 3.32, 3.156, 3.215, 5.129, 5.225, 5.617, 5.641, 6.46, 6.54, 6.83, 6.92, 6.315, 8.59, 9.10, 9.20, 10.76, 10.156, 10.185. In most of these cases we present both readings hypertextually, as described in V.3.2 below. For beta = **Cx** / alpha = **Ax**, see notes to: **Bx.**1.72, 9.132, 10.146, 10.198, 10.416. Only in the first of these cases do we think the evidence compelling enough to present both readings.

large crosses. Still mainly legible are the scribe's marginal instructions for the rubricator as a guide to passus headings, which the rubricator often abbreviated (see IV.2 below).

Schmidt (1995), lxvii-iii, argues that L provides independent witness of the B-text citing the following lines (on which see our notes): **Bx**.14.194, 275, 15.643, 16.28, 18.204, 19.38, 20.6. He postulates that L shares error with R or alpha, where other beta manuscripts offer the correct reading, but in the following lines he discusses we take L + R probably to represent **Bx**: **Bx**.5.267, 10.291 (a **Bx** error), 11.139 (possibly **Bx**), 14.116 (perhaps **Bx**), 18.41 (probably **Bx**). We suppose the following to be easy coincidental error: 13.355 (*or* for *of*), 13.402 (omission of *I* in LR, but possibly a **Bx** error), 18.208 (again omission of *I* in LR). In **Bx**.13.166 alpha and L coincidentally misread *deme* as *sen*, but the L scribe spotted the misreading and corrected it. For fuller discussion see our notes to these lines.

III.2 M: London, British Library, MS Additional 35287, ff. 1r–104r.

Edited Eric Eliason, Thorlac Turville-Petre, and Hoyt N. Duggan, PPEA, vol. 5 (2005) <http://piers.chass.ncsu.edu/texts/M>.

s. xv in.; SW Midl dialect.

The text is divided into verse paragraphs with blank spaces between (as in LWRY), but no coloured paraphs were added. Latin lines are generally boxed in red or in text ink. The original scribe usually punctuated with a mid-line raised point, but the corrector commonly altered this to a punctus elevatus for the first half of the text (up to the middle of passus 13).

M's textual relationships are more complex than the stemma can indicate. For much of the poem its text is relatively independent of other beta witnesses. A good example is **Bx**.5.209 *ware* LMR, supported by **AC**, against *chaffare* in beta1. Yet there are sporadic indications as early as passus 13 and 14 that M inherited errors shared with beta1; see e.g. notes to **Bx**.13.78, 13.296, 13.314, 14.1, 14.158, 16.53. In the last four passus M switches exemplar to a beta2 copy, showing affiliations with CrWHm. Its text has subsequently been very extensively revised, with corrections from a beta2 text and perhaps other copies as well, although the majority of its revisions are spelling changes to bring the forms into line with those used by sophisticated London scribes such as the W scribe (Turville-Petre [2002], 41–65). For the argument that the corrector is the W scribe, see Horobin (2009). Crucially for our purposes, M is independent of L, so that they cannot inherit wrong readings against correct readings in other beta manuscripts. They can, of course, and frequently do, uniquely share right readings with alpha against all other beta manuscripts.

III.3   Cr: The printed editions of Robert Crowley, STC 19906, 19907a, 19907. London 1550.

References are to the first edition (Cr^1). Hailey (2007), 143–70, discusses the alterations in Crowley's second and third editions (listing them on pp. 165–70).

Crowley makes it clear in his Preface that he has consulted manuscripts of the C-version, and the lines he quotes (RK.8.348–9) share the readings of the early 16th-century manuscript, London, BL Royal 18 B.xvii (a text of the P family). For instance, he adds a C-text line after **Bx**.3.30.

Crowley uses syntactic punctuation, with a comma to mark pauses within the line, and sometimes full-stops at the end of the line. The line is indented at the start of a paragraph. The text is the best representative of beta2, but with some contamination from **C**.[7]

III.4   W: Cambridge, Trinity College, MS B.15.17, ff. 1r–130v.

Edited Thorlac Turville-Petre and Hoyt N. Duggan, PPEA, vol. 2 (2000) <http://piers.chass.ncsu.edu/texts/W>.

s. xiv ex. London.

Paraphs (more than in any other text) alternate in red and blue, with a blank line between paragraphs, as in LMRY. Latin lines and words are in enlarged script and usually enclosed in a red box. The scribe uses a very regular raised point in mid line.

W is a fully professional metropolitan production. The presentation of the text, including its spellings and grammatical forms, conforms very systematically to the best London practice, as in the Ellesmere-Hengwrt scribe of the *Canterbury Tales* (see PPEA, vol. 2 [2000], Introduction, Linguistic Description). Horobin and Mooney (2004), 65–112, argue that the scribe of W and Ellesmere-Hengwrt are one and the same, Adam Pinkhurst. For reconsiderations see Roberts (2011), Warner (2015). W's text is a reasonably good beta2 copy, though readings peculiar to W are not infrequent.

---

7 See Hailey (2008), 153 and n. 25.

III.5   Hm, Hm²: San Marino, Huntington Library, MS 128 (olim Ashburnham 130), ff.96r–v, 95r (Hm²), 113r–205r (Hm).

Edited Michael Calabrese, Hoyt N. Duggan, and Thorlac Turville-Petre, PPEA, vol. 6 (2008) <http://piers.chass.ncsu.edu/texts/Hm>.

s. xv in. SW Warwicks. (*LALME*, LP 8040).

There are two main text scribes, hand1 copies up to **Bx**.2.210 and hand2 the rest. Paraphs are in red and blue; the scribes do not leave blank lines. Latin lines are written in text ink without boxing or underlining. Hand1 begins with a raised point at mid line but switches to punctus elevatus at **Bx**.P.177; hand2 generally uses a raised point.

Hm belongs to the beta2 group, with Cr and W. The scribes are often careless, and have corrected their own work quite heavily. In addition, the rubricator of the manuscript has made numerous corrections, and a corrector or correctors has made hundreds of alterations to spelling (see Turville-Petre [2002], 41–65]. A major disruption has caused the reversal of **Bx**.11.445-12.93 and 11.113–226.

III.6   C: Cambridge, Cambridge University Library, MS Dd.1.17, part 3, ff. 1r–31r.

s. xiv/xv.

Latin lines are in enlarged script and often underlined in red. Paraphs are in alternating red and blue. The mid-line punctuation is generally a raised point. With GOC²YBmBoCot, C is a beta4 text.

III.7   G: Cambridge, Cambridge University Library, MS Gg.4.31, ff. 1r–101r.

Edited Judith Jefferson, PPEA, vol. 8 (2011) <http://piers.chass.ncsu.edu/texts/G>.

s. xvi¹.

In later passus, particularly 19–20, the scribe uses a mid-line solidus, and in earlier passus some have been added in brown ink. There are no paraphs, but enlarged capitals, used at the beginning of each passus, also occur fourteen times at significant junctures.

The text is contaminated from **A** and perhaps also from **C**, with such contaminated readings sometimes in clusters: e.g. **Bx.**1.8 *wilne*, G and **A** *kepe*; 1.98 *transgressores*, G and **A** (and the P family of **C**) *trespacers*; 1.102 *wolden al,* G and **A** *asketh þe*; 1.210 *þe*, G and **AC** *syght off thes*; 5.509 *fresshe*, G and the X family of **C** *flessche &*. Table of contents on 101v–103r (Jefferson, 2010).

III.8   O: Oxford, Oriel College, MS 79, part 1, ff. 1r–88r.

Edited Katherine Heinrichs, PPEA, vol. 3 (2004) <http://piers.chass.ncsu.edu/texts/O>.

s. xv[1]. N Herts (*LALME*, LP 6550).

Latin lines are underlined in red and are sometimes placed in the margin, especially after **Bx.**10.119. Paraphs are indicated by "cc" in ff. 1r–17v (up to **Bx.**5.80), sporadically in ff. 18r–38v, and after that not at all. The scribe uses a mid-line punctus elevatus.

III.9   R: London, BL MS Lansdowne 398, ff. 77r–80v, and Oxford, Bodleian Library, MS Rawlinson Poetry 38, ff. 1r–101v.

Edited Robert Adams, PPEA, vol. 7 (2011) <http://piers.chass.ncsu.edu/texts/R>.

s. xiv ex.; SW Worcs relict forms.

Samuels (1985), 232–47, notes its "south-west Worcestershire dialect" relict forms. Hanna (1996), 40, supposes "several stages of copying; in succession: SW Worcestershire, London, Suffolk." It might be observed that this mix could have been achieved by a Suffolk scribe copying an authorial blend of London and SWMidl. dialects, and need not imply a long chain of copies. See Horobin (2017). The punctuation is generally a mid-line punctus elevatus and often a punctus at the end of the line. There are some paraphs in alternating red and blue, but many are indicated only by "cc". A blank space is left between paragraphs (as in LMWY).

R is a professionally produced manuscript by an extremely literal-minded scribe providing a very accurate copy of alpha and rarely tempted to improve on his exemplar, to the extent that he will copy nonsense (e.g. **Bx.**10.291, 17.110), and let an implication of homosexuality stand (**Bx.**5.594). Unfortunately the manuscript has lost the following passages:

Bx.P.1–124, 1.142–2.41, 18.428–20.26. In his edition (2011), Adams provides detailed annotations on the relationships of R's text.

III.10   F: Oxford, Corpus Christi College, MS 201, ff. 1r–93r.

Edited Robert Adams, et al., PPEA, vol. 1 (2000) <http://piers.chass.ncsu.edu/texts/F>.

s. xiv/xv; Essex (*LALME*, LP 6110).

F is written by an Essex scribe, using vellum of very variable quality with many singletons, perhaps indicating a limited supply in the area. Yet it was not a cheap production, since it uniquely has an illustration within the first capital. Paraphs are first in red and green, later in red and blue, others indicated but not executed. The scribe uses a mid-line solidus. He also copied the *Prick of Conscience*, fragments of which are preserved as Ushaw College, Durham, MS 50 (see PPEA, vol. 1 [2000], Appendix, and Doyle [2000]).

The text of *Piers* is a heavily revised version of alpha, so much altered that Skeat discarded it. For a characterisation of the work of the F-Redactor who produced the text that the F scribe copied, see PPEA, vol. 1 (2000), Introduction. The F-Redactor divides the poem into 16 passus, and by discarding the two inner dreams has ten dreams instead of eight (PPEA, vol. 1 [2000], Presentation of Text: Levels of Inscription [4] The F Redaction, chart). We accept the argument made by Schmidt (1995), lxiii–iv, that F is at times contaminated from a text of **A**; **Bx**.1.75 provides a clear example. Contamination is particularly noticeable in Passus 8, with whole lines imported from **A**; see the note to **Bx**.8.18. This, together with the general character of F's text, makes it very difficult to rely on F's agreements with **A** as evidence of alpha readings in sections where R is lost. Schmidt also points to F's line following **Bx**.P.94, which Kane and Donaldson, p. 221 agree is from **A**. In Passus 1, from about l. 177 to the end, is another section where it appears probable that F has derived many readings from an **A**-text, but since R is lost here, it is possible that F presents the alpha reading, which of course might be **Bx**. There are also some indications that F may be contaminated from **C**; e.g. **Bx**.13.363, and for a fuller discussion see V.3.2 below. F tends to "improve" the alliteration, e.g. **Bx**.3.6, 3.10 and (an extreme example) **Bx**.5.92. Invented lines are added for emphasis: an unusually fine example follows **Bx**.5.112.[8]

---

8 For a list of added lines in F, see Kane and Donaldson, pp. 222–3.

III.11   Texts not Regularly Cited

We have relied on Kane and Donaldson's collations of the following texts:

Y: Cambridge, Newnham College, MS 4 (the Yates-Thompson manuscript), ff. 1r–104r.
s. $xv^{2/4}$. London, with underlying N Oxon forms.

C^2: Cambridge, Cambridge University Library, MS Ll.4.14.
s. xv^{2-4}. Ely (*LALME*, LP 673).

Bm: London, BL MS Additional 10574, ff. 1r–99v.
s. xv^{1-4}.

Bo: Oxford, Bodleian Library, MS Bodley 814, ff. 1r–92v.
s. xv^{1-4}.

Cot: London, BL MS Cotton Caligula A.xi, part 2, ff. 170r–286r.
s. xv^{1-4}.

    Bm, Bo, and Cot are so closely related that they are referred to by the common sigil B. Their B-text begins at passus 3; before that their source is a C-text, with a passage also from an A-text.

H: London, BL MS Harley 3954, ff. 92r–123v.
s. xv med. Norfolk (*LALME*, LP 638).

    After **Bx.**5.128 this is an A-text, and its B-text is heavily contaminated from **A**. Schmidt (2008), 135–6, rather oddly calls it "a significant witness" to **B**, while admitting that its "superior" readings could be derived from **A**. At any rate it is of no use for establishing **Bx**.

S: Tokyo, Toshiyuki Takamiya MS 23 (*olim* London, Sion College MS Arc. L. 40).
s.xvi med.

IV   The Character of Bx

IV.1   Language

We can determine very little of the language of the archetype and have made no attempt to reconstruct it here. Scribes can never be trusted to have followed the forms and spellings of their exemplars. Indeed the scribe of W has been shown to have imposed with considerable consistency and intelligence a system reflecting the best London usage (PPEA, vol. 2 [2000], Intro. Linguistic Description; Horobin and Mooney [2004]). The scribe very regularly writes final <-e> for nouns and adjectives where historically justified, distinguishes commonly between infinitives ending in <-e> before a consonant and <-en> before a vowel or <h> so that the syllable is retained, uses the <y-> prefix for past participles, and so on (PPEA, vol. 2 [2000], Linguistic Description, 2.1, 2.2, 2.4, 2.5.1, 2.5.15). Whether or not this restores Langland's own usage and his metre, the system does not appear to be that transmitted by **Bx** (see Duggan [1990], 157–91, esp. 184 n. 61, 188–90.) The careful scribes of L and R certainly took no such liberties; but even if they did reproduce most of the forms of their exemplars, these can represent no more than the usages of the alpha and beta copies, and not necessarily the archetype from which these copies derived.

However, forms that differ from a scribe's usual repertoire may go back to his exemplar, and, where such forms are shared by beta and alpha (in particular L and R), they probably derive from **Bx**. Thus Samuels (1985), 241, observed patterns of distribution in the forms of *any / eny, ȝif / if, come / cam, byȝunde / byȝende* in L and R, concluding that these "must be presumed to be archetypal", and on the basis of spot-checks, Duggan and Hanna (2004), Introduction III.1, confirm these findings. Again, it is telling that *-ende* as the present participle ending only occurs on the same three occasions in L and in R, at **Bx**.17.50, 212, and 20.100 (see note to **Bx**.17.50).

Samuels (1985), 232–47; (1986), 40; (1988), 70–85, argued that Langland's dialect can be placed in SW Worcestershire on the basis of a number of relict spellings, and if this is the case (for reservations see Hanna [1993], 5–8), such forms are necessarily among those transmitted by **Bx**. Some of these can be established as authorial where they satisfy the requirements of an alliterative pattern. We give three examples of words in **Bx** where this consideration applies: words for "she", "they", and "church".[9]

The form *he/heo* occasionally contributes to the alliteration of the line, and in such cases it must be a relict spelling. L and some other scribes write this in alliterative position in place of their regular *she*: at **Bx**.1.75 (with MR), at 3.29 (with MRW), and at 5.546 (with WR, and with M corrected to *she*). At **Bx**.18.175 alliteration requires *he*, as in alpha; but this has been altered in L by the addition of the initial *s-*. In **Bx**.18.156 alliteration supports alpha's *he* over beta's *she*. In **Bx**.20.198 only R has the alliterating form with *h-*. Evidently **Bx** had *h-* forms in all these lines. Where such forms appear in non-alliterating positions, however, they may or may not be archetypal. L has non-alliterating *he(o)* at **Bx**.1.144, 5.317, 5.645–6, 9.56, and 18.170, shared with at least one other ms., sometimes with M revised to *she*. In general, alpha seems to have written *he(o)* for "she" more often than beta. The form is common in R up to the end of passus 5 – it appears eight times between 5.219 and 256, for example – but *heo* is not used after 5.648,

---

9 For fuller analysis of the archetypal language, see now Horobin (2017).

though *he(e)* appears sporadically after this point. This probably means that R was at first copying out the form of his exemplar, later shifting to that in his active repertoire (Benskin and Laing [1981], 66), which suggests that the form was common at least in alpha.

L uses *hij* for "they" on ten occasions:

Bx line	hij	they	Comment
P.43	L	MCrWHmCGOF	M corrected; R lost
P.66 allit	LWC original M	HmGOF, corrected M	Cr *I*; R lost
1.59 allit	LMCrWHmC	GO	R *heo*, F *he*
1.129	LC	MCrWHmGORF	M corrected
1.195 allit	LMWC	CrHmGOF	R lost
3.341	LMCR	CrWHmG	O *he*, F *hem*
5.116	LMCR	CrWHmGO	F *hem*
6.15	LM	CrWHmCGOF	R *a*
9.172	LC	CrMCrWGO	Hm *her neyther*; alpha lost
10.336	LMR	WHmCOF	Cr *the*, G *om*

Bx must have used the <h-> form in the three lines it alliterates, and it seems reasonable to suppose that L, whose own form is *þei*, reproduces beta on all ten occasions. L is usually supported by M (twice corrected to *thei*), but M uses it nowhere else, implying that beta only used *hij* on those ten occasions. The pattern in W is characteristic of the carefully regularising practice of that scribe: he has *hij* only where it alliterates, otherwise altering to *þei*. The form is rarely used in alpha. R has *hij* just three times (3.341, 5.116, 10.336), and once (6.15) has the reduced form *a*. In 9.119 alpha has *he* (perhaps by misunderstanding). Otherwise F never has the *h*- form, and the evidence suggests that alpha generally avoided it. In 20.301 all manuscripts have alliterating *he* (F is absent), though the scribes probably misunderstood it as a sg. form.

Significant patterns emerge in the distributions of *chirche* (OE), in its various spellings, and the synonymous *kirke* (ON). These occur the following number of times in the six most important manuscripts:

Sigil	cherch-	chirch-	chyrch-	church-	kirk-	kyrk-	kerk-
L	56	2	0	0	18	3	0
M	0	1	2	56	7	12	0
W	2	57	0	0	20	0	0
Hm	73	0	2	0	0	5	0
R	64	0	0	0	2	2	3
F	2	62	1	0	2	7	0

Kirke is a word of the Danelaw, restricted to northern and eastern dialects. Chaucer, Gower and *William of Palerne* never use it; *The Wars of Alexander* and the *Gawain*-poet never use *cherche*. Langland uses *kirke* as an alliterative convenience. L has it 21 times, in four cases in final non-alliterating position as *holy-kirke* agreeing with MCrW (15.204, 401, 542,

19.455). As can be seen above, F often avoids it, but unusually has *kyrke* in final position in **Bx**.19.2, where other manuscripts have *cherche*. R is strongly
resistant, and almost always substitutes *cherche*, though in 6.150 R uniquely
has *kerkes* in final position. Of the beta witnesses, Hm avoids *kirke* (once
it has the odd spelling *kurke*). It is also evident that scribes are particular
about the spelling of "church": M has the SW form *churche*, W and F the
Midland/London form *chirche*, and LHmR *cherche*, a Midland form found
especially in eastern counties (*LALME* 1, dot maps 384–6). We cannot identify the spelling used by **Bx** for "church," but we can conclude that many
scribes were uncomfortable with the word *kirke* and tended to substitute
ch-.[10]

No other scribes, not even the careful L and R, are systematic in these
respects. The editors of L point out that the scribe often writes <-e> as a
marker of length in the preceding vowel, so that it no longer has a grammatical function (PPEA, vol. 4 [2004], Intro. III.3.1, Metrical Considerations).
In R adjectives tend to end in <-e> whether or not it is historically justified.

The evidence suggests that L and R reproduced many of the spelling
features of their exemplars, beta and alpha, with some fidelity, and that they
may be closer to the spellings of **Bx** than other copies. It may also be (as
suggested by R's treatment of *heo* and beta's avoidance) that alpha's language
was more distinctively SW Midlands than beta's.

IV.2 Passus Structure and Headings

The **B** witnesses apart from F are unanimous in their division of the poem
into a prologue and 20 passus. Each passus has a heading, and though the
precise wording of these headings varies from one manuscript to another,
we find good evidence to believe that the marginal guidewords left by the
scribe of L for the rubricator originate with **Bx**. From Passus 3 onwards the
rubricator has abbreviated these instructions. The editors of L say: "Presumably, the guides record the form of the exemplar, edited later by the scribe
when he went through the manuscript with red ink to add the actual headings" (PPEA, vol. 4 [2004], I.6). Agreement with other early manuscripts,
in particular M and W, makes it clear that these instructions represent the
headings of beta, but evidence for the headings of alpha is more sketchy:
F follows a unique and idiosyncratic scheme and R misnumbers passus 13–
18 and has lost the headings for the Prologue and passus 19–20. However
there is evidence that R shared the same rubrication scheme with beta,[11]
so this scheme must go back to **Bx**. Furthermore, the "split rubrics" for

---

10 Cr has only the forms *church-* (38x), *kirk-* (12x), and *kyrk-* (31x). The prevalence of the
ON derived forms is noteworthy in such a late copy.

11 See Cornelius (2015).

passus 15 and 19 suggest that they, and by implication the scheme in **Bx**, are authorial.[12]

The headings are set out in Adams (1985), 216–31, and Benson and Blanchfield (1997), *passim*. Below we revise their descriptions of the ten copies LMCrWHmCGORF, in particular to include the guidewords still legible in M.

The heading to the Prologue in L is no longer legible, but Skeat read it as *Incipit liber de Petro Plowman*. F has *Incipit pers þe plowman* in a later hand. R is lost, and most manuscripts including MW have no heading. Hence **Bx** is irrecoverable, and we follow copy-text as read by Skeat for want of anything better.

Passus primus de visione: L (rubric and guide), and MWHmCrC. O omits *de visione*, while R adds *petri plowman*. F has the rubric *Explicit passus Primus Petri Plouhman . Incipit Passus Secundus*. G, which has incipits only for Passus 8, 15 and 20, has *Explicit primus passus de visione* at the end of the Prologue, and continues in the same form, one step ahead of the other texts except for F, up to the explicit for passus 7. L is thus reliably beta here, challenged only by R which may represent alpha.

Passus secundus de visione vt supra: L (rubric and guide), and MWC; HmCr lack *vt supra* here and onwards, and O has merely *Secundus Passus*. R is lost, while F has *Explicit passus secundus de visione Petri Plouhman / Incipit Passus Tercius*, and its incipits continue in this fashion.

Passus tercius de visione vt supra: L guidewords and W, and probably beta. (HmCrC lack *vt supra*). L's rubric is merely *Passus iijus*, as in M which has indications of the erasure of the guidewords. O has *Passus tercius de visione* in the guide, but not including the last two words in the rubric. R has the fullest heading: *Passus tercius de visione petri plowman vt supra & cetera*, which is perhaps alpha.

Passus iiijus de visione vt supra: L guidewords and MW (with *quartus* for *iiijus*), and probably beta. (HmCrC lack *vt supra*). L's rubric is abbreviated to *Passus iiijus*. R again includes *petri plowman*.

Passus quintus de visione vt supra: L guidewords (though with *v* for *quintus*) and W, and probably beta. L's rubric and MHmCrC lack *vt supra*. R again includes *petri plowman*.

Passus vjus de visione vt supra: L guidewords (rubricated *Passus vjus*), MW and R; evidently therefore **Bx**. (HmCrC lack *vt supra*).

Passus vijus de visione vt supra: L guidewords (rubricated as *Passus vijus*), WC and R; evidently therefore **Bx**. (MHmCr lack *vt supra*).

The variants in the *Visio* headings, Passus 1–7, are minor. There is always good support for L's guidewords as the beta headings, and R, perhaps

---

12 See Burrow (2008).

representing alpha, differs only by including *petri plowman*, except in Passus 6–7 where it is identical to beta.

Passus 8 and 9 cause difficulties. It seems clear that the heading *primus de Dowel* for Passus 9 is archetypal, but some scribes have already used that label for passus 8. Therefore Hm and G (in its explicit) call Passus 9 *secundus de Dowel*, and continue numeration in that fashion until Passus 14 *septimus de Dowell*. But in **Bx** passus 8 is both the end of the Visio and "the beginning of the search (*inquisicio prima*) for Dowel" and passus 9 is "the first passus of Dowel" (see Burrow [2008]). O has the passus numbers only, to which R adds *de visione vt supra*. C has the passus number, sometimes with *de visione vt supra* (8, 9, 14), sometimes with *vt supra* (10, 11), sometimes on its own (12, 13).

Passus viijus de visione & hic explicit & incipit inquisicio prima de Dowel: L guidewords.[13] MCr lack *& hic explicit*; L's rubric and WHm have instead *Passus viijus de visione & primus de Dowel*. R's rubric has been overwritten to read *Passus octauus de visione petri plowhman. Incipit Dowel. Dobet. & Dobest*, but originally seems to have read *Passus octauus vt supra*, as does C.[14] G has at the end *Explicit primus passus de dowell*, and continues in this style until Passus 14.

Passus ixus de visione vt supra & primus de Dowel: These are perhaps the very faded guidewords in L, though the editors are rightly more cautious in their reading. The words have support from Cr (which however does not include *vt supra*), and from W, despite its confused *Passus ixus de visione vt supra & primus de Dobet*. Hm, logically, has *Passus nonus de visione et secundus de dowel*. CR have *Passus nonus de visione vt supra*, with M dropping the last two words. L's rubric is simply *Passus nonus*.

Passus xus de visione & ijus de dowel: L guidewords and MCrW. Hm has the same, but advancing by one as described above. L's rubric is *Passus xus*, as O. R has *Passus xus de visione vt supra*.

Passus xjus: L's rubric and guide, as well as WOC, though this may represent an abbreviation of **Bx**. MCr add *de visione*, and Cr continues in this style until Passus 14, but M drops this addition henceforth. As before, R adds *de visione vt supra*, and continues in this style throughout, and Hm has *Passus xjus de visione et iiijus de do weel*.

Passus xijus: L's rubric and guide, as well as MWOC. CrR have their standard additions, and Hm continues as before.

Passus xiijus: L's guide (*Passus terciodecimus* as rubric), as well as MWOC. Cr has its standard additions, but R miscounts from this point, losing one. Hm continues as before.

---

13 On *inquisicio* see Hanna (2005), 243–304, esp. 246–7.

14 Sean Taylor argues that the alteration is in the hand of the scribe of F in "The F Scribe and the R Manuscript of *Piers Plowman* B," *English Studies* 77 (1996): 530–48.

Passus xiiijus: L's rubric and guide, as well as MWO. CrR have their standard additions, and C has the same as R (which continues to miscount). Hm continues as before.

Passus xvus finit dowel & incipit dobet: L's rubric and guide (which lacks *&*). WHmCr and M's guide have the same with minor variations; M's rubric and O have merely *Passus xv*. R, miscounting as before, continues with *Passus xiiij de visione vt supra*.

Passus xvjus & primus de dobet: L's rubric and guide, WCr, and M's guidewords. All these count this as the first Dobet passus, regarding Passus 15 as transitional between the Dowel and Dobet sections. However, HmG both refer to this as the second passus of Dobet. CO and M's rubric abbreviate to *Passus xvjus*. R continues as before.

Passus xvijus & secundus de dobet: L's guide, and W (adding *& c* after the passus number). L's rubric and MOC abbreviate to *Passus xvijus*, to which Cr adds *de visione*; HmG continue as before, but from here R miscounts by two (corrected by a later hand adding *j*): *Passus xvus de visione vt supra*.

Passus xviijus & tercius de dobet: L's guide, and W (adding *& c* after the passus number). What is legible of M's guide suggests it had the same, though the LMCO rubrics abbreviate to *Passus xviijus*, to which Cr adds *de visione*. HmG and R continue as before.

Passus xixus & explicit dobet & incipit dobest: L's guide and W. With this "split rubric" cf. passus 15 and note. M's guide is not visible. L's rubric and OC have just *Passus xixus*, to which Cr adds *de visione*. R is lost. Hm has *Passus vus et vltimus de do bet. Hic incipit passus Ius de do best*, and G has the first part of this as an explicit to passus 18.

Passus xxus de visione & primus de dobest: L's guide and W. L's rubric, M's guide and CrC drop *de visione*. M's rubric and O abbreviate to *Passus xxus*. G has *Incipit primus passus de dobest*, and Hm, with its usual logic, has *Passus ijus et vltimus de do best*. R is lost.

At the end of the text LMWGOCC[2]Y have: *Explicit hic dialogus petri plowman*.[15] There is no serious opposition to this as the beta explicit: Hm has *Explicit visio petri ploughman*. R's *Passus ijus de dobest* (both as guide and rubric) is, as Adams (1985), 214 n. 11, says, "an anomaly," but it appears to be authentically **Bx** for all that, since L also has in the left margin below the last line the guidewords *[Pass]us ijus de Dobest*. It seems that **Bx**, perhaps receiving his copy passus by passus, wrote the guide in expectation of a further section.[16] Both L and R copied the words from their hyparchetypes; L, realising that it made no sense, did not follow it when it came to rubrica-

---

15 On the significance of the description *dialogus*, see Hanna (2005), 243–304, esp. 246–7.

16 This must also have been the case with the C-text manuscript Laud Misc 656 (late 14th c.) which has as its explicit: *Explicit passus secundus de dobest incipit passus tercius*. Seven other manuscripts of C also end with *explicit passus secundus*. See Adams, *YLS* 8 (1994), 84, and Cornelius (2015).

tion; R, acting as so often without thought, rubricated it. The implication is that LR are both very close to **Bx**, and also that L had some other source for his rubricated explicit which became that standard in beta copies. On our principle of following the guidewords in L, we adopt this as the first explicit, and follow that with the rubricated explicit.

IV.3 Paragraphs

All **B** witnesses have some indication of paragraphing.[17] The archetype evidently had paraph signs reinforced by blank lines between paragraphs, as in LWYR, though in R the paraphs have often been left unrubricated. The same arrangement was planned for M, which has the blank lines, though the paraphs are not usually executed. Hm has paraphs but does not leave blank lines. O has "cc" marks at the start, but progressively fewer as the text proceeds. G has sporadic enlarged capitals. Cr has paragraph indents, frequent in Prol. (21 times, corresponding most often to W), but much fewer thereafter. Paragraphs vary in frequency from manuscript to manuscript; figures for Passus 5–7, assembled from Benson and Blanchfield (1997), 316, are: R 257, W 246, L 223, Hm 214, M 209, C 189, Y 184, F 171. From this it can be seen that R and its alpha partner F vary considerably, not so surprisingly in view of F's recasting of the passus structure. R and W have more paragraphs than other manuscripts, with W using them to emphasise the other aspects of his spacious display. L and M are close, both in total number and in position, suggesting, as in other respects, that their paragraphing is a reliable indication of beta's. What does not emerge from the figures, but is very striking when the positioning is examined, is that L's paragraphs are almost invariably confirmed by R's, though, since R has more of them, the reverse is not true. As a result, LR agreement is, as in other aspects of the text, a secure witness to the paragraphing of **Bx**.[18] Where L is not matched by R, there is often an explanation. Both L and R tend to lose a paraph at the top of the page, since there is no blank line to indicate to the rubricator that a paraph is intended. Rather less explicably, R also tends to miss a space and a paraph before the last line on the page; presumably the scribe thought there was no point leaving a blank line so near the foot. R, following alpha if F's witness is anything to go by, tends not to begin a paragraph with "And" where beta has it. Either might represent **Bx**. R less often has a paraph following a Latin line where beta has it. This might be explained by a scribe leaving a gap after the Latin line to allow for red boxing, as in W, so that a rubricator might assume a paraph was needed.

---

17 For discussion of the functions of paragraphs see Burrow, "Punctuation" (2014). For a listing of paraphs, see Benson and Blanchfield (1997), 238–414.

18 See Robert Adams, "The Kane-Donaldson Edition of *Piers Plowman*: Eclecticism's Ultima Thule," *TEXT* 16 (2006): 131–41, at p. 137.

IV.4   Punctuation

The only thing that can be said with certainty about the punctuation of **Bx** is that it marked the caesura, for all manuscripts of **B** have mid-line punctuation (G only sporadically); see Burrow, "Punctuation" (2014). However, the marks used vary between a solidus (as F), a punctus elevatus (as O), and a raised point. R consistently has a mid-line punctus elevatus, perhaps representing alpha, and alpha perhaps also marked line-ends with a point, as R does; but most beta manuscripts have no regular punctuation at line-end. Crowley uses syntactic punctuation, usually a comma, but the manuscripts have it only rarely, and we have not often found it to be archetypal. For details of L's punctuation see V.2.3.

IV.5   Latin Lines

In all manuscripts except Cot the Latin lines, and sometimes individual Latin words, are distinguished in some way, with underlining in black or red, or enclosing in a box, and sometimes written red or in enlarged textura. In LMWR the lines are boxed in red ink and often written in display script, so that it is likely these features were inherited from **Bx**.

IV.6   Alliteration

Our survey of alliterative patterns in all 7217 lines of **Bx** (excluding those entirely or mainly in Latin) shows the expected great preponderance of the "normative" pattern aa/ax. We found this in 5796 lines, 80% of the whole. For the rest, the commonest patterns were as follows:

> aaa/ax 291 lines
> ax/ax 219 lines
> aa/aa 199 lines
> xa/ax 198 lines
> aa/xx 161 lines
> aaa/xx 153 lines
> aa/xa 71 lines.

The frequencies for rare types are: aa/bb 43 lines, xa/aa 26, ax/aa 19, ax/xa 3, aaa/xa 2. There are also 26 lines in which we could see no alliterative pattern at all.

    No two such surveys can be expected to arrive at quite the same results. Although the majority of **Bx** lines show clear and indisputable patterns of alliteration, a sizeable minority are open to more than one possible scansion. **Bx**.19.331 reads "And grace gaue hym þe crosse . with þe croune of þornes." We recorded this as xa/ax, with alliteration on *crosse* and *croune*. Schmidt's text follows **Bx**, but, because he allows what he calls "cognative" alliteration between /g/ and /k/, he scans the line aaa/ax: Schmidt (2008), 460. Like Schmidt, Kane-Donaldson reject xa/ax, as a pattern that Langland did not allow; but, because they do not accept Schmidt's cognative alliterations, they conjecture *garland* for *croune*, giving aa/ax (KD.19.321).[19] For editors of **Bx**, issues concerning the poet's own metrical usage arise only occasionally, as one factor in choosing between manuscript alternatives; but, in order to determine the archetypal patterns, they have to decide what alliterations to recognise. The present editors have allowed those between vowels and /h/, /f/ and /v/, /s/ and /ʃ/, and /w/ and /hw/, but not that between /f/ and /θ/, accepted by both Kane and Donaldson, pp. 132–3, and Schmidt, *The Clerkly Maker: Langland's Poetic Art* (Cambridge, 1987), pp. 40–1 and n. 69; and like Kane and Donaldson, we reject Schmidt's cognative alliterations between voiceless and voiced /p/ and /b/, /t/ and /d/, and /k/ and /g/.

Issues of a different kind arise with those lines that have, or appear to have, three alliterating staves in their first half. We have recorded 153 lines with aaa/xx, having no alliteration after the mid-line pointing. This pattern (generally accepted as authorial) raises no problems: examples are **Bx**.15.383, "Now failleth þe folke of þe flode . and of þe londe bothe," and 19.27, "That knyȝte kynge conqueroure . may be o persone." However, where alliteration is present after the caesura, among the 291 lines here recorded as aaa/ax, there may be uncertainties of interpretation. In many cases it may seem sufficiently clear that the line does indeed have three alliterating staves in its a-verse. Examples are **Bx**.15.440, "Grace sholde growe & be grene . þorw her good lyuynge," or 17.83, "And spes sparklich hym spedde . spede if he myȝte." But what is one to make of a line such as **Bx**.16.7, "Þe blosmes beth boxome speche . and benygne lokynge"? Normal sentence stress would not accent *beth* in this context, so we have registered the line as aa/ax.[20] There are many doubtful cases where it is not easy to decide whether all three alliterating words can claim metrical recognition, and our high count of 291 aaa/ax lines certainly includes many lines that would be read as aa/ax by those who favour two-stress scansion for such so-called "extended" a-verses.

IV.7   Meter

Duggan (1987), 41–70, recapitulates the Metrical Rules that he had identified in b-verses of classical alliterative verse, and lists lines from **Bx** that do not accord to these patterns (and see Duggan [2009]). Rule 5 states that the b-verse requires between four and eight syllables and that one of the dips preceding either lift must be strong and one must be weak. A weak dip

---

19 On xa/ax see Burrow (2011), and on ax/ax see Burrow (2013).

20 On sentence stress in relation to alliterative verse, see Ad Putter, Judith Jefferson, and Myra Stokes, *Studies in the Metre of Alliterative Verse* (Oxford, 2007), pp. 145–216.

is of one syllable, a strong dip is of two or more. In contravention to this rule are archetypal lines with two strong dips: e.g. **Bx**.P.56, P.175, P.203, 1.49, 1.159, 1.161, 162 etc. (Duggan [1987], n. 4). B-verses of the form x / x / (x) are inherently uncommon, since Langland tends to write longer lines than other poets; Duggan identifies 15.413, *in mysbileue*, as archetypal, and another example is discussed below, V.3.5.

Scribes using the forms of their own dialect can often alter the syllable-count of their exemplar, by dropping or supplying an *-e(n)* ending, adopting a syncopated form of a word for the full form or vice versa, and so on. It is often impossible to be sure of the forms of **Bx**, but agreement of the most reliable manuscripts, LMR, is a guide. From this it appears that **Bx** happily transmitted b-verses that contravene Metrical Rule 5. Many of the forms of W are unsupported by LMR and, whether or not they "improve" the metre, they are unlikely to be those of **Bx**; it seems clear that the highly professional London scribe of W has adopted the forms used by metropolitan scribes of Chaucer and Gower and by Hoccleve. It is these forms that we can observe the corrector inserting into M's original copying.

V   Editorial Procedures

V.1   Choice of Copy-Text

Our choice of L as copy-text is really inevitable. It was the basis for Skeat's edition, who was so impressed by the quality of its text and the nature of its corrections that he thought it might even be written by Langland himself, a view which he later retracted (Brewer [1996], 141 and note). Kane-Donaldson, followed by Schmidt, based themselves on W, while admitting that it had more errors than L (Kane and Donaldson, p. 214). They chose W because of its consistent spelling and systematic grammar (Kane and Donaldson, pp. 214–15), although they admitted that "the ideal basic manuscript or copy-text is the one which first provides the closest dialectal and chronological approximation to the poet's language, and then second, most accurately reflects his original in substantive readings" (Kane and Donaldson, p. 214). Later study suggests that the sophistication of W's hand is matched by the sophisticated accidentals of his text, which has been processed for a London audience by imposing standard London spellings and Chaucerian grammar (see PPEA, vol. 2 [2000], Introduction, Linguistic Description; Horobin and Mooney [2004]). The only alternative copy-text is R, but its major losses make it an impractical basis.

We believe that both L and W (and perhaps R as well) are London productions, but L is on a much more modest scale with none of W's consistently imposed spelling system and grammar. While it cannot be relied on to represent the forms of **Bx**, still less of Langland himself, it is clear that many forms significant for alliteration and metre are well preserved. Thus Langland uses the <g-> forms of "give, forgive" for alliteration and the SW Midlands <ȝ-> forms elsewhere; of the fifty occasions on which L has the <g> spelling, all but one alliterate, and that one (**Bx**.19.341) is spelt *gaf* in all manuscripts and therefore must be archetypal. In contrast, Hm very frequently, and W quite often, use the <ȝ> forms in lines alliterating on /g/. Parallels with R, who also preserves many of the spellings of his exemplar, reinforce the impression that L accurately represents **Bx** in this respect. Though the spelling system of L is not an entirely consistent representative of a single dialect, it is probable that **Bx** was also inconsistent, and likely enough that Langland himself, as a London immigrant, wrote forms reflecting his new environs as well as his native dialect.

Copy-text is therefore the text of L as presented in PPEA, vol. 4 (2004). All alterations to the text are enclosed in square brackets, though omissions are not marked. Every emendation is discussed in a note, except for most corrections of straightforward miswriting, such as *tran[s]gressores* in **Bx**.1.98.

V.2 Textual Presentation

V.2.1 Passus Headings

We follow the guide headings of L, our copy-text, which we believe to offer the closest representation of the headings of beta. For reasons explained above IV.2, there is poorer evidence for the headings in alpha. On extra-textual grounds put forward in Burrow, "Structure" (2008), 311, we believe that beta's headings are also those of the archetype, and that these were reduced by alpha.

V.2.2 Paragraphing

Our documentary editions have reproduced as far as possible in print the layout and pointing of the manuscripts, and we have followed the practice here in so far as we can infer the format of **Bx**. We have found no information about its page-breaks, so they are not recorded. There is considerable agreement among the manuscripts as to the division into paragraphs and to the placing of paraphs (see Benson and Blanchfield (1997), 240–313), and the four important witnesses LMWR emphasise these divisions by a blank space between line-groups. We believe this arrangement to be archetypal, and indeed eyeskip from paraph to paraph to be a frequent explanation of major omissions in alpha and beta (see Burrow [2010]; Burrow and Turville-Petre [2012]), and so we have marked the line-groups with blank spaces and with paraphs. L's paragraphs are consistently matched in M, and so give good evidence of beta's scheme. More surprisingly, L's paragraphs are almost invariably matched by R's, and give us confidence that in these cases we are reproducing the arrangement in **Bx** (see earlier, IV.3.). Where L is not supported by R, there is often some identifiable reason for this, suggesting why one of the two scribes might have dropped or supplied a paragraph break. Where we have not followed the scheme in L, we have added a note to explain our reason for departing from it, and also noted where L is not supported by R.

V.2.3   Punctuation

All the early manuscripts of Langland's poem have mid-line pointing, whether it is a solidus, a raised point or a punctus elevatus; see Burrow, "Punctuation" (2014), 9–14. Modern editors, unlike Skeat, do not reproduce the mid-line pointing, and Kane and Donaldson, 138 n. 37, speak of "a subjective element in the reading of verse which may affect identification of the caesural pause." But the manuscripts largely agree in their placement of punctuation, offering evidence of **Bx**'s usage which editors are wrong to neglect. At **Bx**.15.120, for example, all manuscripts that mark the caesura do so after *prestes*:

> Ri3t so many prestes . prechoures and prelates

but Schmidt (2008), 425, says that *prelates* is to be "pronounced with two full stresses," evidently placing the caesura after *prechoures* to give the normative scansion aa/ax. Yet the pointing in the manuscripts provides evidence that the line should be scanned xa/aa, a pattern which both Kane and Donaldson and Schmidt regard as non-authorial.

Our copy text, L, begins with a punctus elevatus, perhaps because it was more formal, but switches to a raised point after P.25, perhaps because it was quicker. The L scribe occasionally uses a punctus elevatus thereafter in particular circumstances. Inserted punctuation is usually by punctus elevatus, presumably because it is clearer (e.g. **Bx**.12.287, 15.237). Where the scribe has placed a raised point too early in the line, he adds a punctus elevatus at the correct position without erasing the earlier punctuation (e.g. 7.143, 19.461). A punctus elevatus is sometimes employed in Latin quotations (e.g. 15.124, 358). We cannot say what form the pointing took in **Bx**, but since we suppose that this pointing was a formal device and part of the *ordinatio* of the page, we have used a mid-line raised point throughout.[21] Relying on the witness of other scribes, we have supplied it in square brackets where the L scribe missed it, which he does about 5% of the time. This is usually straightforward, but see the note to 4.29. Where other witnesses indicate that L has misplaced the punctuation, we have moved it; see the note to

---

21 With one exception, where we retain a punctus elevatus; see note to 8.74.

9.203 for an interesting case. L has double punctuation in 63 lines, but in only four (3.270, 8.74, 11.317, 16.24) does the evidence suggested to us that it goes back to **Bx**; see notes to these lines (and Smith [2008]). L also has raised points at the ends of 24 English lines, but we have not recorded it. There is sporadic end-line pointing in some manuscripts (notably R), but the distribution does not suggest derivation from **Bx**, so we have not recorded it. Latin lines in prose and verse are commonly punctuated, and we have retained the punctuation of copy text.

V.2.4 Marginalia

Beta manuscripts identify the seven sins in Passus 5 in the margin in the scribal hand, formal and boxed in LWHm, and we have presented them in our text. These marginal identifications are not in alpha, though in F the names of the sins are highlighted and underlined in red in the text. We also keep L's interlinear glosses to 6.245, 9.34, 9.172, 15.90 and 15.153, all with beta support. Of course it is possible they are not archetypal. The unusual identification of the quotation in **Bx**.15.605 as Isaiah 3 is in exactly the same form in LRF, strongly suggesting that it is archetypal.

V.3 Choice of Variants

V.3.1 Forms and Spellings

We have almost always retained the forms and spellings of L. So we do not generally alter L's forms of the personal pronouns. **Bx** uses *hij* for "they" in at least three lines where it alliterates (see above, IV.1). The L scribe, whose own form is *þei*, uses *hij* on these occasions and in seven further lines, and we suppose L reproduces beta on all ten occasions. In other lines the attestation suggests that beta uses the *th-* form. There is no evidence to suggest that alpha differs. In all cases, therefore, we take L's form of the third person nominative plural pronoun. For reasons explained above, IV.1, we also follow L's form of the nominative feminine pronoun, except on two occasions where alliteration demands an *h-* form (**Bx**.18.156, 20.198). For example, in **Bx**.1.75 L's *heo* is supported by MR and participates in the alliteration; in 1.77 only R has *he* which is not necessary for alliteration even though the line alliterates on /h/ + vowel, so we do not emend L's *she*; in 1.87, in the same position, R again reads *quod he* against *quod she* in all other manuscripts in a line alliterating on /t/, and again we take L's pronoun. It seems that alpha had the *h-* form for "she" much more often than beta, and we can only determine when **Bx** used the *h-* form where it is necessary for the alliteration. Similarly in **Bx**.3.47, where R uniquely has *a* for "he," we have no reason for thinking that this reduced form was that in **Bx**. L several times has *an* for "and," sometimes in lines that are marked for correction, as **Bx**.5.361 and

6.215; we have left the form to stand. Some nouns have genitives without ending, many presumably inherited from **Bx** and perhaps also representing Langland. In **Bx**.5.550 L has *soules* (gen.) where other reliable manuscripts have the form *soule* (so MHmG + alpha, as in **AC**), but we have not emended L's form. If we were to make alterations in cases of this sort, it would be difficult to know where to stop, and we have recognised that we cannot recreate the spellings of **Bx** with any assurance. Where L is lost, we have adapted the spellings to L's usual forms, so that where beta has lost a passage extant in alpha, we have modified alpha's (usually R's) forms without notice.

V.3.2   Comparison with the A and C Versions

Wherever the reading of **Bx** is in doubt, we compare the readings of **Ax** and/or **Cx** if there is an equivalent line. Our references to **Ax** and **Cx** are inevitably provisional, since neither has yet been established. We therefore rely on our own assessment of the evidence presented by Kane and Russell-Kane, and report in more detail where the evidence is divided. This applies most often to variation between the two great families of **C**, X and P. It follows that references to lines in Kane and Russell-Kane are to our reconstructions of archetypal readings, not to the edited texts.

Readings from **Ax** and **Cx** cannot, of course, be imported when evidence for **Bx** is supported by a consensus of the better **B** manuscripts, in particular L, M and R. We recognise that other texts, especially CrGF, are at times contaminated from **A** and/or **C**, so that their witness can be discounted or at least regarded with suspicion if not confirmed by others. **AC** attestation becomes an important factor, however, where alpha and beta are divided. As a straightforward example: in the a-verse of **Bx**.5.569 beta makes acceptable sense with *Ich haue myn huire wel*, against alpha's *Ich haue my huyre of hym wel*, but **AC** have the line as in alpha, and therefore we conclude that beta has dropped *of hym*. The beta reading in **Bx**.5.185, *bi contenaunce ne bi riȝt* makes poor sense: Repentance instructs Wrath not to reveal privities *by contenance ne by speche* as alpha has it, in a reading supported by **C** (the passage has no parallel in **A**). More uncertain is **Bx**.5.579, in which LR and HmW (but not M) read *a longe tyme þere-after*, attestation that would usually secure **Bx**. However, there is conflicting support from **AC** for the reading of other manuscripts, *a long tyme after*. It is perhaps relevant that this b-verse, though presumably authorial, is unmetrical (x / x / x), so we suppose that either **Bx** or LR and beta2 supplied the necessary syllable. If the former, we should retain *þere*; if the latter we should emend L. In the face of such equal attestation on either side, we follow copy-text. At **Bx**.14.116 LR have the reading *it* against *he* in other beta manuscripts and omission in F. **Cx** has *he* in a revised line, but LR agreement is usually decisive, and we follow it here.

On a number of occasions where the alpha/beta variation is paralleled by A/C variation, and where we think authorial revision within the **B** tradition is a strong possibility, we have presented *both* variants. For an example see **Bx.**1.46. The weighing-up of the evidence — split readings in either **A** or **C**, variation within alpha or beta, the inherent probability of coincidental agreement, and so on — is conducted in a note. After passus 10, where there is no **A**-text to compare, we have used the parallel text in **C** to help determine the reading of **Bx**. In a number of cases this may mean that we have designated an unrevised but authorial variant preserved in beta as an error, and we are thus presenting the revised text as in alpha and **C**, but there is no reason to suppose that revision was much more thorough in the second half of the poem than the very sporadic revision in the first half. We have, of course, discussed the possibilities in individual notes.

The passage from **Bx.**18.428 to 20.26 presents a particular difficulty. Here R has lost a quire, leaving the unreliable F as the only witness to alpha. Since the **C**-text is only lightly revised in the last two passus of the poem, we initially followed the principle that readings of F supported by **Cx** generally represented **Bx**, and we adopted most of those readings against beta. Further considerations, however, caused us to rethink. Kane and Donaldson and Russell-Kane state categorically that **C** is unrevised in its passus 21–2:

> These passus were untouched by the revising poet, and the manuscripts of the two traditions were treated as constituting two great families with an exclusive common ancestor, a single scribal B copy, and as differentiated only scribally. (RK, 118–19)

But it became apparent to us that the **C**-text has indeed undergone a certain amount of revision (see notes to **Bx.**19.150, 245, 257, 259–60, and especially in the final lines **Bx.**20.371, 376, 377, 378, 380), a fact of course obscured by the Athlone's adoption of readings from one tradition into the other. It is also clear, as was to be expected, that **Cx** is at times corrupt. Having found instances of F and **Cx** agreeing in error, we were forced to conclude that we could not unquestioningly regard F/**Cx** agreement as representing **Bx**. Coincidence might account for a number of such agreements, but some were of a character that suggested contamination. There are sporadic indications of F's contamination from a **C**-text elsewhere in the poem: a notable instance is **Bx.**13.361–8 (see notes). Indications of contamination do not extend for the entire section where R is absent, but for most of it, from the beginning of **Bx.**19 up to 20.13. Striking instances are: 19.12 *Pieres* beta, *cristis* F/**Cx**; 19.43 *conquest* beta, *his conquest* F/**Cx**; 19.119 *holy* beta, *onely* F/**Cx**; 19.477 *seke* beta, *tooken* F and **Cx**?; 20.7 *þi bylyf* beta, *lyve by* F/**Cx**.

There is no wholly satisfactory way of restoring **Bx** in these circumstances. Where beta readings and those of F/**Cx** are equally strong, or the differences are trivial, we have preferred beta on our usual grounds that L is copy text. For instances see the notes to **Bx**.19.39, 136, 147, both notes to 228, and 288. In cases where one reading seems to us superior and the variant reading a scribal error as judged by the usual criteria, we have chosen the better reading. So in **Bx**.19.96, 142, 151, 291, 435 and 471 we have judged beta to offer scribal readings, and 19.56–9, 154, and 242b–243a are lines omitted in beta that we have restored. As a result, we may sometimes have rejected an error in **Bx**, though this is perhaps not a high price to pay. For a particularly difficult case see the note to **Bx**.19.493. All such instances have been discussed at length in the annotations, but it is fair to warn the reader that the section where R is absent is the part of our text of which we are least confident.

V.3.3   *Conjectural Emendation*

It might be supposed that conjectural emendation had no place in an edition of the archetype, and was appropriate only in the reconstructed **B**-version. In theory, however, reconstruction of the archetype from its misrepresentation in all extant witnesses must be a possibility. In practice there are very few occasions where we had the confidence to do this. One case is **Bx**.13.92 where, in a line alliterating on /p/, beta reads *wynked* and alpha *bad*. There can be little doubt that the authorial reading was the rather rare and dialectal verb *preynte*, "winked in admonition" as conjectured by Kane and Donaldson. But it was probably also the reading of **Bx**; how can the alpha and beta variation be accounted for otherwise? Beta substituted a common synonym for the movement of the eye, while alpha replaced with a word conveying the intention of the winking. There is a similar situation at **Bx**.11.190, where beta calls Jesus *owre hele*, while R has the nonsensical *oure euel*. We suppose that alpha and **Bx** had *iuel*, meaning "jewel," misread by R and replaced by beta. This is a little more problematical because F replaces it with *helthe*, but we see a **Bx** reading "jewel" as the most probable source of the variants. Again the reading was conjectured by Kane and Donaldson. In 17.337 we are confident that the authorial reading is *þe borre in þe throte*, "the burr in the throat," i.e. "hoarse," as adopted by Kane and Donaldson from **C**. We suppose that, in order to avoid a rare word, alpha altered alliterating *þe borre* to *cowȝe*, "coughing," and beta to *hors*. In conjecturing *þe borre* we are aware of the danger of emending to **B** rather than **Bx**, but it provides an explanation for the variant readings of alpha and beta, neither of which is likely to have given rise to the other. In a quite exceptional case in Passus 19 we introduce a line from **Cx** that is not in any **B** manuscript: see the note to 19.450, and for the particular circumstances affecting this passus, see V.3.2 above.

V.3.4   Alliteration

Irregular alliteration is not sufficient evidence on its own to cast doubt on **Bx** (see IV.6 above), but it may be one factor in the choice of variants. See the variants in **Bx**.11.6, 138, 416, 12.222, 13.205. We have also to consider the possibility that a scribe improved the alliteration on his own initiative, as is quite often the case with F. As in other matters, comparison with parallel lines in **Ax** and **Cx** has been used to guide a choice between variants.

V.3.5   Metrical Criteria

We have of course not corrected an unmetrical b-verse where the distribution of variants suggests that it was the reading of **Bx**. L's unmetrical b-verse in **Bx**.5.610 *or þow beest noȝte ysaued* (x x / x x / x) could easily be "improved" by dropping the *y*- prefix, but it has good support for **Bx** from MR. Although other **B** manuscripts drop the prefix, this presumably reflects the scribal dialects rather than metrical sensitivities. Though **A** manuscripts and the P family of **C** are without the prefix here, the X family has it, as would be standard in their SW Midland dialect (*LALME*, dot map 1195). Exceptionally, we have emended L in **Bx**.10.115 *þei went to helle* (x / x / x), since all other manuscripts have disyllabic *wente(n)*.

V.3.6   Sense

Our aim is to restore the readings of **Bx**, not of the poem that Langland wrote. This means that we are bound at times to preserve a text that we know or suspect to be corrupt if it is what **Bx** wrote, and even, though it goes against the grain for editors to do so, to preserve nonsense. In **Bx**.5.341 we take R's b-verse describing how Robin the roper *arise þe southe* to be another example of that scribe copying exactly what he had before him. F typically rewrites, while beta makes a small adjustment to give superficial sense with *arose bi þe southe*. The evidently correct reading is that offered by C, *aryse they bisouhte*. We follow R's meaningless reading. In **Bx**.10.291 the L scribe first wrote the nonsensical *For goddis worde wolde nouȝt be boste*, then corrected the last word to *loste*, thus agreeing with all other manuscripts except one. In the usual circumstances, we would suppose *boste* to be a mere miswriting. However, R also has *boste*, without correction. We know that R is both accurate and often mindless, copying whatever is in front of him, however nonsensical; we therefore suppose that **Bx** had the reading *boste*, easily corrected by all scribes except R to *loste*. How else could we otherwise account for the agreement of the two most careful scribes? Since L is self-corrected, we record the reading as *[b]oste*. Fortunately, there are not many occasions on which we have to preserve self-evident nonsense.

VI Bibliography

VI.1 Editions

Bennett, J. A. W., ed. *Langland. Piers Plowman. The Prologue and Passus I–VII of the B Text as Found in Bodleian MS. Laud Misc. 581*. Oxford: Clarendon Press, 1972.

Kane, George, ed. *Piers Plowman: The A Version: Will's Visions of Piers Plowman and Do-Well, An Edition in the Form of Trinity College Cambridge MS R.3.14 Corrected from Other Manuscripts, with Variant Readings*. Rev. ed. London: Athlone Press, 1988.

Kane, George, and E. Talbot Donaldson, eds. *Piers Plowman: The B Version: Will's Visions of Piers Plowman, Do-Well, Do-Better and Do-Best. An Edition in the Form of Trinity College Cambridge MS B.15.17 Corrected and Restored from the Known Evidence, with Variant Readings*. Rev. ed. London: Athlone Press; Berkeley and Los Angeles: University of California Press, 1988.

Pearsall, Derek, ed. *Piers Plowman: A New Annotated Edition of the C-Text*. Exeter: Exeter University Press, 2008.

Russell, George, and George Kane, eds. *Piers Plowman: The C Version: Will's Visions of Piers Plowman, Do-Well, Do-Better and Do-Best. An Edition in the Form of Huntington Library MS HM 143, Corrected and Restored from the Known Evidence, with Variant Readings*. London: Athlone Press; Berkeley and Los Angeles: University of California Press, 1997.

Schmidt, A. V. C., ed. *The Vision of Piers Plowman: A Critical Edition of the B-Text Based on Trinity College Cambridge MS B.15.17*. London, Melbourne, and Toronto: J. M. Dent & Sons Ltd.; New York: E. P. Dutton & Co., 1978; 2nd ed., London: J. M. Dent & Sons, Ltd.; Rutland, Vermont: Charles E. Tuttle Co., 1995.

—, ed. *Piers Plowman: A Parallel-Text Edition of the A, B, C and Z Versions: Vol. 2. Introduction, Textual Notes, Commentary, Bibliography and Indexical Glossary*. Kalamazoo: Western Michigan University, 2008.

Skeat, Walter W., ed. *The Vision of William Concerning Piers the Plowman together with Vita de Dowel, Dobet, et Dobest, Secundum Wit et Resoun by William Langland: Part II. The "Crowley" Text; or Text B*. EETS, OS 38. London: N. Trübner, 1869.

—, ed. *The Vision of William Concerning Piers the Plowman, in Three Parallel Texts together with Richard the Redeless*. 2 vols. Oxford: Oxford University Press, 1886.

Piers Plowman Electronic Archive. Vol 1: Corpus Christi College, Oxford MS 201 (F). edited by Robert Adams, Hoyt N. Duggan, Eric Eliason, Ralph Hanna, John Price-Wilkin, and Thorlac Turville-Petre. SEENET Series A.1, Ann Arbor: University of Michigan Press, 2000.

Piers Plowman Electronic Archive. Vol 2: Trinity College, Cambridge MS B.15.17 (W). edited by Thorlac Turville-Petre and Hoyt N. Duggan. SEENET Series A.4, Ann Arbor: University of Michigan Press, 2002.

Piers Plowman Electronic Archive. Vol 3: Oriel College, Oxford MS 79 (O). Ed. Katherine Heinrichs. SEENET Series A.5, Cambridge: for SEENET and the Medieval Academy of America by Boydell and Brewer, 2004.

Piers Plowman Electronic Archive. Vol 4: Bodleian Library MS Laud Misc. 581 (L). edited by Hoyt N. Duggan and Ralph Hanna. SEENET Series A.6, Cambridge: for SEENET and the Medieval Academy of America by Boydell and Brewer, 2004.

Piers Plowman Electronic Archive. Vol 5: British Library MS Additional 35287 (M). edited by Eric Eliason, Thorlac Turville-Petre and Hoyt N. Duggan. SEENET Series A.7, Cambridge: for SEENET and the Medieval Academy of America by Boydell and Brewer, 2005.

Piers Plowman Electronic Archive. Vol 6: Huntington Library Ms Hm 128 (Hm). edited by Michael Calabrese, Hoyt N. Duggan and Thorlac Turville-Petre. SEENET Series A.9, Cambridge: for SEENET and the Medieval Academy of America by Boydell and Brewer, 2008.

Piers Plowman Electronic Archive. Vol 7: London. British Library, MS Lansdowne 398 and Oxford, Bodleian Library MS Rawlinson Poetry 38 (R). edited by Robert Adams. SEENET Series A.10, Cambridge: for SEENET and the Medieval Academy of America by Boydell and Brewer, 2011.

Piers Plowman Electronic Archive. Vol 8: Cambridge, Cambridge University Library, MS Gg.4.31 (G). edited by Judith Jefferson. SEENET Series A.11, Charlottesville: Society for Early English and Norse Electronic Texts, 2013.

VI.2 Studies

Adams, Robert. "The Reliability of the Rubrics in the B-Text of *Piers Plowman.*" *Medium Ævum* 54 (1985): 208–31.

—. "Editing and the Limitations of the *Durior Lectio.*" *YLS* 5 (1991): 7–15.

—. "Langland's Ordinatio: The Visio and the Vita Once More." *YLS* 8 (1994): 51–84.

—. "Evidence for the Stemma of the *Piers Plowman* B Manuscripts." *Studies in Bibliography* 53 (2000): 173–94.

—. "The R/F MSS of *Piers Plowman* and the Pattern of Alpha/Beta Complementary Omissions: Implications for Critical Editing." *TEXT* 14 (2002): 109–37.

Alford, John A. *Piers Plowman: A Glossary of Legal Diction.* Cambridge: D. S. Brewer, 1988.

—. *Piers Plowman: A Guide to the Quotations.* Binghamton: State University of New York, 1992.

Barney, Stephen A. *The Penn Commentary on Piers Plowman.* Vol. 5. Philadelphia: University of Pennsylvania Press, 2006.

Benskin, Michael, and Margaret Laing. "Translations and Mischsprachen in Middle English Manuscripts." In *So Meny People Longages and Tonges: Philological Essays in Scots and Mediaeval English Presented to Angus McIntosh*, eds. Michael Benskin and M. L. Samuels. Edinburgh: Middle English Dialect Project, 1981. 55–106.

Benson, C. David, and Lynne S. Blanchfield with acknowledgements to the work of Marie-Claire Uhart. *The Manuscripts of Piers Plowman: The B-Version.* Cambridge: D. S. Brewer, 1997.

Brewer, Charlotte. *Editing Piers Plowman: The Evolution of the Text.* Cambridge Studies in Medieval Literature 28. Cambridge: Cambridge University Press, 1996.

Burrow, J. A. "Reason's Horse." *YLS* 4 (1990): 139–44.

—. *Thinking in Poetry: Three Medieval Examples.* London: Birkbeck College, 1993.

— (ed.). *Thomas Hoccleve's Complaint and Dialogue.* EETS OS 313. Oxford: Oxford University Press, 1999.

—. "Hoccleve's Questions: Intonation and Punctuation." *Notes & Queries* 49 (2002): 184–8.

—. *Gestures and Looks in Medieval Narrative.* Cambridge: Cambridge University Press, 2002.

—. "Wasting Time, Wasting Words in *Piers Plowman* B and C." *YLS* 17 (2003): 191–202.

—. "The Structure of *Piers Plowman* B XV–XX: Evidence from the Rubrics." *Medium Ævum* 77 (2008): 306–312.

—. "Piers Plowman B XIII 190." *Notes & Queries* 55 (2008): 124–5.

—. "Conscience on Knights, Kings, and Conquerors: *Piers Plowman* B.19.26–198." *YLS* 23 (2009): 85–95.

—. "*Piers Plowman* B: Paragraphing in the Archetypal Copy." *Notes and Queries* 57 (2010): 24–6.

—. "An Alliterative Pattern in *Piers Plowman*." *YLS* 25 (2011): 117–29.

—. "Another Alliterative Pattern in *Piers Plowman* B." *YLS* 27 (2013): 3–13.

—. "The Athlone Edition of *Piers Plowman* B: Stemmatics and the Direct Method." *Notes & Queries* 61 (2014): 339–44.

—. "Punctuation in the B Version of *Piers Plowman*." In *"Truthe is the Beste": A Festschrift in Honour of A. V. C. Schmidt*, ed. Nicolas Jacobs and Gerald Morgan. Bern: Peter Lang, 2014. 5–15.

Burrow, J. A., and Thorlac Turville-Petre. "Editing the B Archetype of *Piers Plowman* and the Relationship Between Alpha and Beta." *YLS* 26 (2012): 98–119.

Cable, Thomas. "Middle English Meter and Its Theoretical Implications." *YLS* 2 (1988): 47–69.

Cornelius, Ian. "Passus secundus de dobet: On the Genesis of a Rubric in the Archetype of *Piers Plowman B*." *Medium Ævum* 84 (2015): 1–15.

Donaldson, E. T. "MSS R and F in the B-Tradition of *Piers Plowman*." *Transactions of the Connecticut Academy of Arts and Sciences* 39 (1955): 177–212.

Doyle, A. I. "Remarks on Surviving Manuscripts of *Piers Plowman*." In *Medieval English Religious and Ethical Literature: Essays in Honour of G. H. Russell*, edited by Gregory Kratzmann and James Simpson. Cambridge: D. S. Brewer, 1986. 35–48.

—. "Ushaw College, Durham, MS 50." In *The English Medieval Book*, edited by A. S. G. Edwards, Vincent Gillespie and Ralph Hanna. London: The British Library, 2000. 43–9.

Duggan, Hoyt N. "Notes Towards a Theory of Langland's Meter." *YLS* 1 (1987): 41–70.

—. "Langland's Dialect and Final -e." *Studies in the Age of Chaucer* 12 (1990): 157–91.

—. "Notes on the Metre of *Piers Plowman*: Twenty Years On." *Leeds Texts and Monographs* n.s. 17 (2009): 159–86.

Galloway, Andrew. "The Rhetoric of Riddling in Late-Medieval England." *Speculum* 70 (1995): 68–105.

—. *The Penn Commentary on Piers Plowman*. Vol. 1. Philadelphia: University of Pennsylvania Press, 2006.

Hanna, Ralph. *William Langland. Authors of The Middle Ages: English Writers of the Late Middle Ages* 3. Aldershot: Variorum, 1993.

—. "Studies in the Manuscripts of *Piers Plowman*." *YLS* 7 (1993): 1–25.

—. *Pursuing History. Middle English Manuscripts and Their Texts*. Stanford, CA: Stanford University Press, 1996.

—. *London Literature, 1300–1380*. Cambridge: Cambridge University Press, 2005.

Hailey, R. Carter. "Robert Crowley and the Editing of *Piers Plowman* (1550)." *YLS* 21 (2007): 143–70.

Horobin, Simon. "Adam Pinkhurst and the Copying of British Library, MS Additional 35287 of the B Version of *Piers Plowman*." *YLS* 23 (2009): 61–83.

—. "Langland's Dialect Reconsidered." In *Pursuing Middle English Manuscripts and their Texts: Essays in Honour of Ralph Hanna*, ed. Simon Horobin and Aditi Nafde. Turnhout: Brepols, 2017. 63–75.

Horobin, Simon, and Linne R. Mooney. "A *Piers Plowman* Manuscript by the Hengwrt/Ellesmere Scribe and its Implications for London Standard English." *Studies in the Age of Chaucer* 26 (2004): 65–112.

Jefferson, Judith A. "Divisions, Collaboration and Other Topics: The Table of Contents in Cambridge, University Library, MS Gg.4.31." In *Medieval Alliterative Poetry*, edited by John A. Burrow and Hoyt N. Duggan. Dublin: Four Courts Press, 2010. 140–52.

Jordan, Richard. *Handbook of Middle English Grammar: Phonology*, trans. and revised Eugene J. Crook. The Hague and Paris: Mouton, 1974.

Kane, George. *Piers Plowman Glossary*. London: Continuum, 2005.

McIntosh, Angus, M. L. Samuels and Michael Benskin, with the assistance of Margaret Laing and Keith Williamson, eds. *A Linguistic Atlas of Late Mediaeval English*. 4 volumes. Aberdeen: Aberdeen University Press, 1986.

Mustanoja, Tauno F. *A Middle English Syntax. Part I: Parts of Speech*. Mémoires de la Société Néophilologique de Helsinki 23. Helsinki: Société Néophilologique, 1960.

Roberts, Jane. "On Giving Scribe B a Name and a Clutch of London Manuscripts from *c.*1400." *Medium Ævum* 80 (2011): 247–70.

Samuels, M. L. "Langland's Dialect." *Medium Ævum* 54 (1985): 232–47. Reprinted in *The English of Chaucer and his Contemporaries*. edited by J. J. Smith. Aberdeen: Aberdeen University Press, 1989. 70–85.

—. "Corrections to 'Langland's Dialect'." *Medium Ævum* 55 (1986): 40.

—. "Dialect and Grammar." In *A Companion to Piers Plowman*, edited by John A. Alford. Berkeley, Los Angeles and London: University of California Press, 1988, 201–21.

Schmidt, A. V. C. *The Clerkly Maker: Langland's Poetic Art*. Cambridge: D. S. Brewer, 1987.

Smith, Macklin. "Langland's Unruly Caesura." *YLS* 22 (2008): 57–101.

Turville-Petre, Thorlac. "Emendation on Grounds of Alliteration in *The Wars of Alexander*." *English Studies* 61 (1980): 302–17.

—. "Putting it Right: The Corrections of Huntington Library MS. HM 128 and BL Additional MS. 35287." *YLS* 16 (2002): 41–65.

—. Review of Galloway (2006). *YLS* (2006): 231–4.

—. "The B Archetype of *Piers Plowman* as a Corpus for Metrical Analysis." In *Yee? Baw for Bokes: Essays on Medieval Manuscripts and Poetics in Honor of Hoyt N. Duggan*, ed. Michael Calabrese and Stephen H. A. Shepherd. Loyola Marymount University, Los Angeles, CA: Marymount Institute Press, 2013, 17–30.

Warner, Lawrence. "Scribes, Misattributed: Hoccleve and Pinkhurst." *Studies in the Age of Chaucer* 37 (2015): 55–100.

Wittig, Joseph S. *Piers Plowman: Concordance*. London: Athlone Press, 2001.

Wordsworth, Iohannes, and White, Henricus Iulianus, eds. *Nouum Testamentum Latine Secundum Editionem Sancti Hieronymi*. Oxford: Clarendon Press, 1911.

VI.3   Abbreviations

K	George Kane and his **A**-text
KD	George Kane and E Talbot Donaldson and their **B**-text
LALME	McIntosh et al. *A Linguistic Atlas of Late Mediaeval English*
MED	*Middle English Dictionary*
OED	*Oxford English Dictionary*
PPEA	*Piers Plowman Electronic Archive*
RK	George Russell and George Kane and their **C**-text
YLS	*Yearbook of Langland Studies*

TEXT

Prologue

Incipit liber de Petro Plowman

In a somer seson · whan soft was the sonne
I shope me in[to] shroudes · as i a shepe were
In habite as an heremite · vnholy of workes
Went wyde in þis world [·] wondres to here
5 Ac on a May mornyng · on Maluerne hulles
Me byfel a ferly · of fairy me thouȝte
I was wery forwandred · and went me to reste
Vnder a brode banke · bi a bornes side
And as I lay and lened · and loked [o]n þe wateres
10 I slombred in a slepyng · it sweyued so merye

[¶] Thanne gan I to meten · a merueilouse sweuene
That I was in a wildernesse · wist I neuer where

---

2 **into**: In the absence of R in **Bx**.P.1–124 and 1.142–2.41, we are obliged to rely on F for alpha readings. This is problematic, partly because of F's eccentricity, and more importantly because its text is evidently contaminated from **A**. (See Introduction, p. 15.) We have therefore been very cautious in adopting readings from F, but have accepted F in agreement with **A** when it offers a superior text, and also taken the agreement of F with AC against beta as evidence in favour of the F reading. In this line, although L has *in*, the agreement of CrWHm (and M revised) with F insecurely establishes *into*, which is confirmed by **Ax** (*into a shroud*) and **Cx**.

9 **on**: As with *into* in l. 2, the reading of MCrWHm and F is supported by **Ax**. LCO have *in*, G *vpon*. **Cx** rewrites.

10 **in a**: The reading of LMCO is challenged by CrWHmG *in-to a* and F *into*. **A** mss. read variously *on a, in a, a, into a, into*. There is no equivalent in **Cx**.

10 **sweyued**: This is probably the beta reading, supported by LCO, and probably original M, where *swei...* (three or four letters erased) has been altered to *sweyed*, in line with beta2 and GF. See *MED sweiven*, "whirl, sweep", a rare verb cited elsewhere only from *Patience* and *Cleanness*. But the noun *sweuene* in the next line might have given rise to the reading. The variant *sweyed* is *MED sweien* v.(1), "sound", or the commoner v.(2), "move along (of water)." There is the same variation in **Ax**.

11–40 **¶**: L has no paraphs on fol. 1r because of the decoration running down the left margin, but it has blank spaces before ll. 11, 23, 25, 31 and 40.

As I bihelde in-to þe est · an hiegh to þe sonne
I seigh a toure on a toft · trielich ymaked
15 A depe dale binethe · a dongeon þere-Inne
With depe dyches & derke · and dredful of sight
A faire felde ful of folke · fonde I there bytwene
Of alle maner of men · þe mene and þe riche
Worchyng and wandryng · as þe worlde asketh
20 Some put hem to þe plow · pleyed ful selde
In settyng and in sowyng · swonken ful harde
And wonnen that [þese] wastours · with glotonye destruyeth

[¶] And some putten hem to pruyde · apparailed hem þere-after
In contenaunce of clothyng [·] comen disgised

25 [¶] In prayers and in penance · putten hem manye
Al for loue of owre lorde · lyueden ful streyte
In hope forto haue · heueneriche blisse
As ancres and heremites · that holden hem in here selles
And coueiten nought in contre [·] to kairen aboute
30 For no likerous liflode · her lykam to plese

[¶] And somme chosen chaffare · they cheuen the bettere
As it semeth to owre sy3t · that suche men thryueth
And somme murthes to make · as mynstralles conneth
And geten gold with here glee · synneles I leue
35 Ac iapers & iangelers · Iudas chylderen
Feynen hem fantasies · and foles hem maketh
And han here witte at wille · to worche 3if þei sholde
That Poule precheth of hem · I nel nought preue it here

---

14 **trielich**: So LWG and original M. A scribes also have trouble with the adverb (from adj. *trie*), and **Cx** rewrites.

19 **þe**: So beta, supported by the P family of C, but F's *this* is supported by the X family.

20 **þe**: Dropped in GF. There is the same variation between *to þe* and *to* in AC.

21 **in** (2): So LHmCG; dropped in others. There is the same variation in AC.

22 **þese**: F has support from AC. Beta manuscripts omit it.

25 **in** (2): Agreement of LMCOF is good support for **Bx**, but it is not in Ax or Cx.

25 **penance**: The plural of WHmF is probably prompted by *prayers*; C mss. are similarly split, but **Ax** has sg. For variation with and without <-s>, see note to **Bx**.14.211.

26 **loue**: Beta2 (CrWHm) and GF have *the loue*. AC mss. are split.

27 **forto haue**: Beta2 (CrWHm) and G read *to haue after*. This is also the reading of two A mss. **Cx** is revised.

29 **kairen**: So LMGOF, supported by Ax and Cx; CrWHm regularly alter to *carien*; e.g. **Bx**.4.23, 5.310.

31 **cheuen**: In all three versions the present tense varies with the past. LMGOF support the present for **Bx**.

35 **Ac**: So LWHm, with GF's regular substitution of *But*. MCrCO have *As*. A mss. split between *Ac* and *But*. **Cx** has no equivalent line.

Qui turpiloquium loquitur · &c

40   [¶] Bidders and beggeres · fast aboute ȝede
With her bely and her bagge · of bred ful ycrammed
Fayteden for here fode · fouȝten atte ale
In glotonye god it wote · gon hij to bedde
And risen with ribaudye · tho roberdes knaues
45   Slepe and sori sleuthe · seweth hem eure

¶ Pilgrymes and palmers · pliȝte[n] hem togidere
To seke seynt Iames · and seyntes in rome
Thei went forth in here wey · with many wise tales
And hadden leue to lye · al here lyf after
50   I seigh somme that seiden · þei had ysouȝt seyntes
To eche a tale þat þei tolde · here tonge was tempred to lye
More þan to sey soth · it semed bi here speche

¶ Heremites on an heep · with hoked staues
Wenten to walsyngham · and here wenches after
55   Grete lobyes and longe · that loth were to swynke
Clotheden hem in copis · to ben knowen fram othere
And shopen hem heremites · here ese to haue

¶ I fonde þere Freris [·] alle þe foure ordres
Preched þe peple · for profit of hem-seluen
60   Glosed þe gospel · as hem good lyked
For coueitise of copis · construed it as þei wolde
Many of þis maistres [·] mowe clothen hem at lykyng

---

39 **&c**: The absence of the b-verse in L, original M, Cr[1]C (F misses the line) suggests that the English completion was added to the Latin phrase from other versions. WHmG *is luciferes hyne* is **Ax**; O's *is lucifers knaue* (which is added in Cr[23]) is **Cx**. A later hand has added *est seruus diaboli* in M.

41 **bely ... bagge**: The distributive sg. as in LM is supported by **Cx**; **A** mss. vary. F misses the line.

41 **of bred ful**: Presumably an error in beta or **Bx** for AC *bretful*.

43 **it**: Supported by LMHmCO though omitted by CrWG and **Ax** (**Cx** rewrites). F's reversed a-verse, *& god woot with glotenye*, also omits it. For a parallel, see **Bx**.4.81.

44 **risen**: **Cx** has *ryseþ*. F's *rysen vp* is **Ax**.

46 **pliȝten**: The form could represent the past tense or the present. LMO with *pliȝted* take it as past, in line with the verbs in ll. 48–61, but the form receives no support from **Ax** or **Cx**.

49 **to**: MGOF's *for to* has limited support from **A** mss. and none from **Cx**.

50–54 These five lines are omitted in F by eyeskip from *after* to *after*.

59 **Preched**: AC have the pres. part., as W, and Hm by correction. Schmidt (1995), 363 explains the source of what is presumably an error in **Bx** as "the unexpectedness of a participle in a sequence of preterites".

62 **maistres**: The reading of FG and **Ax**, meaning "learned professional theologian" (Kane, 2005), cf. **Bx**.13.25. The retention of the pl. form *maistres* in L suggests that *Freris* was an

For here money and marchandise · marchen togideres
For sith charite haþ be chapman · and chief to shryue lordes
65 Many ferlis han fallen · in a fewe ȝeris
But holychirche and hij · holde better togideres
The moste my[s]chief on molde · is mountyng faste

¶ Þere preched a Pardonere · as he a prest were
Brouȝte forth a bulle · with bishopes seles
70 And seide þat hym-self myȝte · assoilen hem alle
Of falshed of fastyng · of vowes ybroken

¶ Lewed men leued hym wel · and lyked his wordes
Comen vp knelyng · to kissen his bulles
He bonched hem with his breuet · & blered here eyes
75 And rauȝte with his ragman · rynges and broches
Thus þey geuen here golde · glotones to kepe
And leneth [it] such loseles · þat lecherye haunten
Were þe bischop yblissed · and worth bothe his eres
His seel shulde nouȝt be sent · to deceyue þe peple
80 Ac it is nauȝt by þe bischop · þat þe boy precheth
For the parisch prest and þe pardonere · parten þe siluer
That þe poraille of þe parisch · sholde haue ȝif þei nere

¶ Persones and parisch prestes · pleyned hem to þe bischop
Þat here parisshes were pore · sith þe pestilence tyme

---

interlinear gloss in beta, but not present in alpha. Cx's explanatory revision "Mony of þise maistres of mendenant freres" (RK.P.60) might imply that the gloss was in his exemplar.

63 **and**: Beta2 (CrWHm) has *and her*. AC show the same variation.

66 **hij**: The form in L, original M, and WC is necessary for alliteration. See Introduction, p. 18.

67 **myschief**: In L the line is marked for correction.

67 **mountyng**: F has *mountynge*. The beta reading is *mountyng wel*, though GO share the reading *vp* with AC. We suppose, with Schmidt (1995), 364, that Bx dropped *vp*, and beta supplied the adverb for the metre. F's final *-e* compensates for the omission of the adverb, avoiding the x / x / x b-verse rhythm, but there is no reason to suppose it represents Bx. See note to l. 104.

71 **of** (2): LMWHmCO in agreement with Cx; CrGF have *and* or *and of*. A mss. vary in the same way.

71 **vowes**: LMCrCO in agreement with Cx; others have *auowes*. A mss. vary in the same way.

75 F follows this with two lines not supported by AC.

77 **it**: Supported by AC as well as by sense. Omitted by LC and original M, presumably taking the verb as *leueth*, "believe": see F's *be-leven on*.

80 F follows this with a line not supported by AC.

82 **poraille**: Not elsewhere in the poem. O expands to *pore porayle* to explain the word; M perhaps originally read *pore peple*, which is the reading of Ax and Cx. F's *pore men* seems a typical avoidance of a difficult word, as is Cr's *pouerty*. However, the reading of Bx lacks alliteration in the b-verse.

85 To haue a lycence and leue · at London to dwelle
    And syngen þere for symonye · for siluer is swete

    ¶ Bischopes and bachelers · bothe maistres and doctours
    Þat han cure vnder criste · and crounyng in tokne
    And signe þat þei sholden · shryuen here paroschienes
90 Prechen and prey for hem · and þe pore fede
    Liggen in London · in lenten an elles
    Somme seruen þe kyng · and his siluer tellen
    In cheker and in chancerye · chalengen his dettes
    Of wardes and wardmotes · weyues and streyues

95 ¶ And some seruen as seruantz · lordes and ladyes
    And in stede of stuwardes · sytten and demen
    Here messe and here matynes · and many of here oures
    Arn don vndeuoutlych · drede is at þe laste
    Lest crist in constorie · acorse ful manye
100 I parceyued of þe power · þat Peter had to kepe
    To bynde and to vnbynde · as þe boke telleth
    How he it left wiþ loue · as owre lorde hight
    Amonges foure vertues · þe best of alle vertues
    Þat cardinales ben called · & closyng ȝatis
105 Þere crist is in kyngdome · to close and to shutte
    And to opne it to hem · and heuene blisse shewe
    Ac of þe cardinales atte Courte · þat cauȝt of þat name
    And power presumed in hem · a Pope to make

---

85 **leue**: LC have *a leue*, induced by *a lycence*. A few **AC** mss. have the same error.

91 **in** (1): Supported by **Cx**. Beta2 and G have *at*, perhaps influenced by the same phrase six lines above. Lines 87–210 are not in **A**.

91 **an**: "and". See Introduction, pp. 29–30. The form has been corrected in L in the line above.

94 **and** (1): LMCrCG, and so likely to be beta. WF have *and of*, which is probably the **Cx** reading. HmO have *of*.

94 F's additional line is from **A** (KProl.95).

98 An entirely different line referring to Sarum Use replaces this and the next line in F.

102 **it left**: This word-order is supported by **Cx**. MCrF reverse.

103 **þe best of alle vertues**: Beta alliterates aa/xa with /f/ + /v/ alliteration. F's reading, *most vertuous of hevene*, might represent alpha. See KD, p. 180, for discussion. It could be that the **Cx** b-verse, *most vertuous of vertues* (RK.P.131), was also **Bx**, with alpha and beta taking different action to avoid the repetition.

104 **closyng**: We have retained L's spelling, though final *-e* as in MWHm would improve the metre; see Duggan (1988), 143 and n. 58, and for the disyllabic ending in Hoccleve, see Burrow (1999), liii. F characteristically rewrites to avoid the short b-verse. Among **C** mss., X has and *closyng ȝates thare*, P has *and closynde yates*.

105 **in**: WHmF have *in his*, not supported by **Cx**.

107 **atte**: "at the", as usual in L. The reading of LMHmCF establishes this as **Bx**, even though *at* in CrWGO is the **Cx** reading.

108 **presumed**: Beta has pa.t. (or ppl.) following from *cauȝt* in l. 107. F's present tense appears to have support from **Cx**, but in **Cx** this follows from *cauȝt han*.

To han þ[e] power þat peter hadde · inpugnen I nelle
110 For in loue and letterure · þe eleccioun bilongeth
For-þi I can and can nauȝte · of courte speke more

¶ Þanne come þere a kyng · knyȝthod hym ladde
Miȝt of þe comunes · made hym to regne
And þanne cam kynde wytte · and clerkes he made
115 For to conseille þe kyng · and þe comune saue

¶ The kyng and knyȝthode · and clergye bothe
Casten þat þe comune [·] shulde hem-self fynde

¶ Þe comune contreued · of kynde witte craftes
And for profit of alle þe poeple · plowmen ordeygned
120 To tilie and [to] trauaile · as trewe lyf askeþ
Þe kynge and þe comune · and kynde witte þe thridde
Shope lawe & lewte · eche [lyf] to knowe his owne

¶ Þanne loked vp a lunatik · a lene þing with-alle
And knelyng to þe kyng · clergealy he seyde
125 Crist kepe þe sire kyng · and þi kyngriche
And lene þe lede þi londe · so leute þe louye
And for þi riȝtful rewlyng · be rewarded in heuene

¶ And sithen in þe eyre an hiegh · an angel of heuene
Lowed to speke in latyn · for lewed men ne coude
130 Iangle ne iugge · þat iustifie hem shulde
But suffren & seruen · for-thi seyde þe angel
Sum Rex sum Princeps · neutrum fortasse deinceps
O qui iura regis · cristi specialia regis
Hoc quod agas melius · iustus es esto pius
135 Nudum ius a te · vestiri vult pietate
Qualia vis metere · talia grana sere
Si ius nudatur · nudo de iure metatur ·

---

109 **þe**: Beta has *þat*, but F is supported by **Cx**.
110 **and**: WF have *and in*, not supported by **Cx**.
119 **of alle**: LCrWCO, and probably beta, but MHmGF drop *alle*. There is no help from the revised line in **Cx**. We retain copy-text.
120 **to trauaile**: All mss. have this second *to* except LCO. For the same pattern with initial *to*, cf. **Bx**.2.83–4, 5.134, etc. This passage is dropped in C.
122 **lyf**: So F. Although the reading could derive from two lines above, it is probable that non-alliterating *man* is a substitution in beta.
125 R begins with this line.
135 **ius**: Alpha picks up *vis* (in the sense "force") from the line below (where it means "you wish", from *volo*), and it is an easy minim error. Beta is supported by **Cx**.
135 **vestiri**: Alpha has *vestire*, but beta is supported by most C mss.
137 **ius**: Alpha again has *vis*. See note to l. 135.

Si seritur pietas · de pietate metas ·

¶ Thanne greued hym a Goliardeys · a glotoun of wordes
140 And to þe angel an hei3 · answeres after
Dum rex a regere · dicatur nomen habere
Nomen habet sine re · nisi studet iura tenere ·

¶ And þanne gan alle þe comune · crye in [a] vers of latin
To þe kynges conseille · construe ho-so wolde
145 Precepta Regis · sunt nobis vincula legis ·

¶ Wiþ þat ran þere a route [·] of ratones at ones
And smale mys with hem [·] mo þen a þousande
And comen to a conseille · for here comune profit
For a cat of a courte · cam whan hym lyked
150 And ouerlepe hem ly3tlich · and lau3te hem at his wille
And pleyde wiþ hem perilouslych · and possed [hem] aboute
For doute of dyuerse dredes · we dar nou3te wel loke
And 3if we grucche of his gamen · he wil greue vs alle
Cracche vs or clowe vs · and in his cloches holde
155 That vs lotheth þe lyf · or he lete vs passe
My3te we wiþ any witte · his wille withstonde
We my3te be lordes aloft · and lyuen at owre ese

¶ A raton of renon [·] most renable of tonge
Seide for a souereygne · help to hym-selue
160 I haue ysein segges quod he · in þe cite of london

---

140 **answeres**: All mss. except LR have the past tense following *greued*, though both MHm probably shared the present before correction. Lines 139–45 are not paralleled in **Cx**.

143 **And**: LRC only; others omit. Although this is strong evidence for **Bx**, it could of course be coincidental error.

143 **a**: "one". R probably represents alpha, obscured by F's rewriting. Beta's omission loses the sense, "one line", referring to **Bx.P.145**.

144 The line is omitted by alpha. The passage differs in **Cx**.

147 **with**: W has *mid*, an interesting case of scribal improvement to the alliteration. **Cx** also has *with*. Cf. **Bx**.1.117 and note.

148 **here**: LMCOR supported by **Cx** against *þe* in others.

149 **courte**: The reading of LCO and alpha is obviously right and supported by **Cx**. Beta2 (CrWHm), joined by G, read *contree*, either a simple misreading or avoidance of a politically sensitive reference. M's *contre* is a correction, but apparently just a respelling.

150 **his**: omitted in F and also **Cx**.

151 **hem** (2): Supported by alpha (though F switches to first-person pronoun in both instances in the line), as well as by MCO. **Cx** includes *hem* in a revised b-verse.

153 **grucche of**: "complain about". Alpha drops *of*, but beta is supported by **Cx**.

158 **¶**: The paraph is in beta and F. The line is at the top of the page in R.

159 L has an otiose paraph. The line is at the top of the page.

159 **hym-selue**: Skeat (1886) translates: "'Said for a sovereign remedy for himself'; i.e. as far as himself was concerned". Alpha's *hem alle* is suspiciously easier, and credits the rat with a community spirit which he probably does not deserve. The line is not in **Cx**.

Beren biȝes ful briȝte · abouten here nekkes
And some colers of crafty werk [·] vncoupled þei wenden
Boþe in wareine & in waste · where hem leue lyketh
And otherwhile þei aren elles-where · as I here telle
165   Were þere a belle on here beiȝ · bi Ihesu as me thynketh
Men myȝte wite where þei went · and awei renne
And riȝt so quod þat ratoun · reson me sheweth
To bugge a belle of brasse · or of briȝte syluer
And knitten [it] on a colere · for owre comune profit
170   And hangen it vp-on þe cattes hals · þanne here we mowen
Where he ritt or rest · or renneth to playe
And ȝif him list for to laike · þenne loke we mowen
And peren in his presence · þer-while hym plaie liketh
And ȝif him wrattheth be ywar · and his weye shonye

175   ¶ Alle þis route of ratones · to þis reson þei assented
Ac þo þe belle was ybouȝt · and on þe beiȝe hanged
Þere ne was ratoun in alle þe route · for alle þe rewme of Fraunce
Þat dorst haue ybounden þe belle · aboute þe cattis nekke
Ne hangen [it] aboute [his] hals · al Engelonde to wynne
180   And helden hem vnhardy · and here conseille feble
And leten here laboure lost · & alle here longe studye

¶ A mous þat moche good · couthe as me thouȝte
Stroke forth sternly · and stode biforn hem alle
And to þe route of ratones · reherced þese wordes
185   Thouȝ we [had] culled þe catte · ȝut sholde þer come an-other
To cracchy vs and al owre kynde · þouȝ we croupe vnder benches
For-þi I conseille alle þe comune · to lat þe catte worthe

---

163 **leue lyketh**: So LCOR. F alters *leue* to the superlative, *best*; beta2 and G corrupt to the common phrase. CrWG switch to the past tense both here and in the previous line; the M corrector alters both verbs from present to past.

169 **it**: LCGO omit, and M adds. Probably lost by beta and supplied by individual scribes. **Cx** also reads *hit*.

170 The line is lost in beta2 (CrWHm) and G.

171–72 Alpha omits two lines as a result of eyeskip.

171 **renneth**: Y has the C reading *rometh*, by contamination or coincidence.

175 **þis** (1): Beta is supported by the X family of C, alpha's *þe* by the P family.

176 **ybouȝt**: Beta2 and G read *(y)brouȝt*. The P family of C have the former, most of the X family the latter.

179 **it**: Omitted by LG and added in M, but supported by **Cx**. As in l. 169 it was probably lost by beta and supplied by individual scribes.

179 **his**: Beta has *þe cattes*, but the alpha reading is supported by **Cx**.

185 **had culled**: Beta2 (CrWHm) and G have the present tense, other beta mss. the past, and alpha the pluperfect, as does **Cx**.

186 **cracchy**: As in **Cx**. M alters to *cacche*, the reading of beta2, G and F.

186 **croupe**: The various spellings of the verb may all be understood as past tense, "crept".

And be we neuer so bolde · þe belle hym to shewe
For I herde my sire seyn · is seuene ȝere ypassed
190 Þere þe catte is a kitoun · þe courte is ful elyng
Þat witnisseth holiwrite · who-so wil it rede
Ve terre vbi puer [est rex] &c
For may no renke þere rest haue · for ratones bi nyȝte
Þe while he caccheþ conynges · he coueiteth nouȝt owre caroyne
195 But fet hym al with venesoun · defame we hym neuere
For better is a litel losse · þan a longe sorwe
Þe mase amonge vs alle · þouȝ we mysse a schrewe
For many mannus malt · we mys wolde destruye
And also ȝe route of ratones · rende mennes clothes
200 Nere þ[e] cat of þ[e] courte · þat can ȝow ouerlepe
For had ȝe rat[ones] ȝowre wille · ȝe couthe nouȝt reule ȝowre-selue
I sey [it] for me quod þe mous · I se so mykel after
Shal neuer þe cat ne þe kitoun · bi my conseille be greued
Ne carpyng of þis coler · þat costed me neure
205 And þouȝ it coste me catel · biknowen it I nolde
But suffre as hym-self wolde · to do as hym liketh
Coupled & vncoupled · to cacche what thei mowe
For-þi vche a wise wiȝte I warne · wite wel his owne

¶ What þis meteles bemeneth · ȝe men þat be merye
210 Deuine ȝe for I ne dar · bi dere god in heuene

¶ Ȝit houed þere an hondreth · in houues of selke
Seriauntz it semed · þat serueden atte barre
Plededen for penyes · and poundes þe lawe
And nouȝt for loue of owre lorde · vnlese here lippes onis
215 Þow myȝtest better mete myste · on maluerne hulles

---

192 **est rex**: The order in HmOR and **Cx**; reversed in others. Scribes tend to copy quotations in the form with which they are familiar. See Alford (1992), 34.

198 **mannus**: The gen. sg. of LMCR is supported by **Cx** against the plural of others.

199 **ȝe**: LMW + alpha; among C mss. the P family has *ȝe* and the X family *þe*.

200 **þe … þe**: So HmGF and **Cx**; MCrW have *þe … þat*, reversed in R; LO have *þat … þat*. No certainty is possible.

201 **ratones**: The form in alpha and G, supported by **Cx** against *rattes* in others.

202 **sey it**: R is supported by **Cx**. F has *sey þis*, and beta drops *it*.

205 **coste**: Beta's *had coste* is not supported by **Cx**.

206 **do as**: F's *slen what* shows his propensity to correct alliteration. The line is rewritten in **Cx**. See Schmidt (1995), 364–5.

208 **For-þi**: The beta reading. R has *For*, F has *&*. The line is not in **AC**.

214 **vnlese**: LR, so good evidence for **Bx**. Formally a different verb from *vnlose* as in others (*MED vnlesen* v.(2) and *unlosen*). **A** mss. also vary, but **Cx** (RK.P.164) has the latter. At **Bx**.17.142 the reading is *vnlosen*.

215 **myste**: So alpha + WG and the X family of **C**. Other mss. supply *þe*, as the scribe of O does. **A** mss. are split.

Þan gete a momme of here mouthe · [er] monoy [be] shewed

¶ Barones an burgeis · and bonde-men als
I seiȝ in þis assemble · as ȝe shul here after
Baxsteres & brewesteres · and bocheres manye
220   Wollewebsteres · and weueres of lynnen
Taillours and tynkeres · & tolleres in marketes
Masons and mynours · and many other craftes
Of alkin libbyng laboreres · lopen forth somme
As dykers & delueres · þat doth here dedes ille
225   And dryuen forth þe dere day · with dieu vous saue dame Emme

[¶] Cokes and here knaues · crieden hote pies hote
Gode gris a gees · go we dyne go we

¶ Tauerners vn-til hem · tolde þe same
White wyn of Oseye · and wyn of Gascoigne
230   Of þe Ryne and of þe Rochel · þe roste to defye
Al þis seiȝ I slepyng · and seuene sythes more

---

216 **er**: LMCO support for *but* suggests this is the reading of beta, though comparison of **AC** versions suggests that the choice lies between alpha *er* and *til* in beta2 and G. The X family of C has the former, but most A mss. read *til*, as does the P family of **C**. We suppose *til* arises by contamination or coincidence.

216 **be**: So beta2, GOF (R has *hem by*), against *were* in LMC. **Ax** seems to have *be* (K.P.89); the P family of C also have *be*, though the X family probably read *wer* (RK.P.166).

223 **alkin**: The beta reading has force in a list of labourers, but it is challenged by alpha's *alle*, shared by Z (Bodley 851). **AC** versions do not have the line.

225 **dere**: The choice is not obvious. The fact that L has *dere* and that M's *longe* is a correction (apparently of a shorter word) suggests the possibility that beta1 derives *longe* by contamination with A or by coincidental error. Alpha is uncertain: F's *fayre day* has no support, but R's *here dayes here* is supported by **Cx** *her days*. See Donaldson (1955), 197. We retain copy-text by default.

225 **vous**: So **Bx**, though omitted by CrWG, **Ax** and the P family of C.

226 Alpha and W here start a paragraph (the line is at the top of the page in M).

227 **a**: "and", as also at **Bx**.7.104, 8.53, 13.88 etc. See *MED a* conj.

227 **gris ... gees**: this order has the support of LMC + alpha, but is challenged by beta2, GO and **AC**.

229 **wyn** (2): Beta reads *red wyn*, making explicit the contrast with *White wyn* in the a-verse. Alpha omits the adjective (R's b-verse, though defective, is also that of the P family of C), as do the **AC** versions.

230 **of** (2): Beta is supported by **AC**.

231 The line is omitted in WF. It is in **AC**.

Passus 1

What this montaigne bymeneth · and þe merke dale
And þe felde ful of folke · I shal ȝow faire schewe
A loueli ladi of lere · in lynnen yclothed
Come down fram a castel · and called me faire
5   And seide sone slepestow · sestow þis poeple
How bisi þei ben · abouten þe mase
Þe moste partie of þis poeple · þat passeth on þis erthe
Haue þei worschip in þis worlde · þei wilne no better
Of other heuene þan here · holde þei no tale

10   ¶ I was aferd of her face · þeiȝ she faire were
And seide mercy Madame · what is þis to mene

[¶] Þe toure vp þe toft quod she · treuthe is þere-Inne
And wolde þat ȝe wrouȝte · as his worde techeth
For he is fader of feith · fourmed ȝow alle
15   Bothe with fel and with face · and ȝaf ȝow fyue wittis
Forto worschip hym þer-with · þe while þat ȝe ben here
And þerfore he hyȝte þe erthe · to help ȝow vchone

---

6 **abouten**: The variation is between trisyllabic *abouten* in L, unrevised M, C and alpha, and *alle aboute* in corrected M, CrWHmG. Both are metrical, the former supported by **Ax** and **Cx**.
8 **wilne**: G has *kepe* from **Ax**.
12 ¶: The paraph in WHm is supported by the new line-group in R (the paraph and first word are lost).
12 **vp**: CrF have *vpon*, WHmG have *on*. Prepositional *vp* is not uncommon, but usually altered to *vpon* by W and later texts: e.g. **Bx**.9.108. Though it is certainly **Bx**, it is not here supported by AC mss.
14 **fourmed**: LMCOR, so **Bx**. Others read *and formed* (WF), *that formede* (HmG), *and former of* (Cr). Cr shares the reading of **Cx**. A mss. vary between *and fourmide* and *that formed*.
16 **þe while þat**: LMCR, contested by WHm *whil þat*. **Ax** and the P family of **C** have *whyle* or *whyles*; the X family has *þe whiles*.

Of wollen of lynnen · of lyflode at nede
In mesurable manere · to make ӡow at ese

20 ¶ And comaunded of his curteisye [·] in comune þree þinges
Arne none nedful but þo · and nempne hem I thinke
And rekne hem bi resoun · reherce þow hem after
That one is vesture · from chele þe to saue
And mete atte mele · for myseise of þi-selue
25 And drynke whan þow dryest · ac do nouӡt out of resoun
That þow worth þe werse · whan þow worche shuldest

¶ For loth in his lifdayes · for likyng of drynke
Dede bi his douӡtres · þat þe deuel lyked
Delited hym in drynke · as þe deuel wolde
30 And lecherye hym lauӡt · and lay bi hem boþe
And al he witt it wyn · þat wikked dede
Inebriamus eum vino · dormiamusque cum eo
Vt seruare possimus de patre nostro semen
Thorw wyn and þorw women · þere was loth acombred
35 And þere gat in glotonye · gerlis þat were cherlis
For-þi drede delitable drynke · and þow shalt do þe bettere
Mesure is medcyne · þouӡ þow moche ӡerne
It is nauӡt al gode to þe goste · þat þe gutte axeþ
Ne liflode to þi likam · [þat lief is to þi soule
40 Leue not þi likam ·] for a lyer him techeth
That is þe wrecched worlde · wolde þe bitraye
For þe fende and þi flesch · folweth þe to-gidere
This and þat see[th] þi soule · and seith it in þin herte
And for þow sholdest ben ywar · I wisse þe þe beste

45 ¶ Madame mercy quod I · me liketh wel ӡowre wordes

---

22 **þow**: Supported by LWCR, against *ӡe* in CrHmOF and in M as an addition. In ll. 13–19 Holychurch addresses her remarks to the world at large; here and in the next lines she directs her attention to Will. **Ax** supports *þow*; **Cx** rewrites.

24 **atte**: "at the" (see **Bx**.19.110, 487, etc.). Supported by LMCR, though **Ax** has *at*, as do CrWHmGOF.

31 **wyn**: LG and alpha, with beta2 and MC reading *þe wyn*. Most A mss. have the former; **Cx** has the latter.

32 **Inebriamus**: ROC correct to the subjunctive, "Let us get him drunk". C mss. vary similarly.

39–40 Supported by **Ax** and **Cx**. LMWHmC dropped the b-verse of l. 39 and the a-verse of l. 40 through eyeskip on *likam*. M is later corrected. Cr dropped l. 39 altogether; FG dropped l. 40.

42 **folweth þe**: WHmG omit *þe*, as do **Ax** and **Cx**. Bx perhaps picked it up from the previous line.

43 **seeth**: The beta reading (L miswrites as *seest*) is supported by **Cx** (RK.1.39), though alpha has *sueth* (F *sewe*). **Ax** has instead *shendith*.

45 **Madame**: F's interjection *A* is in agreement with AC. Probably it is derived from an A text.

Ac þe moneye of þis molde · þat men so faste *holdeth / kepeth*
Telle me to whom Madame · þat tresore appendeth

¶ Go to þe gospel quod she · þat god seide hym-seluen
Tho þe poeple hym apposed · wiþ a peny in þe temple
50 Whether þei shulde þer-with · worschip þe kyng Sesar
And god axed of hem · of whome spake þe lettre
And þe ymage ilyke [·] þat þere-inne stondeth
Cesaris þei seide [·] we sen hym wel vchone

¶ Reddite cesari quod god · þat cesari bifalleth
55 Et que sunt dei deo · or elles ȝe done ille
For riȝtful reson · shulde rewle ȝow alle
And kynde witte be wardeyne · ȝowre welthe to kepe
And tutour of ȝoure tresore · and take it ȝow at nede
For housbonderye & hij · holden togideres

60 [¶] Þanne I frained hir faire · for hym þat hir made
That dongeoun in þe dale [·] þat dredful is of siȝte
What may it be to mene · ma-dame I ȝow biseche

¶ Þat is þe castel of care · who-so cometh þerinne
May banne þat he borne was · to body or to soule
65 Þerinne wonieth a wiȝte · þat wronge is yhote
Fader of falshed · and founded it hym-selue
Adam and Eue · he egged to ille
Conseilled caym · to kullen his brother
Iudas he iaped · with iuwen siluer

---

46 **holdeth / kepeth**: Beta agrees with **Ax**; alpha's *kepeth* is in agreement with **Cx**. See Introduction, pp. 8–10.

47 **Madame**: This is secure for **Bx**, though it is not in F, **Ax** or **Cx**. Its position in the line is
uncertain. It is likely enough, as KD argue (p. 168), that it is caught up from two lines above.
As in that line, F's agreement with **Ax** here may reflect contamination, as Schmidt (1995), 365,
suggests.

53 **Cesaris**: Of those that have a genitive, LOR have the Vulgate form (Matt 22.21), while M
and beta2 (CrWHm) have *Cesares*.

56 **riȝtful**: The adjective seems clearly the **Bx** reading, but W shares the adverb with **Ax** and
Cx. The latter is superior in sense; possibly an independent correction in W.

59 **hij**: The plural in beta, referring to Reason and Kind Wit, probably represents **Bx**. Alpha,
taking the reference to be to Kind Wit alone, alters to the singular, with fem. *heo* in R (perhaps
as alpha), masc. *he* in F as in AC. If **Bx** had read *he*, it would be difficult to understand that
causing confusion.

60 **¶**: The paraph in WHm is supported by a new line-group in alpha.

60 **hir** (2): LMCO and alpha, as in AC. Beta2 and G have *me*.

62 **be to mene**: Schmidt (1995), 365, suggests GF's *bemene* is from AC versions.

69 **iuwen**: CrG and alpha have *Iewes* or *þe Iewys*. There is some variation in **AC**, but *iuwen* is
probably archetypal in all three versions.

70   And sithen on an eller [·] honged hym after
      He is letter of loue · and lyeth hem alle
      That trusten on his tresor · *bitrayeth he / bytrayed aren* sonnest

      ¶ Thanne had I wonder in my witt · what womman *it / she* were
      Þat such wise wordes · of holywrit shewed
75   And asked hir on þe hieȝe name · ar heo þennes ȝeode
      What she were witterli · þat wissed me so faire

      ¶ Holicherche I am quod she · þow ouȝtest me to knowe
      I vnderfonge þe firste · and þe feyth tauȝte
      And brouȝtest me borwes · my biddyng to fulfille
80   And to loue me lelly · þe while þi lyf dureth

      ¶ Thanne I courbed on my knees · and cryed hir of grace
      And preyed hir pitousely · [to] prey for my synnes
      And also ken[n]e me kyndeli · on criste to bileue
      That I miȝte worchen his wille · þat wrouȝte me to man
85   Teche me to no tresore · but telle me þis ilke
      How I may saue my soule · þat seynt art yholden

      ¶ Whan alle tresores aren tried quod she · trewthe is þe best
      I do it on deus caritas · to deme þe soþe
      It is as derworth a drewery · as dere god hym-seluen

90   ¶ Who-so is trewe of his tonge · & telleth none other
      And doth þe werkis þer-with · and wilneth no man ille

---

70 **hym after**: The variation *hym-selue* as in WF is also in **A**. The b-verse is revised in **C**.

72 **bitrayeth he/bytrayed aren**: The beta reading is essentially that of **Cx**, *he bytrayeth*. Alpha's reading *bytrayed aren* is shared with **Ax**. G's reading is presumably contaminated from an **A** source (Schmidt (1995), 365).

73 **it/she**: Beta agrees with **Ax**; alpha's fem. pronoun is in agreement with **Cx**.

75 **asked**: (R *hasked*.) F alone has *halsede*, probably by contamination from **A**; see Schmidt (1995), lxiii. **C** mss. have *halsede* or *halsnede*. The verb does not occur elsewhere in the poem, and it was perhaps obsolescent.

75 **heo**: The form is secure for **Bx**, with LMR support.

76 **she**: R alone has the form *he*. See also l. 87 and note to l. 77.

77 **she**: R again has *he*, as in the previous line. The form is not necessary for the alliteration.

78 **þe feyth**: The apparent agreement of Hm and F recorded by KD, *þe feyþ þe*, is not significant, since Hm's reading results from a misdivision of *feythe*.

79 **brouȝtest**: **Bx** idiomatically lacks the subject pronoun *þow*, added in CrHmGOF, bringing them into line with **AC** versions.

80 **me lelly**: Reversed in alpha. Beta is supported by **Ax**. **Cx** rewrites.

81 **¶**: The paraph is in beta and F. The line is at the bottom of the page in R.

82 **to**: Omitted by beta. Alpha is supported by **Ax** and **Cx**, though the addition of *to* before an infinitive is a common scribalism.

83 **kenne**: L has *kende*, with the line marked for correction.

84 The line is attested by beta and **Ax**, but omitted in alpha and **Cx**, perhaps as a revision.

89 **It**: Alpha's *Þat it* has no support from **AC**.

90 **Who-so**: The beta reading, but alpha has *He* (R) or *He þat* (F). **Ax** supports beta; in **C** the P family begins *For who*, the X family has *For he*.

He is a god bi þe gospel · agrounde and aloft
And ylike to owre lorde · bi seynte lukes wordes
Þe clerkes þat knoweþ þis · shulde kenne it aboute
95 For cristene and vncristne · clameþ it vchone

¶ Kynges & kniȝtes · shulde kepe it bi resoun
Riden and rappe down · in reumes aboute
And taken tran[s]gressores · and tyen hem faste
Til treuthe had ytermyned · her trespas to þe ende
100 And þat is þe professioun appertly · þat appendeth for knyȝtes
And nouȝt to fasten a fryday · in fyue score wynter
But holden wiþ him & with hir · þat wolden al treuthe
And neuer leue hem for loue · ne for lacchyng of syluer

¶ For dauid in his dayes · dubbed kniȝtes
105 And did hem swere on here swerde · to serue trewthe euere
And who-so passed þat poynte · was apostata in þe ordre

¶ But criste kingene kynge · kniȝted ten
Cherubyn and seraphin · suche seuene and an othre
And ȝaf hem myȝte in his maieste · þe murger hem þouȝte
110 And ouer his mene meyne · made hem archangeles
Tauȝte hem bi þe Trinitee · treuthe to knowe
To be buxome at his biddyng · he bad hem nouȝte elles

¶ Lucifer wiþ legiounes · lerned it in heuene
[Til] he brake buxumnesse · his blisse gan he tyne
115 And fel fro þat felawship · in a fendes liknes
In-to a depe derke helle · to dwelle þere for eure
And mo þowsandes wiþ him · þan man couthe noumbre
Lopen out wiþ Lucifer · in lothelich forme

---

97 **down:** This varies in all three versions with *adoun*, though **Ax** has the former and **Cx** the latter.

100 **for:** So LCR, which is good evidence for **Bx**. But AC have the obvious *to*, as in all other mss.

102 **wolden:** G's alliterating *asketh* is from **Ax**. **Cx** rewrites.

103 **And:** The beta reading is supported by AC against alpha's *Ne*.

108 **an othre:** The reference is to the ten orders of angels at Creation; see the comprehensive note in Skeat (1886), ii. 24–5. Beta2 and R (perhaps additionally confused by preceding *and*) miss the point and drop *an*, but AC support *an othre*.

112 **To:** Beta has the support of **Ax** against alpha's *And*. Nevertheless, the latter may be the better reading: "God taught them to know truth and be obedient". Not in C.

113 **¶:** The paraph is in beta and F. The line is at the bottom of the page in R.

114 **Til:** Alpha is supported by **Ax** against beta's *But for*. **Bx** lost the preceding line, "And was þe louelokest of siȝt aftir oure lord" (K.1.110), leaving the argument that Lucifer learned obedience until he lost it. Beta rewrote to avoid nonsense. See Donaldson (1955), 208–09.

117 **wiþ:** As at **Bx.P.147**, W alters to *myd* to create the standard alliterative pattern, on the model of **Bx.4.79**. The line is not in AC. See also **Bx.17.243**.

For þei leueden vpon hym · þat lyed in þis manere
120 Ponam pedem in aquilone · et similis ero altissimo ·

¶ And alle þat hoped it miȝte be so · none heuene miȝte hem holde
But fellen out in fendes liknesse · nyne dayes togideres
Til god of his goodnesse · gan stable and stynte
And garte þe heuene to stekye · and stonden in quiete

125 ¶ Whan thise wikked went out · wonderwise þei fellen
Somme in eyre somme in erthe · & somme in helle depe
Ac lucifer lowest [·] lith of hem alle
For pryde þat he pult out · his peyne hath none ende
And alle þat worche with wronge · wenden hij shulle
130 After her deth-day · and dwelle wiþ þat shrewe
Ac þo þat worche wel · as holiwritt telleth
And enden as I ere seide · in treuthe þat is þe best
Mowe be siker þat her soule · shal wende to heuene
Þer treuthe is in Trinitee · and troneth hem alle
135 For-þi I sey as I seide ere · bi siȝte of þise textis
Whan alle tresores arne ytried · treuthe is þe beste
Lereth it þis lewde men · for lettred men it knowen
Þat treuthe is tresore · þe triest on erþe

¶ ȝet haue I / I haue no kynde knowing quod I · ȝet mote ȝe kenne me better
140 By what craft in my corps · it comseth and where

---

120 **et ... altissimo**: R omits, and F loses the line. Beta is supported by **Cx**.

125 **wonderwise**: Beta2 has *in wonderwise*, as does the P family of **Cx** in a revised line.

126 **eyre ... erthe**: The versions vary, with **Ax** having the order of most beta mss., and **Cx** the order as in MO and alpha. The beta order is more logical.

128 **pult out**: The West Midlands form *pult* appears only in LCr, while R has the spelling *pelt*. **Ax** has *put out* as do the remaining **B** mss; **Cx** has *pokede*. *MED pilten* v., 3(b) glosses the phrase *pult out* as "exhibit (pride), display", though records no other instance of this sense. In **Bx**.8.97 LR again read *pulte/pelte* against *pull* or *putte* in other **B** witnesses. See also note to **Bx**.15.66.

129 **hij**: Only LC, though M's *þei* is a correction. See Introduction, p. 18.

129 Alpha has a new line-group here.

130 **and**: Supported by AC against alpha's *to*.

131 W and alpha have a paraph here.

133 **soule**: Beta2 and G have the plural, and M is altered to that reading. **Ax** supports the distributive sg. **Cx** rewrites ll. 131–6.

134 **troneth**: Alpha has non-alliterating *saue*. Beta's b-verse reproduces **Ax**; **Cx** rewrites.

135 Alpha has a new line-group here.

135 **siȝte of**: Alpha's b-verse is defective; beta is supported by **Ax**. The line is repeated at **Bx**.1.210.

136 **arne**: Beta's form is supported by most **A** mss. **Cx** revises.

137 **it þis**: So LWCO. M is corrected to *it ye*; CrHm read *on thys*; GF have *thys ye*, and R *this*. The variation reflects a **Bx** error, since AC read *it þus*.

139 **ȝet haue I/I haue**: The beta reading is that of **Ax**, whereas alpha (and Cr) is **Cx**.

139 **ȝet mote ȝe kenne me**: Presumably R, *ȝette mote I lerne*, represents alpha, and F repairs the alliteration. For some reason **A** mss. have much trouble with this b-verse, and **C** mss. only

¶ Þow doted daffe quod she · dulle arne þi wittes
To litel latyn þow lernedest · lede in þi ȝouthe
Heu michi qu[od] sterilem duxi vitam iuuenilem

¶ It is a kynde knowyng quod he · þat kenneth in þine herte
145 For to louye þi lorde · leuer þan þi-selue
No dedly synne to do · dey þouȝ þow sholdest
This I trowe be treuthe · who can teche þe better
Loke þow suffre hym to sey · and sithen lere it after
For thus witnesseth his worde · worcheth þow þere-after
150 For trewthe telleþ þat loue · is triacle of heuene
May no synne be on him sene · þat [þat spise vseth]
And alle his werkes he wrouȝte · with loue as him liste
And lered it Moises for þe leuest þing [·] and moste like to heuene
And also þe plente of pees · moste precious of vertues

155 ¶ For heuene myȝte nouȝte holden it · it was so heuy of hym-self
Tyl it hadde of þe erthe · yeten his fylle

¶ And whan it haued of þis folde [·] flessh & blode taken
Was neuere leef vpon lynde · liȝter þer-after
And portatyf and persant · as þe poynt of a nedle
160 That myȝte non armure it lette · ne none heiȝ walles

¶ For-þi is loue leder [·] of þe lordes folke of heuene
And a mene as þe Maire is · bitwene þe kyng and þe comune
Riȝt so is loue a ledere · and þe lawe shapeth
Vpon man for his mysdedes · þe merciment he taxeth
165 And for to knowe it kyndely · it comseth bi myght
And in þe herte þere is þe heuede · and þe heiȝ welle

---

slightly less, though there the X group has the beta reading we take to be **Bx**, while the P
group has *ȝe mot kenne me*, as does W here.
141 This is the last line of the Lansdowne fragment of R; the Rawlinson ms. begins with
Bx.2.42. On editorial policy where R is lacking, see note to **Bx.P.2**.
143 **quod**: The quotation is repeated in this form at **Bx.5.452**. In both cases alpha's *quod* for
beta's *quia* is also the wording in **Cx**. See Alford (1992), 35–6.
144 **he**: "she".
148 LWC have an inappropriate paraph, though possibly it is **Bx**.
149 The line is lost by beta2 (CrWHm) and G. It is in **Ax** but not **Cx**.
151 **þat þat spise vseth**: F's inverted order is metrical, and perhaps authorial, with K.7.137 *þat
no werk vsiþ* (alliterating on /n/) providing a parallel. Even so, it may be a scribal sophistication,
and this is one of the occasions where R is sorely missed. The line is not in **AC**.
154 **plente**: "fullness"; and cf. the proverb "peace maketh plenty" which may have influenced
the **Bx** scribe. Cr's *plant* may have been taken from his C ms.; it is probably also **Ax**. See
Adams (1991), 7–15.
156 **yeten**: "eaten". See Schmidt (1995), 366. Cr's *yoten it-selue* (*MED yeten* v.3, "poured out")
is the reading of **Cx**.

¶ For in kynde knowynge in herte · þere a myȝte bigynneth
And þat falleth to þe fader · þat formed vs alle
Loked on vs with loue · and lete his sone deye
170 Mekely for owre mysdedes · to amende vs alle
And ȝet wolde he hem no woo · þat wrouȝte hym þat peyne
But mekelich with mouthe · mercy he bisouȝte
To haue pite o[n] þat poeple · þat peyned hym to deth

¶ Here myȝtow see ensamples · in hym-selue one
175 That he was miȝtful & meke · and mercy gan graunte
To hem þat hongen him an heiȝ · and his herte þirled

¶ For-thi I rede ȝow riche · haueth reuthe of þe pouere
Thouȝ ȝe be myȝtful to mote · beth meke in ȝowre werkes

¶ For þe same mesur[e] þat ȝe mete · amys other elles
180 Ȝe shullen ben weyen þer-wyth · whan ȝe wende hennes
Eadem mensura qua mensi fueritis · remecietur vobis ·

¶ For þouȝ ȝe be trewe of ȝowre tonge · and trewliche wynne
And as chaste as a childe · þat in cherche wepeth
But if ȝe louen lelliche · and lene þe poure
185 [Of] such goed as god ȝow sent [·] godelich parteth
Ȝe ne haue na more meryte · in masse ne in houres
Þan Malkyn of hire maydenhode · þat no man desireth

¶ For Iames þe gentil · iugged in his bokes
That faith with-oute þe faite · is riȝte no-þinge worthi
190 And as ded as a dore-tre · but ȝif þe dedes folwe
Fides sine operibus mortua est &c

---

173 **on**: MCrHmGO as well as F (= alpha?) are supported by AC versions against *of* in LWC. Yet the latter might be **Bx**; cf. l. 177 for a similar case, and note that MCrHmGOF have *pity on* for *pity of* in **Bx**.5.260.

173 **peyned**: A mss. have predominantly *pinede* (*MED pinen*), as do MHmF, whereas C mss. have *paynede* (*MED peinen*), but the verbs were often confused.

174 **ensamples**: The singular of WCGF varies with the plural in all three versions. For the argument that the plural is "more exact", see Schmidt (2008), 316.

177 **reuthe of**: The beta reading, as in LMWCO. HmCrG have the more usual *ruthe on* (as in **Bx**.4.110, 112, 5.523, 14.180, 15.11), agreeing here with **AC**, by coincidence or contamination. F has *mercy on*.

179 **mesure**: LMWCGO (hence beta) have the plural, but CrHmF have sg., as **AC**. The plural is presumably a beta error, since the word is sg. in the Latin, l. 181.

184 **if**: Dropped by MF, but supported by **Cx**. A mss. vary.

185 **Of such**: *Of* is easily lost, as in beta. F is supported by **AC**.

186 **ne** (1): Dropped by MCrGF, but supported by **AC**.

189 **þe faite**: G reads *dede*, F has *fewte*, and in M the definite article is inserted by the corrector. The article in this phrase is more easily lost than added, and beta probably had it. **Ax** is without the article; **Cx** is divided, though the best representatives of the X family have it. We follow copy-text.

189 **riȝte**: F's omission of the word may represent **Bx**, but the b-verse is corrupt in any case. The **AC** reading is *is feblere þan noȝt*.

¶ For-thi chastite with-oute charite · worth cheyned in helle
It is as lewed as a laumpe · þat no liȝte is Inne

¶ Many chapeleynes arne chaste · ac charite is awey
195 Aren no men auarousere þan hij · whan þei ben auaunced
Vnkynde to her kyn · and to alle cristene
Chewen here charite · and chiden after more
Such chastite wiþ-outen charite · worth cheyned in helle

¶ Many curatoures kepen hem · clene of here bodies
200 Thei ben acombred wiþ coueitise · þei konne nouȝt out crepe
So harde hath auarice · yhasped hem togideres
And þat is no treuthe of þe trinite · but treccherye of helle
And lernyng to lewde men · þe latter for to dele

¶ For-þi þis wordes [·] ben wryten in þe gospel
205 Date & dabitur vobis · for I dele ȝow alle
And þat is þe lokke of loue · and lateth oute my grace
To conforte þe careful · acombred wiþ synne

¶ Loue is leche of lyf · and nexte owre lorde selue
And also þe graith gate · þat goth in-to heuene
210 For-þi I sey as I seide · ere by þe textis
Whan alle tresores ben ytryed · treuthe is þe beste
Now haue I tolde þe what treuthe is · þat no tresore is bettere
I may no lenger lenge þe with · now loke þe owre lorde

---

195 **no men auarousere**: G's *non herder* is by contamination from **AC**. F's *non* for beta's *no men* may be from **A**, but may represent **Bx**.

200 **nouȝt out crepe**: Beta has *nouȝt don it fram hem*, with G's *not cry ovte* an independent improvement or indebted to **AC**, which both have variously *not crepe out* and *not out crepe*. This supports F's *out crepe* (omitting *nouȝt* by oversight), though it may be by contamination.

203 **for to dele**: The beta reading, though G omits *for*, aligning it with most **A** mss. F has *to leve synne*. **C** rewrites.

204 **¶**: L's paraph is shared only with **C**, but the line is at the top of the page in **M** (which marks paraphs only with a blank space).

204 Because of the short line, scribes misplaced the punctus. Only **L** has it awkwardly after *ben*. We follow **MWCO**.

206 **and** (2): Clearly the beta reading, supported by the X family of **C**. CrGF have *þat* (M is revised to that reading), as does **Ax** and the P family of **C**. Again, F may be alpha or an **A** reading.

210 **by þe**: G's alliterating *by syght of thes* is supported by **AC**, but is derived by contamination and is not **Bx**. See KD p. 154, Schmidt (1995), 366. Alpha also omits *siȝte of* in the same b-verse at **Bx**.1.135.

213 **þe with**: In omitting the phrase G again shows contamination from **A**.

213 **now**: Supported by **Ax** though omitted by F and replaced by *but* in G. **Cx** is rewritten.

Passus 2

3et I courbed on my knees · and cryed hir of grace
And seide mercy Madame · for Marie loue of heuene
That bar þat blisful barne · þat bouȝte vs on þe Rode
Kenne me bi somme crafte · to knowe þe fals

5 ¶ Loke vppon þi left half · and lo where he standeth
Bothe fals and fauel · and here feres manye

¶ I loked on my left half · as þe lady me taughte
And was war of a womman · wortheli yclothed
Purfiled with pelure · þe [purest on] erthe
10 Ycrounede with a corone · þe kyng hath non better
Fetislich hir fyngres · were fretted with golde wyre
And þere-on red rubyes · as red as any glede
And diamantz of derrest pris · and double manere safferes
Orientales and ewages · enuenymes to destroye

15 ¶ Hire robe was ful riche · of red scarlet engreyned
With ribanes of red golde · and of riche stones
Hire arraye me rauysshed · suche ricchesse saw I neuere

---

5 **vppon**: Beta shares the C reading. F's *on* is the A reading.

5 **he**: O anticipates the appearance of Mede in l. 8; hence *sche*, so that *her* in l. 6 is perhaps feminine in O, whereas it is plural in other mss. A mss. vary, with masc., fem. and pl.

6 **here**: "their"; clearly **Bx**. **Ax** has *hise*, referring to *fals*. **Cx** rewrites the b-verse, but has *here* in its following line.

8 **wortheli**: G's *wonderslyche* is from A or C.

9 **purest on**: F shares this reading with **Ax**, whereas **Cx** revises to *non puyrere on*. The non-alliterating beta reading *fynest vpon* may of course be a **Bx** error.

10 **Ycrounede**: Beta has support from **Ax**; F's addition of *And* is supported by **Cx** and may represent alpha.

11 **golde wyre**: G's *rynges* is from **A**. **Cx** rewrites. F omits the line.

I had wondre what she was · and whas wyf she were

¶ What is þis womman quod I [·] so worthily atired

20　¶ That is Mede þe Mayde quod she · hath noyed me ful oft
And ylakked my lemman · þat lewte is hoten
And bilowen hire to lordes · þat lawes han to kepe
In þe popis paleys · she is pryue as my-self
But sothenesse wolde nouȝt so · for she is a bastarde

25　¶ For fals was hire fader · þat hath a fykel tonge
And neuere sothe seide · sithen he come to erthe

¶ And Mede is manered after hym · riȝte as kynde axeth
Qualis pater talis filius · bonus arbor · bonum fructum facit
I auȝte ben herre þan she · I cam of a better

30　¶ Mi fader þe grete god is · and grounde of alle graces
O god with-oute gynnynge · & I his gode douȝter
And hath ȝoue me mercy · to marye with my-self
And what man be merciful · and lelly me loue
Shal be my lorde and I his leef · in þe heiȝe heuene

35　¶ And what man taketh Mede · myne hed dar I legge
That he shal lese for hir loue · a lappe of caritatis
How construeth dauid þe kynge · of men þat taketh Mede
And men of þis molde · þat meynteneth treuthe
And how ȝe shal saue ȝow-self · þe Sauter bereth witnesse

40　Domine quis habitabit in tabernac[u]lo tuo &c

---

19 Only L has the punctuation after *womman*.

22 **bilowen hire**: "made herself pleasing to" (*MED biloven*); cf. **Bx**.6.233 where LMR have the -w- form. Both KD and Schmidt emend to *bilowen h[ym]*, "slandered him" (*MED bilien* v.(2)). A has *And lakkide my lore to lordis aboute* (K.2.17); **Cx** has *And lakked hym to lordes þat lawes han to kepe* (RK.2.21, who emend), with *ylow on my lemman* in the previous line.

27 ¶: Only LM indicate a new paragraph here. WHmCF have a paraph in the line above.

28 **bonus**: LMWF treat *arbor* as masc.; the others alter to the more usual feminine. At RK.10.244b the X family of C similarly have *bonus*. F's expansion of the Latin is not supported.

30 ¶: L's paraph is supported by a new line-group in M.

31 **& I**: F has *& y am*, as does **Cx** but in the a-verse.

35 **hed**: MO read *lif*. Presumably this is coincident error in a common phrase. Nevertheless, **Cx** reads *my lif y dar* (or *dar y*) *wedde*. Cf. **Bx**.18.162, *I dar my lyf legge*.

36 **lappe**: This must be the **Bx** reading, with Cr taking *lippe* from a C text. The P group of C have *lappe*, the X group *lippe*. *MED* cites *lippe* n.(2), "a little bit", only from Langland. Probably *lappe* is a scribal substitution of an easier word, as again at RK.11.224 where two mss. read *lappe* in the same context. It is likely enough that the word developed the sense "small piece"; see *MED lap(pe*, 3.

37 F has revised the line to improve the alliteration, though the reversal in the b-verse, *þat Meede taken*, might represent alpha. The line has no parallel in **AC**.

¶ And now worth þis Mede ymaried · to a mansed schrewe
To one fals fikel tonge · a fendes biȝete
Fauel þorw his faire speche · hath þis folke enchaunted
And al is lyeres ledyng · þat she is þus ywedded

45   ¶ To-morwe worth ymade · þe maydenes bruydale
And þere miȝte þow wite if þow wolt · which þei ben alle
That longeth to þat lordeship · þe lasse and þe more
Knowe hem þere if þow canst · and kepe þi tonge
And lakke hem nouȝt but lat hem worth · til lewte be iustice
50   And haue powere to punyschen hem · þanne put forth þi resoun

¶ Now I bikenne þe criste quod she · and his clene moder
And lat no conscience acombre þe · for coueitise of Mede

¶ Thus left me þat lady · liggyng aslepe
And how Mede was ymaried · in meteles me þouȝte
55   Þat alle þe riche retenauns · þat regneth with þe false
Were boden to þe bridale · on bothe two sydes
Of alle maner of men · þe mene and þe riche
To marie þis maydene · was many man assembled
As of kniȝtes and of clerkis · and other comune poeple
60   As sysours and sompnours · Shireues and here clerkes
Bedelles and Bailliues · and brokoures of chaffre
Forgoeres and vitaillers · and vokates of þe arches
I can nouȝt rekene þe route · þat ran aboute mede

65   ¶ Ac symonye and cyuile · and sisoures of courtes
Were moste pryue with Mede · of any men me þouȝte
Ac fauel was þe first · þat fette hire out of boure
And as a brokour brouȝte hir [·] to be with fals enioigned

---

41 **to:** F's reading probably represents alpha, and is supported by **Cx.** Beta must be *al to* since it has the support of LMCO, though *al* is subsequently erased in M. Beta2 reads *vnto.*
42 Here R resumes.
42 **tonge:** The beta reading has support from RK.2.6 over alpha's *of tonge.*
48 **þi:** So LCR, and probably M before correction. It seems likely that other scribes filled out a short line with *þou þi* or *wel þi.* **AC** read *kepe the fro hem alle.*
49 LMCrC have punctuation after *nouȝt* as well or instead.
52 **lat:** Probably R's *at* represents alpha, interpreted by F as *that.* C mss. have *Acombre neuere thy Conscience* or *And acombre thow ....*
56 **þe:** Beta is supported by **Ax** and the X family of C, while R's *þis* (F has *his*) is supported by the P family.
58 **maydene:** The form varies with *mayde* throughout; there is no equivalent line in **AC.** Although *MED* has separate entries, they are different forms of the same word and are listed together by Wittig (2001).
62 After this F adds a line that is obviously scribal.
66 Alpha has a paraph here.

Whan symonye and cyuile · sei3 here beire wille
Thei assented for siluer · to se[i] as bothe wolde
70 Thanne lepe lyer forth · and seide lo here a chartre
That gyle with his gret othes · gaf hem togidere
And preide cyuile to se · and symonye to rede it
Thanne symonye and cyuile · stonden forth bothe
And vnfoldeth þe feffement · þat fals hath ymaked
75 And þus bigynneth þes gomes · to greden ful hei3
Sciant presentes & futuri &c ·

¶ Witeth and witnesseth · þat wonieth vpon þis erthe
Þat Mede is ymaried · more for here goodis
Þan for ani vertue or fairenesse · or any free kynde
80 Falsenesse is faine of hire · for he wote hire riche
And fauel with his fikel speche · feffeth bi þis chartre
To be prynces in pryde · and pouerte to dispise
To bakbite and to bosten · and bere fals witnesse
To scorne and to scolde · and sclaundere to make
85 Vnboxome and bolde · to breke þe ten hestes

¶ And þe Erldome of enuye · and wratthe togideres
With þe chastelet of chest · and chateryng oute of resoun
Þe counte of coueitise · and alle þe costes aboute
That is vsure and auarice · alle I hem graunte
90 In bargaines and in brokages · with al þe borg[h]e of theft

¶ And al þe lordeship of lecherye · in lenthe and in brede
As in werkes and in wordes · and waitynges with eies

---

68 Beta2 has a paraph (a paragraph in Cr), as does R.

68 **beire**: Genitive of *bo*, synonymous with *boþere* in MWO and *bethere* in R.

69 **Thei**: Alpha has *And*, continuing the subordinate clause, but contradicting this syntax with a paraph before the following line. **Cx** has *Thei*.

69 **sei**: Falsely corrected to *se* in L.

70 Here and at l. 73 WHm and alpha have a paraph.

73 **stonden**: The past tense as in MF is also a minority form in **AC**.

74 F omits the line.

79 **or** (1): HmCGO read *of*. The line is not paralleled in **AC**, though C alters to a line with the same structure, *Then for holynesse oþer hendenesse oþer for hey kynde* (RK.2.84).

79 **or** (2): LCrWCG and alpha. The parallel line in **Cx** would give some support to MO *or for*.

85 **Vnboxome and bolde**: Beta's order is supported by **Cx** against alpha's reversal.

87 **chest**: i.e. "strife". Supported by **Cx** against alpha's non-alliterating *gestes*.

87 **resoun**: Again supported by **Cx**. Alpha's reading is probably R's *tyme*. F rewrites the b-verse to alliterate on /dʒ/ in a-verse.

90 **in** (2): The key witnesses LMR are supported by CrWCO. It is omitted by most **C** mss.

90 **borghe**: L writes *borgthe*.

92 **and** (2): So LMCGOR. Yet CrWHm have *and in* as the X family of **C**; F has *in* as the P family.

And in wedes and in wisshynges · and with ydel thou3tes
There as wille wolde · [and] wermanship failleth

95 ¶ Glotonye he gaf hem eke · and grete othes togydere
And alday to drynke · at dyuerse tauernes
And there to iangle and to iape · and iugge here euene-cristene
And in fastyngdayes to frete · ar ful tyme were
And þanne to sitten and soupen · til slepe hem assaille
100 And bredun as burgh-swyn · and bedden hem esily
Tyl sleuth and slepe · slyken his sides
And þanne wanhope to awake hym so · with no wille to amende
For he leueth be lost · þis is here last ende

¶ And þei to haue and to holde · and here eyres after
105 A dwellyng with þe deuel · and dampned be for eure
Wiþ al þe purtenaunces of purgatorie · in-to þe pyne of helle
3eldyng for þis þinge · at one 3eres ende
Here soules to sathan · to suffre with hym peynes
And with him to wonye with wo · whil god is in heuene

110 ¶ In witnesse of *which / þis* þing · wronge was þe first
And Pieres þe pardonere · of paulynes doctrine
Bette þe bedel · of Bokyngham-shire
Rainalde þe Reue · of Rotland sokene

---

93 **wedes**: The reading of beta; C mss. divide between *wedes* and *woldes*. R's *wedynges* is probably alpha's misreading influenced by the general context, although F offers the attractive and
appropriate variant *wenyngis*, glossed "hopes" by Schmidt (1995).
94 **and**: The line is marked for correction in L. Original *wolde and* has been revised by the
addition of *ne* before *wolde* and the subpunction of *and*, giving the reading of C. A couple of
C mss. have the same reading. Possibly the supervisor intended the correction of *wermanship*
instead, though it is not an uncommon spelling and is repeated at this point in the C text by X.
97 **to** (2): Supported by **Cx** against omission in WHmG.
100–3 There is disagreement about number in this passage. Alpha switches to the sg. in l. 100
with *a burgh swyne* and *hym*. In l. 101 alpha is joined by LWCGO in *his*, against *hyr* in CrHm
and corrected M. In 102 alpha + LMCO have *hym* against pl. *hem* in CrWHmG. In the a-verse
of 103 all mss. except CrHm have sg. *he*, while in the b-verse beta has pl. *here* while R has
his and F *þe*. Meanwhile, in the parallel but rewritten passage in **Cx**, there is also a switch in
number, with pl. pronouns throughout except in RK.2.108 (=**Bx**.2.103), *For a leueth be lost
when he his lyf leteth*. It looks as though scribes made rather ineffective attempts to rationalise
number. We follow copy-text, partly on the grounds that it is the least consistent.
106 **purtenaunces**: L and alpha have the aphetic form (initial *a-* is deleted in R). Other beta
mss. vary, as do C mss.
109 **with** (2): Alpha has *in*; beta probably has *with*, though MCO read *in*. Probably this is
reversion to the commoner phrase, as in **Bx**.19.203, though of course this parallel could also
be cited in support of *in*. **Ax** has "þere to wone wiþ wrong" (K.2.71).
110 **which / þis**: Beta is supported by **Ax** and by the alliteration, but alpha's non-alliterating
þis is undoubtedly also the **Cx** reading.
113 **Rotland**: Rutland, according to beta. Alpha's *Rokeland*, also a variant in a few **A** mss., is
Rockland in Norfolk.

Munde þe Mellere · and many moo other
115   In þe date of þe deuel [·] þis dede I assele
Bi siȝte of sire symonye · and cyuyles leue

¶ Þenne tened hym theologye · whan he þis tale herde
And seide to cyuile · now sorwe mot þow haue
Such we[d]dynges to worche [·] to wratthe with treuthe
120   And ar þis weddyng be wrouȝte · wo þe bityde

¶ For Mede is moylere · of amendes engendreth
And god graunteth to gyf · Mede to treuthe
And þow hast gyuen hire to a gyloure · now god gyf þe sorwe
Th[e] tixt telleth þe nouȝt so · treuthe wote þe sothe
125   For dignus est operarius · his hyre to haue
And þow hast fest hire to fals · fy on þi lawe
For al by lesynges þow lyuest · and lecherouse werkes
Symonye and þi-self · schenden holicherche
Þe notaries and ȝee · noyeth þe peple
130   Ȝe shul abiggen it bothe · bi god þat me made
Wel ȝe witen wernardes · but if ȝowre witte faille
That fals is faithlees · and fikel in his werkes
And [as] a bastarde ybore · of belsabubbes kynne
And Mede is moylere · a mayden of gode
135   And myȝte kisse þe kynge · for cosyn an she wolde

¶ For-þi worcheth bi wisdome · and bi witt also
And ledeth hire to londoun · þere lawe is yshewed
If any lawe wil loke · þei ligge togederes
And þouȝ Iustices iugge hir · to be ioigned with fals
140   Ȝet beth war of [þe] weddyng · for witty is truthe
And conscience is of his conseille · and knoweth ȝow vchone
And if he fynde ȝow in defaute · and with þe fals holde
It shal bisitte ȝowre soules · ful soure atte laste

¶ Here-to assenteth cyuile · ac symonye ne wolde

---

115 **I assele**: This must be **Bx**, though HmC *ys aseled* is the **AC** reading.

119 **weddynges**: LC have *wendynges*, but the line is marked for correction in L.

121 **engendreth**: Agreement of LR (together with C) indicates that this is an error in **Bx**, with the obvious correction to *engendred* made by other scribes. A spelling such as *engendrit* as in some **A** mss. could have caused the error in **Bx**.

122 **graunteth**: COF have past tense. There is the same variation in **A**.

124 **The**: Alpha is supported by **Ax** against beta's *Thi*.

128 Alpha has a paraph.

133 **as**: Alpha is supported by **AC** against beta's *was*.

139 **with**: Supported by **Ax** against CrWHmG *to*. **Cx** rewrites.

140 **þe**: Alpha's article is supported by **AC**. The line in L is an addition by another scribe.

145 Tyl he had siluer for his seruise · and also þe notaries

¶ Thanne fette fauel forth · floreynes ynowe
And bad gyle to gyue · golde al aboute
And namelich to þe notaries · þat hem none ne faille
And feffe false witnes · with floreines ynowe
150 For he may mede amaistrye · and maken at my wille

¶ Tho þis golde was gyue · grete was þe þonkynge
To fals and to fauel · for her faire ʒiftes
And comen to conforte [·] fram care þe fals
And seiden certis sire · cesse shal we neuere
155 Til Mede be þi wedded wyf · þorw wittis of vs alle
For we haue Mede amaistried · *with / þorw* owre mery speche
That she graunteth to gon [·] with a gode wille
To Londoun to loke · ʒif þat þe lawe wolde
Iugge ʒow ioyntly · in ioye for euere

160 ¶ Thanne was falsenesse fayne · and fauel as blithe
And leten sompne alle segges · in schires aboute
And bad hem alle be bown · beggeres and othere
To wenden wyth hem to westmynstre · to witnesse þis dede

¶ Ac þanne cared þei for caplus · to kairen hem þider
165 And fauel fette forth þanne · folus ynowe
And sette Mede vpon a schyreue · shodde al newe
And fals sat on a sisoure · þat softlich trotted
And fauel on a flatere · fetislich atired

¶ Tho haued notaries none · annoyed þei were
170 For symonye and cyuile · shulde on hire fete gange

---

147 **to**: So LMCrWCR, hence **Bx**. HmGOF have *go*, the reading of **Ax** and the P group of
C, presumably by coincident variation or contamination. Crowley "improves" with *go* in Cr³.
148 **ne**: Supported by LWCR, but dropped in others. It is not in most **AC** mss.
150 **he**: Established for **Bx** by LRF and probably original M, as well as **AC** against *þei* in others.
The referent is unambiguously plural in MW (*witnesses*), sg. in L (contrast *witnesses* **Bx**.9.77),
and ambiguous in other mss.
156 **with / þorw**: The beta reading is supported by most **A** mss.; alpha's *thorʒ*, though it may
have been picked up from the previous line, is also the reading of **Cx**.
158 **ʒif þat þe**: So LMCOF. Beta2 and G drop *þat*, R drops *þe*. **A** mss. vary similarly; **Cx** has *if*.
163 **hem**: Referring to Fals and Favel. Beta's reading is shared with **Ax** and the P family of C.
Alpha and the X family have *hym*. Beta seems more appropriate.
163 **þis**: Alpha *þe*. **A** mss. similarly split between *þis* and *þe*. The line is not in C.
164 **kairen**: So LM + alpha; other scribes substitute the easier *carien*, as also at **Bx**.P.29, 4.23,
5.310. Note, however, that **Ax** also has *carien*.
166 **vpon**: GF read *on*, as does **Ax**; R has *vppe*.
168 **flatere**: So LF. *MED* distinguishes between *flatour* (OF *flatour*) and *flaterer* (from the
verb).

¶ Ac þanne swore symonye · and cyuile bothe
That sompnoures shulde be sadled [·] and serue hem vchone
And lat apparaille þis prouisoures · in palfreis wyse
Sire symonye hym-seluen · shal sitte vpon here bakkes

175 ¶ Denes and suddenes · drawe ȝow togideres
Erchdekenes and officiales · and alle ȝowre Regystreres
Lat sadel hem with siluer · owre synne to suffre
As [de]uoutrie and deuoses · and derne vsurye
To bere bischopes aboute · abrode in visytynge

180 ¶ Paulynes pryues · for pleyntes in þe consistorie
Shul serue my-self · þat cyuile is nempned
And cartesadel þe comissarie · owre carte shal he lede
And fecchen vs vytailles · at fornicatores

¶ And maketh of lyer a l[a]nge carte · to lede alle þese othere
185 As [fobberes] and faitours · þat on here fete rennen
And thus fals and fauel · fareth forth togideres
And Mede in þe myddes · and alle þise men after

¶ I haue no tome to telle [·] þe taille þat hem folweth
Of many maner man · þat on þis molde libbeth
190 Ac gyle was forgoer · and gyed hem alle

¶ Sothenesse seiȝ h[e]m wel · and seide but a litel
And priked his palfrey · and passed hem alle
And come to þe kynges courte · and conscience it tolde
And conscience to þe kynge · carped it after

---

173 **þis**: FG omit, and R reads *þe*. **A** mss. also vary, but most support beta.

178 **deuoutrie**: The alliterating alpha synonym for beta's easier *auoutrie*. There is no parallel line in **AC**, although **Cx** has *deuoutours* at RK.2.187. R again has *deuoutrie* at **Bx**.12.86. *MED* does not record either *de-* form otherwise, but note *OED devoterer*, with an instance from 1550.

180 **pryues**: "parties to suits" (Alford (1988), 120–1). GF's *peple* is an **A** reading.

184 **lange carte**: The form in WR. Wittig (2001) lists the spelling *lange* once in each of the three versions, for this line only. WR always elsewhere have *longe*, and presumably the archetypal scribes recognised this as a technical expression for the *longa caretta*, a "four-wheeled military cart" (Galloway (2006), 278).

185 **fobberes**: "cheats". Alpha's reading has support from **Cx** *fobbes* (related to *fobben* vb.). Beta's *Freres* is much easier; most **A** mss. have *folis*.

186 W and alpha have a paraph here.

187 **men**: LCrWHmR supported by **Cx**. G has the **Ax** reading *meyny*. Oddly, the disparate group MCOF have *opere*.

189 The line is lost in beta2 and G.

191 **¶**: The paraph is in beta and F. The line is at the bottom of the page in R.

191 **hem**: The beta reading is probably *hym*, though CrWG and alpha have the plural, supported by **AC**.

191 **a litel**: Apparently **Bx**, though omission of *a* in MCrWG is shared with **Cx** and most **A** mss.

195 ¶ Now by cryst quod þe kynge · and I cacche my3te
Fals or fauel · or any of his feres
I wolde be wroke of þo wrecches · þat worcheth so ille
And don hem hange by þe hals · and alle þat hem meynteneth
Shal neure man of molde · meynprise þe leste
200 But ri3te as þe lawe wil loke · late falle on hem alle

¶ And comanded a constable · þat come atte furst
To / *Goo* attache þo tyrauntz · for eny thynge I hote
And fettereth fast falsenesse · for enykynnes 3iftes
And gurdeth of gyles hed · and lat hym go no furthere
205 And 3if 3e lacche lyer · late hym nou3t ascapen
Er he be put on þe pilorye · for eny preyere I hote
And bryngeth Mede to me · maugre hem alle

¶ Drede atte dore stode · and þe dome herde
And how þe kynge comaunded · constables and seriantz
210 Falsenesse and his felawschip · to fettren an to bynden
Þanne drede went wi3tliche · and warned þe fals
And bad hym flee for fere · and his felawes alle

¶ Falsenesse for fere þanne · flei3 to þe freres
And gyle doþ hym to go · agast for to dye
215 Ac marchantz mette with hym · and made hym abide
And bishetten hym in here shope · to shewen here ware
And apparailled hym as a prentice · þe poeple to serue

¶ Li3tlich lyer · lepe awey þanne
Lorkynge thorw lanes · to-lugged of manye
220 He was nawhere welcome · for his manye tales
Ouer al yhowted · and yhote trusse

---

196 **or** (1): Alpha reads *other* / *eyþir*, with R alone reading *other* for the second *or*. AC mss. vary in both instances.

199 **of**: Secure for **Bx**, in L, original M, C and R. The variants *of þis* (corrected M, CrW), *on* (OF), *on thys* (G) and *vpon* (Hm) may be prompted by the oddity of the phrase *man of molde*, as well as by l. 189 above. A mss. vary, but **Cx** has *on þys*.

202 **To / Goo**: Beta shares *To* with **Ax**; alpha's *Goo* is also **Cx**. Cf. the variants in **Bx**.2.147 above. The direct speech of "Goo attache ... I hote" is attractive; perhaps it suggested itself as an authorial or scribal improvement.

202 **thynge**: Presumably an error, but undoubtedly **Bx**. AC have *tresour*.

212 **felawes**: F's *feerys* is probably from A. It is also the reading of **Cx** which however avoids the pun on *fere* by altering the a-verse to *And bad falsenesse to fle* (RK.2.222).

216 **shope**: The distributive sg. is supported by LMCOR. **Ax** has the plural; C mss. vary.

217 **And**: **Ax** is without it, as are CrWHmG; it is the reading of **Cx**.

218 **þanne**: i.e. "from there". Both beta and alpha forms represent *MED thenne* adv.; cf. *LALME* 4.262.

221 **yhowted**: "shouted at". Beta2 has *yhonted*, an easy error, apparently supported by AC, though <u/n> are often indistinguishable. On Crowley's revisions here, see Hailey (2007), 152–4.

Tyl pardoneres haued pite · and pulled hym in-to house
They wesshen hym and wyped hym · and wonden hym in cloutes
And sente hym with seles · on sondayes to cherches
225 And gaf pardoun for pens · poundmel aboute

¶ Thanne loured leches · and lettres þei sent
Þat he sholde wonye with hem · wateres to loke
Spiceres spoke [to] hym · to spien here ware
For he couth o[n] here craft · and knewe many gommes

230 ¶ Ac mynst[r]alles and messageres · mette with hym ones
And helden hym an half3ere · and elleuene dayes

¶ Freres with faire speche · fetten hym þennes
And for knowyng of comeres · coped hym as a frere
Ac he hath leue to lepe out · as oft as hym liketh
235 And is welcome whan he wil · and woneth wyth hem oft

¶ Alle fledden for fere · and flowen in-to hernes
Saue Mede þe Mayde · na mo durst abide
Ac trewli to telle · she trembled for [fere]
And ek wept and wronge · whan she was attached

---

222 **in-to**: This must be **Bx**, supported by the X family of C, despite MHmF support for the **Ax** reading *to*.

223 **cloutes**: Hm and alpha have *clothes*. A mss. vary; **Cx** has *cloutes*, though five C mss. read *clothes*.

228 W and alpha have a paraph.

228 **spoke**: The form *speken* in CrWGR is also past plural; cf. **Bx**.15.286 for a clear instance, where L also has *speken*.

228 **to** (1): The alpha reading is also that of **Cx**; A mss. divide. The beta reading *with* is likely to have been influenced by the line above.

229 **on**: Both **Ax** and **Cx** agree with alpha here against beta's *of*.

231 **an half**: Beta is challenged by alpha *half a*. **Cx** has no article; A mss. vary between all three possibilities.

237 **mo**: R has *man*, as do four A mss.

238 **fere**: Beta's reading *drede* is also that of four A mss., but the others have *fere*, as do alpha and **Cx**.

239 **ek**: The beta reading is supported by **Ax** against alpha's *also*. **Cx** has *bothe*.

Passus 3

Passus tercius de visione vt supra

Now is Mede þe Maide · and namo of hem alle
With bedellus & wiþ bayllyues · brou3t bifor þe kyng
The kyng called a clerke · can I nou3t his name
To take Mede þe mayde · and make hire at ese
5 I shal assaye hir my-self · and sothelich appose
What man of þis [worlde] · þat hire were leueste
And if she worche bi my witte · and my wille folwe
I wil forgyue hir þis *gilte / giltes* · so me god help

¶ Curteysliche þe clerke þanne [·] as þe Kyng hight
10 Toke Mede bi þe Middel · and brou3te hir in-to chaumbre
A[c] þere was myrthe and mynstralcye · Mede to plese

[¶] They þat wonyeth [at] westmynstre · worschiped hir alle

---

2 **wiþ** (2): Supported for **Bx** by LR and WHmC, against MCrGOF (F reverses the half lines). Yet neither **Ax** or **Cx** repeats the preposition (**Cx** has *Thorw Bedeles*).

5 **sothelich**: Beta supported by **AC** though the word (meaning "openly, plainly"? or "effectively"? as glossed by Kane (2005)) causes some problems in all versions. R's *couthliche* is presumably the alpha reading, improved by F to *sotilly*. See Hanna (1996), 227.

6 **worlde**: R's reading is supported by **AC**. The beta reading *molde* is prompted by the common alliterative formula, just as F alters *man* to *wy3e* for the same consideration. Alliteration may fall on *What*.

7 **my**(1): Omitted by beta2 and some **A** mss.; **C** rewrites.

8 **gilte / giltes**: Though beta and **Ax** have the sg., alpha and **Cx** have the pl. Hanna (1996), 228, regards this as "a possible product of Langlandian revision".

10 **brou3te**: F's alliterating *mente* has no parallel in any version. **Cx** rewrites the b-verse. Following this line, F alone has a line without support from other versions.

11 **Ac**: R is supported in the less obvious reading by the X family of **C**. The P family omits the conjunction. Beta and F (where the beginning of the line is revised) read *And*, as do some **A** mss. (varying with *But, Ac, Þan*). Kane (2005), in a subtle entry for *ac*, glosses "moreover" here.

12 **¶**: In L the paraph is indicated by *cc*, but not inserted. The line is at the top of the page.

12 **at**: The reading of MG + alpha is supported by **Ax**. **Cx** rewrites.

12 **worschiped**: So LR and CrHmCO. **C** mss. and **A** mss. also divide between past and the easier present.

Gentelliche wiþ ioye · þe Iustices somme
Busked hem to þe boure · þere þe birde dwelled
15   To conforte hire kyndely · by clergise leue
And seiden mourne nought Mede · ne make þow no sorwe
For we [wil] wisse þe kynge · and þi wey shape
To be wedded at þi wille · and where þe leue liketh
For al conscience caste · [and] craft as I trowe

20   ¶ Mildeliche Mede þanne · mercyed hem alle
Of þeire gret goodnesse · and gaf hem vchone
Coupes of clene golde · and coppis of siluer
Rynges with rubies · and ricchesses manye
The leste man of here meyne · a motoun of golde
25   Thanne lauȝte þei leue · þis lordes at Mede

¶ With that comen clerkis · to conforte hir þe same
And beden hire be blithe · for we beth þine owne
Forto worche þi wille · þe while þow myȝte laste

[¶] Hendeliche heo þanne · bihight hem þe same
30   To loue ȝow lelli · and lordes to make
And in þe consistorie [at] courte · do calle ȝowre names
Shal no lewdnesse lette · þe *leode / clerkes* þat I louye
That he ne worth first auanced · for I am biknowen
Þere konnyng clerkes · shul clokke bihynde

35   ¶ Þanne come þere a confessoure · coped as a Frere
To Mede þe mayde · he mellud þis wordes

---

16 **mourne**: MHmO have *mourne þow*, a minor variant in all three versions.

17 **wil**: The omission in L, original M, and CO is probably a beta error corrected in other mss.

19 **caste and craft**: AC support beta's word-order against alpha's, and alpha's *and* against beta's *or*.

23 **richesses**: As a romance loan ending in a sibilant, alpha's reading without *-s* can also be a pl. form. See notes to **Bx**.3.101, 10.90, 223, 227, 19.73, etc.

28 **þow myȝte laste**: Hm's *thy lyfe lasteth* is the reading of some **A** mss. For *þow myȝte* CrG have *we moune / we may*, the reading of the P family of **C**.

29 **¶**: Though L has no paraph, the scribe leaves a blank line, and WHmC have the paraph. In R the left margin is cropped.

30 **ȝow**: Only LR switch to direct address with this line. M probably did too originally, though the corrector altered to *hem*, the reading of all other **B** mss., and also of **AC**. See note on *ȝowre* in the next line. Cr's additional line is from **C** (RK.3.33).

31 **at**: CrHmOR, supported by **AC**, against *atte* and *at þe* in LMWCG and *in þe* in F. (In L the form *atte* consistently represents "at the".) But cf. **Bx**.P.107n.

31 **ȝowre**: Beta2 and G continue with the 3rd person pl., as does **Ax**. **Cx** has *ȝoure*.

32 **leode / clerkes**: The beta reading (alliterating aa/aa) is shared with **Ax**, but alpha's *clerkes* is shared with **Cx** (alliterating aa/xa), though **Cx** has the sg., whence Cr's *clerke*.

33 **ne**: Beta is supported by **AC** against alpha's omission.

36 **þe**: Beta is supported by **AC** against R's *þis* and F's *þat*.

And seide ful softly · in shrifte as it were
Thei3 lewed men and lered men · had leyne by þe bothe
And false[hede] haued yfolwed þe [·] al þis fyfty wyntre
40   I shal assoille þe my-selue · for a seme of whete
And also be þi bedeman · and bere wel þi message
Amonges kni3tes and clerkis · conscience to torne

¶ Thanne Mede for here mysdedes · to þat man kneled
And shroue hire of hire shrewednesse · shamelees I trowe
45   Tolde hym a tale · and toke hym a noble
Forto ben hire bedeman · and hire brokour als

¶ Thanne he assoilled hir sone · and sithen he seyde
We han a wyndowe a-wirchyng [·] wil sitten vs [ful] heigh
Woldestow glase þat gable · and graue þere-inne þi name
50   Siker sholde þi soule be · heuene to haue

[¶] Wist I that quod þat womman · I wolde nou3t spare
For to be 3owre frende frere · and faille 3ow neure
Whil 3e loue lordes · þat lechery haunteþ
And lakkeþ nou3t ladis · þat loueþ wel þe same
55   It is a frelete of flesche · 3e fynde it in bokes
And a course of kynde · wher-of we komen alle
Who may scape þe sklaundre · þe skaþe is sone amended
It is synne of seuene · sonnest relessed

¶ Haue mercy quod Mede · of men þat it haunte

---

39 **falsehede**: (For the spelling cf. **Bx**.5.300.) R's *falsede* presumably represents alpha (with F reading *Fals*) and is supported by **AC**. Beta reads *falseness*. (F's variants *& þey* and *fyftene* are from **A**.)

46 **hire brokour als**: G's *hyr bavd after* is contamination from **A**.

48 **ful**: Only L has *wel*.

49 **þere-inne**: R's *þere* merits consideration, since it is the reading of some **A** mss. and of **Cx**. Hanna (1996), 228, suggests the reading *þere-inne* arose from dittographic attraction, *þ'in þi-n|ame*.

51–62 In place of these twelve lines in beta, alpha has three lines garbled from two lines of **A** (K.3.50–1). **C** has the expanded passage from **B**, but rewrites **Bx**.3.50–1 as RK.3.53–4. The **Bx** archetype may have had the cancelled **A** lines which had been rendered illegible, with an expanded passage on a separate sheet, followed by beta but for some reason not available to alpha. Or alpha's exemplar may have lost the passage by eyeskip from one paraph to the next. On the other hand Hanna (1996), 316 n.26, suggests that the omission "may be an outright case of shocked scribal censorship with partial restoration", pointing out that "the memorial quality of this reading [in alpha] implies quite precisely that the archetypal scribe had no direct access to a manuscript version of **A**" (217).

51 **¶**: The paraph is attested by alpha and WHmC and an indented line in Cr. It is the first line on the leaf in L, where a paraph is sometimes missed, as on the previous leaf (**Bx**.3.12).

51 **þat womman**: MCr's *þe womman* could be correct, since it is supported by **Ax**. **Cx** rewites.

58 **seuene**: So LMC; beta2 and GO have *þe seuene*. **Cx** has *as of seuene*.

60   And I shal keure ȝowre kirke · ȝowre cloystre do maken
     Wowes do whitten · and wyndowes glasen
     Do peynten and purtraye · and paye for þe makynge
     That eury segge shal se[e]n · I am sustre of ȝowre hous

     ¶ Ac god to alle good folke · suche grauynge defendeth
65   To writen in wyndowes · of here wel-dedes
     On auenture pruyde be peynted þere · and pompe of þe worlde
     For crist knoweþ þi conscience · and þi kynde wille
     And þi coste and þi coueitise · and who þe catel ouȝte

     ¶ For-þi I lere ȝow lordes · leueþ suche werkes
70   To writen in wyndowes · of ȝowre wel-dedes
     Or to greden after goddis men · whan ȝe delen doles
     An auenture ȝe han ȝowre hire here · and ȝoure heuene als
     Nesciat sinistra quid faciat dextra ·
     Lat nouȝte þi left half · late no rathe
75   Wyte what þow worchest · with þi riȝt syde
     For þus bit þe gospel · gode men do here almesse

     ¶ Meires and maceres · that menes ben bitwene
     Þe kynge and þe comune [·] to kepe þe lawes
     To punyschen on pillories · and pynynge stoles
80   Brewesteres and bakesteres · bocheres and cokes
     For þise aren men on þis molde · þat moste harme worcheth
     To þe pore peple [·] þat parcel-mele buggen

     ¶ For they poysoun þe peple · priueliche and oft
     Thei rychen þorw regraterye · and rentes hem buggen

---

63 **eury**: The beta reading, supported by **Cx**. Alpha's *vch a* finds some support in **A** mss.

63 **seen**: Alpha is supported by **Ax** and by the X family of C; the P family has *see* and *seye*. On grounds of sense, *seen* is preferable to beta's *seyn*, "say".

63 **of ȝowre hous**: Beta is supported by **Ax** and by the derived *of ȝoure ordre* in **Cx** against alpha's weak *to ȝow alle*.

67 **crist**: The reading of all except R, whose *god* might have been picked up from l. 64, although it is also the reading of **Cx** (the passage is not in A). K-D argue, perhaps rightly, that R's reading is original, and that F's agreement with beta is the common variation of a more explicit reading (p. 168 and n. 89).

68 **And**: As in the previous line, R's reading (without *And*) is unique in **B** mss. but it is the reading of the P family of C (the X family conflate this line with the previous). Here F has *Boþe þe* for *And þi*.

78 **comune**: F regularly has *comounys* with its political implications (see *MED communes*), e.g. at Bx.P.115, 117, 118, 121, 143, usually joined by Cr. Here F is joined by GO.

79 **on**: Beta supported by **Ax** and the P family of C, against alpha's *vppon* and the X family.

79 **and**: F's *& on* may be from A. Yet C mss. have *and on* or *and vppon*.

81 **on**: Alpha again reads *vppoun*; **A** mss. divide between *on* and *of* (as in HmC); **Cx** rewrites.

83 **For they**: Beta is supported by **Ax** against alpha's *&* or *And also*.

85 With þat þe pore people [·] shulde put in here wombe
For toke þei on trewly · þei tymbred nouȝt so heiȝe
Ne bouȝte non burgages · be ȝe ful certeyne

¶ Ac Mede þe Mayde [·] þe Maire hath bisouȝte
Of alle suche sellers · syluer to take
90 Or presentz withoute pens · as peces of siluer
Ringes or other ricchesse · þe regrateres to maynetene

¶ For my loue quod that lady [·] loue hem vchone
And soffre hem to selle · somdele aȝeins resoun

¶ Salamon þe sage · a sarmoun he made
95 For to amende Maires · and men þat kepen lawes
And tolde hem þis teme · þat I telle thynke
Ignis deuorabit tabernacula eorum qui libenter accipiunt munera &c
Amonge þis lettered ledes · þis latyn is to mene
That fyre shal falle and berne · al to blo askes
100 The houses and þe homes · of hem [þat] desireth
Ȝiftes or ȝeresȝyues · bi-cause of here offices

¶ The kynge fro conseille cam · and called after Mede
And ofsent hir alswythe · with seriauntes manye
That brouȝten hir to bowre · with blisse and with ioye

105 ¶ Curteisliche þe kynge þanne · comsed to telle
To Mede þe mayde · melleth þise wordes
Vnwittily womman · wrouȝte hastow oft
Ac worse wrouȝtestow neure · þan þo þow fals toke
But I forgyue [þe] þat gilte · and graunte þe my grace
110 Hennes to þi deth-day · do so namore

¶ I haue a knyȝte conscience · cam late fro biȝunde
Ȝif he wilneth þe to wyf · wyltow hym haue

---

85 **wombe:** The distributive sg. is supported by **AC**.
87 **burgages:** The plural is supported by **AC** against the sg. in alpha (F *bargayn*).
92 **loue** (1): Beta is supported by **Ax** and by **Cx** (RK.3.119), against alpha's *lord*, perhaps substituted to avoid repetition.
97 Alpha's version of the quotation, omitting the last two words, is not supported by **AC**.
100 **þe:** Omitted by Beta2 and G, but supported by **AC**.
100 **þat:** Omitted in L, although a corrector's mark appears in the margin.
101 **offices:** As a romance loan ending in a sibilant, alpha's *office* may represent a distributive sg. or a plural. See note to l. 23. There is no parallel in **AC**.
104 **That:** W's agreement with **Ax** on *And* is presumably coincidental.
105 **comsed:** R has the present, presumably by attraction to *melleth*, yet it agrees with **Ax**. The verb is past tense in the rewritten passage in **Cx**.
109 **þe** (1): Omitted in L and added in W. Supported by **AC**.
110 The short b-verse of beta is expanded variously in G, R and F. **Ax** has *do þou* for **Bx** *do*.

¶ 3e lorde quod þat lady · lorde forbede elles
But I be holely at 3owre heste · lat hange me sone

115   ¶ And þanne was conscience calde · to come and appiere
Bifor þe Kynge and his conseille · as clerkes and othere
Knelynge conscience · to þe kynge louted
To wite what his wille were · and what he do shulde

¶ Woltow wedde þis womman quod þe kynge · 3if I wil assente
120   For she is fayne of þi felawship · for to be þi make

¶ Quod conscience to þe kynge · cryst it me forbede
Ar I wedde suche a wyf · wo me bityde
For she is frele of hir feith · *fykel / and fykel* of here speche
And maketh men mysdo · many score tymes
125   Truste of hire tresore · treieth ful manye
Wyues and widewes · wantounes she techeth
And lereth hem leccherye · that loueth hire 3iftes
3owre fadre she felled · þorw fals biheste
And hath apoysounde popis · [ap]peired holicherche
130   Is nau3t a better baude · bi hym þat me made
Bitwene heuene and helle · [and] erthe þough men sou3te
For she is tikil of hire taile · talwis of tonge
As comune as a cartwey · to eche a knaue þat walketh

---

113 **forbede**: LCrCGOF are supported by **Ax**; WHm read *forbede it*, and M is corrected to that reading. R's b-verse, *lord it me for-bede*, is that found in **Cx**. It may therefore represent alpha, and an authorial revision to avoid metrical demotion of the verb. However, since F agrees with beta, R's reading is more probably attracted to the b-verse of l. 121 below.

117 W and alpha have a paraph.

123 **fykel / and fykel**: *fykel* is the beta reading, despite Hm; supported by **Ax**. R's *and fykel* is the alpha reading (F has *& fals*), supported by **Cx**.

125 **treieth**: CrWG have *betrayeth*, a reversion to the commoner form. AC are not parallel here.

126 **wantounes**: *MED* records this as a spelling of *wantonness*, and cf. the CrHm spellings of the word at **Bx**.12.6.

128 **fals**: Beta is supported by **Ax**, though three mss. agree with alpha's variant *faire*. The common proverb "Fair behest maketh a fool glad" (*MED bihest(e* 1b.(b)) may have prompted the reading. Cf. **Bx**.11.62 and 20.118 for *faire beheste*. C rewrites.

129 **appeired**: Alpha and most beta mss. read *and (ap)peired*, but L, original M, and C are without *and*, as is **Ax**, which suggests that scribes supplied it for a smoother reading. Most beta mss. have the aphetic form of the verb, but *appeired* is the form in alpha + Hm, supported by **Cx** and the majority of A mss. R's present tense may represent alpha, since it is shared with **Cx**.

131 **and** (2): R's reading appears to represent alpha. It is supported by most A mss. (though five have *in*) and the X family of C (the P family has *alle*). The apparent illogicality of the expression (what lies between heaven, hell and earth?) perhaps prompted beta to revise to *in* and F to revise to *þey men al erthe sowhte*. Schmidt (1995) and Kane (2005) interpret *and* as "if".

132 **tonge**: Beta reads *hir tonge*, prompted by the parallel of *hire taile*, but alpha's omission of the pronoun is paralleled by many A mss. and by **Cx**.

To monkes to mynst[r]alles · to meseles in hegges
135 Sisoures and sompnoures · suche men hir preiseth
Shireues of shires · were shent ȝif she nere
For she doþ men lese here londe · and here lyf bothe
She leteth passe prisoneres · and payeth for hem ofte
And gyueth þe gailers golde · and grotes togideres
140 To vnfettre þe fals [·] fle where hym lyketh
And takeþ þe trewe bi þe toppe · and tieth hym faste
And hangeth hym for hatred · þat harme dede neure

¶ To be cursed in consistorie · she counteth nouȝte a russhe
For she copeth þe comissarie · and coteth his clerkis
145 She is assoilled as sone · as hir-self liketh
And may neiȝe as moche do · in a moneth one[s]
As ȝowre secret seel · in syx score dayes
For she is priue with þe pope · prouisoures it knoweth
For sire symonye and hir-selue · seleth hire bulles

150 ¶ She blesseth þise bisshopes · þeiȝe þey be lewed
Prouendreth persones · and prestes [she] meynteneth
To haue lemmannes and lotebies · alle here lif-dayes
And bringen forth barnes · aȝein forbode lawes
There she is wel with þe kynge · wo is þe rewme
155 For she is fauorable to þe fals · and fouleth trewthe ofte

---

134 **to** (2): R's *and to* may represent alpha (cf. F), joined by Cr. Beta seems to have the support of **AC**, though some mss. have *and*.

138 **prisoneres**: R has *prisons* again at **Bx.**7.30 (together with most **B** mss.), 14.180 and 186, and 15.190 (together with LM). See *MED prisoun*, n. 7. All three versions have both variants here. We follow copy-text.

140 **hym**: Supported by most **AC** mss. against the plural in MC.

141 **þe trewe**: Alpha has *trewthe*, perhaps rightly, but cf. notes to ll. 155 and 247. There is similar variation in **A** and **C** mss. The X family of **C** has *treuthe*, with the P family reading *trewe* or improving to *þe trewe*.

141 **hym**: MWG have plural (cf. l. 140). The sg. is supported by **A** and the X family in **C**.

142 **hym**: MCrWG have plural (cf. ll. 140–1). The sg. is supported by **A** and the X family of **C**.

143 **russhe**: The reading is supported by **AC** against *bene* in beta2 and G. Langland repeats the phrase at **Bx.**11.450.

146 **ones**: Alpha, supported by **Ax** and the X family of **C**, against the probable beta reading *one*.

149 **hire**: LMWCOR, supported by **Cx**, against *þe*. **A** mss. split.

150–51 R's conflation into one line represents loss in alpha, which F makes good by invention.

151 **she**: Alpha, despite the disruption, retains the pronoun, supported against beta by **AC**.

153 **bringen**: The infinitive is supported by most **A** mss., but **Cx** has *bringeth* as does beta2.

155 **þe**: Beta2 and GF are without the article, treating *fals* as a personification. This is attractive and appropriate, and has the support of **Ax** and the P family of **C**. However, the most reliable **B** mss. (LMR) and CO read *þe fals*, with the support of the X family of **C**. Cf. *þe fals* in l. 140 above, and the note to l. 141.

¶ Bi ihesus with here ieweles · ȝowre / þe iustices she shendeth
And lith aȝein þe lawe · and letteth hym þe gate
That feith may nouȝte haue his forth · here floreines go so þikke
She ledeth þe lawe as hire list · and louedayes maketh
160 And doth men lese þorw hire loue · þat lawe myȝte wynne
Þe mase for a mene man · þouȝ he mote hir eure
Lawe is so lordeliche · and loth to make ende
With-oute presentz or pens · she pleseth wel fewe

¶ Barounes and burgeys · she bryngeth in sorwe
165 And alle þe comune in kare · þat coueyten lyue in trewthe
For clergye and coueitise · she coupleth togideres
Þis is þe lyf of that lady · now lorde ȝif hir sorwe
And alle that meynteneth here men · meschaunce hem bityde
For pore men mowe haue no powere · to pleyne hem þouȝ þei smerte
170 Suche a maistre is Mede · amonge men of gode

¶ Thanne morned Mede · and mened hire to the kynge
To haue space to speke · spede if she myȝte

¶ The kynge graunted hir grace [·] with a gode wille
Excuse þe ȝif þow canst · I can namore seggen
175 For conscience acuseth þe · to congey þe for euere

¶ Nay lorde quod þat lady · leueth hym þe worse
Whan ȝe wyten witterly · where þe wronge liggeth
There þat myschief is grete · Mede may helpe
And þow knowest conscience · I cam nouȝt to chide
180 Ne depraue þi persone · with a proude herte
Wel þow wost wernard · but ȝif þow wolt gabbe
Þow hast hanged on myne half · elleuene tymes
And also griped my golde · gyue it where þe liked
And whi þow wratthest þe now · wonder me thynketh
185 Ȝit I may as I myȝte · menske þe with ȝiftes
And mayntene þi manhode · more þan þow knoweste

---

156 **ȝowre / þe**: The beta reading ȝowre is shared with **Ax**; alpha's þe is shared with **Cx**.
161 **hir**: A **Bx** error, dropped by GF, presumably by contamination from **AC** or on grounds of sense. The verb *mote*, "litigate", is intransitive.
163 **wel**: CrR have *ful*, perhaps by alliterative attraction, though it is shared with **Cx** and half the **A** mss.
170 F drops this line.
171 **¶**: The paraph is in beta, with an enlarged rubricated capital in F. The margin is lost in R, and the line is at the bottom of the page.
179 **þow**: So beta and **Ax**; alpha has *þat þow*, reflected in **Cx** *þat*. With *þat þow*, Mede refers back to the previous line.
183 **gyue**: FG *and gyue* is from **AC**. For pp. *gyue*, cf. **Bx.2.151**.

¶ Ac þow hast famed me foule · bifor þe Kynge here
For kulled I neuere no kynge · ne conseilled þer-after
Ne dede as þow demest · I do [it] on þe kynge

190   ¶ In normandye was he nou3te · noyed for my sake
Ac þow þi-self sothely · shamedest hym ofte
Crope in-to a kaban · for colde of þi nailles
Wendest þat wyntre · wolde haue lasted euere
And draddest to be ded · for a dym cloude
195   And hiedest homeward · for hunger of þi wombe

¶ Wiþ-out pite piloure · pore men þow robbedest
And bere here bras at þi bakke · to caleys to selle
There I lafte with my lorde · his lyf for to saue
I made his men meri · and mornyng lette
200   I batered hem on þe bakke · and bolded here hertis
And dede hem hoppe for hope · to haue me at wille
Had I ben Marschal of his men · bi Marie of heuene
I durst haue leyde my lyf · and no lasse wedde
He shulde haue be lorde of þat londe · a lengthe and a brede
205   And also Kyng of þat kitthe · his kynne for to helpe
Þe leste brolle of his blode · a barounes pere

¶ Cowardliche þow conscience · conseiledest hym þennes
To leuen his lordeship · for a litel siluer
That is þe richest rewme · þat reyne ouer-houeth

210   ¶ It bicometh to a kynge · þat kepeth a rewme
To 3iue Mede to men · þat mekelich hym serueth
To alienes and to alle men [·] to honoure hem with 3iftes
Mede maketh hym biloued · and for a man holden
Emperoures and Erlis · and al manere lordes
215   [Thorw] 3iftes han *3onge men / 3oumen* · to [3erne] and to ride

---

188 **kynge**: Mede is answering the accusation of **Bx**.3.128. Beta reads as AC; alpha's *kni3t* perhaps avoids a dangerous topic.

189 **do it on**: "refer it to" (*MED don* 6(f)), as in **Bx**.1.88. The lack of the object in LMC suggests a beta error made good in other mss. It is in **Ax**.

204 **a** (1 & 2): We follow copy-text and CRO (M has been altered in the second case) against the *in* of most other mss. in all three versions. The archetype is not determinable, but preservation of the less usual form (contrast **Bx**.2.91) in the two most reliable mss. is at least a guide.

206 **blode**: Supported by AC against alpha's non-alliterating *lond*.

214 WHm and alpha have a paraph, as do W and alpha for l. 216 and W and R for l. 218. Cf. note to l. 222.

215 **Thorw**: Alpha has firm support from AC against beta's *For*.

215 **3onge men / 3oumen**: These are perhaps just forms of the same word (see *MED yong man* and *yeman*). Beta has the former, agreeing with **Ax**. Alpha has the latter, agreeing with **Cx**.

215 **3erne**: A metathesised form of *renne*, as in OE, used for the alliteration but frequently altered by scribes. Here beta and **Ax** have the non-alliterating form, while alpha and **Cx** have *3erne*.

The pope and alle prelatis · presentz vnderfongen
And medeth men hem-seluen · to meyntene here lawes
Seruauntz for her seruise · we seth wel þe sothe
Taken Mede of here maistre[s] · as þei mowe acorde
220 Beggeres for here biddynge · bidden men Mede
Mynstralles for here murthe · mede þei aske
Þe kynge hath mede of his men · to make pees in londe
Men þat teche chyldren · craue of hem mede
Prestis þat precheth þe poeple · to gode asken mede
225 And masse-pans and here mete · at þe mele-tymes
Alkynnes crafty men · crauen Mede for here prentis
Marchauntz and Mede · mote nede go togideres
No wiȝte as I wene · with-oute Mede may libbe

¶ Quatȝ þe kynge to conscience · bi criste as me thynketh
230 Mede is worthi · þe maistrye to haue

¶ Nay quod conscience to þe Kynge · and kneled to þe erthe
There aren two manere of Medes · my lorde [bi] ȝowre leue
Þat one god of his grace · graunteth in his blisse
To þo þat wel worchen · whil þei ben here
235 The prophete precheth þer-of · and put it in þe sautere
Domine quis habitabit in tabernaculo tuo
Lorde who shal wonye in þi wones · and with þine holi seyntes
Or resten on þi holy hilles · þis asketh dauid

---

216 **alle**: LMCOR, as **Cx**; CrWG supply *the*, Hm *his*. **Ax** has *wiþ his*.

218 **Seruauntz**: Beta2 (CrWHm) + G have *Sergeauntz*, which is a corrected reading in M, as does the P family of **C**. Otherwise **AC** agree on *seruauntz*.

219 **maistres**: The distributive sg. of LOF, though generally to be preferred, is not supported by **AC**.

220 **biddynge**: Alpha's *beggynge* is not supported by **Ax**; **Cx** rewrites.

222 W and alpha have a paraph here, as do W and R at ll. 224 and 226.

224 **to gode**: "to (adopt) good behaviour" (rather than an inflected form of "God", which is not found in L). It is supported by **AC** against alpha + Hm *to/of god*, though in **AC** *Asken mede* begins the next line.

226 **crafty**: Supported by **AC** against *craftes* in CrWG.

230 **worthi**: Beta has *wel worthi*, probably to beef up the alliteration, but the adverb is not supported by **AC**. **Ax** has the a-verse as in R; **Cx** improves the alliteration by adding *me thinketh*.

232 **bi**: Alpha has support from **Ax** against beta's *with*. **Cx** rewrites. The phrase does not recur, though cf. **Bx**.3.15.

237 **and**: Alpha omits; there is no parallel in **AC**, and nothing to choose between the variants.

238 **on**: The reading of LM + alpha; others have *in*. Notice that two lines above F quotes the Vulgate, "in monte sancto eius", memory of which may have prompted the reading of other mss.

238 **asketh**: Alpha has past tense; there is no parallel in **AC**, though the present has the support of the surrounding context.

¶ And dauyd assoileth it hym-self [·] as þe sauter telleth
240 Qui ingreditur sine macula · & operatur iusticiam
Tho þat entren of o colour · and of on wille
And han wrouȝte werkis · with riȝte and with reson
And he þat ne vseth nauȝte · þe lyf of vsurye
And enfourmeth pore men · and pursueth treuthe
245 Qui pecuniam suam non dedit ad vsuram & munera super innocentem &c ·
And alle þat helpeth þe innocent · and halt with þe riȝtful
Withoute mede doth hem gode · and þe trewthe helpeth
Suche manere men my lorde · shal haue þis furst Mede
Of god at a grete nede · whan þei gone hennes

250 [¶] There is an other Mede mesurelees · þat maistres desireth
To meyntene mysdoers · Mede þei take
And þere-of seith þe sauter · in a salmes ende
In quorum manibus iniquitates sunt [·] dextera eorum repleta est
    muneribus
And he þat gripeth her golde · so me god helpe
255 Shal abie it bittere · or þe boke lyeth

¶ Prestes and parsones · þat plesynge desireth
That taketh Mede and mone · for messes þat þei syngeth
Taketh here mede here · as Mathew vs techeth
Amen amen recipiebant mercedem suam ·

260 ¶ That laboreres and lowe folke · taketh of her maistres
It is no manere Mede · but a mesurable hire
In marchandise is no mede · I may it wel avowe
It is a permutacioun apertly · a penyworth for an othre

¶ Ac reddestow neuere Regum · þow recrayed Mede
265 Whi þe veniaunce fel · on saul and on his children

---

243 **ne:** So LCOR; omitted by beta2 and GF.

245 F omits the line.

247 **þe trewthe:** R's *þe trewe* must be alpha (F has *trew men*). There is no parallel in AC. Cf. **Bx.3.141n.**

249 **a:** CrHm read *her*, with M altered to that reading. F has *his* and GO omit.

250 **¶:** The paraph, certainly appropriate, is recorded in WHmC and alpha.

255 **bittere:** FGO *bitterly* is easier and perhaps from A; R expands to *ful bitter*. For the same a-verse see **Bx.18.418**, where FGO again have *bitterly*.

259 **recipiebant:** There is variation in the form of the verb in all three versions (as at K.3.64a). The Vulgate has *receperunt*.

260 **lowe:** Beta, as against alpha and Hm *lewed*. A mss. vary similarly. The a-verse *laboreres and lowe folke* is repeated at **Bx.5.223** (K.5.135, RK.6.227), where there is similar variation in A but not in BC.

262 WHm and R have a paraph.

263 **a (1):** Dropped in alpha, but supported by AC.

God sent to saul · bi samuel þe prophete
Þat agag of amaleke · and al his peple aftre
Shulde deye for a dede · þat done had here aldres

¶ For-þi seid samuel to saul · god hym-self hoteth
270 The · be boxome at [my] biddynge · his wille to fulfille
Wende to amalec with þyn oste · and what þow fyndest þere slee it
Biernes and bestes · brenne hem to ded
Wydwes and wyues · wommen and children
Moebles and vnmoebles · and al þat þow my3te fynde
275 Brenne it bere it nou3te awey · be it neuere so riche
For mede ne for mone · loke þow destruye it
Spille it and spare it nou3te · þow shalt spede þe bettere

¶ And for he coueyted her catel · and þe kynge spared
Forbare hym and his bestes bothe · as þe bible witnesseth
280 Otherwyse þan he was · warned of þe prophete
God seide to samuel [·] þat saul shulde deye
And al his sede for þat synne · shenfullich ende
Such a myschief Mede made [·] saul þe kynge to haue
That god hated hym for euere · and alle his eyres after

285 ¶ The culorum of þis cas · kepe I nou3te to shewe
An auenture it noyed men · none ende wil I make
For so is þis worlde went · wiþ hem þat han powere
That who-so seyth hem sothes · is sonnest yblamed

¶ I conscience knowe þis · for kynde witt me it tau3te
290 Þat resoun shal regne · and rewmes gouerne
And ri3te as agag hadde · happe shul somme

---

270 **The**: Undoubtedly **Bx**; LWM follow it with punctuation in response to the line-break
between verb and object. HmO have *The to*. **AC** instead have *To*. For discussion see Duggan
(1987), 47.

270 **my**: Alpha, against beta's *his*, which arises by attraction to the pronoun of the b-verse
and ignoring the shift to direct speech. The line is revised from **Ax**, with alpha reading as
Cx. Further support for alpha's *my biddynge* is provided by the source, in which Saul says to
Samuel after his disobedience: "Peccavi quia praevaricatus sum sermonem Domini et verba tua"
(1 Kings 15.24).

282 **shenfullich**: The word causes problems to scribes of all versions. Neither the adj. or adv.
occurs elsewhere in the poem.

282 **ende**: The past tense in alpha and Hm occurs in isolated mss. in the other versions.

285 **shewe**: LMCOR, supported by **AC**, against *telle* of Beta2 (CrWHm) and G; F has *expowne*.
There seems no explanation for the variation.

288 **sothes**: Pl. noun, or less probably adverb. WG's *sopest* is easier and prompted by *sonnest*
in the b-verse, although it is the reading of **Cx**. Galloway (2006), 362, cites other versions of
the saying.

289 **me it**: LHmCRF (and unrevised M); *it* is differently placed in other **B** mss. and omitted
in C and most A mss.

Samuel shal sleen hym · and saul shal be blamed
And dauid shal be diademed · and daunten hem alle
And one cristene Kynge · kepen hem alle

295 ¶ Shal namore Mede · be maistre as she is nouthe
Ac loue and lowenesse · and lewte togederes
Þise shul be maistres on molde · treuthe to saue

¶ And who-so trespasseth ayein treuthe · or taketh aȝein his wille
Leute shal don hym lawe · and no lyf elles
300 Shal no seriaunt for here seruyse · were a silke howue
Ne no pelure in his cloke · for pledyng atte barre
Mede of mys-doeres · maketh many lordes
And ouer lordes lawes · reuleth þe rewmes

¶ Ac kynde loue shal come ȝit · and conscience togideres
305 And make of lawe a laborere · suche loue shal arise
And such pees amonge þe peple · and a parfit trewthe
Þat iewes shal wene in here witte · and waxen wonder glade
Þat Moises or Messie · be come in-to þis erthe
And haue wonder in here hertis · þat men beth so trewe

310 ¶ Alle þat bereth baslarde [·] brode swerde or launce
Axe [o]ther hachet · or eny wepne ellis
Shal be demed to þe deth · but if he do it smythye
In-to sikul or to sithe · to schare or to kulter
Conflabunt gladios suos in vomeres &c
315 Eche man to pleye with a plow · pykoys or spade
Spynne or sprede donge · or spille hym-self with sleuthe

¶ Prestes and parsones · with placebo to hunte
And dyngen vpon dauid · eche a day til eue
Huntynge or haukynge · if any of hem vse
320 His boste of his benefys · worth bynome hym after

---

294 **hem alle**: Before correction L read *alle*, and M may have had the same, revised to *hem echone* in line with Cr. R has *hem alle*, as do all others except F which alters inventively. **Bx** is in error (as several times in these lines), repeating the end of the previous line. **AC** read *vs ichone*.
295 LR punctuate after *Mede*, having regard to alliteration; others punctuate after *maistre*, paying more attention to rhythm. The phrase *as she is nouthe* replaces **Ax** *on erþe*, with a metrical revision in **Cx**.
300 **here**: Even if not strictly grammatical, this is clearly **Bx**, as in L, original M, HmOC and R. CrWG have corrected to *his*, followed by the corrector of M. Most **AC** mss. read *þat*.
306 **pees**: So alpha, supported by **Cx**; beta adds the article. **Ax** does not have this or the succeeding lines to the end of the passus.
316 **spille**: Alpha has non-alliterating *lese*. Beta is supported by **Cx**.
318 **eche a**: LMCR and O (corrected), against *eche* WHmG or *euery* CrF. The line is not in **AC**.

Shal neither kynge ne kny3te [·] constable ne Meire
Ouer-lede þe comune · ne to þe courte sompne
Ne put hem in panel · to don hem pli3te here treuthe
But after þe dede þat is don · one dome shal rewarde
325   Mercy or no mercy · as treuthe wil acorde

¶ Kynges courte and comune courte · consistorie and chapitele
Al shal be but one courte · and one baroun be iustice
Thanne worth trewe tonge a tidy man · þat tened me neuere
Batailles shal non be · ne no man bere wepne
330   And what smyth þat ony smyt[hie] · be smyte þer-with to dethe
Non leuabit gens contra gentem gladium &c ·

¶ And er þis fortune falle [·] fynde men shal þe worste
By syx sonnes and a schippe · and half a shef of arwes
And þe myddel of a mone · shal make þe iewes torne
335   And saracenes for þat si3te · shulle synge gloria in excelsis &c
For Makomet & Mede · myshappe shal þat tyme
For melius est bonum nomen quam diuicie multe

¶ Also wroth as þe wynde · wex Mede in a while
I can no latyn quod she · clerkis wote þe sothe
340   Se what salamon seith [·] in sapience bokes
That hij þat 3iueth 3iftes · þe victorie wynneth
& moche worschip had þer-with · as holiwryt telleth
Honorem adquiret qui dat munera &c

¶ I leue wel lady quod conscience · þat þi latyne be trewe
345   Ac þow art like a lady · þat redde a lessoun ones
Was omnia probate · and þat plesed here herte
For þat lyne was no lenger [·] atte leues ende
Had [she] loked þat other half · and þe lef torned
[She] shulde haue founden fele wordis · folwyng þer-after
350   Quod bonum est tenete · treuthe þat texte made

---

328 **Thanne**: Undoubtedly **Bx. Cx** reads *That*.
330 **smythie**: Cx supports alpha's subjunctive. LC's *smyteth* has no support.
334 **torne**: Alpha + G, supported by **Cx**, against beta's *to torne*.
335 **þat si3te**: Beta is supported by **Cx** against alpha's *þe si3te þere-offe*.
341 **hij**: The form is supported by LMCR against *þei* in others. See Introduction, p. 18.
342 **moche**: So LMCO + alpha, supported by **Cx**, against *moost* in beta2 (CrWHm) and G.
342 **had**: CrHmF have the expected present tense. The form in the other mss. may be understood as an absolute past participle: "With much honour gained" (Mustanoja, (1960), 559).
348 **she**: The reading is obviously correct and supported by **Cx**, but here and in the next line the reading of L is *3e* and M's original reading is altered to *she*. This suggests that beta had an ambiguous form for *she*, perhaps even *3e*, recorded in Gloucs. and Worcs. (*LALME*, 4. 8).
349 **She**: See note to previous line.
349 **fele**: CrG have *fel*, as in three C mss.

¶ And so ferde ȝe madame · ȝe couthe namore fynde
Tho ȝe loked on sapience · sittynge in ȝoure studie
Þis tixte þat ȝe han tolde · were gode for lordes
Ac ȝow failled a cunnyng clerke · þat couthe þe lef haue torned
355 And if ȝe seche sapience eft · fynde shal ȝe þat folweth
A ful teneful tixte · to hem þat taketh Mede
And þat is animam autem aufert accipientium · &c ·
And þat is þe taille of þe tixte · of þat þat ȝe schewed
Þat þeiȝe we wynne worschip · and wiþ mede haue victorie
360 Þe soule þat þe soude taketh · bi so moche is bounde

351–58 A series of lines that alliterate irregularly in **Bx**. The lines are omitted or heavily revised in C. F makes several b-verse improvements for the sake of alliteration, but they cannot be regarded as derived from **Bx**. F's reading in 352 is an easy substitution of *seyȝe* for *loked on*; *ȝee takyn nout þe ende* in 353, and *þat ȝe to me pitte* (356) are inspired by 358 which F omits. F also omits l. 357.

358 **ȝe**: Beta2 (CrWHm) + G read *she*, and M is altered to that reading, evidently ending Conscience's speech at l. 354, with the remainder as a narrator's comment. There is no parallel in AC. F omits the line.

359 **mede**: Alpha's *me* is clearly an error.

Passus 4

Passus quartus de visione vt supra

Cesseth sei[de] þe kynge · I suffre ȝow no lengere
ȝe shal sauȝtne for-sothe · and serue me bothe
Kisse hir quod þe kynge · conscience I hote

¶ Nay bi criste quod conscience · congeye me for euere
5   But resoun rede me þer-to · rather wil I deye

¶ And I comaunde þe quod þe Kynge · to conscience þanne
Rape þe to ride · and resoun þow fecche
Comaunde hym þat he come · my conseille to here
For he shal reule my rewme · and rede me þe beste
10 And acounte with þe conscience · so me cryst helpe
How þow lernest þe peple · lered and lewede

¶ I am fayne of þat forwarde · seyde þe freke þanne
And ritte riȝte to resoun · and rowneth in his ere
And seide as þe kynge badde · and sithen toke his leue

15 ¶ I shal arraye me to ride quod resoun [·] reste þe a while
And called catoun his knaue · curteise of speche

---

1 **seide:** The past tense in alpha and Hm is shared with **AC**.

4 **for euere:** This is secure for **Bx**, though **A** has *rather*, as does beta4, with F reading *rather sone*, presumably by contamination or by anticipation of the next line. The three best mss. of the X family of **C** have *are*, "sooner", but all others have *rather*.

9 Following this line, O (supported by Cr²³C²Y) has the line "Of Mede & of moo oþere . & what man schal hir wedde", adopted from **AC** but absent from **Bx**.

11 **lered and lewede:** The reading of R (= alpha?) supported by **Cx**, and by seven A mss. Beta includes the definite article twice, presumably in response to a short b-verse. F has *boþe … & þe*.

14 **seide … badde:** F has *tolde hym as þe kyng seide*. **Cx** has *sayde* for both verbs. **Ax** has *Seide … sente*.

15 L omits punctuation, and its position varies in other mss. W and alpha have it after *resoun*, MO after *ride*.

And also tomme trewe tonge · telle me no tales
Ne lesyng to law3e of · for I loued hem neuere
And sette my sadel vppon suffre · til I se my tyme
20   And lete warrok it wel · with witty wordes gerthes
And hange on hym þe heuy brydel · to holde his hed lowe
For he wil make wehe · tweye er he be there

¶ Thanne conscience vppon his caple · kaireth forth faste
And resoun with hym ritte · rownynge togideres
25   Whiche maistries Mede · maketh on þis erthe

¶ One waryn wisdom · and witty his fere
Folwed hem faste · haued to done
In þe cheker and at þe chauncerie · to be discharged of þinges
And riden fast for resoun [·] shulde rede hem þe beste
30   For to saue hem for siluer · fro shame and fram harmes

¶ And conscience knewe hem wel · þei loued coueitise
And bad resoun ride faste · and recche of her noither
Þere aren wiles in here wordes · and with Mede þei dwelleth
There as wratthe and wranglyng is · þere wynne þei siluer

35   ¶ Ac þere is loue and lewte · þei wil nou3te come þere
Contricio & infelicitas in vijs eorum &c
Þei ne gyueth nou3te of god · one gose wynge
Non est timor dei ante oculos eorum
For wot god þei wolde do more · for a dozeine chickenes

---

20 **it**: The reference is to the saddle securely fastened with girths. This is clearly the reading of **Bx**. Burrow (1990), 139–44, calls the text "hopelessly confused", and discusses the possibility of taking *vppon* in l. 19 as an adverb. Galloway (2006), 381 considers this further. Beta2 and GF smooth by altering *it* to *him*, as in **AC**.

22 **tweye**: The form is supported by LMR; see Adams (2000), 176.

23 **kaireth**: Sound support from LM and alpha against the form *carieth* in beta2 and G. For the same variation, see **Bx**.P.29, 2.164, 5.310.

25 **erthe**: The reversed word-order in alpha is an error; both the alliterative scheme and the order in the revised line in **Cx** support beta.

27 **hem**: The attestation of LMO + alpha, with support from **AC**, guides choice of this reading over CrWHmG *hym*.

27 **haued**: It looks as though **Bx** lost *for þei* before *haued*. The obvious omission is corrected, perhaps partly on the basis of **Ax**, in all but the two most reliable mss., LR. Note, however, that M, also independent at this stage, expands to *for he*, probably by conjecture. The line is marked for correction in L.

28 **and at**: The reading of **Bx** is uncertain. L's *and at* has support from R's *atte*, and LR agreement is usually decisive. However, MGF have *and*, which could be the archetypal reading, expanded differently by other scribes. Yet Beta2 and CO are supported by **Ax** with *and in* (the line is not in C), and also by the same a-verse in **Bx**.P.93 (and RK.P.91).

28 **þe** (2): Not in MHmF. Most **A** mss. have neither instance of *þe* in the line. Cf. the same a-verse in **Bx**.P.93 (without either article) and RK.P.91 (where readings vary).

29 Following the punctuation of CO + alpha. L has nothing and MWHm punctuate after *shulde*.

35 **þere**(1): "where"; beta2 and F have *where*.

40 Or as many capones · or for a seem of otes
Þan for loue of owre lorde · or alle hise leue seyntes
For-þi resoun lete hem ride · þo riche bi hem-seluen
For conscience knoweth hem nouȝte · ne cryst as I trowe

[¶] And þanne resoun rode faste · þe riȝte heiȝe gate
45 As conscience hym kenned · til þei come to þe Kynge

¶ Curteisliche þe kynge þanne · come aȝein resoun
And bitwene hym-self and his sone · sette hym on benche
And wordeden wel wyseli · a gret while togideres

¶ And þanne come pees in-to parlement · and put forth a bille
50 How wronge aȝeines his wille · had his wyf taken
And how he rauisshed Rose · Reginoldes loue
And Margarete of hir maydenhode · maugre here chekis
Bothe my gees & my grys · his gadelynges feccheth
I dar nouȝte for fere of hym · fyȝte ne chyde
55 He borwed of me bayard · he brouȝte hym home neure
Ne no ferthynge þer-fore · for nauȝte I couthe plede
He meyneteneth his men · to morther myne hewen
Forstalleth my feyres · and fiȝteth in my chepynge
And breketh vp my bernes dore · and bereth aweye my whete
60 And taketh me but a taile · for ten quarteres of otes
And ȝet he bet me þer-to · and lyth bi my Mayde
I [am] nouȝte hardy for hym · vneth to loke

¶ The kynge knewe he seide sothe · for conscience hym tolde
Þat wronge was a wikked luft · and wrouȝte moche sorwe

---

42 **resoun**: Alpha omits, losing the alliteration.

44 **¶**: Alpha's paraph finds support from the paragraph in Cr.

54 **hym**: Only WHm have *hem* (*theym* G). There is the same variation in **A** mss.

55 **he** (2): Thus beta, against alpha + CrHm *and*. Most **A** mss. have the alpha reading, as does the P family of **C**, but the X family has the beta reading. We follow copy-text.

56 **nauȝte**: LM + alpha give this strong support for **Bx** against *ought* in all other mss. **AC** also have *nouȝt*.

58 **Forstalleth**: So beta and A*x*; R has *He forstalleth*, and F *& to for-staleþ* (sic). **Cx** begins the line with *And*.

59 **bernes dore**: So LWHmR, against *berne dore* in MCrF, and *berne dores* in GO. **AC** vary similarly.

60 **of otes**: Agreement of LR (together with WCO) suggests that this is perhaps the **Bx** reading, though since A*x* and **Cx** have *otes* only, this could equally represent **Bx**.

62 **am**: LC have *nam* but all others are supported by **AC**. (M originally had *ham*, with *h* altered to *n*). The alliteration of the line is on /h/ and vowel, not /n/. Cf. **Bx**.5.424, 443.

64 **luft**: "evil person". This unusual nominal use (*MED lift* adj. 3(b)) provokes confusion and avoidance among the scribes. **Cx** simplifies to *man*.

64 **wrouȝte moche sorwe**: Perhaps **Cx** inherited R's word order, *muche sorwe wrouȝte*, altering *sorwe* to *wo* for the alliteration.

65 ¶ Wronge was afered þanne · and wisdome he souȝte
    To make pees with his pens · and profered hym manye
    And seide had I loue of my lorde þe kynge · litel wolde I recche
    Theiȝe pees and his powere · pleyned hym eure

    ¶ Þo wan wisdome · and sire waryn þe witty
70 For þat wronge had ywrouȝte · so wikked a dede
    And warned wronge þo · with suche a wyse tale
    Who-so worcheth bi wille · wratthe maketh ofte
    I seye it bi þi-self · þow shalt it wel fynde
    But if Mede it make · þi myschief is vppe
75 For bothe þi lyf and þi londe · lyth in his grace

    ¶ Thanne wowed wronge · wisdome ful ȝerne
    To make his pees with his pens · handi-dandi payed
    Wisdome and witte þanne [·] wenten togideres
    And toke Mede myd hem [·] mercy to winne

80 ¶ Pees put forþ his hed · and his panne blody
    Wyth-outen gilte god it wote · gat I þis skaþe
    Conscience and þe comune · knowen þe sothe

    ¶ Ac wisdom and witte · were about faste
    To ouercome þe kynge · with catel ȝif þei myȝte

85 ¶ Þe kynge swore bi crist · and bi his crowne bothe
    Þat wronge for his werkis · sholde wo þolye
    And comaunded a constable · to casten hym in yrens
    And late hym nouȝte þis seuene ȝere · seen his feet ones

    ¶ God wot quod wysdom · þat were nauȝte þe beste
90 And he amendes mowe make · late meynprise hym haue
    And be borwgh for his bale · and biggen hym bote
    And so amende þat is mysdo · and euermore þe bettere

---

67 **my lorde**: Cr and alpha omit, losing the alliteration. This heavy a-verse is **Ax**, but **Cx** drops *þe kynge*.

68 **hym**: HmR have *hem* (G *theym*). A mss. are split; **Cx** rewrites as *he pleyne(de)*. The more obvious pl. suggest that *powere* was understood as "supporters" (so Kane (2005), s.v.), rather than "legal power" (so Alford (1988), 199).

69 **wan**: So LCR, as well as the parallel a-verse in A (K.4.53); Kane (2005) glosses "profited". M is corrected to *wente*, the reading of the other **B** mss. See Adams (2000), 181. F omits this and the next three lines.

72 **bi**: Supported by **Ax** against the variants *by my* in MO and *my* in C.

73 **þi-self**: So LO + alpha. The a-verse means "I say that with reference to you". M is altered to *my-self*, the reading of CrWHmCG and some **A** mss., on the basis of the phrase recorded in **Bx**.4.139, where it means "I give it as my own opinion".

78 WHm and R have a paraph.

92 **euermore**: The beta reading, supported by AC. R has *euere be*.

¶ Witt acorded þer-with · and seide þe same
Bettere is þat bote · bale adoun brynge
95 Þan bale be ybette · & bote neuere þe bettere

¶ And þanne gan Mede to me[k]en here · and mercy she bisought
And profred pees a present · al of pure golde
Haue þis man of me quod she · to amende þi skaþe
For I wil wage for wronge · he wil do so namore

100 ¶ Pitously pees þanne · prayed to þe kynge
To haue mercy on þat man · þat mys-did hym so ofte
For he hath waged me wel · as wisdome hym tauȝte
And I forgyue hym þat gilte · with a goode wille
So þat þe kynge assent · I can seye no bettere
105 For Mede hath made m[yn] amendes · I may namore axe

¶ Nay quod þe Kynge þo · so me cryst helpe
Wronge wendeth nouȝte so awaye · arst wil I wite more
For loupe he so liȝtly · laughen he wolde
And efte þe balder be · to bete myne hewen
110 But resoun haue reuthe on hym · he shal rest in my stokkes
And þat as longe as he lyueth · but lowenesse hym borwe

¶ Somme men redde Resoun þo · to haue reuthe on þat schrewe
And for to conseille þe Kynge · and conscience after
That Mede moste be meynpernour · resoun þei bisouȝte

115 ¶ Rede me nouȝte quod resoun · no reuthe to haue
Til lordes and ladies · louien alle treuthe
And haten al harlotrye · to heren it or to mouthen it
Tyl pernelles purfil · be put in here hucche
And childryn cherissyng · be chastyng with ȝerdes
120 And harlotes holynesse · be holden for an hyne

---

94 **Bettere**: The beta reading, supported by **AC** against alpha's *þat bettere*.

96 **meken**: The alpha reading, supported by **AC** against beta's *mengen*, which nevertheless makes good sense, "get involved" (*MED* 3(c)).

96 **she**: Clear support as **Bx**, though not in **Ax** or most **C** mss.

105 **myn**: The alpha reading, supported by **AC** against beta's *me*.

106 **cryst**: So beta, against alpha's non-alliterating *god*. In **Ax** the b-verse is *so god ȝiue me blisse* (K.4.91); in **Cx** the line is revised to *Nay by crist quod þe kyng for Consiences sake* (RK.4.99).

117 **it(1)**: So LCO and alpha, as well as the X family of C; erased in M, in line with beta2 + G, together with the P family of C.

119 **chastyng**: "chastisement" (*MED chastiinge*); clearly **Bx**, with HmF *chastised* the easier reading though also that of **Ax**. **Cx** has *chasted*.

120 **an hyne**: lit. "servant", in context something of small consequence. R replaces it with *nauȝte*, F with *vanyte*. Beta is supported by **Ax** but **Cx** revises. For discussion see Galloway (2006), 405–6; Turville-Petre (2006), 233–4.

Til clerken coueitise be · to clothe þe pore and to fede
And religious romares · recordare in here cloistres
As seynt Benet hem bad · Bernarde and Fraunceys
And til prechoures prechyng · be preued on hem-seluen
125 Tyl þe kynges conseille · be þe comune profyte
Tyl bisschopes baiardes · ben beggeres chambres
Here haukes and her houndes · helpe to pore Religious

¶ And til seynt Iames be souȝte · þere I shal assigne
That no man go to Galis · but if he go for euere
130 And alle Rome-renneres · for robberes of byȝende
Bere no siluer ouer see · þat signe of kynge sheweþ
Noyther graue ne vngraue · golde noither siluer
Vppon forfeture of þat fee · who-so fynt hym at Douere
But if it be marchaunt or his man · or messagere with lettres
135 Prouysoure or prest · or penaunt for his synnes

¶ And ȝet quod resoun bi þe Rode · I shal no reuthe haue
While Mede hath þe maistrye · in þis moot halle
Ac I may shewe ensaumples · as I se other-while
I sey it bi my-self quod he · and it so were
140 That I were kynge with crowne · to kepen a Rewme
Shulde neuere wronge in þis worlde · þat I wite myȝte
Ben vnpunisshed in my powere · for peril of my soule
Ne gete my grace [þorw] giftes · so me god saue
Ne for no Mede haue mercy · but mekenesse it make

145 ¶ For nullum malum þe man · mette with inpunitum
And badde nullum bonum · be irremuneratum

¶ Late ȝowre confessoure sire Kynge · construe þis vnglosed
And ȝif ȝe worken it in werke · I wedde myne eres
That lawe shal ben a laborere · and lede a-felde donge
150 And loue shal lede þi londe · as þe lief lyketh

¶ Clerkes þat were confessoures · coupled hem togideres

---

121 **to fede**: Despite the scribal tendency to add *to* with an infinitive, the agreement of LR (+ CO) suggests that this is **Bx**, with other scribes dropping *to* from a b-verse that is already heavy. There is no parallel in **A**, and **C** is revised to *be cloth for þe pore* (RK.4.114).

130 **of**: So LMCOR, supported by **Ax**, revised in **C**.

133 **hym**: i.e. "if anyone catches him". Beta2 corrupts to *it*; **A** mss. vary between the two pronouns, while **C** mss., although split between *hym* and *hem*, effectively support **Bx**.

134 **if**: The agreement of LR and CrWCGO would suggest that this is from **Bx**, though MHmF without it are paralleled by **AC**.

143 **þorw**: Alpha's preposition is supported by **AC** against beta's *for*.

144 **make**: Alpha (with CrHm) has the past tense. **A** mss. are similarly split, and **C** rewrites.

Alle to construe þis clause · and for þe kynges profit
Ac nou3te for conforte of þe comune · ne for þe kynges soule

¶ For I sei3e mede in þe moot halle · on men of lawe wynke
155   And þei lawghyng lope to hire · and lafte resoun manye

¶ Waryn wisdome · wynked vppon Mede
And seide Madame I am 3owre man · what-so my mouth iangleth
I falle in floreines quod þat freke · an faile speche ofte

¶ Alle ri3tful recorded · þat resoun treuthe tolde
160   And witt acorded þer-with · and comended his wordes
And þe moste peple in þe halle · and manye of þe grete
And leten mekenesse a maistre · and Mede a mansed schrewe

¶ Loue lete of hir li3te · and lewte 3it lasse
And seide it so hei3e [·] þat al þe halle it herde
165   Who-so wilneth hir to wyf · for welth of her godis
But he be knowe for a kokewolde · kut of my nose

¶ Mede mourned þo · and made heuy chere
For þe moste comune of þat courte [·] called hire an hore
Ac a sysoure and a sompnoure · sued hir faste
170   And a schireues clerke · byschrewed al þe route
For ofte haue I quod he · holpe 3ow atte barre
And 3it 3eue 3e me neuere · þe worthe of a russhe

¶ The kynge called conscience · and afterwardes resoun
And recorded þat resoun [·] had ri3tfullich schewed
175   And modilich vppon Mede · with my3te þe Kynge loked
And gan wax wrothe with lawe · for Mede almoste had shent it
And seide þorw 3owre lawe as I leue · I lese many chetes
Mede ouer-maistrieth lawe · and moche treuthe letteth
Ac resoun shal rekene with 3ow · 3if I regne any while
180   And deme 3ow bi þis day · as 3e han deserued
Mede shal nou3te meynprise 3ow · bi þe Marie of heuene

---

152 **and**: This has the support of LR and WHmC, though F reads *al* and MCrGO omit,
presumably reacting to its oddity. In both **A** and **C** the b-verses are quite different.

157 **iangleth**: Alpha + WHm have subjunctive, which may be right, but the indicative is not
uncommon in such expressions. See Mustanoja (1960), 468, and cf. "what-euere þe boke
telleth" (**Bx**.5.495). The line is not in **AC**.

158 **þat**: So beta, against alpha's *þe*. Either could be **Bx**. See KD, p. 143.

163 **3it**: Beta is supported by **Cx** against *wel* in Hm and alpha.

171 **he**: F takes the form to be feminine, referring to Mede, and MHm alter to *she*, but the
reference is obviously to the sheriff's clerk.

175 **modilich**: In L a corrector has added <w> to read *mowd-*.

175 Alpha's b-verse, *mi3te þat kyng loke*, is perhaps a response to the clumsy reading of **Bx**, as
recorded by beta. **Cx** patches to "many tyme lokede" (RK.4.167).

I wil haue leute in lawe · and lete be al ȝowre ianglyng
And as moste folke witnesseth wel · wronge shal be demed

¶ Quod conscience to þe kynge · but þe comune wil assent
185   It is ful hard bi myn hed · here-to to brynge it
Alle ȝowre lige leodes · to lede þus euene

¶ By hym þat rauȝte on þe rode · quod resoun to þe kynge
But if I reule þus ȝowre rewme · rende out my guttes
Ȝif ȝe bidden buxomnes · be of myne assente

190   ¶ And I assent [quod] þe kynge · by seynte Marie my lady
Be my conseille comen [·] of clerkis and of erlis
Ac redili resoun [·] þow shalt nouȝte ride fro me
For as longe as I lyue · lete þe I nelle

¶ I am aredy quod resoun · to reste with ȝow euere
195   So conscience be of owre conseille · I kepe no bettere
And I graunt quod the kynge · goddes forbode [he] faile
Als longe as owre lyf lasteth · lyue we togideres

---

183 R's a-verse, *And as alle folke witnesseth*, represents alpha, with F altering *folke* to *wyȝes* for the alliteration.

183 **moste**: There seems nothing to choose between beta and alpha's *alle* except the scribal tendency to exaggerate. There is no parallel line in AC.

186 **lige**: In omitting the adjective, R probably represents alpha, with F's *londys* an attempt to improve alliteration, as in l. 183. Beta is supported by AC.

190 **quod**: Support is strong from alpha + HmGO, together with **Ax**. M's *seith* is a correction. On the other hand, the alliterative pattern would support *seith* as in LCrWC. In C the line is rewritten to alliterate on /w/ (RK.4.183).

191 L misplaces the punctuation after *clerkis*.

194 **aredy**: LMOR have this form; Cr has *redy* (as does **Ax**); WHmCGF have *al redy*.

195 **owre**: M's *yowre* is paralleled in a number of A mss.

196 **he**: R shares this reading with **Ax**. Both F (with *þou*) and beta (with *it*) miss the reference to Conscience.

197 **lasteth**: There is no particular reason to prefer alpha's subjunctive form. For not very precise parallels, cf. **Bx**.6.295, 20.211.

Passus 5

Passus quintus de visione vt supra

The kyng and his knightes · to the kirke wente
To here matynes of þe day · and þe masse after
Þanne waked I of my wynkynge [·] and wo was with-alle
Þat I ne hadde sleped sadder · and yseiȝen more
5   Ac er I hadde faren a fourlonge · feyntise me hente
That I ne myȝte ferther a foot · for defaute of slepynge
And sat softly adown · and seide my bileue
And so I babeled on my bedes · þei brouȝte me a-slepe

¶ And þanne saw I moche more · þan I bifore tolde
10 For I say þe felde ful of folke · þat I bifore of seyde
And how resoun gan arrayen hym · alle þe reume to preche
And with a crosse afor þe kynge · comsed þus to techen

¶ He preued þat þise pestilences · was for pure synne
And þe southwest wynde · on saterday at euene
15 Was pertliche for pryde · and for no poynt elles
Piries and plomtrees · were puffed to þe erthe
In ensample ȝe segges · ȝe shulden do þe bettere
Beches and brode okes · were blowen to þe grounde

---

8 **so I**: Omitted by R, but F has *y bablede so*, and beta is supported by **Ax**. The line is not in **Cx**.
12 **afor**: On five occasions alpha and random beta mss. read the preposition as *byfor*; the others are **Bx**.5.23, 16.46, 17.311, 20.130. Probably this is regression to the commonplace, since *afor* is uncommon in the poem. Only in 12.91 does it have support from both branches. At 14.145 the adverb reads *afore* in beta, but *tofore* in alpha.
13 **was**: LMCOR have this as the plural form. It is also the form in **Cx** (RK.5.115) and some **A** mss. For parallels see **Bx**.13.368, 17.11, 19.47, 19.96.
15 **pryde**: Beta adds *pure* (from l. 13); alpha is supported by AC.
17 **In**: Alpha begins the line with *And in*, but **AC** support beta.
17 **ȝe segges ȝe**: WHm have *þat ye segges*. F's *þat we* is also the reading of **Cx** (RK.5.119). **A** mss. show considerable variation.

[And] torned vpward her taille · in tokenynge of drede
20 Þat dedly synne ar domesday · shal fordon hem alle

¶ Of þis matere I my3te · mamely ful longe
Ac I shal seye as I saw · so me god helpe
How pertly afor þe poeple · resoun gan to preche

¶ He bad wastoure go worche · what he best couthe
25 And wynnen his wastyng · with somme manere crafte

¶ And preyed peronelle · her purfyle to lete
And kepe it in hir cofre · for catel at hire nede

¶ Thomme stowue he tau3te · to take two staues
And fecche filice home · fro wyuen[e] pyne

30 ¶ He warned watt · his wyf was to blame
Þat hire hed was worth halue marke · his hode nou3te a grote
And bad bette kut · a bow other tweyne
And bete betoun þer-with · but if she wolde worche
And þanne he charged chapmen · to chasten her childeren
35 Late no wynnynge [forweny hem] · whil þei be 3onge
Ne for no pouste of pestilence · plese hem nou3te out of resoun

---

19 **And**: Dropped in beta, but alpha is supported by **AC**.

19 **taille**: As often, the distributive sg. is to be preferred. In this case alpha is supported by **AC**.

19 **in**: Dropped by alpha, but supported by **AC**.

23 **afor**: See note to **Bx**.5.12 for variation with *byfor*.

23 **gan**: Strong support from LMR against *bigan*. F's word-order *prechen gan resoun* improves the alliteration of the b-verse, but cannot be archetypal. No doubt the order in **Bx** is a reminiscence of l. 11. The line is not in the other versions.

24 **go**: Only R has *to*, which is, however, the reading of the X family of **C**.

25 **crafte**: **Ax** also has the sg. as beta.

26 **And**: Clear support from LMR and HmCO, against *He* in CrWGF. **A** mss. vary, but **Cx** has *He*, possibly the source for CrG by contamination.

29 **wyuene pyne**: Having lost -*e* (OE -*ena*), beta adds the definite article to correct a short b-verse. A few **AC** scribes do the same.

31 **Þat**: Also the **A** reading. WHm *For* is also the **C** reading (RK.5.133).

31 **halue marke**: LCrCG include the indefinite article, and M is corrected to include it. But alpha and WHmO are without it, as is **Cx**. **Ax** has *a mark*.

31 **his**: CrWHmF have *and his*, as also do **AC**. But probably **Bx** omitted *and*, since it is not attested by LR and CGO. In M it is first added by the corrector and then deleted.

31 **nou3te**: The reading *nou3te worth* looks suspiciously scribal. Six **A** mss. omit *worth*, as do all except one of the **C** mss. But attestation for **Bx** is uncertain: only HmG and R omit it. We follow the readings of R throughout this line.

34 WHm and alpha have a paraph, though it is not particularly appropriate.

34 **chasten**: The form supported for **Bx** by LR and CrCG, as well as **Cx** and five **A** mss. Others have *chastisen*.

35 **forweny hem**: Beta has *hem forweny*. The word-order of alpha is uncertain, since R omits the pronoun, but F's *for-wayne hem* is the order of **AC**.

35 **whil**: R alone has *þe while*, though it is in the X family of **C**.

¶ My syre seyde so to me · and so did my dame
Þat þe leuere childe · þe more lore bihoueth
And Salamon seide þe same · þat sapience made
40 Qui parcit virge odit filium
Þe Englich of þis latyn is · who-so wil it knowe
Who-so spareth þe sprynge · spilleth his children

¶ And sithen he preyed prelatz · and prestes togideres
Þat 3e prechen to þe peple · preue it on 3owre-seluen
45 And doth it in dede · it shal drawe 3ow to good
If 3e lyuen as 3e leren vs [·] we shal leue 3ow þe bettere

¶ And sithen he radde Religioun · here reule to holde
Leste þe kynge and his conseille · 3owre comunes appayre
And ben stuwardes of 3owre stedes · til 3e be ruled bettre

50 ¶ And sithen he conseilled þe kynge · þe comune to louye
It is þi tresore if tresoun ne were · and triacle at þi nede

[¶] And sithen he prayed þe pope · haue pite on holicherche
And er he gyue any grace · gouerne firste hym-selue

¶ And 3e that han lawes to kepe · late treuthe be 3owre coueytise
55 More þan golde or other gyftes · if 3e wil god plese
For who-so contrarieth treuthe · he telleth in þe gospel
That god knoweth hym nou3te · ne no seynte of heuene
Amen dico vobis nescio vos ·

¶ And 3e þat seke seynte Iames · and seintes of Rome
60 Seketh seynt treuthe · for he may saue 3ow alle
Qui cum patre & filio · þat feire hem bifalle
Þat suweth my sermon · and þus seyde resoun

¶ Thanne ran repentance · and reherced his teme
And gert wille to wepe · water with his eyen

65 ¶ Peronelle proude-herte · platte hir to þe erthe

---

42 **spilleth**: Alpha includes the pronoun *he*, but beta is supported by **Cx**. The line is not in **A**.

43 **preyed**: Evidently the beta reading, supported against the variants by **AC**.

46 **leren**: This varies with *lerne* also in **A**, but is supported by **Cx**.

49 **ruled**: An obvious substitution in **Bx** for alliterating *stewed*, "governed", in **AC**.

50 **þe** (2): This is secure for **Bx**, though beta2 *his* is the **Cx** reading (RK.5.180).

51 **ne were**: R's loss of *ne* suggests that alpha may have read *nere*, as in F, which would be a little less clumsy. The line is not paralleled in **AC**.

52 **¶**: The parallel with the paraphs for lines 43, 47 and 50 also beginning *And sithen* supports the paraph recorded in WHmCOR (with a new line-group in M).

55 **or other**: M and beta2 (CrWHm) drop *other*, but it has support from LCHm and alpha. The line is not in **AC**.

And lay longe ar she loked · and lorde mercy cryed

And byhi3te to hym · þat vs alle made   Superbia ·

She shulde vnsowen hir serke · and sette þere an heyre

To affaiten hire flessh · þat fierce was to synne

70   Shal neuere hei3e herte me hente · but holde me lowe

And suffre to be myssayde · and so did I neuere

But now wil I meke me · and mercy biseche

For al þis I haue · hated in myne herte

¶ Þanne lecchoure seyde allas · and on owre lady he cryed

75   To make mercy for his mis-dedes · bitwene god and his soule   Luxuria ·

With þat he shulde þe saterday · seuene 3ere þere-after

Drynke but [with] þe doke · and dyne but ones

¶ Enuye with heuy herte · asked after scrifte   Inuidia

And carefullich mea culpa · he comsed to shewe

80   He was as pale as a pelet · in þe palsye he semed

And clothed in a caurimaury · I couthe it nou3te discreue

In kirtel and kourteby · and a knyf bi his syde

Of a freres frokke · were þe forsleues

And as a leke hadde yleye · longe in þe sonne

85   So loked he with lene chekes · lourynge foule

¶ His body was to-bolle for wratthe · þat he bote his lippes

And wryngy[ed] with þe fiste · to wreke hym-self he þou3te

With werkes or with wordes · whan he seighe his tyme

Eche a worde þat he warpe · was of an addres tonge

90   Of chydynge and of chalangynge · was his chief lyflode

With bakbitynge and bismer · and beryng of fals witnesse

Þis was al his curteisye · where þat euere he shewed hym

---

67 **to:** Supported by **Ax** (K.5.47) and **Cx** (RK.6.5) against MO *vn-to*.

67 The beta scribes have Latin titles for the sins in the main hand in the margin, and marked out by rubrication from other marginal annotations, but the alpha scribes do not have them.

73 **al:** Dropped by alpha, but supported by **AC** and alliterating.

76 **þe saterday:** R's *on þe day* probably represents alpha. Beta is supported by **Ax** and alliteration.

77 **with:** Alpha is supported by **A** and **C** (RK.6.174); elsewhere (e.g. **Bx**.4.79) Langland uses *myd* to provide alliteration. For discussion of this variation, see note to **Bx**.7.26.

79 **shewe:** R has *schrewe*, F has *shryue*, but beta is supported by **Ax**. The line is revised in **Cx**.

83 **þe:** Beta is supported by the majority of **A** mss., but six read *his* with alpha.

84 **hadde:** Beta2 (CrWHm) read *þat hadde*, supported by the majority of **A** mss., though four omit *þat*. It is more probably supplied than dropped. The line is not in **Cx**.

87 **wryngyed:** R (= alpha?). **A** has *wroþliche he wroþ his fest* (K.5.67) and **C** reads *A wroth his fuste vppon wrath* (RK.6.66). Apparently **Bx** misunderstood the pun (*wroth* from *writhen*, and *wrath*), and substituted the past tense of *wringen*. Beta's *wryngynge he 3ede* is an expansion. Elsewhere in **B** the past tense of *wring* is *wrong*, as in F here.

92 F entirely rewrites the line with much more emphatic alliteration. W omits. Lines 91–5 are not in **AC**, and lines 96–121 are not in **C**.

¶ I wolde ben yshryue quod þis schrewe · and I for shame durst
I wolde be gladder bi god · þat gybbe had meschaunce
95 Than þou3e I had þis woke ywonne · a weye of essex chese

¶ I haue a neighbore ney3e me · I haue ennuyed hym ofte
And lowen on hym to lordes · to don hym lese his siluer
And made his frendes ben his foon · thorw my false tonge
His grace and his good happes · greueth me ful sore
100 Bitwene m[eyne] and m[eyne] · I make debate ofte
Þat bothe lyf and lyme · is lost þorw my speche

¶ And whan I mete him in market · þat I moste hate
I hailse hym hendeliche · as I his frende were
For he is dou3tier þan I · I dar do non other
105 Ac hadde I maystrye and my3te · god wote my wille

¶ And whan I come to þe kirke · and sholde knele to þe Rode
And preye for þe pople · as þe prest techeth
For pilgrimes and for palmers · for alle þe poeple after
Þanne I crye on my knees · þat cryste 3if hem sorwe
110 Þat bar awey my bolle · and my broke schete

¶ Awey fro þe auter þanne · turne I myn eyghen
And biholde how [H]eleyne · hath a newe cote
I wisshe þanne it were myne · and al þe webbe after

¶ And of [his] lesynge I laughe · þat liketh myn herte
115 A[c] for h[is] wynnynge I wepe · and waille þe tyme

---

96 **ennuyed**: The spellings *anoyed, noyed, enuyed* are all forms of "annoyed".

100 **meyne and meyne**: We take R's reading ("retinue") to represent alpha, supported by **Ax** *hym & his meyne*. F thus revises, perhaps partly on the basis of **A**; beta regresses to the commonplace.

106 **kirke**: Hm and alpha have non-alliterating *cherche*. See Introduction, pp. 18–19.

108 **and for**: Support from LR and CrWCO, though MHmG lack *for*. F instead lacks *and*, as in **Ax**.

111 The alpha scribes punctuate the line before *þanne*.

112 **Heleyne**: F perhaps notices the unlikelihood of Envy envying a woman's coat, and substitutes *Hervy*. Initial *H-* (as in R) is presumably archetypal: **Ax** has the male name, *Heyne* (cf. **Bx**.5.114–15).

112 **hath**: Alpha's *hath on* is not supported by **Ax**. Following this line F adds rather a vivid line.

114 **his**: **Bx** alters the coatwearer from male (**Ax** has *Heyne*) to female *Heleyne*, and faces scribes with a problem, which they deal with characteristically. Beta and F revise to *mennes*, but R copies his exemplar regardless, ignoring the inconsistency. **Ax** also reads *his*, but there is nowhere evidence that R is contaminated by an **A** text. See notes to ll. 115 and 116.

115 **Ac**: There is the same common variation with *But* in **A** mss., with three reading *And*, as beta does here.

115 **his**: Again R follows his copy-text, and on this occasion F is content to do the same, whereas beta logically replaces with *her*, "their". **Ax** again reads *his*.

¶ And deme [men] þat hij don ille · þere I do wel worse
Who-so vndernymeth me here-of · I hate hym dedly after
I wolde þat vche a wyght · were my knaue
For who-so hath more þan I · þat angreth me sore
120   And þus I lyue louelees · lyke a luther dogge
That al my body bolneth · for bitter of my galle

¶ I my3te nou3te eet many 3eres · as a man ou3te
For enuye and yuel wille · is yuel to defye
May no sugre ne swete þinge · asswage my swellynge
125   Ne no diapenidion · dryue it fro myne herte
Ne noyther schrifte ne shame · but ho-so schrape my mawe

¶ 3us redili quod repentaunce · and radde hym to þe beste
Sorwe of synnes · is sauacioun of soules

¶ I am *sori / euere sory* quod þat segge · I am but selde other
130   And þat maketh me þus megre · for I ne may me venge
Amonges Burgeyses haue I be · dwellynge at Londoun
And gert bakbitinge be a brocoure · to blame mennes ware
Whan he solde and I nou3te · þanne was I redy
To lye and to loure on my neighbore · and to lakke his chaffare
135   I wil amende þis 3if I may · þorw my3te of god almy3ty

¶ Now awaketh wratthe · with two whyte eyen   Ira ·
And nyuelynge with þe nose · and his nekke hangynge

¶ I am wrath quod he · I was sum-tyme a frere
And þe couentes Gardyner · for to graffe ympes
140   On limitoures and listres · lesynges I ymped
Tyl þei bere leues of low speche · lordes to plese
And sithen þei blosmed obrode · in boure to here shriftes
And now is fallen þer-of a frute · þat folke han wel leuere

---

116 ¶: The inappropriate paraph is in LR, with a new line-group in M, and so is apparently a **Bx** error.

116 **men**: Again R is supported by **A**, with F supplying the object *hem* instead. Since beta already has a plural referent, *men* is unnecessary and is therefore dropped.

121 **of**: Probably R's *in* represents alpha (F has *ys*). **Ax** supports *of*.

129 **sory / euere sory**: Beta agrees with **Ax**, while alpha's *euere sory* agrees with **Cx**.

133 **redy**: R has *aredy* which may be right. It is the **Cx** form (RK.6.97). The passage **Bx**.5.131–89 is not in **A**.

134 **chaffare**: Alpha's *ware* presumably arises by eyeskip from l. 132, where F actually reads *to lakke mennys ware*. For the reverse situation see l. 209 and note. **Cx** is rewritten.

138 **wrath**: Alpha's *wrothe* is perhaps here the adjective, "I am angry"; alternatively it is the adjective used as a noun (see *MED wroth*), as in R's spelling in l. 136. The X family of **C** also has this form.

142 **obrode**: Dropped by alpha, but supported by alliteration.

Schewen her schriftes to hem · þan shryue hem to her persones

145　¶ And now persones [han] parceyued · þat Freres parte with hem
Þise possessioneres preche · and depraue freres
And freres fyndeth hem in defaute · as folke bereth witnes
That whan þei preche þe poeple · in many place aboute
I wrath walke with hem · and wisse hem of my bokes
150　Þus þei speken of spiritualte · þat eyther despiseth other
Til þei be bothe beggers · and by my spiritualte libben
Or elles alle riche [·] and riden aboute
I wrath rest neuere · þat I ne moste folwe
This wykked folke · for suche is my grace

155　¶ I haue an aunte to nonne · and an abbesse
Hir were leuere swowe or swelte · þan soeffre any peyne
I haue be cook in hir kichyne · and þe couent serued
Many monthes with hem · and with monkes bothe
I was þe priouresses potagere · and other poure ladyes
160　And made hem ioutes of iangelynge · þat dame Io[n]e was a bastard
And dame Clarice a kniȝtes douȝter · ac a kokewolde was hire syre
And dame Peronelle a prestes file · Priouresse worth she neuere
For she had childe in chirityme · al owre chapitere it wiste

¶ Of wykked wordes I wrath · here wortes I-made
165　Til þow lixte and þow lixte · lopen oute at ones
And eyther hitte other · vnder þe cheke
Hadde þei had knyues bi cryst · her eyther had killed other

145　**persones han**: "Now that parsons have perceived" (as in beta2 and G), rather than, with the word-order in CO and alpha, "Now have parsons perceived". Either order could be **Bx**. L drops the auxiliary, while M drops the phrase, and *persons han* is added above the line in another hand. The line is not in **AC**.

147　**freres**: Alpha drops the word, but the following line refers to the peripatetic activity of friars.

148　**place**: This is probably the beta form. As a romance loan ending in a sibilant, it may be singular or plural.

150　**spiritualte**: Beta2 (and M by correction) and GR supply *my*, by contamination with the next line. It makes no sense here. See note on l. 151.

151　**by my spiritualte**: Hm and alpha drop *my*, by confusion with the previous line. F revises to *by almesse*.

155　**abbesse**: R is supported by **Cx**. Beta's addition of *bothe* and F's of *eek* are responses to the unusually light b-verse.

158　**bothe**: R's *alse* probably represents alpha (F rewrites), but beta is supported by **Cx** (RK.6.131).

159　**priouresses**: LMR and Hm have this form of the genitive, whereas other mss. have the unmarked form, as do most C mss.

160　**Ione**: So MCrO and alpha, as well as C mss. It is the usual feminine form of the name in Middle English. LWHm have *Iohan(n)e*.

164　**I-made**: Past tense; *MED imaken*. The prefix recorded in LOR makes the b-verse regular.

167　**her eyther**: "each of them". LMWR include the genitive pronoun.

¶ Seynt Gregorie was a gode pope · and had a gode forwit
Þat no Priouresse were prest · for þat he ordeigned
170 Þei had þanne ben infamis þe firste day · þei can so yuel hele conseille

¶ Amonge monkes I miȝte be · ac many tyme I shonye
For þere ben many felle frekis · my feres to aspye
Bothe Prioure an supprioure · and owre pater abbas
And if I telle any tales · þei taken hem togyderes
175 And do me faste frydayes · to bred and to water
And am chalanged in þe chapitelhous · as I a childe were
And baleised on þe bare ers · and no breche bitwene
For-þi haue I no lykyng · with þo leodes to wonye
I ete there vnthende fisshe · and fieble ale drynke
180 Ac otherwhile whan wyn cometh · whan I drynke w[el] at eue
I haue a fluxe of a foule mouthe · wel fyue dayes after
Al þe wikkednesse þat I wote · bi any of owre bretheren
I couth it in owre cloistre · þat al owre couent wote it

¶ Now repent þe quod Repentaunce · and reherce þow neure
185 Conseille þat þow cnowest · bi contenaunce ne bi [speche]
And drynke nouȝte ouer-delicatly · ne to depe noyther
Þat þi wille bi cause þer-of [·] to wrath myȝte torne
Esto sobrius he seyde · and assoilled me after
And bad me wilne to wepe · my wikkednesse to amende

190 ¶ And þanne cam coueytise · [I can] hym nouȝte descryue   Auaricia ·
So hungriliche and holwe · sire henri hym loked

---

170 **þe firste day**: Dropped by M, G (in a rewritten line) and O to shorten a long a-verse. Cr replaces with two invented lines. The line is not in **AC**.

176 **And am**: R's *ȝeet*, "furthermore", may be right, even though not in F. It gives good sense and has some support from **Cx** *ȝut am I*.

177 **ers**: Beta is confirmed by **Cx**. R initially read *hers*, altered to the euphemism *bak* by the correcting hand. F also reads *bak*.

180 Alpha has a paraph.

180 **whan** (2): So LMR and G; W has *þanne*, the others read *and* or omit.

180 **wel**: Beta's repetition of *wyn* gives weaker sense, though *wel* is repeated in the following line. Perhaps both alpha and beta are making up for a loss in **Bx**, since **Cx** has *late* instead (RK.6.160).

183 **owre** (2): The distribution of variants is odd here. LM, the two most reliable beta witnesses, are joined by CrW with *owre*; the other mss., including F, have *þe*, except for G with *your* and R which has nothing. It may be that R is faithfully copying a **Bx** error, with other scribes supplying the obvious omission. **Cx** has *þe*.

185 **speche**: Alpha's reading is obviously correct and supported by **Cx** against beta's *riȝte*.

188 **me**: Here and in l. 189 Cr has third person pronouns in line with **Cx**, and M is altered to the same readings.

190 **I can**: Alpha's word-order is supported by **AC**.

191 **henri**: There is reasonable support for this as **Bx** from LR and CG, and possibly M before correction, but **AC** have *heruy*, agreeing with WHmOF. Although F may have derived the

He was bitelbrowed · and baberlipped also
With two blered eyghen · as a blynde hagge
And as a letheren purs · lolled his chekes
195   Wel sydder þan his chyn · þei chiueled for elde
And as a bondman of his bacoun · his berde was bidraueled
With [his] hode on his hed · a lousi hatte aboue
And in a tauny tabarde · of twelue wynter age
Al totorne and baudy · and ful of lys crepynge
200   But if a lous couthe · l[epe] þe bettre
[H]e sholde nouȝte walk[e] on þat welche · so was it thredebare

¶ I haue ben coueytouse quod þis caityue · I biknowe it here
For some-tyme I serued · symme atte stile
And was his prentis ypliȝte · his profit to wayte
205   First I lerned to lye · a leef other tweyne
Wikkedlich to weye · was my furst lessoun
To wy and to wynchestre · I went to þe faire
With many manere marchandise · as my Maistre me hiȝte
Ne had þe grace of gyle [·] ygo amonge my ware
210   It had be vnsolde þis seuene ȝere · so me god helpe
¶ Thanne drowe I me amonges draperes · my donet to lerne
To drawe þe lyser alonge [·] þe lenger it semed
Amonge þe riche rayes · I rendred a lessoun
To broche hem with a bat-nedle · and plaited hem togyderes

---

correction from **A**, it is difficult to see how the other three mss. got it, although Bennett (1972), 163 quotes a parallel from Skelton, possibly an indication that Hervy was a traditional name for a miser.

197 **his**: Alpha's reading is in agreement with **Cx** against beta's indefinite article.

200 **if**: Beta has *if þat*; AC agree with alpha.

200 **lepe**: Comparison with **AC** suggests that R represents **Bx**, with F and beta expanding an uncomfortably short line. **A** mss. show considerable variation in the b-verse, and **Cx** offers a desperate repair: *But ȝif a lous couthe lepe y leue it as y trowe* (quoting Skeat C.7.204).

201 **He**: Whether masc. or fem., alpha's reading is supported by **AC** against beta's *She*.

201 **walke**: Beta's *haue walked* follows on from its reading of the previous line. Alpha's infinitive is supported by **AC**, which, however, have *wandre*.

201 **welche**: "Welsh cloth", the reading of LR and **AC**, but mistranscribed or avoided by the other **B** scribes.

205 WHm and R have a paraph.

209 Only LW punctuate the line after *ygo*.

209 **ware**: A good example of the superiority of LMR (joined by F here), supported in this reading by **AC**, against *chaffare* in other beta mss. (i.e. beta1). See Adams (2000), 176, and for the same variation see l. 134.

214 **bat-nedle**: The form in L and alpha, with M corrected to the majority beta form, *paknedle*. Adams (2000), 181. **A** mss. have the same variation, with the majority reading *p*- (K.5.126). The P family of **C** also has *p*-, but the X family has *b*-, and *plaited* is revised to *bande* so that the line alliterates on /b/ (RK.6.218). *MED* lists only this instance for *bat-nedle*.

215   And put hem in a presse · and pyned hem þerinne
      Tyl ten ȝerdes or twelue · tolled out threttene

      ¶ My wyf was a webbe · and wollen cloth made
      She spak to spynnesteres · to spynnen it oute
      Ac þe pounde þat she payed by · poised a quarter more
220   Than myne owne auncere · who-so weyȝed treuthe

      ¶ I bouȝte hir barly · she brewe it to selle
      Peny ale and podyng ale · she poured togideres
      For laboreres and for low folke · þat lay by hym-selue

      ¶ The best ale lay in my boure · or in my bedchambre
225   And who-so bummed þer-of · *bouȝte / he bouȝte* it þer-after
      A galoun for a grote · god wote na lesse
      And ȝit it cam in cupmel · þis crafte my wyf vsed
      Rose þe regratere · was hir riȝte name
      She hath holden hokkerye · al hire lyf-tyme

230   ¶ Ac I swere now so the ik · þat synne wil I lete
      And neuere wikkedliche weye · ne wikke chaffare vse
      But wenden to walsyngham · and my wyf als
      And bidde þe Rode of bromeholme · brynge me oute of dette

---

215 **pyned**: "subjected to stress" in the *presse*, which is apparently a stretching frame. Schmidt (1995), 72, glosses "tortured". The reading is supported by LW and alpha against the easier and less appropriate *pynned*, glossed as "kept fastened" in Kane (2005). A mss. vary, but **Cx** has *pynned*.

216 **tolled**: LM and alpha, supported by **AC**; other scribes supply *hadde*. *MED* v.(1) interprets *tollen* as "stretch out to" (OE **tollian*), while Kane (2005) glosses "tease, coax". It varies with *tolde* in **A**; in **C** the X family reads *tolde*, the P family has *tilled*.

218 **spynnesteres**: Alpha has the sg. A mss. are split, but **Cx** has the plural. Athlone adopts the sg. in all versions.

219 **poised**: A variant of *peised*, though given a separate entry by *MED*.

219 **quarter**: Beta has *quarteroun* (*MED quartroun*), but alpha is supported by **AC**.

221 **barly**: Though all **B** mss. except for R read *barly malte*, R is supported by **AC**. We assume that the easy addition was made by beta and F, with R as usual reproducing his exemplar.

223 **for** (2): Not in MCrCOF, or in most **AC** mss.

223 **hym-**: LWHmR have sg.: "was set aside on its own", So in **Cx**, while **A** mss. vary with the plural. The odd use of *hym* to refer to a barrel of ale (cf. Cr *it*) perhaps confused scribes.

225 **bouȝte / he bouȝte**: Beta, without the pronoun, agrees with **Ax**; alpha and **Cx**, add the pronoun *he*.

227 **vsed**: Beta's past tense is supported by **AC**.

228 **was**: Beta's past tense is supported by **AC**.

231 **wikke** "dishonest". So LMW. Particularly in context, the *wikked* of alpha and others is likely to be a scribal substitution. **A** mss. exhibit some uncertainty over the word; the line is not in **C**.

¶ Repentestow euere quod repentance · ne restitucioun madest

235 ¶ 3us ones I was herberwed quod he · with an hep of chapmen
I roos whan þei were arest · and yrifled here males

¶ That was no restitucioun quod repentance · but a robberes thefte
Þow haddest better worthy · be hanged þerfore
Þan for al þat · þat þow hast here shewed

240 ¶ I wende ryflynge were restitucioun quod he · for I lerned neuere rede on
boke
And I can no frenche in feith · but of þe ferthest ende of norfolke

¶ Vsedestow euere vsurie quod repentaunce · in alle þi lyf-tyme

¶ Nay sothly he seyde · saue in my 3outhe
I lerned amonge lumbardes · [a lessoun and of iewes]
245 To wey pens with a peys · and pare þe heuyest
And lene it for loue of þe crosse · to legge a wedde and lese it
Suche dedes I did wryte · 3if he his day breke
I haue mo maneres þorw rerages · þan þorw miseretur & comodat

¶ I haue lent lordes · and ladyes my chaffare
250 And ben her brocour after · and bou3te it my-self
Eschaunges and cheuesances · with suche chaffare I dele
And lene folke þat lese wol · a lyppe at euery noble
And with lumbardes lettres · I ladde golde to Rome
And toke it by taille here · and tolde hem þere lasse

---

234 **Repentestow**: Representing the past tense, as more "properly" in WHmR. (See *MED repenten* for pa.t. *repente*). C mss. show the same forms. In **Bx**.5.453 WHm again "improve" to *Repentedestow*, falsely on that occasion. LM (= beta?) treat the verb as reflexive, but *þe* is not in R (= alpha?) or C. HmF include *þe* but drop the subject pronoun. For a similar set of variants see **Bx**.5.453 and note. The passage **Bx**.5.234–308 is not in **A**.

234 **ne**: Another example of LMR presenting a superior reading, here agreeing with **Cx** against *or*. See Adams (2000), 176. The syntax is, however, odd.

236 **yrifled**: The form, though unmetrical (x x / x x / x), is supported by LR against *rifled*.

238 **better**: Although most mss. have *be better*, LR and original M give secure evidence for **Bx**, with *be* in the b-verse governing both *worthy* and *hanged*. Bx might have lost *be* in this context, with other scribes restoring it conjecturally, just as the M corrector did. Adams (2000), 183 judges this instead to be an accidental omission in LR. **Cx** revises the a-verse to "Thow wolt be hanged heye þerfore" (RK.6.238).

240 **quod he for**: Probably in response to the length of the line, MHmGF drop *quod he*, while CGO drop *for*. The line is not in **AC**.

244 **a lessoun and of iewes**: The word-order in alpha is alliteratively correct, and R's reading is shared with **Cx**. Beta simplifies to *and iewes a lessoun*; F revises.

248 **rerages**: Alpha's *regages* is an obvious error.

254 **here**: R alone reads *þere*, presumably by anticipation. Lines 247–51 and 254 have no parallel in **AC**.

255   [¶] Len[t]estow euere lordes · for loue of her mayntenaunce

¶ 3e I haue lent lordes · loued me neuere after
And haue ymade many a kny3te · bothe mercere & drapere
Þat payed neuere for his prentishode · nou3te a peire gloues

¶ Hastow pite on pore men · þat mote nedes borwe

260   ¶ I haue as moche pite of pore men · as pedlere hath of cattes
Þat wolde kille hem yf he cacche hem my3te · for coueitise of here skynnes

¶ Artow manlyche amonge þi nei3bores · of þi mete and drynke

¶ I am holden quod he as hende · as hounde is in kychyne
Amonges my neighbores namelich · such a name ich haue

265   ¶ Now god lene neure quod repentance · but þow repent þe rather
Þe grace on þis grounde · þi good wel to bisette
Ne þine [v]sue after þe · haue ioye of þat þow wynnest
Ne þi excecutours wel bisett · þe siluer þat þow hem leuest
And þat was wonne with wronge · with wikked men be despended
270   For were I frere of þat hous · þere gode faith and charite is
I nolde cope vs with þi catel · ne owre kyrke amende
Ne haue a peny to my pitaunce of þyne [·] bi my soule hele

---

255 ¶: The line is at the top of the page in L, and the rubricator presumably missed the paraph which is in WHmC and alpha, with a new line-group in M, to mark the opening of the speech.

255 **Lentestow**: L's present tense *Lenestow* is not supported by **Cx**.

256 Alpha alone has *quod he* after *lordes*, but it is not in **Cx**. CrHmOF supply the subject pronoun *that* before *loued*, as in **Cx**, but its omission, supported by LMWCGR, is idiomatic.

257 **a**: Not in COR, but in **Cx**.

260 **of** (1): The reading of LR and WC, against *on*, likely to have been prompted by the phrase in the previous line.

260 **pedlere**: Alpha has *þe pedlere*, which is perhaps over-specific. For want of guidance from other versions, we follow copy-text.

267 **vsue**: This is the initial spelling in L, then corrected to *ysue*. R and possibly uncorrected M share the word, against *heires* in all others mss. except F with *houswif*! R spelling *vssue* explains F's reading as an attempt to make sense of *vssue* via *hussie*. Schmidt (1995), lxvii–iii, supposes this is shared error in LR; and see Adams (2000), 181–2. We take it to represent the reading of **Bx**, despite the fact that **Cx** has *heyres*, by error or revision.

271 **nolde**: Beta shares this reading with the P family of C, against alpha's *wolde nou3t*. At RK.7.202 the P family again has *nolde*, as do all **B** mss. (**Bx**.5.578) against *ne wol(d)* in the X family.

271 **kyrke**: Alpha has the non-alliterating *cherche*.

272 **of þyne**: Well supported by LMCOR, though omitted by beta2 and GF, presumably because of its metrical clumsiness. The C reviser's text evidently had the phrase, for the line is rewritten as *Ne take a meles mete of þyn and myn herte hit wiste* (RK.6.289). LC, confused by its clumsiness, punctuate before the phrase; MOR punctuate after it.

272 **bi my soule hele**: Clearly **Bx**, despite its lack of alliteration. Beta2 and G have *so God my soul help*, with W increasing alliteration by altering the verb to *saue*.

For þe best boke in owre hous · þei3e brent golde were þe leues
And I wyst wytterly · þow were suche as þow telle[st]
275 Seruus es alterius · cum fercula pinguia queris
Pane tuo pocius · vescere liber eris ·

¶ Thow art an vnkynde creature · I can þe nou3te assoille
Til þow make restitucioun · and rekne with hem alle
And sithen þat resoun rolle it · in þe regystre of heuene
280 That þow hast made vche man good · I may þe nou3te assoille
Non dimittitur peccatum · donec restituatur ablatum &c

¶ For alle þat hath of þi good · haue god my trouthe
Is hold[ynge] at þe heighe dome · to helpe þe restitue
And who-so leueth nou3te þis be soth · loke in þe sauter glose
285 In miserere mei deus · where I mene treuthe
Ecce enim veritatem dilexisti &c

¶ Shal neuere werkman in þis worlde · þryue wyth þat þow wynnest
Cum sancto sanctus eris · construe me þat on englische

¶ Thanne wex þat shrewe in wanhope · and walde haue hanged himself

---

274 **tellest:** L has *telleth*, though the line is marked for correction. Following this line CO have the line *Or elles þat I kouþe knowe it by any kynnes wise*, and it is supplied in Cr²³. It is the first of four spurious lines recorded by CO in this passus; see notes to **Bx**.5.308, 342, 580.

278 **restitucioun:** Only R adds *quod repentaunce* as a second alliterating stave in the a-verse. The **Bx** reading without it seems to have been the basis for the revision in **C** alliterating on *ymad … myhte … men*.

281 **donec:** Perhaps alpha and Cr alter the reading to *nisi* on the basis of a well-known maxim of canon law; see Alford (1992), 46. In **Bx**.17.316, RK.6.257a and RK.19.290a the quotation is in many mss. abbreviated to *Numquam dimittitur peccatum &c.* (the form recorded in the *Speculum Christiani*), with some mss. expanding to *donec....* and others to *nisi....* On this occasion the former is marginally more appropriate than the latter ("until" vs. "unless"; cf. l. 278 *Til*). Not in **AC**.

282 **hath:** LMR have the sg., "everyone who has", smoothed to the pl. after *alle* in other mss. See next line.

283 **Is:** LMR continue with the sg., as does F, although rewriting the line. Many **C** mss. have *Is* here, though they have the pl. in the previous line.

283 **holdynge:** "obliged", against beta's *holden*. R's curious pres. ppl. form, revised out by F, must represent alpha, since it is also the form in the X family of **C**. Indeed R's whole line is reproduced by that family. See next note.

283 **restitue:** Beta has *to* + infinitive, but R is supported by **Cx**.

284 **þe:** Beta supported by **Cx**, against R's *a*. F has four unsupported lines in place of this one.

286 The line that follows this in alpha, *Þere is no laborere wolde leue with hem . þat knoweth peres þe plowman*, appears to be spurious. Its reference to *peres þe plowman* who has not yet been introduced "relates the immediate discussion to a consideration earlier and subsequently expressed" (KD, p. 193).

287 **Shal:** Alpha begins *For schal*, tying this line to the added line preceding it. There is no parallel for this passage in **AC**.

289 **þat:** Beta, against alpha's *þe*. We follow copy-text.

290 Ne hadde repentaunce þe rather · reconforted hym in þis manere
     Haue mercye in þi mynde · and with þi mouth biseche it
     For goddes mercye is more · þan alle hise other werkes
     Misericordia eius super omnia opera eius &c ·

     ¶ And al þe wikkednesse in þis worlde · þat man myȝte worche or thynke
295 Ne is no more to þe mercye of god · þan in þe see a glede
     Omnis iniquitas quantum ad misericordiam dei · est [quasi] sintilla in
        medio maris

     ¶ For-þi haue mercy in þi mynde · and marchandise leue it
     For þow hast no good grounde · to gete þe with a wastel
     But if it were with thi tonge · or ellis with þi two hondes
300 For þe good þat þow hast geten · bigan al with falsehede
     And as longe as þow lyuest þer-with · þow ȝeldest nouȝte but borwest

     ¶ And if þow wite neuere to whiche · ne whom to restitue
     Bere it to þe bisschop · and bidde hym of his grace
     Bisette it hym-selue · as best is for þi soule
305 For he shal answere for þe · at þe heygh dome
     For þe and for many mo · þat man shal ȝif a rekenynge
     What he lerned ȝow in lente · leue þow none other
     And what he lent ȝow of owre lordes good · to lette ȝow fro synne

     ¶ Now bigynneth glotoun · for to go to schrifte   Gula ·
310 And kaires hym to kirke-ward · his coupe to schewe

     ¶ Ac Beton þe brewestere · bad hym good morwe
     And axed of hym with þat · whiderward he wolde

     ¶ To holicherche quod he · forto here masse
     And sithen I wil be shryuen · and synne namore

315 ¶ I haue gode ale gossib quod she · glotown wiltow assaye
     Hastow auȝte in þi purs · any hote spices

---

290 **reconforted**: R (= alpha?) loses alliteration with *conforted* (as do HmG independently). F
repairs with *reersyd*.
293 The Latin line is only in LMOR. It is translated in l. 292 above (which KD exclude), but
that does not seem sufficient explanation for other mss. to lose it. For the first *eius* (as in the
Vulgate) R reads *domini*, which gives a precise translation of l. 292 and may be right. The verse
is quoted again as **Bx**.17.325, where both R and F read *domini*.
296 **quasi**: Omitted in L and added in M, but in all other **B** and C mss. For the source see
Alford (1992), 47.
302 **restitue**: The form is supported by **Cx** (RK.6.344) against GR *restitute* and CrF *restore*.
See l. 283.
308 The line following this in CO is obviously scribal, to compensate for the error *his goode*
for *owre lordes goode*.
316 W and alpha have a paraph here to mark the start of direct speech.

¶ I haue peper and piones quod he · and a pounde of garlike
A ferthyngworth of fenel-seed · for fastyngdayes

¶ Þanne goth glotoun in · and grete othes after
320 Cesse þe souteresse · sat on þe benche
Watte þe warner · and his wyf bothe
Tymme þe tynkere · and tweyne of his prentis
Hikke þe hakeneyman · and hugh þe nedeler
Clarice of cokkeslane · and þe clerke of þe cherche
325 [Sire Piers of Pridie · and Peronelle of Flaundres
Dawe þe dykere [·] and a dozeine other]
A ribibour a ratonere · a rakyer of chepe
A ropere a redyngkyng · and Rose þe dissheres
Godfrey of garlekehithe · and gryfin þe walsh
330 And vpholderes an hepe · erly bi þe morwe
Geuen glotoun with glad chere · good ale to hansel

¶ Clement þe cobelere · cast of his cloke
And *atte / to þe* new faire · nempned it to selle
Hikke þe hakeneyman · hitte his hood after
335 And badde bette þe bochere · ben on his side
Þere were chapmen ychose · þis chaffare to preise
Who-so haueth þe hood · shuld haue amendes of þe cloke

¶ [Þo] risen vp in rape · and rouned togideres

---

317 **he:** We preserve copy-text's form for "she". It was beta, though, not alpha, since it is the original form in M, and also survives in CrCG (by misunderstanding?).

322 **Tymme:** The probable source of the variants *Tomme* and *Symme*. A and C mss. vary similarly; see note to Kane's *A Version*, p. 443.

322 **prentis:** The plural form of a romance loan ending in a sibilant.

325–6 We follow the order of alpha; beta reverses the two lines. Line 325 is not in **Ax**; **Cx** has the alpha order, although adding a line between these two.

325 **Sire:** Alpha begins *And sire*, but without support from **Cx**.

328 **dissheres:** See *MED disheresse.* Alpha supposes it is genitive of *dishere*, and so adds *douȝter*. AC have *disshere*.

329 **gryfin:** Both this and R's *grifyth* are forms of Welsh Gruffudd. **Ax** and the P family of C have the former, while the X family has the latter.

333 **atte / to þe:** Beta's *atte* is the reading of **Ax** (K.5.169). R's *to þe* is the reading of **Cx** (RK.6.377). F's *in þe* has no support.

333 **nempned:** The reading of R. Beta and F (by convergence?) add the pronoun *he*, but it is not supported by **AC**.

335 **ben:** Alpha's *to ben* is found in some AC mss.

337 **haueth:** WHmO have the past tense, as in AC.

337 **shuld:** M has *shal*, though it is an addition above the line; R has *schul*, which is probably present tense, though *LALME* 4. 41, records examples of this as a past-tense form. AC have the past.

338 **Þo:** The reading of R (= alpha, with F glossing as *Þan*.) Beta reads *Two*. Choice is difficult, since A and C mss. also have both readings, with *Tho* the majority A reading, and *Two* the majority C reading. Perhaps scribes felt the lack of a subject; note that F supplies a pronoun.

And preised þese penyworthes · apart bi hem-selue
340 Þei couth nou3te bi her conscience · acorden in treuthe
Tyl Robyn þe ropere · [arise] þe southe
And nempned hym for a noumpere · þat no debate [w]ere

¶ Hikke þe hostellere · hadde þe cloke
In couenaunte þat Clement [·] shulde þe cuppe fille
345 And haue hikkes hode hostellere · and holde hym yserued
And who-so repented rathest · shulde arise after
And grete sire glotoun [·] with a galoun ale

¶ Þere was laughyng and louryng · and let go þe cuppe
And seten so til euensonge · and songen vmwhile
350 Tyl glotoun had yglobbed · a galoun an a Iille
His guttis gunne to godly · as two gredy sowes
He pissed a potel · in a pater noster while
And blew his rounde ruwet · at his rigge-bon[es] ende
That alle þat herde þat horne · held her nose after
355 And wissheden it had be wexed · with a wispe of firses

¶ He my3te neither steppe ne stonde · er he his staffe hadde
And þanne gan he go · liche a glewmannes bicche
Somme-tyme aside · and somme-tyme arrere
As who-so leyth lynes · forto lacche foules

360 ¶ And whan he drowgh to þe dore · þanne dymmed his eighen
He trembled on þe thresshewolde · an threwe to þe erthe

---

339 **þese**: So beta and the X family of C, but alpha's *þe* is the reading of **Ax** and the P family. We follow copy-text.

339 **hem-selue**: Original M, Hm and alpha have *hym-*, as do a few C mss.

341 **arise þe southe**: Beta has *arose bi þe southe*. R's nonsensical b-verse explains the attempts by F and beta to correct it, but it is a corruption of **Cx** *aryse they bisouhte* (RK.6.387). **Ax** has *was red to arisen* (K.5.178). See KD, p. 90; Hanna (1996), 217.

342 **were**: The reading of HmGR, and probably the alpha reading (F rewrites). It agrees with the majority of **A** mss. and all **C** mss. but one. Beta's *nere* is perhaps due to alliterative attraction.

342 Following this line, a non-alliterating line occurs in Cr²³ and OC.

351 **godly**: The form is supported for **Bx** by LMR, and 11 C mss. have -d- forms. See *MED gothelen*, and the variants for **Bx**.13.95, where LR again have *god(e)le*.

353 **rigge-bones**: Scribes vary in treating one or both parts of the compound as appositive or genitive. Most AC mss. support *rygbones*.

357 **go**: The infinitive without *to*, as in LMC and alpha, is supported by **Cx** and most **A** mss.

360 **And**: R's *Ac* has no support from **AC**, and may be picked up from l. 364.

361 **trembled**: The word is supported for **Bx** by LR, with the M corrector revising to *stombled* in line with beta1 to make better sense in context. The word that lies behind this must be the rare verb *thromblede*, "tripped", as in the X family of C, which causes confusion in all versions. *OED* needlessly divides *thrumble* into two verbs, though it is true that the predominant sense recorded is "to crowd in, to jostle". The line in L is marked for correction, but probably this refers to *an* for *and*.

Clement þe cobelere · cauȝte hym bi þe myddel
For to lifte hym alofte · and leyde him on his knowes
Ac glotoun was a gret cherle · and a grym in þe liftynge
365 And coughed vp a caudel · in clementis lappe
Is non so hungri hounde · in Hertford-schire
Durst lape of þe leuynges · so vnlouely [it] smauȝte

¶ With al þe wo of þis worlde · his wyf and his wenche
Baren hym to his bedde · and brouȝte hym þer-inne
370 And after al þis excesse · he had an accidie
Þat he slepe saterday and sonday · til sonne ȝede to reste
Þanne waked he of his wynkyng · and wiped his eyghen
Þe fyrste worde þat he warpe · was where is þe bolle
His witte gan edwite hym þo · how wikkedlich he lyued
375 And repentance riȝte so · rebuked hym þat tyme

¶ As þow with wordes and werkes · hast wrouȝte yuel in þi lyue
Shryue þe and be [a]shamed þer-of · and shewe it with þi mouth

¶ I glotoun quod þe gome · gylti me ȝelde
[Of] þat I haue trespassed with my tonge · I can nouȝte telle how ofte
380 Sworen goddes soule [and his sydes] · and so [help me god] and halidom
Þere no nede ne was · nyne hundreth tymes

¶ And ouer-seye me at my sopere · and some-tyme at nones
Þat I glotoun girt it vp · er I hadde gone a myle
And yspilte þat myȝte be spared · and spended on somme hungrie

---

367 **þe**: LMR against *þat* or *þo* in other mss. (F rewrites). But **Cx** has *þat*.

367 **leuynges**: R has the sg., as does **Cx**, and may be right. See next note.

367 **it**: Supported by MHm and alpha as well as **Cx**. Presumably other beta scribes altered to plural in concord with the plural subject. See *MED hit* 4a(b) for its use as the grammatical subject relating to an abstract plural.

369 **hym** (1): Beta has *hym home*, but alpha is supported by AC.

372 A paraph would be appropriate here, but only WR have one.

374 **witte**: The reading of all **B** mss. except *wif* in CrW and revised M. **Ax** has *wife*, but **Cx** has *His wyf and his inwit*. See Schmidt (1995), 371, who suggests that **Bx** corrupted the reading represented in **Cx**.

377 **ashamed**: CrHmO and alpha have the prefix, as do the equivalent lines in AC (K.5.206, RK.6.422). There are only two other examples of either form: **Bx**.3.191 *shamedest*, and **Bx**.20.284 *ashamed*.

379 **Of**: In the absence of F which misses the line, the presumed alpha reading which is also that of **Cx**. Beta omits. The passage **Bx**.5.378–89 is not in A.

380 **and his sydes**: R is supported by the X family of C. The P family drops the pronoun as does F, while beta omits the phrase altogether.

380 **so help me god**: Alpha's word-order is also that of **Cx**. M's agreement, with *selpe me god*, is probably coincidental. Otherwise beta, having lost the second alliterating stave in the a-verse, brings the noun forward so that the line alliterates on /g/ rather than /s/.

381 **ne**: Dropped by beta2 (CrWHm), and GF. C mss. vary.

383 **it**: LR and WHmG, but omitted in MCrCO (F rewrites as *vp a-geyn*). The line is not in C.

385   Ouerdelicatly on fastyng-dayes · drunken and eten bothe
      And sat some-tyme so longe þere · þat I slepe and ete at ones
      For loue of tales in tauernes · to drynke þe more I dyned
      And hyed to þe mete er none · whan fastyng-dayes were

      ¶ This shewyng shrifte quod repentance · shal be meryte to þe

390   ¶ And þanne gan glotoun grete · and gret doel to make
      For his lither lyf · þat he lyued hadde
      And avowed fast · for hunger or for thurst
      Shal neuere fisshe on þe fryday · defien in my wombe
      Tyl abstinence myn aunte · haue ȝiue me leue
395   And ȝit haue I hated hir · al my lyf-tyme

      ¶ Þanne come sleuthe al bislabered · with two slym[ed] eiȝen   Accidia
      I most sitte seyde þe segge · or elles shulde I nappe
      I may nouȝte stonde ne stoupe · ne with-oute a stole knele
      Were I brouȝte abedde · but if my taille-ende it made
400   Sholde no ryngynge do me ryse · ar I were rype to dyne
      He bygan benedicite with a bolke · and his brest knocked
      And roxed and rored · and rutte atte laste

      [¶] What awake renke quod repentance · and rape þe to shrifte

      ¶ If I shulde deye bi þis day · me liste nouȝte to loke
405   I can nouȝte parfitly my pater noster · as þe prest it syngeth
      But I can rymes of Robyn hood · and Randolf erle of Chestre
      Ac neither of owre lorde ne of owre lady · þe leste þat euere was made

      ¶ I haue made vowes fourty · and forȝete hem on [morwe]

---

387 **to drynke þe more I dyned**: R and F are flummoxed by the sense, so R alters *drynke* to *ete*. Bennett (1972) translates the line: "I dined in taverns, where I could hear tales, in order to satisfy my thirst more easily". Lines 386–89 have no parallel in **AC**.

390 **grete**: HmR have *to grete*.

392 **fast**: The idiomatic use of infinitive without *to* is found in LRG and original M. Nevertheless, **Ax** has *to faste*. Donaldson (1955), 198, takes *faste* as adverb. There is no parallel in C. See Adams (2000), 182.

393 **þe**: Supported by LR only. AC mss. are split.

396 **slymed**: The form in alpha and many C mss., with beta adopting the commoner form *slymy*. The passage **Bx**.5.396–453 is not in **A**.

398 **a**: HmC and alpha drop the article. C mss. are split (RK.7.3).

401 Alpha has a paraph.

403 **¶**: The paraph in WHmC (with a new line-group in M) and alpha marks the speech-opening. Cf. l. 255.

404 **day**: Alpha adds *quod he*, as in the P family of C. Beta reads as the X family. Schmidt (1995), 372, argues that the phrase is required for its liaison alliteration on /d/. **Cx** has a revised b-verse.

408 **vowes**: This is the form of **Cx**, against *avowes* in WHmF.

408 **on morwe**: O, F (= alpha?) and corrected M have this form, which receives support from **Cx** *amorwe(n)*. R has uniquely *or morwe*, C has *at morwe*, LCrWHmG supply the definite article. L alone has the form *morne*.

I parfourned neure penaunce · as þe prest me hiȝte
410 Ne ryȝte sori for my synnes · ȝet was I neuere
And ȝif I bidde any bedes · but if it be in wrath
Þat I telle with my tonge · is two myle fro myne herte
I am occupied eche day · haliday and other
With ydel tales atte ale · and otherwhile in cherches
415 Goddes peyne and his passioun · ful selde þynke I þere-on

¶ I visited neuere fieble men · ne fettered folke in puttes
I ha[dd]e leuere here an harlotrie · or a somer game of souteres
Or lesynges to laughe [of] · and belye my neighbore
Þan al þat euere Marke made · Mathew Iohan & lucas
420 And vigilies and fastyng-dayes · alle þise late I passe
And ligge abedde in lenten · an my lemman in myn armes
Tyl matynes and masse be do · and þanne go to þe freres
Come I to ite missa est · I holde me yserued
I [am] nouȝte shryuen some-tyme · but if sekenesse it make
425 Nouȝt tweies in two ȝere · and þanne vp gesse I s[ch]ryue me

¶ I haue be prest and parsoun · passynge thretti wynter
Ȝete can I neither solfe ne synge · ne seyntes lyues rede
But I can fynde in a felde · or in a fourlonge an hare
Better þan in beatus vir · or in beati omnes
430 Construe [it] clause[mel] · and kenne it to my parochienes
I can holde louedayes · and here a Reues rekenynge
Ac in canoun ne in þe decretales · I can nouȝte rede a lyne

¶ Ȝif I bigge and borwe it · but ȝif it be ytailled
I forȝete it as ȝerne · and ȝif men me it axe

---

410 **ȝet**: F supplies *soþly* for the alliteration of the b-verse, which **Cx** rewrites.

414 **cherches**: Beta2, G and alpha have the sg., but the plural is supported by **Cx**.

416 **fieble**: There is no support for alpha's non-alliterating *seke*. **Cx** agrees with beta.

417 **hadde**: Alpha is supported by **Cx** against beta's present tense.

418 **of**: Alpha is supported by **Cx**, though in a revised line in which the phrase *to lauhen of* comes finally (RK.7.22). Beta has *at*.

418 **neighbore**: LM and alpha agree on the sg. (though F has *evyncristene*).

419 **Þan**: Beta's conjunction (supported by **Cx**) is necessary to the sense.

424 **am**: Alpha and **Cx** against *nam*, probably beta.

424 **if**: LR and beta2 (CrWHm) and **Cx**, but omitted by MCGOF.

430 **it clausemel**: Beta's *oon clause wel* is prompted by the unusual compound, "clause by clause". KD omit *it*, on the grounds that it lacks a referent (p. 186). Note that the L scribe left spaces for *oon* and *wel* which were later written in, suggesting that he was unable to read or make sense of his copy. **Cx** rewrites, blending **Bx**.5.430 and 432 as one line, RK.7.34.

431 **and**: Alpha reads *or*. **Cx** has *and* in a revised line.

432 **þe**: LMR and G, but omitted in others. **Cx**'s revised line offers no evidence.

433 **it** (1): Despite the *auȝt* of beta2 (CrWHm) and G, **Bx** appears to have read *it*, and shares the reading with the X family of C. The P family has the more specific *ouht*.

435　Sixe sithes or seuene · I forsake it with othes
　　　And þus tene I trewe men · ten hundreth tymes

　　　¶ And my seruauntz some-tyme · her salarye is bihynde
　　　Reuthe is to here rekenynge · whan we shal rede acomptes
　　　So with wikked wille and wraththe · my werkmen I paye

440　¶ ȝif any man doth me a benfait · or helpeth me at nede
　　　I am vnkynde aȝein his curteisye · and can nouȝte vnderstonde it
　　　For I haue and haue hadde · some-dele haukes maneres
　　　I [am] nouȝte lured with loue · but þere ligge auȝte vnder þe thombe

　　　¶ The kyndenesse þat myne euene-cristene · kidde me farnere
445　Sixty sythes I sleuthe · haue fo[r]ȝete it sith
　　　In speche and in sparynge of speche · yspilte many a tyme
　　　Bothe flesche & fissche · and many other vitailles
　　　Bothe bred and ale · butter melke and chese
　　　Forsleuthed in my seruyse · til it myȝte serue noman

450　¶ I ran aboute in ȝouthe · and ȝaf me nouȝte to lerne
　　　And euere sith be beggere · for my foule sleuthe
　　　Heu michi qu[od] sterilem vitam duxi Iuuenilem

　　　¶ Repentest þe nauȝte quod repentance · and riȝte with þat he swowned
　　　Til vigilate þe veille · fette water at his eyȝen
455　And flatte it on his face · and faste on hym criede
　　　And seide ware þe fram wanhope · wolde þe bitraye
　　　I am sori for my synnes · sey so to þi-selue
　　　And bete þi-selue on þe breste · and bidde hym of grace
　　　For is no gult here so grete · þat his goodnesse [i]s more

---

436 **tene I**: So beta; the phrase is reversed in alpha. **C** has *haue y tened* and so offers no grounds for choice.

438 **rekenynge**: So LM and alpha, supported by the X family of **C**. Other **B** mss. and the P family add the definite article.

443 **am**: The form is supported by **Cx**. LMO have *nam*. Cf. ll. 424, 459.

443 **þe**: Alpha omits, as does the P family of **C**. The X family, however, has the article.

451 **be**: So LR and original M. The M corrector inserts *haue*, in line with other mss. (*haue I* in WHmO). **Cx** includes *haue I be* in a reordered a-verse.

452 **quod**: For the same quotation see **Bx**.1.143. In both cases alpha's *quod* for beta's *quia* is also the form in **Cx**. See Alford (1992), 35–6.

453 **Repentest þe**: The reading of alpha and **Cx**. LM presumably record the form of beta, *Repentestow þe*, which the other witnesses simplify by dropping the reflexive pronoun. Cf. the variants at **Bx**.5.234, where we again follow alpha and **Cx**.

456 **fram**: CrWO read *for*, and CrW punctuate after *þe* (1), taking *for* as a conjunction. AC mss. are divided.

457 **so**: LM and alpha, thus secure for **Bx**, but AC are without it.

459 **is** (2): Supported by AC against L, corrected M, and W *nys*. See ll. 424 and 443 for LM's preference for the negative forms of the verb. In l. 474 M alone has the negative.

460 ¶ Þanne sat sleuthe vp · and seyned hym swithe
And made avowe to-fore god · for his foule sleuthe
Shal no sondaye be þis seuene зere · but sykenesse it lette
Þat I ne shal do me er day · to þe dere cherche
And heren matines and masse · as I a monke were
465 Shal none ale after mete · holde me þennes
Tyl I haue euensonge herde · I behote to þe Rode
And зete wil I зelde aзein · if I so moche haue
Al þat I wikkedly wan · sithen I wytte hadde

¶ And þough my liflode lakke · leten I nelle
470 Þat eche man shal haue his · ar I hennes wende
And with þe residue and þe remenaunt · bi þe Rode of chestre
I shal seke treuthe arst · ar I se Rome

¶ Robert þe robbere · on reddite lokede
And for þer was nouзte where-of [·] he wepe swithe sore
475 Ac зet þe synful shrewe · seyde to hym-selue
Cryst þat on caluarye · vppon þe crosse deydest
Tho dismas my brother · bisouзte зow of grace
And haddest mercy on þat man · for memento sake
So rewe on þis robbere · þat reddere ne haue
480 Ne neuere wene to wynne · with crafte þat I [kn]owe
But for þi mykel mercy · mitigacioun I biseche
Ne dampne me nouзte at domesday · for þat I did so ille

¶ What bifel of þis feloun · I can nouзte faire schewe
Wel I wote he wepte faste · water with boþe his eyen
485 And knowleched his gult · to cryst зete eftsones
Þat penitencia his pyke · he shulde polsche newe
And lepe with hym ouer londe · al his lyf-tyme
For he had leyne bi latro · luciferes aunte

---

462 **but**: MHmR have *but зif*, as in the X family of C, but not in **Ax**. F omits the line.
467 **And зete wil I**: Beta is supported by **Ax**. The a-verse is rewritten in C (RK.6.309). R's reading, *What I nam*, apparently represents alpha, revised by F.
470 **shal**: Alpha and HmGO; the presumed beta reading is *ne shal* in LMCrWC, but with little support from AC. Cf. ll. 424, 443, 459 for the preference for an extra negative.
474 All except L punctuate the line after *where-of*.
474 **wepe**: LM and alpha use the strong form of the past tense. (In M it is respelt.) Contrast l. 484, where all mss. have the weak form.
479 **þis robbere**: Certainly Bx, though F has *me Robbere*, and Hm is altered to that reading. Most mss. of **A** have *þis Robert*, though four **A** mss. and the P family of C have *me Robert*, while the X family has simply *Robert* (K.5.241, RK.6.321). See Schmidt (2008), 351.
480 **knowe**: The reading of alpha, **Ax** and **Cx** (from where Cr derives it). Beta has *owe*, glossed *debeo* in L.
485 The line is omitted by alpha, but it is in **AC**.

¶ And þanne had repentaunce reuthe · and redde hem alle to knele
490 For I shal biseche for al synful · owre saueoure of grace
To amende vs of owre mysdedes · and do mercy to vs alle

¶ Now god quod he þat of þi goodnesse · gonne þe worlde make
And of nauȝte madest auȝte · and man moste liche to þi-selue
And sithen suffredest [hym] to synne · a sikenesse to vs alle
495 And al for þe best as I bileue · what-euere þe boke telleth
O felix culpa o necessarium peccatum ade &c

[¶] For þourgh þat synne þi sone · sent was to þis erthe
And bicam man of a mayde · mankynde to saue
And madest þi-self with þi sone · and vs synful yliche
500 Faciamus hominem ad ymaginem et similitudinem nostram
Et alibi qui manet in caritate · in deo manet & deus in eo

¶ And sith with þi self sone · in owre sute deydest
On gode fryday for mannes sake · at ful tyme of þe daye
Þere þi-self ne þi sone · no sorwe in deth feledest
505 But in owre secte was þe sorwe · and þi sone it ladde
Captiuam duxit captiuitatem

¶ Þe sonne for sorwe þer-of · les syȝte for a tyme
Aboute mydday whan moste liȝte is · and mele-tyme of seintes
Feddest [þo] with þi fresche blode · owre forfadres in derknesse
510 Populus qui ambulabat in tenebris · vidit lucem magnam
And thorw þe liȝte þat lepe oute of þe · lucifer [it] blent
And blewe alle þi blissed [þennes] · in-to þe blisse of paradise

¶ Þe thrydde daye after · þow ȝedest in owre sute
A synful Marie þe seighe · ar seynte Marie þi dame
515 And al to solace synful · þow suffredest it so were
Non veni vocare iustos · set peccatores ad penitenciam

---

493 **to**: LR and WHmCO, but not in MCrGF or most C mss. (RK.7.123). **Bx**.5.489–528 are not in A.

494 **hym**: Beta reads *for*, but alpha is supported by **Cx**.

496 **peccatum ade**: The word-order *ade peccatum* in MGO is also recorded in four C mss.

497 **¶**: The paraph has support from WHmCR.

497 **þis**: Better supported for **Bx** than *þe* in MCrG. F omits, as does **Cx**.

505 **þe**: Alpha has *þat*. Without a parallel in C, we follow copy-text.

507 **syȝte**: So LHmCG and alpha, and secure for **Bx**. M (corrected) and CrWO read *light*; if this is an error picked up from the following line, as the alliterative pattern suggests, it nevertheless became **Cx**.

509 **þo**: Alpha's reading is supported both by sense ("at that time fed ...") and by **Cx**.

511 WHm and R have a paraph.

511 **it**: R's reading of the b-verse is supported by **Cx**, which revises the a-verse to avoid the syntactic difficulty (what does *it* refer to?), which is smoothed in different ways by beta and F.

512 **þennes**: Alpha's adverb is included in the revised line in C.

¶ And al þat Marke hath ymade [·] mathew Iohan and lucas
Of þyne douȝtiest dedes · were don in owre armes
Verbum caro factum est et habitauit in nobis
520 And bi so moche [it] semeth · þe sikerere we mowe
Bydde and biseche · if it be þi wille
Þat art owre fader and owre brother [·] be merciable to vs
And haue reuthe on þise Ribaudes · þat repente hem sore
Þat euere þei wratthed þe in þis worlde · in worde þouȝte or dedes

525 ¶ Þanne hent hope an horne · of deus tu conuersus viuificabis [nos]
And blew it with Beati quorum · remisse sunt iniquitates
Þat alle seyntes in heuene · songen at ones
Homines & iumenta saluabis quemadmodum multiplicasti misericordiam
        tuam deus &c ·

¶ A thousand of men þo · thrungen togyderes
530 Criede vpward to cryst · and to his clene moder
To haue grace to go with hem [·] treuthe to seke

¶ Ac þere was wyȝte non so wys · þe wey þider couthe
But blustreden forth as bestes · ouer bankes and hilles
Til late was and longe · þat þei a lede mette
535 Apparailled as a paynym · in pylgrymes wyse
He bare a burdoun ybounde · with a brode liste
In a withewyndes wise · ywounden aboute
A bolle and a bagge · he bare by his syde
An hundreth of ampulles · on his hatt seten
540 Signes of [a-sise] [·] and shelles of galice

---

518 **douȝtiest**: LM and alpha have the superlative; a good example of the superiority of LMR in representing **Bx**. All except four C mss. also have the superlative. See Adams (2000), 177.

520 WHm and R have a paraph.

520 **it**: Alpha's reading, supported by **Cx** against beta's *me*.

523 **reuthe**: Alpha's *mercy* is obviously a substitution.

523 **hem**: Most beta mss. have *hem here*, but we do not include *here* since it is not supported by **Cx**. On the other hand the adverb would easily be dropped from the phrase, and it pertinently foreshadows *in þis worlde*.

524 **in þis worlde**: The inclusion of the phrase, omitted by alpha, gives the usual alliterative pattern. It may, however, represent beta's desire to emphasise *here*, added in the previous line. It is not in the heavily revised line in C.

524 **dedes**: The plural is supported by LWR. The rest have sg., as does C in a revised line.

525 **nos**: Dropped in beta (supplied in CrG); supported by **Cx**. A prayer from the Mass; see Alford (1992), 50.

531 **To haue**: Since beta's reading is supported by **Cx**, alpha (= R?) must have offered a defective a-verse, *Grace to god*, rewritten by F.

532 **¶**: The paraph is in beta only.

538 **bolle**: Beta is supported by **AC** against alpha's *bulle* (K.6.7, RK.7.164).

540 **a-sise**: i.e. Assisi, on which see Skeat (1886), 2. 101. This is R's reading alone, but probably represents alpha. F rewrites, and beta has *synay*. Most **A** mss. have the beta reading, but a few

And many a cruche on his cloke · and keyes of Rome
And þe vernicle bifore · for men shulde knowe
And se bi his signes · whom he souȝte hadde

¶ Þis folke frayned hym firste · fro whennes he come

545   ¶ Fram synay he seyde · and fram owre lordes sepulcre
In bethleem and in babiloyne · I haue ben in bothe
In ermonye in alisaundre · in many other places
Ȝe may se bi my signes · þat sitten on myn hatte
Þat I haue walked ful wyde · in wete and in drye
550   And souȝte gode seyntes · for my soules helth

¶ Knowestow ouȝte a corseint · þat men calle treuthe
Coudestow auȝte wissen vs þe weye · where þat wy dwelleth

¶ Nay so me god helpe · seide þe gome þanne
I seygh neuere palmere · with pike ne with scrippe
555   Axen after hym er [·] til now in þis place

[¶] Peter quod a plowman · and put forth his hed
I knowe hym as kyndely · as clerke doþ his bokes
Conscience and kynde witte · kenned me to his place
And deden me suren hym sikerly · to serue hym for euere
560   Bothe to sowe and to sette [·] þe while I swynke myghte
I haue ben his folwar · al þis fourty wyntre
Bothe ysowen his sede · and sued his bestes
With-Inne and with-outen · wayted his profyt
I dyke and I delue · I do þat [he] hoteth

(including Bodley 851 (Z)) refer to Assisi instead. **Cx** has *syse*. The reference to *synay* in l. 545
may have prompted beta's reading here; alternatively alpha may record an authorial revision.
541 **keyes**: Alpha has the definite article, but it is not supported by **AC**.
550 **soules**: MHmG and alpha have the uninflected genitive, as in **Ax** and most **C** mss. For
the same expression, again with variation of the genitive form, see **Bx**.10.265, 11.239, 12.44.
551 **ouȝte**: CrF have *not* / *nawht*.
552 **auȝte**: LMWR and revised Hm, so presumably **Bx**, repeated from the line above. A few **A**
mss. include the word, but it is not in **C**. The repetition perhaps prompted the other **B** scribes,
CrCGOF, to drop it.
555 **er til**: MF drop *er* and CO drop *til*. L's mispunctuation of the line after *til* suggests why
scribes found one or other otiose. **Ax** has *er* only; **C** mss. divide between *er* and *but*.
556 **¶**: The line is at the top of the page in L, and the rubricator presumably missed the paraph
which is in WHmC and alpha, with a new line-group in M.
559 **hym**(1): Alpha's plural recognises the two characters of the previous line, but receives no
support from **AC**.
560 **þe while**: In dropping *þe*, MGF have the reading of **Ax**; the other mss. have the **Cx** version.
561 **fourty**: LM and alpha, against *fifty* in other mss. Support from **AC** again demonstrates
the superiority of this set of mss. See Adams (2000), 177.
564 **he**: Alpha has some support from the parallel b-verse of K.6.33: *& do what he hiȝte*. The
line is not in **C**. Beta's *treuthe* is likely to have been picked up from l. 567.

KD.5.522–545

565   Some-tyme I sowe · and some-tyme I thresche
      In tailoures crafte and tynkares crafte · what treuthe can deuyse
      I weue an I wynde · and do what treuthe hoteth

      ¶ For þouȝe I seye it my-self · I serue hym to paye
      Ich haue myn huire [of hym] wel · and otherwhiles more
570   He is þe prestest payer · þat pore men knoweth
      He with-halt non hewe his hyre · þat he ne hath it at euen
      He is as low as a lombe · and loueliche of speche
      And ȝif ȝe wilneth to wite · where þat he dwelleth
      I shal wisse ȝow witterly · þe weye to his place

575   ¶ Ȝe leue Pieres quod þis pilgrymes · and profered hym huire
      For to wende with hem · to treuthes dwellyng-place

      ¶ Nay bi my soules [perel] quod pieres · and gan forto swere
      I nolde fange a ferthynge · for seynt Thomas shryne
      Treuthe wolde loue me þe lasse · a longe tyme þere-after
580   Ac if ȝe wilneth to wende wel · þis is þe weye thider

      ¶ Ȝe mote go þourgh mekenesse · bothe men and wyues
      Tyl ȝe come in-to conscience [·] þat cryst wite þe sothe
      Þat ȝe louen owre lorde god · leuest of alle þinges
      And þanne ȝowre neighbores nexte · in non wise apeyre
585   Otherwyse þan þow woldest · he wrouȝte to þi-selue

      ¶ And so boweth forth bi a broke · beth buxum of speche
      Tyl ȝe fynden a forth · ȝowre fadres honoureth
      Honora patrem & matrem &c ·
      Wadeþ in þat water [·] and wascheth ȝow wel þere

---

566 **and:** In the absence of **AC** parallels, R's *in* remains a possibility as the less obvious reading.

569 **of hym:** Alpha's phrase, omitted by beta, is supported by **AC**.

571 **He:** Beta has *He ne*, but it is not supported by **Cx** or by most A mss.

571 **hewe:** Clearly beta's reading, though avoided by CrG, and revised by Hm. Alpha has *men*. See variants at **Bx.4.109** for similar avoidance. The majority **A** reading is *hyne*; **C** mss. have *hewe* and *higne*.

571 **at euen:** Presumably alpha corrupted to *a none*, understood by R as "anon" and very characteristically improved by F to *soone*. Though **Ax** has the same b-verse as beta, **Cx** drops *þat he ne hath it*.

577 **soules perel:** The reading of R (= alpha?), with support from **AC** which both read *bi þe perel of my soule*. The beta reading was probably the commonplace *soule(s) helth* (cf. **Bx.5.550** and note), with *helth* lost in CO, possibly as a result of misunderstanding an endingless genitive. On this assumption, F dropped *perel*, perhaps to accentuate alliteration on /s/.

579 **þere-after:** Supported for **Bx** by LR and WHm and Cr (*therfor after*), although other mss. omit *þere*. But either **Bx** itself or LR and beta2 may have added the word to improve an unmetrical (x / x / x) b-verse, since there is no support from **AC**.

580 CO follow this with a line that is certainly spurious.

586 **of:** Alpha's *of þi* is not supported by **Ax**. **Cx** rewrites the b-verse.

590 And ȝe shul lepe þe liȝtloker · al ȝowre lyf-tyme
 And so shaltow se swere nouȝte · but if it be for nede
 And namelich an ydel · þe name of god almyȝti

 ¶ Þanne shaltow come by a crofte · but come þow nouȝte þere-Inne
 [Þe] crofte hat coueyte nouȝte · mennes catel ne her wyues
595 Ne none of her seruauntes · þat noyen hem myȝte
 Loke ȝe breke no bowes þere · but if it be ȝowre owne

 ¶ Two stokkes þere stondeth · ac stynte ȝe nouȝte þere
 They hat stele nouȝte ne slee nouȝte [·] stryke forth by bothe
 And leue hem on þi left halfe · and loke nouȝte þere-after
600 And holde wel þyne haliday [·] heighe til euen
 Thanne shaltow blenche at a bergh · bere no false witnesse
 He / — is frithed in with floreines · and other f[e]es many
 Loke þow plukke no plante þere · for peril of þi soule

 ¶ Þanne shal ȝe se sey soth · so it be to done
605 In no manere ellis nauȝte · for no mannes biddyng

 ¶ Þanne shaltow come to a courte · as clere as þe sonne
 Þe mote is of mercy · þe manere aboute
 And alle þe wallis ben of witte · to holden wille oute
 And kerneled with crystendome · [þat] kynde to saue
610 Boterased with bileue so · or þow beest nouȝte ysaued

 ¶ And alle þe houses ben hiled · halles and chambres

---

594 **Þe**: Alpha's reading is supported by Cx, although A mss. split between this and beta's reading *That*. We take into account the scribal tendency to emphasise.

594 **mennes catel**: Another very characteristic example of the practices of the two alpha scribes. It appears that R represents alpha in reading *men*, and F rewrote inventively (*neyþir maydins*), no doubt puzzled by the non-scriptural imputation of homosexuality.

596 **ȝe**: R alone (= alpha?) has *þow* (F rewrites), but it is supported by AC. However *ȝowre* in the b-verse in all B witnesses suggests that a-verse *ȝe* is also Bx. The odd, apparently random, switching to the sg. in Piers' speech, when he is speaking to the group, is a feature of all three versions. Ax matches Cx except at K.6.52 (sg.) = RK.7.212 (pl.) = **Bx**.5.585 (sg.). But **Bx** differs from the other two versions with pl. in **Bx**.5.596–7 and 604 (despite the surrounding sg.).

600 L misplaces the punctus after *heighe*.

601 Following this line F alone has a rather competent line.

602 **He / —**: Beta and Ax have the pronoun, but R and Cx are without. F smooths to *It*.

602 **fees**: So WHmCG and alpha supported by Cx as well as most A mss. LMCrO have *foes*, which may be a beta error.

603 **þow**: Alpha has *ȝe*, and R has *ȝoure soules* in the b-verse (F rewrites). Beta is supported by AC. See the note to l. 596, and note the plural in the next line.

609 **þat kynde**: "that essential substance, distinctive feature" (of the *courte*). All B mss. apart from R have *man kynde*, but R has the reading of AC. Both beta and F made the easy error.

610 **ysaued**: Though the prefix creates two long dips in the b-verse (x x / x x / x), it is supported by LMR (and Hm has *be-*). Some C mss. have it also.

Wit[h] no lede but with loue · and lowe speche as bretheren
Þe brugge is of bidde wel · þe bette may þow spede
Eche piler is of penaunce · of preyeres to seyntes
615 Of almes-dedes ar þe hokes · þat þe gates hangen on

¶ Grace hatte þe gateward · a gode man for-sothe
Hys man hatte amende ȝow · *for /* — many man him knoweth
Telleth hym þis tokene · þat treuthe wite þe sothe
I parfourned þe penaunce · þe preest me enioyned
620 And am ful sori for my synnes · and so I shal euere
Whan I þinke þere-on · þeighe I were a pope

¶ Biddeth amende ȝow meke him · t[o] his maistre ones
To wayue vp þe wiket · þat þe womman shette
Tho Adam and Eue · eten apples vnrosted
625 Per euam cuntis clausa est · & per mariam virginem [iterum] patefacta est

¶ For he hath þe keye and þe clikat · þouȝ þe kynge slepe
And if grace graunte þe · to go in in þis wise
Þow shalt see in þi-selue · treuthe sitte in þine herte
In a cheyne of charyte · as þow a c[h]ilde were
630 To suffre hym and segge nouȝte · aȝein þi sires wille

¶ Ac bewar þanne of wrath þe · þat is a wikked shrewe
He hath enuye to hym · þat in þine herte sitteth
And pukketh forþ pruyde [·] to prayse þi-seluen
Þe boldnesse of þi bienfetes · maketh þe blynde þanne
635 And þanne worstow dryuen oute as dew · and þe dore closed
Kayed and clikated · to kepe þe with-outen

---

612 **With**: L has *Wit*, with the line marked for correction. It is the same at **Bx**.20.119.

617 **for /** —: Beta and **Ax** have the conjunction, but alpha and **Cx** are without it.

617 **man** (2): LM and alpha, supported by **AC**. The other mss. have the plural.

618 Alpha has a paraph.

620 **for**: So beta and **Ax**, but alpha and some **C** mss. have, less expectedly, *of*. Cf. **Bx**.5.410, 457.

622 **to**: MGO and alpha, against *til* in LCrWHmC. Although there is total support in favour of *to* from **AC**, that cannot in this case determine the reading of **Bx**. Some mss., notably HmCrGF, commonly have *to* when others have *til* in the sense "to", but R is not generally among them. See **Bx**.9.88, 10.390, 11.390, 17.149, 18.69, 18.417 (where alpha has *to*), and 19.429. In **Bx**.5.144 R has *til* (2x) against *to* in others; in 5.632 CO have *til* against *to* in others.

625 **iterum patefacta est**: Alpha has *iterum*, beta has *patefacta est*, and **Cx** has both. The line is not in **A**. See Alford (1992), 51.

627 **in in**: So the best beta mss., LM, but the second *in* is almost inevitably lost in all others including R (F omits the line). Half the **A** mss. and the majority of **C** mss. are also without it.

631 **þe**: So LWHmGR, but not supported by **AC**, and presumably a result of false division in **Bx** (*wrappe* as in O > *wrap þe*). Note, however, that *wrath* can be reflexive, and that Schmidt (2008), 360–1, adopts the reading.

633 **forþ**: Omitted by alpha (and part of a correction in L), but supported by most **A** mss. and by **Cx**, as well as by sense.

KD.5.591–614

Happily an hundreth wyntre · ar þow eft entre
Þus myght þow lesen his loue · to late wel by þi-selue
And neuere happil[i]che efte entre · but grace þow haue

640   ¶ Ac þere ar seuene sustren · þat seruen treuthe euere
And aren porteres *of / ouer* þe posternes · that to þe place longeth
Þat one hat abstenence · and humilite an-other
Charite and chastite · ben his chief maydenes
Pacience and pees · moche poeple þei helpeth
645   Largenesse þe lady · heo let in ful manye
Heo hath hulpe a þousande oute · of þe deueles ponfolde

¶ And who is sibbe to þis seuene · so me god helpe
He is wonderliche welcome · and faire vnderfongen
And but if 3e be syb · to summe of þise seuene
650   It is ful harde bi myne heued quod Peres · for any of 3ow alle
To geten ingonge at any gate þere · but grace be þe more

¶ Now bi cryst quod a cutpurs · I haue no kynne þere
Ne I quod an apewarde · bi au3te þat I knowe

¶ Wite god quod a wafrestre · wist I þis for sothe
655   Shulde I neuere ferthere a fote · for no freres prechyng

¶ 3us quod Pieres þe plowman · and pukked hem alle to gode
Mercy is a maydene þere · hath my3te ouer hem alle
And she is syb to alle synful · and her sone also
And þoru3e þe helpe of hem two · hope þow none other
660   Þow my3te gete grace þere · bi so þow go bityme

---

640 **sustren**: Beta is supported by AC. R's *3iftes* probably represents an alpha error, smoothed by F to *seruauntys*.

641 **of / ouer**: Beta and Ax have *of*, but R and Cx have *ouer*. F reads *at*.

645 **heo**: Probably the *h*- form is **Bx**, here and in the next line. In both cases R has *he(o)* and M is altered to *she*, the form in other mss. (**AC** omit the pronoun). See Introduction, pp. 17–18.

646 OF punctuate this line of uncertain structure before *oute*. It has no parallel in **AC**.

648 **He**: R has *Heo* and F rewrites with *she*. **Ax** has *He* and **Cx** omits the pronoun.

649 **if**: Omitted by MCrF, and by nine A mss. (the line is not in C).

650 **quod Peres**: Not in **AC**, dropped in G by contamination, and anticipated in the previous line by F.

653 **Ne**: The form is supported by LM and alpha and **AC** against *Nor* in others.

654 **wafrestre**: Ax has *waferer*, as do MGO, but Cx has the female.

654 **for**: R omits, and F is essentially the same. Some mss. of the other versions agree with alpha, but **Ax** and the X family of C have the beta reading.

657 **hem**: Omitted by WHmCGO, but supported by **AC**.

660 **bi**: Omitted by MWG, and treated as the second element of *therby* in CrC. The word is not in **AC**. The phrase *bi so* means "provided that", as at **Bx**.11.76, 12.183.

¶ By seynt Poule quod a pardonere · parauenture I be nouȝte knowe þere
I wil go fecche my box with my breuettes · and a bulle with bisshopes lettres

[¶] By cryst quod a comune womman · þi companye wil I folwe
Þow shalt sey I am þi sustre · I ne wot where þei bicome

---

661 **knowe þere**: Alpha instead reads *welcome*. Neither reading is compelling: beta's is prosaic,
but on the other hand *welcome* is not elsewhere used to end a line. The line is not in **AC**.
663 **¶**: The usual paraph at the start of a speech is supported by WHmC and alpha.

Passus 6

Passus Sextus de visione vt supra

This were a wikked way · but who-so hadde a gyde
That wolde folwen vs eche a fote · þus þis folke hem mened
Quaþ Perkyn þe plouman · bi seynt Peter of Rome
I haue an half acre to erye · bi þe heigh way
5   Hadde I eried þis half acre · and sowen it after
I wil wende with ȝow · and þe way teche

¶ Þis were a longe lettynge · quod a lady in a sklayre
What sholde we wommen · worche þere-whiles

¶ Somme shal sowe [þe] sakke quod Piers · for shedyng of þe whete
10 And ȝe louely ladyes · with ȝoure longe fyngres
Þat ȝe han silke and sendal · to sowe whan tyme is
Chesibles for chapelleynes · cherches to honoure

¶ Wyues and wydwes · wolle & flex spynneth
Maketh cloth I conseille ȝow · and kenneth so ȝowre douȝtres
15 Þe nedy and þe naked · nymmeth hede how hij liggeth
And casteth hem clothes · for so comaundeth treuthe
For I shal lene hem lyflode · but ȝif þe londe faille
Flesshe and bred bothe · to riche and to pore
As longe as I lyue · for þe lordes loue of heuene

---

3 WF have a paraph and R starts a new line group.
6 **wil**: The reading of LR and C. The past tense is to be expected after *Hadde*, and so *wolde* is more likely to be scribal. **Ax** probably has the latter, as do most C mss., but XYJ have *wol*.
8 **þere-whiles:** So LM and alpha; see *MED ther-whiles*. Other mss. have *þe while(s)*, the AC reading. Adams (2000), 177.
9 **þe** (1): Dropped in L, but supported by all **B** mss. except M, which has the plural noun.
15 **hij**: LM. R records the reduced form *a* (its reading *hym* in the next line suggests the scribe took it as a sg.). Other mss. have *þei*.

20   ¶ And alle manere of men · þat þorw mete and drynke lybbeth
      Helpith hym to worche wiȝtliche · þat wynneth ȝowre fode

      ¶ Bi crist quod a knyȝte þo · he kenneth vs þe best
      Ac on þe teme trewly · tauȝte was I neuere
      Ac kenne me quod þe knyȝte · and bi cryst I wil assaye

25   ¶ Bi seynt Poule quod Perkyn · ȝe profre ȝow so faire
      Þat I shal swynke and swete · and sowe for vs bothe
      And oþer labour[er]es do for þi loue · al my lyf-tyme
      In couenaunt þat þow kepe · holikirke and my-selue
      Fro wastoures and fro wykked men · þat þis worlde struyeth

30   ¶ And go hunte hardiliche [·] to hares and to foxes
      To bores and to [b]ockes · þat breketh adown myne hegges
      And go affaite þ[i] faucones · wilde foules to kille
      For suche cometh to my croft · and croppeth my whete

      ¶ Curteislich þe knyȝte þanne · comsed þise wordes
35   By my power Pieres quod he · I pliȝte þe my treuthe
      To fulfille þis forward · þowȝ I fiȝte sholde
      Als longe as I lyue · I shal þe mayntene

      ¶ Ȝe and ȝit a poynt quod Pieres · I preye ȝow of more
      Loke ȝe tene no tenaunt · but treuthe wil assent
40   And þowgh ȝe mowe amercy hem · late mercy be taxoure
      And mekenesse þi mayster · maugre medes chekes
      And þowgh pore men profre ȝow · presentis and ȝiftis
      Nym it nauȝte an auenture · [þow] mowe it nauȝte deserue
      For þow shalt ȝelde it aȝein · at one ȝeres ende
45   In a ful perillous place · purgatorie it hatte

      ¶ And mysbede nouȝte þi bonde-*men / man* · þe better may þow spede
      Þowgh he be þyn vnderlynge here · wel may happe in heuene

---

27 **laboureres**: The misspelling (presumably an otiose abbreviation) is corrected by most beta mss. (visibly in G) to *laboures*. The Hm corrector alters the line to make sense, and F revises similarly. R copies faithfully, as usual.

28 **kirke**: On alpha's non-alliterating *cherche* see Introduction, pp. 18–19.

29 **and fro**: Support from LR and beta2 (CrWHm) + G against *and*. AC mss. vary similarly.

31 **bockes**: "bucks". Beta has the easy error *brockes*, "badgers", perhaps anticipating *br-* in the b-verse. R (= alpha?) is supported by **AC**; F rewrites.

32 **þi**: So also **Cx**. Only LCrG have the definite article.

40 **hem**: Beta's reading is more satisfactory in sense and metre, yet alpha's *men* receives some support from C's a-verse *And when ȝe mersyen eny man* (RK.8.37), where it is needed for the alliteration.

43 **þow**: Alpha is here supported by AC. The pl. forms in ll. 38, 39, 40 and 42 are also in **Cx** (but **Ax** has sg.); F alters to sg. throughout, and R alters to pl. in 41.

46 **-men / -man**: Beta has the **Ax** pl. while alpha has the sg. as **Cx**.

Þat he worth worthier sette · and with more blisse
Amice ascende superius
50 For in charnel a[t] chirche · cherles ben yuel to knowe
Or a kniȝte fram a knaue þere · knowe þis in þin herte
And þat þow be trewe of þi tonge · and tales þat þow hatie
But if þei ben of wisdome or of witt · þi werkmen to chaste
Holde / Holde nauȝt with none harlotes · ne here nouȝte her tales
55 And nameliche atte mete · suche men eschue
For it ben þe deueles disoures · I do þe to vnderstande

¶ I assente bi seynt Iame · seyde þe kniȝte þanne
Forto worche bi þi wordes · þe while my lyf dureth

¶ And I shal apparaille me quod Perkyn · in pilgrimes wise
60 And wende with ȝow I wil · til we fynde treuthe

¶ And cast on me my clothes · yclouted and hole
My cokeres and my coffes · for colde of my nailles
And hange myn hoper at myn hals · in stede of a scrippe
A busshel of bredcorne · brynge me þerinne
65 For I wil sowe it my-self · and sitthenes wil I wende
To pylgrymage as palmers don · pardoun forto haue

¶ Ac who-so helpeth me to erie · or sowen here ar I wende
Shal haue leue bi owre lorde · to lese here in heruest
And make h[y]m mery þere-mydde · maugre who-so bigruccheth it

70 ¶ And alkyn crafty men · þat konne lyuen in treuthe
I shal fynden hem fode · þat feithfulliche libbeth

¶ Saue Iakke þe iogeloure · and Ionet of þe stues

---

50 **in charnel**: R probably represents alpha with the amusing error *in a chanel*, "gutter", sensibly revised to *in a chapel* by F.

50 **at**: LMHm have *atte*, which represents "at the" in L (see **Bx**.P.107, 3.31, 6.55, etc.). CrWGR have *at*, which has some support from C's *At churche in the Charnel*.

50 **cherles**: Supported by C and by alliteration against alpha's *clerkes*.

52 **þi**: Beta is supported by **Ax** and the X family of C against alpha's omission. The P family reads *hys*.

54 **Holde / Holde nauȝt**: Beta agrees with **Ax**, against *Holde nauȝt* in alpha and Cx.

61 **me**: Although attested only by LR, it is more likely to have been lost than added, and has support from the Cx third-person version, *caste on hym his clothes* (RK.8.58). However, Adams (2000), 183, sees *me* as "random convergence".

67 **here**: Good support from LMR and WHm, strengthening the alliteration of the b-verse, though dropped in CrGOCF. A and C have different b-verses.

69 **hym**: Alpha's sg. is supported by AC over beta's plural.

69 **bigruccheth it**: So LMCrW, and so probably beta. The X family of C has *bigruchen hit*, but the P family is without *hit*, as are beta4 and F (in Hm it appears to have been erased). Scribes may have been uncomfortable with two unstressed syllables at line-end. In R and **Ax** the pronoun precedes the verb. We follow copy-text.

And danyel þe dys playere · and denote þe baude
And frere þe faytoure [·] and folke of his ordre
75   And Robyn þe Rybaudoure · for his rusty wordes
Treuthe tolde me ones · and bad me tellen it after
Deleantur de libro viuencium [·] I shulde nouȝte dele with hem
For holicherche is hote [·] of hem no tythe to [aske]
Quia cum iustis non scribantur
80   They ben ascaped good auenture · now god hem amende

¶ Dame worche whan tyme is · Pieres wyf hiȝte
His douȝter hiȝte do riȝte so · or þi dame shal þe bete
His sone hiȝte suffre þi souereynes · to hauen / hauen her wille
Deme hem nouȝte for if þow doste · þow shalt it dere abugge
85   Late god yworth with al · for so his worde techeth

¶ For now I am olde and hore · and haue of myn owen
To penaunce and to pilgrimage · I wil passe with þise other
For-þi I wil or I wende · do wryte my biqueste
In dei nomine amen · I make it my-seluen
90   He shal haue my soule · þat best hath yserued it
And fro þe fende it defende · for so I bileue
Til I come to his acountes · as my cred[e] me telleth / telleth
To haue a relees and a remissioun · on þat rental I leue

¶ Þe kirke shal haue my caroigne · and kepe my bones
95   For of my corne and catel · he craued þe tythe
I payed it hym prestly · for peril of my soule

---

78 The line is punctuated after *hote* in MCrC and alpha, after *hem* in LWO. The former is
supported by the alliterative pattern.

78 **aske**: The reading of R is supported by **AC**. That F agrees with beta *take* makes the **Bx**
reading uncertain, but it is an easy error, typical of F in increasing the alliteration, especially
in a line where the pattern puzzles some scribes, and indeed it is found as a minor variant in
both **A** and **C** mss.

80 **now**: So LM and alpha, supported by **AC**. Others omit it.

83 The line alliterates aaa/xx, which prompts OR to punctuate the line after *suffre* (which F
drops), disregarding the syntactic break after *souereynes*.

83 **to hauen / hauen**: Beta includes *to* as **Ax**, which alpha and **Cx** omit.

87 **þise**: The demonstrative, which seems preferable in terms of sense, is supported by L (but
not M), by CrW (but not Hm), by R (but not F). **AC** mss. vary in the same way.

89–91 These three lines in beta are set out as two in alpha, divided after *soule* and dropping
for so I bileue. **AC** set the lines as beta.

90 **yserued**: LCGOR, and so **Bx**. But M and beta2 have *deserued*, as does **A**. C rewrites the
b-verse.

91 The order of beta's a-verse is reversed in **AC**. RF are both corrupt.

92 **crede**: Alpha's form is supported by **AC**. Beta has *Credo*.

92 **me telleth / telleth**: Beta reads as **Ax**, while alpha and **Cx** omit *me*.

95 **he**: In a clear example of sophistication, CrW alter to *she*, but the following lines confirm
the masculine.

For-thy is he holden I hope · to haue me in his masse
And mengen in his memorye · amonge alle crystene

¶ My wyf shal haue of þat I wan · with treuthe and nomore
100 And dele amonge my douȝtres · and my dere children
For þowgh I deye to-daye · my dettes ar quitte
I bare home þat I borwed · ar I to bedde ȝede

¶ And with þe residue and þe remenaunte · bi þe Rode of Lukes
I wil worschip þer-with · treuthe bi my lyue
105 And ben his pilgryme atte plow · for pore mennes sake
My plow-[p]ote shal be my pyk-staf · and picche atwo þe rotes
And helpe my culter to kerue · and clense þe forwes

¶ Now is perkyn and [þ]is pilgrymes · to þe plowe faren
To erie þis halue acre · holpyn hym manye
110 Dikeres & delueres · digged vp þe balkes
Þere-with was perkyn apayed · and preysed hem faste
Other werkemen þere were · þat wrouȝten ful ȝerne
Eche man in his manere · made hym-self to done
And some to plese perkyn · piked vp þe wedes

115 ¶ At heighe pryme peres · lete þe plowe stonde
To ouersen hem hym-self · and who-so best wrouȝte
He shulde be huyred þer-after · whan heruest tyme come

¶ And þanne seten somme · and songen atte nale
And hulpen erie his half acre · with how trolli lolli

120 ¶ Now bi þe peril of my soule quod Pieres · al in pure tene
But ȝe arise þe rather · and rape ȝow to worche
Shal no greyne þat groweth · glade ȝow at nede

---

98 **mengen:** F adds *me* by contamination from AC.

101 **deye:** Beta's present is supported by AC, though a few mss. in all versions have the past. Cf. l. 123.

101 **dettes ar:** R's sg. is also the reading of the X family of C.

106 **-pote:** Alpha has support from AC (K.7.95, RK.8.64), though in all three versions the second element of the compound is also recorded as *fote*, *bat*, and *staf*. *MED*, recording no other instance, supposes the implement is probably "to remove earth adhering to a plow, or to chop roots" (*plough*, 1c (e)). Kane (2005) glosses as "ploughman's staff used to give added thrust to the coulter".

106 **atwo:** Beta's reading is also that of **Cx**, though two mss. have *at* (as R) and two *away* (as F). Though Kane's A text has *putte at*, both verb and preposition vary widely, though no ms. has *atwo*.

108 **þis:** The X family of C agrees with R. Most A mss. and the P family of C share F's reading *þe*. We suppose that **Bx** *þis* is a slightly more likely source than *þe* of beta's *his*.

116 **To:** R's *And ȝeed to* must represent alpha (cf. F), but it has no support from AC.

119 **hulpen:** There is no support for R's *ho helpen to*.

119 F's additional line is unusually amusing as well as metrical, but it has no parallel in any version of the poem.

And þough ȝe deye for dole · þe deuel haue þat recch[e]

¶ Tho were faitoures aferde · and feyned hem blynde
125　Somme leyde here legges aliri [·] as suche loseles conneth
And made her mone to pieres · and preyde hym of grace
For we haue no lymes to laboure with · lorde ygraced be ȝe

¶ Ac we preye for ȝow pieres · and for ȝowre plow bothe
Þat god of his grace · ȝowre grayne multiplye
130　And ȝelde ȝow of ȝowre almesse · þat ȝe ȝiue vs here
For we may nouȝte swynke ne swete · suche sikenesse vs eyleth

¶ If it be soth quod pieres þat ȝe seyne · I shal it sone asspye
Ȝe ben wastoures I wote wel · and treuthe wote þe sothe
And I am his olde hyne · and hiȝte hym to warne
135　Which þei were in þis worlde · his werkemen appeyred

¶ Ȝe wasten þat men wynnen · with trauaille and with tene
Ac treuthe shal teche ȝow · his teme to dryue
Or ȝe shal ete barly bred · and of þe broke drynke
But if he be blynde [or] broke-legged · or bolted with yrnes
140　He shal ete whete bred · and drynke with my-selue
Tyl god of his goodnesse · amendement hym sende
Ac ȝe myȝte trauaille as treuthe wolde · and take mete & huyre
To kepe kyne in þe felde · þe corne fro þe bestes
Diken or deluen [·] or dyngen vppon sheues
145　Or helpe make morter · or bere mukke afelde

¶ In lecherye and in losengerye · ȝe lyuen and in sleuthe
And al is þorw suffrance · þat venjaunce ȝow ne taketh

¶ Ac ancres and heremytes · þat eten but at nones
And namore er morwe · myne almesse shul þei haue
150　And of my catel to cope hem with · þat han cloistres and cherches

---

123 **deye**: As in the parallel l. 101, R has the past tense, but it is not supported by **AC**.
123 **recche**: Alpha's subjunctive is supported by **AC**.
128 **¶**: The paraph is recorded in LR and marked by a space in M.
130 **of**: Beta2 (CrWHm) and G have *for*, as do a few AC mss.
133 **and**: R's omission is not supported by **Ax**. R has three unique readings in this line.
135 **appeyred**: GR have the present (F has *wolde a-peyre*). The parallel line in A, *Suche wastours in þis world his werkmen distroyeþ* (K.7.124), is too different to offer support.
139 **or** (1): There is no support for L's *and* in any version, though note that *and* probably underlies the correction *or* in M.
142 Hm and alpha have a paraph.
150 **of my**: LM and alpha. Beta2 (CrWHm) and G drop *my*; CO drop both words. This passage is not in **AC**.
150 **cope**: LMR and CO, with F revising to *kouere*. Beta2 (CrWHm) and G read *kepe*. For the collocation with *catel*, "provide resources for clothing", see **Bx.5.271**.

Ac robert renneaboute · shal nou3te haue of myne
Ne posteles but þey preche conne · and haue powere of þe bisschop
They shal haue payne and potage · and make hem-self at ese
For it is an vnresonable Religioun · þat hath ri3te nou3te of certeyne

155 ¶ And þanne gan a wastoure to wrath hym · and wolde haue yfou3te
And to Pieres þe plowman · he profered his gloue
A Brytonere a braggere · a bosted pieres als
And bad hym go pissen with his plow · for-pyned schrewe
Wiltow or neltow · we wil haue owre wille
160 Of þi flowre and of þi flessche · fecche whan vs liketh
And make vs myrie þer-myde · maugre þi chekes

¶ Thanne Pieres þe plowman · pleyned hym to þe kny3te
To kepe hym as couenaunte was · fram cursed shrewes
And fro þis wastoures wolueskynnes · þat maketh þ[is] worlde dere
165 For þo waste and wynnen nou3te · and þat ilke while
Worth neuere plente amonge þe poeple · þer-while my plow liggeth

¶ Curteisly þe kny3te þanne · as his kynde wolde
Warned wastoure · and wissed hym bettere
Or þow shalt abugge by þe lawe · by þe ordre þat I bere

170 ¶ I was nou3t wont to worche quod wastour · and now wil I nou3t bigynne
And lete li3te of þe lawe [·] and lasse of þe kny3te
And sette Pieres at a pees · and his plow bothe
And manaced pieres and his men · 3if þei mette eft-sone

¶ Now by þe peril of my soule quod Pieres · I shal apeyre 3ow alle
175 And houped after hunger · þat herd hym atte firste
Awreke me of þise wastoures quod he · þat þis worlde schendeth

---

151 WHmCF have a paraph.

157 **a bosted**: As one word in all except CrCGOF. Presumably not all scribes recognised this
as "he threatened" but took it as an unparalleled compound verb. **Ax** has *he bostide*. RK.8.152
records *abostede*, but it is questioned by Kane (2005) s.v.

158 **with**: Beta supported by AC. Alpha's *on* tones down the vulgarism.

160 **Of**: Alpha probably read *And of*. Beta is supported by **Ax**, but alpha by the X family of
C; the P family has *Boþe*.

161 **þer-myde**: M is joined by HmCG with *þere-with*. The half-line is repeated from l. 69
where HmC have the variation. **Ax** has *-wiþ*, but the best C mss. read *-myde*. See note to
Bx.7.26, and cf. 15.144.

164 **þis** (2): R represents alpha since F drops the line, and is supported by **Cx** (RK.8.158)
against beta's *þe*. G also has *þis*.

166 **þer-while**: So LMC, and probably beta. R, which may be right, has *þe while* in line with
other mss.; F reads *while*. **Cx** has *and*. Cf. 6.8n.

171 **li3te**: Alpha with Hm have the adverbial form *li3tly*, but beta has the form recorded in **AC**
and elsewhere in the poem.

174 **Now**: Supported by AC, despite alpha's omission.

176 **schendeth**: Plural, as *schende(n)* in alpha.

¶ Hunger in haste þo · hent wastour bi þe mawe
And wronge hym so bi þe wombe · þat [al wattered] his eyen
He buffeted þe Britoner [·] aboute þe chekes
180   Þat he loked like a lanterne · al his lyf after
He bette hem so bothe · he barste nere here guttes
Ne hadde Pieres with a pese lof · preyed hunger cesse
They hadde ben doluen bothe · ne deme þow non other
Suffre hem lyue he seyde · and lete hem ete with hogges
185   Or elles benes and bren · ybaken togideres
Or elles melke and mene ale · þus preyed pieres for hem

¶ Faitoures for fere her-of · flowen in-to bernes
And flapten on with flayles · fram morwe til euen
That hunger was nou3t hardy · on hem forto loke
190   For a potful of peses · þat peres hadde ymaked

[¶] An heep of heremites · henten hem spades
And ketten here copes · and courtpies hem made
And wenten as werkemen · with spades and with schoueles
And doluen and dykeden · to dryue aweye hunger

195   ¶ Blynde and bedreden · were botened a þousande
Þat seten to begge syluer · sone were þei heled
For þat was bake for bayarde · was bote for many hungry
And many a beggere for benes · buxome was to swynke
And eche a pore man wel apayed · to haue pesen for his huyre
200   And what pieres preyed hem to do · as prest as a sperhauke
And þere-of was peres proude · and put hem to werke

---

178 We adopt R's b-verse, which is that of **AC**, and conforms to the standard alliterative pattern, though it is unmetrical (x x / x x / x). If R reproduces alpha, this leaves the question of how F shares the beta reading. In fact four A mss. have the same reading as beta, and five more have the same noun-verb word-order omitting *bothe*. Either F is contaminated, or else the scribe independently corrupted to the easier reading ("prose order", KD, p. 168 n. 89) just as some **A** scribes did.

182 **cesse**: Beta has *to cesse*, and it may be right, but *to* is perhaps supplied to fill a short b-verse. Cf. 3.334, but for a counter-example cf. 1.82. AC have *preyed hym beleue*.

186 **mene**: "inferior" (*MED mene* adj.(1), 3(a)). But CO and alpha have *meyne* which, in R at least, is used only as a spelling of *MED meine* n., "household"; cf. *meine* 1(b) - *bord*, referring to a more humble table. *MED* does not record the compound *meine-ale*. The line is not in AC and is rejected by KD.

189 **hardy**: Beta has *so hardy*, but alpha is supported by **Cx**. A mss. are split.

191 **¶**: The paraph is in WHmC and alpha. In LM the paraph was easily missed since the line is at the top of the page in both. Though evidently **Bx**, it is inappropriate in splitting 190 from 191.

197 **bote for**: So beta and **Cx** (line not in A). R has *bote to*.

199 **eche a**: Supported by LR and WCO, against *eche* in others. A standard variant; cf. **Bx**.3.318n, 5.89, etc. The line is not in AC.

199 **apayed**: Supported by LR and CrWHm, against *paied* in others.

And ȝaf hem mete as he myȝte aforth · and mesurable huyre

¶ Þanne hadde peres pite · and preyed hunger to wende
Home in-to his owne erd · and holden hym þere
For I am wel awroke now · of wastoures þorw þi myȝte
Ac I preye þe ar þow passe · quod Pieres to hunger
Of beggeres and of bidderes · what best be [to] done
For I wote wel be þow went · þei wil worche ful ille
For myschief it maketh · þei beth so meke nouthe
And for defaute of her fode · þis folke is at my wille
[It] are my blody bretheren quod pieres · for god bouȝte vs alle
Treuthe tauȝte me ones · to louye hem vchone
And to helpen hem of alle þinge · ay as hem nedeth
And now wolde I witen of þe · what were þe best
An how I myȝte amaistrien hem · and make hem to worche

¶ Here now quod hunger · and holde it for a wisdome
Bolde beggeres and bigge · þat mowe her bred biswynke
With houndes bred and hors-bred · holde vp her hertis
Abate hem with benes · for bollyng of her wombe
And ȝif þe gomes grucche · bidde hem go swynke
And he shal soupe swettere · whan he it hath deseruid

¶ And if þow fynde any freke · þat *fortune / falshed* hath appeyred
Or any maner fals men · fonde þow suche to cnowe
Conforte h[e]m with þi catel · for crystes loue of heuene
Loue hem and lene hem · so lawe of god techeth
Alter alterius onera portate

---

204 **erd:** The form in LR and original M, from OE *eard*. Beta2 (CrWHm) and revised M have *yerd*, from OE *geard*.

205 **now:** Supported by LMOC and alpha, but omitted by beta2 (CrWHm) and G, as also (coincidentally?) by **Cx**. The line is not in **A**.

206 **to:** Alpha may be right with *þo to*, creating a long dip, as G does independently with *vn-to*. **A** and **C** have two different versions of the b-verse.

207 **be to:** L alone drops *to*. Most C mss. have the subjunctive as in beta; most **A** mss. have the phrase as in F, *what is best to doone*, though five have R's order.

211 **It:** All other mss. have *Þey*, but R is supported by **AC**. For the formal *it* as equivalent to "they", see Mustanoja (1960), 132–3; and cf. **Bx**.6.56, where GF again read *þei* for *it*.

215 **An:** "and".

220 **go swynke:** For the idiom, cf. 5.24 *go worche*, 7.104 *gon faiten*, 9.143 *go shape*. Alpha has *go and swynke*; the same variation is found in **AC**.

221 The line is dropped by alpha. It is attested by **AC**.

222 **And:** R has *Ac*, which may be right. There is the same variation in **AC**.

222 **fortune / falshed:** An interesting case. Alpha's *false* or *falshed* is clearly an error in view of *fals men* in the next line. And yet it was presumably the basis for **Cx**, which reads *þat fals men han apayred* and drops the next line. Beta shares *fortune* with **Ax**.

224 **hem:** Beta probably had *hym*, as in LCrWHm, with MGO correcting. (Note HmO *man* in the line above.) **AC** have the plural, as in alpha.

And alle maner of men · þat þow myȝte asspye
That nedy ben and nauȝty · helpe hem with þi godis
Loue hem and lakke hem nouȝte · late god take þe venjaunce
230   Theigh þei done yuel · late þow god aworthe
Michi vindictam & ego retribuam ·
And if þow wil be graciouse to god · do as þe gospel techeth
And bilow þe amonges low men · so shaltow lacche grace
Facite vobis amicos de mamona iniquitatis

235   ¶ I wolde nouȝt greue god quod piers · for al þe good on grounde
Miȝte I synnelees do as þow seist · seyde pieres þanne

¶ Ȝe I bihote þe quod hunger · or ellis þe bible lieth
Go to Genesis þe gyaunt · þe engendroure of vs alle
In sudore and swynke · þow shalt þi mete tilye
240   And laboure for þi lyflode · and so owre lorde hyȝte
And sapience seyth þe same · I seigh it in þe bible
Piger pro frigore · no felde nolde tilye
And þerfore he shal begge and bidde · and no man bete his hunger

¶ Mathew with mannes face · mouthe[th] þise wordis
245   Þat seruus nequam had a nam · and for he wolde nouȝte chaffare   a besaunt
He had maugre of his maistre · for euermore after
And binam [hym] his Mnam · for he ne wolde worche

---

227 **maner of**: R omits *of*. AC scribes vary, though the most authoritative of C also omit.

230 **þow**: Only in LR; dropped by other scribes perhaps on the basis of l. 85. Presumably it carries the alliteration of the b-verse. The line is not in AC. Adams (2000), 183.

230 **aworthe**: The rare form is supported by LMR.

233 **bilow**: As at **Bx**.2.22, LMR presumably reproduce the spelling of **Bx**. F wrongly takes the verb to be formed on *lowen*, "be humble". The Latin of the next line makes it clear that it means "make (yourself) loved" (*MED biloven*), and beta1 reads *biloue*. The line replaces K.7.212 *Make þe Frendis þermid*. Adams (2000), 178.

237 **þe** (1): Alpha's *god* is not supported by AC, but cf. l. 285.

239 **and swynke**: Alpha has *and in swynke* and beta's reading is uncertain. **Ax** has the reading adopted here, and **Cx** has a Latin line (altered from Genesis) in the form *In sudore & labore* (or vice versa).

241 **it**: Omitted in R (= alpha?) but supported by **Ax**.

242 **nolde**: This seems to be the beta reading (M is corrected), with alpha reading *wolde*, probably the reading of **Ax**. Either could be **Bx**.

244 **moutheth**: Alpha's present tense is that of **Ax**, and is supported by C's *Mathew maketh mencioun* (RK.8.246). Beta's past tense may be unconscious substitution of *-thed* for *-theth*.

245 **nam**: Alpha has *man*, and beta probably here had the spelling *nam* rather than *Mnam*, which WHmC have corrected from Luke 19.24 and from ll. 247–8. Cf. the spelling variants there. The gloss *a besaunt* which appears in LMWHm and as a variant in CrG must have been in beta.

247 **hym**: Not in L and added in M, so probably absent in beta. Other beta scribes make an obvious correction.

247 **ne wolde**: **Ax** has *nolde*, which carries the alliteration, but it is supported for **Bx** only by MG.

And ȝaf þat Mnam to hym · þat ten Mnames hadde
And with þat he seyde · þat holicherche it herde
250   He þat hath shal haue · and helpe þere it nedeth
And he þat nouȝt hath shal nouȝt haue · and no man hym helpe
And þat he weneth wel to haue · I wil it hym bireue

¶ Kynde witt wolde · þat eche a wyght wrouȝte
Or in dykynge or in deluynge · or trauaillynge in preyeres
255   Contemplatyf lyf or actyf lyf · cryst wolde men wrouȝte
Þe sauter seyth in þe psalme · of beati omnes
Þe freke þat fedeth hym-self · with his feythful laboure
He is blessed by þe boke · in body and in soule
Labores manuum tuarum &c ·

260   ¶ Ȝet I prey ȝow quod pieres · par charite and ȝe kunne
Eny leef of lechecraft · lere it me my dere
For somme of my seruauntz · and my-self bothe
Of al a wyke worche nouȝt · so owre wombe aketh

¶ I wote wel quod hunger · what sykenesse ȝow eyleth
265   Ȝe han maunged ouer-moche · and þat maketh ȝow grone
Ac I hote þe quod hunger · as þow þyne hele wilnest
Þat þow drynke no day · ar þow dyne somwhat
Ete nouȝte I hote þe · ar hunger þe take
And sende þe of his sauce · to sauoure with þi lippes
270   And kepe some tyl soper tyme · and sitte nouȝt to longe
Arise vp ar appetit · haue eten his fulle
Lat nouȝt sire surfait [·] sitten at þi borde
Leue him nouȝt for he is lecherous · and likerous of tonge
And after many manere metes · his maw is afyngred

275   ¶ And ȝif þow diete þe þus · I dar legge myne eres
Þat phisik shal his furred hodes · for his fode selle
And his cloke of calabre · with alle þe knappes of golde
And be fayne bi my feith · his phisik to lete
And lerne to laboure with londe · for lyflode is swete

---

252 **wel**: Alpha has *for* and loses the alliteration. Beta has the support of **Ax** and the X family of **C**, though the P family omit *wel to*.

255 **men**: So LMR; beta1 has *þei* and F has *we*. **AC** are different.

256 **þe**: Alpha has *a*, which could be right, since there are several *Beati omnes* psalms. There is similar variation in **A** mss.

260 **par**: The spelling in LWR (and abbreviated in MCG). See note to **Bx**.8.11.

268 **þe** (1): Supported by **Ax**, but R omits, as does **Cx**.

271 **Arise**: So LMR supported by alliteration and **Ax**; F has *But a-ryse*, the others *And ryse*, evidently misinterpreting *A* as "And".

277 **þe**: Alpha omits; **A** mss. vary similarly.

280   [Þer aren mo morareres þan] leches · lorde hem amende
      Þei do men deye þorw here drynkes · ar destine it wolde

      ¶ By seynt Poule quod pieres · þise aren profitable wordis
      Wende now hunger whan þow wolt · þat wel be þow euere
      For þis is a louely lessoun · lorde it þe forȝelde

285   ¶ By-hote god quod hunger · hennes ne wil I wende
      Til I haue dyned bi þis day · and ydronke bothe

      ¶ I haue no peny quod peres · poletes forto bigge
      Ne neyther gees ne grys · but two grene cheses
      A fewe cruddes and creem · and an hauer cake
290   And two loues of benes and bran · ybake for my fauntis
      And ȝet I sey by my soule · I haue no salt bacoun
      Ne no kokeney bi cryst [·] coloppes forto maken
      Ac I haue percil and porettes · and many kole plantes
      And eke a cow and a kalf · and a cart mare
295   To drawe afelde my donge · þe while þe drought lasteth
      And bi þis lyflode we mot lyue · til lammasse tyme
      And bi þat I hope to haue · heruest in my croft
      And þanne may I diȝte þi dyner · as me dere liketh

      [¶] Alle þe pore peple þo · pesecoddes fetten
300   Benes and baken apples · þei brouȝte in her lapp[e]
      Chibolles and cheruelles · and ripe chiries manye
      And profred peres þis present · to plese with hunger

      ¶ Al hunger eet in hast · and axed after more
      Þanne pore folke for fere · fedde hunger ȝerne
305   With grene poret and pesen · to poysoun hunger þei þouȝte

---

280 **Þer aren mo morareres þan leches**: We take R to represent a corrupt **Bx**. We suppose that B read as A does: *Þer arn mo liȝeris þan lechis* (K.7.257). The nonce word *morareres* resulted from dittography of *mo*. F's *moraynerys* (from *moreine*, "death"?) is a desperate attempt to make sense of this. Beta's revision to *For morthereres aren mony leches* is more radical and more sensible. The line is rewritten in C. See Schmidt (1995), 375.

283 **be þow**: R reverses and F alters. A few C mss. agree with R.

285 **By-hote**: GF's *I hoote* is an A reading, introduced to correct the omission of *I* in **Bx**.

287 **forto**: LR and CrCO, challenged by *to* in MWHmG. **Cx** has the former, **Ax** the latter. We follow copy-text.

293 **porettes**: So beta and F; R has sg. *porett*. A mss. vary similarly; **Cx** revises to *poret plontes*.

293 **kole plantes**: Probably R *queynte herbes* represents the alpha b-verse, which F alters to alliterate. Beta is supported by **Ax**; **Cx** revises to improve the alliteration.

299 **¶**: The paraph in HmW and alpha is appropriate here.

300 **lappe**: We prefer the distributive sg. of R, supported by **Cx** and the A witnesses TDCh.

305 **hunger**: Beta2 (CrWHm); G (corrected) and F read *hym*. This is an agreement by coincidence or contamination with **Ax**. The line is not in C.

By þat it neighed nere heruest · newe corne cam to chepynge
Þanne was folke fayne · and fedde hunger with þe best
With good ale as glotoun tau3te · and gerte hunger go slepe

¶ And þo wolde wastour nou3t werche · but wandren aboute
310 Ne no begger ete bred · þat benes Inne were
But of coket or clerematyn · or elles of clene whete
Ne none halpeny ale · in none wise drynke
But of þe best and of þe brounest · þat in borgh is to selle

¶ Laboreres þat haue no lande · to lyue on but her handes
315 *Deyned nou3t / Deyned* to dyne a-day · ny3t-olde wortes
May no peny-ale hem paye · ne no pece of bakoun
But if it be fresch flesch other fische · fryed other bake
And þat chaude or plus chaud · for chillyng of here mawe
And but if he hieghlich huyred · ellis wil he chyde
320 And þat he was werkman wrou3t · waille þe tyme
A3eines catones conseille · comseth he to iangle
Paupertatis onus pacienter ferre memento

¶ He greueth hym a3eines god · and gruccheth a3eines resoun
And þanne curseth he þe kynge · and al his conseille after
325 Suche lawes to loke · laboreres to greue
Ac whiles hunger was her maister · þere wolde none of hem chyde
Ne stryue a3eines his statut · so sterneliche he loked

---

306 Alpha has a paraph.

306 **newe:** Again W (with F here) has a reading which is probably not **Bx** but agrees coincidentally with another version. *& newe* is the reading of **Cx** and of five **A** mss.

309 **wolde wastour nou3t:** Beta is supported by AC against alpha's *wolde no wastour*.

311 **or** (1): R has *or of*; for which AC offer no support.

313 **and of þe:** LR + beta2 (CrWHm), as the X family of C. The P family omits *of þe*, as F. A*x* omits *of*, as MG and O corrected.

315 **Deyned nou3t / Deyned:** See *MED deinen* v.(1) & (2) for the two related verbs meaning "condescend, see fit" and "disdain". In beta it is the former, in alpha, omitting *nou3t*, the latter. A*x* supports beta, but it seems clear that **Cx** supports alpha (with X significantly adding *no3t* as a correction). The only other use in the **B** text is **Bx**.10.82, recorded only in alpha, in the sense "condescend" in F (*deyneþ not vs to here*), but in R in the sense "disdain" (*deyneþ his heres to opne*)! In the corresponding line in C, some mss. read *deyneth nat vs to here*, but as many omit *nat* (RK.11.59).

317 Alpha runs this and the next line together, omitting the b-verse of l. 317 and the a-verse of l. 318.

318 **or:** WHmG have *and*, supported by AC. We rely on LM, and suppose that G is likely to be contaminated and the reading of the WHm ancestor coincidental. In the absence of alpha, certainty is impossible.

318 **here:** R may be right with sg. *his*, which is the reading of four **A** mss. and the X family of C.

319 Only LM have a paraph, and it is not particularly appropriate.

319 **but if:** So LR and CrWG; others drop *if* (M is rewritten). AC vary similarly.

326 **none of hem:** In A the b-verse reads *wolde þere non chide*; C reverses the first two words, *ther wolde non chyde*, with the P family omitting *ther*. Despite the variations, none of the **B** mss. exactly matches any of these.

¶ Ac I warne ȝow werkemen · wynneth while ȝe mowe
For hunger hideward · hasteth hym faste
330   He shal awake with water · wastoures to chaste
Ar fyue [ȝere] be fulfilled · suche famyn shal aryse
Thorwgh flodes and foule wederes · frutes shul faille
And so sayde saturne · and sent ȝow to warne
Whan ȝe se þe sonne amys · and two monkes hedes
335   And a Mayde haue þe maistrie · and multiplied bi eight
Þanne shal deth withdrawe · and derthe be iustice
And dawe þe dyker · deye for hunger
But if god of his goodnesse · graunt vs a trewe

---

329 **hideward**: There is no need to emend L's spelling, since *hideward* is not uncommon. See *MED*. In the other example in **Bx**.18.313, all scribes including L use the regular spelling, although in the C version of the line (RK.20.341) three mss. including X have *hidward*.

329 **faste**: Alpha's *ful faste* is not supported by AC.

330 **water**: A good example of R blindly following his exemplar with *wat*, and F rationalising to make sense by substituting *sumwhat* for *with wat*.

331 **ȝere**: We suppose that beta omitted the word and that HmO supplied it by conjecture. A mss. generally have the word, though oddly five omit it; C revises to *fewe ȝeres*. Alternatively, it is possible that the riddling *fyue* was **AB**, with scribes making what must have seemed an obvious correction.

332 **flodes**: R's sg. has some support from A mss.

332 **and**: LWHm have *and þourgh*. The variant is also found in AC.

335 **multiplied**: The past participle (i.e. "and everything increased eightfold") is in LM and alpha, though it is a correction in M. Probably the other scribes took it as an imperative.

Passus 7

Passus septimus de visione vt supra

Treuthe herde telle her-of · and to peres he sent
To taken his teme [·] and tulyen þe erthe
And purchaced hym a pardoun · a pena & a culpa
For hym and for his heires · for euermore after
5   And bad hym holde hym at home · and eryen his leyes
And alle þat halpe hym to erie · to sette or to sowe
Or any other myster · þat myȝte pieres auaille
Pardoun with pieres plowman · treuthe hath ygraunted

¶ Kynges and knyȝtes · þat kepen holycherche
10 And ryȝtfullych in reumes · reulen þe peple
Han pardoun thourgh purgatorie · to passe ful lyȝtly
With patriarkes and prophetes · in paradise to be felawes

¶ Bisshopes yblessed · ȝif þei ben as þei shulden
Legistres of bothe lawes · þe lewed þere-with to preche
15 And in as moche as þei mowe · amende alle synful
Aren peres with þe apostles · þus pardoun Piers sheweth
And at þe day of dome · atte heigh deyse to sytte

¶ Marchauntz in þe margyne · hadden many ȝeres

---

1 **he**: Omitted in CrHmGO and inserted in L. The support of MWC and alpha establishes it for **Bx**, though it is omitted in **AC**.

12 **felawes**: The plural is supported by LMG and alpha.

14 **bothe lawes**: So alpha and WHmCr (beta2), supported by **Ax** *Bisshopis þat blissen & boþe lawes kenne* (K.8.13). However LM and beta4 (GOC) read *bothe þe lawes*, which could be right.

16 **þus**: LM and alpha, against *þis* in others.

17 **atte**: "at the", as in all beta mss. except M with *at*. R also has *at*, with F reading *on*. MR could be right. **Ax** reads instead *at here deis*.

141

Ac none a pena & a culpa · þe Pope nolde hem graunte
20 For þei holde nouȝt her halida[y] · as holicherche techeth
And for þei swere by her soule · and so god moste hem helpe
Aȝein clene conscience · her catel to selle

¶ Ac vnder his secret seel · treuthe sent hem a lettre
That þey shulde bugge boldely · þat hem best liked
25 And sithenes selle it aȝein · and saue þe wynny[n]ge
And amende mesondieux þere-[with] · and myseyse folke helpe
And wikked wayes · wiȝtlich hem amende
And do bote to brugges [·] þat to-broke were
Marien maydenes · or maken hem nonnes
30 Pore peple and prisounes · fynden hem here fode
And sette scoleres to scole · or to somme other craftes
Releue Religioun · and renten hem bettere
And I shal sende ȝow my-selue · seynt Michel myn archangel
Þat no deuel shal ȝow dere · ne fere ȝow in ȝowre deying
35 And witen ȝow fro wanhope · if ȝe wil þus worche
And sende ȝowre sowles in safte · to my seyntes in ioye

¶ Þanne were Marchauntz mery · many wepten for ioye
And preyseden Pieres þe plowman · þat purchaced þis bulle

[¶] Men of lawe lest pardoun hadde [·] þat pleteden for Mede

---

19 **none a pena**: Beta is supported by **Ax**; alpha's *no pena* is shared with the X family of C; the P family has *a pena*.

19 **nolde**: Following the negative in the a-verse, **Bx** has a second negative in the b-verse, either *nolde* in beta or *wald nauȝt* (F *wille not*) in alpha. Many A mss. also have *nolde*. C mss. have *wolde* or *nolde* depending on whether they include or omit *no* in the a-verse.

20 **haliday**: The distributive sg. of M and alpha is more likely to have given rise to the plural than vice versa. AC show similar variation.

21 **by her soule and**: Replaced in alpha by *ofte*, but supported by AC and by alliteration.

21 **moste**: Omitted by M and alpha, but supported by AC.

24 **liked**: The beta reading, against the present in alpha. Cx supports the past tense; A mss. are divided. In the context of present-tense verbs, the past tense is more likely to have given rise to the present.

25 **wynnynge**: Beta's distributive sg. is shared with most A mss., while most C mss. have alpha's plural.

26 **þere-with**: The alpha reading is supported by the AC versions. Beta's *þere-myde* is perhaps prompted by the alliteration. For similar variation in this situation, cf. **Bx**.5.77 and note, 6.67 (= RK.8.68), 6.161 (= K.7.145 and RK.8.155), 15.144. There appears to be no settled pattern.

27 **hem**: Supported for **Bx** by LMHmO and alpha; dropped in others. Yet Ax has *to*; Cx rewrites.

31 **somme**: Omitted in alpha, but supported by **Ax** and required by alliteration.

33 Alpha has a paraph.

37 **Marchauntz mery · many wepten**: Beta is supported by AC against alpha's *manye marchauntz . þat wopen*.

39 **¶**: The spacing in LM indicates that a paraph was intended, as in WHmC.

39 **hadde**: Alpha ended the line here, with F filling out this line and RF independently supplying a b-verse for *þat pleteden for mede*.

40 For þe sauter saueth hem nouȝte · such as taketh ȝiftes
And namelich of innocentz [·] þat none yuel ne kunneth
Super innocentem munera non accipies
Pledoures shulde peynen hem · to plede for such an helpe
Prynces and prelates · shulde paye for her trauaille
45 A regibus & pryncipibus erit merces eorum

¶ Ac many a iustice an iuroure · wolde for Iohan do more
Þan pro dei pietate · leue þow none other
Ac he þat spendeth his speche [·] and spekeþ for þe pore
Þat is Innocent and nedy · and no man appeireth
50 Conforteth hym in þat cas · with-oute coueytise of ȝiftes
And scheweth lawe for owre lordes loue · as he it hath lerned
Shal no deuel at his ded-day · deren hym a myte
Þat he ne worth sauf and his sowle · þe sauter bereth witnesse
Domine quis habitabit in tabernaculo tuo &c ·

55 ¶ Ac to bugge water ne wynde · ne witte ne fyre þe fierthe
Þise foure þe fader of heuene · made to þis folde in comune
Þise ben treuthes tresores · trewe folke to helpe
Þat neuere shal wax ne wanye · with-oute god hym-selue

¶ Whan þei drawen on to deye · and Indulgences wolde haue
60 H[is] pardoun is ful petit · at h[is] partyng hennes
Þat any Mede of mene men [·] for her motyng taketh
Ȝe legistres and lawyeres · holdeth þis for treuthe
Þat ȝif þat I lye · Mathew is to blame
For he bad me make ȝow þis · and þis prouerbe me tolde
65 Quodcumque vultis vt faciant vobis homines · facite eis

---

41 **ne**: Supported by LWCrG and alpha against omission in others.

42 The Latin line, omitted by alpha, appears in **A**. The passage is revised in **C**.

43 The paraph in WHmC is perhaps prompted by the Latin line above, though R also begins a line group.

43 **an**: "and". Cf. l. 46.

48 WHmC begin with a paraph, and R begins a new line group, as at l. 43.

50 **Conforteth**: Alpha begins *And conforteth*, but beta is supported by **Ax**.

52 **ded-day**: LCGR have this form, though the usual form is *deþ-day*. Cf. l. 127.

59 **on to deye**: LMWCrG have the verb; HmO and R have the noun *deþ*. F's *to þe deþ* is also the reading of **Cx**. *Drawen to (þe) deþ* is common (*MED drauen* 3b (a)), but note *Cleanness* 1329 *drawes to dyȝe*.

60 **His … his**: In the a-verse R shares the sg. with beta4, but only R has the sg. in the b-verse. However Cx has the sg. in both cases. (Ax also has a sg. pronoun, but the context is different, K.8.59.) The plural pronouns are obviously attracted to the pronouns of the surrounding lines, providing the motive for beta and F independently to rationalise.

61 **any**: Omitted only by R, but it is not in **Cx**. Ax supports the reading of all other mss.

62 **Ȝe**: Beta is supported by **Ax** against alpha's *Þe*. (KD report R's *Þe* and *þe* in this line as *Ȝe* and *ȝe*.)

¶ Alle lybbyng laboreres · þat lyuen with her hondes
Þat trewlich taken · and trewlich wynnen
And lyuen in loue and in lawe · for her lowe hert[e]
Haueth þe same absolucioun · þat sent was to peres

70　¶ Beggeres ne bidderes · ne beth nou3te in þe bulle
But if þe suggestioun be soth · þat shapeth hem to begge
For he þat beggeth or bit · but if he haue nede
He is fals with þe fende · and defraudeth þe nedy
And also he gileth þe gyuer [·] ageines his wil
75　For if he wist he were nou3te nedy · he wolde 3iue þat an other
Þat were more ned[ier] þan he · so þe nediest shuld be hulpe
Catoun kenneth men þus · and þe clerke of þe stories
Cui des videto · is catounes techyng
And in þe stories he techeth · to bistowe þyn almes
80　Sit elemosina in manu tua donec studes cui des

¶ Ac Gregori was a gode man · and bad vs gyuen alle
Þat asketh for his loue · þat vs alle leneth
Non eligas cui miserearis · ne forte pretereas illum qui meretur accipere
Quia incertum est pro quo deum magis placeas

85　¶ For wite 3e neuere who is worthi · ac god wote who hath nede
In hym þat taketh is þe treccherye · if any tresoun walke
For he þat 3iueth 3eldeth · and 3arketh hym to reste
And he þat biddeth borweth · and bryngeth hym-self in dette

---

68 **herte**: Alpha's distributive sg. is supported by many **A** mss. There is no parallel in **C**. Cf. l. 20, 10.420.

71 **hem**: R's *hym* is also the reading of the X family of **C**; the P family and **Ax** support beta's plural.

74 **gileth**: R's reading is supported by AC. The form is less common than *bigileth* (elsewhere only 20.125 in **Bx**, where HmO read *bi-*). We assume that beta and F alter to the commoner form, as on several other occasions in this passage.

74 **wil**: Quite possibly a miswriting for *wille*, as in all except LCrG, and as the word is always otherwise spelt in L. Cable (1988), 54, argues on metrical grounds that the difference is substantive.

76 **nedier**: For alpha's double comparative, cf. e.g. **Bx**.11.165 (passage in alpha only) and 15.206. M here reads *nediere* with *-ere* erased.

77 **men**: Beta2 and GO read *me*. The line is not in **AC**.

77 **þe** (2): Established for **Bx** by LM and alpha, but omitted by beta1.

80 **elemosina**: LM and alpha against *elemosina tua* in others. See Alford (1992), 54. F follows with a line of its own. The passage to l. 96 is not in **AC**.

81 **was**: R has *is*; F rewrites.

84 **deum**: This is clearly the **Bx** reading. M corrects *deum* to *deo*, in line with the reading of WHmG. For the quotation see Alford (1992), 54–5.

86 **In**: R has *Alle in*, and F *For in*.

86 **þe**: Omitted by alpha, perhaps correctly.

87 **3iueth**: KD (p. 145) explain alpha's *3ift* as "variation through misreading of an *-eth* suspension". It might also be noted that *MED yeven* records syncopated forms ending *-th* and *-t*.

For beggeres borwen euermo · and her borgh is god almy3ti
90   To 3elden hem þat 3iueth hem · and 3et vsure more
Quare non dedisti peccuniam meam ad mensam vt ego veniens [& cetera] ·

¶ For-þi biddeth nou3t 3e beggeres · but if 3e haue gret nede
For who-so hath to buggen hym bred · þe boke bereth witnesse
He hath ynough þat hath bred ynough · þough he haue nou3t elles
95   Satis diues est qui non indiget pane

¶ Late vsage be 3owre solace · of seyntes lyues redyng
Þe boke banneth beggarie · and blameth hem in þis manere
Iunior fui etenim senui · et non vidi iustum derelictum nec semen eius &c

¶ For 3e lyue in no loue · ne no lawe holde
100   Many of 3ow ne wedde nou3t · þe wommen þat 3e with delen
But as wilde bestis with wehe · worthen vppe and worchen
And bryngeth forth barnes · þat bastardes men calleth
Or þe bakke or some bone · he breketh in his 3outhe
A sitthe gon faiten with 3oure fauntes · for euermore after
105   Þere is moo mysshape peple · amonge þise beggeres
Þan of alle maner men · þat on þis molde walketh

---

89 **For**: Alpha's *Forthi* perhaps anticipates **Bx**.7.92.

91 **veniens & cetera**: So M. L ends *veniens cum vsuris exigerem*, but the variant readings suggest that scribes expanded an abbreviated quotation from Luke 19.23. Alford (1992), 55.

92 **gret nede**: Established for **Bx** by LMR as well as beta2. The others omit the adjective.

97 **hem**: Omitted by beta4. F rewrites.

98 **semen eius &c**: So LW; M ends with *derelictum &c*, R with *iustum*. CrHmCOF complete the verse from Psalm 36.25, ... *nec semen eius querens panem &c*. Evidently scribes expanded a familiar quotation, as in l. 91.

99 **¶**: The paraph in LWHm (with a new line-group in M), though not alpha, is appropriate.

99 **3e**: AC have third person in this passage (K.8.72–3, RK.9.167). Bennett (1972), 221, explains that the following lines "represent an attempt to return to the original theme from which 71–88 [**Bx**.7.75–97] (new in B) are a digression. The digression has involved the use of the 2nd person, which is retained up to 94, though the original 3rd person forms are kept in 93 [**Bx**.7.103]". Though all **B** mss. have second person here, except for F which alters to *beggeres*, the situation is more complicated than Bennett suggests, since scribes altered to bring the pronouns into line. See notes to ll. 100, 103, 104.

100 **of 3ow**: As in the previous line, F alters, reading *man*, and consequently adopting sg. *womman* and *he* in the b-verse. See next note.

100 **wommen**: The plural is supported by LMR as well as CrG. A mss. vary (K.8.73); **Cx** has the plural in a revised line (RK.9.168).

103 **he ... his**: Beta has sg. pronouns, but alpha has plural. A mss. have *his bak, his bon* and *his 3oupe*, but rather oddly many have *þei* rather than *he* at the beginning of the b-verse. **Cx** brings the pronouns into line with the surrounding plurals.

104 **A**: "And".

104 **3oure**: Beta represents **Bx**'s half-hearted attempt to put the passage into the second person; see note to l. 99. O and alpha resolve the difficulty by altering back to third person, thus aligning with AC.

105 **amonge**: WMO and alpha have the form in *-es*. Either could be **Bx**. AC mss. also vary.

[Þo] þat lyue þus here lyf · mowe lothe þe tyme
Þat euere he was man wrou3t · whan he shal hennes fare

¶ Ac olde men & hore · þat helplees ben of strengthe
110 And women with childe · þat worche ne mowe
Blynde and bedered · and broken her membres
Þat taketh þis myschief mekelych · as meseles and othere
Han as pleyne pardoun [·] as þe plowman hym-self
For loue of her lowe hertis · owre lorde hath hem graunted
115 Here penaunce and here purgatorie · here [vp]on þis erthe

¶ Pieres quod a prest þo · þi pardoun most I rede
For I [shal] construe eche clause · and kenne it þe on englich

¶ And pieres at his preyere · þe pardoun vnfoldeth
And I bihynde hem bothe · bihelde al þe bulle
120 Al in two lynes it lay · and nou3t a leef more
And was writen ri3t þus · in witnesse of treuthe
Et qui bona egerunt ibunt in vitam eternam
Qui vero mala in ignem eternum ·

¶ Peter quod þe prest þo · I can no pardoun fynde
125 But dowel and haue wel · and god shal haue þi sowle
And do yuel and haue yuel · hope þow non other
Þat after þi ded-day · þe deuel shal haue þi sowle

¶ And pieres for pure tene · pulled it atweyne
And seyde si ambulauero in medio vmbre mortis · non timebo mala
    quoniam tu mecum es

130 ¶ I shal cessen of my sowyng quod pieres · and swynk nou3t so harde
Ne about my bely-ioye · so bisi be namore
Of preyers and of penaunce · my plow shal ben her-after
And wepen whan I shulde slepe · þough whete bred me faille

¶ Þe prophete his payn ete · in penaunce and in sorwe

---

107 **Þo**: R only, but supported by AC. F adds *For*, while beta has *And þei*.

108 **he was man**: Beta2 reads *þei were men*, but this is not supported by **Ax**.

112 **þis myschief**: The sg. is established for **Bx** by agreement of LMR (F *myssese*) and **Ax**, though **Cx** has the plural.

115 **vpon**: In AC the b-verse reads *vpon þis pur erþe*. **Bx** has lost the alliterating adjective. R retains *vpon*, the alpha reading which F garbles, while beta reads *on*.

117 **shal**: Alpha's reading expressing necessity (cf. *most* in the line above) is more appropriate than the volition expressed by beta's *wil*. Most **A** mss. support alpha. **Cx** has *can* (RK.9.282).

127 **Þat**: LM and alpha, supported by **Ax**. Other beta mss. have *But*. Lines 127–52 are not in **C**.

127 **ded-day**: LCG have this form, though the usual form is *deþ-day*. Cf. note to l. 52 where R also has the form.

132 **penaunce**: For variation with and without <-s>, see note to **Bx**.14.211.

135 By þat þe sauter seith · so dede other manye
     Þat loueth god lelly · his lyflode is ful esy
     Fuerunt michi lacrime mee · panes die ac nocte

     ¶ And but if Luke lye · he lereth vs bi foules
     We shulde nou3t be to bisy · aboute þe worldes blisse
140 Ne solliciti sitis · he seyth in þe gospel
     And sheweth vs bi ensamples · vs-selue to wisse
     Þe foules on þe felde · who fynt hem mete at wynter
     Haue þei no gernere to go to · but god fynt hem alle

     ¶ What quod þe prest to perkyn · peter as me þinketh
145 Þow art lettred a litel · who lerned þe on boke

     ¶ Abstinence þe abbesse quod pieres · myne abc me tau3te
     And conscience come afterward · and kenned me moche more

     ¶ Were þow a prest pieres quod he · þow mi3te preche where þow sholdest
     As deuynour in deuynyte · with dixit insipiens to þi teme

150 ¶ Lewed lorel quod Pieres · litel lokestow on þe bible
     On salomones sawes · selden þow biholdest
     Ecce derisores et iurgia cum eis ne crescant &c

     ¶ Þe prest and perkyn · apposeden eyther other
     And I þorw here wordes awoke · and waited aboute

---

138 **bi foules**: "(instructs us) by birds"; so beta, anticipating ll. 142–3. Alpha's line ending *or
lereþ vs be foles* means "Unless Luke lies or teaches us to be fools", which cannot be the sense
intended. Schmidt accepts beta's *he* in place of alpha's *or*, and alpha's *foles* in place of beta's
foules, and this indeed makes sense in reference to Luke's fool as the man who tells his soul to
rest now he has laid up treasure for it: "Dixit autem illi Deus: Stulte, hac nocte animam tuam
repetunt a te. ... Nolite solliciti esse animae quid manducetis" (Luke 12.20, 22, abbreviated in
l. 140). See Schmidt (1995), 376–7. It is worth noting, however, that *leren* is followed by a *to*
infin. in the closest parallel "alle he lered to be lele" (**Bx.**19.256). A is no help, with the variant
readings *by foules, by birdes, be folis, to ben foles*. We retain copy-text.

142 **on**: Choice is difficult. The LM reading is generally reliable for beta. R's *of* may represent
alpha, but F has *in* as do the remainder of the beta mss. The situation is further complicated by
the apparent corruption of **Bx**; the gospel has *volatilia caeli* (Matt. 6.26), which **Ax** translates
as *foulis in þe firmament* (K.8.115), suggesting that *on þe felde* is a **Bx** error prompting scribes
to improve. We follow copy-text.

142 **at**: Supported by LMWCOR against the repetition of *in* in CrHmF, even though A mss.
have either *in* or *a*.

146 **þe abbesse**: Lost in alpha but supported by **Ax** and necessary for the alliteration.

148 **sholdest**: The beta reading. R's *woldest* is perhaps easier; F revises. **Ax** has *þe likide*.

149 **in**: G and alpha have *of*, perhaps rightly. Cf. *of diuinite Maistres* (**Bx**.15.396). There is no
parallel in **Ax**.

150 **þe**: Supported by **Ax**. R's *þi* is perhaps prompted by *þi* in the same position in the line above.

151 **On**: Beta is supported by **Ax** against R's *And* (F rewrites).

152 **Ecce**: The reading of all **A** and most **B** mss. OF "correct" to *Eice* (KD mistranscribe MR
as *Eice*). For this line from Prov. 22.10, "Eiice ['eject'] derisores ...", see Alford (1992), 57.

155 And seighe þe sonne in þe south [·] sitte þat tyme
Metelees and monelees · on Maluerne hulles
Musyng on þis meteles · [a] my waye ich ȝede
Many tyme þis meteles · hath maked me to studye
Of þat I seigh slepyng · if it so be myȝte
160 And also for peres þe plowman · ful pensyf in herte
And which a pardoun peres hadde · alle þe peple to conforte
And how þe prest impugned it [·] with two propre wordes
Ac I haue no sauoure in songewarie · for I se it ofte faille
Catoun and canonistres · conseilleth vs to leue
165 To sette sadnesse in songewarie · for sompnia ne cures

¶ Ac for þe boke bible · bereth witnesse
How danyel deuyned · þe dremes of a kynge
Þat was nabugodonosor · nempned of clerkis
Daniel seyde sire Kynge · þi dremeles bitokneth
170 Þat vnkouth knyȝtes shul come · þi kyngdom to cleue
Amonges lowere lordes · þi londe shal be departed
And as danyel deuyned [·] in dede it felle after
Þe kynge lese his lordship · and lower men it hadde

¶ And ioseph mette merueillously · how þe mone and þe sonne
175 And þe elleuene sterres · hailsed hym alle
Þanne Iacob iugged · iosephes sweuene
Beau filtz quod his fader · for defaute we shullen
I my-self and my sones · seche þe for nede

¶ It bifel as his fader seyde · in pharaoes tyme
180 Þat ioseph was iustice · egipte to loken
It bifel as his fader tolde · his frendes þere hym souȝte

---

157 **a**: "on": Since AC read *a myle wey*, we conjecture that R's *a my wey*, supported by M's *on my way*, represents the corrupt **Bx**, understood as *and my waye* by L and most scribes, and characteristically expanded by F to *as y my way*.

166 **þe boke bible**: This rather odd expression, variously altered by HmCGOF, is confirmed by **Cx** and paralleled by **Bx**.10.93, though **Ax** reads *þe bible*.

167 **dremes**: Some A mss. have the sg. as in WHmR. The X family of C has the plural, the P family has *dremels* (as in l. 169).

169 **dremeles**: "dream-vision" (sg. or pl.). A word only recorded in Langland. As in **Bx**.13.14 (where F is absent), CrHmCF corrupt to *dremes*.

170 **cleue**: LMGO against easier *cleyme* in beta2 and C, and hence the beta reading. Alpha has *reue*, but the sense of *cleue* is continued in *departed* in the next line, and confirmed by Daniel 5.28, "divisum est regnum tuum". Yet all A mss. except one have *cleyme*. Probably the comparative difficulty of *cleue* (*MED cleven* v.(2), 4, "break up, dismember") led scribes to alter it. The line is not in C.

176 W and Alpha here have a paraph.

181 **þere hym souȝte**: R has the order *hym þere souȝte*, and F has *sowtyn þere*. In **Cx** the equivalent b-verse is *hym for nede souhte* (RK.9.316).

And al þis maketh me · on þis meteles to þynke

¶ And how þe prest preued · no pardoun to dowel
And demed þat dowel · indulgences passed
185   Biennales and triennales · and bisschopes lettres
And how dowel at þe day of dome · is dignelich vnderfongen
And passeth al þe pardoun · of seynt petres cherche

¶ Now hath þe pope powere · pardoun to graunte þe peple
With-outen eny penaunce · to passen in-to heuene
190   Þis is owre bileue · as lettered men vs techeth
Quodcumque ligaueris super terram · erit ligatum et in celis &c ·
And so I leue lelly · lordes forbode ellis
Þat pardoun and penaunce · and preyeres don saue
Soules þat haue synned · seuene sithes dedly
195   Ac to trust to þise triennales · trewly me þinketh
[It] is nou3t so syker for þe soule · certis as is dowel

¶ For-þi I rede 3ow renkes · þat riche ben on þis erthe
Vppon trust of 3owre tresoure · triennales to haue
Be 3e neuere þe balder · to breke þe x hestes
200   And namelich 3e maistres · mayres and iugges
Þat han þe welthe of þis worlde · and wyse men ben holden
To purchace 3ow pardoun · and þe popis bulles
At þe dredeful dome · whan ded shullen rise
And comen alle bifor cryst · acountis to 3elde
205   How þow laddest þi lyf here · and his lawes keptest
And how þow dedest day bi day · þe dome wil reherce
A poke ful of pardoun þere · ne prouinciales lettres
Theigh 3e be founde in þe fraternete · of alle þe *foure / fyue* ordres

---

184 **indulgences**: CR's *indulgence* may also be plural. See note to **Bx**.3.23 and variants in l. 209.

188–96 ¶: O omits the paragraph.

188 RM punctuate the line after *pardoun*, reflecting uncertainty over the very heavy b-verse which F abbreviates.

196 **It**: Alpha's resumed subject is perhaps more likely to have been lost than added. **A** and **C** also vary, though *It* is supported by the X family of **C**.

197 **renkes**: Alpha has no difficulty with the seven other instances of *renk*.

201 **and**: Alpha supported by **AC** over *and for* in LMWHmCr.

203 **rise**: LW and alpha, against *arise* in others. Most **C** mss. have the former, most **A** mss. the latter.

204 **acountis**: Alpha begins the b-verse with *and*, but this is not supported by **AC**.

206 **dedest**: Beta's past tense is supported by **AC** against alpha's present.

207 **poke**: For R's form *pouh3* see *MED pough(e*, but both forms derive from OE *pohha*. R's less common form is paralleled among **A** mss. by V *powhe*, and among **C** mss. by X *pouhe*.

208 **foure / fyue**: Ax supports beta and F with *foure*, but R has *fyue*. Here and twice elsewhere (RK.8.191, 9.344, 15.80) **Cx** refers to the five mendicant orders (the usual four plus the crutched friars). Probably R represents a revision, with F reverting to the more usual number of orders.

And haue indulgences double-folde · but dowel ȝow help
210   I sette ȝowre patentes and ȝowre pardou[n] [·] at one pies hele

¶ For-þi I conseille alle cristene · to crye god mercy
And Marie his moder · be owre mene bitwene
Þat god gyue vs grace here · ar we gone hennes
Suche werkes to werche · while we ben here
215   Þat after owre deth-day · dowel reherce
At þe day of dome · we dede as he hiȝte

---

209 **but:** Alpha is supported by **AC** against beta's *but if*.
210 **pardoun:** The sg. is supported by **Cx**; L's plural is the result of a later correction. F omits the line.
214 **while:** Beta is supported by **Ax** and the P family of C. The X family, however, has *þe while* as alpha.

Passus 8

Passus octauus de visione & hic explicit & incipit inquisicio prima de dowel

Thus yrobed in russet · I rowmed aboute
Al a somer sesoun · for to seke dowel
And frayned ful oft · of folke þat I mette
If ani wiȝte wiste · where dowel was at Inne
5 And what man he miȝte be · of many man I axed

¶ Was neuere wiȝte as I went · þat me wisse couthe
Where þis lede lenged · lasse ne more

¶ Tyl it bifel on a fryday · two freres I mette
Maistres of þe Menoures · men of grete witte
10 I hailsed hem hendely [·] as I hadde lerned
And preyed hem par charitee · ar þei passed forther
If þei knewe any contre · or costes as þei went
Where þat dowel dwelleth · doth me to wytene

---

2 F omits the line.

4 **was:** alpha's subjunctive *were* is not supported by **AC**.

6 **Was:** LMWHm begin a paragraph here. Alpha instead begins *And was* (R) or *But þere was* (F), but beta is supported by **AC**.

6 **as I went:** R's *in þis worlde* is also the reading of **Cx**, and so could possibly represent a revision, but F has the beta reading. Schmidt (1995) conjectures that R's reading is contaminated from **Cx** or is "a coincidental substitution of a familiar phrase" (377). The latter seems likely.

8 ¶: The paraph is in LR (M has a line-space).

9 **Maistres:** Alpha begins *And maistres*, without support from **AC**.

11 **par:** LMWG; HmOF have *pur* (though in fact abbreviated in all except WHm). *MED* treats various forms as the same word (s.v. *par* prep.), and all scribes in all versions vary freely. CrCR have *for*, but this is not supported by **AC**. Cf. **Bx**.6.260, 13.30.

12 **contre:** Alpha's *courte* is a misreading; beta is supported by **AC**. For the reverse error see **Bx**.P.149.

12 **as:** Perhaps a little more pointed in its reference to friars than alpha's *þer*. **AC** have instead *costes aboute*.

¶ For þei ben men on þis molde · þat moste wyde walken
15 And knowen contrees and courtes · and many kynnes places
Bothe prynces paleyses · and pore mennes cotes
And dowel and doyuel · where þei dwelle bothe

¶ Amonges vs quod þe Menours · þat man is dwellyng
And euere hath as I hope · and euere shal here-after

20 ¶ Contra quod I as a clerke · and comsed to disputen
And seide sothli sepcies · in die cadit iustus
Seuene sythes seith þe boke · synneth þe riȝtful
And who-so synneth I seyde · doth yuel as me þinketh
And dowel and do yuel · mow nouȝt dwelle togideres
25 Ergo he nys nauȝt alway · amonge ȝow freres
He is otherwhile ellis-where · to wisse þe peple

¶ I shal sey þe my sone · seide þe frere þanne
How seuene sithes þe sad man · on þe day synneth
By a forbisene quod þe frere · I shal þe faire shewe

30 ¶ Lat brynge a man in a bote · amydde a brode water
Þe wynde and þe water · and þe bote waggynge
Maketh þe man many a tyme · to falle and to stonde
For stonde he neuere so styf · he stombleth ȝif he moeue
Ac ȝit is he sauf and sounde · and so hym bihoueth
35 For ȝif he ne arise þe rather · and rauȝte to þe stiere
Þe wynde wolde wyth þe water · þe bote ouerthrowe

14–17 These four lines omitted in alpha are not paralleled in **Ax** but are in **Cx**. Here the omission can be accounted for as a result of homeoarchy (*dowel* and *dwelle* 8.13, 17) and skipping a paraph.

14 ¶: In the absence of alpha, the paraph is only in LC, with a line-space in M.

14 **on**: The LM reading (supported by G) generally secures beta and hence **Bx** (in the absence of alpha). However, *of* in beta2 and CO is also the reading of **Cx**. We retain copy-text.

18 **Amonges vs**: F has the **Ax** reading *Marye*, and its b-verse is also from **A**. For other lines in this passus which suggest F's contamination from an **A** text, see notes to ll. 25, 28, 38, 43, 45, 49, 74, 76, 78, 79, 87, 100–05, 106, 109, 121, 124.

21 **seide sothli**: The reading of LM is supported by **Cx**. The other beta mss. add a pronoun object. R has no pronoun and loses the alliteration by omitting *sothli*. F drops the line. Since both LM place the punctuation after *sepcies* (R is without punctuation here), that is probably beta or archetypal error.

25 **nys**: LMW against *is* in other mss. AC mss. vary similarly. We retain copy-text.

25 **alway**: F's *alwey at hoom* is the AC reading.

28 **on þe**: LM and alpha, against *on a* in beta1. F's word-order is that of **AC**.

30 **a** (3): LR supported by AC, against *þe* in other mss.

32 **many a**: CrOR have *many*, as do AC.

35 **stiere**: The beta reading, vs. alpha (and Hm) *sterne*. Both words mean "rudder", and are used to translate "clavus" in Prov.23.34 from which the friar's example comes. Neither is used elsewhere in the poem. See *MED ster(e* n.(2) and *stern(e* n.(2). A mss. also vary.

36 **wyth**: R's *and* is probably alpha, altered for sense to *on* by F. Beta is supported by **Ax**.

And þanne were his lyf loste · þourgh lacchesse of hym-self

¶ And þus it falleth quod þe frere · bi folke here on erthe
Þe water is likned to þe worlde · þat wanyeth and wexeth
40   Þe godis of þis grounde aren like · to þe grete wawes
Þat as wyndes and wederes · walweth aboute
Þe bote is likned to owre body · þat brutel is of kynde
Þat þorugh þe fende and þi flessh · and þe frele worlde
Synneth þe sadman · a day seuene sythes

45   ¶ Ac dedly synne doth he nou3t · for dowel hym kepith
And þat is charite þe champioun · chief help a3ein synne
For he strengtheth man to stonde · and stereth mannes soule
[Þat] þowgh þi body bow · as bote doth in þe water
Ay is þi soule sauf · but þi-self wole
50   Do a dedly synne · and drenche so þi soule
God wole suffre wel þi sleuthe · 3if þi-self lyketh
For he 3af þe to 3eres3yue · to 3eme wel þi-selue
And þat is witte a fre wille · to euery wy3te a porcioun

---

38 **And:** F's *Ryght* is from **Ax**.

38 **falleth:** GF's *fareþ* is the AC reading.

40 Scribes vary in their placement of the punctus before or after *aren like*, responding to the awkwardness of the line. The hesitation is visibly expressed in M, with a punctus elevatus erased before the phrase and inserted after it.

41 **walweth:** The LM reading, which is therefore likely to represent beta. It is supported by **Ax** and the better **C** mss. against *walweth* in alpha and four mss. of **C**. KD, 154 and n. 73, argue that in context *walweth* is "an easier reading"; nevertheless it is a rarer word. The primary sense of *walken* is "roll about" (*MED walken* v.(1), 1) rather than "go on foot" (3a). For the same variation see **Bx.9.56**.

43 **þi:** LR, and so presumptively **Bx**. But choice is difficult. F has *oure*, perhaps from the previous line but also the reading of **Cx**, while the other beta mss. have *þe*, the reading of **Ax**. We follow copy-text.

43 **þe frele:** The beta reading. F has *þe false*, which is the **Ax** reading. R has *þis frele*, the reading also of **Cx**. Possibly R's reading is a revision. We follow copy-text.

45 **kepith:** F has the AC reading *helpiþ*.

48 **Þat:** The alpha reading is also that of **Ax**. Beta has *And*. Lines 46–56 are rewritten in **Cx**.

48 **þi:** LMCO and alpha, supported by **Ax**, against *þe* in WHmG.

49 **but:** LMR are supported by **Ax** against *but if* in the others.

49 **þi-self:** M reads *þou þi-seluen* as does **Ax**; WCr alter the word-order to *þow wole þi-selue* to the detriment of the alliteration.

49 Following this line, F introduces a line from A (K.9.45).

50 **soule:** R alone has *selue*, perhaps from the previous line, though it is the reading of all but three A mss.

51 **sleuthe:** Alpha and Hm read *soule*, perhaps picked up from 49–50. F revises to make sense of this. The line is revised from **Ax**.

53 **a** (1): "and" (LM). See note to **Bx.P.227**. KD, pp. 193–4, take **Bx** *And þat is* to be an interpolation, and their emendation makes much clearer sense of *to 3eres3yue* "(wit and free will) as a gift". Hence the variants *two 3eres3evis* in CrF and *a yeres3yue* in WG in l. 52. In M, *wit* is a correction, possibly of *with a fre wille*.

To fleghyng foules · to fissches & to bestes
55 Ac man hath moste þerof · and moste is to blame
But if he worche wel þer-with · as dowel hym techeth

¶ I haue no kynde knowyng quod I · to conceyue alle [þi] wordes
Ac if I may lyue and loke · I shal go lerne bettere
I bikenne þe *cryst / cryst quod he* · þat on þe crosse deyde
60 And I seyde þe same · saue ȝow fro myschaunce
And ȝiue ȝow grace on þis grounde · good men to worthe

¶ And þus I went wide-where [·] walkyng myne one
By a wilde wildernesse · and bi a wode-syde
Blisse of þ[e] briddes · [abide] me [made]
65 And vnder a lynde vppon a launde · lened I a stounde
To lythe þe layes · þ[e] louely foules made
Murthe of her mouthes · made me þere to slepe
Þe merueillousest meteles · mette me þanne
Þat euer dremed wyȝte · in worlde as I wene

70 ¶ A moche man as me þouȝte · and lyke to my-selue
Come and called me · by my kynde name
What artow quod I þo · þat þow my name knowest
Þat þow wost wel quod he · and no wyȝte bettere

---

57 **þi**: Alpha agrees with **Ax** against beta *ȝowre*. **Cx** has *this speche*.

59 W and alpha here supply a paraph, and also (see next note) have *quod he*, recognising that the speaker has changed. It may be, therefore, that the paraph was added to **Bx** to make this clear.

59 **cryst / cryst quod he**: Alpha and WHm are supported by *quod he* in **Cx**, making clear that the friar is the speaker rather than Will. However, most beta mss. are supported by **Ax**. R's plural pronoun is presumably an error, though indeed there are two friars.

64 **þe**: Though this is the reading of most mss., LHmR give strong support to *þo*. However the birds have not been previously mentioned, and *þe* is supported by **AC** (but see next note).

64 **abide me made**: Alpha's reading is obviously correct, since beta's *brouȝte me aslepe* sends the dreamer to sleep too early. Alpha is supported by **Ax** (*made me abide*) and **Cx** (RK.10.63). Beta's reading, anticipating l. 67, is puzzling, since the line is identical to K.9.58. The passage in **A** reads:

> Blisse of þe briddes made me abide
> And vndir a lynde vpon a launde lenide I me a stounde
> To lerne þe laies þat [*var.* þat þe] louely briddes [*var.* foulis] maden
> Blisse of þe [*var.* þise] briddis brouȝte me a slepe (K.9.55–8).

66 **þe** (2): The reading of alpha. The beta reading is uncertain, since LCrWGO have *þo* against *þe* in MHmC. The latter has some support from **A** mss. (see previous note); **Cx** is revised.

66 **louely**: Lost in alpha, but supported by **AC** and necessary for the alliteration.

70 **me þouȝte**: R drops *me*, anticipating the identification as Thought. F replaces the phrase with *he was*. Beta is supported by **AC**.

72 WHmC and alpha have a paraph to mark Will's question. Cf. ll. 59, 73.

72 **þo**: Omitted only by R, though **Cx** and many **A** mss. also omit, so it is perhaps added by beta and F.

73 W and alpha have a paraph to mark Thought's answer.

¶ Wote I what þow art ꝫ þought · seyde he þanne
75 I haue suwed þe þis seuene ȝere · sey þow me no rather

¶ Art þow thought quod I þo · þow couthest me wisse
Where þat dowel dwelleth · and do me þat to knowe

¶ Dowel and dobet · and dobest þe thridde quod he
Aren three faire vertues · and beth nauȝte fer to fynde
80 Who-so is trewe of his tonge · and of his two handes
And þorugh his laboure or þorugh his londe · his lyflode wynneth
And is trusti of his tailende · taketh but his owne
And is nouȝt dronkenlew ne dedeignous · dowel hym folweth

¶ Dobet doth ryȝt þus · ac he doth moche more
85 He is as low as a lombe · and loueliche of speche
And helpeth alle men · after þat hem nedeth
Þe bagges and þe bigurdeles · he hath to-broken hem alle
Þat þe Erl auarous · helde and his heires
And with Mammonaes mone · he hath made hym frendes
90 And is ronne in-to Religioun · and hath rendred þe bible
And precheth to þe poeple · seynt Poules wordes
Libenter suffertis insipientes · cum sitis ipsi sapientes
And suffreth þe vnwise · with ȝow forto libbe
And with gladde wille doth hem gode · for so god ȝow hoteth

95 ¶ Dobest is aboue bothe · and bereth a bisschopes cro[c]e

---

74 **what þow art**: F's *who art þou* is the AC reading.

74 The punctus elevatus before *þought* in LMOR and F (rather than his usual virgule) must
be archetypal, perhaps to indicate the question. LMO also have a punctus following *þought*. On
Hoccleve's use of the punctus elevatus to mark this sort of question, see Burrow (2002), 184–5.

76 **wisse**: F's *telle* is the reading of **Ax**.

77 **þat** (2): The beta reading, where alpha has *hym*. AC have neither pronoun. We follow
copy-text.

78 **quod he**: F's placement of this after *Dowel* is that of **Ax**. In **Cx** it follows *dobet*.

79 The line that follows in F only is from A (K.9.71).

81 **þorugh** (2): Clear support for **Bx** from LMWHmR. It is not in **Ax**. **Cx** rewrites.

83 **dedeignous**: CF have the aphetic form *deygnous*, and R subpuncts initial *de-*. The best X
family mss. of **C** have *dedeynus*, but the P family and **Ax** have *deynous*.

87 **to-broken**: WCO have *to-broke* which improves the metre of the b-verse. There is the same
variation in **C** mss. HmGF have *broke(n)*, as do **A** mss.

89 **And**: Beta's *And þus* is not supported by AC.

90 **in-to**: The reading of LM and alpha against *to*, with support from some **A** mss. and the
best **C** mss. of both families.

91 **precheth**: Beta4 and R have the past tense, but AC support the present.

92 **insipientes**: Several **C** mss. share with alpha the spelling *incipientes* (as if from *incipio*).

92 **sitis ipsi**: Reversed in alpha. **Ax** quotes only the first two words of the verse; many **C** mss.
omit the second clause.

95 **croce**: "crosier", the reading of MO and alpha (OFr *croce*), to be distinguished from *cross*
(OE and ON from Irish) in other mss. The description is clearly that of a crosier rather than

Is hoked on þat one ende · to halie men fro helle
A pyke is on þat potente · to pulte adown þe wikked
Þat wayten any wikkednesse · dowel to tene
And dowel and dobet [·] amonges hem ordeigned
100 To croune one to be kynge [·] to reule hem bothe
Þat ȝif dowel or dobet [·] did aȝein dobest
Þanne shal þe kynge come · and casten hem in yrens
And but if dobest bede for hem · þei to be þere for euere

¶ Thus dowel and dobet · and dobest þe thridde
105 Crouned one to be kynge · to kepin hem alle
And to reule þe Reume · bi her thre wittes
And none other wise · but as þei thre assented

¶ I thonked thouȝt þo · þat he me þus tauȝte
Ac ȝete sauoureth me nouȝt þi seggyng · I coueite to lerne
110 How dowel dobet and dobest · don amonges þe peple

¶ But witte conne wisse þe quod þouȝt · where þo thre dwelle
Ellis wote I none þat can · þat now is alyue

¶ Þouȝte and I thus · thre days we ȝeden
Disputyng vppon dowel · day after other

---

a cross. In **Bx.**15.598, however, the bishop's *crosse* is presumably a pectoral cross, unless a pun is intended on *crosse* in 15.608.

97 **pulte:** The reading in LOR (*MED pilten*), the source of *putte* or *pul* in other mss. There is the same variation in **C** mss. (RK.10.95).

99 R has a paraph (F drops the line).

100b–5a Alpha as represented by R is here deficient, omitting through eyeskip from *kynge* to *kynge* five lines present in beta. The lines in beta are a revised version of **Ax**, K.9.91–8, omitting 9.93 and 95, and replacing 9.98 with 91. F repairs the gap from his **A** text, thus:

> F.6.96 And þus dowel . & dobet . & dobest þe thrydde. (K.9.97)
> F.6.97 Haue crowne oon to be kyng / & be here conseyl wirche (K.9.98)
> F.6.98 & to rewle al þe rewhme / be reed of hem alle. (K.9.99)
> F.6.99 & be non oþir-wyse / but as þey þre wille assente. (K.9.100)
> F.6.100 ¶ For if þat dowel or dobet / dyden a-geyn dobest. (K.9.92)
> F.6.101 & weryn vn-buxum to don his byddyngge / & bown to do Ille. (K.9.93)
> F.6.102 Þanne sholde þe kyng come / & comawnde hem to presoun. (K.9.94)
> F.6.103 & pitte hem þere in penawnce / with-oute pite or grace. (K.9.95)

The lines are rewritten in **Cx**.

100 **to reule hem bothe:** The b-verse (beta only) is defective in alliteration and metre, and is presumably corrupted from K.9.98–9, *Corounid on to be kyng & be here counseil werche / And rewele þe reaum.* **Bx** has reversed the positions of the parallel lines 100 and 105 (= K98 and 91). The reversal is retained in **Cx**, which however repairs the alliteration by completing this line *to kull withoute synne* (RK.10.101).

102 **yrens:** **Ax** has *presoun*, which is also F's reading. See note to ll. 100–05.

106 **bi her thre wittes:** F again follows **Ax** (K.9.99). **Cx** follows **Bx**, despite the defective alliteration.

109 **ȝete:** Lost in R, but supported by **AC**.

109 **I coueite to lerne:** **Bx** has evidently conflated two lines in **A**, which F restores (K.9.102–3).

115 And ar we were ywar · with witte gan we mete
     He was longe and lene · liche to none other
     Was no pruyde on his apparaille · ne pouerte noyther
     Sadde of his semblaunt · and of soft chiere
     I dorste meue no matere · to make hym to iangle
120 But as I bad þou3t þo · be mene bitwene
     And put forth somme purpos · to prouen his wittes
     What was dowel fro dobet · and dobest fram hem bothe

     ¶ Þanne þou3t in þat tyme [·] seide þise wordes
     Where dowel dobet [·] and dobest ben in londe
125 Here is wille wolde ywyte · 3if witte couthe teche hym
     And whether he be man or [no] man · þis man fayne wolde aspye
     And worchen as þei thre wolde · þis is his entente

---

115 **were ywar**: R 's order *war were* may be right, since it is that of **Ax** as well as the X family
of **C**. Beta and F are in line with the P family. We follow copy-text.

121 **And**: Also the reading of **Cx**. F's *To* follows **Ax**.

121 **somme**: Supported by AC against R's *his*.

124 **Where**: R interprets this as *Whether*, which, in this case, it is not.

124 **dowel**: F's *dowel &* may be from **Ax**, but it is also the **Cx** reading.

124 **ben**: Lost in alpha, with F recasting to make sense. It is added above the line in M,
suggesting the possibility that the omission was a **Bx** error, with beta scribes making the
obvious correction.

125 **is**: R (= alpha?) loses this, and F rewrites.

126 **no man**: L's *man* is obviously an error, though it may represent confusion in beta or **Bx**,
with other scribes repairing. Alpha and C have *no man*; most beta mss. have *womman*. The
line is not in **AC**.

126 **fayne**: Dropped in Hm and beta4, and erased in M.

Passus 9

Sire dowel dwelleth quod witte · nouȝt a day hennes
In a castel þat kynde made · of foure kynnes þinges
Of erthe and eyre is it made · medled togideres
With wynde and with water · witterly enioyned
5 Kynde hath closed þere-Inne · craftily with-alle
A lemman þat he loueth · like to hym-selue
Anima she hatte · ac enuye hir hateth
A proude pryker of Fraunce · prynceps huius mundi
And wolde winne hir awey · with wyles and he myȝte

10 ¶ Ac / And kynde knoweth þis wel · and kepeth hir þe bettere
And hath do hir with sire dowel · is duke of þis marches
Dobet is hir damoisele · sire doweles douȝter
To serue þis lady lelly · bothe late and rathe
Dobest is aboue bothe · a bisschopes pere
15 Þat he bit mote be do · he reuleth hem alle
Anima þat lady · is ladde bi his lerynge

¶ Ac þe constable of þat castel · þat kepeth al þe wacche

---

2 **kynnes**: Alpha's non-alliterative *maner* is not supported by AC (K.10.2, RK.10.219)

3 **is it**: The order is reversed in HmOF. AC also vary.

10 **Ac / And**: The beta reading is *Ac*, supported by **Ax**. Alteration to *And* in CrC is character-istic (cf. **Bx.9.17**, 57 etc.). But here the alpha reading is also *And*, and it is in turn the reading of **Cx**.

11 **hath do**: So LMR and GO, as in **Ax** and most C mss.; beta2 and CF have the simple present tense, as in some of the P family of C.

11 **sire**: So **AC**, though omitted by alpha.

11 **is**: Certainly **Bx**, though omitted by GOF and **AC**.

11 **þis**: So **AC**. R has *þe* and F *þat*.

16 **lerynge**: The beta reading (though M is a correction), with the late texts CrG altering as usual to *lerneing*. But alpha also has *lernyng*. The better C mss. have *leryng*.

Is a wys kniȝte with-al · sire Inwitte he hatte
And hath fyue feyre sones · bi his first wyf
20   Sire sewel and saywel · and *herewel / sire herewel* þe hende
Sire worche wel wyth þine hande · a wiȝte man of strengthe
And sire godfrey gowel · gret lordes for-sothe
Þise fyue ben sette · to saue þis lady anima
Tyl kynde come or sende [·] to saue hir for euere

25   ¶ What kynnes thyng is kynde quod I · canstow me telle

¶ Kynde quod witte is a creatour · of alle kynnes þinges
Fader and fourmour · of al þat euere was maked
And þe gret god [·] þat gynnynge had neuere
Lorde of lyf and of lyȝte · of lysse and of peyne
30   Angeles and al þing [·] aren at his wille
Ac man is hym moste lyke · of marke and of schafte
For þorugh þe worde þat he spake · wexen forth bestes
Dixit & facta sunt

¶ And made man likkest · to hym-self one   id est adam
35   And Eue of his ribbe-bon · with-outen eny mene
For he was synguler hym-self · and seyde faciamus
As who seith more mote here-to · þan my worde one
My myȝte mote helpe · now with my speche

---

20 **herewel / sire herewel**: Beta is supported by **Ax**, but alpha's addition of *sire* is also in **Cx**. Beta alliterates aaa/bb, alpha aaa/abb.

22 **gret lordes**: Beta's plural is supported by **AC** against the sg. in alpha.

23 **fyue**: F's *sixe* is from **A**; it includes the constable. **Cx** has five.

23 **þis lady**: Alpha drops *lady*, with F rewriting the b-verse. **Cx** *for to saue Anima* may offer slight support for R's reading. (**Ax** reads *to saue þe castel*.)

24 **saue hir for euere**: Agreement of beta and R confirms this as the **Bx** reading even if corrupt. F's *kepen hire hym-selue* is the **AC** reading, taken by F from his **A** ms.

26 **a**: Clearly established for **Bx**, though omitted by **Cx** and most **A** mss. KD record it as omitted in MR, but in both it is erased. Misunderstanding in **Bx** may have been caused, or further compounded, by reading *creatour* as *creature* (as in HmCO), though the spelling of the two words is often confused; see *MED creatour* and *creature*.

28 **And**: Beta1 reads *And þat is*, supported by **Ax**. M reads *And þis is*. But L originally agreed with R before correcting to the beta1 reading. F rewrites the a-verse. **Cx** rewrites as *The which is*.

29 **lysse**: Alpha spoils alliteration with *blisse*, as does the corrector in M. The two late texts CrG adopt the easier reading to avoid the obsolete synonym.

31 **hym moste**: Alpha reverses, but beta's order is supported by **AC**. From here to the end of the passus C is rewritten or heavily revised.

32 F follows with three unique lines, the third of which is based on K.10.34, and omits Bx.9.33.

34 **id est adam**: This gloss appears above the line in LM, and was incorporated into the text in CrHmF. It was therefore presumably a feature of the archetypal text. In R *man* is an addition in a second hand, perhaps indicating the scribe's confusion.

36 **and**: R (= alpha?) omits, and F has *he*. The passage is not in **AC**.

37 **seith**: CrCGR have subjunctive *sey*. The line is not in **AC**.

Riȝte as a lorde sholde make lettres · and hym lakked parchemyn
40   Þough he couth write neuere so wel · ȝif he had no penne
Þe lettre for al þe lordship · I leue were neuere ymaked

¶ And so it semeth bi hym · as þe bible telleth
Þere he seyde [·] dixit & facta sunt
He moste worche with his worde · and his witte shewe
45   And in þis manere was man made · þorugh myȝte of god almiȝti
With his worde and werkemanschip · and with lyf to laste
And þus god gaf hym a goost · of þe godhed of heuene
And of his grete grace [·] graunted hym blisse
And þat is lyf þat ay shal last · to al [his] lynage after
50   And þat is þe castel þat kynde made · caro it hatte
And is as moche to mene · as man with a soule
And þat he wrouȝt with werke · and with worde bothe
Þorugh myȝte of þe maieste · man was ymaked

¶ Inwit and alle wittes [·] closed ben þer-inne
55   For loue of þe lady anima · þat lyf is ynempned
Ouer-al in mannes body · he walketh and wandreth
Ac in þe herte is hir home · and hir moste reste
Ac Inwitte is in þe hed · and to the herte he loketh
What anima is lief or loth · he lat hir at his wille
60   For after þe grace of god · þe grettest is Inwitte

¶ Moche wo worth þat [wiȝte] · þat mys-reuleth his Inwitte
And þat be glotouns globbares · her god is her wombe
Quorum deus venter est
For þei seruen sathan · her soule shal he haue

---

42 **bible**: Beta4 has *book*.

43 **dixit & facta sunt**: (Psalm 148.5), repeating l. 33. L punctuates after *dixit*, but the punctuation after *seyde* in other mss. is more appropriate. F's *faciamus hominem ad ymaginem &c* (Gen.1.26), is from **A** (K.10.41a), where it follows the line equivalent to **Bx**.9.53. Cf. also **Bx**.9.36.

49 **his**: Lost in beta though independently restored by W on grounds of sense (Cr adds *our* instead). Alpha is supported by **Ax**.

52 **worde**: Alpha's *his word(es)* is not supported by **Ax**.

56 **he**: "she". See Introduction, p. 17.

57 **Ac**: Supported by LO and alpha (since F alters to his usual *But*), and by **Ax** (K.10.45). After this line **AC** offer only sporadic correspondences with **Bx** until l. 191.

58 **he**: Omitted by CrR.

59 **lat**: The variants confirm this as a form of "leads".

61 **wiȝte**: Though not an unusual word, *wiȝte* is sporadically replaced by *man* (e.g. **Bx**.P.208 (R), 5.118 (F), 8.53 (Hm), 8.73 (O)). Alpha's alliterative pattern is aaa/xa (on /w/); beta's *man* gives the standard alliterative pattern aa/ax (on /m/). **Cx** does not help to establish the reading, but indicates dissatisfaction with whatever it was, reversing the b-verse: "And moche wo worth hym þat inwit myspeneth" (RK.10.175).

64 **soule**: The reading of LMR is enough to establish **Bx** against the more obvious plural in other mss. Cf. the distributive sg. again in the next line.

65 Þat liueth synful lyf here · her soule is liche þe deuel
    And alle þat lyuen good lyf · aren like god almiȝti
    Qui manet in caritate in deo manet &c

    ¶ Allas þat drynke shal for-do · þat god dere bouȝte
    And doth god forsaken hem · þat shope [hem] to his liknesse
70 Amen dico vobis nescio vos · & alibi et dimisi eos secundum desideria
        eorum

    ¶ Foles þat fauten Inwitte · I fynde þat holicherche
    Shulde fynden hem þat hem faute[th] · and faderelees children
    And wydwes þat han nouȝte wher-with · to wynnen hem her fode
    Madde men and maydenes · þat helplees were
75 Alle þise lakken Inwitte · and lore bihoueth

    ¶ Of þis matere I myȝte · make a longe tale
    And fynde fele witnesses · amonges þe foure doctours
    And þat I lye nouȝt of þat I lere þe · luke bereth witnesse

    ¶ Godfader and godmoder · þat sen her godchildren
80 At myseise and at mischief · and mowe hem amende
    Shal haue penaunce in purgatorie · but ȝif þei hem helpe
    For more bilongeth to þe litel barne · ar he þe lawe knowe
    Þan nempnyng of a name · and he neuere þe wiser
    Shulde no crystene creature · crien atte ȝate
85 Ne faille payn ne potage · and prelates did as þei shulden
    A Iuwe wolde nouȝte se a Iuwe · go iangelyng for defaute
    For alle þe moebles on þis molde · and he amende it miȝte

    ¶ Allas þat a crestene creature · shal be vnkynde til an other
    Sitthen Iuwes þat we iugge · Iudas felawes

---

66 **like**: The agreement of LR supports this against *like to* in beta1. Both locutions are used elsewhere. M originally read *vnto*, corrected to *to*, and F has *lyk after*.

69 **shope hem**: Beta's *he shope* gives an unmetrical b-verse (x x / x x / x), and the alpha reading is syntactically difficult enough to have generated it. However, KD, p. 143, ascribe the alpha reading to "parallelism induced by preceding *forsaken hem*".

70 **& alibi et dimisi eos secundum desideria eorum**: This (Psalm 80.13) is not in alpha: in fact F drops both quotations. It finds it way into **Cx** at this point (RK.10.165a).

72 **hem** (2): Not in R (F is different).

72 **fauteth**: So CGO and R. LMW have the past tense, but the present seems required by sense.

77 **witnesses**: The form in alpha and CGO is also plural. See note to **Bx**.2.150.

78 **of þat**: Lost in alpha, and F further abbreviates to make sense of the omission.

80 **At** (1): The alpha reading is uncertain: R *Þat is*, F *In*.

80 **at** (2): Not in MCGOF.

84 CO and alpha have a paraph.

85 **Ne ... ne**: Alpha has *And ... and*.

87 **moebles**: HmR *nobles* is a good example of coincidental error.

88 **til**: So LWHmR against *to* in others.

90 Ayther of hem helpeth other · of þat þat hym nedeth
Whi nel we cristene · of cristes good be as kynde
As Iuwes þat ben owre lores-men · shame to vs alle
Þe comune for her vnkyndenesse · I drede me shul abye

¶ Bisschopes shul be blamed · for beggeres sake
95 He is worse þan Iudas · þat ʒiueth a iaper siluer
And biddeth þe begger go · for his broke clothes
Proditor est prelatus cum Iuda · qui patrimonium cristi minus distribuit //
&& alibi
Perniciosus dispensator est · qui res pauperum cristi inutiliter consumit
He doth nouʒt wel þat doth þus · ne drat nouʒt god almiʒty
100 Ne loueth nouʒt salamones sawes · þat sapience tauʒte
Inicium sapiencie timor domini ·

¶ Þat dredeth god he doth wel · þat dredeth hym for loue
And nouʒt for drede of veniaunce · doth þer-fore þe bettere
He doth best þat with-draweth hym · by day and bi nyʒte
105 To spille any speche [·] or any space of tyme
Qui offendit in verbo in omnibus est reus

¶ Lesyng of tyme · treuthe wote þe sothe
Is moste yhated vp erthe · of hem þat beth in heuene
And sitthe to spille speche · þat spyre is of grace
110 And goddes gleman · and a game of heuene
Wolde neuere þe faithful fader · his fithel were vntempred
Ne his gleman a gedelyng · a goer to tauernes

---

90 **Ayther**: Alpha's reading was evidently that of R, *Þat ayther helpeth other of hem þat hym nedeth*, with F making a typical attempt to repair the line. See KD p. 142.

90 **hym**: Beta2, G and F repeat *hem* from the a-verse.

91 Alpha has a paraph.

91 **kynde**: The M corrector uniquely adds *willed* at the end of the line, perhaps to correct the alliterative pattern. See Duggan, *YLS* 1 (1987), 66.

92 **shame**: R (= alpha?) has *to schame*, with F altering to *It is shame*.

100 **Ne**: Beta2 and F repeat *He* from the previous line.

102–3 Beta4 abbreviates these two lines and runs them together.

103 **And nouʒt for drede**: Alpha is derived from the previous b-verse.

103 **doth þer-fore**: Following on from its error in the a-verse, alpha reads *to do*.

106 **verbo**: This is probably **Bx** since it is the reading of LR and probably original M, corrected to *vno* in conformity with James 2.10. Beta1 also has *vno*, while F includes both words, *vno verbo*. The reading *verbo* is presumably Langland's adaptation of the quotation for the context, with some scribes reverting to the biblical text. (The line in L is marked for correction, perhaps significantly.) The quotation also occurs at **Bx**.11.326, where no ms. has *verbo*. While *verbo* must have been present in **Bx**, it may alternatively have been in the form of an interlinear gloss to *vno*. See Donaldson (1955), 198–9; Schmidt (1995), 379–80; Burrow (2003), 191–2.

108 **vp**: Supported by LCR and original M. For prepositional *vp*, cf. **Bx**.5.425.

109 **spyre**: "offspring", as in L, beta4 and R, evidently puzzled other scribes.

¶ To alle trew tidy men · þat trauaille desyren
Owre lorde loueth hem and lent · loude other stille
115   Grace to go to hem · and agon her lyflode
Inquirentes autem dominum non minuentur omni bono

¶ Trewe wedded libbing folk · in þis worlde is dowel
For þei mote worche & wynne · and þe worlde susteyne
For of her kynde þei come · þat confessoures ben nempned
120   Kynges and kniʒtes · kayseres and cherles
Maydenes and martires · out of o man come
Þe wyf was made þe weye · for to help worche
And þus was wedloke ywrouʒt · with a mene persone
First bi þe faderes wille · and þe frendes conseille
125   And sytthenes bi assent of hem-self · as þei two myʒte acorde
And thus was wedloke ywrouʒte · and god hym-self it made
In erthe þe heuene is · hym-self was þe witnesse

¶ Ac fals folke [and] faithlees · theues and lieres
Wastoures and wrecches · out of wedloke I trowe
130   Conceyued ben in yuel tyme · as caym was on Eue
Of such synful shrewes · þe sauter maketh mynde
Concepit in dolore et peperit iniquitatem &c
And alle þat come of þat caym [·] come to yuel ende
For god sent to seem · and seyde bi an angel
135   Þyne issue in þyne issue · I wil þat þei be wedded
And nouʒt þi kynde with caymes · ycoupled ne yspoused

¶ ʒet some aʒein þe sonde [·] of owre saueoure of heuene

---

115 **to hem:** R has *to hem tille* and F has *hem to*. The reversal could be right.

115 **agon:** "earn". W restores the more "correct" form *ofgon* (OE *ofgan*).

119 **þei:** Alpha has the form *he*. See Introduction, p. 18.

120 **cherles:** F's *clerkys* is the A reading (K.10.137).

122 **weye,** "man, husband". Perhaps only F understood the word, for the usual spelling in L and elsewhere is *wye*. However C mss. regularly spell it *wey(e)*.

123b–26a Alpha omits as a result of homoarchy (*And þus was wedloke ywrouʒt* 123a, 126a).

127 **þe heuene is:** The syntax of the a-verse, "the heaven (of wedlock) is on earth", puzzled alpha (*þere / here heuen is*) and CrW (*and in heuene*). M is altered to CrW's reading.

127 **was þe:** WCF have *bereþ*, attracted to the common collocation (**Bx**.2.39, 7.53, 7.93, etc.).

128 **and:** Beta omits. Alpha is supported by **Ax** (K.10.139).

130 **yuel:** Certainly the **Bx** reading, though **Ax** has alliterating *cursid*.

132 **in dolore:** The beta reading is that of **Cx** (RK.10.212a) while alpha (and Hm by correction) have *dolorem*, as do some A mss. (K.10.150). The adaptation of scriptural *dolorem* (Job 15.35, Psalms 7.15) on the model of l. 130 *in yuel tyme* suggests scribal hypercorrection in alpha, as demonstrated directly in Hm. See Alford (1992), 61–2.

136 **caymes:** Alpha has *caym*, but the possessive is supported by **Ax** (K.10.158).

137 **some:** The reading of **Bx**; Cr has *Sem* on the basis of l. 134, and M is corrected to that reading.

Caymes kynde & his kynde · coupled togideres
Tyl god wratthed for her werkis · and suche a worde seyde
140 Þat I maked man · now it me athynketh
Penitet me fecisse hominem

¶ And come to Noe anon · and bad hym nou3t lette
Swithe go shape a shippe · of shides and of bordes
Þiself and þi sones three · and sithen 3owre wyues
145 Buske 3ow to þat bote · and bideth 3e þer-inne
Tyl fourty dayes be fulfilde · þat flode haue ywasshen
Clene awey þe cursed blode · þat caym hath ymaked

¶ Bestes þat now ben · shulle banne þe tyme
Þat euere þat cursed caym · come on þis erthe
150 Alle shal deye for his dedes · bi dales and hulles
And þe foules þat fleeghen · for[th] with other bestes
Excepte oneliche [·] of eche kynde a couple
Þat in þi shyngled shippe · shul ben ysaued
Here abou3t þe barne · þe belsyres gultes
155 And alle for her forfadres · þei ferden þe worse
Þe gospel is here-ageine · in o degre I fynde
Filius non portabit iniquitatem patris & pater non portabit iniquitatem
    filij &c ·

¶ Ac I fynde if þe fader [·] be false and a shrewe
Þat somdel þe sone · shal haue þe sires tacches

160 ¶ Impe on an ellerne · and if þine apple be swete
Mochel merueile me þynketh · & more of a schrewe
Þat bryngeth forth any barne · but if he be þe same
And haue a sauoure after þe sire · selde seestow other
Numquam colligitur de spinis vuas · nec de tribulis fycus

---

139 **for**: The reading of L, beta2 and R; it is perhaps harder than MGOF *with*, which however has some support from **Ax** *was wroþ wiþ* (K.10.161).

140 **athynketh**: LMCO. It may have given rise to R's *þinketh* and the commoner *forþynkeþ* as in WHmCrGF. The form is secure at **Bx**.18.92. Yet **Ax** has *forþinkeþ* (K.10.164). We follow copy-text.

146 **ywasshen**: Beta is supported by AC against alpha's *Iwasted*.

150 **and**: So M and R (=alpha?), supported by **Ax** and most C mss. against *and bi* in L and beta1. F drops the line.

151 **forth**: L has *for*.

153 **þi**: R has *þis* (F omits the line). **Ax** has *þe*; **Cx** supports beta.

157 **& pater non portabit iniquitatem filij &c**: Ezek. 18.20. Alpha abbreviates. We follow copy-text, though it is quite likely that **Bx** ended the quotation at *patris*, as **Cx** does, and as at **Bx**.10.119.

160 **on**: So beta, though Hm has *vpon*, C *in* and G *off*. Alpha has *vp-on*. The line is not in **AC**.

164 **colligitur de spinis vuas**: So LM and R, therefore **Bx**. F has the Vulgate reading "colligunt de spinis uvas" (Matt. 7.19). Other scribes correct to a grammatical reading in which *vua* is subject of *colligitur* (beta2 and corrected M), or *vuas* object of *colligimus* (CGO).

165 [¶] And þus þourw cursed caym · cam care vppon erthe
     And al for þei wrou3t wedlokes · a3ein goddis wille
     For-þi haue þei maugre for here mariages · þat marye so her childeren
     For some as I se now · soth forto telle
     For coueitise of catel [·] vnkyndeliche ben wedded
170 As careful concepcioun [·] cometh of suche mariages
     As bifel of þe folke · þat I bifore of tolde

     ¶ For goode shulde wedde goode · þough hij no good hadde   id est boni,
     I am via & veritas seith cryst · I may auaunce alle   id est bonas

     ¶ It is an oncomely couple · bi cryst as me þinketh
175 To 3yuen a 3onge wenche · to an olde feble
     Or wedden any widwe · for welth of hir goodis
     Þat neuere shal barne bere · but if it be in armes
     Many a peire sithen þe pestilence · han pli3t h[e]m togideres
     Þe fruit þat þei brynge forth · aren foule wordes
180 In ialousye ioyeles · and ianglyng on bedde
     Haue þei no children but cheste · an choppyng hem bitwene
     And þough þei don hem to donmowe · but if þe deuel help

---

165 ¶: There is no paraph in L, but the line appears at the top of the leaf and the rubricator probably missed it. WHmR have a paraph and M a line break.

167 for: Supported by LMR. Other mss. have *of*.

167 þat marye so: R has *as men maryen now*; F rewrites.

170 of suche mariages: R's *to þat mariages* presumably represents alpha, with F altering for sense.

171 þe: Beta is supported by Ax (K.10.185) against alpha's *þat*.

172–3 Both lines are omitted in alpha skipping from paraph to paraph (though R has an erased line after l. 171). They are not present in Ax but are transmitted to Cx (RK.10.254–5). See Hanna (1996), 217.

172 ¶: The paraph, in L alone, is perhaps not archetypal, yet eyeskip from paraph to paraph would account for the loss of ll. 172–3 in alpha. See Burrow (2010), 24–6.

172 goode (1) and (2): Glossed *id est boni* and *id est bonas* above the line in LM in the main hand, suggesting that this was a feature of beta. Although the line is not in alpha, we take this to be derived from Bx and include the glosses in the text. Cf. the gloss above l. 34.

174 an oncomely: L originally wrote *an comely*, but the line is noted for correction and then corrected. F also has *an komely*. M omitted the adjective altogether, then correcting *a* to *an vncomely* above the line.

174 cryst: Alpha has *Ihesus*, but beta is supported by Ax and by the alliteration.

177 if: As in LCrWCOR, though omitted by MHmG (F rewrites) and Ax.

178 hem: L's form *hom* is perhaps a miswriting; the scribe uses it nowhere else.

180 The line is omitted by alpha, but is in AC.

181 cheste: "strife". Beta is supported by AC and alliteration against alpha's synonym *iangelynge*.
181 an: "and".

181 choppyng: "striking". So LCGO. CrW read *clappyng* and Hm *carpynge*. M is revised to *chidynge*. Alpha was probably even more confused, since R has *gaying* (sic), and F omits altogether. AC have *choppes*.

182 LC have a paraph, with a new line-group in M, but it interrupts the argument.

182–4 Beta's readings of these lines on the Dunmow flitch are supported by AC. Lines 182b–4 in RF are clearly scribal replacements. Perhaps they were damaged in alpha and were invented

To folwen after þe flicche · fecche þei it neuere
And but þei bothe be forsworne · þat bacoun þei tyne

185 ¶ For-þi I conseille alle crystene · coueite nouȝt be wedded
For coueitise of catel · ne of kynrede riche
Ac maydenes and maydenes · macche ȝow togideres
Widwe[r]s and widw[e]s · worcheth þe same
For no londes but for loue · loke ȝe be wedded
190 And þanne gete ȝe þe grace of god · and good ynogh to lyue with

¶ And euery maner seculer [·] þat may nouȝt continue
Wysly go wedde · and war hym fro synne
For leccherye in likyng · is lymeȝerde of helle
Whiles þow art ȝonge · and þi wepne kene
195 Wreke þe with wyuynge · ȝif þow wil ben excused
Dum sis vir fortis · ne des tua robora scortis
Scribitur in portis · meretrix est ianua mortis

¶ Whan ȝe haue wyued bewar · and worcheth in tyme
Nouȝt as Adam & Eue · whan caym was engendred
200 For in vntyme trewli · bitwene man & womman
Ne shulde no bourde on bedde be · but if þei bothe were clene
Bothe of lyf and of soule · and in parfyte charitee

---

independently by R and F, but this is unprecedented behaviour for R. Furthermore, although
they are independent, there are enough similarities to suggest a common original. 182b *to
fecche hom here bakon* (R), *& fecche þere bakoun* (F) must be alpha, and it signals the disruption.
183 is quite different in the two mss., but similarities in 184 are *þus þei lyuen in* (R), *lyven þus
in* (F), and *þe deuel* (R), *þe develys* (F).

185 **be**: MCrR read *to be*. AC mss. vary similarly, but while **Ax** is perhaps the latter, **Cx** is
certainly the former.

187 **macche**: Beta, supported by **Ax**. F's *marye* probably reflects dissatisfaction with alpha's
synonym *make* (as in R), yet it is the reading of **Cx**.

188 **Widwers and widwes**: Alpha's word-order has the support of **Ax** and the P family of C,
though the X family has beta's order.

190 **þe grace**: Alpha has *grace*. In the absence of a parallel in **AC**, this could be right, but *þe*
is easily lost after *ȝe*.

191–9 These nine lines are omitted in alpha. They are not in **Ax**, but are transmitted to **Cx**.
The cause of the omission is not obvious. KD, p. 68, suggest eyeskip from *maner... man* 191 *to
man and womman* 200, but this is unconvincing, especially as *man* 191 is their emendation and
not **Bx**. More probably alpha jumped from the paraph at 191, since at the point of resumption
alpha (but not beta) has a paraph.

195 **wil**: For this subjunctive form in L, cf. **Bx**.6.232. The other beta witnesses have the indicative. The line is not in **A**, and the b-verse is revised in C.

200 Alpha has a paraph.

201 **bourde on bedde**: "fun in bed". Beta's reading is the basis of the RF variants, and is
supported by AC *bedbourd* (K.10.203; RK.10.290).

202 **and** (1): L has *& and* in error.

Þat ilke derne dede [·] do noman sholde
And if þei leden þus her lyf · it liked god almiȝti
205 For he made wedloke firste · and him-self it seide
Bonum est vt vnusquisque vxorem suam habeat propter fornicacionem

¶ And þei þat oþergatis ben geten · for gedelynges ben holden
A[nd] false folke fondelynges · faitoures and lyars
Vngracious to gete goode · or loue of þe poeple
210 Wandren and wasten · what þei cacche mowe
Aȝeines dowel þei don yuel · and þe deuel serue
And after her deth-day · shulle dwelle with þe same
But god gyue hem grace here · hem-self to amende

¶ Dowel my frende is · to don as lawe techeth
215 To loue þi frende and þi foo · leue me þat is dobet
To ȝiuen and to ȝemen · bothe ȝonge and olde
To helen and to helpen · is dobest of alle

¶ And [þus is] dowel to drede god · and dobet to suffre
And so cometh dobest of bothe · and bryngeth adoun þe mody
220 And þat is wikked wille · þat many werke shendeth
And dryueth away dowel · þorugh dedliche synnes

---

203 **sholde**: Beta has *ne sholde*, but **Cx** supports alpha (though F is revised) without *ne*. A mss. are divided. Beta needs to lengthen the b-verse as a result of placing the punctuation after *do* rather than before it. See Smith (2008), 90–1.

204 **liked**: The LR reading, supported by F's *wold lyke* against the present tense of other mss. The line is not in **AC**.

206 **propter fornicacionem**: Omitted in alpha, but beta is supported by **Cx**.

207 **¶**: The paraph is in LWHm, with a new line-group in M. In R the line is at the foot of the page.

208 **And**: Alpha is supported by **AC** against beta's *As*.

212 **þe same**: Beta is supported by **Ax**. R (= alpha?) repeats *þe deuel* from the previous line, with F, *here Mayster*, varying the expression. **Cx** has instead *dwellen shollen in helle*.

214–17 Lines omitted in alpha, skipping from *Dowel* to *dowel* and from paraph to paraph. Once again they are not in **Ax**, but are transmitted to **Cx**. Compare the same situation in Bx.9.172–3 and 191–9. In all three instances skipped paraphs are involved.

214 Scribes have understandable uncertainty about the placing of the mid-line punctus.

218 **And þus is dowel**: Alpha's word-order is supported by **Cx**. **Ax** has *Þanne is dowel*.

220 **werke**: Beta's distributive sg. is supported by **Ax**.

Passus 10

Passus decimus de visione & secundus de dowel

Thanne hadde witte a wyf · was hote dame studye
Þat lene was of lere · and of liche bothe
She was wonderly wroth · þat witte me þus tauȝte
And al starynge dame studye · sternelich seyde
5 Wel artow wyse quod she to witte · any wysdomes to telle
To flatereres or to folis · þat frantyk ben of wittes
And blamed hym and banned hym · and badde hym be stylle
With suche wise wordes · to wissen any sottes
And seyde noli mittere man · margerye perlis
10 Amanges hogges þat han · hawes at wille
Þei don but dryuele þer-on [·] draffe were hem leuere
Þan al þe precious perre · þat in paradys wexeth
I sey it bi suche quod she [·] þat sheweth bi her werkes
Þat hem were leuer londe · and lordship on erthe
15 Or ricchesse or rentis · and reste at her wille
Þan alle þe sothe sawes · þat salamon seyde euere

¶ Wisdome and witte now [·] is nouȝt worth a carse
But if it be carded with coueytise · as clotheres kemben here wolle
Who-so can contreue deceytes · an conspire wronges
20 And lede forth a loue-day · to latte with treuthe

---

1 **hote**: Alpha has *called* (R) or *klepid* (F), but beta is supported by **AC** (K.11.1; RK.11.1).
14 **on erthe**: Alpha reads *here*, but beta is supported by **Ax**. The line is rewritten in **Cx**.
15 In this passage F omits ll. 15 and 21–2, and supplies two spurious lines after l. 25.
18 **here**: Omitted by alpha and CGO, perhaps to lighten a heavy b-verse. It is supported by **Ax** and the X family of **C**, though the P family also omit it.
19 **an**: "and".
20 **to latte with**: R's *and letten þe* may be right; **Ax** has *to lette þe treuþe*, and cf. K.3.146 *& lettiþ þe treuþe*. On the other hand, "to hinder truth with (the loveday)" makes excellent and

He þat suche craftes can · to conseille is clepid
Þei lede lordes with lesynges · and bilyeth treuthe

¶ Iob þe gentel [·] in his gestes witnesseth
Þat wikked men þei welden · þe welthe of þis worlde
25 And þat þei ben lordes of eche a londe · þat oute of lawe libbeth
Quare impij viuunt bene est omnibus qui preuaricantur & inique agunt

¶ Þe sauter seyth þe same · bi suche þat don ille
Ecce ipsi peccatores habundantes in seculo optinuerunt diuicias
Lo seith holy letterrure [·] whiche lordes beth þis shrewes
30 Þilke þat god moste gyueth · leste good þei deleth
And moste vnkynde to þe comune · þat moste catel weldeth
Que perfecisti destruxerunt · iustus autem &c ·
Harlotes for her harlotrye · may haue of her godis
And iaperes and iogeloures · and iangelers of gestes

35 ¶ Ac he þat hath holy writte · ay in his mouth
And can telle of Tobye · and of þe twelue apostles
Or prechen of þe penaunce · þat pilat wrou3t
To Ihesu þe gentil · þat Iewes to-drowe
Litel is he loued · þat suche a lessoun scheweth
40 Or daunted or drawe forth · I do it on god hym-self

¶ But þo þat feynen hem folis · and with faityng libbeth
A3ein þe lawe of owre lorde · and lyen on hem-selue
Spitten and spewen · and speke foule wordes
Drynken and dryuelen · and do men for to gape
45 Lickne men and lye on hem · þat leneth hem no 3iftes
Þei conne namore mynstralcye · ne musyke men to glade
Than Munde þe mylnere · of multa fecit deus
Ne were here vyle harlotrye · haue god my treuthe
Shulde neuere Kyng ne kni3t · ne chanoun of seynt Poules

---

slightly more difficult sense, and seems to be the basis of the revision in **Cx**: "And lette with a loueday treuthe and bigile" (RK.11.17).

24 **þei**: Omitted in HmCGOF, though Hm probably included it before erasure. The line is not in **AC**.

25 **of** (1): Hm and R (= alpha?) have *in*; F rewrites. The line is not in **AC**.

28 **diuicias**: Omitted in alpha. C mss. end with *peccatores* or *habundantes*.

30 **god moste**: So LG and alpha. M has *moost good god*; O has *god most good* which is the reading of **Cx**. See next note.

30 **gyueth**: Alpha and C have *greueth*, which loses the sharp contrast with the b-verse. There seems to have been some confusion in **Bx** since, in revising the line for **Cx**, the poet had a text with both verbs, and recast to *Tho þat god most goed 3eueth greueth most riht and treuthe* (RK.11.25). Schmidt restores **B** by including both verbs, but the resultant a-verse seems impossibly heavy; see Schmidt (2008), 386–7. It may be that **Bx** wrote *greueth*, corrected to *gyueth* (in the margin?), with alpha following one and beta the other.

50   Ȝyue hem to her ȝeresȝiue · þe [worth] of a grote

 ¶ Ac murthe and mynstralcye · amonges men is nouthe
 Leccherye [and] losengerye · and loseles tales
 Glotonye and grete othes · þis murthe þei louieth

 ¶ Ac if þei carpen of cryst · þis clerkis and þis lewed
55   Atte mete in her murthes · whan mynstralles ben stille
 Þanne telleth þei of þe trinite · a tale other tweyne
 And bringen forth a balled resoun · and taken Bernard to witnesse
 And putten forth a presumpsioun · to preue þe sothe
 Þus þei dryuele at her deyse [·] þe deite to knowe
60   And gnawen god with þe gorge · whan her gutte is fulle

 ¶ Ac þe careful may crye · and carpen atte ȝate
 Bothe afyngred and a-thurst · and for chele quake
 Is none to nymen hym nere · his noye amende
 But heon on hym as an hounde · and hoten hym go þennes
65   Litel loueth he þat lorde · þat lent hym al þat blisse
 Þat þus parteth with þe pore · a parcel whan hym nedeth
 Ne were mercy in mene men · more þan in riche
 Mendinantz meteles · miȝte go to bedde
 God is moche in þe gorge · of þise grete maystres
70   Ac amonges mene men · his mercy and his werkis
 And so seith þe sauter · I haue yseye it ofte
 Ecce audiuimus eam in effrata · inuenimus eam in campis silue

---

50 **worth**: Alpha is closer to the **Ax** reading *value* (whence perhaps GO), and the alliteration aaa/xx is satisfactory. Beta's *ȝifte* is prompted by alliterative attraction to *ȝeresȝiue*; for the collocation see **Bx**.3.101 and 13.195. The line is not in **Cx**.

52 **and** (1): Supported by **Ax**, but lost in L and (coincidentally?) in CrW.

53 **murthe**: Secure for **Bx**. Both M and F alter for the alliteration. **Ax** has a different b-verse.

54 **¶**: The paraph is in beta and F.

55 **murthes**: The plural is secure for **Bx**, though beta2 shares the sg. with **Ax**.

60 **gutte is fulle**: So LR, and probably M before correction. **AC** read *guttis fullen*, "are full", as do WHm.

62 **a-thurst**: CrW alter to *a-furst* for the alliteration; it is the dominant form in C mss., while A has a different a-verse. The collocation with *afyngred* is repeated at **Bx**.14.174, where most mss. have *A-fyrst*.

63 **nere**: Presumably the meaningless **Bx** reading is a corruption of **Ax** *in ne*, which the M corrector adopts by conjecture or contamination as *In nor*. This and the next line are rewritten in C.

63 **amende**: It is likely that F and beta supply *to* before *amende* in the b-verse to make some sense of the line, and that R's omission (as in **Ax**) represents **Bx**.

64 **heon**: "shout out" (*MED heuen* v.(3)); the reading of L, beta4 and alpha. The commonplace variant *hunten* in Beta2 (CrWHm), with M corrected to that reading, is less appropriate.

69 **gorge**: Alpha has the pl., but beta's sg. is supported by AC (K.11.44; RK.11.39)

71 **yseye**: For the same b-verse see **Bx**.11.455.

72 **eam** (1 & 2): So **AC** against alpha's *eum*. At **Bx**.15.511 (R only), R again has *eum*. See Alford (1992), 64, and Schmidt (1995), 443.

Clerkes and other kynnes men · carpen of god faste
And haue [hym] moche in þe mouthe · ac mene men in herte

75   ¶ Freres and faitoures · han founde suche questiouns
To plese with proude men · sithen þe *pestilence tyme / pestilence*
And prechen at seint poules · for pure enuye of clerkis
Þat folke is nouȝte fermed in þe feith · ne fre of her goodes
Ne sori for her synnes · so is pryde waxen
80   In religioun and in alle þe rewme · amonges riche & pore
Þat preyeres haue no power · þ[is] pestilence[s] to lette
[For god is def now-a-days . and deyneth not vs to here
Þat gerles for here gyltes . he for-grynt hem alle]
And ȝette þe wrecches of þis worlde · is none ywar bi other
85   Ne for drede of þe deth · withdrawe nouȝt her pryde
Ne beth plentyuous to þe pore · as pure charite wolde
But in gaynesse and in glotonye · for-glotten her goode hem-selue
And breken nouȝte to þe beggar · as þe boke techeth
Frange esurienti panem tuum &c ·
90   And þe more he wynneth and welt · welthes & ricchesse
And lordeth in londes · þe lasse good he deleth

¶ Thobye te[ch]eth ȝow nouȝt so · take hede ȝe riche
How þe boke bible · of hym bereth witnesse

---

73 **other kynnes men**: So beta, with alpha dropping *kynnes*. **Ax** has *kete men*, while **Cx** has
knyhtes. Perhaps alpha reproduces **Bx** which has avoided the rare adjective *kete*, with beta then
supplying the alliteration.

74 **hym**: Not in LHm. Easily lost, of course, and four **A** mss. omit it, as does the X family of C.

76 **pestilence tyme / pestilence**: Alpha omits *tyme*. Beta is supported by **Ax**; however **Cx**
reads *pestelences*. Cf. l. 81 below.

79 **is pryde**: Beta's word-order is supported by **Cx**. Lines 77–110 are not in **A**.

81 **þis pestilences**: Beta has *þe pestilence*, presumably understanding the noun as sg., although
the form can also represent the plural (see *MED pestilence*). Alpha and **Cx** have the demonstrative article followed by an unambiguous plural. Cf. l. 76 and note.

82–3 These two lines are in alpha and **Cx**. KD, p. 66, suggest that beta dropped them through
eyeskip (*Þat ... Þat*); censorship is another possible explanation.

82 **not vs to here**: The readings diverge in the b-verse. Most unusually, F is supported by **Cx**,
and so we adopt its reading. It must be observed, however, that R offers the less commonplace
reading. In F *deinen* has the sense "condescend"; in R, *deyneth his heres to opne*, it means
"disdain". See *MED deinen* v.(1) & (2) for these two related verbs, and cf. note to **Bx**.6.315.
The most authoritative C mss. read *deyneth nat vs to here* (i.e. *deinen* (1)) but as many omit *nat*
(i.e. *deinen* (2)), allowing for the possibility that **Bx** was also without *not*.

83 **gerles**: R only. F's *gystys* is probably a misreading. **Cx** has *gode men* instead.

83 **for-grynt**: "grinds to pieces". The compound is not recorded in *MED*; **Cx** has *togrynt*.

87 **in** (2): LCrWHmR; others omit. C mss. divide similarly.

90 **ricchesse**: The form may be sg. or plural. For other examples see notes to **Bx**.3.23, 19.73.

91 **And**: Beta is supported by **Cx** against alpha's *Euere as he*.

92 **techeth**: Alpha is supported by **Cx** against beta's *telleth*.

93 **boke bible**: For the expression, altered by CrHm, beta4 and F, see **Bx**.7.166 and note.

Si tibi sit copia habundanter tribue · si autem exiguum illud impertir[e]
[libenter stude]

95 Who-so hath moche spene manliche · so meneth Thobie
And who-so litel weldeth · reule him þer-after
For we haue no lettre of owre lyf · how longe it shal dure
Suche lessounes lordes shulde · louie to here
And how he myȝte moste meyne [·] manliche fynde
100 Nouȝt to fare as a fitheler or a frere · forto seke festes
Homelich at other mennes house[s] · and hatyen her owne
Elyng is þe halle · vche daye in þe wyke
Þere þe lorde ne þe lady [·] liketh nouȝte to sytte
Now hath vche riche a reule · to eten bi hym-selue
105 In a pryue pa[r]loure · for pore mennes sake
Or in a chambre with a chymneye · and leue þe chief halle
Þat was made for meles · men to eten Inne
And al to spare to spille · þat spende shal an other

¶ I haue yherde hiegh men [·] etyng atte table
110 Carpen as þei clerkes were · of cryste and of his miȝtes
And leyden fautes vppon þe fader · þat fourmed vs alle
And carpen aȝeine clerkes · crabbed wordes
Whi wolde owre saueoure suffre [·] suche a worme in his blisse
Þat bigyled þe womman · and þe man after
115 Þorw whiche wyles and wordes · þei went[en] to helle
And al her sede for here synne · þe same deth suffred

¶ Here lyeth ȝowre lore · þise lordes gynneth dispute
Of þat ȝe clerkes vs kenneth · of cryst by þe gospel
Filius non portabit iniquitatem patris &c ·
120 Whi shulde we þat now ben · for þe werkes of Adam
Roten and to-rende · resoun wolde it neuere

---

94 **impertire libenter stude**: Alpha's form of the infinitive verb is supported by most C mss.,
and the order of the last two words is that of **Cx**. Alford (1992), 64, quotes the last three
words in the verse from Tob.4.9 in the form *impertiri stude libenter*, as in beta.

98 LWCR punctuate after *shulde*; MHmO after *lordes*. F rewrites. Lines 95–110 are not in
AC, and ll. 111–45 are not in C.

100 Beta has a paraph, but it interrupts the argument.

100 LMWOF punctuate the line before *forto*, with *forto* supplying the long dip in the b-verse.
CrHmGR, punctuating after *fitheler*, have *to* instead.

101 **houses**: LF have *house*, probably in error, though possibly derived from the OE unchanged
plural; see *MED*. Elsewhere both scribes use the marked plural.

115 **wenten**: Only LCr have *went*; WHmG have *wente*, the others *wenten*. The second syllable
avoids a b-verse stressed x / x / x. See Introduction, p. 33.

118 **ȝe**: So LMOR against *þe* in CrWHmCGF, which misses the switch back to reported
speech.

121 **to-rende**: LW (*to-rent* Hm); the most probable origin of the variants *rende* MCGOF, *to
reade* Cr, and *to-reue* R.

Vnusquisque portabit onus suum &c
Suche motyues þei moeue · þis maistres in her glorie
And maken men in mysbileue · þat muse moche on her wordes

125 ¶ Ymaginatyf her-after-ward · shal answere to ʒowre purpos

¶ Augustyne to suche argueres · he telleth hem þis teme
Non plus sapere quam oportet
Wilneth neuere to wite · whi þat god wolde
Suffre sathan [·] his sede to bigyle
130 Ac bileue lelly · in þe lore of holicherche
And preye hym of pardoun · and penaunce in þi lyue
And for his moche mercye · to amende ʒow here
For alle þat wilneth to wyte · þe weyes of god almiʒty
I wolde his eye were in his ers · and his fynger after
135 Þat euere wilneth to wite · whi þat god wolde
Suffre sathan · his sede to bigile
Or iudas [þe iuwe] · ihesu bytraye
Al was as [he] wolde · lorde yworschiped be þow
And al worth as þow wolte · what-so we dispute

140 ¶ And þo þat vseth þis hauelounes · to blende mennes wittes
What is dowel fro dobet · now def mote he worthe
Sitthe he wilneth to wyte · whiche þei ben [alle]
But if he lyue in þe lyf · þat longeth to dowel
For I dar ben his bolde borgh · þat dobet wil he neuere
145 Þeigh dobest drawe on hym [·] day after other

---

122 **portabit onus suum**: Alpha has the order *honus suum portabit* cited by Alford (1992), 64, from Gal.6.5.

126 **Augustyne**: The form of the name in **Bx** is not determinable. As at l. 485, LM (so beta?) have the full form, but alpha has the more usual *Austyn*. **Ax** has a quite different line with the short form. Cf. note to l. 485 below.

126 **he … hem**: The two words are omitted by WCGO. Cr omits *hem*.

133 Hm and alpha have a paraph.

133 **weyes**: The reading of LCrWHm and alpha, as well as the **Ax** reading. M, joined by GO and a 16th-century **A** ms., have the reading *whyes* (cf. *whi* in 135). The adoption of the latter reading by K (see K, pp. 163–4), KD and Schmidt is a classic case of modern sensibilities overcoming the logic of attestation. Contrast **Bx**.12.238, where the noun *whyes* is secure, despite variants.

137 **þe iuwe**: Alpha supported by **Ax** against beta's *to þe iuwes*.

138 **he wolde**: Alpha supported by **Ax** against L's *þow wolde*, which the other beta scribes correct to *þow woldest*.

140 **blende**: "mislead". Cr, beta4 and F have the related verb *blinde*.

142 **alle**: Referring to the triad including *dobest* as in l. 145 below. Alpha is supported by **Ax** against beta's *bothe*, which does, however, logically follow from the previous line.

144 **bolde**: Dropped by alpha, but supported by **Ax**.

¶ And whan þat witte was ywar [·] what dame studye tolde
He bicome so confus · he couth nouȝte loke
And as doumbe a[s] deth · and drowe hym arrere

¶ And for no carpyng I couth after · ne knelyng to þe grounde
150   I myȝte gete no greyne · of his grete wittis
But al laughyng he louted · and loked vppon studye
In signe þat I shulde · biseche hir of grace

¶ And whan I was war of his wille · to his wyf gan I loute
And seyde mercy madame [·] ȝowre man shal I worthe
155   As longe as I lyue · bothe late & rathe
Forto / And forto worche ȝowre wille · þe while my lyf dureth
With þat ȝe kenne me kyndely · to knowe what is dowel

¶ For þi mekenesse man quod she · and for þi mylde speche
I shal kenne þe to my cosyn · þat clergye is hoten
160   He hath wedded a wyf · with-Inne þis syx monethes
Is sybbe to þe seuene artz · scripture is hir name
Þei two as I hope · after my techyng
Shullen wissen þe to dowel · I dar [wel] vndertake

¶ Þanne was I also fayne · as foule of faire morwe
165   And gladder þan þe gleman · þat golde hath to ȝifte
And axed hir þe heighe weye · where þat clergye dwelte
And telle me some token quod I · for tyme is þat I wende

¶ Axe þe heighe waye quod she · hennes to suffre
Bothe wel & wo · ȝif þat þow wolt lerne
170   And ryde forth by ricchesse · ac rest þow nauȝt þerinne
For if þow couplest þe þer-with · to clergye comestow neuere

¶ And also þe likerouse launde · þat leccherye hatte
Leue hym on þi left halue · a large myle or more
Tyl þow come to a courte · kepe wel þi tonge
175   Fro lesynges and lither speche · and likerouse drynkes

---

146 **what**: Beta's reading has support from **Cx**, *what studie menede* (RK.11.81). Alpha's reading, *how dame studie tolde*, loses the b-verse alliteration which in **Ax** *how his wif tolde* (K.11.93) is carried by the noun.

156 **Forto / And forto**: Beta's reading is that of **Ax** (K.11.102) while alpha's *And forto* is that of **Cx** (RK.11.88)

163 **wel**: R's reading, which carries the alliteration, is that of **Ax**. That F agrees with beta in reading *it* probably indicates independent substitution, since the R scribe rarely corrects for alliteration. The line is not in **C**.

171 **clergye**: R's odd *cherche* probably represents alpha, with F varying further. Beta is supported by **AC**.

172 **hatte**: Beta's reading is confirmed by **Ax** against *is hote* in alpha.

173 **hym**: So LMHmR and **Ax**; unsurprisingly altered to *it* in other **B** mss.

Þanne shaltow se sobrete · and symplete of speche
Þat eche wiȝte be in wille · his witte þe to shewe
And þus shaltow come to clergye · þat can many þinges

¶ Saye hym þis signe · I sette hym to scole
180　And þat I grette wel his wyf · for I wrote hir many bokes
And sette hir to sapience · and to þe sauter glose
Logyke I lerned hir · and many other lawes
And alle þe musouns in mu[si]ke · I made hir to knowe

¶ Plato þe poete · I put hym fyrste to boke
185　Arestotle and *other moo / other* · to argue I tauȝte
Grammer for gerles · I garte first wryte
And bette hem with a baleis · but if þei wolde lerne
Of alkinnes craftes · I contreued toles
Of carpentrie of keruere[·] and compassed masouns
190　And lerned hem leuel and lyne · þough I loke dymme

¶ Ac theologie hath tened me · ten score tymes
The more I muse þereInne · þe mistier it semeth
And þe depper I deuyne · þe derker me it þinketh
It is no science for-sothe · forto sotyle Inne
195　A ful lethy þinge it were · ȝif þat loue nere
Ac for it let best by loue · I loue it þe bettre
For þere þat loue is leder · ne lacked neuere grace
Loke þow loue lelly · ȝif þe lyketh dowel
For dobet and dobest · ben of loues kynne

200　¶ In other science it seyth · I saye it in catoun

---

176 **speche:** Beta is supported by **Ax** against alpha's *berynge*.
179 **¶:** The paraph is in beta only. In R the line is at the foot of the page.
180 **grette:** The unambiguously past tense form is supported for **Bx** by LMOR. **Ax** has *grete* as does the P family of **C**, but the X family has *grette*.
181 **glose:** Hm (as well as BmBoCot) has the ppl. *glosyd*; this cannot be archetypal, even though AC both have *sauter yglosid*. Cf. **Bx.5.284.**
185 **other moo / other:** Beta has the former, alpha the latter. Beta's reading is that of **Ax**, while alpha's is that of **Cx**.
186 **wryte:** M and Beta2(CrWHm) have *to write*, as do a few mss. in all three versions.
189 **carpentrie of:** The **Bx** reading is also that of **Cx**. GF have the reading of **Ax**, *carpenteris &*.
191 **¶:** The paraph is in beta and F.
194 **sotyle:** Beta's reading is that of **Ax**, while the b-verse is rewritten in **Cx**. Alpha's reading *sauȝtele* (*MED* saughtelen) means "become reconciled, settle".
198 **Loke:** R's *Love* probably reflects an alpha error which F rewrites for sense.
198 **þe lyketh:** Alpha's *þow thenke* is an easy error, but (coincidentally?) it is shared with **Ax** (K.11.144), which itself is deficient in alliteration. The line is revised in **Cx** as *Lerne for to louie yf þe like dowel* (RK.11.132).

Qui similat verbis vel corde est fidus amicus
Tu quoque fac simile · sic ars deluditur arte
Who-so gloseth as gylours don · go me to þe same
And so shaltow false folke [·] and faythlees bigyle
205 Þis is catounes kennyng · to clerkes þat he lereth
Ac theologye techeth nou3t so · who-so taketh [gome]
He kenneth vs þe contrarye [·] a3ein catones wordes
For he bit vs be as bretheren · and bidde for owre enemys
And louen hem þat lyen on vs · and lene hem whan hem nedeth
210 And do good a3eines yuel · god hym-self it hoteth
Dum tempus [est] operemur bonum ad omnes maxime autem ad
        domesticos fidei

¶ Poule preched þe peple [·] þat parfitnesse loued
To do good for goddes loue · and gyuen men þat asked
And nameliche to suche · þat sueth owre bileue
215 And alle þat lakketh vs or lyeth vs · owre lorde techeth vs to louye
And nou3t to greuen hem þat greueth vs · god hym-self for-badde it
Michi vindictam & ego retribuam
For-þi loke þow louye · as longe as þow durest
For is no science vnder sonne · so souereyne for þe soule

220 [¶] Ac astronomye is harde þynge · and yuel forto knowe
Geometrie and geomesye [·] is ginful of speche
Who-so thenketh werche with þo two · thryueth ful late

---

201 **similat**: The spelling of L and alpha is found also in mss. of **A**. Lines 200–31 are not in **C**.
201 **vel**: Alford (1992), 64, quotes the line from Cato with *nec*, the reading of M (corrected from *vel*) CrHmCGO and most **A** mss., but LWR and original M establish **Bx** (at the expense of Cato's meaning).
206 **gome**: "notice". R's rare word is a synonym of beta's *3eme* and F's *heede* (*MED gome* n.(4)). Cf. **Bx**.17.13, where R again has *gome*, supported in that case by C.
211 **est**: The alpha reading is supported by the majority of **A** mss. where the same quotation is given at a later point (K.11.245a). Alford (1992), 64 cites the Vulgate as *habemus*, to which beta corrects.
213 **asked**: Beta has the past tense, (though HmGO have the present); alpha has the present. The past is perhaps slightly less obvious, but it may have been prompted by the verbs of the previous line, just as the present might have been suggested by the next line. There is nothing in **AC** to correspond until l. 220. We follow copy-text.
214 **sueth**: "conform to"; cf. **Bx**.17.113, *as suwen owre werkis*. G and alpha less appropriately have *scheweth*.
215 **vs** (1): Beta must have had *vs* twice in the a-verse, though beta2 (CrWHm) dropped the second. Alpha has the second but not the first.
220 **¶**: The paraph is in WC and alpha. In L, which lacks the usual line-space, the scribe's paraph marker is unrubricated. Cf. ll. 260, 265.
220 **harde**: Alpha's reading without an indefinite article is supported by **Ax** against beta.
221 **is**: Supported by **Ax** against beta2 (CrWHm) *so*.

For sorcerye is þe souereyne boke · þat to þ[o] science longeth

¶ ʒet ar þere fybicches in forceres · of fele mennes makyng
225 Experimentz of alkamye · þe poeple to deceyue
If þow þinke to dowel · dele þer-with neuere
Alle þise science I my-self · sotiled and ordeyned
And founded hem formest · folke to deceyue

¶ Telle clergye þise tokenes · and [to] scripture after
230 To conseille þe kyndely · to knowe what is dowel

¶ I seide graunt mercy madame · and mekeliche hir grette
And went wiʒtlich [my] wey · with-oute more lettynge
And til I come to clergye · I couthe neuere stynte
[I] gret þe good man · as [þe good wif] me tauʒte
235 And afterwardes þe wyf · and worshiped hem bothe
And tolde hem þe tokenes · þat me tauʒte were
Was neuere gome vppon þis grounde · sith god made þe worlde
Fairer vnder-fongen · ne frendeloker at ese
Þan my-self sothly · sone so he wist
240 Þat I was of wittis hous · and with his wyf dame studye
I seyde to hem sothely · þat sent was I þider
Dowel and dobet · and dobest to lerne

¶ It is a comune lyf quod clergye · on holycherche to bileue
With alle þe artikles of þe feithe · þat falleth to be knowe

---

223 **þo science**: This is the R reading, in substance that of F also. The noun is an unmarked plural (see l. 227 below, and variants at **Bx**.13.132 and 15.49). It may also be the reading of beta; note that Hm alters it by adding -*s*, while other beta scribes, apart from W, probably take it as sg. and so misread the plural determiner as *þe*. **Ax** also has the demonstrative pronoun, but the noun is sg., *þat science*. The plural is more appropriate in context.

225 **alkamye**: We keep the form of copy-text, even though the form in **Bx** and **Ax** presumably had the extra syllable, as M's *Alkenamye*. See *MED alkamie*.

227 **science**: Plural; see note to l. 223.

228 **founded**: Beta is supported by **Ax** against alpha's *(by-)fond*.

229 **to**: Alpha's rather awkward preposition is necessary to the alliteration, and was dropped by beta. There is no **Ax** parallel.

230 **to knowe what is**: Beta's wording of the b-verse is supported by the exact parallel of **Bx**.10.157. Cf. also **Bx**.15.2. Alpha has *for to knowe*.

232 **my wey**: Beta has *awey*, but alpha (R only, since F misses the line) is supported by **Ax** *And wente wiʒtly my wey*, as well as **Cx** *Tho wente y my way* (RK.12.134). With *miʒteliche* for *wiʒtlich*, R creates alliteration on /m/, but without support from **AC**.

234 **I**: Only R breaks the series of initial *And*, but it is supported by **Ax** and the X family of C; the P family reads *And ich*.

234 **þe good wif**: Again R is the only witness to the reading of **Bx**, supported both by alliteration and by **Ax** (**Cx** has a different b-verse). Probably F revised to avoid the repetition of both *good* and *wif*, and beta perhaps picked up *studye* from a gloss.

241 **hem**: M and beta4 have *hym*, but cf. l. 236. The line is not in **AC**. Lines 241–313 have no parallel in **A**, and C is heavily revised.

245 And þat is to bileue lelly · bothe lered and lewed
On þe grete god · þat gynnyng had neuere
And on þe sothfaste sone · þat saued mankynde
Fro þe dedly deth · and þe deueles power
Þorwgh þe helpe of þe holy goste · þe whiche goste is of bothe
250 Three [propre] persones · ac nouȝt in plurel noumbre
For al is but on god · and eche is god hym-selue
Deus pater deus filius · deus spiritus sanctus
God þe fader god þe sone · god holigoste of bothe
Maker of mankynde · and of bestes bothe

255 ¶ Austyn þe olde · here-of he made bokes
And hym-self ordeyned · to sadde vs in bileue
Who was his autour · alle þe foure euangelistes
And cryst clepid hym-self so · þe ewangelistes bereth witnesse
Ego in patre & pater in me & qui [me vidit · patrem meum vidit]

260 [¶] Alle þe clerkes vnder cryst · ne couthe þis assoille
But þus it bilongeth to bileue · to lewed þat willen dowel
For had neuere freke fyne wytte · þe feyth to dispute
Ne man had no merite · myȝte it ben yproued
Fides non habet meritum vbi humana racio prebet experimentum

265 [¶] Þanne is dobet to suffre · for þi soules helth
Al þat þe boke bit · by holycherche techyng
And þat is man bi þi miȝte · for mercies sake

---

250 **propre**: Yet again R is the only witness to the reading of **Bx**. All other mss. have dropped the alliterating adjective; F fills out the short a-verse in the usual manner. There is no parallel in **AC**.

255 **he**: L is supported by alpha against omission in other beta mss. The passage is revised in C; the line without *he* appears at RK.11.146, but the b-verse, this time with *he*, is repeated at RK.11.152. See Adams (2000), 183.

258 **ewangelistes**: R's *euaungeliez* is pl. of *MED evangelie*, "gospel". F has the sg. There is no AC parallel.

259 **me** (1): So alpha, and also the P family of C. Beta and the X family correct this very familiar quotation from John 14.9–10 to *me est*. The line is dropped by beta2 (CrHmW).

259 **vidit** (1 & 2): R's less classical spelling is actually that of the pre-Clementine Vulgate text edited by Wordsworth and White (1911), as well as most C mss.

259 **patrem meum vidit**: Alpha's word-order is also that of **Cx**.

260 **¶**: The paraph is in WC and alpha. In L, which lacks the usual line-space, the scribe's paraph marker is unrubricated. Cf. ll. 220, 265.

261 **bilongeth**: Beta is supported by **Cx** against *longeth* in GO and alpha.

263 **merite**: Beta is supported by **Cx** and by the Latin quotation in the following line. Alpha has *mercy*.

264 **prebet experimentum**: R omits the last two words from Gregory's Homily. C mss. break off at different points. After this line **B** is without parallel in **AC** until **Bx.10.314**.

265 **¶**: L has an unrubricated paraph marker, MW have a line-space but no paraph. HmC and alpha have paraphs. Cf. ll. 220, 260.

Loke þow worche it in werke · þat þi worde sheweth
Suche as þow semest in syȝte · be in assay yfounde
270 Appare quod es vel esto quod appares
And lat no-body be · bi þi beryng bygyled
But be suche in þi soule · as þow semest with-oute

¶ Þanne is dobest to be bolde · to blame þe gylty
Sithenes þow seest þi-self · as in soule clene
275 Ac blame þow neuere body · and þow be blame-worthy
Si culpare velis · culpabilis esse cauebis
Dogma tuum sordet · cum te tua culpa remordet
God in þe gospel · grymly repreueth
Alle þat lakken any lyf · and lakkes han hem-selue
280 Quid consideras festucam in oculo fratris tui trabem in oculo tuo &c
Why meuestow þi mode for a mote · in þi brotheres eye
Sithen a beem in þine owne · ablyndeth þi-selue
Eice primo trabem de oculo tuo &c
Whiche letteth þe to loke · lasse other more

285 ¶ I rede eche a blynde bosarde · do bote to hym-selue
For abbotes and for prioures · and for alle manere prelates
As parsones and parissh prestes · þat preche shulde and teche
Alle manere men · to amenden by here myȝte
This tixte was tolde ȝow · to ben war ar ȝe tauȝte
290 Þat ȝe were suche as ȝe seyde · to salue with othere
For goddis worde wolde nouȝt be [b]oste · for þat worcheth euere
If it auailled nouȝt þe comune · it myȝte auaille ȝow-seluen

¶ Ac it semeth now sothly · to þe worldes syght
Þat goddes worde worcheth nauȝte · on lered ne on lewede
295 But in suche a manere as Marke [·] meneth in þe gospel
Dum cecus ducit cecum ambo in foueam cadunt

---

268 **þi:** So beta; R's *þis* points to the ensuing quotation. F has *þe*.
270 **vel:** Alford (1992), 65, quotes this commonplace with the alpha reading *aut*.
271 **bygyled:** Hm and alpha have *be bygiled*.
278 **grymly:** Beta2 and F share the reading *greuously*.
280 Beta breaks off the quotation (Luke 6.41) which alpha completes with *non vides*. The wording is something between Matt. 7.3 and Luke 6.41.
288 **manere:** So LCrWGR. The M corrector adds *of* to come into line with HmCOF. Cf. ll. 286 and 299.
291 **boste:** Though nonsensical, LR share the reading, indicating a corruption in **Bx**. The L scribe subsequently made the obvious correction to *loste*, thereby bringing his text into agreement with all other mss. See Introduction, p. 33.
293 **now:** Probably R represents alpha's *no*, which F unreflectingly expanded to *not*. That M originally wrote *not* is presumably coincidental.
294 **worde:** R has the plural; F omits.
295 Beta (or possibly **Bx**) misplaced the punctuation to follow *manere*, as in LWC. In OR punctuation correctly precedes *meneth*, while MF have it twice.

¶ Lewed men may likne ȝow þus · þat þe beem lithe in ȝowre eyghen
And þe festu is fallen · for ȝowre defaute
In alle manere men · þourgh mansed prestes
300 Þe bible bereth witnesse [·] þat alle þe folke of israel
Byttere abouȝte þe gultes · of two badde prestes
Offyn and Fynes · for her coueytise
Archa dei myshapped · and ely brake his nekke

¶ For-þi ȝe corectoures claweth her-on · and corecteth fyrst ȝow-seluen
305 And þanne mowe ȝe [man]ly seye · as dauid made þe sauter
Existimasti inique quod ero tui similis · arguam te & statuam contra
    faciem tuam ·

¶ And þanne shal borel clerkes ben abasched · to blame ȝow or to greue
And carpen nouȝte as þei carpen now · and calle ȝow doumbe houndes
Canes non valentes latrare
310 And drede to wratthe ȝow in any worde · ȝowre werkemanship to lette
And be prestiore at ȝowre prayere · þan for a pounde of nobles
And al for ȝowre holynesse · haue ȝe þis in herte

[¶ Amonges riȝtful religiouse · þis reule shulde be holde
Gregorie þe grete clerke · and þe good pope
315 Of religioun þe reule · [he] reherceth in his morales
And seyth it in ensaumple · [þat] þei shulde do þere-after
Whanne fisshes failen þe flode · or þe fressh water
þei deyen for drouthe · whanne þei drie ligge
Riȝt so quod Gregori · religioun rolleth
320 Sterueth and stynketh · and steleth lordes almesses

---

305 **manly**: Beta's *saufly* alliterates rather unconvincingly on /s/, and F improves on this with *soply* in the a-verse and *seiþ in* (for *made*) in the b-verse. Both avoid R's difficult adverb, which Kane (2005) glosses "boldly, w. confidence". *MED manli* adv.(1), gives no instance of this sense, though "strongly" is close. Possibly *MED mainli*, which seems to have been used as a loose intensifier, is relevant.

307 **or to greue**: Alpha has lost the last three words of the line.

313–25 These thirteen lines are in alpha only. Lines 314–21 are in Ax (K.11.204–10); ll. 314–15, 317–24, revised in places, are moved to a different context in Cx (RK.5.146–55). Eyeskip from the paraph recorded by R at l. 313 to that at l. 326 is the most likely explanation. See Burrow (2010): 25–6. KD, p. 66, point to homeoteleuton (*al…-nesse…herte, al…-nesse…lerne*). We have altered R's spelling to that of L.

314 **Gregorie**: F begins *Seynt Gregory*, but R is supported by AC.

315 **he**: F is supported by Ax against omission in R.

315 **morales**: *Moralia*. R is supported by Ax against F's *bookis*, though Cx also refers to them as *bokes* (RK.5.146).

316 **it**: R is supported by Ax. F omits.

316 **þat**: F receives some support from Ax, *þat þei shulde do þe betere*. R has *for*.

317 **or**: R is supported by Ax against F *&*; Cx revises.

319 **rolleth**: This seems to be alpha's reading, replaced in F by the partly synonymous *trollyþ*, "wander" (cf. **Bx**.18.305). It is, however, an error for *roileth*, "totter, flop" (so Kane (2005))

þat oute of couent and cloystre · coueyten to libbe
For if heuene be on þis erthe · and ese to any soule
It is in cloistre or in scole · be many skilles I fynde
For in cloistre cometh [no] man · to chide ne to fiȝte
325　But alle is buxomnesse þere and bokes · to rede and to lerne]

¶ In scole þere is [skile · and] scorne but if [he] lerne
And grete loue and lykynge · for eche of hem loueth other
Ac now is religioun a ryder · a rowmer bi stretes
A leder of louedayes · and a londe-bugger
330　A priker on a palfray · fro manere to maner
An heep of houndes at his ers · as he a lorde were
And but if his knaue knele · þat shal his cuppe brynge
He loureth on hym and axeth hym · who tauȝte hym curteisye
Litel had lordes to donn · to ȝyue londe fram her heires
335　To Religious þat haue no reuthe · þough it reyne on here auteres

¶ In many places þer hij persones ben · be hem-self at ese
Of þe pore haue þei no pite · and þat is her [pure] charite
Ac þei leten hem as lordes · her londe lith so brode

¶ Ac þere shal come a kyng · and confesse ȝow religiouses
340　And bete ȝow as þe bible telleth · for brekynge of ȝowre reule
And amende monyales · monkes and chanouns
And putten hem to her penaunce · ad pristinum statum ire
And Barounes with Erles beten hem · þorugh beatus virres techynge
Þat here barnes claymen · and blame ȝow foule
345　Hij in curribus [et] hij in equis ipsi obligati sunt &c

---

in either **Bx** or alpha, and the line is suspiciously short. This and the following line in alpha
expand one line in the other versions. **Ax** has: *Riȝt so be religioun it roileþ* (one ms. *rolleþ*) *and
steruiþ*; **Cx** has *Ryht so religioun roteth and sterueth* (RK.5.150).
322 **on þis**: R is supported by **Cx** against F's *in*.
322 **ese to any**: C mss. have *eny ese to þe* (or *for*) (RK.5.152).
323 **many**: R is supported by **Cx**. F alters to *fele* to increase alliteration.
324 **no**: R's obvious omission is confirmed by **Cx**.
324 **chide ne to fiȝte**: R's b-verse word-order is supported by **Cx**.
325 **þere**: F omits. The line is not in **AC**.
326 **skile and scorne but if he**: R evidently represents alpha, mangled by F. If right, the reading
involves a play on *skilles* three lines above in l. 323. Beta, on this argument, having lost *skile
and*, added *a clerke* in place of *he*. The alliteration is weaker, though KD p. 132 n. 9 cite l. 323
as evidence that /sk/ can alliterate with /k/. **Cx** revises this and the next line to *In scole is loue
and louhnesse and lykyng to lerne* (RK.5.155).
328 **rowmer**: F's *rennere* is the **A** reading.
330 **manere to maner**: Cf. **Ax** *toune to toune* (K.11.213), **Cx** *places to maneres* (RK.5.159).
333 **axeth**: Both F and Hm supply alliteration; the line is not in **Ax** and rewritten in **Cx**.
337 **pure**: Beta omits, but alpha is supported by **Cx** and the b-verse alliteration.
345 **et**: Omitted by LM, so perhaps supplied by other beta scribes on the basis of the Psalm.

¶ And þanne Freres in here freitoure [·] shal fynden a keye
Of costantynes coffres · in which is þe catel
Þat Gregories god-children · han yuel dispended

¶ And þanne shal þe abbot of Abyndoun · and alle [his] issu for euere
350 Haue a knokke of a kynge · and incurable þe wounde

¶ That þis worth soth seke ȝe · þat oft ouer-se þe bible
Quomodo cessauit exactor · quieuit tributum · contriuit dominus baculum
    impiorum et virgam dominancium cedencium plaga insanabili &c

¶ Ac ar þat kynge come · cayme shal awake
Ac dowel shal dyngen hym adoune · and destruyen his myȝte
355 Þanne is dowel and dobet quod I · dominus and kniȝthode

¶ I nel nouȝt scorne quod scripture · but if scryueynes lye
Kynghod ne knyȝthod · by nauȝt I can awayte
Helpeth nouȝt to heueneward · one heres ende
Ne ricchesse riȝt nouȝt · ne reaute of lordes

360 ¶ Poule preueth it inpossible · riche men haue heuene
Salamon seith also · þat syluer is worst to louye
Nichil iniquius quam amare peccuniam
And caton kenneth vs to coueiten it · nauȝt but as nede techeth
Dilige denarium set parce dilige formam
365 And patriarkes and prophetes · and poetes bothe
Wryten to wissen vs · to wilne no ricchesse
And preyseden pouerte with pacience · þe apostles bereth witnesse
Þat þei han heritage in heuene · and bi trewe riȝte
Þere riche men no riȝte may clayme · but of reuthe and grace

370 ¶ Contra quod I bi cryste · þat can I repreue
And preue it bi Peter · and bi poule bothe
Þat is baptized beth sauf · be he riche or pore

¶ Þat is in extremis quod scripture · amonges saracenes and iewes
Þei mowen be saued so · and þat is owre byleue
375 Þat an vncristene in þat cas · may crysten an hethen
And for his lele byleue · whan he þe lyf tyneth

---

349 **his**: Dropped in L.
354 **Ac**: The common *Ac/And/But* variation, with LMHmR attesting to *Ac*. Lines 354–401
are not in C.
363 In MCF the punctuation follows *nauȝt*.
363 **as nede techeth**: LMCrWHm represent beta, with CO reading *as it nedes* and G corrupting
further to *vs neditþe*. Beta's phrase receives some support from **Bx.20.9**. KD reject R (= alpha?)
at pure nede on the grounds that it is "more emphatic" (p. 144). The line is not in **AC**.
372 **he**: MGOF have the plural following the plural *ben* for *is* in their a-verse.

Haue þe heritage of heuene · as any man crystene

¶ Ac crysten men with-oute more · may nou3t come to heuene
For þat cryst for cristen men deyde · and confermed þe lawe
380   Þat who-so wolde and wylneth · with cryste to aryse
Si cum cristo surrexistis &c ·
He shulde louye & lene · and þe lawe fulfille
Þat is loue þi lorde god · leuest aboue alle
And after alle crystene creatures · in comune eche man other
385   And þus bilongeth to louye · þat leueth to be saued
And but we do þus in dede · ar þe daye of dome
I[t] shal bisitten vs ful soure · þe siluer þat we kepen
And owre bakkes þat moth-eten be · and sen beggers go naked
Or delyte in wyn and wylde foule · and wote any in defaute
390   For euery cristene creature [·] shulde be kynde til other
And sithen hethen to helpe · in hope of amendement
God hoteth bothe heigh and lowe [·] þat no man hurte other
And seith slee nou3t þat semblable is · to myne owen liknesse
But if I sende þe sum tokne · and seith non [m]ecaberis
395   Is slee nou3t but suffre · and al for þe beste
[For Michi vindictam & ego retribuam]
For I shal punysshen in purgatorie · or in þe putte of helle
Vche man for his mysdedes · but mercy it lette

¶ Þis is a longe lessoun quod I · and litel am I þe wyser
400   Where dowel is or dobet · derkelich 3e shewen
Many tales 3e tellen · þat theologye lerneth
And þat I man made was · and my name yentred
In þe legende of lyf · longe er I were

---

379 The position of the line-break causes uncertainty, so that L has a punctus after *men* and a
punctus elevatus after *deyde*. WHm have the former punctuation, MCrCO and alpha the latter,
which we follow.

383 **þi lorde god**: For a precise parallel see **Bx**.5.583. Since F omits the line, R's word-order
may represent alpha. Lines 378–89 have no parallel in **AC**.

383 **alle**: Cr and beta4 have *al thyng*.

387 **It**: A corrector has noted the omission of <t> in L.

388 **bakkes**: "clothes", as observed by the L scribe who writes above it *id est panni*. M has a
different gloss: *id est vestes*.

388 **moth**: Alpha has *mote* which F makes sense of with great imagination.

394 **mecaberis**: WHmCG and alpha, supported by **Ax** (K.11.254). L and G have been altered to
necaberis (and CrO more grammatically to *necabis*); M is altered to *occides*. See Luke 18.20: "non
occides, non moechaberis", i.e. "Thou shalt not kill, thou shalt not commit adultery". Langland
has confused *moechari* with *necare*, "to slay". See Skeat (1886), 2.160; Alford (1992), 68–9.

395 **Is**: CO have *I*, and M is altered to that reading.

396 The quotation from Rom. 12.19 is omitted in beta but supported by **Ax** (K.11.255).

397 **punysshen**: Alpha's omission of *hem* is supported by **Ax**.

KD.10.356–381

Or elles vnwriten for somme wikkednesse [·] as holywrit wytnesseth
405 Nemo ascendit ad celum nisi qui de celo decendit

¶ [And] I leue it wel bi owre lorde [·] and on no letterure bettere
For salamon þe sage · þat sapience tauȝte
God gaf hym grace of witte · and alle his godes after
[To reule þe reume · and riche to make]
410 He demed wel & wysely [·] as holy writte telleth
Aristotle & he · who wissed men bettere
Maistres þat of goddis mercy · techen men and prechen
Of here wordes þei wissen vs · for wisest in here tyme
And al holicherche · holdeth hem bothe ydampned

415 ¶ And if I shulde worke bi here werkes [·] to wynne me heuene
Þat for her werkes and witte · now wonyeth in pyne
Þanne wrouȝte I vnwysely · what-so-euere ȝe preche

¶ Ac of fele witty in feith · litel ferly I haue
Þough her goste be vngraciouse · god for to plese
420 For many men on þis molde · more sette here hert[e]
In good þan in god · for-þi hem grace failleth
At here moste myschief · whan þei shal lyf lete
As salamon dede and such other · þat shewed gret wittes
Ac her werkes as holy wrytte seyth · was euere þe contrarye
425 For-þi wyse witted men · and wel ylettred clerkes
As þei seyen hem-self · selden done þer-after

---

404 **vnwriten**: "not recorded", as in AC (K.11.263; RK.11.207). MGOF have *writen*.

404 **wytnesseth**: So beta; alpha has *telleth*, probably picked up from l. 410 below. **Ax** has *as witnessiþ þe gospel*; **Cx** has *as holy writ shewith* (RK.11.207). For the same b-verse as in beta, see **Bx**.11.416; for that as in alpha, see **Bx**.1.130, 3.342, etc.

406 **And**: R only, since F substitutes *For* and beta omits. **Ax** and the X group of C support *And*, but the P group omits it.

406 **wel**: Beta adds *quod I* (in CGO it follows *lord*), but there is no support from **AC**.

408 **his**: Alpha omits, perhaps rightly. The b-verse is rewritten from **Ax**. In **Cx** it is instead *and of goed aftur* (cf. F's *& of alle goodis after*).

409 Beta omits the line. In **Ax** the line reads *For to reule his reaum riȝt at his wille* (K11267); **Cx** has *To reule alle reumes and ryche to make* (RK.11.212). F may therefore be right with *his rewme*, or it may be contamination from the A tradition.

413 **in**: Beta reads *as in*, possibly rightly, but **Cx**, with a different a-verse, has *and wisest in here tyme*. This use of *as in* is not well exemplified in the poem; perhaps the closest is **Bx**.15.609: *ferme as in þe faith*.

416 **witte**: Alpha reads *here witt*, supported by a majority of A mss.; beta is however supported by **Cx**. We follow copy-text.

420 **Cx** supports beta's *men* in the a-verse and alpha's *herte* in the b-verse, which may be regarded as generic sg. or as an unchanged pl. of part of the body. Cf. **Bx**.7.68. Even so, alpha's unmarked form needs to be seen in the context of its sg. *man* in the a-verse. Lines 418–43 are not in **A**.

423 **dede and such other**: Alpha reads *and other dede*, losing the alliteration. There is no parallel in **AC**.

Super cathedra moysy &c ·

¶ Ac I wene it worth of many · as was in Noes tyme
Þo he shope þat shippe · of shides and bordes
430 Was neuere wriȝte saued þat wrouȝt þer-on · ne oþer werkman elles
But briddes and bestes · and þe blissed Noe
And his wyf with his sones · and also here wyues
Of wriȝtes þat it wrouȝte [·] was none of hem ysaued

¶ God lene it fare nouȝt so bi folke · þat þe feith techen
435 Of holicherche þat he[r]berwe is · and goddes hous to saue
And shelden vs fram shame þer-inne · as noes shippe did bestes
And men þat maden it · amydde þe flode adreynten
Þe culorum of þis clause · curatoures is to mene
Þat ben carpenteres holykirke to make · for crystes owne bestes
440 Homines & iumenta saluabis domine · &c ·
[At domes-day þe deluuye worth · of deth and fyre at ones
For-þi I conseille ȝow clerkes · of holy cherche þe wriȝtes
Worcheth ȝe as ȝe se writen · lest ȝe worth nauȝt þerinne]

¶ On gode fridaye I fynde · a feloun was ysaued
445 Þat had lyued al his lyf [·] with lesynges and with thefte

---

427 **cathedra**: C mss. split between abl. *cathedra* (in the X family) and acc. *cathedram* (in the P family). The Vulgate has the latter (Matt. 23.3), although the former is more "correct" (with abl. denoting rest).

429 **and**: This is probably the beta reading, with CrW and alpha reading *and of*. C mss. also split, with the X family having the beta reading, while the P family has that of alpha. We follow copy-text.

433 **wriȝtes**: The line is lost (presumably by eyeskip from l. 430) by beta4 and added in M. Beta2 has *wightes*.

434 **lene**: As usual, this is indistinguishable in L and other mss. from the easier *leue*, as recorded in CrF. G alters to *leve*. Cf. **Bx**.5.265.

438 Alpha has a paraph.

438 **curatoures is**: The b-verse as in beta is the reading of **Cx**.

439 **kirke**: R's non-alliterating form *cherche* may represent alpha, as at **Bx**.5.106, 271, etc., inspiring F to rewrite. See Introduction, pp. 18–19.

441–3 These three lines are preserved in alpha only. The first is in **Cx**, and ll. 442–3 are revised as RK.11.250, with a new line added. We have revised R's spellings to those of L.

441 **fyre**: R's line is supported by **Cx** against F's revisions. R has *feer* as a spelling for "fire" at **Bx**.3.99.

442 **cherche**: It may seem obvious that, as at l. 439, **Bx** had *kirke* for the alliteration. However, **Cx** has *churche* in a line alliterating on /w/, suggesting that Langland revised the line to improve the alliteration of **Bx**.

443 **as**: R's line is verbose and clumsy throughout, here reading *werkes as*. We take *werkes* to be an addition to strengthen alliteration and follow F, while recognising the slightness of the evidence. In **Cx** the line reads: *Worcheth ȝe wrihtus of holy churche as holy writ techeth* (RK.11.250).

443 **worth nought þerinne**: F's *worth ydrenkled*, "are drowned", is more emphatic. Cf. F's reading at l. 437, suggesting that **Bx** might have read *worth adreynte* or similar. Again it is impossible to be confident of either reading.

444 **On**: Alpha begins *For a* (R) or *For on* (F), but beta is supported by **AC**.

And for he biknewe on þe crosse · and to cryste s[h]rof hym
He was sonnere saued · þan seynt Iohan [þe] Baptiste
And or Adam or ysaye · or eny of þe prophetes
Þat hadde yleine with Lucyfer · many longe ȝeres
450 A robbere was yraunceouned · rather þan þei alle
With-outen any penaunce of purgatorie · to perpetuel blisse

¶ Þanne Marye Magdaleyne · what womman dede worse
Or who worse [dede] þan dauid · þat vries deth conspired
Or Poule þe apostle · þat no pitee hadde
455 Moche crystene kynde · to kylle to deth
And ben þise as souereynes · wyth seyntes in heuene
Þo þat wrouȝte wikkedlokest · in worlde þo þei were

¶ And þo þat wisely wordeden · and wryten many bokes
Of witte and of wisdome · with dampned soules wonye
460 Þat salamon seith I trowe be soth · and certeyne of vs alle
S[unt] iusti atque sapientes · & opera eorum in manu dei sunt &c

¶ Þere aren witty and wel libbyng [·] ac her werkes ben yhudde
In þe hondes of almiȝty god · and he wote þe sothe
Wher for loue a man worth allowed þere · and his lele werkes
465 Or elles for his yuel wille · & enuye of herte
And be allowed as he lyued so · for bi lyther men knoweth þe gode

¶ And wherby wote men whiche is whyte · if alle þinge blake were
And who were a gode man · but if þere were some shrewe
For-þi lyue we forth with lither men · I leue fewe ben gode

---

447 **þe**: Lost in LHm, but supported by **AC**.

448 **or** (1): "before". See spelling variants.

453 **worse dede**: Beta drops *dede*, but R (and cf. F) is supported by alliteration and by **Ax** *dede wers*. C rewrites.

455 Alpha omits the line. **AC** have it without *Moche* (K.11.290; RK.11.268). C mss. vary, incorporating an abbreviated version of the line into the previous line, as in X: *Poul þe apostel no pite ne hadde cristene peple to culle to dethe.*

456 Hm begins with rewritten *And ȝit been*; all others have *And now ben* except LR that omit the adverb, and F which reverses the order. The omission is almost certainly an error, since the adverb is in **Cx**, but the combined testimony of LR implies that it was an omission in **Bx**, with other scribes correcting by conjecture or contamination. See Adams (2000), 184.

461 **Sunt**: Beta's *Sine* or *Siue* is an obvious misreading. Alpha is supported by **Cx** and the source (Ecclesiastes 9.1). Lines 462–71 have no parallel in **AC**.

462 **¶**: The paraph is in beta and F.

464 **Wher for**: "whether for". Beta2 and G mistake this as *Wherefore*, and CrW drop *loue*.

465 **&**: L initially read *or*, corrected to *&*. Beta2 has *and for*.

466 **as**: R has *for*; F rewrites the line.

466 **so**: Dropped by Cr and beta4 (O has *þere*).

467 **wote**: So LR, and probably M before correction to conform to CrW *wiste*. Hm may also have had *wote* before revision.

468 **And**: Alpha probably read *Or*, altered by F to *For*.

469 **lither**: Beta2 reads *other* and loses alliteration.

470   For qant oportet vyent en place · yl nyad que pati
       And he þat may al amende · haue mercy on vs alle
       For sothest worde þat euere god seyde · was þo he seyde nemo bonus

       [¶] Clergye þo of crystes mouth · commended was it litel
       For he seyde to seynt Peter · and to suche as he loued
475   Dum steteritis ante Reges et presides &c ·
       Þough ȝe come bifor kynges · and clerkes of þe lawe
       Beth nouȝte abasched · for I shal be in ȝoure mouthes
       And ȝyue ȝow witte at wille · and kunnynge to conclude
       Hem alle þat aȝeines ȝow · of crystenedome disputen

480   ¶ Dauyd maketh mencioun · he spake amonges kynges
       And miȝte no kynge ouercome hym · as bi kunnyng of speche
       But witte ne wisdome · wan neuere þe maystrye
       Whan man was at myschief · with-oute þe more grace

       ¶ Þe doughtiest doctour · and deuynoure of þe trinitee
485   Was augustyn þe olde · and heighest of þe foure
       Sayde þus in a sarmoun · I seigh it writen ones
       Ecce ipsi idioti rapiunt celum · vbi nos sapientes in inferno mergimur ·
       And is to mene to englissh men · more ne lasse
       Aren none rather yrauysshed · fro þe riȝte byleue
490   Þan ar þis cunnynge clerkes · þat conne many bokes

       ¶ Ne none sonner saued · ne sadder of bileue
       Þan plowmen and pastoures · & pore comune laboreres
       Souteres and sheperdes · suche lewed iottes
       Percen with a pater noster [·] þe paleys of heuene

---

473 ¶: The paraph is in WHmR, with a new line-group in M. In L, which lacks the usual line-space, the scribe's paraph marker is unrubricated.

475 **Dum**: Beta2 alters to *Cum*, but **Cx** supports the others.

478 **at**: L is supported by alpha; all others have *and*. The line is revised in **Cx**.

479 **of**: Alpha omits, though F has a different object, *goddis lawe*, for alliteration's sake. Though this is attractive, it might be noted that the verb *disputen* is elsewhere used transitively only at **Bx**.10.260; it is usually *disputen with*.

481 **And**: **Cx** supports beta against R *Al* and F *Þere*.

485 **augustyn**: As at l. 126 above, the form of the name in **Bx** is not determinable. LMG (so beta?) have the full form, but alpha has the more usual *Austyn*. Both **AC** have the abbreviated form. We follow copy-text.

485 **þe** (2): **AC** do not support R's *hem*.

487 **idioti**: **Bx** and most **A** mss. make the fools masculine, though CrCGOF correct to feminine.

490 **conne**: Beta has the support of **Ax** against alpha's *knowe*.

491 ¶: The paraph is in LW (in M the line is at the top of the page).

492 **pore**: W and beta4 read *opere* and lose the alliteration.

493 **suche**: So LR and Cr, as well as the majority of **A** mss. Others have added *and*.

493 **iottes**: A nonce word, variously recorded as *iottes* and *iuttes* by **A** and **B** scribes. It may be the same word as modern *jot*, "small amount".

495 And passen purgatorie penaunceles · at her hennes-partyng
In-to þe blisse of paradys · for her pure byleue
Þat inparfitly here · knewe and eke lyued

¶ 3ee men knowe clerkes · þat han cursed þe tyme
Þat euere þei couth or knewe more · þan credo in deum patrem
500 And pryncipaly her pater noster · many a persone hath wisshed

¶ I se ensamples my-self · and so may many an other
Þat seruauntes þat seruen lordes · selden falle in arrerage
But þo þat kepen þe lordes catel · clerkes and reues
Ri3t so lewed men · & of litel knowyng
505 Selden falle so foule · and so fer in synne
As clerkes of holikirke · þat kepen crystes tresore
Þe which is mannes soule to saue · as god seith in þe gospel
Ite vos in vineam meam

---

496 Here ends comparison with A.
497 **here:** This line is obviously defective in R, which uniquely drops *here*. In the b-verse R's loss of *eke* may represent alpha, since F rewrites. Lines 497–501 are not in C.
498 **þat han cursed:** R alone has *cursen*.
500 **her:** So beta; alpha might equally be right with *þe*.
502 **arrerage:** Beta is supported by **Cx**. F regularly reads *rerage*; cf. esp. **Bx**.11.133, 135 (final position), 138, 14.117.
503 **þe lordes:** R has *lordes*; F has *here*. The line is not in C.
504 **knowyng:** Alpha reads *kunnynge*. **Cx** has *vnderstondyng* in a revised line (RK.11.299).
505 **falle:** So alpha, supported by **Cx**; beta reads *falle þei*.
506 **kirke:** Beta2 and GR alter to *chirche* and lose alliteration.

Passus 11

Passus undecimus

Thanne scripture scorned me · and a skile tolde
And lakked me in latyne · and li3te by me she sette
And seyde multi multa sciunt [·] & seipsos nesciunt
Þo wepte I for wo · and wratth of her speche
5 And in a wynkyng wratth · [til] I [was] aslepe
A merueillouse meteles · mette me þanne
[For] I was rauisshed ri3t þere · and fortune me fette
And in-to þe londe of longynge · allone she me brou3te
And in a myroure þat hi3t mydlerd · she mad me to biholde
10 Sitthen she sayde to me · here my3tow se wondres
And knowe þat þow coueytest · and come þer-to par-aunter

¶ Þanne hadde fortune folwyng hir [·] two faire damoyseles

---

2 **she**: Scripture is female in **Bx**.10.160–1. Alpha reads *he*, either as the feminine pronoun or taking Scripture as a male personification. **Cx** omits the pronoun (RK.11.162). Though she is clearly female in l. 4, in l. 110 Scripture is referred to as *he* by GOCF.

3 MHmO and alpha treat this as a standard alliterative line with medial punctuation.

4 **wo**: Supported by alliteration and **Cx** against alpha's *sorwe*.

5 **til I was**: R's reading is taken to be alpha and **Bx**. Beta has *wex I*. In the a-verse the form *wratth* is pretty clearly a **Bx** error (prompted by the previous line) for *warth*, "entered, fell", where **Cx** has *I warth* (RK.11.165). We assume that beta rewrote the b-verse, supposing that the a-verse meant something like "in an angry sleepiness" or "in a sleepy anger". The b-verse in **Cx** is quite different. F rewrote the whole line and added another five, avoiding the dream within a dream by waking Will up and sending him swiftly back to sleep again.

6 **mette me þanne**: Alpha's *me tydde to dreme* has less satisfactory alliteration. Surprisingly, the verb *tiden* is never used in the poem.

7 **For**: Alpha's reading is confirmed by **Cx** (RK.11.166). Beta has *Þat*.

7 **and**: R's reading *for*, though not supported by F, may be **Bx**, since it is paralleled by the X family of C. The P family has no conjunction.

8 **allone**: Beta and F are supported by the X family of C, although the P family as well as two of the X family (YU) support R's *& loue*. For the collocation of *love* and *longing*, see *MED longing(e* (1) (b) and (c). Either reading could easily have given rise to the other.

Concupiscencia carnis · men called þe elder mayde
And coueytise of eyes · ycalled was þat oþer
15 Pryde of parfyte lyuynge · pursued hem bothe
And badde me for my contenaunce · acounte clergye liȝte

¶ Concupiscencia carnis · colled me aboute þe nekke
And seyde þow art ȝonge and ȝepe · and hast ȝeres ynowe
For to lyue longe · and ladyes to louye
20 And in þis myroure þow myȝte se · myrthes ful manye
Þat leden þe wil to lykynge · al þi lyf-tyme

¶ Þe secounde seide þe same · I shal suwe þi wille
Til þow be a lorde and haue londe · leten þe I nelle
Þat I ne shal folwe þi felawship · if fortune it lyke
25 He shal fynde me his frende · quod fortune þer-after
Þe freke þat folwed my wille · failled neuere blisse

¶ Thanne was þere one þat hiȝte elde [·] þat heuy was of chere
Man quod he if I mete with þe · bi Marie of heuene
Þow shalt fynde fortune þe faille · at þi moste nede
30 And concupiscencia carnis · clene þe forsake
Bitterliche shaltow banne þanne · bothe dayes and niȝtes
Coueytise of eyghe · þat euere þow hir knewe
And pryde of parfyt lyuynge · to moche peril þe brynge

¶ Ȝee recche þe neuere quod recchelesnes · stode forth in ragged clothes
35 Folwe forth þat fortune wole · þow hast wel fer t[o] elde
A man may stoupe tymes ynow · whan he shal tyne þe croune

¶ Homo proponit quod a poete [þo] · and plato he hyght
And deus disponit quod he · lat god done his wille
If trewthe wil witnesse it be wel do · fortune to folwe
40 Concupiscencia carnis · ne coueityse of eyes
Ne shal nouȝt greue þe gretly · ne bigyle þe but þow wolt

---

20 **myrthes:** Beta2's *myȝtes* has no support from **Cx**.

22 **¶:** The paraph is in beta and F.

26 **folwed:** Alpha's present tense might equally represent **Bx**. C has a different line, with present-tense *liketh*.

29 R places the punctuation after *fortune*, thus alliterating aa/ax rather than aaa/xx.

35 **to:** MHmCGO and alpha, supported by **Cx**, against *til* in LCrW. Cf. **Bx**.9.88, 11.83.

36 **tymes:** LMHmR have the plural, presumably representing **Bx**, though the regular adverbial expression is *time enough*, "soon enough"; see *MED time* n.(2), 8c(c). The other **B** mss. and most **C** mss. have the regular singular. See Adams (2000), 179.

37 **þo:** Alpha is supported by **Cx** (RK.11.303).

41 **gretly:** So beta and **Cx**, but it is hard to explain why alpha might have replaced it with *graythly*, "quickly, readily". Yet the only other occurrence of *graythely* in B is **Bx**.18.298, where it causes the scribes no difficulty.

KD.11.13–41

[¶] 3ee farewel phippe quod fauntelte [·] and forth gan me drawe
Til concupiscencia carnis · acorded [til] alle my werkes

¶ Allas eye quod elde · and holynesse bothe
45 Þat witte shal torne to wrecchednesse · for wille to haue his lykyng

¶ Coueityse of eyghes · conforted me anon after
And folwed me fourty wynter · and a fyfte more
Þat of dowel ne dobet · no deyntee me ne þou3te
I had no lykynge leue me if þe leste · of hem au3te to knowe

50 ¶ Coueytyse of eyes · cam ofter in mynde
Þan dowel or dobet [·] amonge my dedes alle
Coueytise of eyes [·] conforted me ofte
And seyde haue no conscience [·] how þow come to gode
Go confesse [þe] to sum frere · and shewe hym þi synnes
55 For whiles fortune is þi frende · Freres wil þe louye
And fe[tt]e þe to her fraternite · and for þe biseke
To her priour prouyncial · a pardoun forto haue
And preyen for þe pol bi pol · 3if þow be peccuniosus
[P]ena pecuniar[i]a non sufficit pro spiritualibus delictis

60 ¶ By wissynge of þis wenche I [dede] · here wordes were so swete
Tyl I for3at 3outhe · and 3arn in-to elde
And þanne was fortune my foo · for al hir faire biheste
And pouerte pursued me · and put me lowe
And þo fonde I þe Frere aferde · and flyttynge bothe

---

42 ¶: The paraph is in WHmC and alpha, with a line-space in M. In L, which lacks the usual line-space, the scribe's paraph marker is unrubricated.

43 til: In beta the verb *acorded* is used most unusually with direct object; alpha has the prepositions *til* (R) and *with* (F). For *acord with* cf. Bx.20.304, 354. Cx supports R.

46–9 Omitted by alpha, an easy case of eye-skip, with the same a-verse in ll. 46 and 50, both lines beginning with a paraph. F then also omits ll. 50–1. It is worth noting that Bx.11.47–52 are absent from C, and this may also be attributable to eye-skip.

48 ne (2): LM only (alpha is absent).

49 þe: LMW; Hm has *thu* and Cr has *ye*.

50 ¶: The paraph is in LR only (F is absent).

50 in: GOR have *in my*. The line is not in Cx.

54 þe: LF omit, but supported by Cx.

56 fette: R (= alpha) with F misreading as *sette*. *MED fetten* notes that "in the ME and Early MnE period *fetten* is gradually replaced by *fecchen*", whence beta's reading. Cx has instead *festene* (RK.12.8). At Bx.18.344 R has *fecchest* for Bx *fettest*.

59 Pena: Alpha is supported by Cx. Presumably beta's *Set pena* is an attempt to link the quotation more closely to the argument. Alford (1992), 72.

60 dede: The choice of reading is difficult. R is supported by Cx. We therefore suppose that beta corrupted to *wrou3te* by alliterative attraction, while F coincidentally included *wrowhte* in a rewritten a-verse, again prompted by the alliteration.

61 3arn: "ran", the form regularly used for alliteration, which HmR lose with *ran*. Cf. Bx.3.215 and note.

65   A3eines owre firste forward · for I seyde I nolde
      Be buryed at her hous · but at my parissh cherche
      For I herde onys · how conscience it tolde
      Þat þere a man were crystened · by kynde he shulde be buryed
      Or where he were parisshene · ri3t þere he shulde be grauen
70   And for I seyde þus to freres · a fool þei me helden
      And loued me þe lasse [·] for my lele speche
      Ac 3et I cryed on my confessoure [·] þat helde hym-self so kunnyng
      By my feith frere quod I · 3e faren lyke þise woweres
      Þat wedde none wydwes · but forto welde here godis
75   Ri3te so by þe Rode · rou3te 3e neuere
      Where my body were buryed · bi so 3e hadde my siluer
      Ich haue moche merueille of 3ow · and so hath many another
      Why 3owre couent coueyteth · to confesse and to burye
      Rather þan to baptise barnes · þat ben catekumelynges
80   Baptizyng and burying · bothe ben ful nedeful
      Ac moche more merytorie · me þynke[th] it is to baptize
      For a baptized man · may as maistres telleth
      Þorugh contricioun come · to þe heigh heuene Sola contricio &c ·

      ¶ Ac a barne with-oute bapteme · may nou3t so be saued
85   Nisi quis renatus fuerit loke 3e lettred men · whether I lye or do nou3te
      And lewte [þo] loked on me · and I loured after
      Wherfore lourestow quod lewte · and loked on me harde
      3if I durste quod I amonges men · þis meteles auowe

---

69 **parisshene**: Alpha adds the indefinite article. There is no parallel in C.

77 **another**: R's *other* has support from CrCGO. The line is not in C, and is rejected by KD.

81 **þynketh**: Only L has *þynke*.

82 L's placing of the punctuation after *man* has the support of MCR, suggesting a **Bx** error. Beta2 (CrWHm) and OF correct by placing it after *may*.

83 **to**: R has *til*, and F has *into*.

83 **&c**: HmCGO extend the "common saying" (Alford (1992), 72) by adding *delet peccatum*. In beta (LMCrWHmO) the Latin follows the English on the same line, either as part of the line (MCr) or separated from the English with a space, in L (boxed in red), W (boxed in red preceded by // to indicate an omission), Hm (with caret to indicate omission), and O (which commonly sets Latin quotations in the right margin, underlined in red). In alpha the Latin is given a separate line. Compare l. 85, where it is clear that **Bx** treats the Latin as the first part of the line.

85 CGO extend the quotation (from John 3.5) but LMCrWR show that **Bx** took the four Latin words as the start of the English line. Cf. 11.83.

86 Hm and F have a paraph and M has a line-space.

86 **þo**: Alpha's reading has some support from the parallel line in **Cx**: *And thenne louhe leaute for y loured on þe frere* (RK.12.23).

87 A paraph would be appropriate here to mark the beginning of direct speech, but it is supported by WR only. In the next line it has stronger support from WHm and alpha, and in l. 89 from W and alpha. W is much more regular than other scribes in paragraphing speech, and his testimony therefore carries less weight.

ȝe bi peter and bi poule quod he · and take hem bothe to witnesse
90 Non oderis fratres secrete in corde tuo · set publice argue illos

¶ Þei wol alleggen also quod I · and by þe gospel preuen
Nolite iudicare quemquam ·

¶ And wher-of serueth lawe quod lewte · if no lyf vndertoke it
Falsenesse ne faytrye · for sumwhat þe apostle seyde
95 Non oderis fratrem · and in þe sauter also seithe dauid þe prophete
Existimasti inique quod ero tui similis &c
It is licitum for lewed men · to segge þe sothe
If hem lyketh and leste · eche a lawe it graunteth
Excepte parsones and prestes · and prelates of holycherche
100 It falleth nouȝte for þat folke · no tales to telle
Þough þe tale were trewe · and it touched synne

¶ Þinge þat al þe worlde wote · wherfore shuldestow spare
And reden it in Retoryke · to arate dedly synne
Ac be neuere-more þe fyrste · þe defaute to blame
105 Þouȝe þow se yuel sey it nouȝte fyrste · be sorye it nere amended
No þinge þat is pryue · publice þow it neuere
Neyther for loue laude it nouȝt · ne lakke it for enuye
Parum lauda vitupera parcius

¶ He seith sothe quod scripture þo · and skipte an heigh & preched
110 Ac þe matere þat she meued · if lewed men it knewe
Þe lasse as I leue · louyen it þei wolde
[Þe bileue [of] þat lord . þat lettred men techeth]

¶ This was her teme and her tyxte · I toke ful gode hede
Multi to a maungerye · and to þe mete were sompned
115 And whan þe peple was plenere comen · þe porter vnpynned þe ȝate
And plukked in pauci priueliche · and lete þe remenaunt go rowme

---

89 **take**: The imperative is supported by the crucial witnesses LMR, as well as G. Others have the easier past tense. See Adams (2000), 179.

93 **lewte**: Cx does not support R's addition of *þanne*.

95 All scribes except F incorporate the Latin quotation into the line. Cf. 11.85.

102 **Þinge**: Alpha may have started the line with *A* (F) or *Ac* (R), but neither is supported by Cx.

103 **And**: Clearly the **Bx** reading, though probably an error for *To* as in WHm and also **Cx**.

104 **be**: HmF add *thu*, as does the P family of C.

107 **laude**: R has *lakke*, anticipating the b-verse, while F rewrites. Cx has *labbe it out*, "blurt it out", for *laude it nouȝt*.

110 **if lewed men it knewe**: R's b-verse *lewed men it knowe* probably represents corruption in alpha (cf. F). Cx supports beta.

112 **of þat lord**: The line is recorded only in alpha, though evidently the a-verse has been corrupted, perhaps simply by omitting *of* as in R. Cx reads *of oure lord* (RK.12.44).

¶ Al for tene of her tyxte · trembled myn herte
And in a were gan I waxe · and with my-self to dispute
Whether I were chosen or nou3t chosen · on holicherche I þou3te
120 Þat vnderfonge me atte fonte · for one of goddis chosne
For cryste cleped vs alle · come if we wolde
Sarasenes and scismatikes · and so he dyd þe iewes
O vos omnes scicientes venite &c
And badde hem souke for synne · sa[ue] at his breste
125 And drynke bote for bale · brouke it who-so my3te

¶ Þanne may alle crystene come quod I · and cleyme þere entre
By þe blode þat he bou3te vs with · and þorugh baptesme after
Qui crediderit & baptizatus fuerit &c
For þough a crystene man coueyted · his crystenedome to reneye
130 Ri3tfulliche to renye · no resoun it wolde

¶ For may no cherle chartre make · ne his catel selle
With-outen leue of his lorde · no lawe wil it graunte
Ac he may renne in arrerage · and rowme fro home
And as a reneyed caityf [·] recchelesly aboute
135 Ac Resoun shal rekne with hym · [and rebuken hym at þe laste
And conscience a-counte with hym ·] and casten hym in arrerage
And putten [hym] after in prisone · in purgatorie to brenne
[And] for his arrerages rewarden hym þere · [ri3te] to þe daye of dome

---

123 **scicientes**: Evidently the **Bx** (and probably **Cx**) spelling for the more formally correct *sicientes*.

124 **saue**: Beta has *saufly*, but Alpha's word is supported by the X family of C; the P family has *sauete* in a rewritten b-verse. Kane (2005) glosses *saue* RK.12.56 as "decoction of herbs taken internally *fig.*". See *MED save* n.(1).

127 **þat**: G, Alpha and a few **C** mss. omit.

129 **reneye**: Beta, supported by sense and by **Cx** against alpha's *receyue*.

133 **rowme**: R repeats *renne*; F has *rayke*. **Cx** supports the verb as in beta, and the omission of *so* as in alpha, added in beta to fill out a short line.

134 **recchelesly**: The L corrector assumes omission of a verb, and supplies *gon*, while Beta2 (CrWHm) repeats *rennen* from the previous line. Alpha has corrupted the a-verse (R has *he renneth* for *a reneyed*), and it appears likely that **Cx** has to make sense of a corrupted exemplar, since the line becomes *As a recheles caytyf or reneyed as hit semeth* (RK.12.65).

135–6 As a result of eyeskip on mid-line *with hym*, beta drops 135b and 136a. Alpha is supported by **Cx**.

137 **hym**: The omission in LMC suggests that the pronoun may have been lost in beta. It is supported by both alpha and **Cx**.

137 **in**: LM and beta2 (CrWHm) have *in a*, but the article is not in alpha or **Cx**.

138 **And**: Beta drops *And*, but alpha is supported by the X family of C. The P family reorders the a-verse.

138 **ri3te**: R supplies the **Bx** reading. The alliterating adverb is supported by **Cx**. F rewrites the b-verse.

But if contricioun w[o]l come · and crye bi his lyue
140 Mercy for his mysdedes · with mouth or with herte

¶ Þat is soth seyde scripture [·] may no synne lette
Mercy alle to amende · and mekenesse hir folwe
For þey beth as owre bokes telleth · aboue goddes werkes
Misericordia eius super omnia opera eius

145 ¶ 3ee baw for bokes quod one · was broken oute of helle
Hi3te troianus had ben a trewe kny3te · toke witnesse at a pope
How he was ded and dampned · to dwellen in pyne
For an vncristene creature [·] clerkis wyten þe sothe
Þat al þe clergye vnder cryste · mi3te me cracche fro helle
150 But onliche loue and leaute · [of] my lawful domes

¶ Gregorie wist þis wel · and wilned to my soule
Sauacioun for [þe] sothenesse · þat he seigh in my werkes
And after þat he wepte · and wilned me were graunted
Grace wyth-outen any bede-byddynge · his bone was vnderfonge
155 And I saued as 3e may se · with-oute syngyng of masses
By loue and by lernyng [·] of my lyuyng in treuthe
Brou3te me fro bitter peyne · þere no biddyng my3te

¶ Lo 3e lordes what leute did · by an Emperoure of Rome
Þat was an vncrystene creature · as clerkes fyndeth in bokes
160 Nou3t þorw preyere of a pope · but for his pure treuthe
Was þat sarasene saued · as seynt Gregorie bereth witnesse
Wel ou3te 3e lordes þat lawes kepe · þis lessoun to haue in mynde
And on troianus treuth to thenke · and do treuthe to þe peple

---

139 **wol**: LR give strong support for *wel*, which could be right ("happily", etc.). More probably both scribes mistake *wol come* for a spelling of *welcome* (see *MED*), and in L the line is marked for correction. **Cx** revises the line.

140 **or**: Well supported for **Bx**, though *and* in WHmF is also the reading of **Cx**.

142 **alle to**: Alpha's *may al* was perhaps the basis for **Cx**, which has the a-verse *Mercy þat he ne may al amende*. However, the syntax is *lette to amende* "prevent from amending".

142 **and mekenesse hir folwe**: R (= alpha?) muddles through with *þat mekenesse he folweth*, but **Cx** supports the b-verse as in beta.

149 **mi3te**: Evidently **Bx** lost *ne*, required for sense and supplied by beta2 (CrWHm), as in **Cx** (RK.12.79).

150 **of**: So alpha, against beta's *and*. The sense is supported by **Cx** *as in my lawes demynge*, which also sets Trajan's love and integrity in relation to his justice.

152 **þe**: Alpha, dropped by beta, but supported by **Cx**.

152 **seigh in**: Beta, supported by **Cx**, against R's *seith of*.

155 **may**: Probably R's *now* is a misreading of an alpha form *mowe*.

156 **By**: Probably dropped by alpha, with F patching. Alpha may have stumbled over the non-expression of the subject pronoun "that" in the next line (where F again patches).

162 **3e**: Beta, supported by **Cx**, against alpha's *þe*.

[¶ Þis matir is merke for mani of ȝow · ac men of holy cherche
165 Þe legend[a] sanctorum ȝow lereth · more larger þan I ȝow telle
Ac þus lele loue · and lyuynge in treuthe
Pulte oute of pyne · a paynym of rome
Yblessed be treuthe · þat so brak helle ȝates
And saued þe sarasyn · fram sathanas and his power
170 Þere no clergie ne couthe · ne konnynge of lawes
Loue and leute [·] is a lele science
For þat is þe boke blessede · of blisse and of ioye
God wrouȝt it and wrot hit · with his one fynger
And toke it moyses vpon þe mount · alle men to lere]

175 [¶]Lawe with-outen loue quod troianus [·] leye þere a bene
Or any science vnder sonne · þe seuene artz and alle
But þei ben lerned for owre lordes loue · loste is alle þe tyme
For no cause to cacche siluer þere-by · ne to be called a mayster
But al for loue of owre lorde · and þe bet to loue þe peple
180 For seynte Iohan seyde it · and soth aren his wordes
Qui non diligit manet in morte

¶ Who-so loueth nouȝte leue me · he lyueth in deth-deyinge
And þat alle manere men · enemys and frendes
Louen her eyther other · and lene hem as her-selue
185 Who-so leneth nouȝte he loueth nouȝte · [oure lorde] wote þe sothe
And comaundeth eche creature · to confourme hym to louye
And souereynelyche pore poeple · and here ennemys after

164–74 Beta omits these 11 lines, perhaps due to eyeskip from paraph to paraph. KD p. 66 suggest an implausible series of homeoarchy. 11.172 is in R alone. The passage is not in C, although **Bx.**11.171–2 lies behind RK.12.97. R's spellings have been altered to those of L.
165 **legenda**: RF write *legende*, but cf. **Bx.**11.229 and 15.280.
167 **Pulte**: From *pilten* (cf. RK.11.206) rather than *pullen, pace* Kane (2005). Cf. **Bx.**1.128, 15.66.
168 **so brak**: F reverses the word-order.
173 **one**: R's *on* is his usual form of "one". F has *owne*.
174 **to**: F supplies an object *it*, perhaps rightly.
175 **¶**: Since we suppose that the beta scribe skipped from one paraph to another, we insert the paraph supplied only in R and Hm. In L the line is at the top of the leaf.
177 **But**: In L the corrector has added *if*, but it is without support.
182 **¶**: The paraph is in beta only. In R the line is at the top of the page.
185 **Who-so**: Alpha begins *For ho-so*, obscuring the parallel with l. 182.
185 **leneth**: Alpha's *leueth* (also Cr) is not appropriate to the argument that follows.
185 **oure lorde**: The reading is very uncertain since it is attested by R alone. Possibly R altered **Bx** *god* for the sake of alliteration, but that would be very untypical behaviour. More probably beta read *god*, coincidentally adopted by F. These lines are not in C. Perhaps reflecting the lack of b-verse alliteration with the reading *god*, all scribes except W, beta4 and R punctuate after each *nouȝte*.
186 **comaundeth**: O and Alpha have the past tense. Either alpha or beta could be right.

For hem þat hateth vs · is owre meryte to louye
And pore peple to plese · here prayeres may vs helpe
190 For owre ioye and owre [Iuwel] · Ihesu cryst of heuene
In a pore mannes apparaille · pursueth vs euere
And loketh on vs in her liknesse · and þat with louely chere
To knowen vs by owre kynde herte · and castyng of owre eyen
Wheþer we loue þe lordes here · byfor owre lorde of blisse

195 ¶ And exciteth vs bi þe euangelye · þat when we maken festes
We shulde nouȝte clepe owre kynne þer-to · ne none kynnes riche
Cum facitis conuiuia nolite inuitare amicos
Ac calleth þe careful þer-to [·] þe croked and þe pore
For ȝowre frendes wil feden ȝow · and fonde ȝow to quite
200 Ȝowre festynge and ȝowre faire ȝifte · vche frende quyteth so other

¶ Ac for þe pore I shal paye · and pure wel quyte her trauaille
Þat ȝiueth hem mete or moneye · and loueth hem for my sake

[¶ God myȝte riche haue made . alle men if he wolde]
[Ac] for þe best ben somme riche · and somme beggers and pore
205 For alle are we crystes creatures · and of his coffres riche
And bretheren as of o blode · as wel beggares as erles
For [at] caluarye of crystes blode · crystenedome gan sprynge
And blody bretheren we bycome þere · of o body ywonne
As quasi modo geniti · and gentil men vche one
210 No beggere ne boye amonges vs · but if it synne made

---

190 **Iuwel**: KD's conjecture, proposed on p. 184, is persuasive as the reading of **Bx**, and fits the alliteration on /j/. R's nonsensical *euel* can hardly have been prompted by the commonplace *hele, helthe* of beta and F, but is more likely to be a misinterpretation of an alpha spelling *iuel*. If so, then beta and F misunderstood or objected to the rare use of "jewel" to refer to Christ. The closest parallel is *Pearl* 795; cf. also **Bx**.18.447.

190 **Ihesu**: Alpha has *is ihesu*, but *Ihesu* is subject of *pursueth* in the next line.

194 **owre**: Strong support from LMR and CO, against *þe* in beta2 and GF.

195 **¶**: Only LR have a paraph.

196 **kynnes riche**: Probably "rich of any sort", translating Luke 14.12 "vicinos divites". R may have confused with *kine-riche*, "kingdom", or interpreted as "rich kin", following *kyn* (Luke's "cognatos") in the a-verse. Cf. also GO, and F's apparent difficulty with the b-verse. It is noteworthy that **Cx**, which has *knyhtes* in the a-verse, has *none kyne ryche*, "no rich kin" in the b-verse (RK.12.103).

200 **ȝifte**: Clearly beta, though beta4 (CGO) has plural, as does alpha.

203 **God myȝte riche haue made alle**: We suppose that F represents alpha and also **Bx**, in a line that is lost in beta. We take F's *a* as "have". R is defective in sense, though KD's emendation based on R is attractive: "Alle myȝte god haue maad riche men if he wolde" (KD.11.197). Lines 202–6 are not in C.

204 **Ac**: So R. Having lost the previous line, beta drops the co-ordinating conjunction. F as usual alters to *But*.

206 **And**: R has *As*, but it is not supported by **Cx**.

207 **at**: Alpha is supported by **Cx** (RK.12.109).

Qui facit peccatum seruus est peccati &c

¶ In þe olde lawe · as [þe] lettre telleth
Mennes sones · men called vs vchone
Of adames issue and Eue · ay til god-man deyde
215 And after his resurreccioun · Redemptor was his name
And we his bretheren þourgh hym ybou3t · bothe riche and pore
For-þi loue we as leue [children] shal · and vche man laughe vp other
And of þat eche man may forbere · amende þere it nedeth
And euery man helpe other · for hennes shal we alle
220 Alter alterius onera portate
And be we nou3te vnkynde of owre catel · ne of owre kunnynge neyther
For noet no man how neighe it is · to be ynome fro bothe
For-þi lakke no lyf other · þough he more latyne knowe
Ne vnder-nym nou3te foule · for is none with-oute faute
225 For what-euere clerkis carpe [·] of crystenedome or elles
Cryst to a comune woman seyde · in comune at a feste
Þat fides sua shulde sauen hir [·] and saluen hir of alle synnes

¶ Þanne is byleue a lele helpe [·] aboue logyke or lawe
Of logyke ne of lawe [·] in legenda sanctorum
230 Is litel allowaunce made · but if bileue hem helpe
For it is ouerlonge ar logyke · any lessoun assoille
And lawe is loth to louye · but if he lacche syluer
Bothe logyke and lawe · þat loueth nou3te to lye
I conseille alle crystene · cleue nou3te þer-on to sore
235 For sum wordes I fynde ywryten · were of faithes techyng
Þat saued synful men · as seynt Iohan bereth wytnesse
Eadem mensura qua mensi fueritis remecietur vobis

---

212 **þe** (2): Alpha is supported by **Cx**. Beta is probably filling out a short b-verse. In **Cx**, this whole line becomes the a-verse, and the next line the b-verse, dropping *vchone*.

217 **children:** Alpha, supported by **Cx**; beta repeats *bretheren* from the previous line.

217 **shal:** Strong support for **Bx** from all except WCrF, which omit as in **Cx**.

217 **vp:** LMCR, against *on* GOF and *of* WHm. The b-verse is revised in **Cx**.

219 **other:** Alpha adds *here*, but **Cx** supports beta.

222 **noet:** Supported by LMCOR against *woot* in others. This passage to l. 237 is not in C.

224 **faute:** So LMCrCGO. Curiously the word is only used once in the three versions, at **Bx**.10.111 (where F reads *defawte*). In contrast, *defaute*, as in WHm and alpha, is common, though generally in the senses "lack, hardship". We follow copy-text.

227 **alle:** So LCrHmR; MGC read *hire*, while WOF omit.

230 **litel allowaunce made:** Although we adopt beta's a-verse, alpha's phrase *litel alowed* has a parallel in **Bx**.14.335 *For lordes alloweth hym litel*.

230 **if:** Omitted by G and alpha. There are plenty of parallels for either reading.

234 **crystene:** For independent scribal addition of *men* in this a-verse, cf. **Bx**.9.185. The a-verse is repeated at **Bx**.7.211 and 15.360.

¶ For-þi lerne we þe lawe of loue · as owre lorde tau3te
And as seynte Gregory seide · for mannes soule helthe
240 Melius est scrutari scelera nostra · quam naturas rerum

¶ Why I moue þis matere · is moste for þe pore
For in her lyknesse owre lorde · ofte hath ben yknowe
Witnesse in þe Paske-wyke · whan he 3ede to Emaus
Cleophas ne knewe hym nau3te · þat he cryste were
245 For his pore paraille · and pylgrymes wedes
Tyl he blessed and brak · þe bred þat þei eten
So bi his werkes þei wisten · þat he was Ihesus
Ac by clothyng þei knewe hym nou3te · ne bi carpynge of tonge

¶ And al was ensample [for-sothe] · to vs synful here
250 Þat we shulde be low · and loueliche of speche
And apparaille vs nou3te ouer-proudly · for pylgrymes ar we alle
And in þe apparaille of a pore man · and pilgrymes lyknesse
Many tyme god hath ben mette · amonge nedy peple
Þere neuere segge hym seigh · in secte of þe riche

255 ¶ Seynt Iohan and other seyntes · were seyne in pore clothynge
And as pore pilgrymes · preyed mennes godis
Ihesu cryste on a iewes dou3ter aly3te · gentil woman þough she were
Was a pure pore mayde · and to a pore man wedded

¶ Martha on Marye magdeleyne · an huge pleynte she made
260 And to owre saueour self · seyde þise wordes
Domine non est tibi cure quod soror mea reliquit me sola ministrare &c

¶ And hastiliche god answered · and eytheres wille folwed
Bothe Marthaes and Maries · as Mathew bereth witnesse
Ac pouerte god put bifore · and preysed it þe bettre

---

238 ¶: The paraph is in beta and F.

245 **paraille**: So LR. C mss. vary. However, cf. l. 252 where (in the absence of F) R alone has
the aphetic form.

249 ¶: The paraph is in beta only.

249 **ensample for-sothe**: R's reading, doubtfully adopted on the basis of **Cx** *ensample sothly*.
The adverb supplies a second alliterative stave for the a-verse. Beta has *in ensample*, although
M shares the reading of F without *in*.

251 **ouer-**: Supported by LMR and WHm (C has *to*), but dropped by CrGOF.

256 **mennes**: In alpha *men* is object of *preyude*, "begged men (for their) goods", and is so
expanded by F.

258 **Was**: R (F drops lines 257–8) repeats *A*, "she" from the previous line, as does Hm *sche*,
but **Cx** is without it.

261 **sola**: So LM and F (R truncates after *cure*), together with some C mss. The accusative
solam is expected, as in other mss.

262 ¶: The paraph is in beta only.

265 Maria optimam partem elegit · que non &c

¶ And alle þe wyse þat euere were · by auȝte I can aspye
Preysen pouerte for best lyf · if pacience it folwe
And bothe bettere and blisseder · by many folde þan ricchesse
Although it be soure to suffre · þere cometh swete after
270 As on a walnot with-oute [·] is a bitter barke
And after þat bitter barke · be þe shelle aweye
Is a kirnelle of conforte · kynde to restore
So is after pouerte or penaunce · pacientlyche ytake
[M]aketh a man to haue mynde in gode · and a grete wille
275 To wepe and to wel bydde · wher-of wexeth mercy
Of which cryst is a kirnelle · to conforte þe soule
And wel sykerer he slepyth · þe [segge] þat is pore
And lasse he dredeth deth · and in derke to be robbed
Þan he þat is riȝte ryche · resoun bereth wytnesse
280 Pauper ego ludo dum tu diues meditaris

¶ Alþough salamon seide · as folke seeth in þe bible
Diuicias nec paupertates &c
Wyser þan salamon was · bereth witnesse and tauȝte
Þat parfyte pouert was · no possessioun to haue
285 And lyf moste lykynge to god · as luke bereth witnesse
Si vis perfectus esse · vade & vende &c
And is to mene to men · þat on þis molde lyuen
Who-so wil be pure parfyt · mote possessioun forsake
Or selle it as seith þe boke · and þe syluer dele
290 To beggeres þat gone and begge · and bidden good for goddes loue

---

265 **non &c**: LMCrW end at this point; R stops after *elegit*, while the others continue *auferetur ab ea*. C mss. show the same variation, though the X family ends with *non &c*.

266 **¶**: The paraph is in beta only.

267 **Preysen**: Only MW have the past tense, following on from *were* in the previous line. However, it must be observed that **Cx** also has the past. See next note.

267 **folwe**: W continues with the past tense, as do six C mss. Alpha's *wolde/welde* is presumably a misreading of *folwede*; two C mss. have the same curious reading.

269 **Although**: The reading of LM and alpha and the X family of C. Other beta mss. have *And though*. See Adams (2000), 179.

274 **Maketh**: Beta begins *For it maketh*, but the clause without subject as in alpha is supported by **Cx**.

277 **segge**: Beta's *man* is a straightforward example of the substitution of an easier reading. **Cx** supports alpha.

281 **¶**: The paraph in L is supported by WF.

281 **folke**: Presumably on this occasion alpha has adopted the easier reading *men*; cf. l. 277. From here to l. 301 there is no parallel in C.

287 MWHmC would support a paraph here, but it is not particularly appropriate and not supported by alpha.

¶ For failled neuere man mete · þat my3tful god serued
As dauid seith in þe sauter · to suche þat ben in wille
To serue god godeliche · ne greueth hym no penaunce
Nichil inpossibile volenti
295 Ne lakketh neuere lyflode · lynnen ne wollen
Inquirentes autem dominum · non minuentur omni bono

[¶] If prestes weren parfyt · þei wolde no syluer take
For masses ne for matynes · nou3te her mete of vsureres
Ne neither kirtel ne cote · þeigh þey for colde shulde deye
300 And þei her deuor dede · as dauid seith in þe sauter
Iudica me deus & discerne causam meam
Spera in deo speketh of prestes · þat haue no spendyng syluer
Þat 3if þei trauaille trewlich · and trusten in god almi3ti
Hem shulde lakke no lyflode · noyther wollen ne lynnen
305 And þe title þat [3e] take ordres by · telleth 3e ben auaunced
Þanne nedeth nou3te 3ow to take syluer · for masses þat 3e syngen
For he þat toke 3ow 3owre tytle · shulde take 3ow 3owre wages
Or þe bisshop þat blesseth 3ow · if þat 3e ben worthy

---

291 **serued**: Despite beta2 (CrWHm), beta probably has the past tense and alpha the present. Either could be right: the past following on from *failled*, or the present anticipating *seith* and the verbs in ll. 293 and 295.

292 Following this line, alpha evidently had the half line *With eny wel or wo*, reproduced by R. F makes a full line by coupling it with l. 292b which he has replaced by a half-line of his own.

293 **hym**: MCr and alpha have pl. *hem*. We follow copy-text.

294 **inpossibile**: Alford (1992), 75, quotes the proverb in this form. Alpha, with *difficile* instead, may have known another form. The *Oxford Dictionary of English Proverbs*, p. 463, cites Heywood (1546) "Nothing is impossible to a willyng hart", and Fergusson (1641) "Nothing is difficile to a well willit man".

295 **neuere**: R has *noyther*; F drops the line.

297 ¶: The rubricator in L misses the paraph since the line is at the top of the page. It is supported by WHmRF and a line-space in M.

297 **parfyt**: Both KD and Schmidt adopt alpha's *wise* for the sake of the alliteration, although Schmidt (1995) considers that alpha gives "less good sense" (p. 386). However, the parallel line in **Cx** (following a divergence from **B** of 190 lines) is *Vch a parfit prest to pouerte sholde drawe* (RK.13.100), which precedes the line parallel to **Bx**.11.302. Perhaps **Bx** *syluer* is an error picked up from that line for *pens*. *Parfit* priesthood is a favourite concept of Langland's; cf. *3if presthod were parfit* (**Bx**.15.566).

300 **dede**: Dropped in alpha, but necessary for the sense, which leads F to revise.

304 **wollen ne lynnen**: WHm reverse the nouns, as in the nearly identical l. 295, thus no doubt correcting a **Bx** error. **Cx**, which only uses the line once, has *lynnen ne wollene*, to alliterate aa/ax.

305 **3e** (1): The reading of R, and also of W's text, but significantly not of the catchword, which has the beta reading *þei*. W's reading is thus an enlightened correction, and it is the **Cx** reading. F revises, but keeping the second person.

306 **nou3te 3ow**: This appears to be the order in beta, reversed to the commonplace in MW; alpha perhaps had *3ow nou3t* as in R. We follow copy-text. **Cx** omits the pronoun, and replaces *take* with alliterating *nyme*.

¶ For made neuere kynge no kny3te · but he hadde catel to spende
310　As bifel for a kni3te · or fonde hym for his strengthe
It is a careful kny3te · and of a caytyue kynges makynge
Þat hath no londe ne lynage riche · ne good loos of his handes
Þe same I segge for sothe · by alle suche prestes
Þat han noyther kunnynge ne kynne · but a croune one
315　And a tytle a tale of nou3te · to his lyflode at myschief
He hath more bileue as I leue · to lacche þorw his croune
Cure · þan for konnyng · or knowen for clene of berynge
I haue wonder & why · and wher-fore þe bisshop
Maketh suche prestes · þat lewed men bytrayen

320　¶ A chartre is chalengeable · byfor a chief iustice
If false latyne be in þa[t] lettre · þe lawe it inpugneth
Or peynted parenterlinarie · parceles ouer-skipped
Þe gome þat gloseth so chartres · for a goky is holden

¶ So is it a goky by god · þat in his gospel failleth
325　Or in masse or in matynes · maketh any defaute
Qui offendit in vno in omnibus est reus &c
And also in þe sauter · seyth dauyd to ouerskippers
Psallite deo nostro psallite quoniam rex terre deus israel psallite sapienter
Þe bisshop shal be blamed · bifor god as I leue
330　Þat crouneth suche goddes kni3tes · þat conneth nou3t sapienter
Synge ne psalmes rede · ne segge a messe of þe day
Ac neuer neyther is blamelees · þe bisshop ne þe chapleyne
For her eyther is endited · and þat of ignorancia
Non excusat episcopos · nec idiotes prestes

335　¶ Þis lokynge on lewed prestes · haþ don me lepe fram pouerte
Þe whiche I preyse þere pacyence is · more parfyt þan ricchesse

¶ Ac moche more in metynge þus · with me gan one dispute
And slepynge I seigh al þis · and sithen cam kynde

---

309 **kynge**: LHm read *no kynge*. Hm subsequently erases the *no* before *knygth*.

312 **no**: Alpha's *noþer* may equally be right. The P family of C have the beta reading, the X family the alpha.

312 **riche**: Omitted by alpha, but supported by **Cx**.

315 **at**: Beta2 (CrWHm) adds *his*. **Cx** ends the line *lyflode as hit were*.

317 The syntactic punctuation after *Cure* is recorded in LMWOF.

321 **þat**: L has *þa*; the line is marked for correction.

322 **parceles**: In beta2 (CrWHm) and F the b-verse begins *or*, but this is not supported by Cx (RK.13.119).

329 LR do not have a paraph here, but it might be added on the basis of MWHmCF.

333 **of**: Beta2 (CrWHm) alters to *is*; F has *ys be*.

337 Instead of this line F has nine lines in which Will wakes, and falls asleep again in the line corresponding to l. 338.

And nempned me by my name · and bad me nymen hede
340 And þorw þe wondres of þis worlde · wytte for to take
And on a mountaigne þat mydelerd hyȝte · as me þo þouȝte
I was fette forth · by ensaumples to knowe
Þorugh eche a creature and kynde · my creatoure to louye
I seigh þe sonne and þe see · and þe sonde after
345 And where þat bryddes and bestes · by here make þei ȝeden
Wylde wormes in wodes · and wonderful foules
With flekked fetheres · and of fele coloures
Man and his make · I myȝte [se bothe]
Pouerte and plente · bothe pees and werre
350 Blisse and bale · bothe I seigh at ones
And how men token Mede · and mercy refused

¶ Resoune I seighe sothly [·] suen alle bestes
In etyng in drynkynge · and in engendrynge of kynde
And after course of concepcioun · none toke kepe of other
355 As whan þei hadde ryde in rotey-tyme · anon riȝte þer-after
Males drowen hem to males · a-mornynges bi hem-self
And in euenynges also · ȝe[de] males fro femeles
Þere ne was cow ne cowkynde · þat conceyued hadde
Þat wolde belwe after boles · ne bore after sowe
360 Bothe horse and houndes · and alle other bestes
Medled nouȝte wyth here makes · þat with fole were

¶ Briddes I bihelde · þat in buskes made nestes
Hadde neuere wye witte · to worche þe leest
I hadde wonder at whom · and where þe pye lerned
365 To legge stykkes · in whiche she leythe and bredeth
Þere nys wriȝte as I wene · shulde worche hir neste to paye

---

340 **wondres:** So beta. R has *wordes*, presumably reproducing alpha, which F improves to *worchynge*.

345 **make:** CrWGF have *makes*, as does the P family of C.

345 **þei:** Well supported for **Bx**, but omitted by WGOF and by the P family of C.

348 **se bothe:** R is supported by **Cx**. Beta reads *bothe byholde*.

350 **at:** Beta2 (CrWHm) has *al at*, not supported by **Cx**.

357 **ȝede:** In the absence of F which omits ll. 355–7, R represents alpha and also **Bx**. On the evidence of L, beta read *ȝe*, which scribes "corrected" to *þe* (or misread *ye*), and lost the alliteration. Beta2 (CrWHm) then smoothed by adding the verb *ben*. See Schmidt (1995), 387. For alliteration of *ȝede* with vowels, cf. **Bx**.20.136 etc. The line is rewritten in **Cx**.

365 **stykkes:** Beta includes the definite article: **Cx** *Lernede to legge stikkes* gives slight support to alpha's omission.

365 **she leythe:** An interesting example of how a minor alpha error (*lenth* for *leith*), faithfully reproduced by R, has prompted F to make sense (but the wrong sense). F interprets *a* as "in" rather than "she", takes the additional minim in *lenth* (for *leith*) as a spelling of "length", and sensibly supposes *bredeth* to be an error for *breede*, "breadth".

366 **nys:** Alpha's *is no* might equally be right; it is shared by C mss. (a few have *nys no*).

If any masoun made a molde þer-to · moche wonder it were

¶ And ʒet me merueilled more · many other briddes
Hudden and hileden · her egges ful derne
370 In mareys and mores · for men sholde hem nouʒt fynde
And hudden here egges · whan þei þere-fro wente
For fere of other foules · and for wylde bestis

¶ And some tr[e]den her makes · and on trees bredden
And brouʒten forth her bryddes so · al aboue þe grounde
375 And some bryddes at þe bille · þorwgh brethynge conceyued
And some kauked I toke kepe · how pekokes bredden
Moche merueilled me · what maister þei hadde
And who tauʒte hem on trees · to tymbre so heigh
Þere noither buirn ne beste · may her briddes rechen

380 ¶ And sythen I loked vpon þe see · and so forth vpon þe sterres
Many selcouthes I seygh · ben nought to seye nouthe

¶ I seigh floures in þe fritthe · and her faire coloures
And how amonge þe grene grasse · grewe so many hewes
And somme soure and some swete · selcouthe me þouʒte
385 Of her kynde and [of] her coloure · to carpe it were to longe

¶ Ac þat moste moeued me · and my mode chaunged
Þat resoun rewarded · and reuled alle bestes
Saue man and his make · many tyme and ofte
No resoun hem folwed · and þanne I rebuked
390 Resoun · and riʒte til hym-seluen I seyde

---

368 **many**: Probably R represents the alpha reading, with F adding *of* to complete the construction with *merueilled*. For the same reason most beta mss. add *how* (though G also has *off*).
Cx supports R with *merueylede more mony of þe briddes*.

373 **treden**: Alpha's present tense is supported by Cx.

374 **brouʒten**: Beta is supported by Cx. R repeats the verb *bredde* from the previous line.

380 **vpon** (1 & 2): Both in the a-verse and in the b-verse, the readings of LMWR support
this as **Bx**, though Cx has *on* for both, as do other **B** mss. (Hm has *vpon* and *yn*.)

385 **of** (2): R is supported by Cx. Beta evidently dropped it (added in Cr); F rephrases the
a-verse.

388 **tyme**: Variation between *many tyme / tymes / a tyme* is unpatterned, except that alpha
shows a tendency to prefer *tymes*, as here: e.g. **Bx**.13.4, 14.4, and (in the same b-verse) 20.26
(where R is out). There is the same variation in AC (e.g. K.8.150, 9.29; RK.4.167, 22.26, etc.).
Here, though the majority of C mss. have *tymes*, seven have *tyme* (RK.13.181).

389 This and the following line are defective in **Bx**. In Cx the lines read: *Resoun reulede hem
nat, noþer ryche ne pore / Thenne y aresonede resoun and ryht til hym y sayde* (RK.13.182–3). F's
line presumably represents an intelligent revision for the alliteration; the reading *rewlyþ* for
folwed must be contamination from C or coincidental, picking up *rewlede* two lines above.

390 In this defective line the punctuation follows *Resoun* in LMCrWOR, with R adding a
second punctuation after *hym*; HmC punctuate after *right*, creating an aa/bb line. F again
revises for the metre.

I haue wonder of þe quod I · þat witty art holden
Why þow ne suwest man and his make · þat no mysfait hem folwe

¶ And resoun arated me · and seyde recche þe neuere
Whi I suffre or nouȝt suffre · þi-self hast nouȝt to done
395   Amende þow it if þow myȝte · for my tyme is to abyde
Suffraunce is a souereygne vertue · and a swyfte veniaunce
Who suffreth more þan god quod he · no gome as I leue
He miȝte amende in a Minute-while · al þat mys-standeth
Ac he suffreth for somme mannes good · and so is owre bettre

400   [¶ Holy writt quod þat wye · wisseth men to suffre
Propter deum subiecti estote omni creature
Frenche men and fre men · affaiteth þus her children
[B]ele vertue est soffrance · mal dire est pety veniance
Bien dire et bien soffrer · fait lui soffrant a bien venir
405   For-þi I rede [þe] quod reson · reule þi tonge bettere
And ar þow lakke my lyf · loke þow be to preyse
For is no creature vnder criste · can formen hym-seluen
And if a man miȝte [·] make hym-self good to þe poeple
Vch a lif wold be lakles · leue þow non other
410   Ne þow shalt fynde but fewe · fayne for to here
Of here defautes foule · by-for hem rehersed]

¶ Þe wyse and þe witty · wrote þus in þe bible
De re que te non molestat noly certare
For be a man faire or foule · it falleth nouȝte forto lakke
415   Þe shappe ne þe shafte · þat god shope hym-selue
For al þat he [wrouȝt] was wel ydo · as holywrit witnesseth
Et vidit deus cunta que fecerat et erant valde bona

400–11 These 12 lines have been lost in beta, probably as a result of eyeskip from one paraph to the next, as so often. Lines 403–09 are paralleled in **Cx**. We follow R, with spellings altered to those of L. There are many differences in F's version.

403 **Bele**: F is supported by **Cx** (RK.13.203). R has *Vele*.

405 **þe quod**: R is without *þe* and F without *quod*. In the b-verse F has *þou rewle* for R's *rewle*. The X family of C has *Forthy quod Resoun y rede thow* while the P family has … *rede þe*.

406 **þow** (2): R has *if þow* where F has *þyn*, perhaps influenced by *þy tunge* in the previous line. **Cx**'s *loke ho is to preyse*, though different, lends support to R's nominative but not to the conjunction.

408 With evident corruption in both mss., it is impossible to recover **Bx**. If R reproduces alpha, F has improved by picking up *lakles*, "without fault", from the following line to replace *goed to þe poeple*. F suggests that the punctuation should follow *miȝte* rather than *make* as in R. If so, **Bx** may have read simply *And if a man miȝte · make hymself good*, with alpha expanding a short line. **Cx** rewrites with much the same sense: *And if creatures cristene couth make hemsulue* (RK.13.208).

412 **¶**: The paraph (following the gap in beta) is in LR, with a new line-group in M.

413 **noly**: R has *nolite*. C mss. vary between *noli*, *nolite* and *noli te* (RK.13.196a).

414 Only LR are without a paraph here.

416 **wrouȝt**: Alpha's reading carries the alliteration. Beta has *did*. This passage is not in C.

¶ And badde euery creature · in his kynde encrees
Al to murthe with man · þat most woo tholye
420 In fondynge of þe flesshe · and of þe fende bothe
For man was made of suche a matere · he may nouȝt wel astert
Þat some-tymes hym bitit · to folwen his kynde
Catoun acordeth þere-with · nemo sine crimine viuit

¶ Tho cauȝte I coloure anon · and comsed to ben aschamed
425 And awaked þer-with · wo was me þanne
Þat I in meteles ne myȝte · more haue yknowen
And þanne seyde I to my-self · and chidde þat tyme
Now I wote what dowel is quod I · by dere god as me þinketh
And as I caste vp myn eyghen · one loked on me and axed
430 Of me what þinge it were · ywisse sire I seide
To se moche and suffre more · certes quod I is dowel

¶ Haddestow suffred he seyde · slepyng þo þow were
Þow sholdest haue knowen þat clergye can · and conceiued more þorugh
    resoun
For resoun wolde haue reherced þe · riȝte as clergye saide
435 Ac for þine entermetyng · here artow forsake
Philosophus esses si tacuisses

¶ Adam whiles he spak nouȝt · had paradys at wille
Ac whan he mameled aboute mete · and entermeted to knowe
Þe wisdom and þe witte of god · he was put fram blisse
440 And riȝt so ferde resoun bi the · þow with rude speche
Lakkedest and losedest þinge · þat longed nouȝt [þe to] done
Þo hadde he no lykynge · forto lere þe more

---

418 ¶: Following the Latin line, only LW have the paraph. It is perhaps not archetypal.
418 euery: R has *to vch a*; F has *ech*.
419 tholye: Infinitive dependent upon *most*, "must". O and Alpha, taking *most* to mean "most", read *tholieth*, but this gives weak sense.
422 Þat: Beta has *Þat ne*, but alpha is supported by **Cx**.
422 tymes: L is supported by R against *tyme* in other mss. C mss. are divided. The -*s* form of *sometimes* is rare and late in Middle English; in L it occurs again only at **Bx**.13.323. See Adams (2000), 184 and note to l. 388.
423 þere-with: Beta is supported by **Cx** against R *with al* and F *þerto*.
433 conceiued: The variants *kend* and *contreued* in beta2 are not supported by **Cx**.
433 þorugh: As in **Cx**, against *bi* in CrHmGF.
437 ¶: The paraph is in beta only.
437 whiles: R has *þe whiles*, as does the X family of C.
438 entermeted: MCGO add *hym*. **Cx** rewrites.
440 þow with: Beta2 (CrWHm) and CF add *thy*. **Cx** rewrites as *for thy rude speche*.
441 nouȝt þe to done: In beta the b-verse probably ends *nouȝt to be done*, though WO have *noȝt to doon* and W adds the pronoun *þe*. W's reading is also that of alpha, "which was not appropriate for you to do", which gives stronger sense than beta's reading. We adopt R's b-verse

¶ Pruide now and presumpcioun · par-auenture wole þe appele
That clergye þi compaignye · ne kepeth nou3t to sue
445 [For] shal neuere chalangynge ne chydynge · chaste a man so sone
As shal shame and shenden hym · and shape hym to amende
For lat a dronken daffe · in a dyke falle
Late hym ligge loke nou3te on hym · til hym lest to ryse
For þough resoun rebuked hym þanne [· reccheth h[e] neuere
450 Of clergie ne of his conseil · he counteth nou3t a rusche
Or for to bete hym þanne] · it were but pure synne
Ac whan nede nymeth hym vp · for doute lest he sterue
And shame shrapeth his clothes · & his shynes wassheth
Þanne wote þe dronken daffe · wherfore he is to blame

455 ¶ 3e seggen soth [by my soule] quod I · ich haue yseyne it ofte
Þere smitte no þinge so smerte · ne smelleth so [foule]
As shame þere he sheweth him · for euery man hym shonyeth
Why 3e wisse me þus quod I · was for I rebuked resoun

¶ Certes quod he þat is soth · and shope hym forto walken
460 And I aros vp ri3t with þat · and folwed hym after
And preyed hym of his curteisye · to telle me his name

---

with its less usual word-order, although we recognise that *þe* may be an alpha addition. The line is not in **Cx**.

444 **to sue**: Alpha sometimes avoids the verb: cf. **Bx**.10.214, 11.352, 392. Here he revises the line, adding *in* before *þi* and ending *efte to sitte*.

445 **For**: Beta omits. Alpha's reading is supported by **Cx**.

449–51 As a result of eyeskip (mid-line *hym þanne* 449 and 451), beta drops ll. 449b–451a. The lines are in **Cx** (RK.13.236–8).

449 **he**: F is supported by **Cx** against R's *hym*.

451 **Or**: Dropped by F. **Cx** begins *To blame hym or to bete*.

455 **by my soule**: Alpha's phrase is also **Cx**.

456 **foule**: The reading of R alone, but it is supported by **Cx**. F rewrites the b-verse, with the sense "upsets no-one so greatly". Beta's *soure* is a simple misreading; G, additionally misreading the verb, adopts an appropriate adverb.

457 **for euery man hym shonyeth**: Cx supports beta's verb with *vch man shoneth his companye*, which is perhaps a revision for the sake of the alliteration. Alpha is quite different from either with *no man loueth his felachippe*, though one might note that "fellowship" is a synonym of "company".

Passus 12

I am ymagynatyf quod he · Idel was I neuere
Þouȝe I sitte bi my-self · in sikenesse ne in helthe
I haue folwed þe in feithe · þis fyue and fourty wyntre
And many tymes haue moeued þe · to þinke on þine ende
5   And how fele fernȝeres are faren · and so fewe to come
And of þi wylde wantounesse · þo þow ȝonge were
To amende it in þi myddel age · lest miȝte þe faylled
In þyne olde elde · þat yuel can suffre
Pouerte or penaunce · or preyeres bidde
10 Si non in prima vigilia · nec in secunda &c
Amende þe while þow myȝte · þow hast ben warned ofte
With poustees of pestilences [·] with pouerte and with angres
And with þise bitter baleyses · god beteth his dere childeren
Quem diligo castigo
15 And dauid in þe sauter seith · of suche þat loueth Ihesus
Virga tua & baculus tuus ipsa me consolata sunt &c
Al-þough þow stryke me with þi staffe · with stikke or with ȝerde
It is but murth as for me [·] to amende my soule
And þow medlest þe with makyng[e] · and myȝtest go sey þi sauter
20 And bidde for hem þat ȝiueth þe bred · for þere ar bokes ynowe

---

2 **ne**: So LMR, defining *neuere*. The *and* of most other mss. is an obvious easier reading, defining the a-verse. See Adams (2000), 179.

7 **faylled**: L and beta2 (CrWHm) have the past subjunctive, "were to fail", which is perhaps less obvious than the present *faile* of all other mss. There is no parallel in C for **Bx**.12.4–61.

12 **pestilences**: Alpha's *penaunce(s)* is a curious error.

15–16 Alpha omits two lines.

19 **makynge**: Alpha has the sg. and all beta mss. except M have the plural. There is a parallel with the John But ending of **A**, presumably derived from this line, *And for he medleþ of makyng he made þis ende* (K.12.109).

211

To telle men what dowel is · dobet and dobest bothe
And prechoures to preue what it is · of many a peyre freres

¶ I seigh wel he sayde me soth · and somwhat me to excuse
Seid catoun conforted his sone · þat clerke þough he were
25   To solacen hym sum-tyme · as I do whan I make
Interpone tuis interdum gaudia curis · &c ·

¶ And of holy men I herde quod I · how þei otherwhile
Pleyden þe parfiter · to be in many places
Ac if þere were any wight · þat wolde me telle
30   What were dowel and dobet · and dobest atte laste
Wolde I neuere do werke · but wende to holicherche
And þere bydde my bedes · but whan ich eet or slepe

¶ Poule in his pistle quod he · preueth what is dowel
Fides spes caritas & maior horum &c
35   Feith hope and charitee · and alle ben good
And sauen men sundry tymes · ac none so sone as charite
For he doth wel with-oute doute · þat doth as lewte techeth
Þat is if þow be man maried · þi make þow louye
And lyue forth as lawe wole · while ȝe lyuen bothe

40   ¶ Riȝt so if þow be Religious · renne þow neuere ferther
To Rome ne to Rochemadore · but as þi reule techeth
And holde þe vnder obedyence · þat heigh wey is to heuene

¶ And if þow be [mayde &] to marye · and miȝte wel contynue
Seke þow neuere seynt forther · for no soule helthe
45   For what made Lucyfer · to lese þe heigh heuene
Or salamon his sapience · or sampson his strengthe

---

23 **and**: R's *ac* may represent alpha, with F substituting *and*, in coincidental agreement
with beta.
24 **Seid**: Alpha begins *And seide*, to the detriment of the syntax.
25 **as**: Alpha has *and*, though in a rewritten b-verse in F.
27 **¶**: The paraph is in LWHm only, perhaps prompted by the preceding Latin line.
27 **herde**: Alpha has the present tense, which may be correct.
28 **places**: R's *a place* may represent alpha. F rewrites.
29 **Ac**: Not in R; F has *Nou.*
34 **&**: Not in alpha. The text cited by Alford (1992), 78–9, has it; the Clementine Vulgate (I
Cor. 13.13) is without it.
35 **and** (2): Following the Latin of the previous line, this is dropped in alpha.
39 **while**: Variation between *while* and *þe while* is common in this position; e.g. **Bx**.1.16, 10.156,
19.342.
40 **¶**: The paraph is in beta and F.
43 **mayde & to marye**: R's reading means "a maid and (due) to marry", which has more point
than beta's *mayden to marye*, and underlines the contrast with l. 38. F confirms alpha's *mayde*,
but simplifies the construction.

Iob þe Iewe his ioye · dere he it abouȝte
Arestotle and other mo · ypocras & virgyle
Alisaundre þat al wan · elengelich ended

50 ¶ Catel and kynde witte · was combraunce to hem alle
Felyce hir fayrnesse · fel hir al to sklaundre
And Rosamounde riȝt so [·] reufully bysette
Þe bewte of hir body · in badnesse she dispended
Of many suche I may rede · of men and of wommen
55 Þat wyse wordes wolde shewe · and worche þe contra[r]ye
Sunt homines nequam bene de virtute loquentes

¶ And riche renkes riȝt so · gaderen and sparen
And þo men þat þei moste haten · mynistren it atte laste
And for þei suffren & se · so many nedy folkes
60 And loue hem nouȝt as owre lorde bytte · lesen her soules
Date & dabitur vobis &c ·
[So catel and kynde witte · acombreth ful many
Wo is hym þat hem weldeth · but he hem w[e]l dispende
Scienti & non facienti variis flagellis vapulabit
65 Sapience seith þe boke · swelleth a mannes soule
Sapiencia inflat &c]

¶ And ricchesse riȝt so · but if þe Rote be trewe
Ac grace is a grasse þer-[fore] · þo greuaunces to abate
Ac grace ne groweth nouȝte · but amonges lowe
70 Pacience and pouerte · þe place is þere it groweth
And in lele lyuynge men · and in lyf-holy
And þorugh þe gyfte of þe holygoste · as þe gospel telleth

---

50 ¶: The paraph is in LC, with a new line-group in M.
53 **badnesse she**: Alpha's *badd vse* is probably avoidance of a noun rare at this date, though strikingly Langland uses neither the noun *badnesse* nor the adjective *bad* elsewhere.
54 **I may**: For support for beta's order in this position, cf. *Matrymonye I may nyme* (**Bx**.16.71).
57 ¶: The paraph is in beta and F.
62–6 Omitted in beta. The first three lines are in **Cx** (RK.14.17–18a). KD, p. 66, very plausibly suggest the omission was caused by homeoteleuton (*soule(s)* ll. 60, 65, followed by a Latin line). We alter the spellings of R to those of L.
63 **but**: As F and **Cx**. R has *but if*.
63 **wel**: As F and **Cx**. R has *wil*.
64 In part loosely based on Luke 12.47. Alford (1992), 79, quoting the form of the citation adopted by Schmidt and KD from the P family of C, does not note the closer parallel in James 4.17, "Scienti igitur bonum facere et non facienti, peccatum est illi". Based on this, F has added *bonum*, but it is not included in R or in mss. of C.
68 **þer-fore**: Alpha is supported by **Cx** and by sense against beta's *þer-of*. For the sense of *grasse*, "healing herb", see *MED gras* n. 2(b).
70 **Pacience**: R begins *Of pacience*. F drops the line, which is not in **Cx**.
72 **þe** (1): Not in R. F rewrites.

Spiritus vbi vult spirat &c
Clergye and kynde witte · comth of siȝte and techynge
75   As þe boke bereth witnesse · to buirnes þat can rede
Quod scimus loquimur quod vidimus testamur
Of quod scimus cometh clergye · [a] connynge of heuene
And of quod vidimus cometh kynde witte [·] of siȝte of dyue[r]se peple
Ac grace is a gyfte of god · and of gret loue spryngeth
80   Knewe neuere clerke how it cometh forth · ne kynde witte [his] weyes
Nescit aliquis vnde venit · aut quo vadit &c
Ac ȝit is clergye to comende · and kynde witte bothe
And namely clergye for crystes loue · þat of clergye is rote
For Moyses witnesseth þat god wrote · for to wisse þe peple
85   In þe olde lawe as þe lettre telleth · þat was þe lawe of iewes
Þat what woman were in auoutrie taken · were she riche or pore
With stones men shulde hir stryke · and stone hir to deth
A womman as we fynden · was gulty of þat dede
Ac cryste of his curteisye · þorw clergye hir saued
90   For þorw [crystes] carectus · þe iewes knewe hem-seluen
Gultier as afor god · and gretter in synne
Þan þe woman þat þere was · and wenten awey for schame
Þe clergye þat þere was · conforted þe womman
Holykirke knoweth þis · þat crystes writyng saued
95   So clergye is conforte · to creatures þat repenten
And to mansed men · myschief at her ende

¶ For goddes body myȝte nouȝte be of bred · with-outen clergye
Þe which body is bothe · bote to þe riȝtful
And deth and dampnacioun · to hem þat dyeth yuel

---

77 **a**: Beta evidently interpreted the indefinite article as a form of *and*. Alpha is supported by the revised line in **Cx** (RK.14.34).

80 **his**: "its", referring to Grace and following on from *it*. R represents alpha, misunderstood by F. Beta has *þe*.

85 **þat was**: R (= alpha?) drops *þat*; F rewrites. Alpha's reading is quite possibly right, but it is ambiguous, appearing to mean "The Jewish Law was in the Old Law", whereas the line has to mean "In the Old Law, which was the Jewish Law".

86 **auoutrie**: R has the unusual *deuoutrie* which may be right. See note to **Bx**.2.178. The line is not in **Cx**.

86 **were she**: Dropped by Cr and beta4. On WF *where she* see KD, p. 183.

88 Alpha omits the line, as a result of homeoteleuton. (Note that R's form of "death" in l. 87 is *dede*).

90 **crystes carectus**: Beta has instead the clumsier *carectus þat cryst wrot*. It is perhaps more likely that beta was influenced by l. 84 above than that alpha was prompted by l. 100 below. The line is not in **Cx**.

94 **saued**: Beta2 (CrWHm) has *saued hire*, and M is corrected to that reading. F has *hire savede*. Cf. l. 89.

100   As crystes carecte conforted [·] and bothe coupable shewed
      Þe womman þat þe iewes brouȝte · þat Ihesus þouȝte to saue
      Nolite iudicare et non iudicabimini &c
      Riȝt so goddes body bretheren · but it be worthily taken
      Dampneth vs atte daye of dome · as [dede] þe carect[e] þe iewes
105   For-þi I conseille þe for cristes sake · clergye þat þow louye
      For kynde witte is of his kyn · and neighe cosynes bothe
      To owre lorde leue me · for-þi loue hem I rede
      For bothe ben as miroures · to amenden owre defautes
      And lederes for lewed men · and for lettred bothe

110   ¶ For-þi lakke þow neuere logyke · lawe ne his custumes
      Ne countreplede clerkes · I conseille þe for eure
      For as a man may nouȝt se · þat mysseth his eyghen
      Namore can no klerke · but if he cauȝt it first þorugh bokes
      Al-þough men made bokes · god was þe maistre
115   And seynt spirit þe saumplarye · and seide what men sholde write
      And riȝt as syȝte serueth a man · to se þe heighe strete
      Riȝt so le[r]eth letterure · lewed men to resoun
      And as a blynde man in bataille · bereth wepne to fiȝte
      And hath none happ with his axe · his enemye to hitte
120   Namore kan a kynde-witted man · but clerkes hym teche
      Come for al his kynde witte · to crystendome and be saued
      Whiche is þe coffre of crystes tresore · and clerkes kepe þe keyes
      To vnlouken it at her lykynge · and to þe lewed peple
      Ȝyue mercy for her mysdedes · if men it wole aske
125   Buxomelich & benygneliche · and bidden it of grace

      ¶ Archa dei in þe olde lawe · leuites it kepten
      Hadde neuere lewed man leue · to leggen honde on þat chest
      But he were preste or prestes sone · patriarke or prophete

---

100 **As**: R's *Ac* may be taken as alpha (F has *But* as often). The sense is "just as Christ's writing both comforted the woman and revealed her to be guilty". But correlative *bothe* is oddly placed.
104 **dede þe carecte**: We follow alpha in the word-order and the sg. noun. Beta has reverted to unmarked order, spoiling the metre. For sg. *carecte*, "writing", altered to pl. by some scribes, cf. l. 100.
110 **¶**: The paraph is in beta and F.
112 **eyghen**: Beta is supported by **Cx** against alpha's *siȝte*.
115 **men**: Alpha and O have *man*, as in the next line, but **Cx** agrees with beta.
117 **lereth**: So alpha, supported by **Cx** (RK.14.49). Beta's *ledeth* makes excellent sense.
120 **kynde-witted**: "with innate intelligence". R's *kende wedded* presumably represents alpha, with F rewriting *lewid* to make sense.
124 **Ȝyue**: Beta is supported by **Cx**. The readings of RF reflect confusion in alpha.
127 **þat**: Evidently the **Bx** reading supported by **Cx**, though MCGO have *þe* and F rewrites.

[¶ Saul for he sacrifised · sorwe hym bitydde
130 And his sones also · for þat synne myscheued
And many mo other men · þat were no leuites
Þat with archa dei ȝeden · in reuerence and in worship
And leyden honde þer-on to liften it vp · and loren her lif after
For-þi I conseille alle creatures · no clergie to dispise
135 Ne sette shorte be here science · what-so þei don hem-selue
Take we her wordes at worthe · for here witnesse be trewe
And medle we nauȝt muche with hem · to meuen any wrathe
Lest cheste chasen vs · to choppe vche man other
Nolite tangere christos meos &c]

140 ¶ For clergye is kepere [·] vnder cryst of heuene
Was þere neuere no knyȝte · but clergye hym made
Ac kynde witte cometh [·] of alkynnes siȝtes
Of bryddes and of bestes · of tastes of treuthe and of deceytes

¶ Lyueres to-forn vs · vseden to marke
145 Þe selkouthes þat þei seighen · her sones for to teche
And helden it an heighe science · her wittes to knowe
Ac þorugh her science sothely · was neuere no soule ysaued
Ne brouȝte by her bokes · to blisse ne to ioye
For alle her kynde knowynges · come but of dyuerse sightes

129–39 Beta drops 11 lines, presumably skipping from paraph to paraph. **Cx** has parallels for all except ll. 131–2. We alter the spellings of R to those of L.

129 **he sacrifised**: R's a-verse is supported by **Cx**. F has his *myssacrifyse*.

132 **ȝeden**: For alliteration of *ȝede* with vowels, see Turville-Petre (1980), 314, and cf. e.g. **Bx**.11.357, 20.136, and 16.178 "And ȝede forth as an ydiote · in contre to aspye", which also has the mute stave *in*. KD instead adopt F's *wentyn* and the b-verse order (based on F) *worship and reuerence*. There is no parallel in **Cx**.

133 The line is not in the P family of **Cx**. In the X family it reads: "And all lewede þat leide hand þeron loren lyf aftir" (RK.14.63). Alpha clearly had *and* before *loren*, spoiling the construction.

134 **to**: R is supported by **Cx** against F's *yee*.

135 **shorte**: R is supported by **Cx** against *lyght* in F.

136 **we**: F omits, but R is supported by **Cx**.

136 **for**: F omits, but R is supported by **Cx**.

136 **witnesse**: A plural form (see *MED*), as unambiguously spelt by F. C mss. split, but the most authoritative have *witnesses*. Cf. **Bx**.2.149, 9.77 (and note), 12.280 (and note).

137 **medle**: Both F and **Cx** omit R's *ne*, but in other respects R's line is supported by **Cx**. F rewrites for the sense.

138 **chasen**: **Cx** has the line as in R, but with *chaufen* "inflame"; *chasen* is surely an alpha or **Bx** error.

140 **kepere**: So beta. R has *kynge and kepere*, F has *keye & kepere*. **Cx** rewrites the line.

144 **marke**: Alpha's *make* is obviously wrong. Beta is supported by **Cx**.

148 **brouȝte**: Beta is supported by **Cx** against alpha's *bouȝte*.

149 **come**: Past tense plural; cf. the form *cam* in alpha and also C mss.

KD.12.116–135

150 ¶ Patriarkes and prophetes · repreued her science
And seiden her wordes ne her wisdomes · [w]as but a folye
As to þe clergye of cryst · counted it but a trufle
Sapiencia huius mundi · stulticia apud deum
For þe heihe holigoste · heuene shal to-cleue
155 And loue shal lepe out after · in-to þis lowe erthe
And clennesse shal cacchen it · and clerkes shullen it fynde
Pastores loquebantur ad inuicem

¶ He speketh þere of riche men riȝt nouȝt · ne of riȝt witty
Ne of lordes þat were lewed men · but of þe hexte lettred oute
160 Ibant magi ab oriente &c

¶ If any frere were founde þere · Ich ȝif þe fyue shillynges
Ne in none beggares cote · was þat barne borne
But in a burgeys place · of bethlem þe best
Set non erat locus in diuersorio [·] & pauper non habet diuersorium

165 ¶ To pastours and to poetes [·] appiered þat aungel
And bad hem go to bethlem · goddis burth to honoure
And songe a songe of solas · gloria in excelsis deo

[¶ Riche men rutte þo · and in here reste were
Þo it shon so to shepherdes · a shewer of blisse]

170 ¶ Clerkes knewe it wel · and comen with here presentz
And deden her homage honourabely · to hym þat was almyȝty

---

150 ¶: The paraph is in LW with a new line-group in M.

150 **repreued**: Alpha's present tense is clearly wrong; **Cx** supports beta.

151 **wisdomes**: Though R has the sg., **Cx** supports beta's plural.

151 **was**: Alpha's alliterating verb is supported by **Cx**; the P family have *ne was*, as of course **Bx** might have had.

153 **stulticia**: MWCGF correct the quotation by adding *est*, as in **Cx**. The medial punctuation, unusual for a non-metrical Latin line (though cf. l. 164), is recorded in LMCrHmF.

154–64 These 11 lines are lost in alpha, jumping from one Latin line to another, and possibly from paraph to paraph, though only WHm record a paraph at l. 154. The lines are paralleled in **Cx**, apart from ll. 159 and 164.

164 **erat**: Beta2 (CrWHm) adds *ei* in line with the source; see Alford (1992), 80.

165 **þat**: So LM. Choice is difficult, since the other beta mss. read *þe*, as does **Cx**, while alpha reads *an*. LM agreement nearly always establishes the beta reading. Perhaps **Bx** *þat* was rejected by other beta scribes and by alpha because it has no antecedent.

167 **songe** (1): R and the P family of C have *syngen*.

168–9 Beta drops 2 lines, both in **Cx**, perhaps skipping from paraph to paraph. We alter the spellings of R to those of L.

168 **and**: R is supported by **Cx** against F's *þat*.

169 R's a-verse is supported by **Cx**. F has *Whan to shepperdis a sterre shon*.

170 ¶: The paraph is in beta only, following its loss of text. See note to ll. 168–9.

170 **Clerkes**: Alpha's addition of *And* is not supported by **Cx**.

171 **honourabely**: L miswrites the word.

171 CGO follow with a spurious line.

Why I haue tolde al þis · I toke ful gode hede
How þow contraryedest clergye · with crabbed wordes
How þat lewed men liȝtloker · þan lettred were saued
175   Þan clerkes or kynde-witted men · of crystene peple

¶ And þow seidest soth of somme · ac se in what manere
Take two stronge men · and in themese caste hem
And bothe naked as a nedle · her none syker þan other
Þat one hath connynge and can [·] swymmen and dyuen
180   Þat other is lewed of þat laboure · lerned neuere swymme
Which trowestow of þo two · in themese is in moste drede
He þat neuere ne dyued · ne nouȝt can of swymmynge
Or þe swymmere þat is sauf · bi so hym-self lyke
Þere his felaw flet forth · as þe flode lyketh
185   And is in drede to drenche · þat neuere dede swymme

¶ Þat swymme can nouȝt I seide · it semeth to my wittes

¶ Riȝt so quod þe Renke [·] resoun it sheweth
Þat he þat knoweth clergye [·] can sonner aryse
Out of synne and be sauf · þough he synne ofte
190   If hym lyketh and lest · þan any lewed lelly
For if þe clerke be konnynge · he knoweth what is synne
And how contricioun with-oute confessioun · conforteth þe soule
As þow seest in þe sauter · in psalme one or tweyne
How contricioun is commended · for it caccheth awey synne
195   Beati quorum remisse sunt iniquitates & quorum tecta sunt &c ·

---

172 **tolde:** So evidently beta, though CGO add *þe*. R also has *þe*, probably representing alpha (F alters to *told þis tale*). Most C mss. have *þe*, though ms. X is without it. It seems easier added than lost.

176 **what manere:** R offers an extreme example of his willingness to reproduce his exemplar with *whanere*. F makes sense of it.

178 **syker:** The agreement of L, original M and R is sufficient to establish **Bx**. Others (including M) make the obvious correction to *sikerer*, "stronger" (*MED siker* 2 (b)), though see KD p. 179, who conjecture an original reading *sadder*. **Cx** has instead *heuegore*, "heavier". See Adams (2000), 179.

180 **swymme:** LWR; as often, scribes tend to add the infinitive marker *to*. In C the X family has it, but the P family is without.

182 **ne** (1): As in LWCO, but not in MCrHmG and alpha. It improves the alliteration, yet may not be **Bx**. **Cx** revises to alliterate on /s/.

186 Alpha drops the line, which is supported by **Cx**. Its loss is easily accounted for if **Bx** had the paraph that is recorded only by L (though MW have a line-space). See Burrow (2010), 25.

189 **be:** CrR have *he be*. It is not supported by **Cx**.

193 **psalme:** The odd sg. is certainly **Bx**; it is the reading of LMR (and F), though M corrects to the more obvious plural. **Cx** has the plural.

195 **&c:** Alpha adds *peccata*. The familiar verse from Psalm 31.1 is quoted in part several times; cf. **Bx**.13.56, 14.103. **Cx** ends with *iniquitates*.

And þis conforteth vch a clerke · and keuereth hym fram wanhope
In which flode þe fende · fondeth a man hardest
Þere þe lewed lith stille · and loketh after lente
And hath no contricioun ar he come to shryfte · & þanne can he litel telle
200 And as his lores-man leres hym · bileueth & troweth
And þat is after person or parisch prest · and parauenture [bothe]
Vnconnynge to lere lewed men · as luk bereth witnesse
Dum cecus ducit cecum &c ·

¶ Wo was hym marked · þat wade mote with þe lewed
205 Wel may þe barne blisse · þat hym to boke sette
Þat lyuynge after letterure [·] saued hym lyf and soule
Dominus pars hereditatis mee [·] is a meri verset
Þat has take fro tybourne · twenti stronge þeues
Þere lewed theues ben lolled vp · loke how þei be saued
210 Þe thef þat had grace of god · on gode fryday as þow speke
Was for he 3elte hym creaunt to cryst on þe crosse · & knewleched hym
        gulty
And grace axed of god · and he is euer redy
Þat boxomeliche biddeth it · and ben in wille to amenden hem
Ac þough þat þef had heuene · he hadde none heigh blisse
215 As seynt Iohan and other seyntes · þat asserued hadde bettere
Ri3t as sum man 3eue me mete · and sette me amydde þe flore
Ich haue mete more þan ynough · ac nou3t so moche worship
As þo þat seten atte syde table · or with þe souereignes of þe halle
But sitte as a begger bordelees · bi my-self on þe grounde
220 So it fareth bi þat feloun · þat a gode fryday was saued

---

196 **keuereth**: Supported by **Cx** (and sense) against alpha's *kenneth*.

199 **þanne**: Beta has support from **Cx** against alpha's omission.

200 **And**: WHm + F have *But*. Although this reading is preferable and is supported by **Cx**, it is unlikely to be the **Bx** reading.

201 **bothe**: Beta drops, and WO expand a short b-verse. Alpha is supported by **Cx**, which, however, indicates that **Bx** broke the line too early. **Cx** reads *paraunter bothe lewede / To lere lewede men* ... (RK.14.123–4).

204 Alpha drops the line, which is preserved in **Cx**.

205 **to boke sette**: Beta is supported by **Cx** and by the alliterative pattern against alpha's *sette to scole*.

210 **speke**: Past tense 2nd sg. (cf. CrCG), misunderstood as present by WHmO. **Cx** reads *toldest*.

211 **creaunt**: MR read *recreaunt*. **Cx** has the shorter form.

211 **on þe crosse**: Not in **Cx**, but certainly in **Bx**, perhaps as a gloss. CrHmF adopt different ways of shortening the line. For the same phrase see l. 234.

212 The line is dropped in alpha. W strengthens the alliteration. **Cx** has *And god is ay gracious to alle þat gredeth to hym* (RK.14.133).

214 Hm and alpha start a new paragraph here.

215 **asserued**: Supported for **Bx** by LR and the majority of **C** mss. against the common *deserued* of other **B** witnesses. See Adams (2000), 184.

He sitte neither with Seynt Iohan · Symonde ne Iude
Ne wyth maydenes ne with martires [·] [ne] confessoures ne wydwes
But by hym-self as a soleyne · and serued on þe erthe
For he þat is ones a thef · is euermore in daungere
225   And as lawe lyketh · to lyue or to deye
De peccato propiciato noli esse sine metu
And forto seruen a seynt · and such a thef togyderes
It were noyther resoun ne riȝt · to rewarde bothe aliche

¶ And riȝt as troianus þe trewe knyȝt · tilde nouȝt depe in helle
230   Þat owre lorde ne had hym liȝtlich oute · so leue I þe thef be in heuene
For he is in þe lowest of heuene · if owre bileue be trewe
And wel loselyche he lolleth þere · by þe lawe of holycherche
Quia reddit vnicuique iuxta opera sua &c

¶ A[c] why þat one thef on þe crosse · creaunt hym ȝelt
235   Rather þan þat other thef · þough þow wolde appose
Alle þe clerkes vnder cryst · ne couthe þe skil assoille
Quare placuit quia voluit

[¶] And so I sey by þe · þat sekest after þe whyes
And aresonedest resoun · a rebukyng as it were

---

221 **Seynt**: Alpha drops the word, but it is necessary for the alliteration and supported by **Cx**.
221 **Symonde**: R begins the b-verse with *ne* perhaps correctly (F rewrites). In C the X family has it, the P family is without.
222 **ne** (3): In this case the support for R's *ne* is stronger (cf. previous line). Though F and Cx revise, they share the *ne* at the start of the b-verse.
223 **þe**: Lost by beta2 (CrWHm).
228 **bothe**: Following R, supported by **Cx** (RK.14.148). MF substitute *hem*, while all beta mss. apart from M have *hem bothe*.
229 **¶**: The paraph is recorded by LW, with M starting a new line-group.
229 **tilde**: Beta2 (CrWHm) has the easier *dwelte*.
230 **thef**: Alpha, reproduced by R, misread *þe þef* and lost the noun; F repairs.
231 **lowest of heuene**: "lowest part of heaven"; so LWHmR and the X family of C. MCrCGO omit *of*, as does the P family.
232 **loselyche**: Commentators take this as a form of *MED losli(e*, "loosely", interpreting "precariously" (Kane (2005)). It is clear that some scribes also took it this way (so CG *lowselyche*, F *loosly*), but the careful beta2 spelling *loselly* suggests instead derivation from *losel*, "worthless person", as in **Bx**.P.77, 10.52, 15.142. C scribes had considerable difficulty with the word, the majority taking it as a form of *loveli*.
233 **Quia reddit**: The beta reading; beta2 (CrWHm) begins *Qui*, and M is altered to that reading. Alpha, represented by R, begins *And reddite*, which may be right, since **Cx** has *Et reddet*. The injunction is phrased variously throughout the Bible: see Alford (1992), 80.
234 **Ac**: The alpha reading, as in R, with F altering to *But* as usual. It is supported by **Cx**.
234 **on**: Beta, together with F, against R's *vpon*. Choice is difficult, since C mss. also vary, but **Cx** probably had *vpon*.
236 **assoille**: Beta supported by **Cx**, against alpha's *telle*.
238 **¶**: The paraph, though not in L, is recorded in beta2 and alpha.

240   [And willest of briddes and of bestes · and of hire bredyng to knowe
      Why somme be alowe and somme alofte · þi lykyng it were
      And of þe floures in þe fryth · and of her feire hewes
      Where-of þei cacche her coloures · so clere and so briȝte]
      And of þe stones and of þe sterres · þow studyest as I leue
245   How euere beste or brydde · hath so breme wittes

      ¶ Clergye ne kynde witte [·] ne knewe neuere þe cause
      Ac kynde knoweth þe cause hym-selue · no creature elles
      He is þe pyes patroun · and putteth it in hire ere
      Þat þere þe þorne is thikkest · [þere] to buylden and brede
250   And kynde kenned þe pecok · to cauken in swich a kynde
      And [kynde] kenned Adam · to knowe his pryue membres
      And tauȝte hym and Eue · to hylien hem with leues

      ¶ Lewed men many tymes · maistres þei apposen
      Why Adam ne hiled nouȝt firste · his mouth þat eet þe apple
255   Rather þan his lykam alow · lewed axen þus clerkes
      Kynde knoweth whi he dede so · ac no clerke elles
      Ac of briddes and of bestes · men by olde tyme
      Ensamples token and termes · as telleth þis poetes
      And þat þe fairest foule · foulest engendreth
260   And feblest foule of flyght is · þat fleegheth or swymmeth
      And þat is þe pekok & þe pohenne proude · riche men þei bitokneth
      For þe pekok and men pursue hym · may nouȝte fleighe heighe
      For þe traillyng of his taille · ouertaken is he sone
      And his flesshe is foule flesshe · and his feet bothe

240–3 The syntax makes it clear that alpha's order is right. Beta reverses it through eyeskip from *it were* in l. 239 to *it were* in l. 241, supplying skipped 240–1 after 242–3. Only **Bx**.12.242 is in **Cx** (RK.14.158).

240 **of** (2): Omitted by CrCGO and supplied in L, but supported by MWHmR.

240 **to**: Dropped in HmCGO.

243 **coloures**: Beta's pl. follows from *hewes* in the previous line, though alpha has the sg. There is no parallel for **Bx**.12.243–82 in **Cx**.

249 **þere** (2): The repetition as in alpha clarifies the syntax and provides b-verse alliteration, though without it the pattern aaa/bb would be satisfactory.

250 **kenned**: The past tense is supported by LMWR; cf. the next line.

251 **kynde**: Easily lost before *kennede* in beta, especially in the context of the punning *kynde* in the previous line. It provides alliteration for the a-verse.

254 **ne**: Supported by LMWR.

261 **þat is**: WHm drop *is*, and Cr drops both words.

261 In LMR the punctuation follows *pohenne proude*. In beta2 and O the punctuation precedes *proude riche*, while C drops *proude*. There is better support for *proude* as qualifying *pohenne* in an aaa/xx line. The usual word-order in Middle English is adj. + n. + adj. rather than adj. + adj. + n.

261 **þei**: Dropped in WHm.

262 **may**: R's *ne may* could be alpha, since F has *he may*, but note that Cr adds *he*.

265   And vnlouelich of ledene · and laith for to here

       ¶ Ri3t so þe riche [·] if he his ricchesse kepe
       And deleth it nou3t tyl his deth-day · þe taille of al sorwe
       Ri3t as þe pennes of þe pecok · payned hym in his fli3te
       So is possessioun payne · of pens and of nobles
270   To alle hem þat it holdeth · til her taille be plukked
       And þough þe riche repente þanne · and birewe þe tyme
       Þat euere he gadered so grete · and gaf þere-of so litel
       Þough he crye to cryst þanne · with kene wille I leue
       His ledne be in owre lordes ere · lyke a pyes
275   And whan his caroigne shal come · in caue to be buryed
       I leue it flaumbe ful foule · þe folde al aboute
       And alle þe other þer it lyth · enuenymed þorgh his attere
       By þe p[o]feet is vnderstonde · as I haue lerned in auynet
       Executoures fals frendes · þat fulfille nou3t his wille
280   Þat was writen and þei witnesse · to worche ri3t as it wolde
       Þus þe poete preues · þat þe pecok for his fetheres is reuerenced
       Ri3t so is þe riche · bi resoun of his godis

       ¶ Þe larke þat is a lasse foule · is more louelich of ledne
       And wel awey of wenge [·] swifter þan þe pecok
285   And of flesch by fele-folde · fatter and swetter
       To lowe-lybbyng men · þe larke is resembled

       ¶ Arestotle þe grete clerke [·] suche tales he telleth
       Thus he lykneth in his logyk · þe leste foule oute

---

267 **taille**: "tally", with a pun on "tail". M is altered to *tail* to conform to Beta2. M also adds *is*, which improves the syntax but is not **Bx**.

268 **payned**: M alters to the expected present tense, in line with CrW, and OF also have the present, but the past is supported by LHmCGR.

274 **pyes**: The M corrector adds *chiteryng* to bring the text in line with Beta2 (CrWHm). Clearly the **Bx** b-verse (attested by LR, original M, as well as CGO) is too short. F rewrites entirely. Schmidt (1995), 389, conjectures misdivision between ll. 273–4, with *I leue* beginning l. 274 and the a-verse ending *be*.

277 **enuenymed**: p.ppl., with "are" understood. The reading of LCrR and probably original M, subsequently corrected to the easier present tense of all other mss.

278 **pofeet**: The L scribe writes the word correctly and then alters it to *profeet*.

280 **witnesse**: A noun, sg. or pl., "they as witness(es)". R is unambiguously plural. See note to **Bx**.12.136.

280 **it**: So beta, against alpha *he*. See KD, p. 146, who explain *it* as referring to "the actual testamentary document".

281 W shows understandable uncertainty over the placing of the half-line break, with punctuation after both *preueþ* and *pecok*; LMR support the former.

287 **Arestotle**: Alpha begins *For aristotel*. We follow copy-text.

288 Only L has a paraph.

288 **logyk**: Beta is supported by the alliteration and by **Cx**; alpha has *glosinge*.

And where he be sauf or nou3t sauf · þe sothe wote no clergye
290 Ne of sortes ne of salamon · no scripture can telle
Ac god is so good I hope · þat sitth he gaf hem wittis
To wissen vs weyes þere-with · þat wissen vs to be saued
And þe better for her bokes · to bidden we ben holden
Þat god for his grace [·] gyue her soules reste
295 For lettred men were lewed men 3ut · ne were lore of her bokes

¶ Alle þise clerkes quod I þo · þat on cryst leuen
Seggen in her sarmones · þat noyther sarasenes ne iewes
Ne no creature of cristes lyknesse · with-outen crystendome worth saued

¶ Contra quod ymagynatyf þo · and comsed for to loure
300 And seyde saluabitur vix iustus in die iudicij

¶ Ergo saluabitur quod he · and seyde namore latyne
Troianus was a trewe kny3te · and toke neuere cristendome
And he is sauf so seith þe boke · and his soule in heuene
[Ac] þere is fullyng of fonte · and fullyng in blode shedyng
305 And þorugh fuire is fullyng · and þat is ferme bileue
Aduenit ignis diuinus non comburens sed illuminans &c ·

¶ Ac trewth þat trespassed neuere · ne transuersed a3eines his lawe
But lyue[d] as his lawe t[au3te] · and leueth þere be no bettere
And if þere were he wolde amende · and in suche wille deyeth
310 Ne wolde neuere trewe god · but [trewe] treuth were allowed
And where it worth or worth nou3t · þe bileue is grete of treuth
And an hope hangyng þer-inne · to haue a Mede for his treuth

---

289 **sauf** (2): CrCGOF omit, but it is supported by **Cx** (RK.14.192).

292 **wissen** (2): A spelling of "wish", influenced by (and punning on) *wissen* in the a-verse.

294 **soules**: Beta's plural is supported by **Cx**.

295 **men** (2): Omitted by CGOF, but supported by **Cx**.

295 **her**: Beta only, since R has *þe* and F omits. **Cx** probably reads *þo clerkes*.

301 **¶**: The paraph is recorded by LR only.

303 **is**: Since this is omitted in R and inserted in L, it is possible that the ellipsis is **Bx**; however the verb is in **Cx**.

304 **Ac**: R (= alpha, F has *But* as usual) is supported by the X family of C (most of the P family omit the conjunction). Schmidt (1995), 457, argues that it "has the force of *Sed* in scholastic debate '(but) now'". However, it might have been picked up from l. 307. For discussion of the passage see Burrow (1993), 13–14.

307 **transuersed**: Though most beta mss. have *trauersed*, the form in LCr and alpha is also in many C mss. and is the **Cx** form at RK.3.446. The two verbs are of the same ultimate origin.

308 **lyued ... tau3te**: Alpha's past tense is supported by **Cx**.

310 **trewe** (2): Beta drops the adjective and F rewrites; R is supported by **Cx**.

311 The a-verse is supported by LMR, with minor variations in the other mss. *Where* and *were* are both forms of "whether" as in W; see *MED whether* adv. & conj. C mss. vary similarly, with the P family reversing the order of *worth nou3t*.

312 **a**: Supported by LWHmR. **Cx** rewrites the b-verse.

For deus dicitur quasi dans vitam eternam · suis hoc est fidelibus
Et alibi si ambulauero in medio vmbre mortis
315 Þe glose graunteth vpon þat vers · a gret mede to treuthe
And witt and wisdome quod þat wye · was somme-tyme tresore
To kepe with a comune · no katel was holde bettere
And moche murth and manhod · and riȝt with þat he vanesched

---

318 **with**: Schmidt adopts R's *mid* for alliteration; see Schmidt (2008), 412. It would be easy
to suppose that this was independently altered by F and beta, but **Cx** has *þerwith* following a
different a-verse.

Passus 13

And I awaked þere-with · witles nerehande
And as a freke þat f[e]re were · forth gan I walke
In manere of a mendynaunt · many ȝere after
And of þis metyng many tyme · moche þouȝt I hadde
5 First how fortune me failled · at my moste nede
And how þat elde manaced me · myȝt we euere meten

¶ And how þat freris folwed · folke þat was riche
And folke þat was pore · at litel prys þei sette
And no corps in her kirkeȝerde · ne in her kyrke was buryed
10 But quikke he biquethe hem auȝte · or shulde helpe quyte her dettes
And how þis coueitise ouercome · clerkes and prestes
And how þat lewed men ben ladde · but owre lorde hem helpe
Þorugh vnkonnyng curatoures · to incurable peynes

¶ And how þat ymagynatyf · in dremeles me tolde
15 Of kynde and of his connyng · and how curteise he is to bestes
And how louynge he is to bestes · on londe and on water
Leneth he no lyf · lasse ne more
Þe creatures þat crepen · of kynde ben engendred

---

2 **fere**: "bold" (*MED fer* adj.(2)). R's reading is likely to represent alpha, and is the basis for
F's misunderstanding *a-feerd*. Beta has instead revised to *fre* which is no more apposite. **Bx** has
presumably corrupted *feye*, "doomed to die", as in **Cx** (and BmBo), alluding to the opening of
the previous passus.
3 **many**: L, Beta2 and F have *many a*, but MR are supported by **Cx**.
4 **tyme**: See note to **Bx**.11.388. C mss. split between *tyme* and *tymes*.
7 **¶**: The paraph is supported by LCR alone.
11 **þis**: LMWHm are supported by **Cx**. R has *þus*.
14–20 Alpha skips a paragraph and loses seven lines. Lines 14–16 and 19–20 are paralleled in
Cx (RK.15.17–19, 21–3).

And sitthen how ymagynatif seyde [·] vix iustus saluabitur
20 And whan he had seyde so · how sodeynelich he passed

¶ I lay down longe in þis þouȝte · and atte laste I slepte
And as cryste wolde þere come conscience · to conforte me þat tyme
And bad me come to his courte · with clergye sholde I dyne

¶ And for conscience of clergye spake · I come wel þe rather
25 And þere I say a maistre · what man he was I neste
Þat lowe louted · and loueliche to scripture

¶ Conscience knewe hym wel · and welcomed hym faire
Þei wesshen and wypeden · and wenten to þe dyner
Ac pacience in þe paleis stode [·] in pilgrymes clothes
30 And preyde mete for charite · for a pore heremyte

¶ Conscience called hym in · and curteisliche seide
Welcome wy[e] go and wasshe · þow shalt sitte sone

¶ Þis maister was made sitte · as for þe moste worthy
And þanne clergye and conscience · and pacience cam after

35 ¶ Pacience and I [·] were put to be m[ett]es
And seten by owre-selue [·] at a syde borde

¶ Conscience called after mete · and þanne cam scripture
And serued hem þus sone · of sondry metes manye
Of austyn of ambrose · of alle þe foure euangelistes
40 Edentes & bibentes · que apud eos sunt
Ac þis maister ne his man · no manere flessh eten
Ac þei ete mete of more coste · mortrewes and potages
Of þat men mys-wonne · þei made hem wel at ese
Ac her sauce was ouer soure · & vnsauourely grounde
45 In a morter post mortem · of many bitter peyne

---

19 **iustus**: Apparently dropped in beta2 and inserted at the end of the line by Hm, though O has it in the same position. Cf. **Bx**.12.300.

24 ¶: The paraph is supported by LR, with a new line group in M.

29 C and alpha here have a not inappropriate paraph.

30 **for** (1): With support from LMCrHmCR, this seems undoubtedly to be the reading of **Bx**, and thus altered independently by WGOF to alliterating *par / pur*. Cf. the almost identical a-verse **Bx**.8.11 (and note) with the same range of variants, and **Bx**.6.260. In C mss. the P family also has *for* in place of the X family's *pur*, but this is in the b-verse where the alliteration is not structural (RK.15.32).

32 **wye**: L's originally correct reading was altered to *wyel ȝe*.

35 **mettes**: Beta has substituted synonymous *macches*, but alpha is supported by **Cx**. Cf. l. 49.

38 **hem**: HmR's *hym* is not supported by **Cx**.

39 **of alle**: Beta2 has *and of*, but it is not supported by **Cx**.

42 **ete**: Beta is supported by **Cx** against alpha's *hadde*.

KD.13.19–44

But if þei synge for þo soules · and wepe salt teres
Vos qui peccata hominum comeditis nisi pro eis lacrimas & oraciones
    effunderitis · ea que in delicijs comeditis · in tormentis euometis

[¶] Conscience ful curteisly þo · comaunded scripture
Bifor pacience bred to brynge · and me þat was his m[ett]e
50 He sette a soure lof to-for vs · and seyde agite penitenciam
And sith he drough vs drynke · dia perseuerans
As longe quod [he] as ly[f] · and lycame may dure
Here is propre seruice quod pacience · þer fareth no prynce bettere

¶ And þanne he brouȝt vs forth a mees of other mete · of Mise[r]ere mei
    deus
55 And he brouȝte vs of Beati quorum [·] of beatus virres makyng
Et quorum tecta sunt peccata [·] in a dissh
Of derne shrifte dixi [·] and confitebor tibi
Brynge pacience some pitaunce · pryueliche quod conscience

¶ And þanne had pacience a pitaunce [·] pro hac orabit omnis sanctus in
    tempore oportuno
60 And conscience conforted vs · and carped vs mery tales
Cor contritum & humiliatum deus non despicies

¶ Pacience was proude [·] of þat propre seruice
And made hym muirth with his mete · ac I morned euere

---

46 **þo**: LWGR supported by the better C mss., against *þe* in other BC mss.
46 **and wepe**: Supported by Cx against alpha's *with many*.
48 **¶**: The paraph is recorded by WHmC and alpha, with a line-space in M.
49 **mette**: As at l. 35, beta reads *macche*, but alpha is supported by Cx.
51 **dia**: Clearly the Bx reading, with M altering to the more obvious *diu*, the reading of GOF. Some C mss. including X also have *dia*. Schmidt (1987), 92, supposes a pun (ME *dia*, "drug", as in **Bx**.20.173). Perhaps, therefore, it might be interpreted "a concoction whose chief ingredient is persevering" (cf. *MED dia-*). Note Cr's *diaperseueraunce* as one word.
52 **he as lyf**: R's reading (F reverses) is supported by Cx against beta's *I as I lyue*.
54 **¶**: Although the paraph is not particularly appropriate, it is evidently **Bx**, supported by LWR and a line-space in M.
54 **vs**: Supported by LMWR, but dropped by others in an unusually long a-verse.
54 **a mees of**: Dropped by beta4 and altered by the Hm corrector.
55 **vs**: Dropped by R; The line is not in C. F, understandably dissatisfied with this and the next line, rewrites them to bring them closer to Psalm 31.1–2, and so is no use in determining alpha.
55 **of** (2): R has *and of*, and *vir his* for *virres*. F rewrites.
56 **Et**: R's *And*, possibly supported by F's *&*, deserves serious consideration, although *Et* is part of the quotation from Psalm 31.1. In R this is a new dish; in beta it is all part of the same dish. There is no parallel in C.
59 **orabit**: Beta adds *ad te*, in line with the Vulgate (once again the Second Penitential Psalm, 31.6), but alpha's omission is supported by Cx. Alpha sets the Latin as a separate line, as does beta4 (CGO), which takes *ybroughte* from C to fill out the English line.
62 **¶**: The paraph is in beta and F.
63 **mete**: R has *mene*, an alpha error which F revises to *mowht* for sense. Cx supports beta.

For þis doctoure on þe heigh dese · dranke wyn so faste
65 Ve vobis qui potentes estis ad bibendum vinum
[And] eet many sondry metes · mortrewes and puddynges
Wombe cloutes and wylde braune · & egges y-fryed with grece
Þanne seide I to my-self so · pacience it herde
It is nouȝt foure dayes þat þis freke · bifor þe den of poules
70 Preched of penaunces · þat poule þe apostle suffred
In fame & frigore · and flappes of scourges
Ter cesus sum & a iudeis quinquies quadragenas &c ·

¶ Ac o worde þei ouerhuppen · at ech a tyme þat þei preche
Þat poule in his pistel · to al þe peple tolde
75 Periculum est in falsis fratribus
Holywrit bit men be war · I wil nouȝt write it here
On englisch an auenture · it sholde be reherced to ofte
And greue þere-with þat good men ben · ac gramarienes shul rede
Vnusquisque a fratre se custodiat [·] quia vt dicitur periculum est in falsis
    fratribus

80 ¶ Ac I wist neuere freke þat as a frere ȝede · bifor men on englissh
Taken it for her teme · and telle it with-outen glosynge
Þei prechen þat penaunce is · profitable to þe soule
And what myschief and malese · cryst for man tholed
Ac þis goddes gloton quod I · with his gret chekes
85 Hath no pyte on vs pore · he perforneth yuel

---

64 þe: HmR have þis, but it is not supported by **Cx**.
66 **And**: R is supported by **Cx**. Following the Latin line, beta adds a paraph and begins *He*.
F, with the same motivation, begins *Þey*.
68 In **Bx** the punctus follows *so*, though it makes better sense to take it as "in such a way that"
as in CO. F has *þat* for *so*.
69 **poules**: R uniquely has *seynt poules*, as does the P family of **C** in a completely revised line.
73 **¶**: The paraph is in beta and F. In R the line is at the top of the page.
73 **a**: Good support for **Bx** from LMWR. Others omit.
75 **est**: Alpha drops the verb. The form of the citation in F is the same as in some of the P
family of **C** and in *Upland's Rejoinder* 329. R's version is unique.
77 **On**: This appears to be beta's reading, and perhaps alpha's too, despite the reading *In* of
CrWR.
78 **þat good men ben**: L and alpha; other beta mss. drop *men*, while beta2 simplifies to *goode*
men.
80 **Ac**: Dropped by alpha, but supported by **Cx**.
80 **a**: Not in R; both F and **Cx** rephrase.
81 **her**: WHmGF and the M corrector pedantically replace with the sg. **Cx** also has the sg.,
but the referent *frere is ycald* prompts it in this case.
82 **Þei**: R begins *Ac þei* (F *But þey*), not supported by **Cx**.

Þat he precheth he preueth nou3t · to pacience I tolde
And wisshed witterly · with wille ful egre
Þat disshes a dobleres · bifor þis ilke doctour
Were moltoun led in his maw · and Mahoun amyddes
90 I shal iangle to þis Iurdan · with his iust-wombe
To telle me what penaunce is · of which he preched rather
Pacience parceyued what I thou3t · and [preynte] on me to be stille
And seyde þow shalt se þus sone · whan he may no more
He shal haue a penaunce in his paunche · and puffe at ech a worde
95 And þanne shullen his guttis godele · and he shal galpen after
For now he hath dronken so depe · he wil deuyne sone
And preuen it by her pocalips · and passioun of seynt Auereys
Þat neither bacoun ne braune · blanmangere ne mortrewes
Is noither fisshe no flesshe · but fode for penaunte[s]
100 And þanne shal he testifye of a trinitee · and take his felawe to witnesse
What he fonde in a freyel · after a freres lyuyng
And but if þe fyrst lyne be lesyng · leue me neuere after
And þanne is tyme to take · and to appose þis doctoure
Of dowel and of dobet · and if dobest be any penaunce

---

86 **he** (2): The beta reading, supported by the P family of C. Alpha has *and*, so that this line completes the previous line: "he performs badly what he preaches", as in many of the X family of C. An original *a* could have been understood as either "he" or "and". See Schmidt (1995), 390.

86 **nou3t**: Dropped by alpha, but necessary for the sense.

88 **a**: "and". See note to **Bx**.P.227.

88 **ilke**: Alpha omits, while F adds *on dees* to correct the alliteration. Perhaps **Bx** was as R, with beta "improving" a defective b-verse. Cx rewrites as "with alle þe deyntees aftur" (RK.15.90).

90 **iust**: Kane (2005) appositely glosses *iust-wombe* as "pot-belly". See *MED iuste* n. Alpha *iuysty* makes an adjective of it, as do a couple of C mss.

91 **rather**: Probably R's reading *þere ay* represents alpha, of which F's *euere* is a revision. The line is not in C.

92 **preynte**: "winked admonishingly"; see Burrow (2002), 103–05. Though this reading is in neither beta nor alpha, conjecturing it as the reading of **Bx** explains the variants and restores alliteration. Beta substitutes the synonym *wynked* and alpha conveys the same sense with *bad*. The word is used again in l. 119 and **Bx**.18.21. See Introduction, p. 32.

95 **godele**: For the form in LR see note to **Bx**.5.351.

97 **by her**: Beta is supported by Cx. R has *here*, the omission perhaps representing alpha, which F corrects to *in þe*.

98 **blanmangere**: Alpha's *ne blaumanger* is supported by the X family of C, beta's omission by the P family. We retain copy-text.

99 **penauntes**: Alpha's plural is supported by Cx.

102 **lyne**: So LM + alpha. Beta1, perhaps encouraged by *lyuyng* and *leue*, must have read the word as *lyue*, leading Beta2 to alter *if þe* to *he*, "unless he first live" to make a modicum of sense. O alters his exemplar's *lif* to *leef*, so by coincidence or contamination arriving at the Cx reading (RK.15.103).

103 **take**: Kane (2005) glosses "seize", which does not seem quite appropriate. Perhaps the sense is "address" (*MED taken* v. 39b (a)). In any case OR alter to easier *talke*, the reading of the P family of C, and F rewrites.

104 **of** (2): So LMR and CrC, dropped by others. C mss. vary.

105   ¶ And I sete stille as pacience seyde · and þus sone þis doctour
     As rody as a rose · rubbed his chekes
     Coughed and carped · and conscience hym herde
     And tolde hym of a trinite · and toward vs he loked

     ¶ What is dowel sire doctour quod I · is do[best] any penaunce

110   ¶ Dowel quod þis doctour · and [dranke after]
     Do non yuel to þine euenecrystene · nouȝt by þi powere

     ¶ By þis day sire doctour quod I [·] þanne be ȝe nouȝt in dowel
     For ȝe han harmed vs two · in þat ȝe eten þe puddyng
     Mortrewes and other mete · and we no mussel hade
115   And ȝe fare so in ȝowre fermorie · ferly me þinketh
     But chest be þere charite shulde be · & ȝonge childern dorste pleyne
     I wolde permute my penaunce with ȝowre · for I am in poynte to dowel

     ¶ Þanne conscience [ful] curteisliche · a contenaunce he made
     And preynte vpon pacience · to preie me to be stille
120   And seyde hym-self sire doctour · and it be ȝowre wille
     What is dowel and dobet · ȝe deuynours knoweth

     ¶ Dowel quod þis doctour · do as clerkes techeth
     And dobet is he þat techeth · and trauailleth to teche other
     And dobest doth hym-self so · as he seith & precheth
125   Qui facit et docuerit magnus vocabitur in regno celorum

     ¶ Now þow clergye quod conscience [·] carpest what is dowel
     I haue seuene sones he seyde · seruen in a castel

---

106 **rubbed**: Evidently the beta reading, and probably also **Bx**, since R has *robbed*. If so, Hm's *rudded* and F's *gan rody* are picked up from the adj. *rody* in the a-verse. But **Cx** has *rodded* (RK.15.107), which could represent *MED rudden*, "rub", or *ruden*, "redden". Possibly, then, **Bx** also had *rodded*, interpreted as synonymous with the much commoner verb *rubben*. See Schmidt (2008), 414.

109 **dobest**: Alpha, supported by **Cx**, against beta's repetition of *dowel*. Cf. l. 104.

110 **dranke after**: R's reading is supported by **Cx** *and he dronke aftur*. Scribes reacted to the short b-verse, with both F and beta expanding in different ways.

115 **And**: "if"; so R, supported by **Cx**. F substitutes *If* as at **Bx**.4.139, 5.93 etc.; beta reads *And if*.

116 **ȝonge**: Dropped by CrCGOF to shorten a long line. R divides the line into two at the caesura.

118 **ful**: Alpha supported by **Cx**. Dropped by beta.

118 **he**: Good support from LM and alpha as well as **Cx**. Others omit.

119 **to** (2): Firm support from LM, beta2 and R. However the word is dropped in **Cx**.

122 **¶**: The paraph at the start of the speech is in beta and F.

122 **do**: **Cx** also has imperative in a revised line (RK.15.124). Cf. R *dos* and F *ys to doon*.

127 **seuene**: It is not certain that **Bx** had the numeral. R omits it and the L corrector supplies it in the margin, though it is in M and F. Perhaps it is most likely that L and R coincidentally omitted it; see Adams (2000), 184. The line is not in **Cx**.

Þere þe lorde of lyf wonyeth · to leren hym what is dowel

¶ Til I se þo seuene · and my-self acorden

130 I am vnhardy quod he · to any wy3t to preue it
For one pieres þe ploughman [·] hath inpugned vs alle
And sette alle sciences at a soppe · saue loue one
And no tixte ne taketh [·] to meyntene his cause
But dilige deum · and domine quis habitabit &c

135 And seith þat dowel and dobet [·] aren two infinites
Whiche infinites with a feith [·] fynden oute dobest
Which shal saue mannes soule · þus seith piers þe ploughman

¶ I can nou3t her-on quod conscience · ac I knowe wel pieres
He wil nou3t a3ein holy writ speken · I dar wel vndertake

140 Þanne passe we ouer til piers come · and preue þis in dede
Pacience hath be in many place · and par-auntre cnoweth
Þat no clerke ne can · as cryst bereth witnesse
Pacientes vincunt &c
A[t] 3owre preyere quod pacyence þo · so no man displese hym

145 Disce quod he doce · dilige inimicos
Disce and dowel · doce & dobet
Dilige and dobest · þus tau3te me ones
A lemman þat I loued · loue was hir name
With wordes and with werkes quod she · and wille of þyne herte

150 Þow loue lelly þi soule [·] al þi lyf-tyme
And so þow lere þe to louye · for þe lordes loue of heuene
Þine enemye in al wyse · euene-forth with þi-selue
Cast coles on his hed · [of] al kynde speche
Bothe with werkes and with wordes [·] fonde his loue to wynne

155 And lay on hym þus with loue · til he laghe on þe
And but he bowe for þis betyng [·] blynde mote he worthe

---

128 **hym:** i.e. the Lord of Life. So LMR; see Schmidt (1995), 391. Others have pl.; CrWO omit.

130 **to** (2): Alpha omits, perhaps rightly. The line is not in **Cx**.

133 M omits the line.

141 **cnoweth:** The beta2 reading *mouthed* is distinctly odd.

142 **ne:** Omitted by alpha.

144 **At:** "in response to". LWHm read *Ac*, probably representing beta, though CGO share alpha's *At*, and M is corrected to that reading.

151 **þow lere þe:** R's muddled *to lere and* probably represents alpha, further misunderstood by F.

153 **of:** R is supported by beta2 and by the corrected reading of M. Beta perhaps read *and*, with beta2 independently altering for sense. **Cx** has *of* in this line, but three lines below has "Conforte hym with thy catel and with thy kynde speche" (RK.15.145). Pearsall (2008), 256, refers to *Ancrene Wisse* (ed. Millett 7.293–301) for the interpretation of the *carbones ardentes* of Rom. 12.20 as the fire of love.

¶ Ac for to fare þus with þi frende · foly it were
For he þat loueth þe lelly · lyte of þyne coueiteth
Kynde loue coueiteth nouȝte · no catel but speche
160   With half a laumpe lyne in latyne · ex vi transicionis

¶ I bere þere-inne aboute · fast ybounde dowel
In a signe of þe saterday · þat sette firste þe kalendare
And al þe witte of þe wednesday · of þe nexte wyke after
Þe myddel of þe mone [·] is þe miȝte of bothe
165   And here-with am I welcome · þere I haue it with me

¶ Vndo it late þis doctour [sen] · if dowel be þer-inne
For bi hym þat me made · miȝte neuere pouerte
Miseise ne myschief [·] ne man with his tonge
Colde ne care [·] ne compaignye of theues
170   Ne noither hete ne haille · ne non helle pouke
Ne noither fuire ne flode · ne fere of þine enemy
Tene þe eny tyme · and þow take it with þe
Caritas nichil timet
[And eke haue god my soule · and þow wilt it craue
175   Þere nys neither emperour ne emperesse · erl kynge ne baroun
Pope ne patriarch [·] þat pure reson ne shal make
Þe maister of alle þo men · þorugh miȝt of þis redeles
Nouȝt þorugh wicche-crafte but þorugh wit · & þow wilt þi-selue
Do kynge and quene · and alle þe comune after
180   Ȝyue þe alle þat þei may ȝiue · as þe for best ȝemere
And as þou demest wil þei do · alle here dayes after
Pacientes vincunt &c ·]

[¶] It is but a dido quod þis doctour · a dysoures tale

---

158 **lyte**: L's form of "little" is supported by R. Neither scribe has the form elsewhere.

158 **coueiteth**: Beta is supported by **Cx** (RK.15.153). Alpha's *desireth* avoids the repetition in the following line (dropped in C).

164 **is þe miȝte**: WHm confuse the issue with *as þe nyght*. On the "middle of the moon" riddle, see Galloway (1995), 68–105, and **Bx**.3.334.

166 **late**: Alpha has *and late*. The passage **Bx**.13.159–82 is rewritten in C.

166 **sen**: The L scribe alters this to *deme*, in line with beta1, thus correcting the alliteration. But alpha reads *se*, which is more probably the reading of **Bx** than coincidental error.

166 **if**: Alpha has *where*, "whether".

174–82 These nine lines are omitted by beta, skipping from one short Latin line to the next. Lines 179 and 181 are also omitted in F. The passage is rewritten in C (RK.15.165–9).

177 **Þe**: "thee". In F it appears more comfortably in the previous line before *make*.

180 **as þe for**: "as to you who are". F's *as þou for* gives the sense "since you are (the best guardian)".

183 **¶**: The L scribe wrote a paragraph marker which the rubricator missed because the scribe did not leave a line-space. The paraph is in WHmC and alpha.

Al þe witt of þis worlde · and wiȝte mennes strengthe
185 Can nouȝt confourmen a pees · bytwene þe pope and his enemys
Ne bitwene two cristene kynges · can no wiȝte pees make
Profitable to ayther peple · and put þe table fro hym
And toke clergye and conscience · to conseille as it were
Þat pacience þo moste passe · for pilgrimes kunne wel lye

190 ¶ Ac conscience carped loude [·] and curteislich seide
Frendes fareth wel · and faire spake to clergye
For I wil go with þis gome · if god wil ȝiue me grace
And be pilgryme with pacience · til I haue proued more

¶ What quod clergye to conscience · ar ȝe coueitouse nouthe
195 After ȝeresȝyues or ȝiftes · or ȝernen to rede redeles
I shal brynge ȝow a bible · a boke of þe olde lawe
And lere ȝow if ȝow lyke · þe leest poynte to knowe
Þat pacience þe pilgryme · parfitly knewe neuere

¶ Nay bi cryste quod conscience to clergye [·] god þe forȝelde
200 For al þat pacience me profreth · proude am I litel
Ac þe wille of þe wye · and þe wille folke here
Hath moeued my mode · to mourne for my synnes
Þe good wille of a wiȝte · was neure bouȝte to þe fulle
For þere nys no tresore þerto · to a trewe wille

205 ¶ Haued nouȝt [Marie] Magdeleigne more · for a boxe of salue
Þan zacheus for he seide · dimidium bonorum meorum do pauperibus
And þe pore widwe [·] for a peire of mytes
Þan alle þo that offreden · in-to gazafilacium

¶ Þus curteislich conscience · congeyde fyrst þe Frere
210 And sithen softliche he seyde · in clergyes ere

---

184 **and**: Beta is supported by the X family of C. Alpha's *ne*, which makes the meaning clearer, is supported by the P family of C.

189 **þo**: Beta2 has *þou*, and M revises to that reading.

192 **ȝiue**: LMW, and so probably beta's form, with other beta mss. and alpha altering to *gyue* as a result of alliterative attraction.

197 **ȝow lyke**: So beta, while alpha has *ȝe liken*. Elsewhere the verb is always constructed as impersonal with a dative pronoun.

201 **wille folke**: LC, original M and R, so secure for **Bx**. Other scribes have *wille of folke*, repeating *wille of* from the a-verse, and M is altered to bring it in line with beta2. But *wille* is the adjective *wil*, "wandering" (so R's spelling), so that the line means "But the wilfulness of this man (the Doctor) and of the errant folk here". Note that *MED wil* adj. records the spellings *will* and *wille*. See Burrow, *N&Q* (2008), 124–5.

203 **a**: Alpha's *vch a / euery* makes poorer sense.

204 **nys**: Supported by LWR against *is* in other mss.

205 **Marie**: Omitted by beta. Alpha is supported by the alliterative pattern (aaa/xx).

209 **fyrst**: Omitted by GO, and (presumably coincidentally) by M.

Me were leuer by owre lorde · and I lyue shulde
Haue pacience parfitlich · þan half þi pakke of bokes

¶ Clergye to conscience · no congeye wolde take
But seide ful sobreliche · þow shalt se þe tyme
215   Whan þow art wery for-walked · wilne me to consaille

¶ Þat is soth seyde conscience · so me god helpe
If pacience be owre partyng felawe · and pryue with vs bothe
There nys wo in þis worlde · þat we ne shulde amende
And confourmen Kynges to pees · and al-kynnes londes
220   Sarasenes and surre · and so forth alle þe iewes
Turne in-to þe trewe feith · and in-til one byleue

¶ Þat is soth quod clergye · I se what þow menest
I shal dwelle as I do · my deuore to shewen
And confermen fauntekynes · and other folke ylered
225   Tyl pacience haue preued þe · and parfite þe maked

¶ Conscience þo with pacience passed · pilgrymes as it were
Þanne had pacience as pylgrymes han · in his poke vittailles
Sobrete and symple speche · and sothfaste byleue
To conforte hym and conscience · if þey come in place
230   Þere vnkyndenesse and coueytise is · hungrye contrees bothe

¶ And as þei went by þe weye · of dowel þei carped
Þei mette with a mynstral · as me þo þou3te
Pacience apposed hym fyrste · and preyed hym he sholde hem telle
To conscience what crafte he couthe · an to what contree he wolde

235   ¶ I am a mynstral quod þat man · my name is actiua vita
Alle ydel ich hatye · for of actyf is my name
A wafrere wil 3e wite · and serue many lordes

---

213 **to**: So LHmCO and probably uncorrected M. CrWG have easier *of*, but the phrase means "offer no farewell to". This sense of *take*, usually followed by a dative pronoun, is common in the poem, e.g. **Bx**.1.57, etc. Alpha's *and/ne* is ruled out by the next line, where the speaker must be Clergy. See Schmidt (1995), 392.

216 **seyde**: So LMR and CrHm. The others have *quod*, perhaps by semi-alliterative association with *Conscience*, or picked up from l. 222.

219 **and** (2): Beta's reading makes better sense than alpha's *of*, which leads to alpha's addition of *And* at the beginning of the next line.

224 **confermen**: "strengthen in faith"; R (= alpha) repeats *conformen*, "make agree", from l. 219, as does G.

231 ¶: The paraph is in beta and F.

231 **of dowel þei**: Beta's b-verse is supported by **Cx**, although alpha's *and of dowel* goes smoothly with the next line.

233 **hym** (2): LMR, so secure for **Bx**, but possibly an error. Others drop the repeated *hym*, although F includes it in a revised b-verse. Cr follows **Cx** with the simplified *prayed he should tel.*

And fewe robes I fonge · or furred gounes
Couthe I lye [and] do men laughe · þanne lacchen I shulde
240 Other mantel or money [·] amonges lordes mynstralles
Ac for I can noither tabre ne trompe · ne telle none gestes
Farten ne fythelen [·] at festes ne harpen
Iape ne iogly · ne gentlych pype
Ne noyther sailly ne saute · ne synge with þe gyterne
245 I haue none gode gyftes · of þise grete lordes
For no bred þat I brynge forth · saue a beneson on þe sonday
Whan þe prest preyeth þe peple · her pater noster to bidde
For peres þe plowman · and þat hym profite wayten
And þat am I actyf · þat ydelnesse hatye
250 For alle trewe trauaillours · and tilieres of þe erthe
Fro mychelmesse to mychelmesse · I fynde hem with wafres

¶ Beggeres and bidderes · of my bred crauen
Faitoures and freres · and folke with brode crounes
I fynde payne for þe pope · and prouendre for his palfrey
255 And I hadde neuere of hym · haue god my treuthe
Noither prouendre ne parsonage · ȝut of the popis ȝifte
Saue a pardoun with a peys of led · and two pollis amydde
Hadde iche a clerke þat couthe write · I wolde caste hym a bille
Þat he sent me vnder his seel · a salue for þe pestilence
260 And þat his blessyng & his bulles · bocches miȝte destroye
In nomine meo demonia eici[e]nt & super egros manus imponent & bene
      habebunt
And þanne wolde I be prest to [þe] peple · paste for to make
And buxome and busy [·] aboute bred and drynke
For hym and for alle his · fonde I þat his pardoun
265 Miȝte lechen a man · as I bileue it shulde
For sith he hath þe powere · þat peter hym-self hadde

239 **and**: Alpha is supported by **Cx**.
243 **iogly**: C mss. split between this and alpha's *iangele*.
246 **brynge**: Beta's present tense has support from **Cx** in a rewritten line.
249 **þat am I**: Beta4 and R have, less satisfactorily, the standard word-order. F has (by coincidence or contamination) *for me*, as does **Cx** (RK.15.213) which follows more smoothly from the previous lines, "prays ... for me".
251 **wafres**: M is corrected to *my wafres* to bring the text in line with CrW.
257 **amydde**: The form is attested by LMCR, against *amyddes* in beta2 and GOF.
258 **iche**: This is the only example of this spelling in L. "I" is elsewhere spelt *ich*, and "each" is *ech(e)*. The former sense is very obviously intended, but the odd confusion of scribes may suggest a **Bx** reading *iche*, or *ech(e)* as in CG, giving rise to F's *euery*.
260 **And**: Alpha drops.
261 **eicient**: L has the present, as M perhaps did before correction, suggesting a beta error.
262 **þe**: Not in LHm, and supplied in M by the corrector. It is therefore likely that it was lost by beta.

He hath þe potte with þe salue · sothly as me þinketh
Argentum & aurum non est michi quod autem habeo tibi do in nomine
    domini surge & ambula

¶ Ac if miȝte of miracle hym faille · it is for men ben nouȝt worthy
270   To haue þe grace of god · & no gylte of þe pope
For may no blyssyng done vs bote · but if we wil amende
Ne mannes masse make pees · amonges cristene peple
Tyl pruyde be purelich fordo · and þat þourgh payn defaute

¶ For ar I haue bred of mele · ofte mote I swete
275   And ar þe comune haue corne ynough · many a colde mornyng
So ar my wafres ben ywrouȝt · moche wo I tholye

¶ Alle Londoun I leue · liketh wel my wafres
And lowren whan þei lakken it · it is nouȝt longe ypassed
Þere was a carful comune · whan no carte come to toune
280   With [bake] bred fro stretforth · þo gan beggeres wepe
And werkmen were agaste a litel · þis wil be þouȝte longe
In þe date of owre dryȝte · in a drye apprile
A þousande and thre hondreth · tweis [twenty] & ten
My wafres þere were gesen · whan chichestre was Maire

285   ¶ I toke gode kepe by cryst · and conscience bothe
Of haukyn þe actyf man · and how he was yclothed
He hadde a cote of crystendome · as holykirke bileueth
Ac it was moled in many places · with many sondri plottes
Of pruyde here a plotte and þere a plotte [·] of vnboxome speche
290   Of scornyng and of scoffyng · and of vnskilful berynge
As in aparaille and in porte · proude amonges þe peple

---

268 **tibi**: Alpha has *hoc tibi*, as does O, in line with the Vulgate. C mss. split.

270 **þe** (1): Alpha's *no* is not supported by **Cx**.

271 **For**: Dropped by R, but supported by **Cx**.

273 **purelich**: Alpha's *priueliche* is not supported by **Cx** (RK.15.229).

273 **þat**: Dropped by MCrWF, and replaced by *alle* in R, but supported by **Cx**.

278 **it** (1): Alpha has *hem*, as do CrW. It is likely that W, at least, was prompted to adopt the plural for grammatical concord and to avoid the repetition of *it*. The passage from **Bx**.13.274–90 has no parallel in **C**.

280 **bake**: Dropped by beta to the detriment of the alliteration.

283 **twenty**: This does not alliterate and is a **Bx** error (the events occurred in 1370); LR correct to the obvious *thretty*. This is a rare instance where LR have corrected rather than copy an obvious mistake. M and Hm both realise the error and correct in different ways. Numerals are easy to confuse and easy to correct.

285 **gode**: Beta has the standard phrase; for that reason alpha's *grete* might be preferred. We follow copy-text.

289 The placing of the punctus causes scribes problems. M has it after each *plotte*, as though first inserting it too early; HmCO and crucially R have it after the second (hence aaa/xx); LCrW have the second *plotte* in the b-verse (aa/ax).

Otherwyse þan he hath · with herte or syȝte shewynge
Hym wil[n]ynge þat alle men wende · he were þat he is nouȝte
For-why he bosteth and braggeth · with many bolde othes
295 And in-obedient to ben vndernome · of any lyf lyuyng
And so syngulere by hym-self · as to syȝte of þe poeple
Was none suche as hym-self · ne none so po[p]e-holy
Yhabited as an hermyte · an ordre by hym-selue
Religioun sanz reule · and resonable obedience
300 Lakkyng lettred men · and lewed men bothe
In lykyng of lele lyf · and a lyer in soule
With Inwit and with outwitt · ymagenen and studye
As best for his body be · to haue a b[ol]de name
And entermeten hym ouer al · þer he hath nouȝt to done
305 Wilnyng þat men wende · his witte were þe best
[Or for his crafty kunnynge · or of clerkes þe wisest
Or strengest on stede · or styuest vnder gerdel
And louelokest to loken on · and lelest of werkes
And non so holy as he · ne of lif clennere
310 Or fairest of feytures · of forme and of shafte
And most sotyl of songe · other sleyest of hondes
And large to lene · loos þere-by to cacche]
And if he gyueth ouȝte pore gomes · telle what he deleth
Pore of possessioun [·] in purse and in coffre
315 And as a lyon on to loke · and lordeliche of speche

---

292 **or:** R has *and*; F, understandably puzzled by the line, rewrites the b-verse, as does **Cx**, *withynne or withouten* (RK.6.31).

293 **wilnynge:** R's reading is perhaps slightly preferable to beta's *willynge* on grounds of sense ("with him being keen that"). It also has support from the parallel line in **Cx** (RK.6.32), and from the variants at l. 305, where some scribes corrupt to *willynge*. Mustanoja (1960), 115, quotes this instance of the absolute construction. F corrupts to *wenynge*.

296 Only L + alpha preserve 296b and 297a, all others (including M) skipping from *hymself* (296) to *hymself* (297). Both lines are in **Cx**.

297 **pope-holy:** Probably beta read *pompe-holy* (as do a few C mss.), corrected by several scribes.

302 **with** (2): Not in alpha or Cr.

303 **bolde:** Alpha's reading is obviously preferable to beta's (?) *badde* (written over an illegible erasure in L).

306–12 Seven lines are omitted by beta; 306–8 and 310 are represented in revised form in **Cx** (RK.6.42–6). There seems no obvious reason for omission, though KD, p. 66, suggest resumption at the wrong point prompted by *to loken on* (308) and *on to loke* (315).

307 **vnder:** R is supported by **Cx** against F's *gyrt with*.

312 **loos:** "repute". R has *losse*, listed by *MED* as a possible spelling of *los* n.(2), but R elsewhere spells it as *los* (**Bx.**11.311) and *loos* (**Bx.**13.471) so may here have misunderstood the word as "loss". F's *looþ* (in a-verse) perhaps suggests that alpha had the form *loos*.

313 **pore:** All except LR have *to pore*.

314 **coffre:** Beta evidently misplaced the punctus after *purse*, prompting the addition of *bothe* in all mss. except LR. (F omits the line.) It is significant that M shares the beta1 error.

315 **on:** R's omission could be right but is not supported by F, which has it after the verb.

¶ Baldest of beggeres [·] a bostour þat nouȝt hath
In towne and in tauernes · tales to telle
And segge þinge þat he neuere seigh · and for soth sweren it
Of dedes þat he neuere dyd · demen and bosten
320 And of werkes þat he wel dyd · witnesse and seggen
Lo if ȝe leue me nouȝt · or þat I lye wenen
Axeth at hym or at hym · and he ȝow can telle
What I suffred and seighe · and some-tymes hadde
And what I couth and knewe · and what kynne I come of
325 Al he wolde þat men wiste [·] of werkes and of wordes
Which myȝte plese þe peple · and praysen hym-seluen
Si hominibus placerem cristi seruus non essem
Et alibi nemo potest duobus dominis seruire

¶ Bi criste quod conscience þo · þi best cote haukyn
330 Hath many moles and spottes · it moste ben ywassh

¶ Ȝe who-so toke hede quod haukyn · byhynde and bifore
What on bakke and what on body half · & by þe two sydes
Men sholde fynde many frounces · and many foule plottes

[¶] And he torned hym as tyte · and þanne toke I hede
335 It was fouler by felefolde · þan it firste semed
It was bidropped with wratthe · and wikked wille
With enuye and yuel speche [·] entysyng to fyȝte
Lyinge and la[kk]ynge · [a] leue tonge to chyde
Al þat he wist wykked · by any wiȝte tellen it
340 And blame men bihynde her bakke · and bydden hem meschaunce
And þat he wist bi wille · tellen it watte
And þat watte wiste · wille wiste it after
And made of frendes foes · þorugh a false tonge
Or with myȝte of mouthe [·] or þorugh mannes strengthe
345 Auenge[d] me fele tymes · other frete my-selue

---

325 **of** (2): Alpha omits.

332 **and what on**: Probably the beta reading, though MC drop *and*, and GO drop *what*. Alpha also drops *what*. **Bx**.13.329–39 have no parallel in C.

334 **¶**: In L the scribe indicated the paraph but forgot to leave a line-space, so the rubricator missed it. It has support from WCR.

338 **lakkynge**: Alpha's reading is greatly preferable to beta's *laughynge* on grounds of sense.

338 **a**: R only, but apparently alpha since F expands to *& with a*. Beta thus interpreted **Bx** *a* as "and". Cf. note to l. 88 above. The b-verse "a tongue eager to chide" defines *lakkynge*.

341 **watte**: LMWCG, hence the beta reading, with CrHmO and alpha reading *to watte*. The parallel b-verse in **Cx** is RK.6.71, *tolde hit wille aftur*, rather than RK.6.70, *to watekyn he tolde hit*.

345 **Auenged**: Despite lack of support from other **B** mss., R's past tense is preferable on grounds of syntax, and is supported by **Cx**. Hence *frete* is also past tense, as in **Cx**.

Wyth-inne as a shepster shere · I shrewed men & cursed
Cuius maledictione os plenum est & amaritudine sub lingua eius labor &
    dolor
& alibi filij hominum dentes eorum arma & sagitte & lingua eorum
    gladius acutus

¶ Þere is no lyf þat I louye · lastyng any while
350 For tales þat I telle · no man trusteth to me
     And whan I may nou3t haue þe maistrye · [swich] malencolye I take
     Þat I cacche þe crompe · þe cardiacle some-tyme
     Or an ague in suche an angre · and some-tyme a feure
     Þat taketh me al a twelf-moneth · tyl þat I dispyse
355 Lechecrafte or owre lorde · and leue on a wicche
     And segge þat no clerke ne can · ne cryste as I leue
     To þe souter of southwerke · or of shordyche dame emme
     And segge þat no goddes worde · gaf me neuere bote
     But þorw a charme had I chaunce · & my chief hele

360 ¶ I wayted wisloker · and þanne was it soiled
     With lykyng of lecherye · as by lokyng of his eye
     For vche a mayde þat he mette · he made hir a signe
     Semynge to synne-ward · and some-tyme he gan taste
     Aboute þe mouth or bynethe · bygynneth to grope
365 Tyl eytheres wille waxeth kene · and to þe werke 3eden
     As wel fastyng-days & frydayes · and forboden ny3tes
     And as [lef] in lente as oute of lente · alle tymes ylyche

---

346 **I shrewed**: Interpreted by Skeat and *MED shreuen* as past participle, but this is syntactically impossible. Kane (2005) and Schmidt (1995) take *ishrewed* as past tense, but *MED* does
not record a verb *ishrewen*. See F's rewriting, and cf. **Cx** past tense *shrewed* (RK.6.75).
349 ¶: The paraph is in beta only, following the Latin lines.
349 **I louye**: KD, p. 148, argue for the CrW reading *me loueth*, but it cannot be **Bx**.
351 **swich**: The spelling of F probably represents **Bx**. R misread as *which*. Beta apparently
misread as *with*, though CrW have *such* (by conjecture?) and MHm are both visibly altered to
that reading. The **Cx** reading is also *such*. L retains the spelling *swich* only in **Bx**.15.17.
355 **or**: So LR. Clearly an error for *of*, with the obvious correction (supported by **Cx**) made
by all other scribes.
360 **it**: F has *he*, emphasising that *I* in the a-verse refers to Will. R's *I* is perhaps prompted
by the alpha reading *myn* for *his* in the next line.
361 **as**: A number of scribes (Hm, beta4 and R) have the easier *and*.
361 **his**: Alpha's *myn* is obviously an error, suggesting a muddle over the speaker here. See note
to l. 363.
363 In F, ll. 361–8 are in the first person, as they are in **Cx** where they are part of the confession
of lechery (RK.6.176–84). In this line F's *& summe y gan* is a C-text reading and suggests
contamination.
366 **wel**: Beta has *wel in* anticipating the following line, but alpha is supported by **Cx**
(RK.6.182).
367 **lef**: Beta's *wel* is prompted by the preceding line. Alpha is supported by the alliteration
and **Cx**.

Suche werkes with hem · was neuere oute of sesoun

Tyl þei my3te namore · and þanne had merye tales

370 And how þat lechoures louyen · lau3en an iapen

And of her harlotrye and horedome · in her elde tellen

¶ Thanne pacience parceyued [·] of poyntes his cote

Was colmy þorw coueityse · and v[n]kynde desyrynge

More to good þan to god · þe gome his loue caste

375 And ymagyned how · he it my3te haue

With false mesures and mette · and with false witnesse

Lened for loue of þe wedde · and loth to do treuthe

And awaited þorwgh whi[ttes] [·] wey[es] to bigile

And menged his marchaundyse · and made a gode moustre

380 Þe worste with-in was · a gret witte I lete hit

And if my neighbore had an hyne · or any beste elles

More profitable þan myne · many sleightes I made

How I my3te haue it · al my witte I caste

And but I it had by other waye · atte laste I stale it

385 Or pryuiliche his purse shoke · vnpiked his lokkes

Or by ny3t or by day · aboute was ich euere

Þorwgh gyle to gadren [·] þe good þat ich haue

¶ 3if I 3ede to þe plow · I pynched so narwe

Þat a fote londe or a forwe · fecchen I wolde

390 Of my nexte neighbore · nymen of his erthe

And if [I] rope ouer-reche · or 3af hem red þat ropen

To seise to me with her sykel · þat I ne sewe neure

¶ And who-so borweth of me · aboute þe tyme

---

368 **was:** We retain L's plural form, though other mss. have *were*. See note to **Bx.5.13**.

371 **her** (1): Not in F or R, which begins *Or herlotrie*. **Bx**.13.370–8 have no parallel in C.

372 **his:** All except LR supply *of* (added in M), but *his cote* is subject of *was* in the following line: "his coat was grimy with stains".

378 **whittes weyes:** R's spelling *whitus weyus* suggests the cause of confusion in beta: **Bx** presumably had the spelling <wh> for /w/ (as sometimes in SW), preserved but perhaps not understood as "wits" by R, and desperately altered to *which* by beta, who consequently understood *wey* as "way". R has his usual spelling of *weye*, "man". For once, F gets it more or less right.

381 **an:** Alpha is supported by **Cx** (RK.6.262). Beta anticipates *any* in the b-verse.

384 **but I it:** LMW, so beta, supported by the X family of C (the P family has Hm's order). R omits *it* and F rewrites.

390–1 Alpha loses the b-verse of 390 and the a-verse of 391.

391 **I:** Dropped by L, though the line is marked for correction.

391 **rope:** "reaped" (*MED repen* v.(1)); the past tense is supported by **Cx**.

391 **ropen:** Cr and alpha have *repen*, which may also be a pa.t.pl. form.

392 **To:** Supported by **Cx** against *And* in MCrCGO.

393 **aboute:** A spelling of *abou3te*, "bought, paid for", preserved by LGR and altered by the correctors of MHm. It was evidently misunderstood as "about" by F, who revised.

With presentes priueliche · or payed somme certeyne
395 So walde he or nouȝt wolde he · wynnen I wolde
And bothe to kyth and to kyn · vnkynde of þat ich hadde

¶ And who-so cheped my chaffare · chiden I wolde
But he profred to paye · a peny or tweyne
More þan it was worth · and ȝet wolde I swere
400 Þat it coste me moche more · swore manye othes

¶ In halydayes at holicherche · whan ich herde masse
Hadde [I] neuere wille wot god · witterly to biseche
Mercye for my mysdedes · þat I ne morned more
For losse of gode leue me · þan for lykames giltes
405 As if I had dedly synne done · I dred nouȝt þat so sore
As when I lened and leued it lost · or longe ar it were payed
So if I kydde any kyndenesse · myn euen-cristene to helpe
Vpon a cruel coueityse · my [conscience] gan hange
And if I sent ouer-see · my seruauntz to Bruges
410 Or in-to Pruslonde my prentys · my profit to wayten
To marchaunden with monoye · and maken her eschaunges
Miȝte neuere me conforte · in þe mene-tyme
Noither messe ne matynes · ne none manere siȝtes
Ne neuere penaunce perfourned · ne pater noster seyde
415 Þat my mynde ne was more · on my gode in a doute
Þan in þe grace of god · and his grete helpes
Vbi thesaurus tuus · ibi & cor tuum

[Ȝet glotoun with grete othes · his g[ar]nement hadde soyled

---

395 **he** (2): Omitted by WR. For *nouȝt wolde he*, beta4 and F have *he nolde*.

398 **profred**: CGO and rewritten Hm add *me*.

400 **me**: In beta only; alpha may be right to omit. The line is not in C.

402 I: LR, the two best witnesses, coincidentally omit the pronoun, which is necessary for the sense and supported by **Cx** (RK.6.273). The line is marked for correction in L.

404 **lykames**: So R, supported by **Cx**; all other mss. have *my lykames*, following on from *my mysdedes* in the previous line.

408 **conscience**: Alpha's reading corrects the aa/bb alliteration of beta's *herte*. The line is not in C.

411 **eschaunges**: Alpha has *chaunges*, but beta is supported by **Cx**.

412 **tyme**: Confirmed by **Cx**. Beta2 has *while*.

418–27 These lines are omitted by beta. Probably the scribe skipped from one paraph to the next, though alpha does not record the expected paraph at 418 following the Latin line. Lines 420 and 422 have some parallel in the C text, but are there transferred to the confession of Gluttony (RK.6.428 and 430).

418 **glotoun**: R's reading is surprising enough to have prompted F's revision to *þat goome*. Compare the other sins attributed to Hawkin: lechery (361), covetousness (373), sloth (426), though they are not personified as here. On the other hand R's *glotoun* is possibly a reminiscence of **Bx**.5.319 and 10.53, "Glotonye and grete othes".

And foule beflobered it · as with fals speche
420　As þere no nede ne was · godes name an ydel
Swore þere-by swithe ofte · and al byswatte his cote
And more mete ete and dronke · þen kynde miȝt defie
And cauȝte sekenesse sum-tyme · for my [surfai]tes ofte
And þanne I dradde to deye · in dedlich synne
425　Þat in-to wanhope he w[or]the · and wende nauȝt to be saued
Þe whiche is sleuthe so slow · þat may no sleightes helpe it
Ne no mercy amenden · þe man þat so deyeth]

¶ [Ac] which ben þe braunches · þat bryngeth a man to sleuth
His woman morneth nouȝte for his mysdedes · ne maketh no sorwe
430　Ac penaunce þat þe prest enioigneth · perfourneth yuel
Doth none almes-dede · dret hym of no synne
Lyueth aȝein þe bileue · and no lawe holdeth
Vch day is haliday with hym · or an heigh ferye
And if he auȝte wole here · it is an harlotes tonge
435　Whan men carpeth of cryst · or of clennesse of soule
He wexeth wroth & wil nouȝte here · but wordes of myrthe
Penaunce and pore men · and þe passioun of seyntes
He hateth to here þere-of · and alle þat it telleth
Þise ben þe braunches beth war · þat bryngeth a man to wanhope
440　Ȝe lordes and ladyes · and legates of holicherche
Þat fedeth fol[e]-sages · flatereres and lyeres
And han likynge to lythen hem · to do ȝow to lawghe
Ve vobis qui ridetis &c
And ȝiueth hem mete and Mede · and pore men refuse

---

423 **surfaites**: R's *forfetes* is a misreading of alliterating *surfetys*, as in F.

425 **worthe**: R's *wrathe* could be a metathesised form but is probably an error (cf. **Bx**.11.5). F revises to synonymous *wente*.

428 **Ac**: Dropped by beta following the loss of text. For *Ac which*, F has *Þese*. R is supported by **Cx** (RK.7.69).

429 **His woman**: Evidently the **Bx** reading, recorded in LR, original M, and CG. Beta2 and F recognise it as nonsense and so emend by conjecture to *He þat* or *Þat*; O, *Is whanne a man*, has the reading of the P family of C, by conjecture or contamination (RK.7.70). In C these lines are transferred to the confession of Sloth.

430 **Ac**: The reading of LO and probably original M, while G has its usual substitution *But*. The others have *And* (*Ne* in F). **Cx** has *The*.

435 **of** (2): Dropped by CGOF, but supported by authoritative C mss. of both families.

435 **soule**: The sg. is supported by **Cx**.

437 **and** (1): As in **Cx**. WF have *of*.

441 **fole-sages**: "wise fools, jesters". R is supported by **Cx** (RK.7.82). Beta reads *foles sages*, i.e. a pl. noun followed by an adj. with a French pl. inflection (Mustanoja (1960), 277). F has *folis sage*.

442 **to** (3): GR omit, as does **Cx**, but GR are unmetrical (x / x /) whereas **Cx** is expanded to x / x x x / by the addition of *in hope*. Perhaps, though, **Cx** has preserved the reading that **Bx** has dropped, leading beta and F to add *to* for the metre. So Schmidt (1995), 392.

445 In 30wre deth-deyinge · I drede me sore
     Lest þo thre maner men · to moche sorwe 30w brynge
     Consencientes & agentes pari pena punientur
     Patriarkes & prophetes · and prechoures of goddes wordes
     Sauen þorw her sarmoun · mannes soule fram helle
450 Ri3t so flateres and foles · aren þe fendes disciples
     To entice men þorw her tales [·] to synne and harlotrye
     Ac clerkes þat knowen holywryt · shulde kenne lordes
     What dauid seith of suche men · as þe sauter telleth
     Non habitabit in medio domus mee · qui facit superbiam qui loquitur iniqua
455 Shulde none harlote haue audience · in halle ne in chambres
     Þere wise men were · witnesseth goddes wordes
     Ne no mysproude man · amonges lordes ben allowed

     [¶ Clerkes and kni3tes · welcometh kynges mynstralles
     And for loue of [her] lorde · litheth hem at festes
460 Muche more me thinketh · riche men shulde
     Haue beggeres byfore hem · þe whiche ben goddes mynstralles
     As he seyth hym-self · seynt Iohan bereth witnesse
     Qui vos spernit me spernit
     For-thi I rede 30w riche · at reueles whan 3e maketh
465 For to solace 30ure soules · suche minstralles to haue
     Þe pore for a fol-sage · syttynge at þe table
     And a lered man to lere þe · what oure lorde suffred
     For to saue þi soule · fram sathan þin enemy
     And fithel þe with-out flaterynge · of gode friday þe storye
470 And a blynd man for a bourdeoure · or a bedrede womman
     To crie a largesse by-for oure lorde · 30ure gode loos to shewe
     Þise thre maner mynstralles · maketh a man to laughe

---

445 **sore**: Beta adds *ful*, but **Cx** is without it.

447 **punientur**: Alpha has *puniendi sunt*, but beta is supported by **Cx**. Alford (1992), 86, quotes beta's form.

448 WHmR here have a paraph.

449 **sarmoun**: Beta2 has the more obvious plural, as does the P family of C.

450 **flateres**: Here, as elsewhere (and in C mss.) the form varies with *flaterers*. Cf. l. 477 below. We follow copy-text.

454 **qui** (2): Beta has *& qui*, but this is supported neither by **Cx** nor the Vulgate. F drops the last phrase.

455 **chambres**: CrWGF have the sg., as does **Cx**.

458–76 This block of 19 lines is omitted by beta. The lines are pretty well exactly reproduced in C (RK.7.96–113), usually supporting R over F.

459 **her**: F is supported by **Cx** against R's *þe*.

464 **at**: Evidently the reading of alpha, but not in **Cx**.

466 **þe** (2): So F; R has *þe hey3*; perhaps rightly, but perhaps an uncharacteristic addition, since **Cx** has *þy*.

469 **storye**: **Cx** has *feste*.

And in his deth-deyinge · þei don hym grete conforte
Þat bi his lyue lythed hem · and loued hem to here
475 Þise solaseth þe soule · til hym-selue be falle
In a welhope · amonges worthi seyntes]
[Þere] flateres and foles [·] þorw her foule wordes
Leden þo þat loue[d] hem · to luciferes feste
With turpiloquio a lay of sorwe · and luciferes fithele
480 Thus haukyn þe actyf man · hadde ysoiled his cote
Til conscience acouped hym þere-of · in a curteise manere
Whi he ne hadde wasshen it · or wyped it with a brusshe

---

474 **lythed:** So R, against F's *he lystned*. But the X family of C has *lened* and the P family *loueþ*.

476 **welhope:** Alpha or **Bx** has presumably lost *for a wrouhte so* as in **Cx**, leading F to expand.

477 **Þere:** "where". Alpha is supported by **Cx**. Following the loss of the preceding passage, beta has *Ac* with a paraph.

478 **loued:** Alpha's past tense is supported by **Cx**'s probable reading *lythed*, though some mss. of the P family have the present.

Passus 14

I Haue but one hatere quod haukyn · I am þe lasse to blame
Þough it be soiled and selde clene · I slepe þere-inne on niȝtes
And also I haue an houswyf · hewen and children
Vxorem duxy & ideo non possum venire
5 Þat wolen bymolen it many tyme · maugre my chekes

¶ It hath ben laued in lente · and oute of lente bothe
With þe sope of sykenesse · þat seketh wonder depe
And with þe losse of catel · loth forto agulte
God or any gode man · bi auȝte þat I wiste
10 And was shryuen of þe preste · þat gaue me for my synnes
To penaunce pacyence · and pore men to fede
Al for coueitise of my crystenedome · in clennesse to kepen it

¶ And couthe I neuere by cryste · kepen it clene an houre
Þat I ne soiled it with syȝte · or sum ydel speche
15 Or þorugh werke or þorugh worde · or wille of myn herte
Þat I ne flober it foule · fro morwe tyl eue

¶ And I shal kenne þe quod conscience · of contricioun to make
Þat shal clawe þi cote · of alkynnes filthe
Cordis contricio &c

---

1 **one:** L and alpha. Other mss. (including M) add *hool*, which KD (but not Schmidt) adopt on the basis that this is Haukyn's *best cote* (**Bx.**13.329). With the exception of the b-verse of l. 32, lines 1–42 have no parallel in C.

5 **tyme:** G and alpha have *tymes*. See note to **Bx.**11.387 where there is the same variation.

9 F rewrites to repair the alliteration.

13 **neuere:** Alpha has *nouȝt*.

15 **þorugh worde:** CGO omit *þorugh*, but it motivates alpha's non-alliterating *thouȝt*. F has *þoruh* in the b-verse.

20 Dowel wasshen it and wryngen it · þorw a wys confessour
 Oris confessio &c
 Dobet shal beten it and bouken it · as briȝte as any scarlet
 And engreynen it with good wille · and goddes grace to amende þe
 And sithen sende þe to satisfaccioun · for to so[nn]en it after
25 Satisfaccio dobest

 ¶ Shal neuere myste bimolen it · ne moth after biten it
 Ne fende ne false man [·] defoulen it in þi lyue
 Shal none heraude ne harpoure · haue a fairere garnement
 Þan haukyn þe actyf man · and þow do by my techyng
30 Ne no mynstral be more worth · amonges pore & riche
 Þan Haukynnes wyf þe wafrere · w[hic]h is actiua vita

 ¶ And I shal purueye þe paste quod pacyence · þough no plow erie
 And floure to fede folke with · as best be for þe soule
 Þough neuere greyne growed · ne grape vppon vyne
35 Alle þat lyueth and loketh · lyflode wolde I fynde
 And þat ynough shal none faille · of þinge þat hem nedeth
 We shulde nouȝt be to busy · abouten owre lyflode
 Ne solliciti sitis &c [·] volucres celi deus pascit &c [·] pacientes vincunt &c

 ¶ Þanne laughed haukyn a litel · and liȝtly gan swerye
40 Who-so leueth ȝow by owre lorde · I leue nouȝte he be blissed

 ¶ No quod pacyence paciently · and out of his poke hente
 Vitailles of grete vertues · for al manere bestes
 And seyde lo here lyflode ynough · if owre byleue be trewe

For lente neuere was [þere] lyf · but lyflode were shapen
45 Wher-of or wherfore · [and] where-by to lybbe

¶ Firste þe wylde worme · vnder weet erthe
Fissch to lyue in þe flode · and in þe fyre þe crykat
Þe corlue by kynde of þe eyre · moste clennest flesch of bryddes
And bestes by grasse and by greyne · and by grene rotis
50 In menynge þat alle men · my3te þe same
Lyue þorw lele byleue and loue · as god witnesseth
Quodcumque pecieritis in nomine meo &c & alibi
Non in solo pane viuit homo set in omni verbo quod procedit de ore dei

¶ But I loked what lyflode it was · þat pacience so preysed
55 And þanne was a pece of þe pater noster · fiat voluntas tua

¶ Haue haukyn quod pacyence · and ete þis whan þe hungreth
Or whan þow clomsest for colde · or clyngest for dr[outh]e
[And] shal neuere gyues þe greue · ne grete lordes wrath
Prisone ne peyne · for pacientes vincunt
60 Bi so þat þow be sobre · of sy3te and of tonge
In etynge and in handlyng · and in alle þi fyue wittis
Darstow neuere care for corne · ne lynnen cloth ne wollen
Ne for drynke ne deth drede · but deye as god lyketh
Or þorw honger or þorw hete · at his wille be it
65 For if þow lyuest after his lore · þe sho[r]ter lyf þe better
Si quis amat cristum mundum non diligit istum

¶ For þorw his breth bestes wexen · and abrode 3eden

---

44 **þere**: Supported by R alone, since F rewrites the line and beta drops the word, but C mss. have either *here* or more commonly *þere* (RK.15.238).

45 **and**: Beta has *or*, though O reads *&*. F loses the line, but R's *and* is supported by **Cx**.

50 **my3te**: Misunderstanding the syntax (*þe same*, "similarly"), scribes add *do* (MCrGOF) or *se* (C), but LWHmR are supported by **Cx**.

52 **pecieritis**: Beta adds *a patre*. The P family of C reads *patrem*, the X family omits as does alpha. Biblical texts vary; see Alford (1992), 87.

54 **lyflode it**: Beta is supported by **Cx** (though in a b-verse) against alpha's *þat liflode*.

55 **was**: LWCG read *was it*, as in **Cx**, supplying a **Bx** omission preserved in MO before correction and in alpha. Cr has *it was* and Hm *þat was*.

57 **drouthe**: The alpha reading is supported by **Cx** against beta's *drye*. However, the latter is a good reading (cf. **Bx**.5.549), and it is possible that the alpha reading is a revision.

58 **And**: R (=alpha?) is supported by **Cx**, though beta omits and F has *Þere*.

58 **gyues**: "shackles". **Cx** supports beta. Alpha substitutes non-alliterating *feytoures*, "deceivers"; presumably this was a misreading of a gloss *feteres*, "fetters" in **Bx**. For another case of a gloss being included in the text, cf. note to **Bx**.15.25.

60 L's paraph is unsupported except for the line-space in M.

65 **better**: Alpha has *leuere*, perhaps by alliterative attraction; beta is supported by **Cx**.

67 **wexen**: L's forms are inf. *wax(en)*, pr. 3 sg. *wexeth, waxeth*, pr. pl. *wexeth*, pa. sg. *wex*, pa. pl. *wexen, woxen*, ppl. *waxen, woxen*. The readings of other beta mss. confirm that *wexen* is here past tense, as is *3eden*. R has the present; the most authoritative C mss. have the past.

Dixit & facta sunt &c ·
Ergo þorw his breth mowen · men & bestes lyuen
70 As holywrit witnesseth · whan men segge her graces
Aperis tu manum tuam · & imples omne animal benediccione

¶ It is founden þat fourty wynter · folke lyued with-outen tulying
And oute of þe flynte spronge þe flode · þat folke & bestes dronke
And in Elyes tyme · heuene was yclosed
75 Þat no reyne ne rone · þus rede men in bokes
Þat many wynt[er] men lyueden · and no mete ne tulyeden

[¶] Seuene slepe as seith þe boke · seuene hundreth wynter

And lyueden with-oute lyflode · and atte laste þei woken
And if men lyued as mesure wolde · shulde neuere-more be defaute
80 Amonges cristene creatures · if crystes wordes ben trewe
Ac vnkyndnesse carestia maketh · amonges crystene peple
And ouer-plente maketh pruyde · amonges pore & riche
Ac mesure is so moche worth · it may nouȝte be to dere
For þe meschief and þe meschaunce · amonges men of sodome
85 Wex þorw plente of payn · & of pure sleuthe
Ociositas & habundancia panis peccatum turpissimum nutriuit
For þei mesured nouȝt hem-self · of þat þei ete and dronke
Diden dedly synne [·] þat þe deuel lyked
So vengeaunce fel vpon hem · for her vyle synnes
90 Þei sonken in-to helle · þo citees vchone

¶ For-þi mesure we vs wel · and make owre faithe owre scheltroun
And þorw faith cometh contricioun · conscience wote wel
Whiche dryueth awey dedly synne · and doth it to be venial
And þough a man myȝte nouȝte speke · contricioun myȝte hym saue
95 And brynge his soule to blisse · by so þat feith bere witnesse
Þat whiles he lyued he bileued · in þe lore of holycherche
Ergo contricioun feith and conscience · is kyndelich dowel

---

70 **graces**: Beta's plural is supported by **Cx**.

75 **ne**: Omitted by MHmF and the P family of C.

75 **rede men**: This word-order is supported by **Cx** against the reversal in MF.

76 **wynter**: There is the usual variation between the marked and unmarked forms of the plural. Here **Cx** supports CrR.

77 **¶**: WHmR have a paraph here which in L has slipped to the next line.

79 **more**: Although in alliterative position, this is omitted by all C mss. as well as by beta4 and F presumably by coincidence in a revised b-verse.

86 R ends the quotation at *panis*, and F omits altogether. Lines 81–110 have no parallel in C.

90 **þo**: So LM and F, but R joins the others with *þe*. Either could be a substitution for the other.

95 **by**: LCr + alpha; MW substitute *for* and others drop. For the idiom *by so*, "provided that", cf. **Bx.11.76**.

And surgienes for dedly synnes · whan shrifte of mouth failleth

¶ Ac shrifte of mouth more worthy is · if man be i[n]liche contrit
100 For shrifte of mouth sleeth synne · be it neuere so dedly
Per confessionem to a prest · peccata occiduntur
Þere contricioun doth but dryueth it doun · in-to a venial synne
As dauid seith in þe sauter · et quorum tecta sunt peccata
Ac satisfaccioun seketh oute þe rote · and bothe sleeth and voideth
105 And as it neuere had ybe · to nou3t bryngeth dedly synne
Þat it neuere eft is seen ne sore · but semeth a wounde yheled

¶ [3e] where woneth charite quod haukyn · I wiste neuere in my lyue
Man þat with hym spake · as wyde as I haue passed

¶ Þere parfit treuthe and pouere herte is · and pacience of tonge
110 Þere is charitee þe chief chaumbrere [·] for god hym-selue

¶ Whether pacien[c]e pouerte quod haukyn · be more plesaunte to owre
      dri3te
Þan ricchesse ri3tfulliche ywonne · and resonablelich yspended

¶ 3e quis est ille quod pacience · quik laudabimus eum
Þough men rede of richchesse · ri3t to þe worldes ende
115 I wist neuere renke þat riche was · þat whan he rekne sholde
Whan it drow to his deth-day · þat he ne dred hym sore
And þat atte rekenyng in arrerage fel · rather þan oute of dette

¶ There þe pore dar plede · and preue by pure resoun

---

98 **synnes**: Apparently beta, though CrHm agree with alpha on the sg. We follow copy-text.
99 **inliche**: R reproduces alpha, as shown by F's error *with* (for *within*). MO also have *ynlich*, presumably a scribal restoration since other beta mss. have *iliche*.
107 **3e**: Alpha only, but an opening discourse-marker that is characteristically Langlandian; cf. l. 113 below, **Bx**.11.145 etc.
109 **¶**: The paraph at the start of the speech is in beta and F. Cf. l. 107 above, and l. 111 below.
110 **chaumbrere**: The form *chambre* in MHmCG and alpha could represent **Bx**, corrected by other scribes. See note to *laborere* in l. 338.
111 **pacience pouerte**: This, rather than *paciente pouerte* in LCrWO, is likely to be the beta reading, as in CG and MHm before correction. Scribes were understandably puzzled, not realising that Pacience is a term of address (as in l. 292). Evidence that W's exemplar may have read *pacience* is that W nowhere else spells *paciente* with final /e/. On this analysis, alpha, equally puzzled, added *and*, to read *pacience and pouerte*. Yet alpha's reading has support from **Cx**, *pouerte and pacience* (RK.15.277).
111 **dri3te**: The difficult word is misread by C and replaced by *lorde* by G and alpha. **Cx** has instead "plese more god almyhty".
112 **yspended**: Beta2 alters to *dispended*.
116 **it**: L's agreement with R against the easily adopted *he* (as in the b-verse) in the other beta mss. would be secure for **Bx** except that **Cx** reads *he drow to þe deth*. F omits the pronoun. See Introduction, p. 30.
117 **þat**: The beta reading, but easily lost as in MGR.

KD.14.89–109

To haue allowaunce of his lorde · by þe lawe he it cleymeth
120 Ioye þat neuere ioye hadde · of riȝtful iugge he axeth
And seith lo briddes and bestes · þat no blisse ne knoweth
And wilde wormes in wodes · þorw wyntres þow hem greuest
And makest hem welnyegh meke · and mylde for defaute
And after þow sendest hem somer · þat is her souereigne Ioye
125 And blisse to alle þat ben · bothe wilde and tame
Þanne may beggeres as bestes · after bote waiten
Þat al her lyf han lyued · in langour and in defaute
But god sent hem some-tyme · some manere ioye
Other here or elles-where · kynde wolde it neuere
130 For to wrotherhele was he wrouȝte · þat neuere was ioye shaped

¶ Angeles þat in helle now ben · hadden ioye some-tyme
And diues in deyntees lyued · and in douce vye
Riȝte so resoun sheweth · þat þo men þat were riche
And her makes also · lyued her lyf in murthe

135 ¶ Ac god is of a wonder wille · by þat kynde witte sheweth
To ȝiue many men his mercymonye · ar he it haue deserued
Riȝt so fareth god by some riche · reuthe me it þinketh
For þei han her hyre here · an heuene as it were
And is gret lykyng to lyue · with-oute laboure of body
140 And whan he deyeth ben disalowed · as dauid seith in þe sauter
Dormierunt & nichil inuenerunt
And in an other stede also · velud sompnum surgencium domine in
     ciuitate tua & ad nichilum rediges
Allas þat ricchesse shal reue · and robbe mannes soule
Fram þe loue of owre lorde · at his laste ende

145 ¶ Hewen þat han her hyre afore · aren euermore nedy
And selden deieth out of dette · þat dyneth ar he deserue it

---

126 **as**: So L, corrected M, CrW. Certainly a more meaningful reading than *and* in beta4 and alpha, and supported by the X family of C, though some of the P family also have *and*.

130 **was ioye**: The word-order is supported by alliteration and **Cx**, against the reversal in Hm and alpha.

133 **þo**: Beta2 has, less appropriately, *þe*. Lines 133–40 are not in C.

133 **þat were riche**: The phrase is lost in alpha. F repairs.

138 **an**: "and". The fact that the form is also in M may indicate that it is beta's.

139 **is**: "it is". Dropped by beta2 and F, and erased in M.

142 **& ad**: Scribes have corrected this familiar quotation (Psalm 72.20). F reads *sompnium*, "dream", in place of *sompnum*, "sleep", and adds *ymaginem*, both as in the Vulgate. Alpha's *ad* for beta's *& ad* is probably a similar correction. **Cx** ends the quotation at *surgencium*.

145 **afore**: Alpha has *to-fore* and **Cx** *byfore*. See note to **Bx**.5.12.

146 **deieth**: Beta adds the pronoun *he*, but R (F rewrites) is supported by **Cx** in postponing the subject until the b-verse.

146 **he**: Beta supported by the X group of C, while alpha's plural has support from the P group. The plural is probably prompted by the previous line.

And til he haue done his deuor · and his dayes iourne
For whan a werkman hath wrou3te · þanne may men se þe sothe
What he were worthi for his werke · and what he hath deserued
150   And nou3t to fonge bifore · for drede of disalowynge

¶ So I segge by 3ow riche · it semeth nou3t þat 3e shulle
Haue [two] heuene[s] in 3owre here-beyng · and heuene her-after
Ri3t as a seruaunt taketh his salarye bifore · & sitth wolde clayme more
As he þat none hadde · and hath huyre atte laste
155   It may nou3t be 3e riche men · or matheu on god lyeth
De delicijs ad delicias · deficile est transire

¶ Ac if [3]e riche haue reuthe · and rewarde wel þe pore
And lyuen as lawe techeth · done leute to alle
Criste of his curteysie · shal conforte 3ow atte laste
160   And rewarde alle dowble ricchesse · þat reuful hertes habbeth
And as an hyne þat hadde · his hyre ar he bygonne
And whan he hath done his deuor wel · men doth hym other bounte
3yueth hym a cote aboue his couenaunte · ri3te so cryst 3iueth heuene
Bothe to riche and to nou3te riche · þat rewfullich lybbeth
165   And alle þat done her deuor wel · han dowble hyre for her trauaille
Here for3yuenesse of her synnes · and heuene blisse after

---

151 **nou3t**: Lost by alpha making nonsense; F rewrites the b-verse to improve the sense.

152 **two heuenes**: Alpha is supported by **Cx** against *heuene*. Probably beta misunderstood the sense of a line which causes scribes problems in other respects also. It involves an unusual disjuncture after the first stress: "(You shall not) have two heavens: (one) in your present existence and (another) in heaven afterwards". In **Cx** the line is simplified by dropping the b-verse: "(You shall not) have two heavens in return for your present existence" (RK.16.9).

152 **in**: Though R's *for* is shared with **Cx**, it makes no sense in the context of the line as in **Bx**.

152 **here-beyng**: Only recorded here and in C by *MED*, *her* adv. 7(a). Beta2 and G corrupt to *here beryng* (? *OED harbouring*), prompting W to guess at *here dwellyng*.

152 **her-after**: This is perhaps **Bx**, though it could have been prompted by *here* in the a-verse. WGR have *þere-after*.

153 R (reproducing alpha) divides the line at the end of the unusually heavy a-verse, but is left with an impossibly short line. F therefore expands freely. Hm divides at the same point as alpha, and then fills out the following line independently. Alpha's *huire* for beta's *more* anticipates **Bx** *huyre* in l. 154. The passage up to l. 169 is dropped in C.

154 **huyre**: Alpha's *heuene* is a consequence of its muddle in the previous line.

156 **transire**: Alford (1992), 89, quotes Jerome in support of this reading rather than *ascendere* in alpha, who still has his eye on *heuene*.

157 **¶**: The paraph, following the Latin line, is in beta and F.

157 **3e**: LMCrGF *þe* is an easy misreading. It may, however, represent **Bx**, with WHmCOR making an obvious correction.

158 **alle**: All beta mss. except L have *hem alle* (referring to the poor) but *alle* is probably the alpha reading, as in R, with F expanding a short b-verse to *his brothir*. On M's agreement with beta1, see Introduction, p. 11.

164 **rewfullich**: Cf. l. 160. Alpha adopts the easier reading *ri3tfullich*.

¶ Ac it nys but selde yseyn · as by holy seyntes bokes
Þat god rewarded double reste · to any riche wye
For moche murthe is amonges riche · as in mete and clothyng
170 And moche murthe in Maye is · amonges wilde bestes
And so forth whil somer lasteth · her solace dureth

[¶] Ac beggeres aboute Midsomer · bredlees þei soupe
And ȝit is wynter for hem worse · for wete-shodde þei gange
Afyrst sore and afyngred · and foule yrebuked
175 And arated of riche men · þat reuthe is to here
Now lorde sende hem somer · and some manere ioye
Heuene after her hennes-goynge · þat here han suche defaute
For alle myȝtest þow haue made · none mener þan other
And yliche witty & wyse · if þe wel hadde lyked
180 And haue reuthe on þise riche men · þat rewarde nouȝte þi prisoneres
Of þe good þat þow hem gyuest · ingrati ben manye
Ac god of þi goodnesse · gyue hem grace to amende
For may no derth ben hem dere · drouth ne weet
Ne noyther hete ne haille · haue þei here hele
185 Of þat þei wilne and wolde · wanteth hem nouȝt here

¶ Ac pore peple þi prisoneres · lorde in þe put of myschief
Conforte þo creatures · þat moche care suffren
Þorw derth þorw drouth · alle her dayes here
Wo in wynter tymes · for wantyng of clothes
190 And in somer tyme selde · soupen to þe fulle
Conforte þi careful [·] cryst in þi ryche
For how þow confortest alle creatures · clerkes bereth witnesse
Conuertimini ad me & salui eritis

167–71 These five lines are lost in alpha, jumping from *Ac* to *Ac* and paraph to paraph.
167 **bokes**: M shares the error *liues* with O.
172 **¶**: An appropriate paraph, recorded by WHm and alpha.
172 **Ac**: Alpha must have had this reading, though R omits it. F has (as usual) *But*.
179 **þe wel**: In L the scribe has first written *þi* followed by five letters; the /i/ has been altered to /e/ followed by *wel* and a punctus. There can be little question that L's original reading was *þi wille* as in MCGOF. Rather doubtfully we follow L's corrected reading, supported by beta2 (CrWHm) and R, on the grounds that *þe wel* was more likely to have been mistaken for *þi wille* than vice versa. **Cx** revises the b-verse and offers no guide.
180 Alpha's paraph is not appropriate.
180 **prisoneres**: For R's form *prisones*, see note to **Bx**.3.138 and l. 186 below. Here and elsewhere we follow copy-text. Lines 180–209 are not in C.
186 **lorde**: R has *lore*, either as a spelling of *lorde* as at **Bx**.5.407, 18.61, or as the ppl. "lost". Perhaps the form represents alpha, since F supposes it to be a verb, reading *lyȝn*, "lie". Note also the addition of final /d/ in O's *lord*.
189 **wynter tymes**: Alpha has *wyntres tyme*. In the same a-verse in C at RK.9.78, the X family has beta's reading, the P family has *wynter tyme*. Cf. *somer tyme* in the next line.
191 **ryche**: Beta2 corrupts to *rychesse*, and M is altered to that reading.

¶ Þus in genere of his genitrice · Ihesu cryst seyde
195 To robberes and to reueres · to riche and to pore
[To hores to harlotes . to alle maner poeple]
Þow tauȝtest hem in þe Trinitee · to take baptesme
And be clene þorw þat crystennynge · of alle kynnes [synnes]
And vs fel þorw folye · to falle in synne after
200 Confessioun and kne[w]lechyng [·] & crauyng þi mercy
Shulde amende vs as many sithes · as man wolde desire
Ac if þe p[ouke] wolde plede here-aȝeine · and punyssh vs in conscience
He shulde take þe acquitance as quik · and to þe qued schewe it
Pateat &c per passionem domini
205 And putten of so þe pouke · and preuen vs vnder borwe
Ac þe perchemyn of þis patent · of pouerte be moste
And of pure pacience · and parfit bileue
Of pompe and of pruyde · þe parchemyn decorreth
And principaliche of alle peple · but þei be pore of herte
210 Ellis is al an ydel · al þat euere we writen
Pater nostres and penaunce · and pilgrimage to Rome
But owre spences and spendyng sprynge · of a trewe welle

---

194 **in genere of his genitrice**: "by the very nature of his nobility". Alpha must have had *alle his*, as R, but beta copies apart from L have neither word.

196 The line is in alpha only, beta missing the second line beginning *To*. For *to* (2) F has *& to*, possibly correctly, since R uniquely drops *&* in the parallel position in the line above. F's b-verse is, however, rather meaninglessly inclusive.

198 **synnes**: Dropped by L after *kynnes*. W alone has the sg.

199 **And**: "if". Alpha underlines the sense with *And if*, adopted also by CrW. In M a word is first inserted and then erased.

200 **Confessioun and knewlechyng**: Reversed in alpha.

202 **Ac**: Beta2, C and alpha have *And*.

202 **pouke**: Beta's *pope* is an odd error, especially in view of l. 205. KD, p. 147 suggest "a preferred villain substituted".

202 **here-aȝeine**: Alpha has *þere-aȝeine*, adopted also by G.

203 **He**: Either Christ, or more probably "the one affected". R's *Ho* is perhaps an alpha error, altered by F to *We* for the sense.

208 The paraph in W and alpha is not adopted.

211 **Pater nostres**: CrCGOR have the singular. Cx has *preyeres* (RK.16.38).

211 **penaunce**: Here and elsewhere, romance loans ending in a sibilant may be unchanged in the plural, hence frequent variations between *penaunce* and *penaunces*, e.g. Bx.P.25, 7.132, 15.153, 16.39. Here Hm and alpha have the marked plural, as does the X family of C. It is worth observing that of 44 instances of *penaunce* from the C text in Wittig's *Concordance*, 16 are emendations of *penaunces* in the X family.

211 **pilgrimage**: CrWG have the plural, as do most C mss. See Bx.15.189 and 19.387 for a similar situation.

212 **But**: "unless". Beta is supported by Cx. R has *And*; F begins *With* in a rewritten a-verse.

212 **spendyng**: R has *oure spendynge*, as the X family of C.

212 The punctuation follows *sprynge* (aaa/xx) in LR and probably in original M, though there another punctus appears before *springe*, as in other mss. (aa/ax).

212 **welle**: The obviously superior reading is supported by Cx over *wille* in CrWCO (G corrects).

Elles is al owre laboure loste · lo how men writeth
In fenestres atte freres · if fals be þe foundement
215   For-þi crystene sholde ben in comune riche · none coueitouse for
        hym-selue

        ¶ For seuene synnes þat þere ben · assaillen vs euere
        Þe fende folweth hem alle · and fondeth hem to helpe
        Ac wiþ ricchesse þ[o] ribaude[s] · rathest men bigyleth
        For þere þat richesse regneth · reuerence[s] folweth
220   And þat is plesaunte to pryde · in pore and in riche
        And þe riche is reuerenced · by resoun of his richchesse
        Þere þe pore is put bihynde [·] and par-auenture can more
        Of witte and of wysdom · þat fer [w]ey is better
        Þan ricchesse or reaute · and rather yherde in heuene
225   For þe riche hath moche to rekene · and riȝte softe walketh
        Þe heigh waye to heuene-ward · oft ricchesse letteth
        Ita possibile diuiti &c

        ¶ Þere þe pore preseth bifor þe riche · with a pakke at his rugge
        Opera enim illorum sequntur illos
230   Batauntliche as beggeres done · and baldeliche he craueth
        For his pouerte and his pacience · a perpetuel blisse
        Beati pauperes · quoniam ipsorum est regnum celorum

        ¶ And pryde in ricchesse regneth · rather þan in pouerte

---

216 **þat**: Dropped in CO, and postponed to the b-verse in WGF. **Cx** has *þat* in both positions.
218 **þo ribaudes**: Alpha, supported by **Cx**, referring to the sins. Beta has *þat Ribaude* referring to the devil.
219 **reuerences**: i.e. expressions of deference. Alpha has the plural, as do the best **C** mss. Beta's form might be construed as plural without ending, as often with romance loans ending in a sibilant. See note to l. 211.
221 **And**: Beta supported by the X family of C against alpha's *Ac/But*. The P family has no conjunction.
223 **fer wey**: R only, since the line is lost in F, but supported by **Cx** against beta's *fer awey*. Neither phrase occurs elsewhere in the poem.
225 **riȝte softe**: Corruption in beta2 leads CrW to invent and Hm to correct. Perhaps beta2 read *ofte*, and lost the word in the next line.
226 **heigh**: Alpha and G repeat *riȝt* from the previous line. Beta's a-verse is as in **Cx**.
226 **ricchesse**: Beta against alpha's *riche*. The b-verse is rewritten in C.
227 **possibile**: "It is as (*ita*) possible for a rich man etc." Quoted in this form also in RK.11.201a. MW alter to *impossibile*, in view of Matt. 19.23 which has "quia dives difficile ...".
228 **preseth**: Beta is supported by **Cx**. Alpha has *precheth* (R) or *procheth* (in both cases <p> with abbreviation).
228 **þe riche**: Certainly **Bx**, though **Cx** omits, as does F by contamination or coincidence.
231 **his (2)**: Omitted by MCGO, as in the P family of C. (F loses ll. 229–31).
233 **And**: Alpha has *Ac* (F *But*); **C** mss. have *And* or *Also*. Cf. l. 221.

[Or] in þe Maister [or] in þe man · some mansioun he hath
235 Ac in pouerte þere pacyence is · pryde hath no myȝte
Ne none of þe seuene synnes · sitten ne mowe þere longe
Ne haue powere in pouerte · if pacyence it folwe
For þe pore is ay prest · to plese þe riche
And buxome at his byddyng · for his broke loues
240 And buxomenesse and boste · aren euer-more at werre
And ayther hateth other · in alle manere werkes
If wratthe wrastel with þe pore · he hath þe worse ende
For if þey bothe pleyne · þe pore is but fieble
And if he chyde or chatre · hym chieueth þe worse
245 [For lowelich he loketh · and loueliche is his speche
Þat mete or money · of other men mote asken
And if glotonye greue pouerte · he gadereth þe lasse
For his rentes wol nauȝte reche · no riche metes to bugge
And þouȝ his glotonye be to gode ale · he goth to cold beddynge
250 And his heued vnhiled · vnesily ywrye
For whan he streyneth hym to strecche · þe strawe is his shetes
So for his glotonye and his grete sleuthe · he hath a greuous penaunce
Þat is welawo whan he waketh · and wepeth for colde
And sum-tyme for his synnes · so he is neuere merye
255 Withoute mornynge amonge · and mischief to bote]

¶ And [þouȝ] coueitise wolde cacche þe pore · þei may nouȝt come togideres
And by þe nekke namely · her none may hente other
For men knoweth wel þat coueitise · is of a kene wille
And hath hondes and armes · of a longe lengthe
260 And pouerte nis but a petit þinge · apperetth nouȝt to his naule
And louely layke was it neuere · bitwene þe longe and þe shorte
And þough auarice wolde angre þe pore · he hath but litel myȝte
For pouerte hath but pokes · to putten in his godis

---

234 **Or … or:** Beta has *Arst … þan,* but alpha is supported by **Cx.** Beta supposes that the master would have more pride than his man, but Skeat (1886), ii, 211 explains that by *man* Langland refers to "the arrogant manners of the retainers in a great household".

234 **he:** Omitted by R, but supported by **Cx.**

242 A paraph might be expected here, as for the other sins, but only WCF have one.

245–55 These eleven lines are lost in beta, probably by eyeskip from *And if* 244 to ¶ *And if* (in beta only) 256. **Cx** is closely parallel except for the last two lines, and generally supports R over F.

247 The paraph in F marks the introduction of gluttony.

248 **wol:** R has *ne wol.* **Cx** has neither *ne* in the a-verse nor *no* in the b-verse.

251 **shetes: Cx** supports R's plural.

255 **mischief:** The b-verse in **Cx,** "so meschief hym folleweth" (RK.16.78) offers no support to F's *myche myschef.*

256 **þouȝ:** Alpha is supported by **Cx** against *if* in beta.

256 **wolde:** Only L + alpha, but supported by **Cx** "wolde with þe pore wrastle".

Þere auarice hath almaries · and yren-bounde coffres
265 And whether be liȝter to breke · lasse boste it maketh
A beggeres bagge · þan an yren-bounde coffre

¶ Lecherye loueth hym nouȝt · for he ȝeueth but lytel syluer
Ne doth hym nouȝte dyne delycatly · ne drynke wyn oft
A strawe for þe stuwes · it stode nouȝt I trowe
270 Had þei none but of pore men · her houses were vntyled

¶ And þough sleuthe suwe pouerte · and serue nouȝt god to paye
Mischief is his maister · and maketh hym to thynke
Þat god is his grettest helpe · and no gome elles
And [he is] seruaunt as he seith · and of his sute bothe
275 And where he be or be nouȝte · he bereth þe signe of pouerte
And in þat secte owre saueoure · saued al mankynde
For-thi al pore þat paciente is · may claymen and asken
After her endynge here · heuene-riche blisse

¶ Moche hardier may he axen · þat here myȝte haue his wille
280 In londe and in lordship · and likynge of bodye
And for goddis loue leueth al · an lyueth as a beggere
And as a mayde for [a] mannes loue · her moder forsaketh
Hir fader and alle her frendes · and folweth hir make
Moche is suche a mayde to louie · of hym þat such one taketh
285 More þan a mayden is · þat is maried þorw brokage
As bi assent of sondry partyes · and syluer to bote
More for coueitise of good · þan kynde loue of bothe

---

265 **lasse boste it**: M alters its reading to agree with CrW; **Cx** supports the other mss.
269–70 The lines are in beta only, but supported by **Cx**. Perhaps alpha censored them, though KD, p. 68, suggest eyeskip from *A...stuwes* 269 to *And...suwe* 271.
270 **none**: **Cx** has alliterating *noen haunt*. We suppose that **Bx** or beta lost *haunt*, with L preserving the reading *none*, beta1 altering to *no þing* for sense, and G further altering to *noght*. If so, then M is perhaps dependent on beta1.
270 **were**: All beta mss. except L read *stoode*, perhaps repeated from the previous line. **Cx** loses the b-verse.
273 **his**: Omitted by R and misplaced by F, but supported by **Cx**.
274 **he is**: The reading of R alone, but supported by **Cx** (RK.16.97). The beta reading, as in L, original M, and HmGOC, appears to have been *his*. CrWF make an obvious correction to *he his*, and this is followed by the M corrector. The sense is that Poverty is a servant in God's retinue.
275 **where**: "whether", the spelling of LR.
277 **pore**: CrCGO have *pouertie*, influenced by l. 275. **Cx** supports *pore*.
277 **may claymen and asken**: The b-verse does not alliterate. **Cx** has instead *of puyr rihte may claymen*.
280 **In londe**: F's reading *As a lorde* shows that R's *In lorde* is an alpha error.
282 **a** (2): R is supported by **Cx** against omission in all other **B** mss.
284 **suche a mayde**: LMHmCO are supported by **Cx** (RK.16.107). Alpha reads *þat mayde*, G drops *suche*, and CrW reflect a corrupt exemplar anticipating *more* in the following line.
284 **hym**: **Cx** has *a man* to carry the alliteration.

¶ So it fareth bi eche a persone · þat possessioun forsaketh
And put hym to be pacient · and pouerte weddeth
290   Þe which is sybbe to god hym-self · and so [neighe is pouerte]

¶ Haue god my trouthe quod Haukyn · ʒe preyse faste pouerte
What is pouerte pacience quod he · proprely to mene

¶ Paupertas quod pacience · est odibile bonum
Remocio curarum · possessio sine calumpnia · donum dei · sanitatis mater
295   Absque solicitudine semita · sapiencie temperatrix · negocium sine dampno
Incerta fortuna · absque solicitudine felicitas ·

¶ I can nouʒt construe al þis quod haukyn · ʒe moste kenne þis on englisch
In englisch quod pacyence it is wel harde · wel to expounen
Ac somdel I shal seyne it · by so þow vnderstonde
300   Pouerte is þe first poynte · þat pryde moste hateth
Thanne is it good by good skil · al þat agasteth pryde
Riʒte as contricioun is confortable þinge · conscience wote wel
And a sorwe of hym-self · and a solace to þe sowle
So pouerte propreliche [·] penaunce and ioye
305   Is to þe body [·] pure spiritual helthe
Ergo paupertas est odibile bonum
And contricioun confort [·] & cura animarum

---

290 **Þe which:** Supported by **Cx** against R *Which* and Cr *Such.*

290 **so neighe is pouerte:** This is the reading of R and presumably of alpha, which F attempts to clarify by altering *pouerte* to *þat persone.* Beta is quite different, *so to his seyntes,* which makes superficial but inappropriate sense and can hardly have given rise to alpha. The readings of this b-verse and that of the next line suggest that **Bx** was damaged or unclear. **Cx** has a rather feeble repair: "The whiche is syb to Crist sulue and semblable bothe" (RK.16.113), and drops the next line.

291 **ʒe preyse faste pouerte:** Beta's b-verse at least makes sense but it lacks alliteration. R, *þat huyre faste preyse pouerte,* is nonsense, and F skilfully rewrites. It may be that **Bx** read *ʒe herie faste pouerte,* with *preyse* as a gloss to avoid confusion with "hear", a gloss then incorporated by the scribes. It may be also that **Bx** was only partly legible; see previous note.

292 **pacience:** R only, but supported by **Cx**, where Actyf is addressing Patience. F drops the word and beta has *with pacience.* Cf. l. 111 for similar confusion.

293 **¶:** The paraph in LWHm introduces four Latin lines.

294 **sanitatis:** CrWC and original M have erroneous *sanitas,* as again at l. 326; R anticipates *semita.*

295 **solicitudine:** O and Alpha have the error *solitudine,* as again at l. 331. Many C manuscripts have the same error.

297 **al:** Dropped by Hm and beta4, but supported by **Cx**.

297 **kenne:** Scribes add *me* (WR) or alter to *telle* (Hm) or *say* (beta4).

298 MWHmCF mark the start of Patience's speech with a paraph or line-space.

298 **wel** (2): Lost by CrHmG who move the punctuation to follow *pacyence.* F also loses the word and expands the b-verse.

307 Alpha has a paraph which beta more logically postpones to l. 308.

307 CGO add *þe second,* no doubt incorporated from a marginal note. But cf. l. 314.

¶ Selde sitte pouerte · þe sothe to declare
Or as iustyce to iugge men · enioigned is no pore
310 Ne to be a Maire [ouer] men · ne mynystre vnder kynges
Selden is any pore yput · to punysshen any peple
Remocio curarum
Ergo pouerte and pore men · parfornen þe comaundement
Nolite iudicare quemquam þe þridde

315 ¶ Selde is pore [riȝt] riche · but of [his] riȝtful heritage
Wynneth he nauȝt with weghtes fals · ne with vnseled mesures
Ne borweth of his neghbores · but þat he may wel paye
Possessio sine calumpnia ·

¶ Þe fierthe [it] is a fortune · þat florissheth þe soule
320 Wyth sobrete fram al synne · and also ȝit more
It affaiteth þe flesshe · fram folyes ful manye
A collateral conforte · crystes owne ȝifte
Donum dei

¶ Þe fyfte [it] is moder of helthe [·] a frende in alle fondynges
325 And for þe la[w]d[e] euere a leche · a lemman of al clennesse
Sanitatis mater

---

309 **Or**: CrW read *For*, and M is altered to that reading. Hm takes *Or as* to be Latin, so writes *horas justicie* in display script. Many C scribes are puzzled by the syntax at this point.

309 **enioigned is no pore**: The b-verse has been lost in alpha, with F patching.

310 **a**: Dropped by beta2 and G, as by some C scribes.

310 **ouer**: Probably alpha as in R, misread as *on* in F. It has support from **Cx** against beta's *aboue*.

311 **any** (1): Beta supported by **Cx**. R's nonsensical *enemye* presumably reproduces alpha, revised to *þe* by F.

314 **þe þridde**: Supported by all **B** mss., though not in **Cx** and quite possibly incorporated from a marginal note. Cf. l. 307.

315 **pore riȝt**: Alpha is supported by **Cx** and alliteration over beta's *any pore*, picked up from l. 311.

315 **his**: Omitted by all except R (rephrased in F), but supported by **Cx**.

316 **weghtes**: Alpha must have had *wittes* as in R but revised in F. C mss. show some confusion, the majority reading *wihtes*, "weights", but with variants including *wittes, whittus* and *whites* (RK.16.130).

319 **it**: Omitted by all except R, but it is in the most reliable mss. of C, and easily lost. Cf. ll. 324, 327, 334, 338, 342, where R again uniquely reads *it*.

324 **it**: Omitted by all except R; cf. note to l. 319. C mss. have instead *ȝut is hit* or *ȝut hit is*.

325 **lawde**: The range of variants suggests that this spelling (as in CR) or possibly *laude* was the reading of **Bx**. Schmidt (1995), 394, plausibly proposes that it was an error for *lowe*, "humble people". Most beta scribes suppose the intended reading to be *lande*, but GO take it as the northern spelling of *lewde*. F's *lawe* presumably means "law" rather than "low", which is *lowe, lowh, lowhȝ*. **Cx** rewrites (RK.16.138)

325 **a leche**: Alpha's *a-liche / y-lyche*, though adopted by KD, is an obvious error. In its rewritten line **Cx** has *of foule eueles leche*.

326 **Sanitatis**: For the error *Sanitas* in CrWC and uncorrected M and G, cf. l. 294.

¶ Þe sexte [it] is a path of pees · ȝe þorw þe pas of altoun
Pouerte myȝte passe · with-oute peril of robbyng
For þere þat pouerte passeth · pees folweth after
330 And euere þe lasse þat he bereth · þe hardyer he is of herte
For-þi seith seneca · paupertas est absque solicitudine semita
And an hardy man of herte · amonge an hepe of þeues
Cantabit paupertas coram latrone viator

¶ Þe seueneth [it] is welle of wisdome · and fewe wordes sheweth
335 For lordes alloweth hym litel · or lysteneth to his reson
He tempreth þe tonge to treuthe-ward · [þat] no tresore coueiteth
Sapiencie temperatrix

¶ The eigteth [it] is a lele laborere · and loth to take more
Þan he may wel deserue · in somer or in wynter
340 And if [he] chaffareth he chargeth no losse · mowe he charite wynne
Negocium sine dampno

¶ The nyneth [it] is swete to þe soule · no sugre is swettere
For pacyence is payn · for pouerte hym-selue
And sobrete swete drynke · and good leche in sykenesse
345 Þus lered me a le[r]ed man · for owre lordes loue
Seynt austyn a blissed lyf · with-outen bysynesse
For body and for soule · absque solicitudine felicitas
Now god þat al good gyueth · graunt his soule reste
Þat þus fyrst wrote to wyssen men · what pouerte was to mene

---

327 **it**: Omitted by all except R; cf. note to l. 319. Most C mss. have it.

330 **he** (2): R drops and **Cx** rewrites. The line is lost in F.

331 **solicitudine**: See note to l. 295.

333 **Cantabit**: Cr and alpha have the imperfect *cantabat* in error. (KD and Schmidt wrongly record *Cantabit* as F's reading).

334 **it**: Omitted by all except R; cf. note to l. 319. Most C mss. have it.

336 **þat**: Alpha is supported by **Cx** against beta's easier *and*.

337 The Latin tag (from l. 295) is recorded only in beta and is not in C.

338 **it**: Omitted by all except R; cf. note to l. 319. Most C mss. have it.

338 **laborere**: The form has strong support for **Bx** from LCr and alpha, though **Cx** has *labour*. *MED labour* 6 gives the sense "laborer", with examples almost entirely from **A** mss, and it is quite a frequent variant in all three versions. Cf. *flateres* for *flaterers* in **Bx.**13.450 and 477, and MHmCG + alpha *chambre* for *chaumbrere* in **Bx.**14.110.

340 **he** (1): Omitted in L, where the line is marked for correction.

342 **it**: Omitted by all except R; cf. note to l. 319. Most C mss. have it.

345 **lered** (2): Alpha supported by **Cx**. To avoid the repetition, beta adopts *lettred*, while a number of **C** mss. have, oddly, *lewid*.

345 **loue**: Supposing an omission, WCr and F add *of heuene* on the model of **Bx.**6.19, 13.151, etc. **Cx** ends *lordes loue seynt Austyn* (RK.16.153), taking up the first words of the following line.

346 **bysynesse**: CrW add *ladde* to complete the b-verse, and M is corrected to that reading. **Cx** redivides ll. 345–7, so that this line becomes "A blessed lyf withoute bisinesse bote onelyche for þe soule" (RK.16.155).

349 **þus**: Beta2 has *þis*, but **Cx** reads *þus*.

350 ¶ Allas quod haukyn þe actyf man þo · þat after my crystendome
I ne hadde ben ded and doluen · for doweles sake
So harde it is quod haukyn · to lyue and to do synne
Synne suweth vs euere quod he · and sori gan wexe
And wepte water with his eyghen · and weyled þe tyme
355 Þat euere he dede dede · þat dere god displesed
Swowed and sobbed · and syked ful ofte
Þat euere he hadde londe or lordship · lasse other more
Or maystrye ouer any man · mo þan of hym-self
I were nou3t worthy wote god quod haukyn · to were any clothes
360 Ne noyther sherte ne shone · saue for shame one
To keure my caroigne quod he · and cryde mercye faste
And wepte and weyled · and þere-with I awaked

---

350 **þe actyf man þo:** Lost in alpha. These lines to the end of the passus are not in **Cx**.
353 **suweth:** Alpha's error *scheweth* prompts F to rewrite.

Passus 15

Passus quindecimus finit dowel & incipit dobet

Ac after my wakyng · it was wonder longe
Ar I couth kyndely · knowe what was dowel
And so my witte wex and wanyed · til I a fole were
And somme lakked my lyf · allowed it fewe
5   And leten [me] for a lorel · and loth to reuerencen
Lordes or ladyes · or any lyf elles
As persones in pellure · with pendauntes of syluer
To seriauntz ne to suche · seyde nou3te ones
God loke 3ow lordes · ne louted faire
10   Þat folke helden me a fole · and in þat folye I raued
Tyl resoun hadde reuthe on me · and rokked me aslepe
Tyl I seigh as it sorcerye were · a sotyl þinge with-al
One with-outen tonge and teeth · tolde me whyder I shulde
And wher-of I cam and of what kynde · I coniured hym atte laste
15   If he were crystes creature · for crystes loue me to tellen

¶ I am crystes creature quod he · and crystene in many a place

---

1–14 The lines have no parallel in C.
1 **wakyng**: R's *walkynge* is an obvious error.
5 **me**: Dropped by beta, though supplied on grounds of sense by CrW and inserted by the M corrector.
8 **ne**: The beta reading against *and* in alpha.
8 **suche**: R adds *and*; F reads *swiche men* followed by an erasure.
8 **seyde**: The M corrector inserts *I* in line with CrWHm.
12 **sorcerye**: R has *of sorserie*; F has *a syght of sorsery3e*.
14 **and of what kynde**: Beta4 omits *of*, and F has simply *kendely*. R drops the whole phrase and rewrites ll. 13–14 as three lines.
15 **for crystes loue**: Beta2 presumably lost the phrase. CrW patch with *anoon*, Hm with *leue*. Here comparison with **Cx** recommences (RK.16.166).
16 **a**: Dropped by R only, though it appears to be the **Cx** reading.

In crystes courte I-knowe wel · and of his kynne a partye
Is noyther peter þe porter · ne poule with his fauchoune
Þa[t] wil defende me þe dore · dynge ich neure so late
20   At mydny3t at mydday · my voice [is so] yknowe
Þat eche a creature of his courte · welcometh me fayre

¶ What ar 3e called quod I in þat courte · amonges crystes peple
Þe whiles I quykke þe corps quod he · called am I anima
And whan I wilne and wolde · animus ich hatte
25   And for þat I can and knowe · called am I mens
And whan I make mone to god · memoria is my name
And whan I deme domes · and do as treuthe techeth
Þanne is racio my ri3t name · resoun an englissh
And whan I fele þat folke telleth · my firste name is sensus
30   And þat is wytte and wisdome · þe welle of alle craftes
And whan I chalange or chalange nou3te · chepe or refuse
Þanne am I conscience ycalde · goddis clerke and his notarie
And whan I loue lelly · owre lorde and alle other
Þanne is lele loue my name · and in latyn amor
35   And whan I fl[e]e fro þe flesshe · and forsake þe caroigne
Þanne am I spirit specheles · and spiritus þanne ich hatte
Austyn and ysodorus [·] ayther of hem bothe
Nempned me þus to name · now þow my3te chese
How þow coueitest to calle me · now þow knowest alle my names
40   Anima pro diuersis accionibus diuersa nomina sortitur · dum viuificat
     corpus anima est · dum vult animus est · dum scit mens est · dum
     recolit memoria est · dum iudicat racio est · dum sentit sensus est ·
     dum amat amor est · dum negat vel consentit consciencia est · dum
     spirat spiritus est

---

18 **his:** The beta reading with which F agrees, supported by the P family of C. R's *þe* has the support of the X family, and could be right.

20 **is so:** The reading of alpha, CrHm, and **Cx**. Other beta mss. reverse the word-order.

22 **quod I in þat courte:** The word-order is reversed in MHm and beta4. The line is not in **Cx**.

23 WHmR have a paraph.

23 **quykke:** CrW read *quykne*, but **Cx** has *quyke* (RK.16.183). Hm and beta4 have *quyk was yn*.

25 **mens:** R, presumably reproducing his exemplar as usual, adds *thou3t*, set out as a gloss between punctus. **Cx** misunderstood it as part of the line, so that most mss. read *mens thouhte* or *mannes þou3te*.

35 **flee:** L's *flye* may represent the beta reading, also in CO; M's *flee* is a correction. But **Cx** supports alpha and beta2.

36 **and:** L and alpha only, but supported by **Cx**.

39 **alle:** W adds *for* at the beginning of the b-verse and drops *alle*. G also drops *alle*, but it is in **Cx**.

40 L sets this as two lines, F as six and R as ten. Cf. **Bx**.15.124.

¶ Ʒe ben as a bisshop quod I · al bourdynge þat tyme
For bisshopes yblessed · þei bereth many names
Presul and pontifex · and metropolitanus
And other names an hepe [·] episcopus & pastor

45 ¶ Þat is soth seyde he · now I se þi wille
Þow woldest knowe and kunne · þe cause of alle her names
And of myne if þow myʒtest · me þinketh by þi speche

¶ Ʒe syre I seyde [·] by so no man were greued
Alle þe sciences vnder sonne · and alle þe sotyle craftes
50 I wolde I knewe and couth · kyndely in myne herte

¶ Þanne artow inparfit quod he · and one of prydes knyʒtes
For such a luste and lykynge · lucifer fel fram heuene
Ponam pedem meum in aquilone & similis ero altissimo

¶ It were aʒeynes kynde quod he · and alkynnes resoun
55 Þat any creature shulde kunne al · excepte cryste one
Aʒein such salomon speketh · and dispiseth her wittes
And seith sicut qui mel comedit multum non est ei bonum
Sic qui scrutator est maiestatis opprim[a]tur a gloria
To englisch men þis is to mene · þat mowen speke & here
60 Þe man þat moche hony e[et] · his mawe it engleymeth
And þe more þat a man · of good mater hereth
But he do þerafter · it doth hym double scathe
Beatus est seith seynt Bernard · qui scripturas legit
Et verba vertit in opera · fullich to his powere

---

42 þei: Dropped in MCGO, but supported by most C mss.

43 metropolitanus: Alpha has *metropolanus*, as in eight C mss., including X. It may, therefore, be an archetypal error.

48 With the short a-verse, the placing of the punctus causes scribes uncertainty. WR put it after *seyde*; F reads *y* for *by* and puts it after that. In HmO it follows *so*; in M it follows *man*. LC omit it.

49 sciences: COR have the plural without ending.

52 F alone adds a line after this.

55 kunne: Alpha and Cr have *kenne* in the sense "know" (*MED kennen* v.(1), 3), but Cx supports beta.

58 opprimatur: R is supported by Cx in the present subjunctive, "let him be overwhelmed". Beta has the present indicative, while F corrects to the future as in the Clementine Vulgate (Prov. 25.27). See Schmidt (1995), 395.

59 WHmCF begin the line with a paraph, with a line-space in M.

60 eet: Beta's *eteth* is indisputably present, but alpha's *eet*, which is supported by Cx, is probably past tense. Cf. Bx.5.386, 6.303, 13.66, etc.

60 it engleymeth: Most C mss. support beta against alpha's *is/mote be englaymed*.

64 verba vertit: This order, which is reversed in Hm and alpha, is supported by Cx (RK.16.223).

65 Coueytise to kunne [·] and to knowe science
    Pulte out of paradys · Adam and Eue
    Sciencie appetitus hominem inmortalitatis gloriam spoliauit
    And ri3te as hony is yuel to defye · and engleymeth þe mawe
    Ri3t so þat þorw resoun [·] wolde þe rote knowe
70 Of god and of his grete my3tes · his graces it letteth
    For in þe lykyng lith a pryde · and a lycames coueitise
    A3ein crystes conseille · and alle clerkes techyng
    That is non plus sapere quam oportet sapere

    [¶] Freres and fele other maistres · þat to þe lewed men prechen
75 3e moeuen materes inmesurables · to tellen of þe Trinite
    Þat ofte tymes þe lewed peple · of her bileue douten
    Bettere byleue were mony · doctoures such techyng
    And tellen men of þe ten comaundementz · and touchen þe seuene synnes
    And of þe braunches þat burgeouneth of hem · and bryngeth men to helle
80 And how þat folke in folyes · myspenden her fyue wittes
    As wel freres as other folke · folilich spenen
    In housyng in haterynge · in to hiegh clergye shewynge

---

65 **science:** WF understand this as plural, and write *sciences* as in **Cx**. Cf. l. 49 note.

66 **Pulte:** "thrust", the reading of LR and M before correction. As at **Bx**.1.128, 8.97, other scribes adopt easier *Putte*. But **Cx** has *Potte*.

67 **gloriam:** The form cited by Alford (1992), 92–3. Beta 2, corrected O, and some C scribes alter to *gloria*, taking it as the expected ablative.

70 **graces:** HmCGOF have the more obvious singular. The line is rewritten in C.

71 **a** (2): Lost by beta2 and F.

74 **¶:** A paraph is warranted by the syntax and supported by MWHmC and alpha.

74 **fele other:** It is possible that beta (apart from G) has added *fele* (not in alpha) to "improve" the alliteration, but obscuring alliteration on /m/. But **Cx** has the word in a revised line (RK.16.231).

74 **þe:** Omitted by WOF.

75 **inmesurables:** Post-positional French adjectives may have a plural inflection, altered by CrWF. (Mustanoja (1960), 277.) *MED* citations suggest that the negative prefix is more commonly *vn-*, as in WG and alpha. **Cx** rewrites the line.

76 Alpha drops the line, perhaps as a result of the repeated *bileue* in l. 77. **Cx** revises (RK.16.233).

77 **Bettere byleue were mony:** "It would be better for many doctors to drop such teaching". This is the reading of LCrHm, and probably that of M before correction, but it caused considerable confusion. The lack of alliteration suggests the line is corrupt. If it is authorial, Langland is presumably punning on the noun *bileue* (l. 76) and *MED bileven* v. (1), "abandon", which some scribes take as *MED bileven* v. (2), "believe". The M corrector rearranged the words as *Bettre were many doctours . bileu..*, but subsequently alters the last word to *leue*, giving the reading "Bettre were many doctours leue suche techinge", which makes good sense. W hits on a similar reading. R (= alpha?) alters *were* to *by* and drops *such* in the b-verse. F revises in his usual uncompromising manner. The line is not in **Cx**.

81 **spenen:** LR (and CrC) agree against *spenden* in other mss., which is no doubt prompted by *myspenden* in the line above. However, **Cx** has *spenden*. The two verbs (*MED spenden* and *spenen*) have the same origin and mean the same thing.

82 **in to:** Perhaps "in displaying too arrogant a learning". So alpha; beta has *and in to*. **Cx** has *in*.

More for pompe þan for pure charite · þe poeple wote þe sothe
Þat I lye nouȝt loo · for lordes ȝe plesen
85   And reuerencen þe riche · þe rather for her syluer
Confundantur omnes qui adorant scul[p]tilia · & alibi
Vt quid diligitis vanitatem & queritis mendacium
Go to þe glose of þe verse · ȝe grete clerkes
If I lye on ȝow to my lewed witte · ledeth me to brennynge
90   For as it semeth ȝe forsaketh · no mannes almesse   nota de fratribus
Of vsureres of hores · of auarous chapmen
And louten to þis lordes · þat mowen lene ȝow nobles
Aȝeine ȝowre reule and Religioun · I take recorde at Ihesus
Þat seide to his disciples · ne sitis [acceptores personarum]

95   ¶ Of þis matere I myȝte · make a longe bible
Ac of curatoures of crystene peple · as clerkes bereth witnesse
I shal tellen it for treuth sake · take hede who-so lyketh

¶ As holynesse and honest[e] [·] oute of holicherche spredeth
Þorw lele libbyng men · þat goddes lawe techen
100 Riȝt so out of holicherche · alle yueles spredeth
There inparfyt presthod is · prechoures and techeres
And se it by ensample [·] in somer tyme on trowes
Þere somme bowes ben leued · and somme bereth none
Þere is a myschief in þe more · of suche manere bowes
105 Riȝt so parsones and prestes · and prechoures of holy cherche
[Is þe] rote of þe riȝte faith · to reule þe peple
Ac þere þe rote is roten · reson wote þe sothe
Shal neure floure ne frute · ne faire leef be grene
For-þi wolde ȝe lettred leue · þe leccherye of clothynge

---

90 **nota de fratribus**: In L this is in the scribal hand and boxed in red. Since it is also in M, it is probably at least beta.

91 **of** (3): R has *and*; F has *& of*. The line is not in C.

94 **acceptores personarum**: Beta reverses the order, but alpha is supported by **Cx**.

95 **longe**: Alpha probably read *grete*, as R, with F increasing the alliteration by altering to *mychil*. There is no guidance from C.

99 **lawe**: Alpha has the plural. There is no parallel line in C.

101 **prechoures**: Beta is supported by **Cx** (RK.16.247). Alpha reads *and prechoures*, perhaps anticipating l. 105.

102 **And**: Beta2 has *I*, but this is not supported by **Cx**.

105 **cherche**: R's plural has no support from **Cx**.

106 **Is þe**: R is supported by **Cx**. Beta alters to *Þat aren* to correct the syntax; F rewrites. The form *is* can be used for the plural (as at **Bx**.16.241), but here presumably agrees with *rote* rather than the nouns in the previous line.

107 **Ac**: The common variation between *Ac/But/And*. The better C mss. support *Ac*.

109 Alpha and Hm have a paraph, and in L the line is at the top of the page where it is sometimes missed.

109 **ȝe**: Alpha has *þe*, as does the P group of C. Cf. l. 111 *ȝowre*, altered by F to *here*.

110   And be kynde as bifel for clerkes · and curteise of crystes goodes
Trewe of ȝowre tonge · and of ȝowre taille bothe
And hatien to here harlotrye · and [a]uȝt to vnderfonge
Tythes of vntrewe þinge · ytilied or chaffared

¶ Lothe were lewed men · but þei ȝowre lore folwed
115   And amenden hem þat mysdon · more for ȝowre ensamples
Þan forto prechen & preue it nouȝt · ypocrysie it semeth
For ypocrysie in latyn · is lykned to a dongehul
Þat were bysnewed with snowe · and snakes wyth-inne
Or to a wal þat were whitlymed · and were foule wyth-inne
120   Riȝt so many prestes · prechoures and prelates
Ȝe aren enblaunched with bele paroles · and with clothes
Ac ȝowre werkes and ȝowre wordes þere-vnder · aren ful [wol]uelich

¶ Iohannes crysostomus · of clerkes speketh and prestes
Sicut de templo omne bonum progreditur · sic de templo · omne malum
    procedit Si sacerdocium integrum fuerit · tota floret ecclesia · si autem
    corupt[a] fuerit · omnium fides marcida est · Si sacerdocium fuerit in

---

112 **auȝt**: R's b-verse depends on *wolde ȝe … hatien*, so "hate under any circumstance to take tithes", and presents aaa/ax alliteration. Beta's *nouȝt* depends, perhaps less plausibly, directly on *wolde ȝe*: "if you would not take tithes" (*to* is used when the auxiliary is separated from the infinitive, as here; see Mustanoja (1960), 522). In beta the pattern is aaa/xx. F rewrites. **Cx** simplifies the line (RK.16.260), with a couple of scribes even so misunderstanding the syntax and adding a negative.

113 **of vntrewe**: Obviously better than CrW *but of trewe* and G + alpha *of trewe*. Perhaps the mistake is prompted by l. 111 *Trewe* in the context of the syntactic difficulty shown by the readings in the line above. **Cx** revises (RK.16.261).

114 ¶: The paraph in LHm and alpha (line-break in M) evidently represents **Bx**, yet the sentence beginning at l. 109 with a series of conditionals must be completed here in the main clause.

115 **mysdon**: **Bx** means "(those) who do wrong amend themselves", but could be misunderstood to mean "amend those who do wrong". R's reading *þei misdon* makes it clearer that *hem* is reflexive, "amend themselves of what they do wrong". **Cx** clarifies with *amenden (hem) of here mysdedes* (RK.16.263).

117 **dongehul**: Cf. "a donghel besnewed" (*Aȝenbit of Inwit*, 81/9–10, translating *Somme le Roi*). Alpha's *dongoun* misses the allusion.

119 The paraph in L and the line-space in M are clearly not appropriate, and may represent a beta error.

119 The line is lost in HmCG, through eyeskip on *wyth-inne*.

121 **and with clothes**: So R. **Cx** has *and with bele clothes*. To repair the archetypal loss of the repeated *bele*, beta lengthens the b-verse with *also* and F supplies alliteration.

122 **woluelich**: Evidently R has the alpha reading, for which F substitutes *foxly*. Beta misreads as *vnlouelich*. **Cx** has an entirely different line, but it ends *as wolues* (RK.16.271).

123 ¶: The paraph is recorded by LR only.

124 Set as four lines in L, nine in R and three in F. Cf. l. 40.

124 **progreditur**: Alpha anticipates *procedit*.

124 **corupta**: Since this is the form in alpha and most C mss., it is presumably archetypal. Beta corrects to *coruptum*, referring to *sacerdocium* rather than *ecclesia*, as in Alford (1992), 93.

124 **sacerdocium** (2): Alpha has *sacerdos*.

peccatis · totus populus co[n]uertitur ad peccandum Sicut cum videris
arborem pallidam & marcidam · inteligis quod vicium habet in radice
Ita cum videris populum indisciplinatum · & irreligiosum sine dubio
sacerdocium eius non est sanum

125 ¶ If lewed men wist · what þis latyn meneth
And who was myn auctor · moche wonder me þinketh
But if many a prest bere · for here baselardes and here broches
A peyre bedes in her hande · and a boke vnder her arme
Sire Iohan & sire Geffray · hath a gerdel of syluer
130 A basellarde or a ballokknyf · with botones ouergylte
Ac a portous þat shulde be his plow · placebo to segge
Hadde he neure seruyse to saue syluer þer-to · seith it with yvel wille
Allas ȝe lewed men · moche lese ȝe on prestes
Ac þinge þat wykkedlich is wonne · and with false sleigthes
135 Wolde neuere witte of witty god · but wikked men it hadde
Þe which aren prestes inparfit · and prechoures after syluer
Sectoures and sudenes · somnoures and her lemmannes
Þis þat with gyle was geten · vngraciouslich is spended
So harlotes and hores · ar hulpen with such goodis
140 And goddes folke for defaute þer-of · forfaren and spillen

¶ Curatoures of holykirke · a[nd] clerkes þat ben auerouse
Liȝtlich þat þey leuen · loselles it habbeth
Or dyeth intestate · and þanne þe bisshop entreth

---

124 **peccandum:** Alpha has *peccatum*.

127 **many a:** MR have the equally common construction without *a*. **Cx** has no parallel for ll. 125–32.

127 **baselardes … broches:** Reversed in R (= alpha?). F corrupts amusingly.

128 **peyre:** The idiom is supported by LCGR (cf. **Bx.**12.22). The others have *peire of.*

128 **and:** Alpha has *or.*

132 **saue:** R reads *haue* (which could be right), while F abbreviates the long a-verse.

132 **yvel:** The reading of L and alpha, and so presumably **Bx.** Schmidt (1995) translates *with yvel wille* as "with a bad grace". The phrase occurs elsewhere in the sense "malice". KD adopt *wyth ydel wylle* in other beta mss., which Kane (2005) glosses "perfunctorily", though there are no parallels. O's *for spendyng at ale* is an inspired invention simplifying a puzzling line. As Skeat explains it, the priest expects to be paid for saying a mass in addition to (*þer-to*) the Placebo, so that *Hadde he neure* means "If he did not have".

135 **witte:** Scribes are puzzled, with W substituting *þe wit* and Hm *þe wylle.* CGO revise further. For *witte of witty god,* "the wisdom of wise God", **Cx** reads *oþerwyse god.* Langland seems to mean that since good men should not benefit from goods obtained wickedly (ll. 112–13), wicked men must enjoy them.

135 **hadde:** Alpha reads *maked,* but beta is supported by **Cx.**

138 **spended:** R has *spened,* agreeing with the X family of C. Cf. l. 81 note.

140 **And:** R (= alpha) has *Ac* (with F reading *But* as usual). Cf. the variants at ll. 107, 131 etc. The line is not in **Cx.**

141 **and:** Alpha is supported by **Cx** against beta's *as,* which, however, gives good sense.

And maketh murthe þere-with · and his men bothe
145 And seggen he was a nygarde · þat no good my3te asspare
To frende ne to fremmed · þe fende haue his soule
For a wrecched hous he helde · al his lyf-tyme
And þat he spared and bispered · spene we in murthe

¶ By lered by lewed · þat loth is to spende
150 Þus gone her godes · be þe goste faren
Ac for good men god wote · gret dole men maken
And bymeneth good mete-3yueres · and in mynde haueth
In prayers and in penaunces · and in parfyt charite   quid est caritas

¶ What is charite quod I þo · a childissh þinge he seide
155 Nisi efficiamini sicut paruuli · non intrabitis in regnum celorum
With-outen fauntelte or foly · a fre liberal wille

¶ Where shulde men fynde such a frende · with so fre an herte
I haue lyued in londe quod I · my name is longe wille
And fonde I neuere ful charite · bifore ne bihynde
160 Men beth mercyable · to mendynantz & to pore
And wolen lene þere þei leue · lelly to ben payed

¶ Ac charite þat poule preyseth best · and most plesaunte to owre saueoure
As non inflatu[r] non [est] ambiciosa non querit que sua sunt
I seigh neuere such a man · so me god helpe
165 That he ne wolde aske after his · and otherwhile coueyte
Þinge þat neded hym nou3t · and nyme it if he my3te

---

144 **men**: Support for *meyne* comes from HmF alone. Lines 143–62 are rewritten in C.

148 **spene**: The form in LMR. For variation with *spende*, cf. ll. 81, 138, 149 and 340.

149 **spende**: Cf. the previous line. In this case only R has *spene*.

152 **haueth**: Alpha has *hem haueth*, which may be right. There is no parallel in C.

153 **penaunces**: For variation of the plural with and without <-s>, see note to **Bx**.14.211.

153 **quid est caritas**: Written in the right-hand margin in the main hand in LM, so probably beta.

157 **¶**: The paraph in LW (with a new line-group in M) marks the start of Will's speech.

158 Alpha and Hm mistake this as the beginning of Will's speech, with a paraph here rather than at l. 157. But the line is certainly notable. A later annotator in L writes: "nota the name of thaucto[r]". R has "Longe Wylle" in display script in red in the right margin; in M a later annotator has scribbled "longe will".

158 **I** (2): Beta2 reads *he*.

162 **¶**: The paraph is in LM only and may be spurious. WHmCF have a paraph at l. 164 instead.

162 **owre saueoure**: Evidently beta, despite WCr's *oure lord*. Alpha presumably had R's *god*.

163 **As**: Beta2 has *Is*, and M is altered to that reading. The word is dropped by CG and is not in **Cx**.

163 **inflatur**: Perhaps beta had the error *inflatus*, retained by L and corrected in M.

163 **est**: Not in L and added in M and Hm, again suggesting that beta was perhaps in error.

166 **neded hym**: Supported by **Cx** against alpha's reversal and the present tense in CGO.

¶ Clerkis kenne me þat cryst · is in alle places
Ac I seygh hym neuere sothly · but as my-self in a miroure
[Hic] in enigmate tunc facie ad faciem
170   And so I trowe trewly · by þat men telleth of charite
It is nou3t championes fy3te · ne chaffare as I trowe

¶ Charite quod he ne chaffareth nou3te · ne chalengeth ne craueth
As proude of a peny · as of a pounde of golde
And is as gladde of a goune · of a graye russet
175   As of a tunicle of tarse · or of trye scarlet
He is gladde with alle gladde · and good ty[l] alle wykked
And leueth and loueth alle · þat owre lorde made
Curseth he no creature · ne he can bere no wratthe
Ne no lykynge hath to lye · ne laughe men to scorne
180   Al þat men seith he let it soth · and in solace taketh
And alle manere meschiefs · in myldenesse he suffreth
Coueiteth he none erthly good · but heuene-riche blisse

¶ Hath he any rentes or ricchesse · or any riche frendes

¶ Of rentes ne of ricchesse · ne reccheth he neuere
185   For a frende þat fyndeth hym · failled hym neuere at nede
Fiat voluntas tua [·] fynt hym euer-more
And if he soupeth et[eth] but a soppe [·] of spera in deo
He can purtreye wel þe pater noster · and peynte it with aues
And other-while is his wone · to wende in pilgrymage

---

168 **a**: Alpha omits. The line is not in **Cx**.

169 **Hic**: M and alpha are supported by **Cx** against *It* in L, *Ita* in CGO, and omission in beta2. In 1 Cor. 13.12 the word is *nunc*.

177 **And**: Alpha has *He*. Lines 177–87 are rewritten in C.

177 **leueth**: R clearly reads *leueth* (though not recorded by KD), and F's *belev*þ supports this as alpha's reading. Cr has *leueth* and in G *lenithe* is altered to *levithe*, as is to be expected in these late texts. In all other beta mss. it is impossible to determine whether the reading is *u* or *n* (though it looks more like *u* in O). Our transcriptions followed KD in reading *leneth* (though with a note of caution in W). We should probably have followed Skeat, who read L as *leueth*, with a note glossing it "believes; answering to *let it soth*" (l. 180).

182 **good**: Alpha has *godes*.

185 **fyndeth**: The evidence supports this as the **Bx** form in this line against R's monosyllabic *fynt*, whereas **Bx** evidently had *fynt* in the next line.

187 **soupeth**: Only MCGO have subjunctive *soupe*.

187 **eteth**: The present tense is required by the sense. L's *ette* must be past, and R's *eet* (= alpha?) may be. See note to l. 60 above. Hm and beta4 have *he eteþ*.

188 **aues**: Beta's plural is supported by **Cx** (RK.16.323).

189 **is his wone**: LMHm (R drops *his*). CrW, beta4 and F have *he is woned*, but **Cx** has *his wone is*.

189 **in pilgrymage**: Only LM have *in*, though this is the **Cx** reading. **Bx** clearly had sg. *pilgrymage*, though WCF have the plural, as does **Cx**. See **Bx**.14.211 and 19.387 for a similar situation.

190　Þere pore men and prisones liggeth · her pardoun to haue
　　　Þough he bere hem no bred · he bereth hem swetter lyflode
　　　Loueth hem as owre lorde biddeth · and loketh how þei fare

　　　¶ And whan he is wery of þat werke · þanne wil he some-tyme
　　　Labory in a lauendrye · wel þe lengthe of a myle
195　And ȝerne in-to ȝouthe · and ȝepliche s[eche]
　　　Pryde with al þe appurtenaunce · and pakken hem togyderes
　　　And bouken hem at his brest · and beten hem clene
　　　And leggen on longe · with laboraui in gemitu meo
　　　And with warme water at his eyghen · wasshen hem after
200　And þanne he syngeth whan he doth so · & some-tyme seith wepyng
　　　Cor contritum & humiliatum deus non despicies

　　　¶ By cryst I wolde þat I knewe hym quod I · no creature leuere

　　　¶ With-outen helpe of Piers plowman quod he · his persone seestow neuere

　　　¶ Where clerkes knowen hym quod I · þat kepen holykirke

205　¶ Clerkes haue no knowyng quod he · but by werkes and bi wordes
　　　Ac piers þe plowman · parceyueth more depper
　　　Þat is þe wille and wherfore · þat many wyȝte suffreth
　　　Et vidit deus cogitaciones eorum
　　　For þere ar ful proude-herted men · paciente of tonge
210　And boxome as of berynge · to burgeys and to lordes
　　　And to pore peple · han peper in þe nose
　　　And as a lyoun he loketh · þere men lakketh his werkes

　　　¶ For þere ar beggeres and bidderes · bedmen as it were
　　　Loketh as lambren · and semen lyf-holy
215　Ac it is more to haue her mete · [on] such an esy manere
　　　Þan for penaunce and parfitnesse · þe pouerte þat such taketh

---

190 **prisones**: The form has good support for both **Bx** and **Cx**. See note to **Bx**.3.138.
194 **a** (1): In LR only, though **Cx** has þe.
195 **seche**: Alpha is supported by **Cx** (as well as sense) against beta's *speke*.
196 **appurtenaunce**: The choice is between this and alpha's *purtenaunce*. This could represent the plural, as MCrWGF unambiguously do. C mss. have the same variation.
200 **And**: Beta is supported by the X family of C, but alpha's omission has support from the P family.
203 **plowman**: MR have *þe plowman*; F drops the two words. Cf. l. 206. Lines 202–24 are heavily revised in C, with few parallels.
207 **Þat**: This odd reading, supported by L and alpha, evidently puzzled the scribes. M is altered to *What*, the reading of beta2, while CGO have *Where*. There is no parallel in C.
207 **þe**: Lost in alpha, prompting F to alter *wil* to *why*.
215 **on**: Alpha's reading gives the required sense. LMCrW suggest that beta had *with*, although Hm and beta4 have *in*.

¶ Þere-fore by coloure ne by clergye · knowe shaltow hym neuere
Noyther þorw wordes ne werkes · but þorw wille one
And þat knoweth no clerke · ne creature in erthe
220   But piers þe plowman · petrus id est cristus
For he ne is nouȝte in lolleres · ne in lande-leperes hermytes
Ne at ancres þere a box hangeth · alle suche þei faiten
Fy on faitoures · and in fautores suos
For charyte is goddis champioun · and as a good chylde hende
225   And þe meryest of mouth · at mete where he sitteth
Þe loue þat lith in his herte · maketh hym lyȝte of speche
And is compenable and confortatyf · as cryst bit hym-selue
Nolite fieri sicut ypocrite tristes &c
For I haue seyn hym in sylke · and somme-tyme in russet
230   Bothe in grey and in grys · and in gulte herneys
And as gladlich he it gaf · to gomes þat it neded

¶ Edmonde and Edwarde · eyther were kynges
And seyntes ysette · [so] charite hem folwed

¶ I haue seyne charite also · syngen and reden
235   Ryden and rennen · in ragged wedes
Ac biddyng as beggeres · bihelde I hym neuere
Ac in riche robes · rathest he walketh
Ycalled and ycrimiled · and his crowne shaue
And in a freres frokke · he was yfounde ones
240   Ac it is ferre agoo · in seynt Fraunceys tyme
In þat secte sitthe · to selde hath he be knowen

¶ Riche men he recomendeth · and of her robes taketh
Þat with-outen wyles · leden her lyues

---

219 **in**: Beta probably had *in*, altered by beta2 (the line is omitted by Hm) to the more usual
on. F also reads *on*, though R has the unusual form *an*.
221 **ne is**: LM. In practice there is no distinction between this and *nys* in WHmR. We follow
copy-text.
224 Alpha has a paraph.
228 R alone has the word-order *tristes fieri sicut* as in **Cx**. Perhaps beta and F reverted to the
Vulgate order, since it was a well-known quotation used as an antiphon on Ash Wednesday.
See Alford (1992), 94.
229 Hm and alpha have a paraph. In L the line is at the top of the page where a paraph is
sometimes missed.
233 **so**: Alpha's alliterating reading means "so much did they practice charity". Beta's *tyl* makes
no sense, prompting the reading *for* in CrW, and the alteration to that reading in MHm. KD
and Schmidt (1995), 396, oddly conjecture *stille*, though the latter has an elaborate explanation.
238 Following this beta4 has an additional line. It is not in C.
240 **ferre**: Though beta2 and F have *fern*, which might be considered difficilior (it occurs
nowhere else in any version), **Cx** has *fer* in a revised a-verse.
241 **knowen**: Clearly the **Bx** reading. Unusually, W's *founde* is shared with **Cx**, presumably by
coincidence.

Beatus est diues · qui &c

245 ¶ In kynges courte he cometh ofte · þere þe conseille is trewe
Ac if coueityse be of þe conseille · he wil nouȝt come þer-Inne
In courte amonge iaperes · he cometh but selde
For braulyng and bakbytyng · and beryng of fals witnesse

¶ In þe constorie bifor þe comissarie · he cometh nouȝt ful ofte
250 For her lawe dureth ouer-longe · but if þei lacchen syluer
And matrimoigne for monye · maken & vnmaken
And þat conscience and cryst · hath yknitte faste
Þei vndon it vnworthily · þo doctours of lawe

[¶ Amonges erchebisshopes and oþer bisshopes · and prelates of holy
cherche
255 Forto wonye with hem · his wone was sum-tyme
And cristes patrimoigne to þe pore · parcel-mele dele
Ac auarice hath þe keyes now · and kepeth for his kynnesmen
And for his sectoures & his seruantz · & somme for here children]

¶ Ac I ne lakke no lyf · but lorde amende vs alle
260 And gyue vs grace good god · charite to folwe
For who-so myȝte mete with hym · such maneres hym eyleth
Noyther he blameth ne banneth · bosteth ne prayseth
Lakketh ne loseth · ne loketh vp sterne
Craueth ne coueiteth · ne crieth after more
265 In pace in idipsum dormiam &c ·
Þe moste lyflode þat he lyueth by · is loue in goddis passioun
Noyther he biddeth ne beggeth · ne borweth to ȝelde
Misdoth he no man · ne with his mouth greueth

¶ Amonges cristene men · þis myldnesse shulde laste
270 In alle manere angres · haue þis at herte
Þat þough þei suffred al þis · god suffred for vs more
In ensample we shulde do so · and take no veniaunce
Of owre foes þat doth vs falsenesse · þat is owre fadres wille
For wel may euery man wite [·] if god hadde wolde hym-selue

247 **but**: LMGR are supported by **Cx** against *noȝt but*.
254–8 These five lines are lost by beta, skipping from one paraph to the next. Lines 254 and 257 are distantly related to RK.16.366–7. We follow R, with spellings altered to those of L. Comparison with **Cx** begins again with l. 290 and then l. 297.
258 **here**: The kinsmen's. F's *hise* weakens the point.
259 ¶: The paraph is in beta, following its loss of text. See note to ll. 254–8.
263 This is transposed with the following line in beta4.
265 The Latin line is lost in alpha. CrHmG extend the verse. It is repeated at **Bx**.18.191–2.
266 **þat**: Supported by LWHmR.
274 **wel may euery man**: Beta's word-order gives a better alliterative pattern than alpha's.
274 **hadde**: Dropped by G and alpha. The b-verse means "if God had followed his own wishes".

275 Sholde neuere Iudas ne iuwe · haue Ihesu don on Rode
Ne han martired peter ne Poule · ne in prisoun holden
Ac he suffred in ensample · þat we shulde suffre also
And seide to suche þat suffre wolde · þat pacientes vincunt

¶ Verbi gratia quod he · and verrey ensamples manye
280 In legenda sanctorum · þe lyf of holy seyntes
What penaunce and pouerte · and passioun þei suffred
In hunger in hete · in al manere angres
Antony and Egidie · and other holi fadres
Woneden in wildernesse · amonge wilde bestes
285 Monkes and mendynauntz · men bi hem-selue
In spekes an spelonkes · selden speken togideres
Ac noyther antony ne Egidy · ne hermite þat tyme
Of liouns ne of leoperdes · no lyflode ne toke
But of foules þat fleeth · þus fynt men in bokes
290 Excepte þat Egydie · after an hynde cryede
And þorw þe mylke of þat mylde best · þe man was susteyned
A[c] day by day had he hir nouȝt · his hunger forto slake
But selden and sondrie tymes · as seith þe boke and techeth

¶ Antony adayes · aboute none-tyme
295 Had a bridde þat brouȝte hym bred · þat he by lyued
And þough þe gome hadde a geste · god fonde hem bothe

¶ Poule primus heremita · had parroked hym-selue
Þat no man miȝte hym se · for mosse and for leues
Foules hym fedde · fele wynteres with-alle
300 Til he founded freres · of austines ordre
Poule after his prechyng · panyers he made
And wan with his hondes · þat his wombe neded
Peter fisched for his fode · and his felawe andrewe

---

275 **ne**: Alpha, reading þe (R) or þat (F), takes no account of the following line.
286 **an**: "and". The attestation of MCr and R (as well as beta4) favours omitting LWHmF *in*.
289 **foules**: Alpha includes the definite article, perhaps rightly. We follow copy-text.
291 **mylde**: F omits, while R has *meke*, perhaps prompted by its spelling *melke* for "milk".
292 **Ac**: The sense seems to call for R's reading, against beta's *And*. F omits.
293 **tymes**: See Bx.12.36. Alpha's *tyme* is possible. Discussed by KD, p. 143.
294 **adayes**: The form does not occur elsewhere in the poem. Alpha has *on a day*. We follow copy-text.
295 **bred**: R probably represents alpha, with punctuation after *hym* and the addition of *his* before *bred* (F has *his* later in the line). Either could be right, though b-verse alliteration on *by* is perfectly good.
296 **fonde**: "provided for". Alpha's *fedde* is likely to be scribal. Cf. l. 299.
297 **parroked**: Cx (RK.17.13) does not support alpha's addition of *in*.
300 **of austines**: There is liaison alliteration on /f/ which F improves by altering to *of fraunces*.

Some þei solde and some þei sothe · and so þei lyued bothe
305 And also Marie Magdeleyne · by mores lyued and dewes
Ac moste þorw deuocioun · and mynde of god almiȝty
I shulde nouȝt þis seuene dayes · seggen hem alle
Þat lyueden þus for owre lordes loue · manye longe ȝeres
Ac þere ne was lyoun ne leopart · þat on laundes wenten
310 Noyther bere ne bor · ne other best wilde
Þat ne fel to her feet · and fauned with þe tailles
And if þei couth han ycarped · by cryst as I trowe
Þei wolde haue fedde þat folke · bifor wilde foules
[For alle þe curteisye þat bestes kunne · þei kidde þat folke ofte
315 In likkyng and in lowynge · þere þei on laundes ȝede]
Ac god sent hem fode bi foules · and by no fierse bestes
In menynge þat meke þinge · mylde þinge shulde fede
As who seith religious · ryȝtful men shulde fynde
And lawful men to lyfholy men · lyflode brynge
320 And þanne wolde lordes and ladyes be · loth to agulte
And to take of her tenauntz · more þan treuth wolde
Fonde þei þat Freres · wolde forsake her almesses
And bidden hem bere it · þere it was yborwed
For we ben goddes foules · and abiden alwey
325 Tyl briddes brynge vs · þat we shulde lyue by
For had ȝe potage and payn ynough · and peny-ale to drynke
And a messe þere-mydde · of o manere kynde
Ȝe had riȝt ynough ȝe Religious · and so ȝowre reule me tolde
Nunquam dicit Iob rugi[e]t on[a]ger cum [habuerit herbam] · aut mugiet
boscum ante plenum presepe steterit · brutorum animalium natura te

---

304 **sothe**: Past tense, from *MED sethen* v. (1). W *sode* is merely a variant spelling. Alpha has
the easier *eeten*, but beta is supported by **Cx**.
305 **lyued and**: Alpha's omission of the verb is attractive following *lyued* in l. 304, but beta
has support from **Cx**.
308 **manye longe ȝeres**: Beta and **Cx**. Alpha's b-verse is repeated from l. 284.
311 **tailles**: R's singular has no support from **Cx**.
314–15 Two lines lost by beta. The whole passage is heavily revised in C, and there is no trace
of these lines. We follow R, with spellings altered to those of L.
318 **fynde**: WF pick up *fede* from the previous line.
319 **brynge**: WF have *sholde brynge*, repeating the construction of the previous two lines.
322 **almesses**: LWHm mark the plural form. The form of the other scribes can also be understood as plural. There is similar variation in the parallel line in C (RK.17.47), though most
scribes have the unmarked form.
327 **a**: i.e. "one", as is clearer in alpha. "And one main dish of just one kind".
328 **reule**: Alpha substitutes non-alliterating *ordre*.
329 **Nunquam**: Supported by **Cx**. F's *Numquid*, which makes much better sense, is a correction
in line with the Vulgate (Job 6.5).
329 **rugiet**: The Vulgate's future tense is supported by alpha and **Cx**.
329 **habuerit herbam**: Beta reverses the word-order, but alpha's order, which is that of the
Vulgate, is supported by **Cx**.

condempnat ·quia cum eis pabulum comune sufficiat · ex adipe prodijt
iniquitas tua

330 ¶ If lewed men knewe þis latyn · þei wolde loke whom þei ȝeue
And auyse hem bifore · a fyue dayes or sexe
Or þei amortesed to monkes · or chanouns her rentes
Allas lordes and ladyes · lewed conseille haue ȝe
To ȝyue fram ȝowre eyres · þat ȝowre ayeles ȝow lefte
335 And ȝiueth to bidde for ȝow · to such þat ben riche
And ben founded and feffed eke · to bidde for other

¶ Who perfourneth þis prophecye · of þe peple þat now lybbeth
Dispersit dedit pauperibus &c
If any peple perfourme þat texte · it ar þis pore freres
340 For þat þei beggen abouten · in buildynge þei spene
And on hem-self sum · and such as ben her laboreres
And of hem þat habbeth þei taken · and ȝyue hem þat ne habbeth

¶ Ac clerkes & knyȝtes · and comuneres þat ben riche
Fele of ȝow fareth · as if I a forest hadde
345 Þat were ful of faire trees · and I fonded and caste
How I myȝte mo þer-inne · amonges hem sette
Riȝt so ȝe riche · ȝe robeth þat ben riche
And helpeth hem þat helpeth ȝow · and ȝiueth þere no nede is
As who-so filled a tonne [ful] · of a fressh ryuer
350 And went forth with þat water · to woke with themese
Riȝt so ȝe riche · ȝe robeth and fedeth
Hem þat han as ȝe han · hem ȝe make at ese

¶ Ac Religious þat riche ben · shulde rather feste beggeres
Þan burgeys þat riche ben · as þe boke techeth
355 Quia sacrilegium est res pauperum non pauperibus dare

---

329 **brutorum ... sufficiat:** Alpha omits but it is in **Cx**.

331 **a:** "a period of". Alpha and GO omit. Lines 331–71 offer few parallels with C.

335 **ȝiueth:** CrWF supply the object *it*.

335 **such þat:** MCr and alpha have (slightly easier?) *such as*.

340 **spene:** The form in LMO, but alpha and others have *spende*. See notes to ll. 81, 148. Beta2 and CF add *it*.

342 **ne:** Beta2 omits, puzzled by the irony.

347 **robeth:** "provide robes for" (as in L, corrected M, WC) but with a pun on the phrase "rob the rich". Already puzzled by the ironic tone earlier in the passage, other scribes write *robbeth*, leading F to alter *ryche* to *not ryche*. See l. 351.

349 **ful:** Called for by the alliteration, though preserved only in R. Alpha also has *ful* in the b-verse, replacing *fressh* in beta.

351 **robeth:** So LWC; the others have *robb-*. See note to l. 347.

353 **¶:** The paraph is in beta only.

353 **feste:** Alpha picks up the weaker *fede* from l. 351.

Item [idem] peccatoribus dare · est demonibus immolare
Item monache si indiges et accipis pocius das quam accipis
Si autem non eges & accipis · rapis
Porro non indiget Monachus · si habeat quod nature sufficit

360 For-þi I conseille alle cristene · to confourmen hem to charite
For charite with-oute chalengynge · vnchargeth þe soule
And many a prisone fram purgatorie · þorw his preyeres he delyureth
Ac þere is a defaute in þe folke · þat þe faith kepeth
Wherfore folke is þe feblere · and nou3t ferme of bilieue

365 As in lussheborwes is a lyther alay · and 3et loketh he lyke a sterlynge
Þe merke of þat mone is good · ac þe metal is fieble
And so it fareth by some folke now · þei han a faire speche
Croune and crystendome · þe kynges merke of heuene
Ac þe metal þat is mannes soule · with synne is foule alayed

370 Bothe lettred and lewede · beth allayed now with synne
That no lyf loueth other · ne owre lorde as it semeth
For [what] þorw werre and wykked werkes · and wederes vnresonable
Wederwise shipmen · and witti clerkes also
Han no bilieue to þe lifte · ne to þe lore of philosofres

375 ¶ Astrymyanes alday · in her arte faillen
Þat whilum warned bifore · what shulde [bi]falle after
Shipmen and sheperdes · þat with shipp & shepe wenten
Wisten by þe walkene · what shulde bityde
As of wederes and wyndes · þei warned men ofte

380 Tilieres þat tiled þe erthe · tolden her maistres
By þe sede þat þei sewe · what þei selle mi3te
And what to leue and to lyue by · þe londe was so trewe
Now failleth þe folke of þe flode · and of þe londe bothe
Sheperdes and shipmen · and so do þis tilieres

---

356 **idem**: i.e. "from the same source again" (viz. Peter Cantor; see Alford (1992), 96). It is omitted by beta.

357–8 These lines are omitted in alpha.

361 **þe soule**: R omits.

362 **prisone**: For the variation with *prisoner* see note to l. 190.

362 **he delyureth**: Alpha has instead *is deliuered*, which could be right.

363 A paraph as in Hm and alpha would be appropriate.

370 The line is dropped by CGF.

372 **what**: Omitted by beta, but alpha is supported by **Cx** (RK.17.86).

375 **Astrymyanes**: L has the same spelling in l. 386, but in **Bx**.19.250 has *astronomyenes*. The forms probably reflect **Bx**; cf. R's spellings. **C** mss. have similar variation.

376 **bifalle**: R's unique reading is supported by **Cx**. All other **B** mss omit the prefix, but it should be noted that F shows a tendency to alter *bifalle* to *falle*: **Bx**.7.179, 8.8, 11.309.

379 **and**: Alpha has *and of*. The line is not in C.

380 A paraph as in WHm and alpha would be appropriate.

382 **to** (2): The reading of LM and alpha supported by **Cx**. Beta1 has *what to*.

385 Noither þei kunneth ne knoweth · one cours bi-for an other
Astrymyanes also · aren at her wittes ende
Of þat was calculed of þe [c]lement · þe contrarie þei fynde
Gramer þe grounde of al · bigyleth now children
For is none of þis newe clerkes · who-so nymeth hede
390 Þat can versifye faire · ne formalich enditen
Ne nouȝt on amonge an hundreth · þat an auctour can construe
Ne rede a lettre in any langage · but in latyn or in englissh
Go now to any degre · and but if gyle be mayster
And flaterere his felawe · vnder hym to fourmen
395 Moche wonder me thynketh · amonges vs alle
Doctoures of decres · and of diuinite Maistres
Þat shulde konne and knowe · alkynnes clergye
And answere to argumentz · and also to a quodlibet
I dar nouȝt seggen it for shame · if suche weren apposed
400 Þei shulde faillen in her philosofye · and in phisyk bothe
Wher-fore I am afered · of folke of holikirke
Lest þei ouerhuppen as other don · in offices & in houres
Ac if þei ouerhuppe as I hope nouȝte · owre byleue suffiseth
As clerkes in corpus cristi feste · singen & reden
405 Þat sola fides sufficit · to saue with lewed peple

¶ And so may sarasenes be saued · scribes and iewes
Allas þanne but owre loresmen · lyuen as þei leren vs
And for her lyuynge þat lewed men be · þe lother god agulten
For sarasenes han somwhat · semynge to owre bileue
410 For þei loue and bileue · in o parsone almiȝty

---

387 **þe clement**: Alpha drops the article; beta reads *þe element*. The right reading is certainly that of **Cx** (RK.17.107), *þe clymat* (*MED climat*, "a region of the earth"). Beta replaced the corrupt **Bx** with much easier and non-alliterating *þe element*, "the weather". Alpha drops the definite article to make some sense: "calculated by [Pope?] Clement". At this date *clement* can only be a proper name; cf. **Bx**.5.344, 365 (in both cases R has small <c> but F a capital). It is possible, too, that **Bx** itself read *þe clemet* correctly and was differently misinterpreted by alpha and beta.

390 The line is omitted by beta2. **Cx** has it.

395 **Moche**: Alpha adds *And*, but the sense is better without it: "It will surprise me greatly if Guile isn't in command and Flatterer working under him amongst everyone".

400 **faillen in**: LMG and alpha, supported by **Cx** against *faillen of* in beta2 and CO.

402 **offices**: The form without ending in MWGF may also be plural. Cf. note to **Bx**.3.101.

403 **Ac**: Good support from LMR, with the usual variants *And* and *But*.

403 **if**: R has *þouȝ*, which may be alpha and may be right. It probably lies behind F's *þey oon hippe* ... (*þey* is F's usual form of "though") and is included in **C** which reworks as two lines (RK.17.118–19).

403 **suffiseth**: Either beta englishes the Latin or alpha supplies the Latin equivalent in antic-ipation of l. 405. **Cx** in a reworked line has the English form, altered by one scribe to *sufficit*.

408 **be**: L and alpha punctuate after *be*, the others after *men*.

And we lered and lewede · in on god bileueth
[Cristene and vncristene . on one god bileueth]
Ac one Makometh · a man in mysbileue
Brouȝte sarasenes of surre · and se in what manere
415 Þis Makometh was a crystene man · and for he moste nouȝte be a pope
In-to surre he souȝte · and þorw his sotil wittes
Daunted a dowue · and day and nyȝte hir fedde
Þe corne þat she cropped · he caste it in his ere
And if he amonge þe poeple preched · or in places come
420 Þanne wolde þe coluer come · to þe clerkes ere
Menynge as after meet · þus Makometh hir enchaunted
A dide folke þanne falle on knees · for he swore in his prechynge
Þat þe coluer þat come so · come fram god of heuene
As messager to Makometh · men forto teche
425 And þus þorw wyles of his witte [·] and a whyte dowue
Makometh in mysbileue · men and wommen brouȝte
Þat lered þere and lewed ȝit · l[e]uen on his lawes

¶ And sitth owre saueoure suffred · þe sarasenes so bigiled
Þorw a crystene clerke · acursed in his soule
430 Ac for drede of þe deth · I dar nouȝt telle treuthe
How englissh clerkes a coluer feden · þat coueityse hatte
And ben manered after Makometh · þat no man vseth treuth

¶ Ancres and hermytes · and monkes and freres

---

412 The line is omitted by beta as a result of eyeskip from the identical b-verse of l. 411. We
follow R as usual. F begins the line *And so*, which is perhaps scribal emphasis. For R's *on*, F
has *in*, as in the previous b-verse. The repetition might be an argument for or against. Lines
406–15 have no parallel in C.
413 **Ac**: LR only. F has *But*, others *And*. Cf. first note to l. 403.
415 **a crystene man**: The alliterating noun is supported by L and alpha, but alpha is without
the article, perhaps rightly. Beta1 seems to have read *a cristene*, as MWHm, though CrGO drop
the article and C has pa. ppl. *cristend*. **Cx**, in a different line, has *a man ycristened* (RK.17.165).
415 **a (2)**: The variation is unpatterned: LWCOR have the article, but the others are without it.
419–20 Two lines omitted by alpha, through eyeskip on *ere*. The lines form the basis of
RK.17.174–5.
421 **enchaunted**: Beta is supported by **Cx** against alpha's *chaunted*.
422 **A**: "And". See note to Bx.P.227.
424 **As**: Supported by the syntax over alpha's *And*.
427 **lered þere and lewed**: The reading of LR, and possibly M's original version. F revises
lered þere to *leernede men*; Hm (corrected) reverses the adjectives; beta4 drops *þere*, and CrW
have *lyued þo þere and lyue*, with M altered to that reading. A further difference is that alpha
punctuates after *lewed*. In **Cx** the line reads: *And on his lore thei lyuen* [or *leuen*] *ȝut, as wel lered
as lewed* (RK.17.182).
427 **leuen**: Only L has *lyuen*. There is some evidence that beta used the form *leuen* also for
"live", causing some scribes to hypercorrect; cf. notes to ll. 571 and 615.
430 **Ac**: LR (F has *But* as usual). See note to l. 413. Lines 429–513 are not paralleled in C.

Peren to apostles · þorw her parfit lyuynge
435 Wolde neuere þe faithful fader · þat his ministres sholde
Of tyrauntz þat teneth trewe men · taken any almesse
But done as Antony did · dominik and Frlaunceys
Benet & Bernarde · þe which hem firste tau₃te
To lyue bi litel & in lowe houses · by lele mennes almesse
440 Grace sholde growe & be grene · þorw her good lyuynge
And folkes sholde fynde · þat ben in dyuerse sykenesse
Þe better for her byddynges · in body and in soule
Her preyeres and her penaunces · to pees shulde brynge
Alle þat ben at debate · and bedemen were trewe
445 Petite & accipietis &c
Salt saueth catel · seggen þis wyues
Vos estis sal terre &c ·
Þe heuedes of holicherche · and þei holy were
Cryst calleth hem salt · for crystene soules
450 Et si sal euanuerit · in quo salietur
Ac fressh flessh other fissh · whan it salt failleth
It is vnsauory for soth · ysothe or ybake
So is mannes soule sothly · þat seeth no good ensaumple
Of hem of holycherche · þat þe heigh weye shulde teche
455 And be gyde and go bifore · as a good baneoure
And hardy hem þat bihynde ben · and ₃iue hem good euydence

¶ Elleuene holy men · al þe worlde torned
In-to lele byleue · þe li₃tloker me thynketh
Shulde al maner men · we han so manye Maistres
460 Prestes and prechoures · and a pope aboue
Þat goddes salt shulde be · to saue mannes soule

---

434 **Peren:** "become equals with". Alpha takes this as a noun, upsetting the syntax.
437 **and:** Alpha has *or*.
438 **&:** Alpha again has *or*.
439 **almesse:** Beta's reading may be prompted by the same word at the end of l. 436. On the other hand, alpha's synonym *fyndynge* may have its origin in visual similarity with *lyuynge* at the end of l. 440, together with *fynde* in l. 441 (so KD, p. 143). KD opts for beta's reading, Schmidt (1995) for alpha's.
440 **good:** Alpha picks up *lele* from the previous line, thus losing alliteration.
441 **folkes:** HmC and alpha have the sg.
443 **brynge:** Alpha has *hem brynge*, anticipating the object of l. 444.
446 Hm and alpha record a paraph.
446 **catel:** Beta2 and F add the definite article or personal pronoun.
447–514 These lines are omitted by F.
449 **calleth:** R's past tense is both easier and less appropriate.
451 **Ac:** So LMHmOR. See note to l. 413.
453 **ensaumple:** R has the apheticform *saumple*.
455 **a:** Omitted by R.

¶ Al was hethenesse some-tyme · Ingelond and wales
Til Gregory gerte clerkes · to go here and preche
Austyn at Caunterbury · crystened þe kynge
465 And þorw myracles as men may rede · al þat marche he torned
To cryst and to crystendome · and crosse to honoure
And fulled folke faste · and þe faith tauȝte
More þorw miracles · þan þorw moche prechynge
As wel þorw his werkes · as with his holy wordes
470 And seyde hem what fullynge · and faith was to mene

¶ Cloth þat cometh fro þe weuyng · is nouȝt comly to were
Tyl it is fulled vnder fote · or in fullyng stokkes
Wasshen wel with water · and with taseles cracched
Ytouked and ytented · & vnder tailloures hande
475 And so it fareth by a barne · þat borne is of wombe
Til it be crystened in crystes name · and confermed of þe bisshop
It is hethene as to heueneward · and helpelees to þe soule

¶ Hethene is to mene after heth · and vntiled erthe
As in wilde wildernesse · wexeth wilde bestes
480 Rude and vnresonable · rennenge with-out [k]eperes

¶ Ȝe [mynnen] wel how matheu seith · how a man made a feste
He fedde hem with no venysoun · ne fesauntes ybake
But with foules þat fram hym nolde · but folwed his whistellynge
Ecce altilia mea & omnia parata sunt &c
485 And wyth calues flesshe he fedde · þe folke þat he loued
Þe calfe bytokeneth clennesse · in hem þat kepeth lawes

---

463 **gerte**: R's *and grete* is much inferior.

463 **here and**: Beta4 and R have *and to*, losing the emphasis on England and Wales.

464 **kynge**: R's addition of *þere* may be a consequence of the loss of *here* in the previous line.

467 **faste**: Possibly a beta addition, since R omits it.

469 **with**: MCrHm repeat *þoruȝ* from the a-verse.

472 **is**: So LMR. Others have the subjunctive *be* as all copies have at l. 476.

474 **hande**: R and corrected Hm have the plural, less appropriately.

475 **of**: M and beta2 have *of a*.

480 **keperes**: The reading of R. Beta probably read *creperes*, as LGO, altered to *cropers* in M, beta2 and C, in order to make some sort of sense. Of course animals are not restrained by "cruppers". It is difficult to see how beta's reading could have derived from the commonplace "keeper". It may be that *crepere* has some technical sense not recorded; for example, in *Morte Arthure* 3667 it seems to refer to a grapnel. KD p. 146 rather implausibly suggest that "the *r* was induced by the alliteration".

481 **mynnen**: Only MW preserve the **Bx** reading, with other scribes avoiding or misreading a word that was mainly northern by this time. It never occurs in L nor elsewhere in **Bx**, though KD conjecture it four times. It is used twice in **C** (RK.17.210, 19.233) with similar variants.

481 **how** (1): GR have *whate*, avoiding the repetition.

KD.15.443–466

¶ For as þe cow þorw kynde mylke · þe calf norissheth til an oxe
So loue and lewte · lele men susteyneth
And maydenes and mylde men mercy desiren
490 Riȝt as þe cow calf · coueyteth swete mylke
So don riȝtful men · mercy & treuthe
[And by þe hande-fedde foules · [i]s folk vnderstonde
Þat loth ben to louye · with-outen lernynge of ensaumples
Riȝt as capones in a court · cometh to mennes whistlynge
495 In menynge after mete · folweth men þat whistlen
Riȝt so rude men · þat litel reson conneth
Louen and byleuen · by lettred mennes doynges
And by here wordes and werkes · wenen and trowen
And as tho foules to fynde · fode after whistlynge
500 So hope þei to haue · heuene þoruȝ her whistlynge
And by þe man þat made þe feste · þe maieste bymeneth
Þat is god of his grace · gyueth al men blisse
With wederes and with wondres · he warneth vs with a whistlere
Where þat his wille is · to worschipen vs alle
505 And feden vs and festen vs · for euere-more at ones]

¶ Ac who beth þat excuseth hem · aren persounes and prestes
Þat heuedes of holycherche ben · þat han her wille here
With-oute trauaille þe tithe del · þat trewe men biswynkyn
Þei wil be wroth for I write þus · ac to witnesse I take
510 Bothe Mathew and Marke · and Memento domine dauid
[Ecce audiuimus e[a]m in effrata &c ·]
What Pope or prelate now · perfourneth þat cryst hiȝte
Ite in vniuersum mundum & predicate & c ·

¶ Allas þat men so longe · on Makometh shulde byleue
515 So many prelates to preche · as þe Pope maketh
Of Nazareth of Nynyue · of Neptalim and damaske

---

487 ¶: The paraph is in LC, with a new line-group in M.

488 **loue ... lele**: R's version of the line, *doth loue & lewte and lele*, is equally probable.

492–505 These 14 lines are omitted by beta, jumping to the next paraph. Since F omits ll. 447–514, and furthermore there is no parallel in **Cx**, we are here entirely dependent upon R.

492 **is**: R has *his*, probably as a spelling for *is* rather than an error.

506 **aren**: Beta has *þat aren*, but the syntax is much better without, as in R: "those who excuse themselves are parsons".

507 **holycherche**: R's plural is less appropriate.

511 **eam**: The line is lost in beta, so R, reading *eum*, is the sole authority for citing the Psalm "Memento Domini" (131.6). It was previously cited at **Bx**.10.72, where alpha again has *eum* for beta's *eam* as in the Vulgate. See note there, and for explanation of the reference in that line see Schmidt (1995), 443.

Þat þei ne went as cryst wisseth · sithen þei wil a name
To be pastours and preche · þe passioun of Ihesus
And as hym-self seyde · so to lyue and deye
520 Bonus pastor animam suam ponit & c
And seyde it in sauacioun · of sarasenes & other
For crystene & vncristene · cryst seide to prechoures
Ite vos in vineam meam ·
And sith þat þis sarasenes · scribes & Iuwes
525 Han a lippe of owre byleue · þe liȝtloker me thynketh
Þei shulde torne who-so trauaille wolde · to teche hem of þe Trinite
Querite & inuenietis &c

¶ It is reuth to rede · how riȝtwis men lyued
How þei defouled her flessh · forsoke her owne wille
530 Fer fro kitth and fro kynne · yuel yclothed ȝeden
Badly ybedded · no boke but conscience
Ne no richchesse but þe Rode · to reioyse hem Inne
Absit nobis gloriari nisi in cruce domini nostri &c ·

¶ And þo was plente & pees · amonges pore & riche
535 And now is routhe to rede · how þe red noble
Is reuerenced or þe Rode · receyued for þe worthier
Þan crystes crosse þat ouer-cam · deþ and dedly synne

¶ And now is werre and wo · and who-so why axeth
For coueityse after crosse · þe croune stant in golde
540 Bothe riche and religious · þat Rode þei honoure
Þat in grotes is ygraue · and in golde nobles
For coueityse of þat crosse · men of holykirke
Shul tourne as templeres did · þe tyme approcheth faste

---

517 **a**: A good example of the superiority of LR. The other beta scribes took this to be a reduced form of "have". F realised it was the article, clarifying the sense by altering to *þe*. In **Cx** (RK.17.191) it is also revised to *þe*, perhaps again for the sake of clarity.

518 L, starting a new leaf, begins with an inappropriate paraph.

519 **so**: Omitted by WGF preceding *to*. Hm omits the line.

522 **For**: As KD point out (p. 146), the alpha variant *To cristene and to vncristene* makes poor sense.

525 **me thynketh**: Supported by **Cx** (RK.17.253) against alpha's *it semeth*.

526 **trauaille wolde**: Beta2 have *trauailed*, and M is altered to that reading, but **Cx** agrees with LCGO and alpha.

528–67 These forty lines are in beta only. Adams (2002), 118–22, discusses alpha's omission here and beta's loss of ll. 575–92, positing that the passages were on opposite sides of an inserted leaf in **Bx**, and the alpha and beta scribes each failed to incorporate one side of the leaf. KD argue that distinct from this is a major dislocation of text that antedated the losses in alpha and beta, and they move **Bx**.15.568–97 to precede 528 (pp. 176–8).

535 **And**: The reading *Ac* in Hm, though tempting, is in the hand of the reviser, who has erased one line to write in this line and the next. In any case, **Cx** has *And* (RK.17.200).

¶ Wyte ȝe nouȝt wyse men · how þo men honoured
545 More tresore þan treuthe · I dar nouȝt telle þe sothe
Resoun & riȝtful dome · þo Religious demed
Riȝt so ȝe clerkes · for ȝowre coueityse ar longe
Shal þei demen dos ecclesie · and ȝowre pryde depose
Deposuit potentes de sede &c ·

550 ¶ ȝif knyȝthod & kynde wytte · and comune conscience
Togideres loue lelly · leueth it wel ȝe bisshopes
Þe lordeship of londes · for euere shal ȝe lese
And lyuen as leuitici [·] as owre lorde ȝow techeth
Per primicias & decimas

555 ¶ Whan costantyn of curteysye · holykirke dowed
With londes and ledes · lordeshipes and rentes
An Angel men herde · an heigh at Rome crye
Dos ecclesie þis day · hath ydronke venym
And þo þat han petres powere · arn apoysoned alle

560 ¶ A medecyne mote þer-to · þat may amende prelates
Þat sholden preye for þe pees · possessioun hem letteth
Take her landes ȝe lordes · and let hem lyue by dymes
If possessioun be poysoun · & inparfit hem make
Good were to dischargen hem · for holicherche sake
565 And purgen hem of poysoun · or more perile falle

¶ ȝif presthod were parfit · þe peple s[h]olde amende
Þat contrarien crystes lawe · and crystendome dispise
For al paynym prayeth · and parfitly bileueth
In þe holy grete god · and his grace asken
570 And make her mone to makometh · her message to shewe

---

544 **wyse**: Beta2 and G have *ye wise*, but **Cx** is without the pronoun (RK.17.210), though in a revised a-verse.

546 **þo**: Supported by most C mss. against *þe* in beta2.

550 **comune conscience**: This must be the beta reading; the line is not in alpha. Cr and W, understanding the knighthood / commons pairing, take *comune* as a noun, so following it with *by conscience*, and M is altered to that reading. Presumably beta is a corruption of the reading of **Cx**, *ȝif knyhthed and kynde wit and þe comune and conscience* (RK.17.216) which adds a kind-wit / conscience pairing.

552 **londes**: W adds *youre* here and drops *ȝow* in the next line.

552 **shal ȝe**: Reversed by beta4. **Cx** has *lese ȝe shal for euer* (RF.17.218).

568 **paynym**: Only L has the distributive sg., but it is supported by the X family of C (RK.17.255). Alpha is now present.

568 **and parfitly bileueth**: Beta's b-verse is supported by **Cx**. Alpha's *to on persone to helpe* looks like censorship, as in the next line.

569 **In þe holy grete god**: Cx has *In þe grete god*. Again alpha objects to allowing so much to pagan beliefs, reading *On o god þei greden*.

569 **asken**: Beta's pronoun *þei* is not supported by **Cx**.

Þus in a faith lyueth þat folke · and in a false mene
And þat is routhe for [þe] riȝtful men · þat in þe Rewme wonyen
And a peril to þe pope · and prelatis þat he maketh
Þat bere bisshopes names · of Bedleem & [of] babiloigne
575 [Whan þe hieȝe kynge of heuene · sent his sone to erthe
Many miracles he wrouȝte · man for to turne
In ensaumple þat men shulde se · þat by sadde resoun
Men miȝt nouȝt be saued · but þorw mercy and grace
And þorw penaunce and passion · and parfit byle[ue]
580 And bycam man of a mayde · and metropolitanus
And baptised and bishined · with þe blode of his herte
Alle þat wilned and wolde · with Inwitte byleue it
Many a seint sithen · hath suffred to deye
Al for to enf[e]rme þe faith · in fele contreyes deyeden
585 In ynde and in alisaundre · in ermonye in spayne
In delfol deth deyeden · for hire faith sake
In sauacioun of þe faith · seynt [thomas] was martired
Amonges vnkynde cristene · for cristes loue he deyede
And for þe riȝt of al þis reume · and al reumes cristene
590 Holy cherche is honoured · hieȝliche þorw his deyinge
He is a forbisene to alle bisshopes · and a briȝt myroure

---

571 **lyueth**: So LCr and alpha, with HmG both altering to *leue-*, the reading of MWCO. **Cx** supports *lyueth*. Schmidt (1995), 397, considers that there is a pun with *leueth* implied in the b-verse: "believe in a false intercessor". Cf. note to l. 427.

572 **þe** (1): Although only in R, **C** mss. have either *þe* or *þo*.

573 **prelatis**: R has *to prelates*. F omits the line and **Cx** rewrites it.

574 **of** (2): This was perhaps not in beta since LMW lack it, but alpha has support from the revised line in **Cx**, *of Ninue and of damaske* (the X family omits *and*).

575–92 These 18 lines are lost in beta, probably (as KD suggest, p. 66) through eyeskip (*bere bisshopes names* 574, *bisshopes … bereth þe name* 591–2). The lines are in **Cx** (RK.17.262–78). See note to **Bx**.15.528–67. The text is based on R, with spellings altered to L's forms.

579 **byleue**: R's *byle* is an obvious miswriting.

580 **metropolitanus**: F adds *after*, but it is not in **Cx**.

581 **bishined**: "illuminated". Not especially uncommon, but evidently C scribes were confused, perhaps because of the weak form of the past tense. Most have *bisshoped*.

582 **Inwitte**: R is supported by **Cx** against F's *wit*.

583 **to deye**: So alpha, but **Cx** has *deth also*.

584 **enferme**: A few C mss. have *enforme*, "teach", as in R, but the best have *enferme*, "strengthen" (RK.17.271), lending support to F's *ferme*.

584 **deyeden**: R's past tense is obviously right, and confirmed by **Cx**.

585 **and in**: F is without *and*, and may be right. Most C mss. have it, but a few do not. See next note.

585 **in** (4): So F, supported by most (and the most reliable) **C** mss. Yet others have *and* or *and in*, as R does. See previous note.

586 The line is entirely rewritten in **Cx**.

587 **thomas**: The name has been erased in R, as in several C mss.

591 **forbisene**: R is supported by **Cx**.

KD.15.507–527

And souereyneliche to suche · þat of surrye bereth þe name]
[And nauȝt to] hippe aboute in Engelonde · to halwe mennes auteres
And crepe [in] amonges curatoures · [and] confessen ageyne þe lawe
595 Nolite mittere falcem in messem alienam &c

[¶] Many man for crystes loue · was martired [amonges Romaynes]
Er crystendome [were] knowe þere · or any crosse honoured

¶ Euery bisshop þat bereth crosse · by þat he is holden
Thorw his prouynce to passe · and to his peple to shewe hym
600 Tellen hem and techen hem · on þe Trinite to bileue
And feden hem with gostly fode · and [nedy folke to fynden
Ac ysaie of ȝow speketh · and ozias bothe
Þat no man shuld be bisshope · but if he hadde bothe
Bodily fode and gostly fode · to] gyue þere it nedeth
605 In domo mea non est panis neque vestimentum et ideo nolite constituere
       me regem · ysaie 3
Ozias seith for such · þat syke ben and fieble
Inferte omnes decimas in oreum meum vt cibus in domo mea

¶ Ac we crystene creatures · þat on þe crosse byleuen
Aren ferme as in þe faith · goddes forbode elles
610 And han clerkes to kepen vs þer-Inne · and hem þat shal come after vs

¶ And iewes lyuen in lele lawe · owre lorde wrote it hym-selue

---

593 **And nauȝt to:** Here beta resumes, but alpha's start of the a-verse is supported by Cx
(RK.17.279). Beta's *Þat* represents smoothing after the omission.

593 **aboute:** Alpha adds *here*, but beta is supported by **Cx.**

593 **mennes:** Omitted by Hm and alpha, but supported by **Cx.**

594 **in:** Beta omits, but alpha is supported by **Cx.**

594 **and:** Beta omits, though W adds it for the sense. Alpha is supported by **Cx.**

596 **¶:** L omits an appropriate paraph here, recorded by WHm and alpha.

596 **man:** The majority of C mss. support beta, but three have *a man* as alpha.

596 **amonges Romaynes:** The reading of R alone, but supported by **Cx.** F revises to *in grete
roome,* and beta has *in Romanye.*

597 **Er:** The beta reading was probably the nonsensical *Er ar any* LC, giving rise to *Er any*
MCrWG, *Er þan* Hm and *Er þan any* O. Alpha is supported by **Cx** (RK.17.282).

597 **were:** The subjunctive as in alpha is supported by **Cx.**

597 **crosse:** R's repetition of *þere* is not supported by **Cx.**

598 **he:** R omits. **Cx** has a different b-verse.

600 **techen:** Alpha picks up non-alliterating *schewen* from the previous line.

601–4 Beta drops ll. 601b-604a, by eyeskip on *gostly fode.* We follow R, altering the forms to
those of L. Up to l. 614 **Cx** is heavily revised.

605 **ysaie 3:** The reference was in **Bx,** since it is preserved in L and alpha in the hands of the
main scribes.

607 **vt:** CrO add *sit,* as in Malachi 3.10. See Alford (1992), 99.

608 **¶:** The paraph, following the Latin line, is in LWHmF.

609 **ferme:** Alpha has *for me* (R) or *formed* (F).

610 **vs (2):** Preserved in LMWR, but lost elsewhere.

In stone for it stydfast was · and stonde sholde eure
Dilige deum & proximum · is parfit iewen lawe
And toke it moyses to teche men · til Messye come
615 And on þat lawe þei l[e]uen · and leten it þe beste
And ȝit knewe þei cryst · þat crystendome tauȝte
[And] for a parfit prophete · þat moche peple saued
Of selcouth sores · þei seyne it ofte
Bothe of myracles & meruailles · and how he men fested
620 With two fisshes an fyve loues · fyue thousande peple
And bi þat maungerye [þei] miȝte wel se · þat Messye he semed
And whan he luft vp lazar · þat layde was in graue
And vnder stone ded & stanke · with styf voys hym called
Lazare veni foras ·
625 Dede hym rise and rowme [·] riȝt bifor þe iuwes
Ac þei seiden and sworen · with sorcerye he wrouȝte
And studyeden to stroyen hym · and stroyden hem-self
And þorw his pacyence her powere · to pure nouȝt he brouȝte
Pacientes vincunt

630 ¶ Danyel of her vndoynge · deuyned and seyde
Cum [veniat sanctus sanctorum &c.]
And ȝet wenen þo wrecches · þat he were pseudo-propheta
And þat his lore be lesynges · and lakken it alle
And hopen þat he be to come · þat shal hem releue
635 Moyses eft or Messye · here maisteres ȝet deuyneth

¶ Ac pharesewes and sarasenes · Scribes & Grekis
Aren folke of on faith · þe fader god þei honouren

---

614 **men**: Alpha has non-alliterating *it hem*.

615 **leuen**: LW and original Hm have *lyuen*, perhaps a beta error picked up from l. 611. The
better C mss. have *leue*, though a number have *lyue*, some altering *on* to *in* to make better sense
(RK.17.297). Cf. also ll. 427, 571. Beta adds *ȝit*, which makes very good sense (the Jews *still*
live under mosaic law), but it is not in alpha or **Cx**.

616 L has a paraph and M a line-space, perhaps a beta error since a paraph is not appropriate.

617 **And**: Dropped by beta, but included in **Cx**.

620 **an**: "and".

621 **þei**: Alpha is more satisfactory as referring specifically to the Jews. Beta perhaps picks up
men from l. 619. Cf. variants at l. 614. The a-verse is rewritten in C.

621 **wel**: Dropped by CrGOF.

623 **ded & stanke**: Presumably R's reversal represents alpha, which F revises. Lines 623–32
are rewritten in C.

631 **Cum veniat sanctus sanctorum & c.**: Beta reverses the verb and subject and completes the
familiar quotation used as a lesson in Advent. In **Bx**.18.113 where the prophecy is repeated,
there is the same alpha/beta variation, except that beta has *veniat sanctus*. At RK.20.112a,
despite considerable variation, it seems that **Cx** had this same form of the quotation.

635 **ȝet**: Alpha has this at the beginning of the b-verse. **Cx** omits it.

636 **Grekis**: WHm read *Iewes*, perhaps recalling ll. 406 and 524. Cf. Schmidt (1995), 398.

And sitthen þat þe sarasenes · and also þe iewes
Konne þe firste clause of owre bileue · credo in deum patrem omnipotentem
640   Prelates of crystene prouynces · shulde preue if þei myȝte
Lere hem litlum & lytlum [·] & in ihesum cristum filium
Tyl þei couthe speke and spelle · et in spiritum sanctum
And re[d]en it & recorden it · with remissionem peccatorum
Carnis resurreccionem · et vitam eternam amen ·

---

639 **omnipotentem**: Omitted by CrCGO (Cr also omits *patrem*), and by **Cx**, but it seems secure for **Bx**.

641 **Lere**: CrW begin *To lere*, and M is altered to that reading.

643 **reden**: This seems undoubtedly the **Bx** reading, despite L's *rendren*, "recite". The reading of **Cx** is less certain: the X family has *Recorden hit and reden hit*, where the P family has *rendren* for *reden*, which does make good sense in this order, "remember and recite". Schmidt (1995), lxvii, 398, follows KD in adopting L's *rendren*, though has difficulty in explaining how it arose.

Passus 16

Passus sextus decimus & primus de dobet

Now faire falle ʒow quod I þo · for ʒowre faire shewynge
For haukynnes loue þe actyf man [·] euere I shal ʒow louye
Ac ʒet I am in a were · what charite is to mene

¶ It is a ful trye tree quod he · trewly to telle
5 Mercy is þe more þer-of · þe myddel stokke is reuthe
Þe leues ben lele wordes · þe lawe of holycherche
Þe blosmes beth boxome speche · and benygne lokynge
Pacience hatte þe pure tre · and pore symple of herte
And so þorw god and þorw good men · groweth þe frute charite

10 ¶ I wolde trauaille quod I þis tree to se · twenty hundreth myle
And forto haue my fylle of þat frute · forsake al other saulee
Lorde quod I if any wiʒte wyte · whider oute it groweth

¶ It groweth in [a] gardyne quod he · þat god made hym-seluen
Amyddes mannes body · þe more is of þat stokke
15 Herte hatte þe erber · þat it in groweth
And liberum arbitrium · hath þe londe to ferme
Vnder Piers þe plowman · to pyken it and to weden it

---

1 F prefaces the passus with two lines in which the dreamer falls asleep again. Lines 1–27 are quite different in C.

4 **trewly**: Alpha has *treuthe*. There is no close parallel elsewhere for either.

8 **pore**: Beta1 repeats *pure*.

9 **þorw** (2): So LMW, and presumably therefore beta (note Hm misreads as *pure*), but other beta texts and alpha are without it, perhaps rightly.

11 **forto**: Alpha and beta4 have *to*, which could equally be right.

11 **saulee**: "food". L first wrote *soule*, as R, then added the gloss "id est edulium".

12 **it**: R has þat it.

13 **a**: Omitted by L.

17 **Vnder**: Alpha begins *And vnder*, perhaps as **Bx**.

17 **to** (2): Omitted by beta4 and F.

Piers þe plowman quod I þo · and al for pure ioye
Þat I herde nempne his name · anone I swouned after
20 And laye longe in a loue-dreme · and atte laste me þou3te
Þat Pieres þe plowman · al þe place me shewed
And bad me toten on þe tree · on toppe and on rote
With þre pyles was it vnder-pi3te · I perceyued it sone
Pieres quod I · I preye þe · whi stonde þise piles here

25 ¶ For wyndes wiltow wyte quod he · to witen it fram fallyng
Cum ceciderit iustus non collidetur · quia dominus supponit manum suam
And in blowyng tyme abite þe floures · but if þis piles helpe
Þe worlde is a wykked wynde · to hem þat wolden treuthe
Coueityse cometh of þat wynde · and crepeth amonge þe leues
30 And forfret neigh þe frute · þorw many faire si3tes
Þanne with þe firste pyle I palle hym down · þat is potencia dei patris
Þe flesshe is a fel wynde · and in flourynge tyme
Þorw lykyng and lustes · so loude he gynneth blowe
Þat it norissheth nice si3tes · and some-tyme wordes
35 And wikked werkes þer-of · wormes of synne
And forbiteth þe blosmes · ri3t to þe bare leues

¶ Þanne sette I to þe secounde pile · sapiencia dei patris
Þat is þe passioun and þe power · of owre prynce Ihesu
Þorw preyeres and þorw penaunces · and goddes passioun in mynde
40 I saue it til I se it rypen · & somdel yfruited
And þanne fondeth þe fende · my fruit to destruye
With alle þe wyles þat he can · and waggeth þe rote
And casteth vp to þe croppe · vnkynde neighbores

---

22 **toten**: Beta2 and C have *to toten*.

24 **I** (2): Dropped by MR. The punctuation separating the repeated pronoun is established as **Bx** by LWHmOF, with a comma in Cr.

25 **witen**: "guard", punning on *wyte*. Alpha substitutes non-alliterating *kepen*.

28 **wynde**: Alpha skips to *wynde* in the next line, dropping l. 28b and l. 29a. The lines are both in **Cx** in a revised form.

28 **wolden**: All beta mss. except L have *willen*, but **Cx** has *wolde* (RK.18.31).

31 **Þanne**: So beta. R has *And* while F rewrites the line. **Cx** also begins this line *And*, but begins the next line *Thenne*. Since this section of the passus is so heavily revised in C, it must be used with caution as evidence for **Bx**.

31 **pyle**: In this long line LR have double punctuation, after *pyle* and *down* (Cr has commas). F abbreviates radically.

31 **palle**: "strike". Hm and beta4 have *pulle*, and F has *call* in its rewritten line.

32 WHmC and alpha here have a paraph marking the transition from World to Flesh.

39 **Þorw** (1): Alpha has *With*.

39 **þorw** (2): Omitted by beta4 and F.

39 **penaunces**: For variation with and without -*s*, see note to **Bx**.14.211.

Bakbiteres breke-cheste · brawleres and chideres
45 And leith a laddre þere-to · of lesynges aren þe ronges
And feccheth away my floures sumtyme · afor bothe myn eyhen
Ac liberum arbitrium · letteth hym some-tyme
Þat is lieutenant to loken it wel · by leue of my-selue
Videatis qui peccat in spiritum sanctum numquam remittetur &c
50 Hoc est idem qui peccat per liberum arbitrium non repugnat ·
Ac whan þe fende and þe flesshe · forth with þe worlde
Manasen byhynde me · my fruit for to fecche
Þanne liberum arbitrium [·] laccheth þe thridde plan[k]e
And palleth adown þe pouke · purelich þorw grace
55 And helpe of þe holy goste · and þus haue I þe maystrie

¶ Now faire falle ȝow Pieres quod I · so faire ȝe discryuen
Þe powere of þis postes · and her propre myȝte
Ac I haue þouȝtes a threue · of þis þre piles
In what wode þei woxen · and where þat þei growed
60 For alle ar þei aliche longe · none lasse þan other
And to my mynde as me þinketh · on o More þei growed
And of o gretnesse · and grene of greyne þei semen

¶ Þat is soth seide Pieres [·] so it may bifalle
I shal telle þe as tite · what þis tree hatte
65 Þe grounde þere it groweth · goodnesse it hiȝte
And I haue tolde þe what hiȝte þe tree · þe trinite it meneth
And egrelich he loked on me · & þer-fore I spared
To asken hym any more ther-of · and badde hym ful fayre

---

44 **breke-cheste**: "fomenters of quarrel". Beta2 misunderstands and writes *breke þe cheste*. R may represent alpha with the more transparent (though equally unique) compound *brewe-cheste*. F smooths to *& boosteris*. For the sense of the verb, cf. **Bx.18.374**, *þe bitternesse þat þow hast browe*. **Cx** drops the compound altogether.

45 After this F adds a rather good line about false executors.

46 **afor**: So beta. The reading *byfore* in CG and alpha is also that of **Cx** which always has *byfore* in place of *afore* (e.g. **Bx.17.311**, 20.130). See note to **Bx.5.12** for support of beta's reading.

47 **hym**: HmR have *hem*, but the antecedent is *þe fende*.

51 **whan**: Alpha's *what* is a misunderstanding of the syntax.

53 **thridde**: So L and alpha. All beta mss. except L read *firste*, though *thridde* is obviously correct (cf. ll. 31, 37) and supported by **Cx** (RK.18.50). This provides a clear example of agreement of M with beta1 in this part of the poem.

53 **planke**: So alpha. Beta reads *plante*, prompted, so KD (p. 146) suggest, by the flowers and fruit of ll. 46 and 52. **Cx** has the synonym *shoriere*.

54 **purelich**: "entirely". Alpha has *priueliche*.

57 **myȝte**: WHmF have the plural.

58 **threue**: "multitude". Only here in the poem. HmF corrupt to *þrowe*.

62 Only O places the punctus after *grene* where it would be expected.

63 **seide**: All beta mss. apart from L alter to non-alliterating *quod*.

63 **it**: GR omit.

To discreue þe fruit · þat so faire hangeth

70 ¶ Here now bineth quod he þo · if I nede hadde
Matrymonye I may nyme · a moiste fruit with-alle
Þanne contenence is nerre þe croppe · as calwey bastarde
Þanne bereth þe croppe kynde fruite · and clenneste of alle
Maydenhode angeles peres · and rathest wole be ripe
75 And swete with-oute swellyng · soure worth it neuere

 ¶ I prayed pieres to pulle adown · an apple and he wolde
And suffre me to assaye · what sauoure it hadde

 ¶ And pieres caste to þe croppe · and þanne comsed it to crye
[A] wagged wydwehode · and it wepte after
80 And whan [he] meued Matrimoigne · it made a foule noyse
Þat I had reuth whan Piers rogged · it gradde so reufulliche
For euere as þei dropped adown · þe deuel was redy
And gadred hem alle togideres · bothe grete and smale
Adam & abraham · and ysay þe prophete
85 Sampson and samuel · and seynt Iohan þe baptiste
Bar hem forth boldely · no-body hym letted
And made of holy men his horde · in lymbo inferni
There is derkenesse and drede · and þe deuel Maister

 ¶ And Pieres for pure tene · þat o pile he lauȝte
90 And hitte after hym · happe how it myȝte
Filius bi þe fader wille · and frenesse of spiritus sancti
To go robbe þat raggeman · and reue þe fruit fro hym

 ¶ And þanne spakke spiritus sanctus · in Gabrieles mouthe
To a mayde þat hiȝte Marye · a meke þinge with-alle
95 Þat one Ihesus a iustice sone · moste iouke in her chambre

---

72 **nerre**: The forms *neer* and *nere* in other mss. may also be comparative; so Kane (2005), s.v. *neer, ner* prep.

78 **¶**: The paraph is in beta only.

79 **A**: "He". Beta and F have *And*, but R is supported by **Cx** (RK.18.108) where the antecedent is Elde rather than Piers.

80 **he**: Alpha is supported against beta's *it* by **Cx**, which again begins the line *A*, "He". See previous note.

81 **Þat**: Support from LMOGR. Cr omits, WHm have *And*, and F has *Þan*. The line is omitted in C.

81 **rogged**: "tugged, shook". R (= alpha?) oddly has *rused*, "drove", which F alters to the equally inappropriate *rusched*.

86 **hym**: GOR and original M have *hem*, repeated from the a-verse. The sg. is supported by **Cx** (RK.18.114).

89 **¶**: The paraph is in beta and F.

89 **o pile**: Beta2 evidently had *a pil* as in W, misunderstood by CrHm as "apple".

90 **And**: LMGO and alpha, supported by **Cx**. Beta2 begins *He*.

Tyl plenitudo temporis · [tyme] comen were
Þat Pieres fruit floured · and fel to be ripe
And þanne shulde Ihesus iuste þere-fore · [&] bi iuggement of armes
Whether shulde fonde þe fruit · þe fende or hym-selue

100 ¶ Þe mayde myldeliche þo · þe messager graunted
And seyde hendelich to hym · lo me his hande-mayden
For to worchen his wille · with-outen any synne
Ecce ancilla domini fiat michi &c
And in þe wombe of þat wenche · was he fourty wokes

105 Tyl he wex a faunt þorw her flessh · and of fiȝtyng couthe
To haue yfouȝte with þe fende · ar ful tyme come
And Pieres þe plowman · parceyued plenere tyme
And lered hym lechecrafte · his lyf for to saue
Þat þowgh he were wounded with his enemye · to warisshe hym-self

110 And did hym assaye his surgerye · on hem þat syke were
Til he was parfit practisoure · [i]f any peril fulle
And souȝte oute þe syke · and synful bothe
And salued syke and synful · bothe blynde & crokede
And comune wommen conuerted · and to good torned

115 Non est sanis opus medicus set [male habentibus]
Bothe meseles & mute · and in þe menysoun blody
Ofte he heled suche · he ne helde [it] for no maistrye
Saue þo he leched lazar [·] þat hadde yleye in graue
Quatriduanus quelt · quykke did hym walke

120 Ac as he made þ[at] maistrye · mestus cepit esse

---

96 **tyme**: So alpha and **Cx**. Beta alters to non-alliterating *fully*.

98 **&**: With R's reading, supported by **Cx**, *iuste þere-fore* applies to both clauses: "Then Jesus would joust for it, and by judgement of arms [joust for] whether the devil or he himself should taste the fruit." Beta and F drop *&* which is simpler.

99 **fonde**: "test", i.e. "taste" (*MED fonden* 3). Established for **Bx** by L, original M and CR. Scribes were puzzled and altered (as M does visibly) to *fonge*. **Cx** has *fecche*.

103 **&c**: HmGF complete the quotation from Luke. **Cx** has just the first three words.

107 **parceyued plenere**: So beta. R (and alpha?) has *parseyued þe plener*; F has *y parseuede in þat plener*. Lines 107–17 are not in C.

111 **if**: L's *of* is an obvious mistake.

111 **fulle**: The western spelling of "fell" in LHmR, and so probably in **Bx**.

112 **synful**: MOF have *þe synful*.

115 **medicus**: The word must have been abbreviated in **Bx**, hence the variety of endings, including G's *medicine*. See next note for further uncertainties.

115 **male habentibus**: Alpha's quotation is from Matt. 9.12 (see Alford (1992), 103). Beta was probably damaged, with the quotation ending in three minims (representing the first letter of *male*?) which LWHmCG transcribe as *in*. O reasonably guesses that *in* is for *infirmis*, while MCr solve the problem by dropping *in*.

117 **it**: The alpha reading. The omission in LMC suggests *it* was lost in beta but supplied by beta2 and GO.

120 **þat**: Alpha is supported by **Cx** *þat miracle* (RK.18.145) against beta's *þe*.

And wepte water with his eyghen · þere seyen it manye
Some þat þe siȝte seyne · saide þat tyme
Þat he was leche of lyf · and lorde of heigh heuene
Iewes iangeled þere-aȝeyne · [þat] iugged lawes
125   And seide he wrouȝte þorw wicchecrafte · & with þe deueles miȝte
Demonium habes &c

¶ Þanne ar ȝe cherles quod [ihesus] · and ȝowre children bothe
And sathan ȝowre saueoure · ȝow-selue now ȝe witnessen
For I haue saued ȝow-self · and ȝowre sones after
130   Ȝowre bodyes ȝowre bestes · and blynde men holpen
And fedde ȝow with fisshes · and with fyue loues
And left baskettes ful of broke mete · bere awey who-so wolde
And mysseide þe iewes manliche [·] and manaced hem to bete
And knokked on hem with a corde · and caste adown her stalles
135   Þat in cherche chaffareden · or chaungeden any moneye
And seyde it in siȝte of hem alle · so þat alle herden
I shal ouertourne þis temple · and adown throwe
And in thre dayes after · edifye it newe
And make it as moche other more · in alle manere poyntes
140   As euere it was and as wyde · wher-fore I hote ȝow
Of preyeres and of parfitnesse · þis place þat ȝe callen
Domus mea domus oracionis vocabitur
Enuye and yuel wille · [aren] in þe iewes
Thei casten & contreueden · to kulle hym whan þei miȝte
145   Vche daye after other · þeire tyme þei awaited
Til it bifel on a fryday · a litel bifor Paske
Þe þorsday byfore [·] þere he made his [cene]
Sittyng atte sopere · he seide þise wordes
I am solde þorw [sum] of ȝow · he shal þe tyme rewe

---

124 **þat:** R (F has *þo þat*) makes much better sense than beta's *and*. Lines 123–58 are thoroughly revised in **C**.

127 **ihesus:** Beta's obviously erroneous *ich* is likely to derive from the abbreviation *ihc*, as in R. F reads *crist*.

129 **self:** Beta follows this with *seith cryst* in order to clarify the speaker after the error in l. 127.

131 **fisshes:** Recalling Matt. 14, beta2 and F read *two fisshes*, and M is altered to that reading.

143 **aren:** The reading of the B-text seems to have been alliterating *arne*, "ran", south-western past tense of *rennen*, as in Cx (RK.18.163). R's *aren*, "are", reproduces the corrupt **Bx**, altered to *was* by both beta and F, realising that a past tense is called for. See KD, p. 186.

147 **cene:** So alpha, where beta has *maundee*. Either could be a substitution of the other, but it is more likely that to increase the alliteration of an ax/ax line beta substituted the fairly common phrase *made his maundee*, "celebrated the Last Supper" (*MED maunde* n. (2) (b)). Langland uses neither word elsewhere.

148 **atte:** "at the"; see note to **Bx**.P.107.

149 **sum:** "a certain one"; cf. Mark 14.18: "unus ex vobis me tradet". Beta alters to the unambiguous *one*, losing the alliteration.

150 Þat euere he his saueoure solde · for syluer or elles

¶ Iudas iangeled þere-a3ein · ac Ihesus hym tolde
It was hym[-self] sothely · and seide tu dicis
Þanne went forth þat wikked man · and with þe iewes mette
And tolde hem a tokne [·] how to knowe with ihesus
155 [Þe] which tokne to þis day · to moche is yvsed
Þat is kissyng and faire contenaunce · & vnkynde wille
And so was with iudas þo · þat Ihesus bytrayed
Aue raby quod þat ribaude · and ri3t to hym he 3ede
And kiste hym to be cau3t þere-by · and kulled of þe iewes

160 ¶ Þanne Ihesus to Iudas · and to þe iewes seyde
Falsenesse I fynde · in þi faire speche
And gyle in þi gladde chere · and galle is in þi lawghyng
Þow shalt be myroure to manye [·] men to deceyue
Ac þe wors and þi wikkednesse · shal worth vpon þi-selue
165 Necesse est vt veniant scandala · ve homini illi per quem scandalum venit
Þow I bi tresoun be ytake · at 3owre owne wille
Suffreth my postles in pays · & in pees gange
On a thoresday in thesternesse · þus was he taken
Þorw iudas and iewes · ihesus was his name
170 Þat on þe fryday folwynge · for mankynde sake
Iusted in ierusalem · a ioye to vs alle
On crosse vpon caluarye · cryst toke þe bataille
A3eines deth and þe deuel · destruyed her botheres my3tes
Deyde and deth fordid · and daye of ny3te made

---

152 **hym-self**: Perhaps the beta reading was *hym* as in L and original M, with other scribes making the obvious correction.

155 **Þe**: Beta's *And* is repeated from the previous line.

159 **of**: Beta has some support from **Cx** which has *cau3t of* (RK.18.169). Alpha reads *þoru3*.

163 **manye · men**: Punctuation as in R, which must be right. L's omission of punctuation may indicate uncertainty. In other beta mss. it follows *myroure*; in F it follows *merour after*.

164 **þi**: So LCrWCG. Repetition of *þe* as in alpha and other beta mss. is the easier error and makes rather poorer sense. In a revised line **Cx** has *thy wyles* (RK.18.174).

166 **at**: This, the beta reading, may refer back to *ytake*, "captured at your wish", or forward "freely allow my apostles". Perhaps there is elision alliteration on *at 3owre*. R has *and* instead; F has *and þorgh*. **Cx** has *and to 3oure will*, which can only refer back.

167 **my postles**: Though other mss. have *myn apostles*, LR are supported by the X family of C.

167 **in pays & in pees**: These may be variant spellings of "peace" but with different senses, as Schmidt (2008), 437, suggests. Kane (2005) derives *pays* from OFr *pais*, "country", though *MED* does not record it. C mss. show similar confusion.

168 **On**: Alpha has *In*.

169 **his name**: The reading of all mss. except F, which has *þan taken*. KD, p. 185, conjecture an original (and archetypal) reading *ynome*, misread as a "pointless homoeograph", but Schmidt (2008), 437, argues for "the importance of the *name* of Jesus", and sees F's reading as induced by *taken* in the previous line. C is revised in this passage.

175 ¶ And I awaked þere-with · & wyped myne eyghen
And after piers þe plowman · pryed and stared
Estwarde and westwarde · I [w]ayted after faste
And ȝede forth as an ydiote · in contre to aspye
After Pieres þe plowman · many a place I souȝte
180 And þanne mette I with a man · a mydlenten sondaye
As hore as an hawethorne · and Abraham he hiȝte
I frayned hym first · fram whennes he come
And of whennes he were · and whider þat he þouȝte

¶ I am feith quod þat freke · it falleth nouȝte [me] to lye
185 And of Abrahames hous · an heraud of armes
I seke after a segge · þat I seigh ones
A ful bolde bacheler · I knewe hym by his blasen

[¶] What bereth þat buirn quod I þo · so blisse þe bityde

¶ Þre leodes in o lith · non lenger þan other
190 Of one mochel & myȝte · in mesure and in lengthe
Þat one doth alle doth · & eche doth by his one
Þe firste hath miȝte and maiestee · maker of alle þinges
Pater is his propre name · a persone by hym-selue
Þe secounde of þat sire is · sothfastnesse filius
195 Wardeyne of þat witte hath · was euere with-oute gynnyng
Þe þridde hatte þe holygoost · a persone by hym-selue
Þe liȝte of alle þat lyf hath · a londe & a watre
Confortoure of creatures · of hym cometh al blisse
So þre bilongeth for a lorde · þat lordeship claymeth
200 Myȝte and a mene · to knowe his owne myȝte
Of hym[-selue] & of his seruaunt · and what suffre[th hem] bothe
So god þat gynnyng hadde neure · but þo hym good þouȝte
Sent forth his sone [·] as for seruaunt þat tyme
To occupien hym here · til issue were spronge
205 Þat is children of charite · & holicherche þe moder

---

175 Following this line F invents two lines to end its Passus 12 and another to begin Passus 13.
177 **wayted**: L alone has *awayted*. There is variation in the parallel line in **Cx** (RK.18.180).
184 **me**: Omitted by beta. R's order is supported by **Cx**.
188 **¶**: At this and the next line a paraph is marked by WHm and alpha to begin two speeches.
L has a paraph at l. 189 only.
194–6 These three lines are omitted in F by eyeskip from *hym-selue* to *hym-selue*.
197 **hath**: Alpha loses the verb and muddles the a-verse.
200 **a**: Omitted by WHmCO, but supported by **Cx** (RK.18.201).
200 **knowe**: Omitted by alpha. **Cx** has *se*.
201 **hym-selue**: The alpha reading carries alliteration and is supported by **Cx** against beta's *hym*.
201 **suffreth hem**: Whatever the b-verse means in alpha, it is supported by **Cx** against *þei suffre* in beta. See Schmidt (2008), 437.

KD.16.167–197

Patriarkes & prophetes · and aposteles were þe chyldren
And cryst and crystenedome · and [alle] crystene holycherche
In menynge þat man moste · on o god bileue
And þere hym lyked & loued · in þre persones hym shewed
210 And þat it may be so & soth · manhode it sheweth
Wedloke and widwehode · with virgynyte ynempned
In toknynge of þe Trinite · was taken oute of o man
Adam owre aller fader · Eue was of hym-selue
And þe issue þat þei hadde · it was of hem bothe
215 And either is otheres ioye · in thre sondry persones
And in heuene & here · one syngulere name
And þ[u]s is mankynde or manhede · of matrimoigne yspronge
And bitokneth þe Trinite · and trewe bileue

¶ Miȝte is [in] matrimoigne · þat multiplieth þe erthe
220 And bitokneth trewly · telle if I dorste
He þat firste fourmed al · þe fader of heuene
Þe sone if I it durst seye · resembleth wel þe wydwe
Deus meus deus meus vt quid dereliquisti me
Þat is creatour wex creature · to knowe what was bothe
225 As widwe with-oute wedloke · was neure ȝete yseye
Na-more myȝte god be man · but if he moder hadde
So wydwe with-oute wedloke · may nouȝte wel stande
Ne matrimoigne withoute moillerye · is nouȝt moche to preyse
Maledictus homo qui non reliquit semen in israel &c
230 Þus in þre persones · is perfitliche [pure] manhede

---

206 **chyldren**: Alpha's *barnes* is an attractive reading, and it is easy to suppose that beta is
repeating *children* in the previous line. But **Cx** also reads *childrene*.

207 **alle**: Easily lost in beta. Alpha is supported by the X family of **C**, though the P family
supports beta.

208 **on**: Cr and Alpha read *in*. Lines 208–27 are not in **C**.

212 **o**: "one". In LHmCOR, but dropped by MCrWG and F (which reads *mankynde*). CrW
reverse the word-order of the b-verse.

213 **aller**: "of us all", of which *alþer* in O is another form. The variants are interesting: Hm's
aldre is ambiguous, though *aldre-fader* suggests "ancestor" (see *MED eldre* and *eldre-fader*).
This is modernised by Cr as *olde father*. F reads *forme fader*.

217 **þus**: The reading of all beta mss. except L *þis*. But possibly L preserves the beta reading
since alpha has *þat*.

218 Beta4 omits the line.

219 **in**: Beta's omission leads CrW to alter the noun *Miȝte* to the adjective *Mighty*.

221 **He**: Altered to the more "correct" form *Hym* in beta2 and F.

222 **it**: As in LW and alpha, but unsurprisingly lost in the others. For *if I it*, CGO read *is if
I*, and alter the b-verse accordingly.

230 **pure**: So R (=alpha?); F rewrites as *þorghȝ*. R has support from **Cx** (*is puyrlich bote o
mankynde*, RK.18.233), and improves the alliteration. Having dropped the third stave, beta
misplaces the punctus, although since alpha does so as well it is probable that the misplacement
was in **Bx**, thus encouraging the omission of *pure* in beta.

KD.16.198–220

Þat is man & his make · & moillere her children
And is nouȝt but gendre of o generacioun · bifor Ihesu cryst in heuene
So is þe fader forth with þe sone · and fre wille of bothe
Spiritus procedens a patre & filio
235   Which is þe holygoste of alle · and alle is but o god
Þus in a somer I hym seigh · as I satte in my porche
I ros vp and reuerenced hym · & riȝt faire hym grette
Thre men to my syȝte · I made wel at ese
Wesche her feet & wyped hem · and afterward þei eten
240   Calues flesshe & cakebrede · and knewe what I thouȝte
Ful trewe tokenes bitwene vs is · to telle whan me lyketh
Firste he fonded me · if I loued bettere
Hym or ysaak myn ayre · þe which he hiȝte me kulle
He wiste my wille by hym · he wil me it allowe
245   I am ful syker in soule þer-of · and my sone bothe
I circumcised my sone · sitthen for his sake
My-self and my meyne · and alle þat male were
Bledden blode for þat lordes loue · and hope to blisse þe tyme
Myn affiaunce & my faith · is ferme in þis bilieue
250   For hym-self bihiȝte to me · and to myne issue bothe
Londe and lordship · and lyf with-outen ende
To me and to myn issue · more ȝete he me graunted
Mercy for owre mysdedes · as many tyme as we asken
Quam olim abrahe promisisti & semini eius
255   And sith he sent me to seye · I sholde do sacrifise
And done hym worshipe with bred · and with wyn bothe
And called me þe fote of his faith · his folke forto saue
And defende hem fro þe fende · folke þat on me leneden
Þus haue I ben his heraude · here and in helle
260   And conforted many a careful · þat after his comynge wayten
And þus I seke hym he seide · for I [herde] seyne late
Of a b[ui]rn þat baptised hym · Iohan Baptiste was his name

---

231 **her**: Support from Cx shows as usual that agreement of L and alpha is sufficient to establish
Bx. Dropped in the others.
232 **o**: Supported by LWCR as well as sense, although lost by MCrHmGOF.
232 **cryst**: To shorten a long line, GF drop *cryst* and Cr drops *in heuene*.
257 **þe**: Dropped by all except L, beta2 and R.
258 **leneden**: "leaned". Cr unambiguously has *leueden*, and F has *beleveþ* (G is altered to *leved*).
These three scribes regularly read "leave" for *lenen* in the sense "grant". The others may be read
as <-u-> or <-n->, but "leaned" is fitting where Abraham is *þe fote*. See Schmidt (1995), 400.
259 F omits the next two lines.
261 **herde**: L omits; the corrector notes the omission.
262 **buirn**: So alpha for beta's inappropriate *barne*.

KD.16.221–250

Þat to patriarkes and to prophetes · and to other peple in derknesse
Seyde þat he seigh here · þat sholde saue vs alle
265 Ecce agnus dei &c ·

¶ I hadde wonder of his wordes · and of his wyde clothes
For in his bosome he bar a thyng · [and] þat he blissed euere
And I loked on his lappe · a lazar lay þere-Inne
Amonges patriarkes and profetes · pleyande togyderes

270 [¶] What awaytestow quod he · and what woldestow haue

[¶] I wolde wyte quod I þo [·] what is in ȝowre lappe

¶ Loo quod he and lete me se · lorde mercy I seide
Þis is [a] present of moche prys · what Prynce shal it haue

[¶] It is a preciouse present quod he · ac þe pouke it hath attached
275 And me þere-[with] quod þat [wy] · may no wedde vs quite
Ne no buyrn be owre borwgh · ne bryng vs fram his daungere
Oute of þe poukes pondfolde · no meynprise may vs fecche
Tyl he come þat I carpe of · cryst is his name
Þat shal delyure vs some daye · out of þe deueles powere
280 And bettere wedde for vs legge · þan we ben alle worthy
Þat is lyf for lyf · or ligge þus euere
Lollynge in my lappe · tyl such a lorde vs fecche

---

263 **to** (2): Lost in beta4 and F.

263 **to** (3): Lost in beta4.

264 **seigh:** Beta is supported by Cx (and sense) against alpha's *seyde*.

264 **sholde saue vs:** Beta is supported by Cx against alpha's *schal sauen hem*.

267 **For:** Beta is supported by Cx (RK.18.270) against alpha's *And*.

267 **and:** Alpha is supported by Cx against beta's omission.

268 **on:** Support from LMCGOR confirms this as the **Bx** reading, even though beta2 and F have *in*, as in **Cx**.

269 **pleyande:** The present participle ending varies suggestively. Alpha, and perhaps **Bx**, may have had *-ende*, as in F, miscopied by R as *-ede*. *LALME* records this in Gloucs as well as East Anglia. HmG have *-eng(e)*, which is scattered but mainly south eastern. L's *-ande*, though often regarded as northern, is also found in London. See *LALME*, dot maps 345–8, and vol. 4, 105–7. And see Introduction, p. 17

270 **¶:** The paraph marking direct speech is supported by WHmC and alpha.

271 **¶:** The paraph marking the change of speaker is supported by WC and alpha.

273 **a:** Omitted in L.

274 **¶:** The paraph marking the change of speaker is supported by WHmC and alpha.

275 **with:** So alpha and Cx, and needed for the alliteration. Beta presumably had *myde*, altered as elsewhere to the commoner *wyþ* in HmCG (see **Bx**.6.69 and 15.324).

275 **wy:** So alpha and **Cx**, and needed for the alliteration. Beta alters to *man*.

277 The line is omitted by alpha. It is in **Cx**.

277 **pondfolde:** The form as in LWC is influenced by *MED pound(e* n. (2). Others have *pynfold*.

¶ Allas I seyde þat synne · so longe shal lette
Þe myȝte of goddes mercy · þat myȝt vs alle amende
285   I wepte for his wordes · with þat sawe I an other
Rapelich renne forth · þe riȝte waye he went
I affrayned hym fyrste · fram whennes he come
[W]hat he hiȝte & whider he wolde · and wightlich he tolde

283–6 These four lines are only in beta; alpha has three quite different lines, though beginning *Allas*, suggesting eyeskip following the word. Beta is supported throughout by **Cx**. KD explain it as "homoeoarchy" (*Allas I … I*) with the spurious lines added to bridge the gap in sense (p. 68).

287 **affrayned:** The form is supported for **Bx** by LWCR. Others have *frained*.

288 **What:** Beta begins the line *And what*. Alpha is supported by **Cx**, though notice that there the previous line begins *And*.

Passus 17

Passus septimus decimus et secundus de dobet

I am spes [a spye] quod he · and spire after a kny3te
That toke me a maundement [·] vpon þe mounte of synay
To reule alle rewmes [þere-]with · I bere þe writte here

[¶] Is it asseled I seyde · may men se þi lettres

5   [¶] Nay he sayde I seke hym · þat hath þe sele to kepe
And þat is crosse and crystenedome · and cryst þere-on to hange
And whan it is asseled so · I wote wel þe sothe
Þat Lucyferes lordeship · laste shal no lenger

[¶] Late se þi lettres quod I · we mi3te þe lawe knowe

10   ¶ [A] plokked forth a patent · a pece of an harde roche
Wher-on was writen two wordes · on þis wyse yglosed

---

1 a spye quod he: Alpha's word-order is supported by Cx (RK.19.1).

1 and: Omitted by R, but supported by Cx.

3 þere-: Omitted by beta, but supported by Cx.

4 ¶: A paraph is indicated by MW and alpha.

4 asseled: The form is supported by Cx against CrWG enseled.

4 þi: Supported by LWHmR. MCrCGOF have þe. Cx is split.

5 ¶: The paraph is supported by WC and alpha. L misplaces it at the start of the following line.

7–8 Beta's two lines are supported by the revised lines in Cx (RK.19.9–10). R reflects a corrupt alpha, conflating the two lines into one and adding a half-line for a smooth transition to l. 9: "And whan it is aseled so sathanas power schal last no lenger / And þus my lettre meneth". F typically fills out the orphan half-line: "& whan it ys a-selyd soo sathenas haþ lost his power / & þus myn lettre meneþ men mowe knowe yt alle". KD adopt F's expanded line.

7 asseled: Supported by Cx. CrWG again have enseled.

9 ¶: The paraph is supported by WHmC and alpha.

9 þi lettres: Beta is supported by Cx against alpha's þat lettre.

10 A plokked: So alpha. Beta begins Þanne plokked he, but is not supported by Cx. The form A, "He" (cf. F & he) is in C mss. and may represent Bx. See note to Bx.16.79.

11 was: L and alpha, supported by Cx, but altered to were in other beta mss. as elsewhere. Cf. Bx.5.13, 13.368, 19.47, 19.96.

Dilige deum & proximum tuum &c
Þis was þe tixte trewly · I toke ful gode [gome]
Þe glose was gloriousely writen · with a gilte penne

15 In hijs duobus mandatis [pendet] tota lex & prophetia

¶ Is here alle þi lordes lawes quod I · ȝe leue me he seyde
And who-so worcheth after þis writte · I wil vndertaken
Shal neuere deuel hym dere · ne deth in soule greue
For þough I seye it my-self · I haue saued with þis charme

20 Of men & of wommen · many score þousandes

¶ He seith soth seyde þis heraud · I haue yfounde it ofte
Lo here in my lappe · þat leued on þat charme
Iosue and Iudith · and Iudas Macabeus
[A]nd sexty þousande bisyde-forth · þat ben nouȝt seyen here

25 ¶ Ȝowre wordes aren wonderful quod I tho · which of ȝow is trewest
And lelest to leue on · for lyf and for soule
Abraham seith þat he seigh · holy þe Trinite
Thre persones in parcelles · departable fro other
And alle þre but o god · þus abraham me tauȝte

30 And hath saued þat bileued so · and sory for her synnes
He can nouȝte segge þe somme · and some aren in his lappe
What neded it þanne · a newe lawe to b[rynge]
Sith þe fyrst sufficeth · to sauacioun & to blisse

¶ And now cometh spes and speketh · þat hath aspied þe lawe
35 And telleth nouȝte of þe Trinitee · þat toke hym his lettres
To byleue and louye · in o lorde almyȝty
And sitthe riȝt as my-self · so louye alle peple

---

13 **gome**: "heed" (*MED gome* n. (4)), with citations from Robert of Gloucester and elsewhere.
The reading of R, with F substituting easier *keepe* and beta the cognate *ȝeme*. In C *gome* has
strong support, with *ȝeme*, *kepe* and *hede* as easier variants. Cf. **Bx**.10.206.

15 **pendet tota lex**: This is R's order, as in most C mss., with the other **B** mss. correcting to
the Vulgate order. See next note.

15 **prophetia**: "prophesy"; so LWHmR. The other mss. correct to *prophete*, "prophets", as in
Matt. 22.40.

16 **Is**: LRF supported by Cx (though note that F consequently alters *lawes* to sg.). Other
scribes correct to *Ben*.

16 **me**: Beta adds *wel*, but CrG and alpha and Cx are without it.

21 **He**: Supported by Cx against WHm *Ye*.

21 **seyde**: As in Cx. MO repeat the present tense.

24 **And**: Beta begins *ȝe and*, which is idiomatic but not supported by Cx.

25 **tho**: Dropped by beta4 and F and by the majority of C mss.

27 Puzzled by the alliterative pattern, CrWO punctuate after *seiþ*, with O having a second
punctuation after *seyȝ*.

30 **bileued**: G and alpha have the present, but beta is supported by most C mss.

32 **brynge**: Alpha is supported by Cx against beta's *begynne*.

37 **alle**: MCrF have *alle þe*. The C text is revised.

¶ Þe gome þat goth with o staf · he semeth in gretter hele
Þan he þat goth with two staues · to syȝte of vs alle
40   And riȝte so by þe Rode · resoun me sheweth
It is lyȝter to lewed men · a lessoun to knowe
Þan for to techen hem two · and to harde to lerne þe leest
It is ful harde for any man · on abraham byleue
And welawey worse ȝit · for to loue a shrewe
45   It is liȝtor to leue · in þre louely persones
Þan for to louye and lene · as wel lorelles as lele

[¶] Go þi gate quod I to spes · so me god helpe
Þo þat lerneth þi lawe · wil litel while vsen it

[¶] And as we wenten þus in þe weye · wordyng togyderes
50   Þanne seye we a samaritan · sittende on a mule
Rydynge ful rapely · þe riȝt weye we ȝeden
Comynge fro a cuntre · þat men called Ierico
To a iustes in iherusalem · he chaced awey faste
Bothe þe heraud and hope · and he mette at ones   id est cristus
55   Where a man was wounded · and with þeues taken
He myȝte neither steppe ne stonde · ne stere fote ne handes
Ne helpe hym-self sothely · for semiuyf he semed
And as naked as a nedle · and none helpe aboute

¶ Feith had first siȝte of hym · ac he flegh on syde
60   And nolde nouȝt neighen hym · by nyne londes lengthe

38–48 Eleven lines omitted by alpha, probably skipping a paraph. The C text is heavily revised, running parallel again from **Bx.**17.47.

47 ¶: The paraph is in WHmC, with a new line group in M. Alpha is not present.

47 **to**: Omitted by beta4, but supported by **Cx**.

47 **so**: MCr have *for so*, but this has no support from **Cx**.

48 **wil**: Supported by **Cx** against MCrHm *wel*.

49 ¶: Alpha resumes. The paraph is in alpha. In LM it has been missed at the top of the page. See note to ll. 38–48 and see Burrow (2010), 26.

49 **þus**: This is presumably the placement of the word in **Bx**, though CrF and **Cx** postpone it to the start of the b-verse.

50 **sittende**: This form of the present ppl. is shared by LRF, and so is probably that of **Bx**. All mss. generally have -*yng(e)*. L has -*ende* just three times, -*enge* once, -*ande* twice, and all these forms occur from **Bx.**16.269. R has -*ende* on the same three occasions, -*ande* once, and -*ynde* (a south-west midland form) once, in l. 52 below. M and W never have these forms. See variants at ll. 51 and 212 below. For distribution see *LALME* 1, dot maps 345–9.

51 **Rydynge**: F's *Rydende* may represent alpha, giving rise to R's *Ryden*. See note to l. 50.

54 **id est cristus**: This is written in the margin by the main hand in LMR. Hm has it in the margin in another hand.

58 **aboute**: Beta adds *hym*, as does the P family of C, but alpha is supported by the most reliable X family mss. It is easier to see why the word was added than how it might have been lost.

59 **of**: Again the C mss. are divided, with the best of the X family supporting beta, while the others have alpha's *on*.

¶ Hope cam hippyng after · þat hadde so ybosted
How he with Moyses maundement · hadde many men yholpe
Ac whan he hadde si3te of þat segge · a-syde he gan hym drawe
Dredfully by þis day [·] as duk doth fram þe faucoun

65   ¶ Ac so sone so þe samaritan · hadde si3te of þis lede
He li3te adown of lyard · and ladde hym in his hande[s]
And to þe wye he went · his woundes to biholde
And parceyued bi his pous · he was in peril to deye
And but if he hadde recourere · þe rather · þat rise shulde he neure
70   [And breyde to his boteles . and bothe he atamede]
Wyth wyn & with oyle · his woundes he wasshed
Enbawmed hym and bonde his hed · & in his lappe hym layde
And ladde hym so forth on lyard · to lex cristi a graunge
Wel six myle or seuene · biside þe newe market
75   Herberwed hym at an hostrye · and to þe hostellere called
And sayde haue kepe þis man · til I come fro þe iustes
And lo here syluer he seyde · for salue to his woundes
And he toke hym two pans · to lyflode as it were
And seide what he speneth more · I make þe good hereafter
80   For I may nou3t lette quod þat leode · & lyarde he bistrydeth
And raped hym to iherusalem-ward · þe ri3te waye to ryde

¶ Faith folweth after faste · and fonded to mete hym
And spes spa[r]klich hym spedde · spede if he my3te
To ouertake hym and talke to hym · ar þei to toun come

85   ¶ And whan I sey3 þis I soiourned nou3te · but shope me to renne
And suwed þ[e] samaritan · þat was so ful of pite
And graunted hym to ben his grome · gramercy he seyde
Ac þi frende and þi felawe quod he · þow fyndest me at nede

---

64 Only L punctuates after *duk*.

66 **handes**: Alpha's rather more difficult plural is supported by **Cx**.

69 **if**: Dropped by CrWGF and the P family of C, but supported by the best of the X family.

69 **recourere**: L's form is supported by R. Both LR follow the word with a punctus.

70 The line, the last of a series beginning *And*, is lost in beta. R's wording is supported by **Cx**, with *breyde to* revised as *vnbokelede*.

75 **to**: The beta reading; alpha is without it. The line is revised in **Cx**.

82 **folweth**: The agreement of LR is generally sufficient to secure the **Bx** reading, and the alteration to the past tense in all other mss. is easily explained as influence of the surrounding verbs. Nevertheless, **Cx** in a revised line (RK.19.80) also has *folewede*.

83 **sparklich**: "quickly." So alpha, a metathesised form of *MED sprakli*, and cf. *sprak*; a rare word, for which beta substitutes synonymous *spaklich* (*MED spakli*, and cf. *spak* and *spake*). Both are ON. See **Bx**.18.12 and note there.

86 **þe**: So alpha, which is supported by the same a-verse in **Cx** against beta's *þat*.

87 **grome**: It would be logical to adopt alpha's *gome* as difficilior, and that might be right. And yet *gome* appears 18 times in **Bx**, and is not a word avoided by either alpha or beta, whereas *grome*

¶ And I thanked hym þo · and sith I hym tolde
90 How þat feith fleigh awey · and spes his felaw bothe
For siȝte of þe sorweful man · þat robbed was with þeues

[¶] Haue hem excused quod he · her help may litel auaille
May no medcyn [vnder] molde · þe man to hele brynge
Neither feith ne fyn hope · so festred ben his woundis
95 With-out þe blode of a barn · borne of a mayde
And be he bathed in þat blode · baptised as it were
And þanne plastred with penaunce · and passioun of þat babi
He shulde stonde and steppe · ac stalworth worth he neure
Tyl he haue eten al þe barn · and his blode ydronke
100 For went neuere wy in þis worlde [·] þorw þat wildernesse
Þat he ne was robbed or rifled · rode he þere or ȝede
Saue faith & his felaw · spes and my-selue
And þi-self now · and such as suwen owre werkis

¶ For outlaw[e is] in þe wode · and vnder banke lotyeth
105 And may vch man se · and gode merke take[th]
Who is bihynde and who bifore · and who ben on hors
For he halt hym hardyer on horse · þan he þat is a-fote
For he seigh me þat am samaritan · suwen feith & his felaw
On my caple þat hatte caro · of mankynde I toke it
110 He was vnhardy þat harlot · and hudde hym in inferno

is used only here, where the sense "servant, attendant" is particularly appropriate, especially in view of the contrast with "friend" and "fellow" in the next line. There is no **Cx** parallel.

89 **sith**: F adds *þus*, which KD adopt on metrical grounds (p. 173). But F lost elision alliteration on *sith I* by altering to *sytthyn*. The line is not in C.

92 ¶: The paraph has been omitted from L at the top of the page, but is supported by MWHm and alpha.

93 **vnder**: Alpha's reading is supported by **Cx** against beta's *on*. The readings are discussed by KD, pp. 111–12.

96 **And be he**: "And if he be"; supported by LWHm. The other beta mss. have *And he be*, where *And* means "If". Alpha loses *he*, necessary for the syntax.

97 **passioun**: Alpha adds the definite article, creating a b-verse with two long dips.

98 O has lost 17.98–354.

103 **now**: All mss. punctuate after *now*, rather than after *such*. **Cx** has no parallel up to l. 127.

104 **outlawe is**: Misled by the lack of an article, beta misreads as pl. *outlawes* and F adds *an*. It is, however, to be taken as a proper name. See notes to next line.

105 **may**: The **Bx** reading is altered to pl. *mowe(n)* by MWHmCG following their misunderstanding of the previous line. Alpha naturally retains *may*, as does L, typically following his copy, and also Cr, for whom it was the standard pl. form.

105 **taketh**: So alpha. Again it is likely that beta altered the sg. verb to pl. *take*, though it works very well as an infinitive.

107 **a-fote**: L's form is also that of R. Others have *on foote*.

108 **seigh**: G and alpha have *seith*, but it makes poor sense.

110 **vnhardy þat harlot**: Alpha, copied blindly by R, skips from -*har* to *har*-, hence *vnharlot*. F makes sense of this with *but an harlot*.

Ac ar þis day þre dayes · I dar vndertaken
Þat he worth fettred þat feloune · fast with cheynes
And neure eft greue [g]ome · þat goth þis ilke gate
[O mors ero mors tua &c]

115   ¶ And þanne shal feith be forester here · and in þis fritth walke
And kennen out comune men · þat knoweth nou3te þe contre
Which is þe weye þat ich went · and wherforth to iherusalem
And hope þe hostelleres man shal be · þere þe man lith an helynge
And alle þat fieble and faynt be · þat faith may nou3t teche
120   Hope shal lede hem forth with loue · as his lettre telleth
And hostel hem and hele · þorw holicherche bileue
Tyl I haue salue for alle syke · and þanne shal I retourne
And come a3ein bi þis contree · and confort alle syke
Þat craueth it or coueiteth it · and cryeth þere-after
125   For þe barne was born in bethleem · þat with his blode shal saue
Alle þat lyueth in faith · and folweth his felawes techynge

¶ A swete syre I seyde þo · wher I shal byleue
As feith and his felawe · enfourmed me bothe
In þre persones departable · þat perpetuel were euere
130   And alle þre but o god · þus abraham me tau3te
And hope afterwarde · he bad me to louye
O god wyth al my good · and alle gomes after
Louye hem lyke my-selue · ac owre lorde aboue alle

¶ After abraham quod he · þat heraud of armes
135   Sette faste þi faith · and ferme bileue
And as hope hi3te þe · I hote þat þow louye
Thyn euene-crystene euermore · euene-forth with þi-self
And if conscience carpe þere-a3ein · or kynde witte oyther
Or heretykes with argumentz · þin honde þow h[e]m shewe

---

113 **gome:** In this case L's *grome* is shared only with C. The only other occurrence of *grome* in L is l. 87 above; see note there.

114–26 Line 114 is only in alpha and ll. 115–26 are only in beta. The whole passage, **Bx.**17.104– 26, is without parallel in **Cx**, which runs parallel again from **Bx.**17.127.

114 The line is only in alpha, and possibly not **Bx.** Cf. **Bx.**18.37. F expands the quotation.

115–26 Twelve lines only in beta: alpha has skipped from paraph to paraph.

116 **out:** Lost in beta4. For *kennen out*, "guide out", see *MED kennen* v. (1), 1b (c).

122 **retourne:** WHm have synonymous *turne*.

127 **I seyde:** Supported by **Cx**. CrHmGF reverse the word-order.

127 **I shal:** So LWR; the others reverse the word-order. **Cx** is different.

135 **faste:** WHm read *fully*.

136 **hi3te:** Alpha's *behi3t* avoids the repetition of the verb in the b-verse, but its usual sense in the poem, "vow, promise", is not appropriate here (cf. l. 131).

139 **hem:** So alpha supported by **Cx**, with beta presumably reading *him*, corrected by WHm.

140 For god is after an hande · yhere now and knowe it

¶ Þe fader was fyrst as a fyst · with o fynger fold[en]
Tyl hym loued and lest · to vnlosen his fynger
And profre[d] it forth as with a paume · to what place it sholde
Þe paume is purely þe hande · and profreth forth þe fyngres
145 To mynystre and to make · þat my3te of hande knoweth
And bitokneth trewly · telle who-so liketh
Þe holygost of heuene · he is as þe paume
Þe fyngres þat fre ben · to folde and to serue
Bitokneth sothly þe sone · þat sent was til erthe
150 Þat toched and tasted · a[t] techynge of þe paume
Seynt Marie a Mayde · and mankynde lau3te
Qui conceptus est de spiritu sancto &c
Þe fader is þanne as a fust · with fynger to touche
Quia omnia traham ad me ipsum &c
155 Al þat þe paume parceyueth · profitable to fele
Thus ar þei alle but one · as it an hande were
And þre sondry si3tes · in one shewynge
Þe paume for he putteth forth fyngres [·] and þe fust bothe
Ri3t so redily · reson it sheweth
160 How he þat is holygoste · sire & sone preueth
And as þe hande halt harde · and al þynge faste
Þorw foure fyngres and a thombe · forth with þe paume
Ri3te so þe fader and þe sone · & seynt spirit þe þridde
Halt al þe wyde worlde · with-in hem thre
165 Bothe welkne and þe wynde · water and erthe

---

141 **folden:** The past ppl. as in alpha is supported by the revised line in **Cx** (RK.19.115), and by **Bx**.17.171.

142 **hym loued:** Clearly the beta reading, though Hm alters to *hym lykede*, which is also the reading of **Cx**. On impersonal uses of personal verbs see Mustanoja (1960), 436. *MED* does not record impersonal use of *louen*, but cf. **Bx**.16.209, *hym lyked & loued*; the WCr reading in 13.349, *me loueþ* as against *I louye* in others. Alpha may have had the same reading as beta, with R misreading as *hym leued* and F altering to *he lyþed*, perhaps (very oddly) influenced by the collocation *lithe* and *lust* (*MED lithen* v. (3)).

143 **profred:** Beta has the infinitive, but alpha's past tense is supported by **Cx**.

150 **Þat:** Alpha makes weaker sense with *And* (R) or *& þorgh3* (F). The line in **Cx** is as beta's, but without *Þat*.

150 **at:** Beta is supported by **Cx**. Only L has *atte*, "at the". Alpha has *and*.

156 **hande:** Supported by **Cx** and by alliteration. Alpha repeats *fust* from l. 153.

158 **he:** WF have *it*; R repeats *þe paume*. There is no parallel in **Cx** until l. 171.

164 **Halt:** W moves the verb to the end of the line; Cr does the same, also reversing the a- and b-verses, and M is revised to match Cr.

164 **with-in:** Alpha reads *with*, and F adds *to-gydres* at line-end to make up for the loss.

165 **welkne:** CrHmGF add the definite article.

Heuene & helle · and al þat þere is Inne
Þus it is · nedeth no man · to trowe non other
That thre þinges bilongeth · in owre lorde of heuene
And aren serelepes by hem-self · asondry were neure
170   Namore þan [may an hande] [·] meue with-outen fyngeres

¶ And as my fust is ful honde · yfolde togideres
So is þe fader a ful god · formeour and shepper
Tu fabricator omnium &c
And al þe my3te myd hym is [·] in makyng of þynges

175   ¶ The fyngres fourmen a ful hande · to purtreye or peynten
Keruynge and compassynge · as crafte of þe fyngres
Ri3t so is þe sone · þe science of þe fader
And ful god as is þe fader · no febler ne no better
Þe paume is purelich þe hande · hath power bi hym-selue
180   Otherwyse þan þe wrythen fuste [·] or werkmanschip of fyngres
For þe paume hath powere [·] to pu[l]t oute þe ioyntes
And to vnfolde þe fuste [· for hym it bilongeth
And receyue þat þe fyngres recheth · and refuse bothe
Whan he feleth þe fuste · and] þe fyngres wille
185   So is þe holygoste god · nother gretter ne lasse
Þan is þe sire [or] þe sone · & in þe same my3te
And alle ar þei but o god · as is myn hande & my fyngres
Vnfolden or folden · my fuste & myn paume

---

166 **þere is Inne**: L's word-order is supported by alpha.
167 **is**: Dropped by Hm, beta4 and alpha. LW both clarify the syntax by punctuating after *is*.
167 **to**: Attested by L and alpha, but dropped by others.
169 **were**: All except L and alpha read *were þei*. The line is marked for correction in L, with the corrector perhaps supposing that a pronoun is missing.
170 **may an hande**: So alpha. Beta's possessive pronoun, *myn hande may*, anticipates the next line.
170 **fyngeres**: Following on from the a-verse, beta mss. apart from LHm add *my*.
174 L omits the punctus, MCrHm punctuate after *hym*, but WC agree with alpha in putting it after *is*.
176 **and**: Alpha reads *or*, probably following the construction of the previous b-verse. The line is not in **Cx**.
176 **as**: Alpha (together with Cr) reads *is*, adopted by both KD and Schmidt without comment.
180 **wrythen**: Alpha's misunderstanding *writen* is shared with three C mss. (RK.19.142).
181 **pult**: *MED pilten*, 3 "extend". R is supported by the X family of C, though as elsewhere most mss. alter to *putte* as beta does here. Cf. notes to **Bx**.1.128, 8.97, 11.167, 15.66.
181 **þe (2)**: Beta reads *alle þe*, but alpha is supported by **Cx**.
182 **fuste**: Beta has *folden fuste*, but **Cx** supports alpha. Beta, skipping from *fuste* to *fuste*, then drops the b-verse of l. 182, l. 183, and the a-verse of l. 184.
182 **for hym it bilongeth**: R's form of the b-verse (lost in beta) is supported by **Cx**.
183 **bothe**: **Cx** reads *yf hym liketh*.
184 **and**: So alpha. Beta's *at* (as in beta4) links 182a with 184b. The line is revised in **Cx**.
186 **or**: Alpha is supported by **Cx** against beta's *and*.

Al is [it] but an hande · how-so I torne it
190 Ac who is herte in þe hande · euene in þe myddes
He may receyue riȝt nouȝte · resoun it sheweth
For þe fyngres þat folde shulde · and þe fuste make
For peyne of þe paume · powere hem failleth
To clicche or to clawe · to clyppe or to holde

195 ¶ Were þe myddel of myn honde · ymaymed or ypersshed
I shulde receyue riȝte nouȝte · of þat I reche myȝte
Ac þough my thombe & my fyngres [·] bothe were to-shullen
And þe myddel of myn hande · with-oute male-ese
In many kynnes maneres · I myȝte my-self helpe
200 Bothe meue and amende · þough alle my fyngres oke
Bi þis skil [he seide] · I se an euydence
Þat who-so synneth in þe seynt spirit [·] assoilled worth he neure
Noither here ne elles-where · as I herde telle
Qui peccat in spiritu sancto &c
205 For he prikketh god as in þe paume · þat peccat in spiritu sancto
For god þe fader is as a fuste [·] þe sone is as a fynger
The holy goste of heuene · is as it were þe pawme
So who-so synneth [aȝeins þe] seynt spirit · it semeth þat he greueth
God þat he grypeth with · and wolde his grace quenche

210 ¶ [For] to a torche or [to] a tapre · þe trinitee is lykned
As wex and a weke · were twyned togideres
And þanne a fyre flaumende · forth oute of bothe
And as wex and weyke · and [warme] fyre togyderes
Fostren forth a flaumbe · and a feyre leye
215 So doth þe sire & þe sone · & also spiritus sanctus

---

189 **it** (1): Lost in beta. Alpha is supported by **Cx**, though several C mss. also omit it.

189 **how-so I torne it**: 189b and 190a are lost in beta mss. apart from LCr, skipping from *hande* to *hande*. The M corrector adds the missing words, which are in **Cx**.

191 Beta4 drops this line, and F loses 191b-196a through eyeskip.

195 **ypersshed**: "pierced" (R has *ypersed*). The other beta mss. have *perisshed* etc., which *MED percen* lists as a variant spelling, though it seems more probable that scribes took it to be *perishen*. Lines 195b-8a are not in **Cx**.

197 **to-shullen**: This is evidently the beta reading, with M altering to the easier *to-swollen* in agreement with Hm and alpha. *MED* ?*toshellen*, "shatter", cites no other instances.

201 **he seide**: Alpha is supported by alliteration and the reading of **Cx** against beta's *me þynketh*.

204 **in spiritu sancto**: Bx has ablatives here and in l. 205, as does the X family of C, which other C mss. "correct" to accusative. See Schmidt (1995), 401, and cf. **Bx**.16.49.

208 **aȝeins þe**: Beta's *in* (with MWC adding *þe*) is a literal translation of ll. 204-05. Alpha is supported by **Cx**.

210 **For**: Beta has *And*, but alpha is supported by **Cx**.

210 **to** (2): Omitted by beta, but supported by **Cx**.

212 **flaumende**: The unusual present ppl. form is shared by LR. See note to l. 50 above.

213 **warme**: Alpha's reading, supported by alliteration and by **Cx**. Beta has *hote*.

Fostren forth amonges folke · loue & bileue
Þat alkyn crystene [·] clenseth of synnes
And as þow seest some-tyme [·] sodeynliche a torche
The blase þere-of yblowe out · ȝet brenneth þe weyke
220 With-oute leye or liȝte · þat þe macche brenneth
So is þe holygost god · & grace with-oute mercy
To alle vnkynde creatures · þat coueite to destruye
Lele loue other lyf · þat owre lorde shapte

¶ And as glowande gledes · gladieth nouȝte þis werkmen
225 Þat worchen & waken [·] in wyntres niȝtes
As doth a kex or a candel · þat cauȝte hath fyre & blaseth
Namore doth sire ne sone · ne seynt spirit togyderes
Graunte no grace · ne forȝifnesse of synnes
Til þe holi goste gynne · to glowe and to blase
230 So þat þe holygoste · gloweth but as a glede
Tyl þat lele loue · ligge on hym & blowe
And þanne flaumbeth he as fyre [·] on fader & on filius
And melteth her myȝte in-to mercy · as men may se in wyntre
Ysekeles in eueses [·] þorw hete of þe sonne
235 Melteth in a mynut-while · to myst & to watre
So grace of þe holygoste · þe grete myȝte of þe trinite
Melteth to mercy · to mercyable & to non other
And as wex with-outen more · on a warme glede
Wil brennen & blasen · be þei to-gyderes
240 And solacen hem þat may se · þat sitten in derkenesse
So wole þe fader forȝif [·] folke of mylde hertes
Þat reufulliche repenten · & restitucioun make
In as moche as þei mowen · amenden & payen
And if it suffice nouȝte for assetz · þat in suche a wille deyeth
245 Mercy for his mekenesse · wil make good þe remenaunte

---

216 The line is omitted by WHm.

224–50 These 27 lines are omitted by alpha, skipping from paraph to paraph. The passage as in beta is almost identical in Cx.

224 **glowande:** The *-ande* form of the present ppl. is used only once elsewhere in L, *pleyande* **Bx**.16.269. See note to l. 50 above.

228 **Graunte:** L has the *-eth* ending of the present plural, but the infinitive (as in all other mss. and **Cx**) is required after *doth*.

234 **eueses:** The form is supported by LMCrHm. WCG have *euesynges*, which is the form in C mss.

237 **to** (1): L has *in-to*, picked up from l. 233. **Cx** supports *to*.

239 **be þei:** Supported by **Cx** against *all* in MCr.

240 **may:** Clearly an error for *may not* as in **Cx** (RK.19.203). In the absence of alpha, it is impossible to determine whether beta or **Bx** is responsible for the mistake.

244 **assetz:** "reparation" (sg.). The form in CrHmC ending *-eth* is a variant spelling.

And as þe weyke and fyre · wil make a warme flaumbe
For to myrthe men with · þat in merke sitten
So wil cryst of his curteisye · and men crye hym mercy
Bothe forȝiue & forȝete · & ȝet bidde for vs
250 To þe fader of heuene · forȝyuenesse to haue

¶ Ac hew fyre at a flynte · fowre hundreth wyntre
Bot þow haue [tacche] to take it with · tondre or broches
Al þi laboure is loste · and al þi longe trauaille
For may no fyre flaumbe make · faille it his kynde
255 So is þe holy gost god · & grace with-outen mercy
To alle vnkynde creatures · cryst hym-self witnesseth
Amen dico vobis nescio vos &c ·

¶ Be vnkynde to þin euene-cristene · and al þat þow canst bidden
Delen & do penaunce · day & nyȝte euere
260 And purchace al þe pardoun [·] of Pampiloun & Rome
And indulgences ynowe · & be ingratus to þi kynde
Þe holy goste hereth þe nouȝt · ne helpe may þe by resoun
For vnkyndenesse quencheth hym · þat he can nouȝte shyne
Ne brenne ne blase clere · for blowynge of vnkyndenesse
265 Poule þe apostle [·] preueth wher I lye
Si linguis hominum loquar &c
For-thy beth war ȝe wyse men · þat with þe wo[r]lde deleth
That riche ben & resoun knoweth · reuleth wel ȝowre soule
Beth nouȝte vnkynde I conseille ȝow · to ȝowre euene-crystene
270 For many of ȝow riche men · bi my soule men telleth
Ȝe brenne but ȝe blaseth nouȝte · [&] þat is a blynde bekene
Non omnis qui dicit domine domine intrabit &c ·

¶ Diues deyed dampned · for his vnkyndenesse
Of his mete & his moneye [·] to men that it neded
275 Vch a riche I rede · rewarde at hym take
And gyueth ȝowre good to þat god · þat grace of ariseth

---

247 **with**: Supported by **Cx**. CrW have *myd*. W alone has *myd* at **Bx**.P.147, 1.117, 15.261.
251 **at a**: Beta is supported by the X family of *C*, while the P family has *of a*.
252 **tacche**: Alpha is supported by **Cx**, with confusion among some scribes. *MED tach(e* n.
(2), "tinder", has no other citations of the word. Beta has *towe*, "flax".
261 **ingratus**: The X family of *C* generally supports this beta reading, while the P family
supports alpha's *ingrat*.
261 **kynde**: Beta is supported by **Cx** against alpha's *kynne*.
265 **wher**: "whether".
267 **worlde**: The corrector has noted the error in L.
271 **&**: Alpha is supported by **Cx** against beta's omission of the word.
274 **& his**: So LMC. The reading is uncertain. The other beta copies have *and of his*, R has
and, and F rewrites. *C* mss. are split between the two beta versions.

For þat ben vnkynde to his · hope I none other
But þei dwelle þere diues is · dayes with-outen ende
Þus is vnkyndenesse þe contrarie · þat quencheth as it were
280 Þe grace of þe holy gooste · goddes owne kynde
For þat kynde dothe vnkynde fordoth · as þese cursed theues
Vnkynde cristene men · for coueityse & enuye
Sleeth a man for his moebles · wyth mouth or wyth handes
For þat þe holygoste hath to kepe · þo harlotes destroyeth
285 Þe which is lyf & loue · þe leye of mannes bodye
For euery manere good man · may be likned to a torche
Or elles to a tapre · to reuerence þe Trinitee
And who-[so] morthereth a good man · me thynketh by myn Inwyt
He fordoth þe leuest lyʒte · þat owre lorde loueth

290 ¶ Ac ʒut in many mo maneres · men offenden þe holygoste
Ac þis is þe worste wyse · þat any wiʒte myʒte
Synnen aʒein þe seynt spirit · assenten to destruye
For coueityse of any kynnes þinge · þat cryst dere bouʒte
How myʒte he axe mercy · or any mercy hym helpe
295 Þat wykkedlich & willefullich · wolde mercy anynte
Innocence is nexte god · & nyʒte and day it crieth
Veniaunce veniaunce · forʒiue be it neuere
That shent vs & shadde owre blode · forshapte vs as it [semed]
Vindica sanguinem iustorum
300 Thus veniaunce veniaunce [·] verrey charite asketh
And sith holicherche & charite [·] chargeth þis so sore
Leue I neure that owre lorde [·] wil loue þat charite lakketh
Ne haue pite for any preyere · þere þat he pleyneth

¶ I pose I hadde synned so · and shulde now deye
305 And now am sory þat [I] so · þe seint spirit agulte
Confesse me & crye his grace · god þat al made
And myldliche his mercy axe · myʒte I nouʒte be saued

---

277 **þat**: WHmCG have *þei þat* (F *þo þat*). The P family of C also add a pronoun, with *ʒe þat* (RK.19.253).

281 LWHmCG punctuate after **fordoth**, R after *deth*, while MF punctuate at both points.

288 **who-so**: LW have *who*, perhaps representing the beta reading, with MCr reading *who þat*. However HmCG and alpha and **Cx** agree on *who-so*.

294 The line is omitted in beta3 and beta4 but attested in **Cx**.

298 **vs** (1): Dropped by alpha, but attested in **Cx**.

298 **semed**: Beta has *were*, but R is supported by most C mss., with a few reading *semeth* as in F.

305 **now**: Alpha's *nouʒt* is an obvious misreading, perhaps of archetypal *nouthe*.

305 **I**: The placement of the pronoun is supported by **Cx**. However, it may not represent **Bx**. L omits it entirely, R postpones it to the b-verse, MWHm have it twice in the a-verse. It is possible that **Bx** omitted it, as in L.

¶ ʒus seide þe Samaritan · so þow myʒte[st] repente
Þat riʒtwisnesse þorw repentance · to reuthe myʒte torne
310 Ac it is but selden yseye · þere sothenesse bereth witnesse
Any creature [be] coupable · afor a kynges iustice
Be raunsoned for his repentaunce · þere alle resoun hym dampneth
For þere þat partye pursueth · þe pele is so huge
Þat þe kynge may do no mercy · til bothe men acorde
315 And eyther haue equite · as holywrit telleth
Numquam dimittitur peccatum &c
Þus it fareth bi suche folke · þat falsely al her lyues
Euel lyuen & leten nouʒte · til lyf hem forsake
[Drede of desperacioun · þanne dryueth awey grace
320 Þat mercy in her mynde · may nauʒt þanne falle]
Good hope þat helpe shulde · to wanhope torneth
Nouʒt of þe nounpowere of god · þat he ne is myʒtful
To amende al þat amys is · and his mercy grettere
Þan alle owre wykked werkes · as holiwrit telleth
325 Misericordia eius super omnia opera eius
Ac ar his riʒtwisnesse to reuthe tourne · some restitucioun bihoueth
His sorwe is satisfaccioun [·] for hym þat may nouʒte paye

¶ Thre þinges þere ben · þat doth a man by strengthe
Forto fleen his owne hous · as holy wryt sheweth
330 Þat one is a wikked wyf · þat wil nouʒt be chasted

---

308 **so þow myʒtest**: Construed with *þat* in the next line: "in such a way that". Alpha is supported by **Cx**. Beta has *so wel þow myʒte* (subjunctive).

309 **þorw**: Beta is supported by **Cx** against alpha's *to*.

311 **be**: Alpha supported by **Cx**. Beta is presumably trying to smooth a difficult construction with *þat is*.

311 **afor**: This is apparently the beta reading, with MCr and alpha regressing to the commonplace *bifore* as elsewhere. See note to **Bx**.5.12 for other examples. Nevertheless the reading of **Bx** is doubtful, since **Cx** has *bifore*.

312 **repentaunce**: Beta, as in **Cx**. Lost by R (= alpha), with F repairing with *gilt*.

313 **pele**: "accusation". So L + alpha, supported by **Cx**'s *apele*. Cr has *plee*, with M altered to that reading; the other beta mss. have nonsensical *peple*.

317 **lyues**: Alpha has the distributive sg., perhaps rightly. The b-verse is rewritten in **Cx**.

319–20 These two lines omitted by beta are supported by **Cx** (RK.19.293–4).

319 **þanne**: F's placement at the start of the b-verse is supported by **Cx**. R has it before *grace*.

319 **awey**: Supported by the P family of **Cx**; the X family is without it.

322 **nounpowere**: "impotence", beta as **Cx**. Alpha mistakes it for *nounper*, "umpire".

325 **eius (1)**: So beta, supported by **Cx** and its source, Psalm 114.9. This may, however, be a correction, since alpha has *domini*, as previously in **Bx**.5.293 (where F is lacking). See that note.

327 The line is in beta only. It lacks b-verse alliteration. The revised line in **Cx** has *suche as* or *suche þat* for beta's *hym þat*.

330 **chasted**: So LCR, supported by **Cx** against *chastised* in others. See again l. 341. The form (*MED chasten*) appears earlier than *MED chastisen*.

Her fiere fleeth hyr · for fere of her tonge
And if his hous be vnhiled · and reyne on his bedde
He seketh and seketh · til he slepe drye
And whan smoke & smolder [·] smyt in his sy3te
335　It doth hym worse þan his wyf · or wete to slepe
For smoke & smolder · sm[er]teth his eyen
Til he be blerenyed or blynde · and [þe borre] in þe throte
Cougheth and curseth · þat cryst gyf h[y]m sorwe
Þat sholde brynge in better wode · or blowe it til it brende

340　¶ Þise thre þat I telle of · [þus ben] vnderstonde
The wyf is owre wikked flesshe · wil nou3t be chasted
For kynde cleueth on hym euere · to contrarie þe soule
And þowgh it falle it fynt skiles · þ[at] frelete it made
And þat is li3tly for3euen · and for3eten bothe
345　To man þat mercy asketh · and amende þenketh

¶ The reyne þat reyneth · þere we reste sholde
Ben sikenesses & [other] sorwes · þat we suffren [ou3te]
As Powle þe Apostle · to þe peple tau3te
Virtus in infirmitate perficitur &c ·
350　And þowgh þat men make · moche deol in her angre
And [be] inpacient in here penaunce · pure resoun knoweth
Þat þei han cause to contrarie · by kynde of her sykenesse
And li3tlich owre lorde · at her lyues ende

---

331 **fleeth**: Beta has *fleeth fro*. Alpha, with the transitive verb as two lines above, is supported by the X family of **C**, while beta shares the reading with the P family.

336 **smerteth**: Beta repeats *smyteth* from l. 334, or anticipates l. 355. Alpha is supported by **Cx**.

337 **blerenyed**: The form (though misdivided in L) is supported by R's *blereneyed*. See *MED blere-eied*.

337 **þe borre**: This is clearly the authorial reading, attested by **Cx**. *MED burre* n.(1), 2(b), "hoarsness", cites only this instance of the phrase. Beta's *hors* and alpha's *cow3he* avoid a difficult phrase, and F restores alliteration by adding *a bold*.

338 **Cougheth**: R begins *He*, and F rewrites, but **Cx** supports beta.

338 **hym**: Beta probably read *hem*, corrected by MCG, but alpha is supported by **Cx**.

340 **þus ben**: So R. Beta has *ben þus to*, and F has *þus ben to*, with *vnderstonde* therefore infinitive rather than past ppl. In C the X family supports R, the P family supports F.

341 **wil**: Only R omits the relative *þat*, which is partly prompted by the same b-verse in l. 330. Although a number of **C** mss. have *þat*, the best do not.

341 **chasted**: LMCrCR supported by **Cx**. See note to l. 330.

343 **þat**: LHm read *þe*, but sense requires *þat*, which is the reading of **Cx**.

347 **sikenesses**: The form without *-es* in CrWCG may also be plural.

347 **other**: The reading depends on R alone, with the support of **Cx**.

347 **ou3te**: Alpha is supported by the more reliable **C** mss., though many have beta's easier reading *oft*. Confusion is likely, since *oft* is a possible spelling of "ought" in south-western texts. See Jordan (1974), para. 196, remark, and para. 294.

351 **be**: So alpha and **Cx**, but apparently lost by beta, and added on grounds of sense by beta2.

352 **cause**: Alpha repeats *resoun* from the previous line and loses the alliteration.

Hath mercy on suche men · þat so yuel may suffre

355   ¶ Ac þe smoke and þe smolder [·] þat smyt in owre eyghen
      Þat is coueityse and vnkyndenesse · þat quencheth goddes mercy
      For vnkyndenesse is þe contrarie · of alkynnes resoun
      For þere nys syke ne sori · ne non so moche wrecche
      Þat he ne may louye & hym lyke · and lene of his herte
360   Goed wille good worde · bothe wisshen and wil[n]en
      Alle manere men · mercy & forʒifnesse
      And louye hem liche hym-self · and his lyf amende
      I may no lenger lette quod he · and lyarde he pryked
      And went away as wynde · and þere-with I awaked

355 Here O resumes.
356 **is**: R drops the verb and consequently drops the relative in the b-verse. Beta4 has *Is* for
Þat is. LMF and beta2 are supported by **Cx**.
359 **lene**: Cr has *leue*; the others are ambiguous.
360 **wille**: Beta reads *wille &*, but alpha is supported by **Cx**.
360 **wilnen**: Alpha is supported by **Cx** against beta's *willen*.
361 **men**: Lost in MCr, which read *of*.
362 **hem**: MCr have *hym*.

Passus 18

Passus duodevicesimus & tercius de dobet

Wolleward and wete-shoed · went I forth after
As a reccheles renke · þat of no wo reccheth
And ȝede forth lyke a lorel · al my lyf-tyme
Tyl I wex wery of þe worlde · and wylned eft to slepe
5 And lened me to a lenten · and longe tyme I slepte
And of crystes passioun and penaunce · þe peple þat of-rauȝte
Rested me þere and rutte faste · tyl ramis palmarum
Of gerlis & of gloria laus · gretly me dremed
And how osanna by orgonye · olde folke songen

10 ¶ One semblable to þe samaritan · & some-del to Piers þe plowman
Barfote on an asse bakke · botelees cam pryke
Wyth-oute spores other spere · sp[r]akliche he loked
As is þe kynde of a knyȝte · þat cometh to be dubbed
To geten h[y]m gylte spores · or galoches ycouped

15 ¶ Þanne was faith in a fenestre · and cryde a fili dauid
As doth an Heraude of armes · whan aunturos cometh to iustes
Olde iuwes of ierusalem · for ioye þei songen
Benedictus qui venit in nomine domini

---

2 **reccheth:** WG's past tense is not supported by **Cx**.
4 **to:** Possibly not in **Bx**. It is added by the main scribe in L, omitted by R and by eight C mss.
6 **þat of-rauȝte:** As KD p. 176 argue, the line lacks sense in this position. They move it to follow l. 9, so that it depends upon *dremed*. Beta4 and F revise to make sense. It is not in **Cx**.
10 **þe** (2): Dropped by HmCGOF and the P family of C.
11 **pryke:** Cr and R (= alpha?) have the present participle as do many C mss. The infinitive after *comen* was becoming rarer; see Mustanoja (1960), 536–7.
12 **sprakliche:** As at **Bx**.17.83, beta reads *spakliche*. Here **Cx** supports alpha.
14 **hym:** Only L has *hem*.
14 **or:** This is confirmed as **Bx** by LMWHmR. Alerted by the unsatisfactory sense, F alters to *on* and beta4 to *and*. **Cx** also reads *and*.

¶ Þanne I frayned at faith · what al þat fare be-ment
20 And who sholde iouste in Iherusalem · Ihesus he seyde
And fecche þat þe fende claymeth · Piers fruit þe plowman
Is Piers in þis place quod I · & he preynte on me
Þis ihesus of his gentrice · wole iuste in piers armes
In his helme & in his haberioun · humana natura
25 Þat cryst be nou3t biknowe here · for consumatus deus
In Piers paltok þe plowman · þis priker shal ryde
For no dynte shal hym dere · as in deitate patris

[¶] Who shal iuste with ihesus quod I [·] iuwes or scribes

¶ Nay quod [faith but þe] fende · and fals dome [to deye]
30 Deth seith he shal fordo · and adown brynge
Al þat lyueth or loketh · in londe or in watere
Lyf seyth þat he likthe · and leyth his lif to wedde
Þat for al þat deth can do · with-in þre dayes
To walke and fecche fro þe fende · piers fruite þe plowman
35 And legge it þere hym lyketh · and lucifer bynde
And forb[i]te and adown brynge [·] bale deth for euere
O mors ero mors tua

¶ Þanne cam pilatus with moche peple · sedens pro tribunali
To se how doughtilich deth sholde do · & deme her botheres ri3te
40 Þe iuwes and þe iustice · a3eine ihesu þei were
And al [þe] courte on hym cryde · crucifige sharpe

---

20 **sholde**: Dropped by R, but supported by **Cx**.

21 **fecche**: R's third person is not supported by **Cx**.

22 A paraph, as in WHmC with a line-space in M, would be appropriate, but is not indicated in L or alpha.

23 **gentrice**: (*MED gentrise*), as in **Cx**. CrHm and alpha substitute *gentrie*.

25 **biknowe**: LW and alpha, against *knowen* or *yknowe* in others. However **Cx** has *yknowe*.

28 **¶**: The paraph marking Will's question is omitted in L but supported by WHmC and alpha and the line-space in M.

29 **faith but þe**: So alpha supported by **Cx**. Beta has *he þe foule*.

29 **to deye**: So alpha supported by **Cx**. Beta has *& deth*.

31 **or** (1): W and alpha read *and*, but this is not supported by **Cx**.

32 **likthe**: "is lying". Since this is the spelling in L and alpha, it was probably **Bx**'s form of *MED lien* v.(2). Cf. **Bx**.5.165 *lixte*. See Adams (2000), 186.

36 **forbite**: "bite through". R's rather odd reading was rejected by other B scribes, who read *forbete* or *for to bete*, but it is supported by the P family and three of the X family of C. It reflects *morsus tuus ero* in Osee 13.14, quoted by F and many C mss. in the next line. See Barney (2006), 25, citing Schmidt (1995), 402.

36 **adown**: Supported by **Cx** against *doun* in MCrHmG and alpha.

41 **þe**: LR have *her*, which is probably coincident error, since **Cx** has *þe* and there is no apparent reason for the other **B** scribes to corrupt.

[¶] Tho put hym forth a piloure · bifor pilat & seyde
This ihesus of owre iewes temple · iaped & dispised
To fordone it on o day · and in thre dayes after
45 Edefye it eft newe · here he stant þat seyde it
And ʒit maken it as moche · in al manere poyntes
Bothe as longe and as large · [a-]loft & by grounde

¶ Cru[ci]fige quod a cacchepolle · I warante hym a wicche
Tolle tolle quod an other · and toke o[f] kene þornes
50 And bigan of kene thorne · a gerelande to make
And sette it sore on his hed · and seyde in envye
Aue rabby quod þat Ribaude · and þrew redes at hym
Nailled hym with þre nailles · naked on þe Rode
And poysoun on a pole · þei put vp to his lippes
55 And bede hym drynke his deth yuel · his dayes were ydone
And ʒif þat þow sotil be · help now þi-seluen
If þow be cryst & kynges sone · come downe of þe Rode
Þanne shul we leue þat lyf þe loueth · and wil nouʒt lete þe deye

¶ Consummatum est quod cryst · & comsed forto swowe
60 Pitousliche and pale · as a prisoun þat deyeth
Þe lorde of lyf & of liʒte · þo leyed his eyen togideres
Þe daye for drede with-drowe · and derke bicam þe sonne
Þe wal wagged and clef [·] and al þe worlde quaued
Ded men for that dyne · come out of depe graues
65 And tolde whi þat tempest · so longe tyme dured
For a bitter bataille · þe ded bodye sayde
Lyf and deth in þis derknesse · her one fordoth her other
Shal no wiʒte wite witterly [·] who shal haue þe maystrye
Er sondey aboute sonne rysynge · & sank with þat til erthe

---

42 ¶: A paraph is appropriate, although it is only in Hm and alpha. In L the line is at the top of the page where a paraph is sometimes missed.

43 iewes: Dropped by alpha, but wanted for the alliteration and supported by Cx.

44 on: MG and alpha have *in* anticipating *in thre dayes*, but this is not supported by Cx.

47 a-loft: R (= alpha) and Cx; F has *on lofte*. Beta's *bi lofte* anticipates *by grounde*.

49 of: L's spelling *o* is probably a slip since the scribe does not use the form elsewhere.

52 þat Ribaude: Cx supports beta against R's *þe ribaudes* and F's *þo rybawdis*. Alpha's plural represents the two catchpoles.

53 þre: F has *fowre*, which the R corrector writes in the margin without deleting *thre* in the text. Cx has *thre*. For the opposing views of whether Christ's feet were nailed together or separately, see Geoffrey Shepherd (ed.), *Ancrene Wisse* (London, 1959), p. 57.

53 on: Supported by the P family of C, though the X family support R's *vp-on*.

54 vp: Not in R, nor in F in a recast line. Again C mss. are split, the X family supporting beta (RK.20.52).

61 Þe: Supported by Cx against *Til* (R), *Tyl þe* (F).

64 depe: Required for the alliteration and supported by Cx against alpha's *here*.

70 Some seyde þat he was goddes sone · þat so faire deyde
  Vere filius dei erat iste · &c
  And somme saide he was a wicche · good is þat we assaye
  Where he be ded or nouȝte ded · doun er he be taken

  ¶ Two theues also · tholed deth þat tyme
75 Vppon a crosse bisydes cryst · so was þe comune lawe
  A cacchepole cam forth · and craked bothe her legges
  And her armes after · of eyther of þo theues
  Ac was no boy so bolde · goddes body to touche
  For he was knyȝte & kynges sone · kynde forȝaf þat tyme
80 Þat non harlot were so hardy · to leyne hande vppon hym

  ¶ Ac þere cam forth a knyȝte · with a kene spere ygrounde
  Hiȝte longeus as þe lettre telleth · and longe had lore his siȝte
  Bifor pilat & other peple · in þe place he houed
  Maugre his many tethe · he was made þat tyme
85 To take þe spere in his honde · & iusten with ihesus
  For alle þei were vnhardy · þat houed on hors or stode
  To touche hym or to taste hym · or take hym down of Rode
  But þis blynde bacheler [·] þa[t] bar hym þorugh þe herte
  Þe blode spronge down by þe spere · & vnspered þe kniȝtes eyen
90 Þanne fel þe knyȝte vpon knees · and cryed [ihesu] mercy
  Aȝeyne my wille it was lorde · to wownde ȝow so sore
  He seighed & sayde · sore it me athynketh
  For þe dede þat I haue done · I do me in ȝowre grace
  Haue on me reuth riȝtful ihesu · & riȝt with þat he wept

95 ¶ Thanne gan faith felly · þe fals iuwes dispise
  Called hem caytyues · acursed for euere
  For þis foule vyleynye · veniaunce to ȝow alle
  To do þe blynde bete hym ybounde · it was a boyes conseille

---

72 **þat we:** R omits both words, and F omits *þat*. Beta is supported by **Cx**.

76 **A:** R (= alpha?) begins *Ac a* and F *But a*; there is no support from **Cx**, and it anticipates l. 78.

79 **tyme:** Beta is supported by **Cx**. Alpha's synonym *throwe*, though not an uncommon word, is used nowhere else in the poem. Both KD and Schmidt adopt it.

80 **hande:** R has *an hand* and F has plural *hondys*. The line is not in **Cx**.

86 **stode:** Alpha replaces with *stede*, not supported by **Cx**.

87 **hym** (1): Dropped by Cr and alpha but supported by **Cx**.

87 **hym** (3): Dropped by M and beta2, but supported by **Cx**.

88 **þat:** MCrW omit, LHm and beta4 have *þanne* (all except C before the punctuation). Beta has missed the construction *alle* (l. 86) ... *But*. Alpha is supported by **Cx**.

89 **vnspered:** Alpha substitutes the non-alliterating and easier synonym *opned*. **Cx** reads as beta.

90 **ihesu:** R (= alpha?) is supported by **Cx**. F has *crist* and beta *hym*.

96 **acursed:** Alpha adds *hem*, making the verb past tense. **Cx** supports beta.

97 **alle:** WHmG read *falle*, perhaps prompted by the alliteration, or perhaps resisting the notion that all Jews were condemned; see Schmidt (1995), 402. The reading *alle* seems securely

Cursed caytyue[s] · kni3thod was it neuere
100 To mysdo a ded body · by day or by ny3te
Þe gree 3it hath he geten · for al his grete wounde

¶ For 3owre champioun chiualer [·] chief kny3t of 3ow alle
3elt hym recreaunt rennyng · ri3t at ihesus wille
For be þis derkenesse ydo · deth worth [yvenkeshed]
105 And 3e lordeynes han ylost · for lyf shal haue þe maistrye
And 3owre Fraunchise þat fre was · fallen is in thraldome
And 3e cherles & 3owre children · chieue shal 3e neure
Ne haue lordship in londe · ne no londe tylye
But al bareyne be · & vsurye vsen
110 Which is lyf þat owre lorde · in alle lawes acurseth
Now 3owre good dayes ar done · as Danyel prophecyed
Whan cryst cam her kyngdom · þe croune shulde [lese]
Cum veniat sanctus sanctorum

¶ What for fere of þis ferly · & of þe fals iuwes
115 I drowe me in þat derkenesse · to de[s]cendit ad inferna
And þere I sawe sothely · secundum scripturas
Out of þe west coste · a wenche as me thou3te
Cam walkynge in þe wey · to helle-ward she loked
Mercy hi3t þat mayde · a meke þynge with-alle
120 A ful benygne buirde · and boxome of speche

¶ Her suster as it semed · cam softly walkyng
Euene out of þe est · and westward she loked

Bx, even though Cx (RK.20.97) also reads *falle* (P family) or *bifalle* (X family). WHmG may possibly be contaminated from a C text; see note to l. 394.

99 **caytyues**: So alpha and Cx. Beta probably had the sg., presumably referring (obviously wrongly) to Longeus. M hesitates, first adding -s and then erasing; CrHmO make the obvious correction.

104 **deth worth yvenkeshed**: The alpha reading is supported by Cx against beta's *his deth worth avenged*.

112 **her**: So L and beta4. Beta2 reads *of hire*, and M is corrected to that reading. The alpha reading is uncertain, with R *þe* and F *to his*. See next note.

112 **lese**: The beta reading is *cesse*, but since *cesse* is not a transitive verb, beta2 adds *of*, and M is corrected to that reading: "the crown (i.e. authority) of their kingdom should come to an end". L realises something is wrong, and leaves out the last word while waiting for further guidance. But *cese* is probably a beta error picked up from *cessabit* in the next line (only cited in beta), and alpha is right with *lese*. Cx rewrites the line.

113 **sanctorum**: Beta completes the quotation with *cessabit vnxio vestra*. Cf. **Bx**.15.631 for the same variation. Cx also varies: the P family has the full quotation (RK.20.112a).

114 **þe**: R's *þo* is not supported by Cx.

118 **þe**: R's *þat* is not supported by Cx.

121 **¶**: The paraph is in beta only.

121 **softly**: Supported by Cx. MW *soþly* is an odd misreading, with Cr *worthely* probably an attempt to make sense of that.

A ful comely creature · treuth she hiȝte
For þe vertue þat hir folwed · aferd was she neuere

125 ⁋ Whan þis maydenes mette · mercy and treuth
Eyther axed other · of þis grete wonder
Of þe dyne & of þe derknesse · and how þe daye rowed
And which a liȝte and a leme · lay befor helle
Ich haue ferly of þis fare · in feith seyde treuth
130 And am wendyng to wyte · what þis wonder meneth

⁋ Haue no merueille quod mercy · myrthe it bytokneth
A mayd[e] þat hatte marye · and moder with-out felyng
Of any kyn[de] creature · conceyued þorw speche
And grace of þe holygoste · wex grete with childe
135 With-outen wem · in-to þis worlde she brouȝt hym
And þat my tale be trewe · I take god to witnesse
Sith þis barn was bore · ben thretty wynter passed
Which deyde & deth þoled · þis day aboute mydday
And þat is cause of þis clips · þat closeth now þe sonne
140 In menynge þat man shal · fro merkenesse be drawe
Þe while þis liȝte & þis leme · shal Lucyfer ablende
For patriarkes & prophetes · han preched her-of often
Þat man shal man saue · þorw a maydenes helpe
And þat was tynt þorw tre · tree shal it wynne
145 And þat deth doun brouȝte · deth shal releue

⁋ Þat þow tellest quod treuth · is but a tale of waltrot
For Adam & Eue · & abraham with other
Patriarkes & prophetes · þat in peyne liggen
Leue þow neuere þat ȝone liȝte · hem alofte brynge
150 Ne haue hem out of helle · h[o]lde þi tonge mercy
It is but trufle þat þow tellest · I treuth wote þe sothe
For þat is ones in helle · out cometh it neuere
Iob þe prophete patriarke · reproueth þi sawes
Quia in inferno nulla est redempcio

---

125 ⁋: The paraph is in beta only.
125 **Whan**: Alpha's *And whan* is not supported by **Cx**.
128 **which**: Alpha's *swich* is not supported by **Cx**.
132 **mayde**: CrG and alpha are supported by **Cx** against beta's *mayden*.
133 **kynde**: "natural"; so alpha against beta's *kynnes*. The X family of C has *kynde*, the P family *kynde of*.
141 **while**: MCrHmF read *which*, but **Cx** supports the others.
147 **with**: GF read *and*. MCr drop *and* (2) and have it here. **Cx** supports *with*.
150 **holde**: L reads *helde*.
151 **trufle**: Beta has *a trufle*, but **Cx** supports R. F has the plural.
151 **I**: Dropped by alpha, but supported by **Cx**.
152 **þat**: WHmF add *he*, and the same mss. have *he* for *it* in the b-verse. **Cx** begins *That thyng*.

155 ¶ Þanne mercy ful myldly · mouthed þise wordes
Thorw experience quod [he] · I hope þei shal be saued
For venym fordoth venym · & þat I proue by resoun
For of alle venymes · foulest is þe scorpioun
May no medcyne helpe · þe place þere he styngeth
160 Tyl he be ded & do þer-to · þe yuel he destroyeth
Þe fyrst venymouste · þorw ve[rtue] of hym-self
So shal þis deth fordo · I dar my lyf legge
Al þat deth dyd furste · þorw þe deuelles entysynge
And riȝt as þorw gyle · man was bigyled
165 So shal grace þat bigan · make a good sleighte
Ars vt artem falleret

¶ Now suffre we seyde treuth · I se as me þinketh
Out of þe nippe of þe north · nouȝt ful fer hennes
Riȝtwisnesse come rennynge · reste we þe while
170 For he wote more þan we · he was er we bothe

¶ That is soth seyde mercy · and I se here bi southe
Where [cometh pees] playinge · in pacience yclothed
Loue hath coueyted hir longe · leue I none other
But he sent hir some lettre [·] what þis liȝte bymeneth
175 Þat ouer-houeth helle þus · [he] vs shal telle

¶ Whan pees in pacience yclothed · approched nere hem tweyne
Riȝtwisnesse hir reuerenced · for her riche clothyng
And preyed pees to telle hir · to what place she wolde
And in her gay garnementz · whom she grete þouȝte

---

156 **he**: "she", as at l. 170. The form in Cr and alpha; supported by **Cx** and required for the alliteration. See Introduction, pp. 17, 29.

161 **vertue**: Alpha is supported by **Cx**. Beta repeats *venym*, not implausibly.

162 **fordo**: Beta supported by **Cx** against alpha's *do*.

163 **dyd**: WHm take *fordide* from the previous line. In KD's listing of WHm agreements (pp. 38–9), over half occur in passus 17–19, indicating a different genetic relationship (beta3, so not including Cr) in the last part of the poem (see KD, p. 49). In passus 18 WHm uniquely agree in error at ll. 108, 209, 214, 222, 230, 256, 278, 338, 339, 441.

165 **sleighte**: The sense is poor, and comparison with **Cx** suggests that **Bx** has lost a line after *good*, skipping to *good* in the line that follows (RK.20.164–5). KD supply "[end / And bigile þe gilour, and þat is good]". See Schmidt (1995), 402–03. G's *end* (shared with Y) is by conjecture or contamination.

171 **¶**: The paraph marking the start of speech is in beta and F.

172 **cometh pees**: R's order is supported by **Cx**. Beta and F reverse to prose order.

175 **he**: The L scribe added an initial <s>, to agree with all other beta mss., but alliteration and **Cx** support alpha's form. See Introduction, p. 17.

178 **she**: In this case neither alliteration nor **Cx** supports alpha's *he*. Cf. notes to ll. 156 and 175.

179 **she**: In this case neither alliteration nor **Cx** supports alpha's *he*. Cf. notes to ll. 156, 175 and 178.

180 ¶ My wille is to wende quod she · and welcome hem alle
Þat many day myȝte I nouȝte se · for merkenesse of synne
Adam & Eue [·] & other moo in helle
Moyses & many mo · mercy shal haue
And I shal daunce þer-to · do þow so sustre
185 For ihesus iusted wel · ioye bygynneth dawe
Ad vesperum demorabitur fletus · & ad matutinum leticia ·
Loue þat is my lemman · suche lettres me sente
That mercy my sustre & I · mankynde shulde saue
And þat god hath forgyuen · & graunted me pees & mercy
190 To be mannes meynpernoure · for euere-more after
Lo here þe patent quod pees · in pace in idipsum
And þat þis dede shal dure · dormiam & requiescam

¶ What rauestow quod riȝtwisnesse [·] or þow art riȝt dronke
Leuestow þat ȝonde liȝte · vnlouke myȝte helle
195 And saue mannes soule · sustre wene it neure
At þe bygynnynge god · gaf þe dome hym-selue
Þat Adam & Eue · and alle þat hem suwed
Shulde deye doune-riȝte · and dwelle in p[e]yne after
If þat þei touched a tre · and þe fruite eten
200 Adam afterward · aȝeines his defence
Frette of þat fruit · & forsoke as it were
Þe loue of owre lorde · and his lore bothe
And folwed þat þe fende tauȝte · & his felawes wille
Aȝeines resoun I riȝtwisnesse · recorde þus with treuth
205 Þat her peyne be perpetuel · & no preyere hem helpe
For-þi late hem chewe as þei chose · & chyde we nouȝt sustres
For it is botelees bale · þe bite þat þei eten

---

180 **she**: Alpha has *he*. **Cx** rewrites. Cf. notes to ll. 156, 175, 178 and 179.

184 The line is preserved in beta only; it is in **Cx**.

187 **me**: R's *he me* has support from the X family of C, but the P family is without *he*.

188 **my sustre**: Dropped by alpha, but supported by **Cx** and by alliteration.

195 **wene**: Alpha's *wene þow* is not supported by **Cx**.

198 **peyne**: Alpha is supported by **Cx** and ll. 205, 208. Beta has *pyne*, "torment" (see *MED pein(e* and *pine* n.(1)).

199 **þe fruite**: This seems undoubtedly the **Bx** reading, despite the lack of alliteration. Hm *þe trees fruyt* corrects the alliteration. F *of þe frut* is the **Cx** reading, presumably by coincidence, influenced by l. 201.

204 **I**: The line is omitted by alpha, and beta mss. apart from L read *and*. The three best C mss. of the X family agree with L; other C mss. have *and* (RK.20.204). Schmidt (1995), 403, ascribes the error to "variation to the stock phrase, and misconstruction of the mood of *recorde* as imperative". Omission of *I* might be a **Bx** error, as at l. 208, with the correction conjectured by L, but such activity is untypical of the L scribe.

¶ And [I] shal pre[i]e quod pees · her peyne mote haue ende
And wo in-to wel · mowe wende atte laste
210 For had þei wist of no wo · wel had þei nouȝte knowen
For no wiȝte wote what wel is · þat neuere wo suffred
Ne what is hote hunger · þat had neuere defaute
If no nyȝte ne were · no man as I leue
Shulde wite witterly · what day is to mene
215 Shulde neuere riȝte riche man · þat lyueth in reste & ese
Wyte what wo is · ne were þe deth of kynde
So god þat bygan al · of his good wille
Bycam man of a mayde · mankynde to saue
And suffred to be solde · to see þe sorwe of deyinge
220 The which vnknitteth al kare · & comsynge is of reste
For til modicum mete with vs · I may it wel avowe
Wote no wiȝte as I wene · what is ynough to mene

¶ For-þi god of his goodnesse · þe fyrste gome Adam
Sette hym in solace · & in souereigne myrthe
225 And sith he suffred hym synne · sorwe to fele
To wite what wel was · kyndelich to knowe it
And after god auntred hym-self · and toke Adames kynde
To wyte what he hath suffred · in þre sondri places
Bothe in heuene & in erthe · & now til helle he þynketh
230 To wite what al wo is · þat wote of al ioye

¶ So it shal fare bi þis folke · her foly & her synne
Shal lere hem what langour is · & lisse with-outen ende
Wote no wighte what werre is · þere þat pees regneth
Ne what is witterly wel · til weyllowey hym teche

235 ¶ Thanne was þere a wiȝte · with two brode eyen
Boke hiȝte þat beupere · a bolde man of speche

---

208 **I**: Easily lost (see l. 204), but the agreement of LR suggests it might be a **Bx** error with
the obvious correction made by other scribes (note F has *I* for *And I*).
208 **preie**: Alpha is supported by **Cx** against beta's *preue*.
210 **had** (1): Omitted by alpha (added in F). **Cx** supports beta.
215 L has an unrubricated paraph marker but no blank line. It is inappropriate and not supported by other mss. Possibly it was intended for l. 213, where WHmR have a paraph.
219 **to** (2): Alpha reads *and*, but beta is supported by **Cx**.
221 **mete**: CrHmCGO and alpha have pa.t., as do a good many C mss.
222 **is ynough**: R's *is nouȝte* probably reproduces alpha, with F altering to make sense. **Cx**
supports beta.
223 **¶**: The paraph is in beta only.
224 **myrthe**: **Cx** supports beta against alpha's *ioye*, picked up from l. 230.
226 **was**: **Cx** supports beta against alpha's *is*, which is perhaps again picked up from l. 230.
232 **lisse**: Supported by **Cx** (RK.20.243) and alliteration over GR's *blisse*. F loses l. 232b and
l. 233a.

By godes body quod þis boke · I wil bere witnesse
Þat þo þis barne was ybore · þere blased a sterre
That alle þe wyse of þis worlde · in o witte acordeden
240   That such a barne was borne · in bethleem [þe] Citee
Þat mannes soule sholde saue · & synne destroye
And alle þe elementz quod þe boke · her-of bereth witnesse
Þat he was god þat al wrouȝte · þe walkene firste shewed
Þo that weren in heuene · token stella comata
245   And tendeden hir as a torche · to reuerence his birthe
Þe lyȝte folwed þe lorde · in-to þe lowe erthe
Þ[e] water witnesse[th] þat he was god · for he went on it
Peter þe apostel · parceyued his gate
And as he went on þe water · wel hym knewe & seyde
250   Iube me venire ad te super aquas
And lo how þe sonne gan louke · her liȝte in her-self
Whan she seye hym suffre · þat sonne & se made
The erthe for heuynesse · that he wolde suffre
Quaked as quykke þinge · and al biquash[e] þe roche
255   Lo helle miȝte nouȝte holde · but opened þo god þoled
And lete oute symondes sones · to seen hym hange on Rode
And now shal lucifer leue it [·] thowgh hym loth þinke
For gygas þe geaunt · with a gynne engyned
To breke & to bete [adown] · þat ben aȝeines ihesus
260   And I boke wil be brent · but ihesus rise to lyue

---

239 **wyse:** Supported by **Cx** and alliteration over alpha's *men*. Did alpha understand it as *wyes* as in a few C mss.?

239 **of:** Beta is supported by **Cx** against alpha's *in*.

239 **acordeden:** **Cx** supports the past tense as in LHmOR.

240 **þe:** WR are supported by **Cx**. Without it the b-verse would have the metrical form x / x / x usually avoided. Possibly beta had dropped it and W restored it on metrical grounds. R presumably represents alpha, with F dropping the article.

247 **Þe:** **Cx** supports CrWO and alpha against *Þat* in LMHmC (G has *Þat þe*).

247 **witnesseth:** Most C mss. support the present tense as in GO and alpha against the past tense in others.

251 **louke:** "lock". Alpha's spellings represent "look". **Cx** supports beta.

252 **se:** Beta is supported by **Cx** against alpha's *mone*.

254 **biquashe:** Probably Langland wrote *al biquashe þe roches* (plural: "all the rocks shatter"; cf. "petrae scissae sunt", Matt. 27.51), as in the X family of C, *al toquasch þe roches* (RK.20.257), but **Bx** obviously read *roche*. Alpha reproduces the verb, presumably taking it as the third-person present sg. with assimilated -*s* ending, though the ending is nearly always -*eth* in the **B** tradition. Beta "corrects" the verb form by making it past, *biquasht*, influenced by the context of past-tense verbs (though G has *byquassethe*). The P family of C also has the past tense, *toquasched*, but retains the plural noun.

257 **leue:** Beta is supported by **Cx** against F's *leese*. R omits the word.

258–9 These two lines preserved only in beta are supported by **Cx**.

259 **adown:** **Cx** supports MWHmCO against *dounn* in LCrG. The line is lost in alpha.

In alle my3tes of man · & his moder gladye
And conforte al his kynne · & out of care brynge
And al þe iuwen ioye · vnioignen & vnlouken
And but þei reuerencen his Rode · & his resurexioun
265 And bileue on a newe lawe · be lost lyf & soule

¶ Suffre we seide treuth · I here & se bothe
[A] spirit speketh to helle · & bit vnspere þe 3atis
Attollite portas &c
A voice loude in þat li3te [·] to lucifer cryeth
270 Prynces of þis place · vnpynneth & vnlouketh
For here cometh with croune · þat kynge is of glorie

[¶] Thanne syked sathan · & seyde to he[lle]
Suche a ly3te a3eines owre leue · Lazar it fette
Care & combraunce · is comen to vs alle
275 If þis kynge come in · mankynde wil he fecche
And lede it þer [Lazar is] · & ly3tlych me bynde
Patriarkes & prophetes · han parled her-of longe
Þat such a lorde & a ly3te · sh[al] lede hem alle hennes

¶ Lysteneth quod Lucifer · for I þis lorde knowe
280 Bothe þis lorde & þis li3te · is longe ago I knewe hym
May no deth [þis lorde] dere · ne no deueles queyntise
And where he wil is his waye · ac war hym of þe periles
If he reue me [of] my ri3te · he robbeth me by maistrye

---

261 **man**: Alpha has *a man*. The line is not in **Cx**.

264 **but**: MCrF have *but if*, but the others are supported by **Cx**.

265 Beta4 has an additional line following this. It is patently scribal and is not in **Cx**.

267 **A**: So alpha, supported by **Cx**. Beta begins *How a*.

268 Alpha treats the two Latin words as the beginning of l. 269. In C four of the X group do the same, while four of the P group place them at the end of the previous line.

269 **cryeth**: Beta4 has the past tense; **Cx** has *saide*.

272 **¶**: The paraph is not in L, but is appropriate and supported by WHmC and alpha, and the line-space in M.

272 **helle**: Alpha is supported by **Cx**. Probably beta was puzzled by the unusual personal use, which derives from the *Gospel of Nicodemus*, in which a devil is named "Inferus", generally translated as Hell (e.g. *MED helle* 1 (c)).

276 **it**: that is, *mankynde*. Beta is supported by **Cx** against alpha's *hem*.

276 **Lazar is**: Alpha is supported by **Cx**. Beta's *hym lyketh* is probably sheer inattention rather than objection to the implication that Lazarus is in heaven. Cf. l. 421.

278 **shal**: Alpha is supported by **Cx** against beta's *shulde*.

281 **þis lorde**: Alpha is supported by **Cx** against beta's *hym*.

283 **of**: Alpha is supported by **Cx** against beta's omission.

283 **he robbeth**: Beta is supported by **Cx** against alpha's *& robbe*, though the subjunctive, parallel to *reue* makes excellent sense, making the whole line conditional, explaining the *periles* (sc. of lawlessness) of l. 282.

KD.18.256–277

For by ri3t & bi resoun · þ[e] renkes þat ben here
285   Bodye & soule ben myne · bothe gode & ille
For hym-self seyde [·] þat sire is of heuene
3if Adam ete þe apple · alle shulde deye
And dwelle with vs deueles · þis þretynge he made
And he þat sothenesse is [·] seyde þise wordes
290   And [I] sitthen I-seised · seuene hundreth wyntre
I leue þat lawe nil nau3te · lete hym þe leest

¶ That is sothe seyde Sathan · but I me sore drede
For þow gete hem with gyle · & his gardyne breke
And in semblaunce of a serpent · sat on þe appeltre
295   And eggedest hem to ete · Eue by hir-selue
And toldest hir a tale · of tresoun were þe wordes
And so þow haddest hem oute [·] & hider atte laste
It is nou3te graythely geten · þere gyle is þe Rote
For god wil nou3t be bigiled · quod Gobelyn ne bi-iaped
300   We haue no trewe title to hem · for þorwgh tresoun were þei dampned
Certes I drede me quod þe deuel · leste treuth wil hem fecche

¶ Þis þretty wynter as I wene · [he wente aboute] & preched
I haue assailled hym with synne · & some-tyme [I] asked
Where he were god or goddes sone · he gaf me shorte answere
305   And þus hath he trolled forth · þis two & thretty wynter
And whan I seighe it was so · slepyng I went
To warne pilates wyf · what dones man was ihesus
For iuwes hateden hym · and han done hym to deth

---

284 **þe**: Beta2, C and alpha are supported by **Cx** against *þo* in LMGO.
287 **3if**: Alpha begins *Þat 3if*. The equivalent line in **Cx** has a different construction, beginning "That Adam and Eve" (RK.20.303).
290 **I sitthen I-seised**: "I being then in possession", an absolute construction. This is R's reading, with F simplifying the presumed alpha reading. Beta has dropped *I*, probably taking ppl. *I-seised* as pronoun + past tense. **Cx** has instead *we haen ben sesed* (RK.20.309).
290 **seuene**: Alpha adds *þise*, but it has no support from **Cx**.
297 **so**: Alpha's *al-so* is without support from **Cx**.
301 The line that follows in beta4 is evidently scribal. It is added in the Crowley revisions, Cr[2] and Cr[3].
302 **Þis**: For numeral + *wynter* treated as sg. cf. **Bx**.3.39, 5.561, 18.305. Here CrWC "correct" it to pl. with *Thise*.
302 **he wente aboute**: Alpha is supported by **Cx** and alliteration against beta's *hath he gone*.
303 **some-tyme**: Beta is supported by **Cx** against alpha's *some*.
303 **I asked**: Beta has the ppl. *yasked*, but alpha's pronoun + past tense is supported by **Cx**. Cf. l. 290.
305 **hath he**: Beta's word-order is supported by **Cx** against alpha's reversal.
306 **slepyng**: Beta2 reads non-alliterative *lepynge*, and M is altered to that reading. Perhaps the scribe didn't know the story.
307 **dones**: "sort of". For the form, see *OED done* ppl. a. (n.); Mustanoja (1960), 86.

I wolde haue lengthed his lyf · for I leued ʒif he deyede

310   That his soule wolde suffre · no synne in his syʒte

For þe body whil it on bones ʒede · aboute was euere

To saue men fram synne · ʒif hem-self wolde

And now I se where a soule · cometh hiderward seyllynge

With glorie & with grete liʒte · god it is I wote wel

315   I rede we flee quod he · faste alle hennes

For vs were better nouʒte be · þan biden his syʒte

For þi lesynges Lucifer · loste is al owre praye

Firste þorw þe we fellen · fro heuene so heigh

For we leued þi lesynges · [we loupen oute alle

320   And now for thi last lesynge ·] ylore [haue we] Adam

And al owre lordeship I leue · alonde & a water

Nunc princeps huius mundi eicietur foras

¶ Efte þe liʒte bad vnlouke · & Lucifer answered

What lorde artow quod lucifer · *quis est iste*

325   *Rex glorie* · þe liʒte sone seide

[Þe] lorde of myʒte & of mayne · & al manere vertues · *dominus virtutum*

Dukes of þis dym place · anon vndo þis ʒates

That cryst may come in · þe kynges sone of heuene

---

309 **I** (1): Alpha begins *And I*, but beta is supported by **Cx**.

309 **leued**: Alpha's present tense is not supported by **Cx**.

310 **wolde**: Alpha has *walde nauʒt*, and Hm *nolde*. There is no equivalent line in **Cx**.

314 **with** (2): Omitted by O and alpha, but **Cx** has it.

318 W and alpha have a paraph, perhaps prompted by *Firste*.

319–20 Beta loses 319b and 320a through eyeskip (*lesynges ... lesynge*). The X family of C does the same.

319 **we loupen oute alle**: Alpha only. R adds *with þe*, perhaps rightly, but it is unnecessary to the sense and metrically clumsy. **Cx** is rewritten.

320 **haue we**: Beta reverses to prose order. **Cx** is rewritten: *þere losten we blisse* (RK.20.347).

323–6 It seems evident that the quotations from Psalm 23.10 have become disordered in **Bx**. This would most easily have happened if at some earlier stage they were to the right of each line:

> Efte þe liʒte bad vnlouke · & Lucifer answered · *quis est iste*
> What lorde artow quod lucifer · þe liʒte sone seide · *Rex glorie*
> The lorde of myʒte & of mayne · & al manere vertues · *dominus virtutum*

All **B** mss. agree on the arrangement of l. 324, with *quis est iste* as the b-verse. Evidently, despite some rearrangement by F, **Bx**.18.325 began with *Rex glorie*. As the b-verse R (= alpha?) amalgamates and abbreviates 325b with 326; F abbreviates still further. LWC have *dominus virtutum* to the right of 326; MCrHmGO have it as a line on its own (with Hm expanding); R has it to begin 327, and F drops it altogether. **Cx** does not include the Latin phrases (RK.20.359–61).

326 **þe**: So alpha and **Cx**. Beta's *And* appears to be a consequence of the disordering; see previous note.

326 **mayne**: Supported by **Cx**. WR have *man*.

327 **Dukes**: Alpha has the sg. The C mss. are also divided: the P group has the sg., the X group the plural. But l. 270 has *Prynces*, and this is supported by the source, the *Gospel of Nicodemus*, which has *principes*.

And with þat breth helle brake · with Beliales barres
330 For any wye or warde · wide opene þe ȝatis

¶ Patriarkes & prophetes · populus in tenebris
Songen seynt Iohanes songe · ecce agnus dei
Lucyfer loke ne myȝte · so lyȝte hym ableynte
And þo þat owre [lorde] loued · in-to his liȝte he lauȝte
335 And seyde to sathan · lo here my soule to amendes
For alle synneful soules · to saue þo þat ben worthy
Myne þei be & of me · I may þe bette hem clayme
Al-þough resoun recorde [·] & riȝt of my-self
That if þei ete þe apple · alle shulde deye
340 I bihyȝte hem nouȝt here · helle for euere
For þe dede þat þei dede · þi deceyte it made
With gyle þow hem gete · agayne al resoun
For in my paleys paradys · in persone of an addre
Falseliche þow fettest þere · þynge þat I loued

345 ¶ Thus ylyke a lusarde · with a lady visage
Theuelich þow me robbedest · þe olde lawe graunteth
Þat gylours be bigiled · & þat is gode resoun
Dentem pro dente & oculum pro oculo
Ergo soule shal soule quyte · & synne to synne wende
350 And al þat man hath mysdo · I man wyl amende [it]
Membre for membre · bi þe olde lawe was amendes
And lyf for lyf also · & by þat lawe I clayme
Adam & al his issue · at my wille her-after
And þat deth in hem fordid · my deth shal releue
355 And bothe quykke & quyte · þat queynte was þorw synne
And þat grace gyle destruye · good feith it asketh
So leue it nouȝte lucifer [·] aȝeine þe lawe I fecche hem

---

329 **brake**: Beta is supported by **Cx** against alpha's *braste*.
330 **opene**: Alpha has the past tense verb, as does W and corrected Hm. The P family of C has the same, while the X family has the adjective.
334 **lorde**: Omitted by L.
350 **it**: Alpha has the pronoun, though F has it before the verb. R is supported by **Cx** in a slightly revised b-verse (RK.20.389). Note that in l. 352 beta has line-terminal *it* where alpha does not; see next note.
352 **clayme**: Beta has *clayme it*, but the object is *Adam* in the next line. See note to l. 350. The line is not in **Cx**.
355 **quykke**: M and beta2 have *quykene, quikne* (*MED quikenen*), but **Cx** supports the others.
356 **destruye**: "should destroy". Cr and alpha have the indicative. The line is rewritten in **Cx**.
357 **it**: L and alpha are obviously right and supported by **Cx**. Beta1 had *I*, which the M reviser corrects to *thow*, bringing it into line with G.
357 **nouȝte**: Beta is supported by **Cx** against alpha's *neuere*.

But bi riȝt & by resoun · raunceoun here my lyges
Non veni soluere legem · sed adimplere
360 Þow fettest myne in my place · aȝeines al resoun
Falseliche & felounelich · gode faith me it tauȝte
To recoure hem thorw raunceoun [·] & bi no resoun elles
So þat with gyle þow gete · þorw grace it is ywone
Þow Lucyfer in lyknesse · of a luther addere
365 Getest by gyle · þo that god loued

¶ And I in lyknesse of a leode · þat lorde am of heuene
Graciouslich þi gyle haue quytte · go gyle aȝeine gyle
And as Adam & alle · þorw a tre deyden
Adam & alle þorwe a tree · shal torne to lyue
370 And gyle is bigyled · & in his gyle fallen
Et cecidit in foueam quam fecit
Now bygynneth þi gyle · ageyne þe to tourne
And my grace to growe · ay gretter & wyder
Þe bitternesse þat þow hast browe · [now] brouke it þi-seluen
375 Þat art doctour of deth · drynke þat þow madest

¶ For I þat am lorde of lyf · loue is my drynke
And for þat drynke to-day · I deyde vpon erthe
I fauȝte so me þrestes ȝet · for mannes soule sake
May no drynke me moiste · ne my thruste slake
380 Tyl þe vendage falle · in þe vale of iosephath
Þat I drynke riȝte ripe must · resureccio mortuorum
And þanne shal I come as a kynge · crouned with angeles
And han out of helle · alle mennes soules

¶ Fendes and fendekynes · bifore me shulle stande
385 And be at my biddynge · where-so-eure me lyketh

---

358 **by**: Not in beta4 or alpha. The X family of C has *thorw* but the P family is without it, perhaps rightly.

360 **al**: Lost in R (= alpha), and F makes up for it by supplying *ryght &*.

363 **with**: So L and alpha, supported by the X family of C. Beta1 anticipates *þoruȝ*, as does the P family of C.

363 **is**: Beta is supported by Cx against alpha's *was*.

365 **þo**: Perhaps alpha's *þinge* is a recollection of the similar b-verse of l. 344, but the parallel might instead lead one to prefer it. There is no parallel in **Cx**.

369 **torne**: Beta adds *aȝeine*, providing vowel alliteration, and perhaps influenced by l. 372, but alpha is supported by **Cx**.

373 **wyder**: This must be the beta reading, though M originally repeated *gretter*, as in alpha. Cx has non-alliterating *wyddore and wyddore* (RK.20.400).

374 **now**: Alpha is supported by Cx. The line is lost in W.

378 **þrestes**: L and alpha share the very unusual *-s* inflexion, which may be a relict form. See also *answeres* P.140. *LALME*'s survey of the form covers the northern area only.

A[c] to be merciable to man · þanne my kynde it asketh
For we beth bretheren of blode · but nouȝte in baptesme alle
Ac alle þat beth myne hole bretheren · in blode & in baptesme
Shal nouȝte be dampned to þe deth · þat is with-outen ende
390 Tibi soli peccaui &c ·
It is nouȝt vsed in erthe · to hangen a feloun
Ofter þan ones · þough he were a tretour
And ȝif þe Kynge of þat kyngedome · come in þat tyme
There þe feloun thole sholde · deth or otherwyse
395 Lawe wolde he ȝeue hym lyf · [and] he loked on hym

¶ And I þat am kynge of kynges · shal come suche a tyme
There dome to þe deth · dampneth al wikked
And ȝif lawe wil I loke on hem · it lithe in my grace
Whether þei deye or deye nouȝte · for þat þei deden ille
400 Be it any þinge abouȝte · þe boldenesse of her synnes
I may do mercy þorw riȝtwisnesse · & alle my wordes trewe
And þough holiwrit wil þat I be wroke · of hem þat deden ille
Nullum malum inpunitum &c
Thei shul be clensed clereliche · & wasshen of her synnes
405 In my prisoun purgatorie · til parce it hote
And my mercy shal be shewed · to manye of my bretheren
For blode may suffre blode · bothe hungry & akale
Ac blode may nouȝt se blode · blede but hym rewe
Audiui archana verba que non licet homini loqui
410 Ac my riȝtwisnesse & riȝt [·] shal reulen al helle
And mercy al mankynde · bifor me in heuene

---

386 **Ac**: So R (= alpha), supported by **Cx**, with F altering to *But* as usual.

386 **to be**: Lost in alpha, with F repairing. Supported by **Cx**.

386 **þanne**: R (= alpha?) postpones until after the noun (F has *may not aske* for *þanne it asketh*). Beta is supported by **Cx**.

386 **it**: Clearly **Bx**, though dropped in WO (F rewrites). It is also dropped in **Cx**.

391 **in**: The phrase *in erthe*, "on earth", is found in **Bx**.15.219 (but see variants) and 18.229. R alone has *on* and is probably a reversion to the usual phrase, but since **Cx** also has *on* it may be right.

394 **otherwyse**: Beta3 (i.e. WHm) and C[2] read *oþer Iuwise*, "another judicial punishment", and G has a muddled and corrected *Iovnesse*. Beta3's reading is clearly superior and, crucially, it agrees with **Cx**, but it can hardly be **Bx**. It is too difficult to be coincidental, so it must be derived by contamination, as G's is likely to be. There is very little evidence of beta3 deriving readings from **Cx**, though see note to l. 97, and see Schmidt (1995), 403. Cr, evidently puzzled, reads *els*, and M is corrected to that reading.

395 **and**: Alpha is supported by **Cx** against beta's *if*.

396 **¶**: The paraph is in LHmF.

401 **may**: L and alpha are supported by **Cx** against omission in beta1.

402 **þat** (1): Dropped by alpha and G, but supported by **Cx**.

408 **blode** (2): Alpha's *his blode* is not supported by **Cx**.

For I were an vnkynde Kynge · but I my ky[n] holpe
And namelich at such a nede · þer nedes helpe bihoueth
Non intres in iudicium cum seruo tuo
415 Þus bi lawe quod owre lorde · lede I wil fro hennes
Þo þat [I] loued · & leued in my comynge
And for þi lesynge lucifer · þat þow lowe til Eue
Thow shalt abye it bittre · & bonde hym with cheynes
Astaroth and al þe route · hidden hem in hernes
420 They dorste nou3te loke on owre lorde · þe boldest of hem alle
But leten hym lede forth what hym lyked · and lete what hym liste

¶ Many hundreth of angeles · harpeden & songen
Culpat caro purgat caro · regnat deus dei caro

¶ Thanne piped pees · of poysye a note
425 Clarior est solito post maxima nebula phebus · post inimicitias &c ·
After sharpe[st] shoures quod pees · moste shene is þe sonne
Is no weder warmer · þan after watery cloudes
Ne no loue leuere · ne leuer frendes
Þan after werre & wo · whan loue & pees be maistres
430 Was neuere werre in þis worlde · ne wykkednesse so kene
Þat loue & hym luste [·] to laughynge ne brou3te
And pees þorw pacience · alle perilles stopped
Trewes quod treuth · þow tellest vs soth bi ihesus
Clippe we in couenaunt [·] & vch of vs cusse other

---

412 **kyn**: Beta repeats *kynde* from the a-verse. Alpha is supported by **Cx**.

412 **holpe**: Cx supports the past subjunctive as in LG and alpha, against the present in others.

415 The paraph in WHmCF, with the line-space in M, is prompted by the Latin line above, but is not in LR.

415 **owre**: MCr have *þis*, but the others are supported by **Cx**.

416 **I**: Alpha supported by **Cx**. Beta with *me* harmonises the subjects of *loued* and *leued*. F goes about it in his inimitable way, with *þei me be-leueden*.

417 **lowe**: "lied". This 2 sg. form is shared with alpha.

417 **til**: Beta supported by **Cx** against alpha's *to*.

425 The "proverbial" verses (Alford (1992), 113) are abbreviated by the more reliable beta mss. and set out as one line. Beta4 agrees with alpha in including *clarior est et amor* and setting over two lines. **Cx** does not offer clear guidance: the X family sets as one line and all but four C mss. abbreviate by dropping *post maxima nebula phebus* (RK.20.451a).

426 **sharpest**: Alpha's superlative is supported by **Cx** and translates *maxima*.

428 From this point R is defective until **Bx.20.27**. We do not always comment on an F variant if it has no support from **Cx**.

431 **Þat**: Most beta mss. have *Þat ne*, though CrC omit *ne* and it is erased in M. In the absence of R the alpha reading is uncertain, though F omission has the support of **Cx** (RK.20.457). See Schmidt (2008), 453.

431 **ne**: F reads *he* and Hm has *it*, but perhaps these may be supplied to fill out a short b-verse since **Cx** omits. See previous note.

432 **stopped**: M alters to the present, bringing it into agreement with WF. There is the same variation in C mss., but the majority have the past. F's addition of *he* has no support from **Cx**.

435 And lete no peple quod pees · perceyue þat we chydde
      For inpossible is no þyng · to hym þat is almyȝty

¶ Thow seist soth seyde ryȝtwisnesse · & reuerentlich hir kyste
      Pees & pees here · per secula seculorum
      Misericordia & veritas obuiauerunt sibi iusticia & pax osculate sunt
440 Treuth tromped þo & songe · te deum laudamus
      And thanne luted loue · in a loude note
      Ecce quam bonum & quam iocundum · &c

¶ Tyl þe daye dawed · þis damaiseles [carol]ed
      That men rongen to þe resurexioun · & riȝt with þat I waked
445 And called kitte my wyf · and kalote my douȝter
      Ariseth & [go] reuerenceth · goddes ressurrexioun
      And crepeth to þe crosse on knees · & kisseth it for a iuwel
      For goddes blissed body · it bar for owre bote
      And it afereth þe fende · for suche is þe myȝte
450 May no grysly gost · glyde þere it shadweth

---

435 **And**: Beta is supported by **Cx** against F's *ȝee*.

435 **chydde**: Only LCrW have the past tense. C mss. are divided: XYJ of the X family have the past, the others have the present.

437 **seyde**: LM against *quod* in the others. Choice is difficult. Is alliteration on /s/ (aaa/xx) or /r/ (xa/ax)? Most C mss. have *quod*, but XJ have *saide*. For other examples of such variation see **Bx**.4.190, 13.216 (*seyde* LMCrHmR, *quod* WCGOF), 16.63 (*seide* LRF, *quod* others), etc. In a-verses *seith sothe quod* occurs at **Bx**.11.109 and 11.455, *seith soth seyde* at 17.21.

438 **per**: CrG add *omnia* to the formula, as do a few C scribes. Since F is missing, the line is only in beta.

439 F truncates the verse, but **Cx** has it in full.

440 **songe**: F adds to the alliteration with *treblide*. It has no support from **Cx**.

443 **caroled**: F's *carolden* is the reading of the X family of C; the P family agrees with beta's *daunced*. The latter is easier, and perhaps motivated by the alliteration.

446 **go reuerenceth**: Beta drops *go*, but F is supported by **Cx**. Most C mss. have *reuerence*, the infinitive or uninflected imperative plural. Imperative *go* may be followed by either infinitive or imperative (Mustanoja (1960), 476, 535).

447 **þe**: L has *þe the* in error.

447 **to þe crosse on knees**: Beta is supported by the X family of C. F (= alpha?) and the P family reverse the order.

Passus 19

Passus vndevicesimus & explicit dobet & incipit dobest

Thus I awaked & wrote · what I had dremed
And diȝte me derely · & dede me to [kirke]
To here holy þe masse · & to be houseled after
In myddes of þe masse · þo men ȝede to offrynge
5   I fel eftsones a-slepe · & sodeynly me mette
That Pieres þe plowman · was paynted al blody
And come in with a crosse · bifor þe comune peple
And riȝte lyke in alle lymes · to owre lorde ihesu
And þanne called I conscience · to kenne me þe sothe
10 Is þis ihesus þe iuster quod I · þat iuwes did to deth
Or it is Pieres þe plowman · who paynted hym so rede
Quod conscience & kneled þo · þise aren Pieres armes

---

1 See Introduction, pp. 31–32 for discussion of the relationship between **Bx** and **Cx**, and F and **Cx**, in this passus.

2 **kirke**: Doubtfully adopting the CrF reading as the minority form. On the distribution of *kirke / cherche* see Introduction, pp. 18–19. RK's text has *kyrke*, recording no variants, though in fact P (as printed by Skeat) has *churche*.

3 Beta4 drops ll. 3b–4a.

4 **ȝede**: MCr and F have *wente*, but this is not supported by **Cx**.

5 **me mette**: Supported by **Cx** against F's *y drempte*. We shall not regularly note such instances of F's unique variants.

9 **And**: LWHm are supported by **Cx**. Other beta mss. drop it; F has *A-non*.

11 **it is**: Supported by the X family of C. The reverse order as in G and F (*ys he*) is supported by the P family.

11 **þe**: Omitted by F and the P family of C.

12 MWHmC here have a paraph.

12 **Pieres**: The beta reading, and clearly preferable on grounds of sense: "These are Piers' arms, but (*ac*) he who comes is Christ". This is confirmed by **Bx**.18.23–7. Perhaps *quod* contributes to aaa/xx alliteration, as again in l. 15 (aaa/bb). However, F's *cristis* is also the reading of **Cx**. RK, p. 123, suggest it is an error prompted by the alliteration; if so, F's reading is by coincidence or contamination. The alternative is that *cristis* is archetypal (if not original), corrected by beta.

His couloures & his cotearmure · ac he þat cometh so blody
Is cryst with his crosse · conqueroure of crystene

15   ¶ Why calle 3e hym cryst quod I · sithenes iuwes calle[d] hym ihesus
Patriarkes & prophetes · prophecyed bifore
Þat alkyn creatures · shulden knelen & bowen
Anon as men nempned · þe name of god Ihesu
Ergo is no name · to þe name of ihesus

20   Ne none so nedeful to nempne · by ny3te ne by daye
For alle derke deuelles · aren adradde to heren it
And synful aren solaced · & saued bi þat name
And 3e callen hym cryst · for what cause telleth me
Is cryst more of my3te · & more worth[ier] name

25   Þan ihesu or ihesus · þat al owre ioye come of

      ¶ Thow knowest wel quod conscience · and þow konne resoun
That kny3te kynge conqueroure · may be o persone
To be called a kni3te is faire · for men shal knele to hym
To be called a Kynge is fairer · for he may kny3tes make

30   Ac to be conquerour called · þat cometh of special grace
And of hardynesse of herte · & of hendenesse
To make lordes of laddes · of londe þat he wynneth
And fre men foule thralles · þat folweth nou3t his lawes

      ¶ The iuwes þat were gentil men · ihesu þei dispised
35   Bothe his lore & his lawe · now ar þei lowe cherlis
As wyde as þe worlde is [·] wonyeth þere none
But vnder tribut & taillage · as tykes & cherles
And þo þat bicome crysten · by conseille of þe baptis[m]e
Aren frankeleynes fre men · þorw fullyng þat þei toke

---

13 **ac**: Dropped in F to remove an illogicality created by the reading *cristis* in the line above. CrC have *and*, as does the P family of **C**.

15 **called**: With the past tense this refers to **Bx**.18.40–3. Hm and beta4 have past tense, as does **Cx**. Note also the past tense of F's *named*. The best beta mss. have the present tense as in the a-verse, and this might be a **Bx** error.

18 **name of god**: As **Cx**. MCr read *hei3e name of*, and F has *name of þat Ientyl*.

18 The Latin line that follows in F only is a variant of l. 82 and is not in **Cx**.

24 **worthier**: F's multiple comparative is supported by **Cx** (where a few scribes correct it) against beta's *worthy*. Cf. **Bx**.7.76 and note.

31 **hendenesse**: CO add *bothe* (Cf. F's *also*). Neither is supported by **Cx**.

32 **of laddes**: Supported by **Cx**, against Cr *or ladyes* and HmGF *and ladys*.

36 **þe**: Supported by **Cx** against HmGF.

36 **þere none**: As in **Cx**. Cr adds *therin*, supplied in turn by the M reviser. W reverses the order. L misplaces the punctuation to follow *wonyeth*.

38 **þe baptisme**: An obvious error in **Bx**, corrected in L to *baptiste* as in **Cx**. F smooths by dropping *þe*. Hm omits 38b-39a.

39 **fre**: OF as well as **Cx** have *& fre*.

40   And gentel men with ihesu · for Ihesus was yfolled
      And vppon caluarye on crosse · ycrouned kynge of iewes

      ¶ It bicometh to a Kynge · to kepe and to defende
      And conquerour of conquest · his lawes & his large
      And so ded Ihesus þe iewes · he iustified & tauȝte hem
45   Þe lawe of lyf · that last shal euere
      And fended fram foule yueles · feueres & fluxes
      And fro fendes þat in hem was [·] & fals bileue
      Þo was he ihesus of iewes called · gentel prophete
      And kynge of her kyngdome · & croune bar of þornes

50   ¶ And þo conquered he on crosse · as conquerour noble
      Myȝt no deth hym fordo · ne adown brynge
      That he ne aros & regned · and rauysshed helle
      And þo was he conquerour called · of quikke & of ded
      For he ȝaf Adam & Eue · and other mo blisse
55   Þat longe hadde leyne bifore · as lucyferes cherles

      [¶ And toke [Lucifer the lothelich] · þat lorde was of helle
      And bonde [him] as [he is bounde] · with bondes of yren
      Who was hardier þanne he · his herte blode he shadde
      To maken alle folke fre · þat folweth his lawe]

---

43 KD, p. 133, scan this line aaa/bb, with two staves on *conquerour*; but its sense is also questionable. Schmidt (1995), taking the line to be dependent on l. 42, translates: "And (it befits) a conqueror to maintain and guard his laws and his munificence by virtue of his act of conquest" (p. 327). Yet it is only kings who, in the following ll. 46–7 "keep and defend" these people, as at **Bx.20.258**. The verbs are not applicable to a conqueror such as Christ here in ll. 50–62, for he carries "his laws and his munificence" into his newly conquered territory, binding some and freeing others at the Harrowing of Hell. It may be that something was lost at an early stage between 43a and 43b, leaving the line as it stands in **Bx**. **Cx** differs only by having *his* before *conquest* and the synonym *layes* for *lawes*.

46 **fended**: Supported by **Cx** against beta2 *defended*.

46 **fram**: HmO have *hem fro(m)*, G has *ytt fro* and F *fram hem*. This indicates that the pronoun was variously added to **Bx** by scribes who sensed an omission. **Cx** has *hem fro*.

47 **was**: LF are supported by **Cx**. As elsewhere, other scribes alter to *were*. See note to **Bx.17.11**.

49 **her**: MCrF omit, but **Cx** has it.

52 **ne aros**: So L as in **Cx**; MCrW have *naroos*, HmG *ne ros*, O *no roos* and CF *aros*.

56–9 These four lines from F were omitted in beta, perhaps skipping from one paraph to the next. They are essential to the narrative and are confirmed by **Cx**, which offers corrections at several points.

56 **And**: F's *& þanne* is not supported by **Cx**.

56 **Lucifer the lothelich**: As in **Cx**. F has *lotthly lucifer*.

57 **him as he is bounde**: This is the reading of **Cx** (a few mss. omit *him*). F has the nonsensical *his as his bondeman*, though *his* might be emended to *him*.

58 **his**: So **Cx**; F has *þat his*.

59 **lawe**: F has the plural, but **Cx** has sg.

60 ¶ And sith he [ʒiueth] largely · alle his lele lyges
Places in paradys · at her partynge hennes
He may wel be called conquerour · & þat is cryst to mene

¶ Ac þe cause þat he cometh þus · with crosse of his passioun
Is to wissen vs þere-wyth · þat whan þat we ben tempted
65 Þer-with to fyʒte & fenden vs · fro fallyng in-to synne
And se bi his sorwe · þat who-so loueth ioye
To penaunce & to pouerte [·] he moste putten hym-seluen
And moche wo in þis worlde · willen & suffren

¶ Ac to carpe more of cryst · and how he come to þat name
70 Faithly forto speke · his firste name was ihesus
Tho he was borne in bethleem [·] as þe boke telleth
And cam to take mankynde · kynges and aungeles
Reuerenced hym [riʒt] faire · with richesse of erthe
Angeles out of heuene · come knelyng & songe
75 Gloria in excelsis deo &c

¶ Kynges come after · kneled & offred
Mirre & moche golde · with-outen mercy askynge
Or any kynnes catel · but knowlechyng hym soeuereigne
Bothe of sonde sonne & see · & sithenes þei went
80 In-to her kyngene kyth · by conseille of angeles
And there was þat worde fulfilled · þe which þow of speke
Omnia celestia terrestria flectantur in hoc nomine Ihesu
For alle þe angeles of heuene · at his burth kneled

---

60 **ʒiueth**: F's present is the reading of the X family of **Cx** and follows logically from *folweth* in the previous line. Beta's past tense, though supported by the P family, is perhaps prompted by its omission of lines 56–9, and *he ʒaf* in l. 54. For the appropriateness of the present "as referring to Christ's continuing grant of heaven to the just", see Schmidt (2008), 454.

63 **crosse of his**: So LWO. MCr have *cros of þe*, HmCG have *cros of*; F reads *his cros of his*. **Cx** is no guide, since the X family reads *his cros and his* and the P family *croys and hus*.

64 **þat whan þat**: So beta. **Cx** has *þat whan*; F just has *whan*.

65 **fenden**: WHmF have *defenden*, as do a few C mss. Cf. l. 46.

68 **willen**: F and most C mss. have *wilnen*, perhaps correctly.

73 **riʒt**: Lost in beta. F is supported by **Cx** and the alliteration.

73 **richesse**: This may be sg. or plural. W and a few C mss. have the marked pl. form. See note to **Bx**.3.23.

77 **mercy**: Evidently the reading of both **Bx** and **Cx**. Cr is naturally puzzled and alters to *mede*, as does the M corrector (overwriting *muche gold*). F, also dissatisfied, alters *with-outen* to *with myche*, and adds *Ensens* to complete the three gifts (as in l. 88). One C scribe, similarly motivated, begins *Rechels Golde & myr*. See Schmidt (2008), 454–5.

78 **knowlechyng**: So apparently beta, though MCr have *knoweliche*, and G has past tense as in **Cx**. F has *þey knowlechid*, possibly representing alpha.

79 **sonde**: Supported by **Cx** against *londe* in beta2.

80 **conseille of angeles**: Supported by **Cx** against F's *kennynge of an angel*.

81 **þow of**: As **Cx**. F's *first þou* is probably motivated by alliteration with *ful-fyld*.

And al þe witte of þe worlde · was in þo þre kynges
85   Resoun & riȝtfulnesse · & reuth þei offred
Wherfore & whi · wyse men þat tyme
Maistres & lettred men · Magy hem called

¶ That o kynge cam with resoun · keuered vnder sense
Þe secounde kynge sitthe · sothliche offred
90   Riȝtwisnesse vnder red golde [·] resouns felawe
Golde is likned to leute · þat last shal euere
And resoun to riche golde · to riȝte & to treuthe
The þridde kynge þo cam · [and] knel[ed] to ihesu
And presented hym with pitee · apierynge by myrre
95   For mirre is mercy to mene · & mylde speche of tonge
[Erthe]liche honest þinges · was offred þus at ones
Þorw þre kynne kynges · knelynge to ihesu

¶ Ac for alle þise preciouse presentz [·] owre lorde prynce ihesus
Was neyther kynge ne conquerour · til he gan to wexe
100 In þe manere of a man · & þat by moche sleight
As it bicometh a conquerour · to konne many sleightes
And many wyles & witte · þat wil ben a leder
And so did ihesu in his dayes · who-so had tyme to telle it
Sum-tyme he suffred · & sum-tyme he hydde hym
105 And sum-tyme he fauȝte faste · & fleigh otherwhile
And some-tyme he gaf good · & graunted hele bothe
Lyf & lyme · as hym lyste he wrought
As kynde is of a conquerour · so comsed ihesu

---

84 **kynges**: Supported by **Cx** against F's *þynges*.

85 **riȝtfulnesse**: So LC. Though C mss. are split, this is evidently the reading of **Cx**. All other B mss. have *riȝtwisnesse / rightuousnes*, which may, of course, be right, even if not archetypal. In l. 90 below *Riȝtwisnesse* is secure and supported by **Cx** and it may have prompted scribes to adopt it here. See Schmidt (2008), 455.

89 **sitthe sothliche**: Cr has *sothly sithens he*, as does M, with *he* added as an alteration. F also has *he*, as does the P family of C, but the X family is without it. There is no metrical need for the pronoun, since *-liche* is disyllabic.

90 F drops ll. 90b and 91a.

92 **riche golde**: Clearly an error (since justice is likened to gold), but the reading of both **Bx** and **Cx**. F rewrites the a-verse and W drops the line altogether. Schmidt (1995) conjectures *richels*, "incense", calling this "one of the stronger indications that B¹ was the basis of the C revision" (p. 405).

93 **and kneled**: F is supported by **Cx**. Compare the actions of the two other kings, also in past tense (ll. 88–9). The phrase *cam knelyng* in beta is perhaps picked up from l. 74.

96 **Ertheliche**: F is supported by **Cx** and by superior sense. Beta's *Thre yliche*, though possible, appears likely to be a misreading.

96 **was**: LF only, but supported by **Cx**. Other B mss. have *were*. For other examples of pl. *was* preserved by L and alpha, see l. 47 and note to **Bx**.17.11.

99 **gan to**: Certainly **Bx**, though **Cx** has alliterating *comsed*.

101 **konne**: F's *knowe* is not supported by **Cx**.

103 **had tyme to**: Certainly **Bx**, though **Cx** has alliterating *durste*.

Tyl he had alle hem · þat he fore bledde

110 ¶ In his iuuente þis ihesus · a[t] iuwen feste
Water in-to wyn tourned · as holy writ telleth
And þere bigan god · of his grace to dowel
For wyn is lykned to lawe · & lyf of holynesse
And lawe lakked þo · for men loued nou3t her enemys
115 And cryst conseilleth þus · & comaundeth bothe
Bothe to lered & to lewed · to louye owre enemys
So atte feste firste [·] as I bifore tolde
Bygan god of his grace [·] & goodnesse to dowel
And þo was he cleped & called [·] nou3t holy cryst but Ihesu
120 A faunt[k]yn ful of witte · filius marie

¶ For bifor his moder marie · made he þat wonder
Þat she furste & formest · ferme shulde bilieue
That he þorw grace was gete · & of no gome elles
He wrou3t þat bi no witte · but þorw worde one
125 After þe kynde þat he come of · þere comsed he dowel
And whan he was woxen more · in his moder absence
He made lame to lepe · & 3aue li3te to blynde
And fedde with two fisshes · & with fyue loues
Sore afyngred folke · mo þan fyue thousande

---

110 **at**: L's *atte* represents "at the", which is supported here only by O. **Cx** has *at*. See the variants at l. 117.

111 **Water in-to wyn tourned**: So beta. F has *he turnede* at the end of the previous line, with some support from **Cx** where the a-verse is *Turned watur into wyn*. Perhaps the standard prose order of F and **Cx** is more likely to be scribal, as argued by RK, p. 123. For the contrary view see Schmidt (2008), 455.

112 **to**: F's omission, shared with beta4, is not supported by **Cx**.

113 **is lykned**: F has *y lykne*, but this is not supported by **Cx**.

113 **lyf of holynesse**: This seems clearly the reading of **Bx**. However, W agrees with **Cx** on *lifholynesse*, which we must suppose is a coincidental variant. So Schmidt (2008), 455.

115 **And** (1): F has *But*. This and other F variants in the line are not supported by **Cx**.

115 **þus**: The reading *vs* in beta4 is shared with a few C mss. including XY. F has *þus vs*.

116 **Bothe**: Apparently beta, though omitted by WHmF to avoid the repetition. Most of the X family of C have it, though the others omit.

117 **atte feste**: WHm have *at þat feeste*, as do the majority of C mss.

119 **holy**: This is the beta reading. Yet CrF have *onely*, and M is altered to that reading, agreeing with **Cx**. On the face of it, *onely* does not give appropriate sense, since Langland's scheme is that Jesus was not called Christ until he became a conqueror. Kane (2005) interprets *onely* as an adj. "peerless", but see Barney (2006), 121, who conjectures *nou3t cryst but onely Ihesu*, "not Christ but rather Jesus". The sense of *holy* is straightforward, even if it reads like a line-filler, to introduce a long dip into the b-verse. For further discussion see Burrow (2009), 90–1.

120 **fauntkyn**: L's form *fauntfyn* shows the source of the error in beta, leading other scribes to interpret as *faunt fyn*. F agrees with **Cx**.

121 **¶**: The paraph is in LM only.

121 **For**: Supported by **Cx**, though dropped by MCr and replaced by *&* in F.

122 **ferme shulde**: F reverses the order, as does **Cx**. RK, p. 123, note this as "variation to prose order".

130 Þus he conforted carful · & cauȝte a gretter name
Þe whiche was dobet · where þat he went
For defe þorw his doynges · & dombe speke [& herde]
And alle he heled & halpe · þat hym of grace asked
And þo was he called in contre [·] of þe comune peple
135 For þe dedes þat he did · fili dauid ihesus
For dauid was douȝtiest · of dedes in his tyme
The berdes þo songe · Saul interfecit mille · et dauid decem milia ·
For-þi þe contre þere ihesu cam · called hym fili dauid
And nempned hym of nazereth · & no man so worthi
140 To be kaisere or kynge · of þe kyngedome of iuda
Ne ouer iuwes iustice · as ihesus was hem þouȝte

¶ Where-of [hadde caiphas] enuye · & other of þe iewes
And forto doun hym to deth · day & nyȝte þei casten
Kulleden hym on crosse-wyse · at caluarie on [a] fryday
145 And sithen buryden his body · & beden þat men sholde
Kepen it fro niȝt-comeres · with knyȝtes yarmed
For no frendes shulde hym fecche · for prophetes hem tolde
Þat þat blessed body · of burieles shulde rise
And gone in-to galile · and gladen his apostles
150 And his moder Marie · þus men bifore demed

¶ The knyȝtes þat kepten it · biknewe[n] hem-seluen
Þat angeles & archangeles · ar þe day spronge

---

130 **carful**: Supported by Cx against CrF *þe carefull*.

132 **& dombe speke & herde**: F supported by Cx (though mss. XYU have *he* for *&* (2)). Beta has *to here & dombe speke he made*, imposing a more obvious order and perhaps not recognising *speke* as a past tense form.

135 **fili dauid ihesus**: This word order is supported by Cx. CGOF have *Ihesu fili dauid*.

136 **douȝtiest**: F and Cx supply the definite article.

137 **The berdes þo**: Supported by Cx against beta4 (*þat* for *þo*) and F's revision to *Þerfore men sungen*.

142 **Where-of**: F has *Þerfore*; Cx has *Hereof*.

142 **hadde caiphas**: So F and Cx. Beta reverses to prose order.

142 **other of þe**: The beta reading; F has *oþire konynge*. Both could be additions to lengthen a short b-verse, since Cx has just *other*.

143 **And**: F (and Hm) omit, but beta is supported by Cx.

144 **Kulleden**: F and Cx begin with *&*, easily supplied for a smooth transition.

144 **a**: CrHmF are supported by Cx. However, all could be independent additions.

147 **frendes**: Beta has the pl.; F shares the sg. with Cx.

147 **hym**: So beta, though F and Cx have *it* as in the previous line. Cf. also l. 151.

148 **shulde rise**: The word-order, reversed in WHm, is supported by Cx. For *rise*, **Bx** may have read *arise* as in MCr supported by Cx. F has *vp ryse*.

150 **demed**: Secure for **Bx**, though Cx has *deuyned*.

151 **it**: Supported by Cx. Beta4 reads *hym*, and Hm is altered to that reading, following on from l. 147.

151 **biknewen**: F agrees with Cx. Beta, having lost the final syllable of the verb, provides the long dip by adding *it*, thus anticipating the clause of the next line.

Come knelynge [·] to þe corps & songen
[Cristus resurgens · and he ros after]
155 Verrey man bifor hem alle · & forth with hem ȝede

¶ The iewes preyed hem pees · & bisouȝte þe knyȝtes
Telle þe comune þat þere cam · a compaignye of his aposteles
And bywicched hem as þei woke · & awey stolen it

¶ Ac Marie Magdeleyne · mette hym bi þe wey
160 Goynge toward galile · in godhed & manhed
And lyues & lokynge · & she aloude cryde
In eche a compaignye þere she cam · cristus resurgens
Þus cam it out þat cryst ouer-cam · rekeuered & lyued
Sic oportet cristum pati & intrare &c ·
165 For þat wommen witeth · may nouȝte wel be conseille

¶ Peter parceyued al þis · & pursued after
Bothe iames & Iohan · Ihesu for to seke
Tadde & ten mo · with Thomas of ynde

---

153 þe: F and Cx have þat.

153 & songen: In beta this is followed by *cristus resurgens*, but both F and Cx postpone the Latin to the start of the following line. F characteristically supplies *konyngly* to fill out a short b-verse and provide alliteration. But the caesura follows *knelynge*, though all B scribes take it to follow *corps*. This is the reading of Cx, with F providing crucial, if characteristically "improved" support. Our argument is that both F and beta reacted to the short line with its uncertain placement of the caesura: F added the adverb *konyngly* to provide b-verse alliteration, and beta took the Latin from the next line, dropping the detached b-verse of l. 154 as a consequence.

154 Cristus resurgens · and he ros after: See note to previous line. Beta has taken the Latin as the end of the line above, and perhaps assumed the English to be a scribal gloss, thus losing this whole line. But *and he ros after* is necessary to the narrative: "after that he rose, true man ...". F offers the reading of Cx with characteristic elaboration, extending the Latin quote with *a mortuis* and adding the adverb *a-noon*. For F's *he*, Cx reads *it*; see note to l. 151.

155 ȝede: In L the scribe has inserted *he*, bringing it into line with other beta mss. that have lost *he* in the line above, but Bx was probably without it, as suggested by the agreement of F and Cx.

156 pees: F and Cx read *of pees*. In view of the variations of the b-verse in both F and Cx (see next note), we follow beta throughout the line.

156 & bisouȝte þe knyȝtes: F supplies alliteration with *alle þo propre knyghtis*, but this has no support from Cx, which reads *& preyed þo knyhtes*, suggesting that Bx may have avoided the repetition of the verb.

160 &: F and the X family of C repeat the preposition *in*, but beta and the P family omit it.

161 lyues: The adjectival gen. "alive" (only here in the poem) causes some scribes difficulty, but it is supported by Cx.

161 she: F has *he* for "she", as in the next line; see Introduction, pp. 17–18. The X family of C omit the pronoun.

164–5 These two lines are omitted by F but are in Cx.

165 þat: MWHmCO supply a second *þat*; only LCrG are without it (the line is lost in F). A few C mss. also have *þat þat*, but it seems clear that Cx had *þat*.

166 al: Inserted by the L scribe and omitted by MCr, but supported by Cx.

167 for: Secure for Bx, but not in Cx.

And as alle þise wise wyes · weren togideres
170 In an hous al bishette · & her dore ybarred
Cryst cam in & al closed · bothe dore & ʒates
To peter & to his apposteles · and seyde pax vobis
And toke Thomas by þe hande · and tauʒte hym to grope
And fele with his fyngres · his flesshelich herte

175 ¶ Thomas touched it · & with his tonge seyde
Deus meus & dominus meus
Thow art my lorde I bileue · god lorde ihesu
Þow deydest & deth þoledest · and deme shalt vs alle
And now art lyuynge & lokynge · & laste shalt euere

180 ¶ Crist carped þanne · and curteislich seyde
Thomas for þow trowest þis · & trewliche bileuest it
Blessed mote þow be · & be shalt for euere
And blessed mote þei be · in body & in soule
That neuere shal se me in siʒte · as þow doste nouthe
185 And lellich bileuen al þis · I loue hem & blesse hem
Beati qui non viderunt [& crediderunt]

¶ And whan þis dede was done · dobest he tauʒte
And ʒaf Pieres power · and pardoun he graunted
To alle manere men · mercy & forʒyfnes
190 Hym myʒte men to assoille · of alle manere synnes

---

176 **Deus meus & dominus meus**: CrF reverse the nouns to the order of John 20.28 perhaps
as a correction of **Bx**. Cf. *lorde … god* in the next line. **Cx** also has the Vulgate order. F's
additional b-verse *& doun he fel to grownde* gives a good line, but has no support from **Cx**.
177 F's b-verse is not supported by **Cx**.
178 F's variants are not supported by **Cx**.
179 F's a-verse is not supported by **Cx**.
183 **þei**: Beta evidently had *þei alle*, obscuring the parallel with the previous a-verse, but GF
are supported by **Cx**.
184 **doste**: This must be the reading of **Bx**, though it does not alliterate. Cr reads *hast*, while O
alone has *seest*, the reading of **Cx**, presumably by conjecture. Cf. l. 156 where **Bx** again seems
to avoid repetition of the verb.
186 **& crediderunt**: Hm, beta4 and F are supported by **Cx**. It may be, of course, that scribes
expanded beta's abbreviation of the quotation.
187 **tauʒte**: Neither beta or F *took sone* is supported by **Cx**, which reads *thouhte*. But *tauʒte*
makes excellent sense; see Burrow (2009), 93 n. 15.
189 **manere**: The majority of C mss. read *maner of*, as do CrCF, but the best texts of the X
family read *maner*. F commonly expands to *manere of*, as in the following line.
190 **Hym myʒte men to**: LC are supported by the best mss. of the X family of C. Other
scribes in both traditions take various actions to avoid a construction they fail to understand,
as do KD (pp. 120–1) and RK (pp. 134–5). But ll. 188–90 mean: "He gave Piers power, and
granted pardon, mercy and forgiveness to all sorts; [granted] him power to absolve men of all
kinds of sins." For an interpretation of the archetypal reading see Barney (2006), 128.
190 **manere**: F again has *manere of*, as do CrG, not supported by **Cx**.

In couenant þat þei come · & knewleche to paye
To pieres pardon þe plowman · redde quod debes

¶ Thus hath pieres powere · be his pardoun payed
To bynde & vnbynde · bothe here & elles
195 And assoille men of alle synnes · saue of dette one

¶ Anone after an heigh · vp in-to heuene
He went & wonyeth þere · & wil come atte laste
And rewarde hym riȝte wel · þat reddit quod debet
Payeth parfitly [·] as pure trewthe wolde
200 And what persone payeth it nouȝt · punysshen he þinketh
And demen hem at domes-daye · bothe quikke & ded
Þe gode to þe godhede · & to grete ioye
And wikke[de] to wonye · in wo with-outen ende

[¶] Þus conscience of crist · & of þe crosse carped
205 And conseilled me to knele þer-to · & þanne come me þouȝte
One spiritus paraclitus · to Pieres & to his felawes
In lyknesse of a liȝtnynge · he lyȝte on hem alle
And made hem konne & knowe · alkyn langages

[¶] I wondred what þat was · & wagged conscience
210 And was afered of the lyȝte · for in fyres lyknesse
Spiritus paraclitus · ouer-spradde hem alle

¶ Quod conscience & kneled · þis is crystes messager
And cometh fro þe grete god · & grace is his name
Knele now quod conscience · & if þow canst synge

---

191 **knewleche**: The past tense in WHm is actually the reading of **Cx**, though a few C mss. have the present, as **Bx** clearly does.

194 **&**: L alone has *& to*. C mss. are divided, with the X family reading *& to*.

194 **elles**: Agreement of LF, together with **Cx**, secures this as the **Bx** reading against *elles-where* in other B mss.

198 **And**: LG have *And wil*, without support from **Cx**.

200 **Cx** offers no support for F's b-verse.

201 Again F has a unique b-verse, which is presumably designed to offer a more regular alliterative pattern.

203 **wikkede**: The form in all mss. except L is supported by **Cx**. For similar variation with *wikke*, see **Bx**.5.231.

204 **¶**: The paraph is in WHmCF, and is entirely appropriate.

206 **to** (2): Not in F; beta has the support of most C mss.

207 **he**: Omitted in some C mss., but none support F's *&*.

208–11 F drops four lines through eyeskip on *hem alle*. The lines are in **Cx**.

209 **¶**: In L there is an unrubricated paraph marker, missed because the scribe failed to leave a line-space. M has a line-space and HmC a paraph.

210 **of**: So beta (F out). **Cx** has *for*.

213 **&**: So beta, but dropped by F and **Cx**.

215   Welcome hym & worshipe hym · with veni creator spiritus

¶ Thanne songe I þat songe · and so did many hundreth
And cryden with conscience · help vs god of grace
And þanne bigan grace · to go with piers plowman
And conseilled hym & conscience · þe comune to sompne
220   For I wil dele to-daye · & dyuyde grace
To alkynnes creatures · þat kan h[is] fyue wittes
Tresore to lyue by · to her lyues ende
And wepne to fy3te with · þat wil neure faille
For antecryst & his · al þe worlde shal greue
225   And acombre þe conscience · but if cryst þe helpe

¶ And fals prophetes fele · flatereres & glosers
Shullen come & be curatoures · ouer kynges & erlis
And pryde shal be pope · prynce of holycherche
Coueytyse & vnkyndenesse · cardinales hym to lede
230   For-þi quod grace er I go · I wil gyue 3ow tresore
And wepne to fi3te with · whan antecryst 3ow assailleth
And gaf eche man a grace · to gye with hym-seluen
That ydelnesse encombre hym nou3t · envye ne pryde
Diuisiones graciarum sunt &c ·

235   ¶ Some he 3af wytte · with wordes to shewe
Witte to wynne her lyflode with · as þe worlde asketh
As prechoures & prestes [·] & prentyce of lawe
Þei lelly to lyue · by laboure of tonge
And bi witte to wissen other · as grace hem wolde teche

240   ¶ And some he kenned crafte · & kunnynge of sy3te
With sellyng & buggynge · her bylyf to wynne

---

216 **Thanne songe I**: Cx begins *And y sange*. F drops this and the following line.
216 **and**: Dropped by WHm, but supported by Cx.
218 **þanne**: Dropped by F but supported by the X family of C. The P family begins *Tho*.
220 **dele**: Omitted by F, but supported by Cx.
220 **dyuyde**: Supported by Cx against the variants in WHm (*3yue diuine*) and in F.
221 **kan**: LF supported by Cx and alliteration. Beta1 (including M) corrupts to *han*.
221 **his**: F is supported by Cx. Beta alters to pl. *her* for concord, as do a few C mss.
222 Beta4 omits 222b–231a by eyeskip.
227 **erlis**: F's *knyghtis* has no support from Cx.
228 **pryde shal**: F and Cx read *þanne shal pryde*.
228 **prynce**: F and Cx read *& prince*.
232 **gye**: As in Cx. CrW have *gide*; beta4 reads *go*.
233 **envye**: F and Cx have *ne envy3e*.
235 **Some**: Secure for Bx. The X family of C reads *Som men*, the P family *To somme men* (cf. Cr).
236 The a-verse is revised in Cx, avoiding the repetition of *witte*.
241 **bylyf**: "subsistence". MCr, Hm (altered) and F read *liflode*. Many C scribes also have difficulty with the word.

And some he lered to laboure [· on londe and on water
And lyue by þat labour] · a lele lyf & a trewe
And somme he tauȝte to tilie · to dyche & to thecche
245 To wynne with her lyflode · by lore of his techynge
And some to dyuyne & diuide · noumbres to kenne
And some to compas craftily · & coloures to make
And some to se & to saye · what shulde bifalle
Bothe of wel & of wo · telle it or it felle
250 As Astronomyenes þorw astronomye · & philosophres wyse

¶ And some to ryde & to recoeure · þat vnriȝtfully was wonne
He wissed hem wynne it aȝeyne · þorw wightnesse of handes
And fecchen it fro fals men · with foluyles lawes

[¶] And some he lered to lyue · in longynge to ben hennes
255 In pouerte & in p[acie]nce · to preye for alle crystene
And alle he lered to be lele · & eche a crafte loue other
And forbad hem alle debate · þat none were amonge hem

---

242 **laboure:** Beta drops 242b and 243a through eyeskip (*laboure … labour*). F is supported
by **Cx**.

243 **a** (2): Omitted by beta4 and F, but supported by **Cx**.

244 **thecche:** Beta4 has *hegge*, F has *þresche*, both probably misreadings. Most C mss. read *to
teche and to coke*, but some make the obvious correction of *teche* to *theche*. See KD, pp. 174–5;
RK, p. 125.

245 **Cx** has an entirely different line here.

246 **&:** M's *and to* is shared with some of the X family of C.

247 **And some to compas craftily:** Cx omits *some* and *craftily*.

249 **telle it or it felle:** In Cx the b-verse is *and be ywaer bifore*.

251 **ryde & to:** Supported by the P family of C, while Hm and beta4 have *ryde and summe to*
as in the X family. F's *rekne &* has no support.

251 **recoeure:** So L; cf. F's *rekewre*. See *MED recuren* (Lat *recurare*), formally different from
MED recoveren (OFr), as in the other mss. Cf. 18.362 for the same variation.

251 **vnriȝtfully:** Supported by **Cx** against *wrongfully* in W. The odd *riȝtfully* in Hm perhaps
reflects puzzlement with the ironic reference to *foluyles lawes* in l. 253.

252 **hem:** Cx reads *men*. F omits the line.

252 **wynne:** As in Cx, against *to wynne* in W, with *to* inserted in O.

252 **wightnesse:** Supported by **Cx**; misunderstood by HmC (*wytnesse*) and G (*ryghtyovsnes*).

253 L alone has a paraph at the top of the page. Presumably it was meant to precede *And* in
the next line.

254 **¶:** The paraph, misplaced at the head of the previous line in L, is supported by WHm.
Cf. the parallels in ll. 235, 240 and 251; though apparently not ll. 242 (W only), 244 and 246
(WHm only).

254 **lered:** CrHmGF read *lerned*, a common variation; cf. e.g. **Bx**.1.148, 153, and l. 256 below.
C mss. also vary.

255 **pacience:** HmF are supported by **Cx**, though three C mss. read *penaunce*. The beta reading
must be *penaunce*, so how did Hm come by the right reading? Both *penaunce* and *pacience* are
frequently collocated with *pouerte*; cf. especially **Bx**.14.231 and 19.67.

257 In **Cx** the line reads "Ne no boest ne debaet be among hem alle" (RK.21.251). For the
suggestion of **Cx** revision here and in ll. 259–60, see Barney (2006), 143.

Thowgh some be clenner þan somme · ȝe se wel quod grace
Þat he þat vseth þe fairest crafte · to þe foulest I couth haue put hym
260 Þinketh alle quod grace · þat grace cometh of my ȝifte
Loke þat none lakke other · but loueth alle as bretheren

¶ And who þat moste maistries can · be myldest of berynge
And crouneth conscience kynge · & maketh crafte ȝowre stuward
And after craftes conseille · clotheth ȝow & fede
265 For I make Pieres þe plowman · my procuratour & my reve
And Regystrere to receyue · redde quod debes
My prowor & my plowman · Piers shal ben on erthe
And for to tulye treuthe · a teme shal he haue

¶ Grace gaue Piers a teme · foure gret oxen
270 Þat on was Luke a large beste · and a lowe-chered
And marke & mathew þe þrydde · myghty bestes bothe
And ioigned to hem one Iohan · most gentil of alle
Þe prys nete of Piers plow · passyng alle other

¶ And grace gaue pieres · of his goodnesse foure stottis
275 Al þat his oxen eryed · þey to harwe after
On hyȝte Austyne · & ambrose an other
Gregori þe grete clerke · & Ierome þe gode
Þise foure þe feithe to teche · folweth pieres teme
And harwed in an handwhile · al holy scripture
280 Wyth two [aithes] þat þei hadde · an olde & a newe
Id est vetus testamentum & nouum

¶ And grace gaue [Pieres] greynes · cardynales vertues

259–60 Replaced by one line in **Cx**: "That all craft and connyng cam of my ȝefte" (RK.21.253).
259 Followed in F by four sanctimonious lines with defective alliteration. See KD, p. 223.
260 **alle**: F has *alle now*. The line is omitted by beta4.
261 **alle**: Not in **Cx**.
262 **who**: **Cx** reads *he*.
265 **þe**: GF are without it. C mss. vary.
267 **prowor**: "overseer". Supported by **Cx**, though some scribes stumble over it.
269 **foure**: W supplies *of*, as does the P family of C.
274 **And**: F has *& ȝit*; **Cx** has *And sethe*.
274 **gaue pieres · of his goodnesse**: The word-order in F, *of his goodnesse / gaf peers* is supported by **Cx**. It is perhaps a revision, but could be an error in **Cx**, or in beta influenced by l. 269. See RK, p. 123, who adopt the beta reading.
275 **harwe**: MCrF supply *it*, as do a couple of C mss.
280 **aithes**: This is the reading of **Cx**. *MED eithe* (OE *egþe*, "harrow") records no other instance. F preserves it in the form *hayȝtes*. Beta and some C mss. have the much easier synonym *harwes*, picked up from the verb in the previous line.
281 **nouum**: F's addition of *testamentum* has no support from **Cx**.
282 **Pieres**: Easily lost in beta. F is supported by **Cx**.
282 **cardynales**: Beta supplies the definite article, but it is not supported by F or **Cx**.

And sewe it in mannes soule · & sithen he tolde her names
Spiritus prudencie · þe firste seed hy3te
285 And who-so eet þat · ymagyne he shulde
Ar he did any dede · deuyse wel þe ende
And lerned men a ladel bugge · with a longe stele
Þat cast for to kepe a crokke · to saue þe fatte abouen

¶ The secounde seed hi3te [·] spiritus temperancie
290 He þat ete of þat seed · hadde suche a kynde
Shulde neuere mete ne [myschief] · make hym to swelle
Ne sholde no scorner ne scolde · oute of skyl hym brynge
Ne wynnynge ne welthe · of wordeliche ricchesse
Waste worde of ydelnesse · ne wykked speche meue
295 Shulde no curyous clothe · comen on hys rugge
Ne no mete in his mouth · þat maister Iohan spiced

¶ The thridde seed þat Pieres sewe · was spiritus fortitudinis
And who-so eet of þat seed [·] hardy was eure
To suffre al þat god sent · sykenesse & angres
300 My3te no lesynge[s] ne lyere · ne losse of worldely catel
Maken hym for any mournynge · þat he nas merye in soule
And bolde & abydynge · bismeres to suffre
And pl[e]yeth al with pacyence · & parce michi domine
And couered hym vnder conseille · of catoun þe wyse
305 Esto forti animo cum sis dampnatus inique

---

283 **sewe it**: WHm alter to *sew hem* on grounds of concord; F reads *he sew it*. Neither has support from **Cx**.

283 **he**: Hm and beta4 omit as do some C mss., but **Cx** has it.

284 Only HmF mark a new paragraph here, corresponding to those at the other members of the numbered set, ll. 289, 297 and 306.

285 **And**: Perhaps a beta error. F and **Cx** read less obvious *Þat*.

285 **þat**: F's *of þat frut* has no support from C, though the P family has *þat seede*.

288 **Þat**: LMCrCG are supported by **Cx** against *And* in WHm, *To* in O, and *For he* in F.

288 **kepe**: So Bx, though **Cx** has *kele*, "cool".

288 **to** (2): F and **Cx** read *&*.

288 **saue**: F repeats *keepe* to strengthen the aaa/xx alliteration, as do two C scribes.

289 **hi3te**: So **Cx**, against F's *þat he sew was*. O is absent from this line to l. 369.

291 **myschief**: i.e. starvation. Beta is understandably puzzled and replaces with *mochel drynke*. F is supported by **Cx**.

292 **ne scolde**: F and **Cx** omit, to the detriment of the alliteration.

293 **welthe**: W's *wele* is not supported by **Cx**. Beta4 drops the line.

298 **was**: The beta reading is supported by **Cx**. WHm have *was he*; F has *he was*.

300 **lesynges ne lyere**: Only L has sg. *lesynge*, which could nevertheless be right. For *ne*, F reads *of*. C mss. have instead *lyare with lesynges*, though X and three other mss. have sg. *lesynge*.

303 **pleyeth**: "plead in court", *MED pleien* v. (2), from *ple*. LCr *playeth* is a misunderstanding of the uncommon verb. F has the easier and unambiguous verb *pleted*. **Cx** has *plede*, which could be either present or past tense. See RK, p. 123 and n. 42; Barney (2006), 151.

304 **couered**: CrCGF have the present tense, but **Cx** has the past.

¶ The fierthe seed þat pieres sewe · was spiritus iusticie
And he þat eet of þat seed · shulde be euere trewe
With god & nou3t agast · but of gyle one
For gyle goth so pryuely · þat good faith other-while
310   May nou3te ben aspyed · for spiritus iusticie

¶ Spiritus iusticie · spareth nou3te to spille
Hem þat ben gulty · & forto correcte
Þe Kynge 3if he falle · in gylte or in trespasse
For counteth he no kynges wratthe · whan he in courte sitteth
315   To demen as a domes-man · adradde was he neure
Noither of duke ne of deth · þat he ne dede þe lawe
For present or for preyere · or any prynces lettres
He dede equite to alle · euene-forth his powere

¶ Thise foure sedes pieres sewe · and sitthe he did hem harwe
320   Wyth olde lawe and newe lawe · þat loue my3te wexe
Amonge þ[ise] foure vertues · and vices destroye

¶ For comunelich in contrees · kammokes & wedes
Fouleth þe fruite in þe felde · þere þei growe togyderes
And so don vices · vertues worthy
325   Quod Piers harweth alle þat kunneth kynde witte · bi conseille of þis
         doctours
And tulyeth after her techynge · þe cardinale vertues

¶ A3eines þi greynes quod grace · bigynneth for to ripe

---

307 **euere:** Cx has *euene*.

308 **With god &:** F's *& of god* is not supported by Cx.

310 **for:** Cx has *thorw*.

311 **¶:** LWHm have a paraph, not entirely appropriately in the middle of the account of the
fourth seed. That it was in beta at least is further suggested by M's misplacement of a paraph
marker at the next line, which is at the top of the leaf.

311 KD, p. 119, and RK, p. 133, detect misdivision and padding in this and the next two lines
in both **Bx** and **Cx**.

312–13 Among C mss., X has "Hem þat ben gulty · and forto corecte the kyng / And the kyng
falle in any a gulte", while P divides the line after *corecte*.

313 **falle:** F's a-verse has no support from **Cx**. See previous note.

314 F's a-verse has no support from **Cx**.

316 **þe:** So LF and **Cx**. Dropped by beta1.

318 **powere:** Cx reads *knowyng*.

320 **olde:** F twice adds the definite article in the a-verse, without support from **Cx**.

321 **þise:** Uncertain. F is supported by **Cx**. LMCrCG have *þe*; WHm have *þo*.

322 **¶:** The paraph is appropriate, though indicated in LM only. F begins *&*, but *For* is
supported by **Cx**.

324 **worthy:** In Cx this reads *forþi quod Peres*, and it is clear that **Bx** has misdivided the line.
F characteristically expands a short line.

Ordeigne þe an hous Piers · to herberwe in þi cornes

¶ By god grace quod Piers · 3e moten gyue tymbre
330 And ordeyne þat hous · ar 3e hennes wende

¶ And grace gaue hym þe crosse · with þe croune of þornes
That cryst vpon caluarye · for mankynde on pyned
And of his baptesme & blode · þat he bledde on Rode
He made a maner morter · & mercy it hi3te
335 And þere-with grace bigan · to make a good foundement
And watteled it and walled it · with his peynes & his passioun
And of al holywrit · he made a rofe after
And called þat hous vnite · holicherche on englisshe
And whan þis dede was done · grace deuised
340 A carte hy3te cristendome · to carye [home] pieres sheues
And gaf hym caples to his carte · contricioun & confessioun
And made presthode haywarde · þe while hym-self went
As wyde as þe worlde is · with pieres to tulye treuthe
[And þe [londe] of bileue · þe lawe of holychirche]

345 ¶ Now is Pieres to þe plow · & pruyde it aspyde
And gadered hym a grete oest · to greuen he þinketh
Conscience and al crystene · and cardinale vertues
Blowe hem doune & breke hem · & bite atwo þe mores

---

328 **Piers**: So **Cx**. Probably beta read *quod Piers* (picked up from the following line), retained by LMCr, with WHm making an obvious correction by dropping *quod*, and beta4 dropping both words. F moves *Peers* to the beginning of the line.

329 **god**: F misunderstands as genitive. Beta is supported by **Cx**.

329 **gyue**: F and **Cx** read *gyve me*.

331 **with**: F's *&* is not supported by **Cx**.

332 **on pyned**: Beta is supported by **Cx** against F's *kawhte*.

334 **&**: F omits; beta is supported by **Cx**.

336 **watteled ... walled**: Reversed in MCr, without support from **Cx**. F rewrites the line.

336 **peynes**: Supported by **Cx** against W's sg. and F's *woundis*.

337 **made**: Supported by **Cx**. F substitutes *wroghte* to alliterate with *writ*.

340 **home pieres**: As in **Cx**. Beta drops *home* while F drops *pieres* (but supplies it in the next line), perhaps both simplifying for metrical reasons.

344 The line is preserved only by F, but it is in **Cx**. For *londe* as in **Cx**, F reads *loore*, but cf. *londe of longynge* **Bx**.11.8. F also supplies *&* to begin the b-verse, but **Cx** does not have it. There seems nothing to have prompted beta's omission, except that the line was at the end of the paragraph, so it may be an addition in C.

345 **&**: Secure for **Bx**, but not in **Cx**.

346 **to greuen**: So LMC, and presumably beta. W has *for to greven*, and Hm *for greuyn*. CrG, reading *to greue him*, misunderstand the construction with the object in the next line, making the same mistake, has *greven hym*. **Cx** reads simply *greue(n)*, with a few mss. adding *to* or *hym*. It is likely enough that **Bx** read *greuen*, with scribes reacting to the short b-verse.

348 **þe mores**: "roots". F rewrites the b-verse as *& beetyn doun here maneres*. The P family of C alters to *rotes*.

And sent forth surquydou[re]s · his seriaunt of armes
350 And his spye spille-loue · one speke yuel byhynde
Þise two come to conscience · and to crystene peple
And tolde hem tydynges · þat tyne þei shulde þe sedes
That Pieres þere hadde ysowen · þe cardynal vertues
And Pieres berne worth broke · & þei þat ben in vnite
355 Shulle come out & conscience · & ȝowre two caples
Confessioun & contricioun · and ȝowre carte þe byleue
Shal be coloured so queyntly · and keuered vnder owre sophistrie
Þat consci[ence] shal nouȝte · knowe by contricioun
Ne by confessioun · who is cristene or hethen
360 Ne no maner marchaunt · þat with moneye deleth
Where he wynne wyth riȝte · with wronge or with vsure

¶ With suche coloures & queyntise · cometh pryde yarmed
With þe lorde þat lyueth after · þe luste of his body
To wasten on welfare · and on wykked kepynge
365 Al þe worlde in a while · þorw owre witte quod pruyde

¶ Quod conscience to alle crystene þo · my conseille is to wende
Hastiliche in-to vnyte · & holde we vs þere
And preye we þat a pees were · in Piers berne þe plowman
For witterly I wote wel · we beth nouȝte of strengthe
370 To gone agayne pryde · but grace were with vs

---

349 **surquydoures**: "arrogant one" (for this form in F see *MED surquidrous*), which both F and **Cx** interpret as plural (but cf. l. 351), and so read *sergawntys* in place of *seriaunt*. Beta has the commoner form *surquidous*. See Schmidt (2008), 460.

353 In C, the X family begins *That sire Peres sewe*. The P family ends the previous line with *sholde* and therefore begins *The seedes that syre Peers sewe*, a satisfactory a-verse. **Bx** must also have been defective as a result of mislineation, and perhaps the a-verse read *That Piers sewe*, with beta and F expanding in different ways. See Schmidt (2008), 460.

355 **&** (1): So beta and **Cx**. Dropped in F, so that *conscience* is a term of address rather than part of a group subject of *Shal* in l. 357. LCrW punctuate for syntax after *out*.

356 **þe**: F has *of*; most C mss. omit.

357 **owre**: So L and most beta mss. Cr has *your*, perhaps from the line above, while WF omit, perhaps to shorten a heavy b-verse. There is the same variation in C mss., with most reading *oure*.

358 **conscience**: L reads *conscioun*, with the line marked for correction. **Cx** supports beta's version of the line; F tries to improve sense and alliteration.

361 **riȝte**: CrF follow this with *or*, but it is not in **Cx**.

362 **& queyntise**: Supported by **Cx** against MCr *and coueityse* and F *y-peyntid*.

364 **on** (2): This is the beta reading, though W has *in*, as do most C mss., and G omits. F's b-verse *wikkednesse he meyntiþ* has no support.

364 **kepynge**: There is no support for W's *lyuyng*.

366 **to** (2): **Cx** has instead *we* or *þat we*. F's b-verse is *y conseyle þe to wende*.

367 **in-to**: Beta is supported by the P family of C, but F's *to* has support from the X family.

370 O resumes.

¶ And þanne cam kynde wytte · conscience to teche
And cryde & comaunded · al crystene peple
For to deluen a dyche · depe aboute vnite
That holycherche stode in vnite · as it a pyle [were]

375 ¶ Conscience comaunded þo · al crystene to delue
And make a muche mote · þat myȝte ben a strengthe
To helpe holycherche · & hem þat it kepeth

¶ Thanne alkyn crystene · saue comune wommen
Repenteden & refused synne · saue they one
380 And fals men flateres · vsureres and theues
Lyeres and questmongeres · þat were forsworen ofte
Wytynge and willefully · with þe false helden
And for syluer were forswore · sothely þei wist it

¶ Þere nas no crystene creature · þat kynde witte hadde
385 Saue schrewes one · suche as I spak of
That he ne halpe a quantite · holynesse to wexe
Somme þorw bedes byddynge · and some þorw pylgrymage
And other pryue penaunce · and some þorw penyes delynge

¶ And þanne welled water · for wikked werkes
390 Egerlich ernynge · out of mennes eyen
Clennesse of þe comune · & clerkes clene lyuynge
Made vnite holicherche · in holynesse to stonde

---

373 **For to**: Secure for **Bx**; **Cx** begins *To*.
373 **a dyche**: LMWG, and so presumably the beta reading, supported by the X family of C. HmCOF have instead *and dike/dych* (Cr *and digge*). The P family of C has *and dike a deop diche*.
373 **aboute**: Beta is supported by the X family of C. F's *alle abowte* is supported by the P family.
374 **in vnite**: This makes sense as a pun, "united". F's *strong* develops the sense of this, looking forward to l. 376 and adding alliteration with *stoode*. **Cx** reads instead *in holinesse*, alluding to the moat that is to be dug, but this is perhaps picked up from RK.21.380 (= **Bx**.19.392).
374 **were**: L omits, with the line marked for correction. For **Bx** *a pyle were*, **Cx** reads *were a pyle*.
380 **flateres**: The form in LF against *flaterers* in others, as also at **Bx**.2.168 and 13.450. See *MED flatour*. This line is not in **Cx**.
381 **Lyeres and questmongeres**: **Cx** has instead *A sysour and a sompnour*. For *questmongere* see Alford (1988), 124.
383 F's puzzling b-verse has no support from **Cx**.
385 **Cx** drops this line. F characteristically expands a short line.
387 **some**: In beta and the P family of C, but not in F or the X family.
387 **þorw** (2): Secure for **Bx**, but Cr and **Cx** have *bi*, carrying the b-verse alliteration.
387 **pylgrimage**: Only W has the plural. It is, however, the reading of **Cx**.
388 **penaunce**: For variation with and without <-s>, see note to **Bx**.14.211. There is similar variation in C mss. MCr have *peines*. F reverses a- and b-verses.
389 **welled**: The reading *walmede* in F suggests that **Bx** might have had the form *walled* (*MED wallen* v.(1)), as in **Cx**.
391 **of þe**: WHm repeat *out of* from the line above.
392 **to stonde**: So beta. **Cx** is without *to*, as **Bx** may have been, since in F the b-verse reads *holylyche stoonde*.

[¶] I care nou3te quod conscience · þough pryde come nouthe
Þe lorde of luste shal be letted · al þis lente I hope
395   Comeþ quod conscience · 3e cristene and dyneth
Þat han laboured lelly · al þis lente tyme
Here is bred yblessed · and goddes body þer-vnder
Grace þorw goddes worde · gaue Pieres power
My3tes to maken it · & men to ete it after
400   In helpe of her hele · onys in a moneth
Or as ofte as þey hadden nede · þo þat hadde ypayed
To pieres pardoun þe plowman · redde quod debes

¶ How quod al þe comune · þow conseillest vs to 3elde
Al þat we owen any wy3te · ar we go to housel

405   ¶ That is my conseille quod conscience [·] & cardynale vertues
[Or] vche man for3yue other · and þat wyl þe pater noster
Et dimitte nobis debita nostra · &c ·
And so to ben assoilled · & sithen ben houseled

¶ 3e bawe quod a brewere · I wil nou3t be reuled
410   Bi ihesu for al 3owre ianglynge · with spiritus iusticie
Ne after conscience by cryste · whil I can selle
Bothe dregges & draffe · and drawe it at on hole
Þikke ale and þinne ale · for þat is my kynde
And nou3te hakke after holynesse · holde þi tonge conscience
415   Of spiritus iusticie · þow spekest moche an ydel

¶ Caytyue quod conscience · cursed wrecche
Vnblessed artow brewere · but if þe god helpe

---

393 ¶: The paraph is in WHm, with a line-space in M.
397 þer-vnder: F, reading þere-Inne, is perhaps uncomfortable with the theological use, *MED*
ther-under 2 (b).
398 Pieres: Cx has *Peres the ploughman*.
399 My3tes: Beta2 and F begin *And*, with support from the P family of Cx. Though the noun
is the more obvious sg. in CrCF, as in Cx, beta had the plural.
399 to ete it after: Cx reads *for to eten it*.
404 ar: As in the P family of C. F's *er þat* has support from the X family.
406 Or: "Or, in other words, …". F agrees with Cx on much the harder reading. Probably
beta altered it, as do a few C mss. Beta has support for the rest of the a-verse.
408 ben (2): Supported by most of the P family of C. Beta4 and F repeat *to been*, with support
from the X family. Perhaps that is more likely to be scribal.
410 with: Cx has *aftur*, as in the next line. F's form of the line is not supported.
411 whil I can: C mss. vary between *y couth* and *for y couthe*. F's b-verse is not supported.
412 it: This is the beta reading; F's b-verse is too different to reveal alpha. O makes a sensible
correction by dropping the pronoun (since the object is in the following line), and thereby
agrees with Cx. Cf. l. 346 for a similar instance of scribes reading line by line.
413 for: Not in F. Cx has *and*. Perhaps both *for* and *and* are scribal expansions.
415 F rewrites the b-verse to increase the alliteration.
417 þe god: F reverses to *god þe*, agreeing with the P family of C.

But þow lyue by lore · of spiritus iusticie
Þe chief seed þat Pieres sewe · ysaued worstow neure
420 But conscience þe comune fede · and cardynale vertues
Leue it wel þei ben loste · bothe lyf & soule

¶ Thanne is many man ylost [·] quod a lewed vycory
I am a curatour of holykyrke · and come neure in my tyme
Man to me þat me couth telle · of cardinale vertues
425 Or þat acounted conscience · at a cokkes fether or an hennes
I knewe neure cardynal · þat he ne cam fro þe pope
And we clerkes whan þey come · for her comunes payeth
For her pelure and her palfreyes mete · & piloures þat hem folweth
Þe comune clamat cotidie · eche a man to other
430 Þe contre is þe curseder · þat cardynales come Inne
And þere they ligge and lenge moste · lecherye þere regneth
For-þi quod þis vicori · be verrey god I wolde
That no cardynal come · amonge þe comune peple
But in her holynesse · holden hem stille
435 At Auynoun amonge iuwes · cum sancto sanctus eris &c
Or in Rome as here rule wole · þe reliques to kepe

---

418 **lore:** F adds the definite article, as do some of the P family of C.

420 **þe comune fede:** "feed the people". The beta reading (with GO corrupting *fede* to *seede*). Beta is supported by the P family of C. F's reading *be þyn comoun foode* makes good sense addressed to the brewer, but it is exactly paralleled in only one C ms. The X family is divided, with one group reading *þy comune fode* and the other *be comune fode*. KD and RK emend to *be þy comunes*; see the discussion in RK, p. 126, where they argue that the adj. *comoun* "did not seem to have been used in the exact sense required, namely 'customary, day-to-day'". For further evaluation of the readings, see Barney (2006), 167. See notes to next line.

421 **it:** F's *me* has no support from **Cx.**

421 **þei ben:** The beta reading, referring to the people (*comune*, l. 420), treated as pl. also in l. 465. F has *þou art* addressed to the brewer, continuing the sense of its previous line. Cx's has instead *we been*, which avoids any difficulty. See note to l. 420.

422 **many:** Among B mss. only L omits *a*, but L has the support of most C mss.

424 **to me þat me couth:** F simplifies to *þat cowde me*, but beta is supported by Cx (although the P family drop the second *me*).

425 **at a:** Beta is supported by some C mss., where *at* is perhaps added to fill out a b-verse shortened by loss of the final phrase (see next note). However, **Cx** seems to have been without the preposition, as F.

425 **or an hennes:** Omitted by F and some C mss., but in **Cx.** See previous note.

428 **her pelure and:** Lost in F, but supported by **Cx.**

429 **to:** WHmF have *til*, but it is not supported by **Cx.**

430 **þat:** F shares the easier *þere* with the P family of C. Note repeated *þere* in the next line.

431 **moste:** In MCrCGO the punctuation follows *lenge*, with *moste* as adj. qualifying *lecherye*, but with the punctuation in LWHmF it is an adverb.

432 Note that WHmCF have a paraph.

434 **holden:** Supported by most C mss. against past tense *helden* in CrWCG.

435 **iuwes:** Beta has *þe iuwes*, but the definite article is easily added and the generalised sense as in F and **Cx** is appropriate.

KD.19.405–423

And þow conscience in kynges courte · & shuldest neure come þennes
And grace þat þow gredest so of · gyour of alle clerkes
And Pieres with his newe plow · & eke with his olde
440 Emperour of al þe worlde · þat alle men were cristene

¶ Inparfyt is þat pope · þat al peple shulde helpe
And sendeth hem þat sleeth suche · as he shulde saue
And wel worth piers þe plowman · þat [pur]sueth god in doyng
Qui pluit super iustos · & iniustos at ones
445 And sent þe sonne to saue · a cursed mannes tilthe
As bryȝte as to þe best man · & to þe beste woman
Riȝte so Pieres þe plowman · peyneth hym to tulye
As wel for a wastour · & wenches of þe stuwes
As for hym-self & his seruauntz · saue he is firste yserued
450 [So blessed be Pieres þe plowman · þat peyneth hym to tulye]
And trauailleth & tulyeth · for a tretour also sore
As for a trewe tydy man · al tymes ylyke
And worshiped be he þat wrouȝte al · bothe good & wykke
And suffreth þat synful be · til some-tyme þat þei repente
455 And god amende þe pope · þat pileth holykirke
And cleymeth bifor þe kynge · to be keper ouer crystene
And counteth nouȝt þough crystene ben · culled & robbed
And fynt folke to fyȝte · and cristene blode to spille
Aȝeyne þe olde lawe & newe lawe · as Luke [bereth] witness
460 Non occides michi vindictam &c

---

438 **gyour**: F's *sholde be gyȝere* is not supported by **Cx**. The P family has *were gyour*.

439 **Pieres**: F moves *with his newe plowh* to the b-verse and adds *plowman* for the alliteration, but it is not in **Cx**.

439 **eke with his olde**: F has *þe olde* (though with *also* in the a-verse). In C the X family has *also his olde*; the P family ends the line *hus olde boþe*.

441 **peple**: L only, with all others adding *þe*. Quite possibly L dropped the article on the model of the previous b-verse. However, the X family of C is also without *þe*. Instead of *peple*, CrW read *the world* (cf. l. 440).

443 **pursueth**: Both **Bx** and **Cx**. In L it is altered by erasure to *sueth*.

446 **&**: Evidently the beta reading, though CrW agree with F and **Cx** in reading *or*, which is equally possible.

448–50 F omits these three lines. See note to l. 450.

448 **& wenches**: The beta reading (F out). **Cx** has *or for a wenche*.

450 This line from **Cx** (RK.21.437) is not in any ms. of **B**. We presume it must have been in **Bx** to account for the loss in F of ll. 448–50 by eye-skip on *peers plowhman peyneþ hym to tylye*. It is important to note that three C mss. make the same error. On this argument, beta retained ll. 448–9 but skipped the following line thinking he had already copied it. So KD, p. 90 ("omission caused by homoteleuton").

459 **newe lawe**: So beta; F reads *þe newe*, losing the alliteration. C mss. have several variants.

459 **bereth witness**: For the b-verse exactly as in F and **Cx**, see Bx.9.78 and 11.285, and cf. 2.38, 7.93, 10.367, 11.236, 11.263 etc. which all end "X bears witness". Beta has *þer-of witnesseth*.

460 F's completion of the quotation is not supported by **Cx**.

It semeth by so · hym-self hadd his wille
That he ne reccheth ri3te nou3te · of al þe remenaunte
And cryst of his curteisye · þe cardinales saue
And tourne her witte to wisdome · & to wele of soule
465 For þe comune quod þis curatour [·] counten ful litel
Þe conseille of conscience · or cardinale vertues
But if þei sow[n]e as by sy3te · somwhat to wynnynge
Of gyle ne of gabbynge · gyue þei neuere tale
For spiritus prudencie · amonge þe peple is gyle
470 And alle þo faire vertues · as vyces þei semeth
Eche man sotileth a sleight · synne to hyde
And coloureth it for a kunnynge · and a clene lyuynge

¶ Thanne loughe þere a lorde · & by þis li3te sayde
I halde it ry3te & resoun · of my reue to take
475 Al þat myne auditour [·] or elles my stuwarde
Conseilleth me by her acounte · & my clerkes wrytynge

¶ With spiritus intellectus · they seke þe reues rolles
And with spiritus fortitudinis · fecche [it] I wole

---

461 Scribes show uncertainty about the placing of punctuation, with L having it after both *semeth* and *so*, F after *so* and *hym-selue*, and HmGO after *hym-sylf*. Our punctuation follows WMC.

461 **his**: OF add *owne* to fill out a b-verse shortened by mispunctuation; see previous note. It is not in **Cx**.

462 **That he**: Beta is supported by the P family of C with *Þat he* or *Þat hym*. F begins *He*; the X family begin *He* or *Hym*.

462 **al**: The reading of beta; F's b-verse is too much altered to be sure of the alpha reading. The X family of C does not have the word; the P group has *al þe oþer*, as does O.

464 **wele**: The beta reading, supported by the X family of C. The P family has *welþe*, as do WF. For the reverse situation see l. 293. See RK, p. 126, who defend *welþe* on the grounds it is less likely in context.

464 **of**: **Cx** has instead *for þe*. F's b-verse is not supported.

467 **sowne**: "relate to". F is supported by **Cx**. L's *sowe* is a simple misreading or mistranscription; the other beta mss. have forms of the verb "see". The verb is not used elsewhere in the B-text.

471 **Eche**: Beta is supported by the P family of C. The X family begins *For vche*, giving partial support to F's *For euerey*.

471 **to**: F is supported by **Cx**. Beta reads *forto* for the metre, as do a few C mss., but *synne* is disyllabic. Cf. **Bx**.2.177, 18.241, and see Duggan (1990), 175.

477 **¶**: Supported only by LM.

477 **seke**: Beta's reading makes excellent sense and provides ax/ax alliteration. F has *tooken*, which is the reading of the P family of C and a few of the X family, but the X family reading appears to be *cote* as in XYU, meaningless in context (for the verb, meaning "clothe", see RK.3.181). Others of the X family alter this to *cutt* or *counte*. Probably, then, *toke* is also a conjectural revision of a **Cx** error. It makes poor sense, and Kane (2005) unconvincingly interprets it as *MED tuken* in the sense "find fault with". For objections, see the discussion in Barney (2006), 181.

478 **fecche it I wole**: Apparently the beta reading, though L loses *it* (the line is marked for correction), and W adds *after*. F's reading is fanciful, but perhaps indicates dissatisfaction with

¶ And þanne come þere a kynge · & bi his croune seyde
480 I am Kynge with croune · þe comune to reule
And holykirke & clergye · fro cursed men to defende
And if me lakketh to lyue by · þe lawe wil I take it
Þere I may hastlokest it haue · for I am hed of lawe
For ȝe ben but membres · & I aboue alle
485 And sith I am ȝowre aller hed · I am ȝowre aller hele
And holycherche chief help · & chiftaigne of þe comune
And what I take of ȝow two · I take it atte techynge
Of spiritus iusticie [·] for I iugge ȝow alle
So I may baldely be houseled · for I borwe neuere
490 Ne craue of my comune · but as my kynde asketh

¶ In condicioun quod conscience · þat þow konne defende
And rule þi rewme in resoun · riȝt wel & in treuth
[Þat þou þine askyng haue ·] as þi lawe asketh
Omnia tua sunt ad defendendum set non ad depredandum
495 Þe vyker hadde fer home · & faire toke his leue
And I awakned þere-with · & wrote as me mette

---

a short b-verse. **Cx** has *fecche hit wolle he null he*. Schmidt (1995), 408 argues that **Bx** might have lost the last phrase, with the line then conjecturally repaired.

481 **to defende**: Supported by **Cx**. The b-verse is shortened by OF (dropping *to*), and by WHm (reading *fende / fonde*).

483 **hastlokest it haue**: Although the P family of C follows the order of Hm, the variants of CrGF are not supported.

484 **For**: Evidently the reading of **Bx**, though W *And* agrees with **Cx**.

487 **atte**: "at the", as usual in L. C mss. have *at þe, at* and *of* (cf. MCr).

488 L alone places the punctuation after *I*.

489 **I may**: Reversed by MCr, but supported by **Cx**.

491 **konne**: The reading of most C mss. RK adopt the minority reading *þe comune*.

492 **in** (1): Supported by **Cx** against the easier reading *by* in MCrHmO.

492 **riȝt wel**: Supported by **Cx** against easier *in riȝt* HmF.

493 **Þat þou þine askyng haue**: "(and on condition) that you take what you want (in the way the law decrees)". Though this may seem acceptable as a restoration of the authorial **B** reading, it is harder to justify as the reading of **Bx**. However, the argument is this. The beta a-verse, *Take þou may in resoun*, seems obviously scribal: it lacks alliteration, partially repeats the previous a-verse, and has no support from **Cx**, which has *That thow haue al thyn askyng*. This gives reasonable support for F's reading, except for non-alliterating *lykyng*. In fact the scribe has written the word over an erasure, and we suppose he substituted a synonym to avoid the repetition of *asken* in the b-verse. The reading of **Bx** may, of course, been exactly that of **Cx**, with F reordering and omitting *al*. See RK, p. 127.

493 **þi**: CrOF have *þe*. C mss. are also split, with *þe* in the P family.

494 **tua sunt**: F and **Cx** reverse the order.

Passus 20

Passus vicesimus de visione & primus de dobest

[And] as I went by þe way · whan I was þus awaked
Heuy-chered I ȝede · and elynge in herte
I ne wiste where to ete · ne at what place
And it neighed nyeghe þe none · & with nede I mette
5 That afronted me foule · and faitour me called
Coudestow nouȝte excuse þe · as dede þe Kynge & other
Þat þow toke to þi bylyf · to clothes and to sustenance
As by techynge & by tellynge · of spiritus temperancie
And þow nome namore · þan nede þe tauȝte
10 And nede ne hath no lawe · ne neure shal falle in dette
For þre thynges he taketh · his lyf forto saue

---

1 **And**: F is supported by **Cx** (though otherwise F rewrites the line). Beta has *Thanne* as a more appropriate opening for a passus (as **Bx**.10.1, 11.1), but Langland often plunges *in medias res*; see especially **Bx**.13.1.

3 **I**: So beta, but F and **Cx** begin *For I*. RK, p. 123, reject the F + **Cx** readings of ll. 3, 7 and 9 as coincidental error, describing *For* here as a "more explicit substitution". See also l. 11.

6 **Coudestow**: L is supported by F and **Cx** against *Kanstow* in other beta witnesses.

7 **þi bylyf**: So beta, though F's *lyve by* is also the reading of **Cx**. Athough the noun is a favourite of Langland's, it appears to have been obsolescent, and *MED* has no citations after c. 1300 apart from *Piers Plowman*. Scribes of C are particularly prone to avoid it; e.g. at RK.16.338 substitutions are *liflode, lyvyng* and *breed*. See note to **Bx**.19.241 (= RK.21.235), where *bylyf* is altered by MCrHmF to *lyflode*. See RK, p. 123.

8 **As by**: "according to". LMCr are supported by the P family of C. WHmCGO read *And*, which makes poor sense. The construction is "excuse yourself that you took according to the teaching of *spiritus temperancie*". F has *& þat was*; the X family of C has *Was*, meaning "excuse yourself that what you took ... was by the teaching ...".

8 **by** (2): Omitted by beta4, F and the P family of **Cx**.

9 **And**: "provided that" (so RK, p. 123). F and **Cx** also make good sense with *& þat*.

10 **And**: Supported by the X family of C; the P family omits. F's *For* has no support.

10 **ne** (1): LWHmCG are supported by some of the X family of C. Other scribes omit.

11 **he**: The reading of beta, though F and **Cx** read *þat he*.

That is mete whan men hym werneth · & he no moneye weldeth
Ne wyght none wil ben his borwe · ne wedde hath none to legge
And he cauȝte in þat cas · & come þere-to by sleighte
15   He synneth nouȝte sothelich · þat so wynneth his fode
And þough he come so to a clothe · and can no better cheuysaunce
Nede anon-riȝte · nymeth hym vnder meynpryse
And if hym lyst for to lape · þe lawe of kynde wolde
That he dronke at eche diche · ar he for thurste deyde
20   So nede at grete nede · may nymen as for his owne
Wyth-oute conseille of conscience · or cardynale vertues
So þat he suwe & saue · spiritus temperancie

¶ For is no vertue by fer [·] to spiritus temperancie
Neither spiritus iusticie · ne spiritus fortitudinis
25   For spiritus fortitudinis · forfaiteth ful oft
He shal do more þan mesure · many tyme & ofte
And bete men ouer bitter · and somme [body] to litel
And greue men gretter · þan goode faith it wolde

¶ And spiritus iusticie · shal iuggen wol he nol he
30   After þe kynges conseille · & þe comune lyke
And spiritus prudencie · in many a poynte shal faille
Of þat he weneth wolde falle · if his wytte ne were
Wenynge is no wysdome · ne wyse ymagynacioun
Homo proponit & deus disponit · & gouerneth alle
35   Good vertues [and] nede is next hym · for anon he meketh

---

13 L has an inappropriate paraph (the line is at the top of the page).

13 **none wil ben**: The beta reading, against F's *þat wille ben*. In **C**, ms. X reads *þat now wol be*, though others in the X family have *none* for *now*. The P family begins the line *And wot that non wol be*.

13 **ne wedde hath none**: Beta reading is preferable since alliteration is on /w/ not /n/. Yet F's *ne no wed haþ* is that of the X family of **C**; the P family reads *noþer haþ wed*.

14 **cauȝte**: i.e. "stole". **Cx** has present tense; F has *caste*.

23 **by fer to**: F has *by-fore*, as do a few C mss.

26 **tyme**: F has *tymes*, with similar variation among C mss. See note to **Bx**.11.387 for alpha's tendency to prefer *tymes*.

27 **body**: Here R resumes, to provide this reading, supported by **Cx** and alliteration. F has the plural. Beta reads *of hem*.

28 **it**: Dropped by HmCGO, as by the P family of **C**.

34 **& gouerneth alle**: In alpha the line-break occurs after *alle*; in beta it is after *good vertues*. Alpha's arrangement is supported as **Bx** and **Cx** by the P family of C, which has *god gouerneth alle*. The X family sets the Latin on its own, but then breaks the lines after *hym* and *lombe*. KD and Schmidt break after *disponit, vertues, meketh*. The problem is caused by the short line *God gouerneth all good vertues*, compounded by the replacement in **Bx** of *God* by *&*.

35 **and**: R is supported by the X family of C against beta's *Ac*. F and the P family rearrange in different ways.

And as low as a lombe · for lakkyng þat hym nedeth

[¶ For nede maketh nede · fele nedes lowe-herted]
[Philosophres] forsoke wel[th]e · for þey wolde be nedy
And woneden [wel elengly] · & wolde nouȝte be riche

40 ¶ And god al his grete ioye · gostliche he left
And cam & toke mankynde · and bycam nedy
So [he was nedy] as seyth þe boke · in many sondry places
Þat he seyde in his sorwe · on þe selue Rode
Bothe fox & foule · may fleighe to hole & crepe
45 And þe fisshe hath fyn · to flete with to reste
Þere nede hath ynome me · þat I mote nede abyde
And suffre sorwes ful sowre · þat shal to ioye tourne
For-þi be nouȝte abasshed · to byde and to be nedy
Syth he þat wrouȝte al þe worlde · was wilfullich nedy
50 Ne neuer none so nedy · ne pouerere deyde

¶ Whan nede had vndernome þus · anon I felle aslepe
And mette ful merueillously · þat in mannes forme
Antecryst cam þanne · and al þe croppe of treuthe
Torned it vp-so-doune · and ouertilte þe rote
55 And [made] fals sprynge & sprede · & spede mennes nedes
In eche a contre þere he cam · he cutte awey treuthe
And gert gyle growe þere · as he a god were

[¶] Freres folwed þat fende · for he ȝaf hem copes
And religiouse reuerenced hym · and rongen here belles

---

36 **þat**: Alpha is supported by most C mss., though some have *of þat*, as in beta.

37 Beta omits the line, which Barney (2006), 202, suggests may be a late addition. R's form of the line is supported by the X family of C.

38 **Philosophres**: Though alpha is supported by Cx, beta has a good line, with *Wyse men* alliterating on /w/. Perhaps this is a case of revision, or alpha contamination from C. See notes to ll. 37 and 39.

38 **welthe**: Alpha is supported by Cx against *wele* in beta.

39 **wel elengly**: Alpha's reading, supported by Cx, may be a revision of beta's *in wilderness*.

42 **So he was nedy**: R's order is supported by the X family of C; F's prose order, *He was so needy*, by the P family. Beta has *So nedy he was*.

45 **to** (2): Alpha has *or to*, taking *reste* as a verb, but it is not supported by Cx or by sense: Kane (2005) glosses *reste* as "safety".

48 **byde**: Beta4 and R have *bidde*, as does the P family of C. The X family supports *bide*, which follows on from l. 46.

51 **vndernome**: All except OR have the object *me*, though it is inserted in M. In C it is in all mss. except XYU, the three most authoritative of the X family. Cf. l. 46, which probably prompted the addition.

55 **made**: Alpha supported by Cx. Beta omits.

58 **¶**: The paraph is in WHm and alpha. In L the line is at the top of the page.

60 And al þe couent cam · to welcome [a] tyraunt
    And alle hise as wel as hym · saue onlich folis
    Which folis were wel [gladd]er [·] to deye þan to lyue
    Lengore sith le[ute] · was so rebuked
    And a fals fende antecriste · ouer alle folke regned
65 And þat were mylde men & holy · þat no myschief dredden
    Defyed al falsenesse · and folke þat it vsed
    And what Kynge þat hem conforted · knowynge hem [gy]le
    They cursed and her conseille · were it clerke or lewed

    ¶ Antecriste hadde thus sone · hundredes at his banere
70 And Pryde it bare · boldely aboute
    With a lorde þat lyueth · after lykynge of body
    That cam aȝein conscience · þat kepere was & gyoure
    Ouer kynde crystene · and cardynale vertues

    ¶ I conseille quod conscience þo · cometh with me ȝe foles
75 In-to vnyte holy cherche · and holde we vs there
    And crye we to kynde · þat he come & defende vs
    Foles · fro þis fendes lymes · for Piers loue þe plowman
    And crye we [on] alle þe comune · þat þei come to vnite
    And þere abide and bikere · aȝein beliales children

80 ¶ Kynd conscience þo herde · and cam out of þe planetes
    And sent forth his foreioures [·] feures and fluxes
    Coughes and cardiacles · crampes and tothaches
    Rewmes & radegoundes · and roynouse scalles
    Byles and bocches · and brennyng agues
85 Frenesyes & foule yueles · forageres of kynde

---

60 **cam**: Beta has *forth cam*, F has *cam holly*. Neither has support from C. R is supported by the X family of C; the P family has *þo cam*.

60 **a**: R is supported by the most reliable of the X family of C. The reading is a little more difficult than *þat*, as in beta and F, as well as the P family of C.

62 **wel**: Omitted by alpha and the P family of C, but supported by the X family.

62 **gladder**: Alpha is supported by **Cx** against beta's *leuer*.

63 **leute**: Alpha is supported by **Cx**. Beta read *lenten*, with the obvious error corrected in Cr, and visibly corrected in Hm by the revising hand.

65 **were**: Beta is supported by **Cx**. Alpha's *we* is an obvious error.

67 **hem gyle**: "them to deceive"? R probably preserves the **Bx** reading, where **Cx** has *here gyle*. Beta revises to *hem any while* to make better sense.

70 **it bare**: Clearly the reading of **Bx** as well as **Cx**. Hm, F and the P family of C all expand in different ways. See RK, p. 130 and n. 50.

77 The punctuation after *Foles* is in LWOF, and so is perhaps archetypal.

78 **on**: Alpha is supported by **Cx** against beta's *to*.

83 **scalles**: "skin diseases". W has *scabbes*, an easier reading, but it is also the reading of **Cx**. See RK, p. 121.

KD.20.60–85

Hadde yprykked and prayed [·] polles of peple
Largelich a legioun · lese her lyf sone

¶ There was harrow and help · here cometh kynde
With deth þat is dredful · to vndone vs alle

90 ¶ The lorde that lyued after lust · tho alowde cryde
After conforte a knyghte · to come and bere his banere
Alarme alarme quod þat lorde [·] eche lyf kepe his owne

¶ Þanne mette þis men · ar mynstralles myȝte pipe
And ar heraudes of armes · hadden descreued lordes

95 ¶ Elde þe hore · he was in þe vauntwarde
And bare þe banere bifor deth · by riȝte he it claymed
Kynde come after [hym] · with many kene sores
As pokkes and pestilences · and moche poeple shente
So kynde þorw corupciouns · kulled ful manye

100 ¶ Deth cam dryuende after · and al to doust passhed
Kynges & Knyȝtes · kayseres and popes
Lered ne lewed · he le[f]t no man stonde
That he hitte euene · þat euere stired after
Many a louely lady · and lemmanes knyghtes
105 Swouned and swelted · for sorwe of dethes dyntes

¶ Conscience of his curteisye · to kynde he bisouȝte
To cesse & suffre · and see where þei wolde
Leue pryde pryuely · and be parfite cristene

¶ And kynde cessed tho · to se þe peple amende
110 Fortune gan flateren thenne · þo fewe þat were alyue
And byhight hem longe lyf · and lecherye he sent

---

86 **peple**: MCrCGOF add the definite article, but it is not in **Cx**.

87 **Largelich**: Beta's *Þat largelich* is not supported by **Cx**.

87 **lese**: Probably past, though R's *lose* is present. **Cx** has *lees*.

91 **conforte a**: R (= alpha) omits; F expands speculatively to make up the loss.

93 **Þanne**: So alpha, supported by **Cx**; beta has *And þanne*.

95–6 Beta4 omits these two lines.

95 **hore**: Beta is supported by **Cx**. F reads the rare *horel*, "fornicator", and R is apparently corrected to that reading.

97 **hym**: Alpha is supported by **Cx**; beta omits.

100 **dryuende**: Note that L and alpha have this form of the present participle. See note to **Bx**.17.50.

100 **passhed**: Beta is supported by **Cx**. F has *daschede*, and in R *paschte* is corrected to *daschte*.

102 **left**: Alpha is supported by **Cx** against beta's *let*.

103 **þat euere stired**: The wording of LWR is supported by **Cx**.

104 **lemmanes knyghtes**: "lover-knights". So R. Beta misunderstands and adds *of*. F rewrites, but its inclusion of *hire* could perhaps indicate that **Bx** read as **Cx**, which reads *here lemmanes knyhtes*.

KD.20.86–111

Amonges al manere men · wedded & vnwedded
And gadered a gret hoste · al agayne conscience

¶ This lecherye leyde on · with laughyng chiere
115 And with pryue speche · and peynted wordes
And armed hym in ydelnesse · and in hiegh berynge
He bare a bowe in his hande · and manye blody arwes
Weren fethered with faire biheste · and many a false truthe
Wit[h] vntydy tales · he tened ful ofte
120 Conscience and his compaignye · of holi[kirke] þe techeres

¶ Thanne cam coueityse · and caste how he my3te
Ouercome conscience · and cardynal vertues
And armed hym in auaryce · and hungriliche lyued
His wepne was al wiles · to wynnen & to hyden
125 With glosynges and gabbynges · he gyled þe peple
Symonye hym se[ude] · to assaille conscience
And preched to þe peple · and prelates þei hem maden
To holden with antecryste · her temperaltes to saue
And come to þe kynges conseille · as a kene baroun
130 And kneled to conscience [·] in courte afor hem alle
And gart gode feith flee · and fals to abide
And boldeliche bar adown · with many a bri3te noble
Moche of þe witte and wisdome · of westmynster halle
He iugged til a iustice · and iusted in his ere

---

114 **¶**: The paraph is in beta and F.

114 **with**: Beta has *with a*, but alpha is supported by **Cx**.

117 **blody**: With support from LMCr, beta4 and R, this is presumably the reading of **Bx**. However, WHmF *brode* is also the reading of **Cx**, and is better in context. Schmidt (1995), 409, conjectures that **Bx** had the form *blode*, independently corrected by beta3 and F.

119 **With**: L's *Wit* is marked for correction, as at **Bx**.5.612. Beta has *With his*, but alpha without *his* is supported by **Cx**.

120 **kirke**: Cr and alpha. Beta and **Cx** read non-alliterating *cherche*. See Introduction, pp. 18–19.

123 **hungriliche**: *MED* records R's *vngriseliche* as a unique instance. Presumably alpha had F's form *vngryly*, "hungrily", misread by R.

125 **and**: Beta must have had *and with* (though beta4 drops *with*). Alpha presumably had *and*, as in R, supported by **Cx**, with F adding *with*.

126 **seude**: "followed" (*MED seuen* v.(1)). R is supported by **Cx**. The form was easily misread as *sende* (pa.t.), altered to *sent(e)* by both beta and F. See Schmidt (1995), 409.

127 **hem**: Omitted by MCr. **Cx** is without it, following a different a-verse *And presed on þe pope*. See Barney (2006), 214, for discussion of the versions.

130 **kneled to**: **Cx** reads *knokked*.

130 **afor**: Beta4 and alpha have *before*, as does **Cx**. For discussion of these variants, see note to **Bx**.5.12.

132 **bri3te**: Beta is supported by alliteration and **Cx**. Alpha has *rede*.

134 **iugged til**: W has *Iogged to*, as does **Cx**. The sense of the verb is uncertain: see *OED jug* v.4, *jag* v., *jog* v; Kane (2005) *s.v. iogged* glosses "thrust his way". **Bx** may have misunderstood it as "judged", i.e. "condemned".

135 And ouertilte al his treuthe · with take þis vp amendement
And [in-]to þe arches in haste · he ȝede anone after
And torned Ciuile in-to symonye · and sitthe he toke þe official
For a [menyuere mentel] · he made lele matrimonye
Departen ar deth cam · & [a] deuos shupte

140 ¶ Allas quod conscience & cried þo · wolde criste of his grace
That coueityse were cristene · þat is so kene [to fiȝte]
And bolde and [a]bidyng · [þe] while his bagge lasteth

¶ And þanne lowgh lyf · and leet dagge his clothes
And armed hym in haste · in harlotes wordes
145 And helde holynesse a iape · and hendenesse a wastour
And lete leute a cherle · and lyer a fre man
Conscience and conseille · he counted it folye

¶ Thus relyed lyf · for a litel fortune
And pryked forth with pryde [·] preyseth he no vertue
150 [Ne] careth nouȝte how kynde slow · and shal come atte laste
And culle alle erthely creature · saue conscience one
Lyf leep asyde · and lauȝte hym a lemman
Heel & I quod he · and hieghnesse of herte
Shal do þe nouȝte drede · noyther deth ne elde
155 And to forȝete sorwe · and ȝyue nouȝte of synne

---

135 **vp:** Cx has *on.*

136 **in-to:** Alpha and Hm; perhaps a little more appropriate than beta's *to.* C mss. are similarly divided: the P family agrees with beta.

138 **menyuere mentel:** Alpha is supported by Cx. Beta has *mentel of menyuere.*

139 **a:** Dropped by beta, but alpha is supported by Cx.

140 **þo:** Dropped by F and the P family of C.

140 **his:** In Cx; dropped in R.

141 **to fiȝte:** Alpha is supported by Cx against beta's *a fiȝter.*

142 **abidyng:** So alpha and CrHmO, against *bidyng* in the others. C mss. are also split, with the X family and some of the P family reading *abidyng.* There is support for *abidyng* from the same a-verse in **Bx.**19.302.

142 **þe:** Not in beta, and Cx is also split, but alpha is supported by the best of both families of C.

147 **folye:** Beta4 and R, supported by Cx. LMHm (hence beta?) have *a folye,* Cr *at foly,* W *at a flye*; F has *but folye.*

149 **pryked:** Bx clearly has past tense, though W has the present, as do the most reliable C mss.

150 **Ne:** Beta has *He* (*A* in L), though Hm has *and,* and W has *Ne,* agreeing with alpha and Cx.

151 **culle:** Supported by Cx against alpha's *calle.*

151 **creature:** LR and original M have the distributive sg. against the plural in others. Cx is also split.

152 **leep asyde:** Beta is supported by Cx against alpha's curious reading *seith occide.*

155 **sorwe:** MCr read *deþ* from the line above. Cx has instead *ȝowthe.*

¶ This lyked lyf · and his lemman fortune
And geten in her glorie · a gadelyng atte laste
One þat moche wo wrouȝte · sleuthe was his name
Sleuthe wex wonder ȝerne · and sone was of age
160 And wedded one wanhope · a wenche of þe stuwes
Her syre was a sysour · þat neure swore treuthe
One Thomme two tonge · ateynte at vch a queste

¶ This sleuthe was war of werre · and a slynge made
And threwe drede of dyspayre · a dozein myle aboute
165 For care conscience þo · cryed vpon elde
And bad hym fonde to fyȝte · and afere wanhope

¶ And elde hent good hope · and hastilich he shifte hym
And wayued awey wanhope · and with lyf he fyȝteth
And lyf fleigh for fere [·] to fysyke after helpe
170 And bisouȝte hym of socoure · and of his salue hadde
And gaf hym golde good woon · þat gladded h[er] herte[s]
And þei gyuen hym agayne [·] a glasen houve
Lyf leued þat lechecrafte · lette shulde elde
And dryuen awey deth · with dyas and dragges

175 ¶ And elde auntred hym on lyf · and atte laste he hitte
A Fisicien with a forred hood · þat he fel in a palsye
And þere deyed þat doctour · ar thre dayes after
Now I see seyde lyf · þat surgerye ne Fisyke
May nouȝte a myte auaille · to medle aȝein elde
180 And in hope of his hele · gode herte he hente
And rode so to reuel · a ryche place and a merye
The companye of conforte · men cleped it sumtyme

---

158 **wo:** Omitted by alpha.
163 **This:** Beta is supported by **Cx.** R has *þus* and F omits.
163 **was:** Beta4 has *wex*, but this is not supported by **Cx.**
163 **war:** Cx has *sley.*
166 **hym:** Omitted by alpha, but beta is supported by **Cx.**
167 **shifte:** "got moving" (refl.). Cx has instead *shroef.*
171 **her hertes:** Beta has *his herte*, following the sg. in the a-verse. R alone has the plural, but is supported by the best C mss., six of which also have *here* for *his* in l. 170. See next note.
172 **þei:** F alters to *he*, following the sg. pronouns of ll. 170–1. Schmidt (2008), 467, explains that the distinction is between the art of Fysyke and its practitioners. See previous note.
174 **dryuen:** Alpha has *to driue*, as do some of the P family of C, but the rest omit *to.*
174 **dyas:** "remedies". Beta is supported by **Cx** against alpha's *dayes.*
176 **a (3):** As in **Cx.** MCrC have *þe* (inserted in M). O omits.
180 **he:** Omitted by R, but **Cx** has it.
182 **conforte:** Beta4 corrupts to *court.*

And elde anone after [hym] · and ouer myne heed ȝede
And made me balled bifore · and bare on þe croune
185 So harde he ȝede ouer myn hed · it wil be seen eure

¶ Sire euel ytauȝte elde quod I · vnhende go with the
Sith whanne was þe way · ouer men hedes
Haddestow be hende quod I · þow woldest haue asked leue

¶ ȝe leue lordeyne quod he · and leyde on me with age
190 And hitte me vnder þe ere · vnethe may ich here
He buffeted me aboute þe mouthe · & bett out my [wange-]tethe
And gyued me in goutes · I may nouȝte go at large
And of þe wo þat I was in · my wyf had reuthe
And wisshed [wel] witterly · þat I were in heuene
195 For þe lyme þat she loued me fore · and leef was to fele
On nyȝtes namely · whan we naked were
I ne myght in no manere · maken it at hir wille
So elde and [he] · [it hadden] forbeten

¶ And as I seet in þis sorwe · I say how kynde passed
200 And deth drowgh niegh me · for drede gan I quake
And cried to kynde · out of care me brynge
Loo elde þe hoore · hath me biseye
Awreke me if ȝowre wille be · for I wolde ben hennes

¶ ȝif þow wilt ben ywroken · wende in-to vnite
205 And holde þe þere eure · tyl I sende for þe
And loke þow conne somme crafte [·] ar þow come þennes

[¶] Conseille me kynde quod I · what crafte [be] best to lerne

---

183 **hym**: Alpha supported by **Cx** against beta's *me*. Beta fails to understand that the reference is to *Lyf*.

187 **men**: L alone has the uninflected gen., but RK record the C reading as *menne*.

191 **wange-tethe**: Beta drops *wange*, though it is included in **Cx**, which has the b-verse as in R. Beta must have had *& bett out my tethe* as in LMCr, with variations in WHm and beta4.

194 **wel**: R alone, but supported by **Cx**. Beta has *ful*, F has *often*.

198 **he**: "she". Only R has the *h*- form, but it is necessary for the alliteration and is supported by **Cx**. See Introduction, p. 17. Beta reads *she sothly*, lengthening a short a-verse, but neither R or **Cx** has the adverb. F rewrites the a-verse.

198 **it hadden**: R's order is supported by **Cx**, altered to prose order in all other **B** mss.

199 **as**: Beta is supported by **Cx** against alpha's *was*.

200 **niegh**: MCrF have *neer* (from OE comparative), but it is not supported by **Cx**.

202 **me**: Beta is supported by **Cx** against alpha's *my lif*.

202 **biseye**: 'dealt with'; *MED bisen* 4(b). Supported by **Cx** against variants in CrGR.

207 **¶**: The paraph to mark the dreamer's words is in WHmC and alpha, with a line-space in M.

207 **be**: R's subjunctive is supported by **Cx** against *is* in beta. F rephrases.

[¶] Lerne to loue quod kynde · & leue alle othre

¶ How shal I come to catel so · to clothe me and to fede

210 [¶] And þow loue lelly · lakke shal þe neure
[Wede] ne wordly [mete] · whil þi lyf lasteth

¶ And þere by conseille of kynde · comsed to rowme
Thorw contricioun & confessioun · tyl I cam to vnite
And þere was conscience constable · cristene to saue
215 And biseged sothly · with seuene grete gyauntz
Þat with Antecrist helden · hard aȝein conscience

¶ Sleuth with his slynge · an[d] hard saut he made
Proude prestes come with hym [· passyng an hundreth]
In paltokes & pyked shoes · & pisseres longe knyues
220 Comen aȝein conscience · with coueityse þei helden

¶ By [þe] Marie quod a mansed preste · [was] of þe marche of yrlonde
I counte namore conscience · bi so I cacche syluer
Than I do to drynke · a drauȝte of good ale
And so seide sexty [·] of þe same contreye
225 And shoten aȝein with shotte · many a shef of othes
And brode hoked arwes · goddes herte & his nayles
And hadden almost vnyte · and holynesse adowne

---

208 **¶**: In L the scribe left a line-space but the rubricator did not supply the paraph to mark Kynde's words. It is in WHmC and alpha, with a line-space in M.

208 **leue**: Alpha and Cr are supported by **Cx** in omitting *of*. Beta perhaps avoids the x / x / x rhythm of the b-verse, as F does by adding *craftys*.

209 **to** (3): Supported by **Cx**, though dropped by HmGF and erased in M.

210 **¶**: Though lacking in LR and therefore somewhat doubtful, the paraph to mark Kynde's words is in WHmCF, with a line-space in M.

210 **lelly**: Beta adds *quod he*, but it is not in alpha or **Cx**.

211 **Wede … mete**: Alpha's order is supported by **Cx**. Beta reverses. Note the spelling *wordly* for "worldly" in LR, perhaps archetypal.

212 **comsed**: So R. Beta has *I comsed*, F has *he comsede*. In **Cx** the line reads: *And y bi conseil of kynde comsed to Rome*, though eight mss. move the pronoun to the b-verse. Evidently *þere* is a **Bx** error for *I*, the omission of which is supplied in the b-verse by all scribes except R.

214 **conscience**: Dropped in alpha; F patches.

217 **and**: Probably an archetypal error for *an*. MCrCR have *and*, as do five C mss. including X (misreported by RK). All other scribes in both versions make the necessary and obvious correction to *an*; M is corrected by adding *an*.

217 **saut**: LHm and alpha are supported by **Cx** against *assaut*. Cf. variants at l. 301.

217 **he**: LWHm and alpha supported by **Cx**. Other mss. omit.

218 **passyng an hundreth**: Alpha is supported by **Cx** and alliteration against beta's *moo þan a thousand*.

221 **þe** (1): In R only, but supported by **Cx**. *MED* cites no other examples of this form of the oath, though cf. *by þe holy Marie* etc.

221 **was**: Omitted by beta. Alpha is supported by **Cx**.

¶ Conscience cryed helpe · clergye or ellis I falle
Thorw inparfit prestes · and prelates of holicherche
230   Freres herden hym crye · and comen hym to helpe
Ac for þei couth nou3te wel her craft · conscience forsoke hem

¶ Nede neghed tho nere · and conscience he tolde
That þei come for coueityse · to haue cure of soules
And for þei arn poure par-auenture · for patrimoigne hem failleth
235   Thei wil flatre to fare wel · folke þat ben riche
And sithen þei chosen chele · and cheytifte pouerte
Lat hem chewe as þei chese · and charge hem with no cure
For lomer he lyeth · þat lyflode mote begge
Þan he þat laboureth for lyflode · & leneth it beggeres
240   And sithen Freres forsoke · þe felicite of erthe
Lat hem be as beggeres · or lyue by angeles fode

¶ Conscience of þis conseille þo · comsed for to laughe
And curtei[s]lich conforted hem · and called in alle freres
And seide sires sothly · welcome be 3e alle
245   To vnite and holicherche · ac on thyng I 3ow preye
Holdeth 3ow in vnyte · and haueth none envye
To lered ne to lewed · but lyueth after 3owre rewle
And I wil be 3owre borghe · 3e shal haue bred and clothes
And other necessaries anowe · 3ow shal no thyng [lakke]
250   With þat 3e leue logyk · and lerneth for to louye
For loue laft þei lordship · bothe londe and scole
Frere Fraunceys and Dominyk · for loue to ben holy

¶ And if 3e coueyteth cure · kynde wil 3ow te[ll]e
That in mesure god made · alle manere thynges
255   And sette it at a certeyne · and at a syker noumbre

---

233 **coueityse**: Alpha misunderstands Nede's advice and adds *no*.

236 **cheytifte**: As in LWR and **Cx**, though other beta mss. alter the noun to the adj. *cheitif*, and F reads *chastite &*. For the suggestion that *poverte* was a marginal gloss incorporated into the text in **Bx** and **Cx**, see RK, p. 136.

238–9 Two lines omitted by alpha but attested by **Cx**. The likely explanation for the omission is eyeskip from *For* (238) to *For* (240), suggesting that alpha's exemplar began l. 240 with *For* rather than **Bx** *And* (see note).

240 **And**: Supported by **Cx** against alpha's *For*.

240 **þe**: Beta is supported by **Cx**, though it is dropped by G and alpha.

242 **þo**: Dropped by alpha and by some of the P family of C.

243 **curteislich**: The line in L is marked for correction.

249 **lakke**: Alpha is supported by **Cx** against beta's *faille*, which is perhaps picked up from l. 234. For *3ow*, F has *3ee* as subject, as do a few C mss. R's *þow* is odd in context.

253 **telle**: Alpha is supported by **Cx** against beta's *teche*.

255 **it**: Supported by **Cx** against *hem* in CrWF.

And nempned [hem] names newe · and noumbred þe sterres
Qui numerat multitudinem stellarum

¶ Kynges & knyghtes [·] þat kepen and defenden
Han officers vnder hem · and vch of hem certeyne
260   And if þei wage men to werre · þei write hem in noumbre
Wil no tresorere [taken] hem [wages] · trauaille þei neure so sore
Alle other in bataille · ben yholde bribours
Pilours and pykehernois · in eche a p[arisch] [a]cursed

¶ Monkes and monyals · and alle men of Religioun
265   Her ordre and her reule wil · to han a certeyne noumbre
Of lewed and of lered · þe lawe wol and axeth
A certeyn for a certeyne · saue onelich of freres
For-þi quod conscience by cryst · kynde witte me telleth
It is wikked to wage ȝow · ȝe wexeth out of noumbre
270   Heuene hath euene noumbre · and helle is with-out noumbre
For-þi I wolde witterly · þat ȝe were in þe Registre
And ȝowre noumbre vndre notarie sygne · & noyther mo ne lasse

¶ Enuye herd þis · and heet freres go to scole
And lerne logyk and lawe · and eke contemplacioun

---

256 **hem**: Omitted by beta, but alpha is supported by **Cx**. See next note.

256 **newe**: Not in **Cx** at all, and presumably a **Bx** error, since it makes poor sense in either position in the line. In **Bx** it was probably in the a-verse, prompting beta to drop *hem* to lighten a heavy verse, and alpha to move it into the b-verse to qualify *numbred*, with no better sense.

257 **stellarum**: Alpha evidently agreed with **Cx** in omitting *& omnibus eis &c*, and F struggles to complete the familiar quotation.

258 ¶: The paraph is in beta and F, following the Latin line.

258 **kepen**: Oddly, R's illogical past tense is supported by three of the best of the X family of C. It could therefore be archetypal error.

259 **certeyne**: WHmOF have *a certein* as in **Cx**, but LR and CrCG omit the article. This is evidently a **Bx** error, with scribes making an obvious correction, as the M scribe does visibly.

261 **taken hem wages**: Beta alters to *hem paye*, shortening a long a-verse but losing the alliteration. Alpha is supported by **Cx**. For *hem* R uniquely reads *hym* as in l. 259. In **Cx** this line is followed by *Bote by ben nempned in þe nombre of hem þat been ywaged* (RK.21.261), necessary to complete the sense. Its loss in **Bx** causes WHm to move l. 261 to the end of the paragraph to follow l. 263, and C² to invent a new line: *but he kunne rekene ariȝt her names in his rollis*. Cr, followed by revised M, more simply begins the line *Or they wil*, and F has *Ellys wille*.

263 **parisch**: Beta has *place*, but alpha is supported by **Cx**.

263 **acursed**: MCrCGO and alpha are supported by **Cx** against *ycursed* in LWHm.

264 ¶: The paraph is in beta and F.

265 **Her ordre and**: Presumably alpha dropped *ordre*, with R faithfully copying *Her and* as *heraude*, and F characteristically revising to make sense.

269 **out of**: Beta and **Cx**. R's *of on* is probably the alpha reading, revised by F to *ouer ony* for sense.

272 **notarie**: MCrWCO's gen. is not supported by **Cx**.

273 ¶: The paraph is in beta and F.

273 **go**: LWC have *to go*, not supported by **Cx**.

275 And preche men of plato · and preue it by seneca
     Þat alle þinges vnder heuene · ou3te to ben in comune

     ¶ [H]e lyeth as I leue · þat to þe lewed so precheth
     For god made to men a lawe · and Moyses it tau3te
     Non concupisces rem proximi tui
280 And euele is þis yholde · in parisches of engelonde
     For parsones and parish prestes [·] þat shulde þe peple shryue
     Ben curatoures called · to knowe and to hele
     Alle þat ben her parisshiens · penaunce enioigne
     And be[n] ashamed in her shrifte · ac shame maketh hem wende
285 And fleen to þe freres · as fals folke to westmynstre
     That borweth and bereth it þider · and þanne biddeth frendes
     3erne of for3ifnesse · or lenger 3eres leue

     ¶ Ac whil he is in westmynstre · he wil be bifore
     And make hym merye [·] with other mennes goodis
290 And so it fareth with moche folke · þat to freres shryueth
     As sysours and execcutours · þei [shul 3eue] þe freres
     A parcel to preye for hem · & make hem myrye
     With þe residue and þe remenaunt · þat other men biswonke
     And suffre þe ded in dette · to þe day of dome

295 ¶ Enuye herfore · hated conscience
     And freres to philosofye · he fonde hem to scole
     The while coueytise and vnkyndenesse · conscience assailled
     In vnite holycherche · conscience helde hym
     And made pees porter · to pynne þe 3ates

---

277 **He:** So alpha and **Cx.** Beta begins *And 3it he.*

283 **penaunce:** Probably plural; alpha has *penaunces.* For variation with and without <-s>, see note to **Bx.**14.211. There is similar variation in C mss.

283 **enioigne:** All except R read *to enioigne,* which has minority support from C mss.

284 **ben:** For once F probably represents alpha and is supported by **Cx.** R takes infin. *ben* as pres. pl., altering to *beth.* Beta clarifies with *shulden be(n).*

287 **leue:** The reading of LR and probably alpha (F's rewrite includes *bleve*), supported by **Cx.** Beta1 has *loone,* adopted by RK, p. 128, who explain the financial arrangement. For *leue,* "dispensation", see Alford (1988), 88.

289 **make:** Beta's infinitive is supported by **Cx** against alpha's *maketh.*

289 **mennes:** For R's gen. pl. *men,* cf. l. 187 and note. Some C scribes have the same form.

290 **to:** Alpha supported by **Cx** against beta's *to þe* (though Cr also has *to*).

290 **shryueth:** WOF have *hem shryueþ,* as do some of the P family of C.

291 **shul:** Alpha is supported by **Cx** against beta's *wil.*

291 **3eue þe:** The L scribe omitted the verb, and the omission was subsequently miscorrected.

292 **hem** (2): R is supported by **Cx** against *hem-self* in beta. F rewrites the b-verse to pad it out, but that then involves rewriting the next line to avoid repetition.

293 **þe** (1 & 2): The definite article is omitted by R in both cases, and the first of them is added by the corrector in M. F has both in a rewritten line. **Cx** drops *þe residue and.*

300 Of alle taletellers · and tyterers [a]n ydel
Ypocrisye and he · an hard saut þei made
Ypocrysie atte ȝate · hard gan fiȝte
And wounded wel wykkedly · many [a] wise techer
Þat with conscience acorded · and cardinale vertues

305 [¶] Conscience called a leche · þat coude wel shryue
Go salue þo þat syke [were] · [and] þorw synne ywounded
Shrifte shope sharpe salue · and made men do penaunce
For her mysdedes [·] þat þei wrouȝte hadden
And þat piers were payed · redde quod debes

310 ¶ Somme lyked nouȝte þis leche · and lettres þei sent
Ȝif any surgien were [in] þe sege · þat softer couth plastre
Sire l[i]f to lyue in leccherye · lay þere and groned
For fastyng of a fryday · he ferde as he wolde deye
Ther is a surgiene in þis sege · þat soft can handle

315 And more of phisyke bi fer · and fairer he plastreth
One frere flaterere [·] is phisiciene and surgiene
Quod contricioun to conscience · do hym come to vnyte
For here is many a man herte · þorw ypocrisie

¶ We han no nede quod conscience · I wote no better leche
320 Than persoun or parissh prest · penytancere or bisshop
Saue Piers þe plowman · þat hath powere ouer alle

---

300 **an**: So R, supported by the X family of C. Beta has *in*, F has *of ydelte*. In L the phrase is elsewhere always *an ydel* (Bx.5.592, 14.210, 19.415).

301 **he**: The *h*- form is necessary for the alliteration. Presumably **Bx** took it to be sg., but **Cx** understands that it must be plural and alters to *they*. See Introduction, p. 18.

301 **saut**: LHmOR supported by **Cx** against *assaut* in MCrWCG. Cf. l. 217. F omits the line.

303 **a**: CrW and alpha are supported by **Cx**. Most beta scribes omit it.

305 **¶**: The paraph is in WHmC and alpha. In L the line is at the top of the page.

306 **Go**: The reading of LCrHmGOR and original M, supported by the X family of C, against *To* in CF and revised M, supported by the P family, and *To go* in W. See next note.

306 **were**: Alpha is supported by **Cx** against *ben* in beta, who takes *Go* as an indication of direct speech.

306 **and**: CrWHm and alpha are supported by **Cx**, against omission in others. It is added in M.

309 **piers**: So **Bx**. **Cx** has *Peres pardon*.

311 **in þe sege**: "among the besiegers". Alpha is supported by **Cx** against beta's *þe segge*, "the man". (L is apparently corrected to *þe sege*.)

312 **lif**: Alpha (and CrHm) supported by **Cx** against beta's *lief*. However, beta's reading is attractive ("Sir Happy-to-Live-in-Lechery"), and is adopted by KD.

314 Only LR are without a paraph at this point. It aptly marks the start of Conscience's speech, otherwise unmarked. Perhaps **Bx** lacked it.

318 The punctuation is after *herte* in LHmORF, before it in MWC, and in both positions in G. Alliteration is on /h/ and the vowel.

321 **alle**: G and alpha are supported by **Cx**. Beta has *hem alle*.

And indulgence may do · but if dette lette it
I may wel suffre seyde conscience · syn ȝe desiren
That frere flaterer be fette · and phisike ȝow syke

325 ¶ The Frere her-of herde · and hyed faste
To a lorde for a lettre · leue to haue to curen
As a curatour he were · and cam with his lettres
Baldly to þe bisshop · & his brief hadde
In contrees þere he come · confessiouns to here
330 And cam þere conscience was · and knokked atte ȝate

¶ Pees vnpynned it · was porter of vnyte
And in haste asked · what his wille were
In faith quod þis frere · for profit and for helthe
Carpe I wolde with contricioun · & þerfore come I hider

335 ¶ He is sike seide pees · and so ar many other
Ypocrisie hath herte hem · ful harde is if þei keure

[¶] I am a surgien seide þe [frere] · and salues can make
Conscience knoweth me wel · and what I can do bothe
I preye þe quod pees þo · ar þow passe ferther
340 What hattestow I preye þe · hele nouȝte þi name

¶ Certes seyde his felow [·] sire penetrans domos

[¶] Ȝe go þi gate quod pees · bi god for al þi phisyk
But þow conne [any] crafte · þow comest nouȝt her-Inne
I knewe such one ones · nouȝte eighte wynter passed
345 Come in þus ycoped · at a courte þere I dwelt
And was my lordes leche · & my ladyes bothe
And at þe last þis limitour · þo my lorde was out
He salued so owre wommen · til somme were with childe

[¶] Hende speche het pees [þo] · opene þe ȝates
350 Late in þe frere and his felawe · and make hem faire chere

---

323 **seyde:** CrHmF have *quod*, as does the P family of **Cx**.

325 **faste:** MCrF add *full* to lengthen the b-verse. It is not in **Cx**.

327 **lettres:** Beta's plural is supported by the P family of C, alpha's sg. by the X family. The sg. seems more logical in view of the sg. in the previous line; however that might have been a motive for altering the plural. We follow copy-text.

329 **come:** Beta has *come in*, but alpha is supported by **Cx**.

337 **¶:** The paraph to mark the surgeon's words is in WHmC and alpha, with a line-space in M.

337 **frere:** Beta's *segge* increases the alliteration, but alpha is supported by **Cx**.

342 **¶:** The paraph to mark Pees's reply is in WHmCR, with line-spaces in MF.

343 **any:** R is supported by **Cx**. Beta has *somme*, F has *more*.

349 **¶:** The paraph is in WHm and alpha, with a line-space in M.

349 **þo:** Omitted by beta, but alpha is supported by **Cx**.

He may se and here [here] · so may bifalle
That lyf þorw his lore [·] shal leue coueityse
And be adradde of deth · and with-drawe hym fram pryde
And acorde with conscience · and kisse her either other

355 [¶] Thus thorw hende speche [·] entred þe frere
And cam in to conscience · and curteisly hym grette
Þow art welcome quod conscience [·] canstow hele syke
Here is contricioun quod conscience · my cosyn ywounded
Conforte hym quod conscience [·] and take kepe to his sores
360 The plastres of þe persoun · and poudres [ben] to sore
[And] lat hem ligge ouerlonge · and loth is to chaunge hem
Fro lenten to lenten · he lat his plastres bite

¶ That is ouerlonge quod this limitour · I leue I shal amende it
And goth gropeth contricioun · and gaf hym a plastre
365 Of a pryue payement · and I shal praye for ȝow
For alle þat ȝe ben holde to · al my lyf-tyme
And make ȝow my lady · in masse and in matynes
As freres of owre fraternite · for a litel syluer

¶ Thus he goth and gadereth · and gloseth þere he shryueth
370 Tyl contricioun hadde clene forȝeten · to crye & to wepe
And wake for his wykked werkes · as he was wont to done
For confort of his confessour · contricioun he lafte
Þat is þe souereynest salue · for alkyn synnes

¶ Sleuth seigh þat · and so did pryde
375 And come with a kene wille · conscience to assaille
Conscience cryde eft · and bad clergye help hym

---

351 **here here so**: F has *er so* after a revised a-verse; Beta has *here so it*. R is supported by **Cx**.
355 **¶**: The paraph is in WHmR, with line-spaces in MF.
357 **syke**: Alpha supported by **Cx**. Beta has *þe syke*.
360 **ben**: So R, supported by **Cx**. However, beta and F read *biten*. This is attractive, though too emphatic for an unstressed position. It is probably picked up from l. 362.
361 **And**: Again R alone is supported by **Cx**. Beta and F substitute the subject *He*, otherwise unexpressed.
364 **goth**: Beta and F read the easier *goth and*, as do a few C mss. mainly of the P family, but R agrees with **Cx** in omitting *and*.
366 **For alle**: Cx reads instead *And for hem*. Cr, beta4 and F agree on *And*, but **Bx** is clearly without it.
367 **make ȝow my lady**: The reading is also that of **Cx**. For discussion of the crux see RK, p. 136; Barney (2006), 244, Schmidt (2008), 469.
368 **freres**: WHmO alter to the singular, to refer to *my lady* above.
371 **to done**: Cx has instead *bifore*. From here to the end of the poem there are significant differences between **Bx** and **Cx**.
376 **and bad clergye**: Cx has instead *Clergie come*.

And also contricioun · forto kepe þe ȝate

[¶] He lith and dremeth seyde pees · and so do many other
The Frere with his phisik · þis folke hath enchaunted
380 And plastred hem so esyly · þei drede no synne

¶ Bi cryste quod conscience þo · I wil bicome a pilgryme
And walken as wyde · as al þe wordle lasteth
To seke Piers þe plowman · þat pryde m[yȝte] destruye
And þat freres hadde a fyndyng · þat for nede flateren
385 And contrepleteth me conscience · now kynde me auenge
And sende me happe and hele · til I haue piers þe plowman
And sitthe he gradde after grace · til I gan awake

Explicit hic dialogus petri plowman

---

377 **also ... forto:** Cx has instead *baed Contricioun to come to helpe.*
378 **¶:** The paraph is in HmCR, with line-spaces in WMF.
378 **and dremeth:** Cx has instead *adreint.*
379 **hath:** Alpha reads *hath so,* but beta is supported by Cx.
380 **plastred ... þei:** In Cx this reads *doth men drynke dwale þat men.*
382 **al:** Omitted by CrWOF, but apparently in **Bx.** Cx instead reads *as þe world regneth.*
382 **wordle:** Not an error but a recognised spelling of "world". See note to l. 211.
383 **myȝte:** Beta has *may,* but alpha is supported by Cx.
387.1 **Explicit hic dialogus petri plowman:** Supported by LMWGOC. See Introduction, pp. 22–23.

CPSIA information can be obtained
at www.ICGtesting.com
Printed in the USA
LVHW09*0119280818
588352LV00005B/56/P